International Community Psychology

History and Theories

International Community Psychology

History and Theories

Edited by

Stephanie M. Reich, Ph.D.
University of California, Irvine
Irvine, California, USA

Manuel Riemer, Ph.D.
Vanderbilt University
Nashville, Tennessee, USA

Isaac Prilleltensky, Ph.D.
University of Miami
Coral Gables, Florida, USA

Maritza Montero, Ph.D.
Universidad Central de Venezuela
Caracas, Venezuela

 Springer

Stephanie M. Reich
Department of Education
University of California, Irvine
2001 Berkeley Place
Irvine, CA 92697-5500

Library of Congress Control Number: 2007922442

ISBN 978-0-387-49499-9   e-ISBN 978-0-387-49500-2

Printed on acid-free paper.

9 8 7 6 5 4 3 2 1

springer.com

*To all the community psychologists around the world
who struggle to promote well-being and liberation from
oppressive forces*

Contents

About the Editors

Stephanie M. Reich, Ph.D., is an Assistant Professor of Education at the University of California, Irvine. Born in the United States of America, Dr. Reich's graduate education has been in community psychology, child development, and program evaluation with a specific emphasis on quantitative methods. She is the recipient of the Newbrough Award for academic writing, a fellowship from the National Institute of Mental Health for children's mental health services research, as well as the Julius Seeman award for academic and professional excellence. Dr. Reich's research interests focus on social interventions for children and families, applied and theoretical models of program evaluation, definitions and applications of community theory, and historical underpinnings to social inequality.

Manuel Riemer, Ph.D., is a research associate at Peabody College of Vanderbilt University. Prior to coming to the United States, Dr. Riemer, who was born and raised in Germany, was a student of clinical, cultural, and critical psychology at the Free University of Berlin where he researched and published on the history of critical psychology in Germany. While Dr. Riemer's training in the United States has been in quantitative methods of psychology and applied social psychology, he has always had a strong interest in community psychology as his research interests focus on understanding, modeling, evaluating, and changing complex human behavioral systems as well as issues of power, oppression, and inequality. Dr. Riemer is currently the director of research and system development in a large-scale multisite study on organizational change in mental health as well as a lecturer in the Community Action and Research Program at Vanderbilt University.

Isaac Prilleltensky, Ph.D., is dean of the School of Education at the University of Miami. Prior to that he was director of the Doctoral Program in Community Research and Action at Peabody College of Vanderbilt University. Isaac was born in Argentina and has studied and worked in Israel, Canada, Australia, and the United States. He has lectured widely in South America, Europe, North America, Australia, and New Zealand. Dr. Prilleltensky is concerned with value-based ways of promoting personal, relational, and collective well-being. He is the author, co-author or co-editor of several books, including *Community Psychology: In Pursuit of Liberation and Well-Being, Doing Psychology Critically, Critical Psychology, Promoting Family Wellness and Preventing Child Maltreatment,* and *The Morals and Politics of Psychology*. He recently completed with his wife, Dr. Ora Prilleltensky, a book entitled *Promoting Well-Being: Linking Personal, Organizational, and Community Change*.

Maritza Montero, Ph.D., is a professor of social psychology and coordinator of the Doctorate Course in Psychology at the Universidad Central de Venezuela. She has lectured extensively throughout Latin America and in the United States, Great Britain, France, Spain, and Australia. Her 1985 book *Ideología, alienación e identidad nacional* ("Ideology, Alienation and National Identity") received the Central University of Venezuela Faculty Association (APUCV) award. Dr. Montero is on the editorial boards of several community and social psychology journals, among which are the *American Journal of Community Psychology* (associate editor) and *Community, Work and Family*. Dr. Montero has won several national and international scientific awards, among which are the Interamerican Society of Psychology (1995) and the Venezuelan National Science Award (2000). She has served as president of the International Society of Political Psychology (2006) and as vice president for South America of the Interamerican Psychology Society (1997–1999). Her latest publication is a trilogy published in Spanish, in Argentina: *Teoría y práctica de psicología communitaria* ("Theory and Practice of Community Psychology"), 2003; *Introducción a la psicología comunitaria* ("Introduction to Community Psychology"), 2004; and *Hacer para transformer. El método en la Psicología comunitaria* ("To Do and to Transform. Method in Community Psychology"), 2006. Dr. Montero has contributed numerous papers and book chapters published in Spanish, English, Portuguese, and French. Her research interests focus on community and political psychology; and the theoretical, epistemological, and methodological aspects in social psychology.

About the Contributors

Charity S. Akotia, Ph.D., is a senior lecturer and head of the Psychology Department, University of Ghana, Legon. She earned her master's degree at Wilfrid Laurier University, Waterloo, Canada, and doctoral degree from the University of Ghana. Besides academic interests, Dr. Akotia is involved in consulting for a number of business and research organizations in Ghana. Her primary interest is to create awareness of the relevance of community psychology in Ghana and to "convert" students to community psychology. Her research primarily focuses on community mental health, suicide and suicide prevention, women and work and personal responsibility.

Cinzia Albanesi, Ph.D., is an assistant professor at the Faculty of Psychology of the University of Bologna, Italy, where she teaches "Work Techniques for Groups within Communities." She is a community psychologist with an academic background in social psychology. Her primary research interests include adolescents' sense of community and psychosocial well-being, community-based participatory research, health promotion, and self-help groups.

Holly L. Angelique, Ph.D., is an associate professor of community psychology and is the coordinator of the community psychology & social change master of art (M.A.) program at Penn State Harrisburg. She has been an active member of the Society for Community Research and Action for many years, acting as the chair of the Women's Committee, co-editor of the women's column in *The Community Psychologist*, secretary of the executive committee, and she is currently a member of the Council for Education Programs. Her research interests focus on feminist and environmental activism.

Caterina Arcidiacono, M.Sc., is an associated professor of social and community psychology at the University Federico II of Naples. From 1994 to 1999, she was president of the Italian Association of Community Psychology and is a founder of ENCP and ECPA (European Community Psychology Association). Her current research area is that of city and sense of community with reference to grounded theory and qualitative research. Trust as a key factor in community orientation and community-based participatory research are her more recent research topics. Further research areas concern the woman–man relationship with special reference to asymmetry of gender, social identities, and intercultural dialogue.

Kofi B. Barimah, Ph.D., obtained his B.A. (Hons) in psychology from the University of Ghana; M.A. in community psychology from Wilfrid Laurier University, Canada; M.Sc. in rural extension studies from University of Guelph, Canada; and Ph.D. in public health from University of Aberdeen, Scotland. He was a lecturer at Ryerson University, Canada, in health promotion and community development where he was involved in community economic development for more than 10 years. Currently he is a senior lecturer at the Catholic University College of Ghana. His current research interests are focused on traditional medicine, health policy, health promotion, and community empowerment.

Jarg Bergold, Ph.D., was born in Nuernberg/Germany. After high school he studied law and psychology and graduated in 1966 in clinical psychology. He worked in Munich, studied behavior therapy at the Institute of Psychiatry, London, and worked as a consultant for behavior therapy at the Psychiatric Outpatient Clinic in Berne, Switzerland. In 1974, he became a full professor of clinical psychology at the Free University of Berlin, teaching clinical psychology based on community psychology. His main research interests include psychosocial/psychiatric institutions, counseling, crisis intervention, evaluation and qualitative research methods. He instigated the qualitative Internet journal *Forum Qualitative Research* (FQS). He retired in 2004.

Arvin Bhana, Ph.D., is a director of research in the Child, Youth, Family and Social Development (CYFSD) research program of the Human Sciences Research Council (HSRC) and is an adjunct associate professor in the School of Psychology at the University of KwaZulu-Natal. He obtained his Ph.D. from the University of Illinois at Urbana-Champaign. He is a clinical/community psychologist by training. He currently heads the Durban office for the Child, Youth, Family and Social Development research program of the HSRC. His research interests include adolescent risk and resilience with a focus on prevention and mental health promotion, particularly community-based ecological interventions.

Sangeeta Bhatia received her Ph.D. from University of Delhi, India. Her doctoral work was on family care-giving in chronic illness and she is currently pursuing postdoctoral work on formulating interventions at the community level to enhance resiliency in individuals/families with an individual who has a disability. She has been author/co-author of papers on mental health and has several publications in reputed national and international journals. Dr. Bhatia has also participated in several research projects in the area of family studies and community psychology. She joined the psychology department at Gargi College, Delhi University, in 1990, where she currently teaches undergraduate courses.

Rolv Mikkel Blakar, Cand. Psych., is a professor of social psychology at the University of Oslo, Norway, specializing in communication and the psychology of language. He has written extensively on power and values in communication and language usage. He has studied power and ideology in various contexts ranging from personal communication to the mass media. For many years he organized a multidisciplinary research program focusing on conflicts in family communication. Lately he has conducted research in the field of ethical dimensions and dilemmas embedded in ideologies, communication, and language usage. He has extensive administrative experience and has served on several editorial boards.

Anna Bokszczanin, Ph.D., is an associate professor at Opole University, Opole, Poland. She earned her Ph.D. in social psychology from Wroclaw University in 1997. Dr. Bokszczanin has been teaching courses in developmental psychology, stress and coping, and community psychology. Her primary research interests concern the impact of major life events and traumatic stress on children's and adolescents' coping resources and psychological wellbeing. Her scholarly work has appeared in many Polish and international journals. Recently, she authored a book about psychological reactions of children and adolescents to natural disaster based on her longitudinal investigation of the 1997 Polish flood.

Stephanie Boyle, Ph.D., is a clinical psychologist working with children and families for Birmingham Children's Hospital NHS Trust in Birmingham, United Kingdom. After completing her first degree in psychology in 1990, she contributed to positivist research on primary/secondary school transfer and the impact of the sinking of the cruise ship *Jupiter* on teenage passengers. She subsequently undertook clinical psychology training on a course that had a social constructionist orientation. From an interest in the concept of resilience and the prevention of emotional and behavioral problems in children and young people, Dr. Boyle is moving towards an emphasis on contexts, systems, and communities.

Lauren Breen is a Ph.D. (psychology) candidate due to graduate from Edith Cowan University in 2007. In her thesis, she examined the grief experience for people bereaved through road traffic crashes in Western Australia, with a particular emphasis on the role of contextual factors on the resulting grief experiences. From 2001 to 2005, Lauren was a part-time associate lecturer in the School of Psychology at Edith Cowan University. Lauren is an active member of the Western Australian section of the Australian Psychological Society's College of Community Psychologists and previously served as a student representative on the national committee.

Melissa Asma Browne, B.A., is a graduate of George Washington University in Washington, D.C. She received her B.A. in psychology, with an interest in cross-cultural psychology, industrial/organizational psychology, and international affairs. She has spent the past 2 years exploring her interest in development and event planning at Boston's Jewish Community Day School and planning events with local Boston nonprofits. In 2007, Melissa will return her attention to West Africa and participate in the Tostan Internship Program in Senegal. Melissa is very interested in exploring ideas of colonialism across the African Diaspora, as well as the effects of culture on cognition.

Mark Burton, Ph.D., is the head of a large public sector service for intellectually disabled people. His work in human services has emphasized the social participation of disadvantaged people and the development of a culture of enquiry, while his written work crosses the fields of health and social care, social policy, and alternative approaches in psychology. Outside paid work, Mark maintains the Community Psychology UK website at www.compsy.org.uk and is active in solidarity with social struggles in the majority world, which also offer a source of learning and inspiration both practically and conceptually. He is a visiting professor at Manchester Metropolitan University.

Erik Carlquist, M.Sc., is a clinical and social psychologist and also holds a business management degree. He is currently working as a psychotherapist and is affiliated with the ideology project at the University of Oslo in Norway as a researcher and teacher. His clinical and research interests include language and communication theory, ideology, identity, and psychodynamic theory and practice. He was previously a senior research officer at the Transport Economics Institute, Oslo, where he was responsible for several cross-disciplinary research projects related to urban planning.

Sheung-Tak Cheng received his Ph.D. in clinical/community psychology from the State University of New York at Buffalo. His primary research areas cover various issues related to successful aging and the environmental conditions that support it. He is a consultant to the Hong Kong government and to the United Nations on national and international policies on aging. He is co-editor of the special issue on international community psychology of the *American Journal of Community Psychology*.

Marci R. Culley, Ph.D., is an assistant professor at Georgia State University. She received her bachelor's degree from Michigan State University and master's degree in community psychology from the Pennsylvania State University. In 2004, she received her Ph.D. from the University of Missouri–Kansas City. Her scholarly interests are grounded in community organizing related to environmental issues and the links between individual transformation and larger community and social change processes. Her research is informed by theories of power and empowerment, ecology, action research, and feminism. These related theoretical domains provide the conceptual context for her program of research and community collaborations.

Serdar M. Degirmencioglu, Ph.D., is an associate professor at the Department of Psychology, Beykent University, in Istanbul. He served as associate editor for the *Turkish Journal of Psychology* and assumed several roles at the Turkish Psychological Association, including the vice-presidency. He served as the coordinator of Children's Rights Coalition of Turkey and as president of NGO/UNICEF Regional Network for Children. He is currently a member of the executive committee of the International Society for the Study of Behavioural Development. He is a long-time member of SCRA and president-elect of the international committee. He is a founding member of the European Community Psychology Association.

Ana Gloria Ferullo, Ph.D., is a psychologist and specialist in methodology of scientific and technological research. She is a professor of theories and techniques about groups in the Faculty of Psychology University of Tucumán and professor of the academic and scientific committees of postgraduate courses in National Universities. She is director of CONICET (Consejo Nacional de Investigaciones Científicas y Técnicas) doctorate and postdoctorate thesis in psychology, director of research programs and projects, and assessor of research projects and of researchers at national, regional, and province levels. Her areas of specialization include social community psychology; institutional psychology, and psychology of groups.

Mariana Fidalgo, lic., has recently graduated with a degree in psychology from Porto University in Portugal. During her training, she was particularly interested in the field of community psychology and deviant behaviors. She worked as a psychologist at a victim support association and is currently doing a postgraduate course in the field of forensics.

Donata Francescato, Ph.D., is professor of community psychology at the University La Sapienza in Rome, Italy. She is the author of 20 books on women's issues, community psychology, and online learning, some of which have been translated into French, Spanish, Portuguese, and Japanese. She is currently involved in research on women in politics and the effects of laughter on health and social capital as well as evaluation of the efficacy of face to face and computer supported collaborative learning in promoting sociopolitical empowerment.

Francis Nkwenti Fru, M.A., obtained the master of education (1999) in adult education and community development from the University of Ibadan, Nigeria. He was an assistant head of the Department of Adult Education and Community Development and is acting head at the Bamenda University of Science and Technology (BUST), where he taught from 2000 to 2004. His professional work experience has been in community-based projects in Nigeria and Cameroon. He is the founding partner of the Cameroon NGO, the National Adult Literacy and Sanitation Program, and is the current project coordinator for Cameroon's Mother Teresa Association for the Old and Needy.

Saúl Fuks, Ph.D., is regular professor in clinical psychology at the Rosario National University in Argentina in the postgraduate programs. Author of several publications, he has worked in the field of community psychology and health community programs for many years and is currently director of the Centro de Asistencia a la Comunidad (CeAC) in the University of Rosario. He is the director of research programs, projects, and graduate committees and assessor of research projects and of researchers at national, regional, and province levels. His areas of specialization include health community, organizational psychology, and systemic facilitation of group and community development.

Víctor Giorgi, M.Sc., is a professor assigned to the area of health, Psychology Faculty, at the University of the República Oriental del Uruguay. He has been a university professor since 1980. He is the former president of the Executive Commission Programs APEX-CERRO (community program) and author of several books and articles on sanitary themes of psychology, community, and issues of the childhood and professional formation of the psychologist. He is also the dean of the Psychology Faculty of the University of the República Oriental del Uruguay.

Heather Gridley, M.A., coordinates one of Australia's two postgraduate programs in community psychology, at Victoria University in Melbourne. Her interest in community psychology stemmed from her work in community health, where she became aware of the limitations of interventions directed solely at individuals. Heather has held national positions in the Australian Psychological Society's College of Community Psychologists and Women and Psychology Interest Group, and has served two terms on the APS board of directors. She recently accepted a part-time management position with APS in the domain of public interest/social issues. Heather also sings with the Brunswick Women's Choir.

Carl Harris, D. Clin. Psy., has worked as a clinical psychologist in the National Health Service in Birmingham, United Kingdom, since 1996. His experience of community psychology has been through working in the Family Well-being Project, an action-research project in a local community regeneration program (2001–present). He holds a B.Sc. in political economy (1985); M.Phil. in political theory and philosophy (1987); Dip. Psych (1990) and D. Clin. Psy (1996). This chapter is his first experience of being involved in writing a "history."

Carolyn Kagan, Ph.D., is professor of community social psychology at Manchester Metropolitan University where she is the director of the Research Institute for Health and Social Change. She combines qualifications in social work and counseling psychology in her community practice. Her work includes prefigurative action research with those marginalized by the social system (in the United Kingdom and other places), and she has worked for many years supporting public and voluntary service developments and citizen advocacy projects. MMU has a group of eight staff with community and critical psychology interests and offers the only M.Sc. community psychology in the United Kingdom.

Krzysztof Kaniasty, Ph.D., studied psychology in Poland and the United States. Since 1990, he has been teaching undergraduate and graduate courses in research methodology, social psychology, and stress and coping at Indiana University of Pennsylvania where he is a professor of psychology. He also teaches at Opole University in Poland. He conducted and collaborated on several large-scale longitudinal studies investigating social support exchanges, individual and communal coping, and psychological well-being after natural disasters and other major stressors (e.g., criminal victimization, job loss) in the United States, Mexico, and Poland. He is co-editor of *Anxiety, Stress and Coping: An International Journal.*

Antonio Lapalma, Ph.D., is a professor of Strategies of Community Intervention at the Faculty of Psychology, University of Buenos Aires. Specialized in social and community psychology, he has been an advisor on numerous projects in the areas of health education and social development. He has worked for several years as a consultant in rural development, both in State and non-governmental organizations. He has written various articles and papers on community psychology and social planning.

Francine Lavoie, Ph.D., is a professor of community psychology at Université Laval, Québec, Canada. She has been teaching at l'École de psychologie since 1979. Over the years, she has received provincial and federal grants on the topics of marital violence, dating violence, and mutual aid groups. She has also developed and evaluated a prevention program on dating violence that is used in all high schools of the province of Québec. She served as a senior editor of the *Canadian Journal of Community Mental Health* and is a fellow of The Society for Community Research and Action (American Psychological Association).

Jorge S. López, Ph.D., is a professor of community psychology at the Autonomous University of Madrid, Spain. After completing graduate studies in medicine and psychology, he worked as an assistant professor and coordinator of community programs in South Brazil universities. He earned his doctorate in social psychology in 1997 at the Autonomous University of Madrid and has been involved in various research and intervention projects related to health psychology and risk behaviors in young people. He has been visiting professor in different Brazilian universities and is still working with Latino American academic institutions in the field of social intervention and postgraduate training.

Winnie W.S. Mak, Ph.D., is an assistant professor at the Chinese University of Hong Kong. She obtained her Ph.D. in clinical psychology at the University of California, Santa Barbara. Having lived in the United States since childhood, she returned to Hong Kong, her birthplace, in 2002 with aspirations to promote mental health in the community. Her research interests include stigma of social minorities (e.g., immigrants, individuals with mental illness, lesbians/gays/bisexual individuals/transgendered individuals, people with HIV/AIDS), sociocultural influences on illness behaviors, and topics related to cultural diversity and community psychology. She is currently working on developing stigma reduction programs in the community.

Terri Mannarini, Ph.D., is an assistant professor at the Faculty of Education of the University of Lecce, Italy, where she teaches community psychology and social psychology. Her main research interests focus on gender issues, political psychology, and community-based participatory processes.

Antonio Martín, Ph.D., is a professor of community psychology at the Autonomous University of Madrid, Spain. He studied science education and psychology in college and earned his doctoral degree in psychology at Salamanca University. A member of the Psychology Faculty of the Autonomous University of Madrid since its foundation, he helped promote the introduction of community psychology within its graduate studies. He was also responsible for the implementation of different academic exchange programs with European and Latin American universities. He has edited *Psicología Comunitaria* (Visor, 1988), in cooperation with F. Chacón and M. Martínez, and *Psicología Comunitaria: Fundamentos y aplicaciones* (Síntesis, 1998).

Athanassios Marvakis, Dr. rer. soc., is since 2007 associate professor in social psychology at the Department of Primary Education of the Aristotle University of Thessaloniki/Greece. His current research interests include psychology and its relation to the various forms of social inequalities and social exclusion (like racism, nationalism, ethnicism, and multiculturalism), youth as a social group, solidarity as a theoretical and practical issue in the social sciences, and the critical psychology of the "schooling-complex."

Bridgette Masters-Awatere, B.Soc.Sc, MSoc.Sc., P.G.Dip.Psych(Com), is Māori with affiliations to Te Rarawa and Ngai Te Rangi iwi. She connects to Ngati Porou by marriage and through her son Tahu. Bridgette has a background in community psychology, research, and evaluation. Her areas of interest include Māori development, public health, health promotion, evaluation research, training and implementation methods. Her research interests

include using applied research methods toward developing culturally appropriate program evaluation processes for Māori (specifically within the areas
of public health promotion programs).

Isabel Menezes, Ph.D., is an associate professor at the Faculty of Psychology
and Education Sciences of Porto University. She has been involved in the
teaching of community psychology since the 1990s and has supported the
implementation of community intervention projects as a consultant with
psychologists, educators, and social workers. Since 1998, she has been coordinating research projects in the field of community and political psychology with a particular emphasis on the role of civic and political
participation in the empowerment of marginalized or discriminated groups
on the basis of gender, sexual orientation, ethnicity, immigrant status, or
disability.

Terry Mitchell, Ph.D., is an assistant professor in the Department of
Psychology at Wilfrid Laurier University. She has a Ph.D. in community psychology from the University of Toronto. Her research and advocacy work is
focused largely on Aboriginal and women's health. Terry was the principal
investigator of a study on the psychosocial impacts of Dragon Boating
among women with breast cancer and on the health of vulnerable populations. She was also the principal investigator of a study on the community
and volunteer impacts of the Swissair Flight 111 disaster.

Hilde Eileen Nafstad, Cand. Psych., is an associate professor of social and
developmental psychology at the University of Oslo, Norway. She is affiliated with the university's ethics program as a supervisor and in undertaking research on ethics in various professions as well as the developing area
of ethics of psychology and the social sciences. She was formerly a senior
research fellow at the Institute of Applied Social Research, Oslo, where she
undertook community research on behalf of the Norwegian government.
She has published books and articles on quality of life and public policy;
ideologies and value systems; minorities; and human development of empathy and altruism.

Geoffrey Nelson, Ph.D., is a professor of psychology and a faculty member
in the graduate program in community psychology at Wilfrid Laurier
University, Waterloo, Ontario. He has served as senior editor of the *Canadian
Journal of Community Mental Health* and as chair of the Community
Psychology Section of the Canadian Psychological Association. Professor
Nelson has held a senior research fellowship from the Ontario Mental Health
Foundation, and he was the recipient with the Canadian Mental Health
Association/Waterloo Branch in 1999 of the Harry MacNeill award for
innovation in community mental health from the American Psychological
Foundation and the Society for Community Research.

A. Bame Nsamenang, Ph.D., is an associate professor of psychology and learning sciences at Yaoundé University, Cameroon, and director of the Human Development Resource Centre. He was a fellow at Stanford University's CASBS (2002–2003), Baroda University, India (2001), and NICHD (1987–1990). He is ad hoc adviser to the ISSBD and on the editorial boards of the *International Journal of Psychology* and the online *Child Health and Education*. He has published five books in psychology and education and more than 50 articles and/or book chapters. His research interest is on early childhood and adolescent development, with keen focus on responsible intelligence in African children.

Inge Petersen, Ph.D., is an associate professor and has served as head of the School of Psychology at the University of KwaZulu-Natal. She obtained her Ph.D. from the University of Cape Town in South Africa. She has published locally and internationally on community mental health and mental health policy development, with a specific focus on health systems reform for integrated primary mental health care and community mental health. Her most recent work focuses on developing community-based models of prevention.

Amiram Raviv, Ph.D., is a professor at the Psychology Department, Tel Aviv University, Israel, and has served as head of the Psychology Department. He has published more than 80 articles and chapters and has co-edited and written four books about children in stressful situations. He served as head psychologist at the School Psychology Service in the Ministry of Education in Israel and has been active in various areas of primary prevention. His research interests are school psychology, children's cognitive development, help-seeking, media psychology, and social cognition. He has written and consulted in preparing enrichment books for children and guidance literature for parents.

Neville Robertson, Ph.D., M.Soc.Sc., B.A., Dip.Psych.(Com) is a Pakeha of Scottish descent. He is a senior lecturer in psychology at the University of Waikato where he convenes the Graduate Programme in Community Psychology. His professional work focuses on men's violence against women and children. He facilitates stopping violence programs and provides consultancy and training. His research focuses on community and institutional responses to domestic violence. Other aspects of Dr. Robertson's work include anti-racism and Treaty of Waitangi education and the evaluation of health and social service programs.

Tamsen Rochat, M.A., is a clinical psychologist and chief researcher at the Child, Youth, Family and Social Development Programme of the Human Sciences Research Council in South Africa. Recently, she has been working in poor rural communities developing and overseeing psychological services and therapeutic and crisis care clinics. In 2005, she was awarded the prestigious ZERO TO THREE Leadership Development Initiative International

Fellowship for her contribution to advancing early child development in South Africa. Her research examines the care and development of young children living with HIV/AIDS and those living in families and communities affected by poverty and HIV/AIDS.

Alicia Rodríguez, M.Sc., is a pscychologist and assistant professor in the area of community psychology of the Faculty of Psychology at the University of the Republic of Uruguay. She was the lead in several research projects on "characteristics of the professional practice of the psychologists in the community" (1998–2000) and "The processes of dislodge and rehousing: The perception of the involved actors " (1999–2004) (master's thesis). She has worked as a community psychologist in public and private institutions and is advisory in the management of communitarian projects in non-governmental organizations and in the context of agreements between the state and the civil society.

Susana Rudolf, M.Sc., is a pscychologist and assistant head of the Health Department, Faculty of Psychology at the Universidad de la República Oriental del Uruguay. She is the director of the University Programme called "Apex - Cerro" (university program of learning and extension that works with an approach of community health) and is the author of different publications and lectures about psychology of health and community psychology.

Enrique Saforcada, Ph.D., is a consultant professor of public health/mental health in the Faculty of Psychology of the University of Buenos Aires (UBA). He was founder and director of the Centre of Research in Social Psychology in the Universidad Nacional de Córdoba (UNC), where, with his team, he developed the field of sanitary psychology in 1970. Sanitary psychology is a specialty recognized by the Federation of Psychologists of República Argentina and is taught in various universities. He is the author of *Sanitary Psychology: Critical Analysis of the Systems of Health Care* and *The Human Factor in Public Health: A Psychological Approach to Collective Health.*

Nandini Sethi, M.A., received her master's in clinical psychology from Delhi University. Her research projects focus on physical disabilities and their role on personal and social resources and health. Currently, she is taking courses in counseling skills and cognitive behavior therapy to expand her interests in adult psychotherapy and family therapy.

Toshiaki Sasao, Ph.D., is currently professor of psychology, International Christian University, Tokyo, Japan, and a fellow of the American Psychological Association (Division 27). His current research interests include cultural issues in program evaluation, school violence prevention in multicultural contexts, psychological sense of community, graduate training issues in community psychology, and faculty development in higher education.

Dr. Sasao currently serves on the editorial boards of the *American Journal of Community Psychology, Japanese Journal of Community Psychology, Asian Journal of Social Psychology, Japanese Journal of Social Psychology,* and *Japanese Journal of Educational Psychology.*

Mike Seckinger, Ph.D., was born in Germany in 1965. After high school he studied psychology in Munich. After university he worked for a short period as a management consultant and started in 1992 as a researcher at the German Youth Institute (DJI). He received his doctorate in 2002. His main research interests include cooperation between institutions, promotion of participation in social services, and structures and changes of the child and youth welfare system.

Keren Sharvit, M.A., is a doctoral student at the Psychology Department, Tel Aviv University, Israel. Her research explores the relationship between societal beliefs and coping with stress in the context of the intractable Israeli–Palestinian conflict. She is working under the supervision of Prof. Amiram Raviv and Prof. Daniel Bar-Tal.

Małgorzata Szarzyńska, M.Sc., is a licensed clinical psychologist in Poland and is currently the chief of clinical psychology in the Opole Province. In her various published works, research projects, and clinical work, she has studied gender issues in the workplace and across history and cultures, eating disorders (especially anorexia and bulimia), and long-term outcomes among youth leaving foster care (including orphanages). In the past few years, she has become active in community psychology in Europe, the Americas, and Asia. She was a key organizer of the Sixth European Conference on Community Psychology held in Opole in October 2006.

Pedro M. Teixeira, M.Sc., received his degree in psychology from Porto University where he also completed a master's degree on higher education students' political development and citizenship. He has worked in learning disabilities and vocational rehabilitation centres and is currently a Ph.D. student with a grant from the Portuguese Science and Technology Foundation. His research focuses on disability issues, specifically the application of empowerment theory to the rehabilitation field in Portugal.

Sofia Triliva, Psy.D., is currently an assistant professor of psychology at the University of Crete in Greece. Her current research interests include the social and emotional adjustment of children, adolescents, and families and the development, application, and evaluation of social and emotional skill-building programing within schools and wider community settings.

Nelson Varas-Díaz, Ph.D., holds a doctoral degree in social-community psychology from the University of Puerto Rico. He is currently an assistant professor at the Graduate School of Social Work at the same institution. His publications include books and journal articles on issues related to AIDS stigma, the social construction of illness, and the emotional aspect of the process of stigmatization. He recently edited a book on community psychology entitled *Psicología Comunitaria: Implicaciones, Retos y Nuevos Rumbos* ("Community Psychology: Implications, Challenges and New Directions").

Tomoyuki Yasuda, Ph.D., is a research associate at the Faculty of Human Sciences at Waseda University, Japan. He received his Ph.D. in educational psychology from Pennsylvania State University and an M.A. in educational research and psychology from University of Missouri–Kansas City. His research interests include program evaluation, prevention and promotion, empowerment of community-based organizations, and applied measurement and psychometrics. His current research focuses on the Japanese elderly's public participation and cross-cultural issues in community-based organizations. He has authored or co-authored several journal articles on applied measurement, prevention research, and public participation.

Mira Zeira, M.A., was born in 1974 in Kibbutz Yagur in the north of Israel and currently lives in Tel Aviv. She received her M.A. degree in clinical psychology from Tel Aviv University. Her master's thesis studied the subjective well-being of Kibbutz and city residents in Israel. She has worked for several years as a counselor for 'Perach,' which is an Israeli nationwide project of tutoring children from impoverished neighborhoods by university students. She is currently a clinical psychology intern with the student counseling services at the Hebrew University of Jerusalem.

An Introduction to the Diversity of Community Psychology Internationally

STEPHANIE M. REICH, MANUEL RIEMER, ISAAC PRILLELTENSKY, AND MARITZA MONTERO

Whereas some may consider community psychology (CP) a young field developed in the United States in the 1960s, it actually has a long history internationally. As one can learn in the Greek chapter of this book, for example, ideas such as community and political consciousness and their connections to social and psychological well-being can be traced all the way back to ancient philosophers such as Aristotle and Plato. In the contributions from Africa and Australasia, we learn that principles of CP have been part of the family and societal structures there for a very long time, disturbed only by the colonization of the past century. The chapters from Latin America demonstrate a history of the field based on liberation and social justice rather than a traditional psychology orientation. Today, CP is well established as a discipline in a few countries, whereas in others it is in its early infancy. Although it is growing in some regions, it is on the decline in several other countries. The uneven development and changing status of CP throughout the world lead to many questions such as: What are the contextual factors that facilitated the development of CP in these different countries? What factors are hindering its development? How similar is CP in these countries and to what degree are they different? What are the unique theories and methods that emerged or are emerging in these countries?

There are multiple resources for learning more about the development of CP, such as the growing number of introductory textbooks and a few books focusing on CP in Australia, Britain, New Zealand, South Africa, and some Latin American countries. To our knowledge, there is no book available, however, whose primary purpose is to describe the history and theories of CP internationally, and no effort has been made to compare the development of CP in other countries comprehensively; a gap that is surprising considering the field's strong emphasis on contextualism, diversity, and cultural perspectives.

Our aim in editing this book is to help fill this gap and increase knowledge about CP around the world, promote international collaboration, enhance theory utilization and development, identify biases and barriers in our field, help ensure critical mass for our often fringe discipline, and minimize the pervasive U.S.-centric view of the field. While we acknowledge that these are

1

lofty goals, we hope the reader agrees with us that these are beneficial aims and that this book is a step in the right direction. Before we describe the potential benefits and limitations as well as the structure of this book in more detail, we would like to provide you with a short history about how this endeavor originated.

A (Somewhat) Brief History of This Book

It is impossible to compile a book about the history of CP around the world without first describing the history of this project. The seeds for this edited book were planted at the Society for Community Research and Action (SCRA) biennial conference in Las Vegas, New Mexico (USA), in 2003. However, the seeds were developed in the mind of a somewhat frustrated doctoral student of community psychology in the United States.

Despite its general values and intentions, studying CP in the United States tends to be very U.S.-focused and ethnocentric. A U.S. education in CP involves reading the works of CP's recognized U.S. forefathers (not fore-mothers), studying U.S. social action in the 1900s, the community mental health movement, Swampscott Conference, and formalization of the field. As a student, one learns about the handful of "core" CP theories (e.g., empowerment, sense of community, prevention) and CP principles and values. What is often lacking from this education is the history of intellectual thought that contributes to the theoretical development of this field (e.g., Aristotle, Dewey, Fals Borda, Freire, Hegel), acknowledgment of the work occurring outside the U.S. borders as well as outside the mainstream (e.g., feminist theories, indigenous knowledge, liberation theology), and theory-driven practice (rather than practice-driven theories). Although learning about the history of CP in the United States is important, many influential components are omitted.

Thus, the seeds for this book were produced by the frustration Stephanie Reich, who was a graduate student in community psychology during the first 5 years of the 21st century, experienced with the well-intentioned but somewhat ethnocentric and a-theoretical doctoral education she was receiving. This hunger for a more diverse and inclusive education led to several poignant conversations at the SCRA biennial with people from Australia, Puerto Rico, Scotland, and Venezuela. Although these conversations focused on different aspects of the practice and utilization of CP, they all shared one common element: a dissatisfaction with the impression at the conference that SCRA members viewed CP as created by the United States and that its practices elsewhere were derived solely from the work and theories of the United States.

Each of the non–U.S. psychologists seemed surprised by a U.S.-student's sincere interest in the practices of their countries as well as the student's disappointment of not being exposed to international theories, practices, and history. From three of these conversations, Stephanie Reich (United States), Heather Gridley (Australia), and Nelson Varas Diaz (Puerto Rico) decided to write a paper about international psychology to submit to the *American Journal of Community Psychology* (the SCRA journal) that would describe some of these countries' historical developments and acknowledge the growing ethnocentrism of CP in the United States.

When Stephanie returned to Nashville, she recounted her experience to Manuel Riemer, another doctoral student (at this time). Manuel, an international student (from Germany) shared similar concerns about the under-exposure of U.S. students to the rich theories and contributions from other counties and was thrilled at the idea of such an article. He suggested a piece about German CP be included as well. Realizing that one article would not be enough space for the history of four countries (it was not realistically enough space for the history of just two countries), Stephanie and Manuel began to question whether editing a special issue of the *American Journal of Community Psychology* on "International CP," which would include more countries, would be possible. Within an hour of brainstorming, the two realized what was needed was an edited book that provided a space for multiple countries to be included. Given that the two were graduate students with no idea how to set such an ambitious plan into motion, they went to see Isaac Prilleltensky for advice and the off-chance that he would want to collaborate. They approached Isaac because he had extensive publishing experience and had lived and taught in numerous countries (e.g., Canada, Argentina, United States, Israel, and Australia) and would be unlikely to share the ethnocentric view of CP that many of their colleagues at the biennial had endorsed.

Upon hearing about the book idea, Isaac was very supportive, offering to collaborate and directing the two students on what was needed to write a book proposal. Soon, Stephanie, Manuel, and Isaac were meeting about how to identify contributors from other countries, what each chapter should include, and how to obtain a book contract. They also began e-mailing community psychologists from around the world and sending book proposals to several publishers. (Within 1 week of shopping for publishers, the three were contacted by Sharon Panulla at Kluwer Publishing (now Springer), who was very excited about the project.

With a book contract in the works and e-mails and letters traveling around the world, Stephanie, Manuel, and Isaac began to reflect on how to structure the book and the weakness of their plan: Although they were from different countries, they were all U.S.-based community psychologists, at the same institution in the South, and therefore highly prone to the ethnocentrism they were trying to avoid. This prompted the unanimous decision to invite Maritza Montero (from Venezuela) to join the endeavor. Maritza brought to the project a vast experience in publishing, a non–U.S. perspective, and access to more community psychologists around the world for the snowball sample of contributors. Similar to Isaac, Maritza had experienced CP in many different countries firsthand.

Thus, a casual conversation at a conference led to this collaborative effort with four editors, 60 authors, and 38 countries represented. We have learned a lot in the process of editing this book, and the four of us hope that the reader will benefit from it as well. For us, the contributions by the authors from around the world have significantly enriched our knowledge and understanding of CP, and we are certain that it will influence the way we teach, research, and practice CP for many years to come. Below, we list several benefits that we see this book could have for the reader as well as the field of CP at large.

Potential Benefits

Increased Knowledge

Community psychology is a relatively new field, although many of its principles, values, and goals are ancient. The impetus of CP to promote individual and collective well-being transcends geographical boundaries. However, as practitioners, we are limited by our lack of knowledge of the work being done in other countries, advances made in theory and practice, as well as the detriments and deficits of our current practices. By presenting the history and theories of CP in different countries, we hope to increase each other's knowledge of what is being done, what works, what harms, and where to go from here.

Research Design and Practice

Unfortunately, oppression and inequality are international problems and every country is afflicted with these conditions. Around the world there are community psychologists working to address these issues, often in isolation. Instead of learning from what has been done before and how it benefited or hurt people in need, we tend to work in seclusion rather than collaboratively developing, learning about, and utilizing a variety of research designs, practices, and theories. One of our goals for this book is to provide information about the types of work, theories, and innovations around the world. While the United States, United Kingdom, and Canada provide numerous outlets for its work (e.g., professional journals, listserves, books), other countries are making meaningful contributions that are not as readily available. Thus, this book is one more avenue for sharing information about research and practice in other countries.

Variety and Complexity of Social Issues

As community psychologists, we tackle complex social issues. As such, we work with a variety of stakeholders, environments, and other disciplines. Throughout the world, some practices are more successful, some collaborations more effective, some theories more applicable, and some contexts more amenable to change than others. This book provides space for community psychologists to discuss the work being done in their own countries, the collaborations under way, the barriers and facilitators to their work, and the theories that have the most utility to their context. Hopefully, this will inform other community psychologists working in similar contexts of new and effective ways to help communities in their own country.

Learn from History

It is difficult to know where you are heading without knowing where you are coming from. As Robert Penn Warren (1929) wrote, "History cannot give us a program for the future, but it can give us a fuller understanding of ourselves, and of our common humanity, so that we can better face the future." As a field focused on context, we often ignore our own historical context. When we do consider history, we tend to look solely at the development of the field within our own country rather than across countries. However, the development of CP in many countries has been greatly influenced by the development of the field in other countries (sometimes in support from and other times as a reaction to).

By looking at the development of CP across the world, we can better understand our field, identify common facilitators and barriers to our development, acknowledge important contributors to this development, recognize some of our own biases and prejudices, and realize where we are headed in our practice, theory development, research methods, values, and beliefs. As Aristotle wrote, "If you would understand anything, observe its beginning and its development."

Critical Mass

Community psychology tends to be a fringe discipline, perpetually fighting for legitimacy, space, and support—especially in the academic context. This is a common theme across the chapters included in this book, with no country perceiving their field as having equal footing as other large branches of psychology such as clinical and social. By identifying CP work happening in 38 countries, this book aims at acknowledging the strength of CP. By noting how truly international this field is, the breadth of work being done, and the tenacity of those working in the field, we hope to offer evidence of our legitimacy as a field, help identify areas of support, and note that there is a critical mass to our profession.

Power Issues, Shortcomings, and Limitations

Whereas this book has many potential benefits, it is also necessary to focus on the many limitations of this endeavor as well as our naiveté in tackling this task. First, we would like to acknowledge that "there is no history of mankind, there is only an indefinite number of histories of all kinds of aspects of human life" (Popper, 1973, p. 25). As such, this book provides one perspective on the history of each country or region and not *the* history of the countries that are included.

Related to this is the second limitation in this endeavor: the need to narrow the book to something that can be considered community psychology. As a book on the history and theories of CP internationally, it is important that each contribution can be related to CP. But, what is CP? In many countries, there is not even a word or phrase that would translate to community, let alone an established field that could be identified as CP. As such, this project imposed boundaries on what was considered CP and the types of work that fell under this umbrella.

Third, as editors of a book about the history and theories of community psychology internationally, we must acknowledge the tremendous power we have held in the process, from determining which countries to include, how much space each contributor received, which topics to include or exclude in this telling of history, and whether some countries were combined by theoretical commonalities regardless of actual borders.

Although these power issues are unavoidable given the task at hand, they no doubt created a biased text. In light of this, we tried structuring this book with an awareness of some of the power dynamics at play when undertaking such a task. We included multiple authors for each country from different intellectual generations, asked each contributor to provide their own definitions for CP, and had chapter authors judge how established CP is in their respective countries (which helped to determine allocated chapter length). We also added a section at the end of most chapters where the authors themselves could compare their country with others. Although we tried to add flexibility into the process and continuously reflected on our role as editors, we acknowledge that we did not eliminate these problems completely and we probably could have done even more. That is why we encourage the reader to keep these issues in mind when learning about the histories and theories of other countries as they are presented in this book.

Below is a description of how the book is structured and some of our efforts, as editors, to distribute power among the contributors.

Structure of the Book

Chapter Size

The book is divided into two types of chapters. The first type is represented by full-length chapters in which the contributors viewed CP in their countries to be well established. The second type of chapter is short (emerging) chapters, in which the authors viewed the field to be present but rather nascent in their country. Rather then determine which countries were established or in their infancy, we asked the contributors to make this determination about their own countries. However, in Latin America, we found the field to be well established but with a centralized view that was not segmented by national borders. After talking with several Latin American community psychologists, we opted for a large Latin American chapter including 16 countries and a smaller Argentinian and Uruguayan chapter (because these two countries had a later start than the rest of the continent). Thus, these chapters do not describe the development of CP specifically in each country but rather country-specific developments that contributed to the field of social-community psychology in the region.

Authorship

In order to provide space for nonconventional ideas as well as unique perspectives, we requested that every chapter be written by at least one senior and one junior person. Our hope was to limit age and prestige biases into the story telling of the discipline as well as provide different perspectives, as people have different vantage points depending on their location within the field. Chapters could include as many authors as they liked but had to have at least two contributors at different levels in their professional career. In some cases, chapters were coauthored by senior and junior academics as well as practitioners.

In selecting contributors to this project, we were limited to those community psychologists with international connections. We identified potential contributors through attendance at international conferences, e-mails with practitioners working internationally, and snowball sampling in which we asked contributors in other countries to name people they knew working in different countries. Thus, those practitioners that do not collaborate internationally, attend conferences internationally, or publish in international journals could not be included in this project. Thus, there is a significant bias in this book as to which countries are included and which authors were invited to write each chapter.

Content

In our letter of invitation to each contributor, we offered suggestions of the type of information each chapter could include (e.g., informal historical roots, theoretical roots, formal recognition, country-specific theories, and professionalization such as organizations, courses and journals). However, we encouraged each group of authors to begin their story where they thought the beginning should be and focus the tale on the elements they thought were most important. For instance, some chapters focused on economic and/or political conditions that formed the context of the field (e.g., Hong Kong, Germany, South Africa), others focused on the period of their country's founding (e.g., Aotearoa/New Zealand, Argentina/Uruguay), whereas others discussed CP's relationship to the dominant field or practice of psychology (e.g., Australia, Greece, India).

British English

Although this volume is published through a U.S.-branch of an international publishing house, we felt it was important to leave the style of writing to the discretion of the contributors. Because the majority of the world uses British English (when writing in English), we left the contributions in their natural styles. As such, only the U.S. chapter is written in American English.

Integrative Conclusions

When editing a book, the editors must undertake the task of integrating the material presented. While we attempt this feat in the conclusion chapter, we feared that by only presenting our summary after each section, we would overshadow differences and commonalties between countries, impose our ethnocentric views on the information provided, and ignore culturally important information provided in this text. To avoid some of these concerns, we asked each contributor of a full-length chapter to write an integrative conclusion to their chapter. As each manuscript was written, it was posted to a private Web site, allowing authors to read the work of one another. Our hope was to make the task of integrating collaborative, in which each author could highlight the components they found most interesting. Our aim was to help distribute the power that normally the editors hold in having the last word when they choose how to compare and contrast each chapter. However, we must acknowledge that we still held this power throughout the editing process and in writing the concluding chapter.

Defining Terms

An unexpected challenge in editing this book was defining what *community psychology* is and how best to define it. Rather than impose our rigid structure as to what CP is and who qualifies as a practitioner of it, we asked each group of authors to define the term for themselves. While each contributor included a definition of CP, CP principles, and CP values, there was little agreement about who qualifies as a community psychologist, with the contributors from Great Britain noting that, "not all CP is being done by those who take the label of community psychologist."

Perspective

Lastly, when inviting community psychologists to contribute, we tried to include males and females as well as contributors from the dominant racial groups and well as those from indigenous and minority groups. However, each chapter is limited to the historical perspective of the people writing it. Thus, we encourage you as a reader to consider how this text would be different if each chapter were written by a person of a different gender, race, ethnicity, amount of power, level of prestige, age, sexual orientation, physical ability, or context of practice. In considering who tells the story, we challenge you to consider the influence of when the tale was told. Would this telling of history be different if it were told 20 years ago or 20 years in the future? It is the inevitable problem with history that it is dependent on who tells it and when they tell it. As Hesseltine (1945) warns, "writing intellectual history is like trying to nail jelly to the wall" (p. 4).

A Humble Beginning

We view this book as a contribution to understanding our field better, promoting communication, and providing references for learning about the theories and practices in other countries. It is an effort, an inevitably faulty one, to bridge some of the gaps in our discourse of the field. Clearly our histories are too rich, the world is too big, and this volume too small to do this task justice. Additionally, we, as editors, are limited to seeing the world through our own lenses and will undoubtedly bias what is included, how it is presented, and how it is summarized. Nonetheless, we feel this is a worthy endeavor. Hopefully, this book will help bridge the work of community psychologists around the world, expose practitioners to new theories and methods, identify our shortcomings as a field, note our successes, and provide a less ethnocentric telling of the field for students, teachers, researchers, and practitioners everywhere.

References

Hesseltine, W. (1945, May 9). Atrocities then and now. *Progressive,* p. 4.

Popper, K. R. (1973). *The Open Society and Its Enemies Volume 2: Hegel and Marx.* 5th Edition. (Originally published 1945). Milton Park: Routledge and Kegan Paul.

Warren, R. P. (1929). *John Brown: The Making of a Martyr.* New York: Payson and Clarke.

THE AMERICAS

1
The History and Theories of Community Psychology in Canada

GEOFFREY NELSON*, FRANCINE LAVOIE*, AND TERRY MITCHELL

Abstract

The authors provide a brief portrait of the socio-political-historical context of community psychology (CP) in Canada identifying linguistic, geographical, gender, and racial challenges, as well as the progressive social policies that have advanced the development and expression of CP in Canada. The growth of CP is mapped out over four decades punctuated by the development in the 1970s and 1980s of three university-based CP training programs and the recent emergence of two new Ph.D. programs in CP. The chapter provides an annotated history of CP research and action in Canada highlighting the values, theories, and main areas of practice that are linked to specific practitioners, programs, and published articles. The rich and varied expression of community psychology in Canada is structured as a discussion of six main areas of research and practice: values and ethics, community mental health, health promotion and prevention, social network intervention and mutual aid, promotion of inclusion and diversity, and social intervention and community economic development. The chapter ends with a summary of CP theory, research, values, and practice, making comparisons with CP in other countries and highlighting the challenges and related opportunities of addressing specific issues of oppression and resilience in Canada now and into the future.

Introduction

The purpose of this chapter is to review the history and theories of community psychology (CP) in Canada. We begin by providing a brief history of CP in Canada, including a review of CP training. We then highlight several areas of CP research and action in Canada, noting the theoretical viewpoints that underlie this work. We conclude by reflecting on the past and envisioning the future

*The first two authors contributed equally to this chapter

of CP in Canada. The chapter is based on published material and our knowledge about CP in Canada and thus is limited by the fact that it does not systematically review the practice of CP in Canada. Many Canadian community psychologists view CP in much the same way that it has been defined by Dalton, Elias, and Wandersman (2001): "Community psychology concerns the relationships of the individual to communities and society. Through collaborative research and action, community psychologists seek to understand and to enhance quality of life for individuals, communities, and society" (p. 5).

Historical Development of Community Psychology in Canada

The Canadian Context

Canada covers an immense landmass, second only in the world to Russia. Canada is politically structured with 10 provinces and two territories and is the northern neighbor of the United States, sharing the world's longest undefended international border. Canada, however, has a relatively small population of 32 million people. Canada was colonized by France and Britain and as a result is a country with an English majority and a contentious official French/English language policy. The largest Francophone (French-speaking) population resides in the province of Québec, which has made persistent efforts to secede from Canada in the past two decades. However, up to one-third of Canadians are of neither French nor English ethnic origin. Canada is emerging as a very visible, multicultural country with 18% of the current population being foreign born and more than 200 ethnic groups residing in Canada (Statistics Canada, 2005). Significantly, Canada also has an Aboriginal population of 1 million first peoples. The socioeconomic conditions of this indigenous population, the history of forced assimilation, and outstanding Native land claims are a mar on Canada's image as a wealthy, liberal, social democracy that celebrates diversity (Bennett, 1982). The development, expression, and focus of CP in Canada has been informed and shaped by the country's historical, social, cultural, political and geographic makeup, a point that we take up throughout the chapter.

The Roots of Community Psychology in Canada

Pols (2000) has traced the roots of CP in Canada back to Professor Edward A. Bott, who was the first chair of the Psychology Department at the University of Toronto (U of T), serving in that role from 1926 to 1956. Under Bott, the Psychology Department at U of T focused on human development and mental health. Psychology faculty members had strong ties to the Canadian National Committee for Mental Hygiene (now the Canadian Mental Health Association) and its founder Dr. Clarence Hincks. In 1951, William Line of the Psychology Department of U of T was the first psychologist to use the term *community psychology* (Babarik, 1979). Line served as President of the Canadian Psychological Association (CPA) in 1945 and President of the World Federation for Mental Health from 1951 to 1952. Bott, Line, and their colleagues worked in the field of mental health and developed school-based and community-based prevention projects (Babarik, 1979; Pols, 2000), areas that continue to be the focus of work by community psychologists today. Motivated by their experiences both during and after the two World Wars, Bott, Line, and colleagues were concerned with developing a psychology that served the interests of society. Over time, the Psychology Department at U of T shifted its focus away from CP and towards cognitive psychology.

There is no document tracing the origins of CP in Québec or in the Francophone community in the rest of Canada. As is the case of Anglophone (English-speaking) universities, experimental and clinical psychology dominated the scene in the post–World War II period. In the early years, psychologists at the Université de Montréal, like those at U of T, had a particular interest in child development and the school environment. Likewise, the need to adapt measurement and intervention tools to the French language was accompanied by consideration of cultural identity and adaptation. In his presidential address to CPA in 1964, Adrien Pinard questioned the traditional training of psychologists. He made criticisms of clinical psychology that were similar to those voiced by emerging CP proponents in the United States: focusing on disease rather than mental health and on intrapsychic factors rather than community factors. The foundations were set in Québec for the emergence of a new kind of practice, but it was only at a later date that discussions related to CP would arise.

The Growth of Community Psychology in Canada

The 1970s

The 1970s saw the emergence of CP training and practice in Canada. From 1973 to 1976, Ed Bennett of Wilfrid Laurier University chaired the Public Policy Committee of CPA's Applied Division and organized several CP events at the annual CPA conference. As well, Bennett founded the Laurier M.A. program in CP in the early 1970s, and this program formally started in 1976. Also, during the 1970s, the late Park Davidson was active in developing training in clinical–community psychology at the doctoral level at the University of British Columbia (Davidson, 1981).

At the same time, community psychologists trained in Canada and the United States were hired in Québec universities. As early as 1975, discussions about CP were taking place within the Ordre Professionnel des Psychologues du Québec (i.e., College of Psychologists), and a correspondence course was offered in the form of a text on CP by Margaret C. Kiely and Denise Moreau (1975).

Graduate training in CP in Québec also began during the 1970s. Community psychologist Margaret C. Kiely was hired by Université de Montréal in 1973. The first Ph.D. program in CP in Canada was started in

1976 at the Université du Québec à Montréal (UQAM) by Camil Bouchard and Gérard Malcuit. Very early on, Michel Tousignant, who was interested in social epidemiology, joined the team. At Université Laval, CP was first introduced in 1977–1978 with the work of Jean-Louis Campagna, who established the first suicide prevention centre in the province of Québec, and by Jérôme Guay. In 1979, the latter assumed responsibility for undergraduate and graduate training at Laval with Francine Lavoie. At the time there were no CP programs per se at this university; students received a general diploma in psychology and some completed practica in clinical psychology.

Why did CP develop in Canada during the 1970s? A major influence on Canadian CP was the emergence of CP in the United States during the 1960s and 1970s. It was during this time that Anglophone community psychologists who had been trained in the United States (some Canadians and some U.S. citizens who immigrated to Canada) were hired in Canadian universities (Walsh, 1988). As well, Davidson (1981) noted that ". . . developments common to both countries (the community mental health movement, alternatives to institutionalization, prevention programs, etc.) . . . (p. 315)" also influenced the growth of CP in Canada.

But there were also unique factors in the Canadian context that shaped the expression of CP in Canada. Bibeau, Sabatier, Corin, Tousignant, and Saucier (1989) noted some issues that influenced research on social factors and mental health in Québec: a European ethnographic perspective reconstructing the meaning of an event or the daily lives of individuals or groups and widespread interest in the identification of macro-sociological processes. Davidson (1981) identified three antecedents to CP in Canada: (a) federal health care policies, (b) the relative absence of inner-city poverty (compared with the United States), but a vast land mass that restricts people's access to services in remote communities, and (c) psychology training programs that were less dominated by traditional clinical psychology than those in the United States. We elaborate on these points later in the chapter when we examine the areas of practice of CP in Canada.

The 1980s

CP became more firmly established in Canada in the 1980s. As momentum for CP in Canada grew, Bruce Tefft of the University of Manitoba conducted a national survey of community psychologists in Canada and began to create a national CP network (Tefft, Hamilton, & Théroux, 1982). This led to the formation of the CP Section of CPA in 1982, which was spearheaded by Tefft and Pierre Ritchie of the University of Ottawa. Currently, CPA still holds an annual conference, and the CP Section Chair typically coordinates CP events.

In 1982, community psychologists Ed Bennett and Maurice Payette, along with a social work colleague, created a bilingual (French and English) journal with an interdisciplinary emphasis, the *Canadian Journal of Community Mental Health* (CJCMH). The second issue was devoted to CP in Canada

(Tefft, 1982) and included surveys of CP training (Nelson & Tefft, 1982) and CP internships (Théroux & Tefft, 1982), as well as other topical issues in Canadian CP. The CJCMH is the primary Canadian publication outlet for Canadian community psychologists, and several community psychologists have played a prominent role on its editorial board and in editing special issues. In Québec, the *Santé Mentale au Québec* journal, founded in 1976, plays a major role, addressing issues such as deinstitutionalization and alternative resources in mental health, as did the publication of an undergraduate teaching manual in CP during the 1980s (Guay, 1987).

As well, a graduate program in CP was founded in 1984 at the Ontario Institute for Studies in Education at the University of Toronto (OISE/U of T), which provided training at both the master's level and doctoral level. During the 1980s, the CP programs at Laurier and OISE/U of T held three conferences for their students and faculty.

1990 to the Present

From 1990 to the present, CP training became more concentrated in and strengthened at a few universities. Since 2003, both Laval and Laurier have developed free-standing Ph.D. programs in CP and have added faculty members in CP. At Laval, there are currently three CP professors and some contributing colleagues, all of them women. The new Ph.D. program leads to recognition by the Ordre des Psychologues de la Province de Québec (O.P.Q.), which is the regulatory body of the profession. The Laval CP program has granted 111 master's degrees (research, 54; professional, 57) and six doctoral degrees. For the Laurier program, there are currently seven CP faculty members, a full-time Director of Community Service Learning, and several affiliated faculty. There have been 189 graduates of the Laurier M.A. program. The other free-standing training program in CP in Canada is at UQAM, also recognized by the O.P.Q., where there are now five professors responsible for CP training. At UQAM, there have been 15 master's-level graduates and 35 doctoral-level graduates.

The program at OISE/U of T provided the only Ph.D. training in CP in English-speaking Canada until the Laurier program began in 2003. Due to the restructuring of U of T, CP faculty members were moved to other programs within OISE/U of T, and the CP stream ceased to exist as a standalone program around 1994, 10 years after it began. While it was in operation, the OISE CP program graduated 36 master's-level and 32 doctoral-level students.

The theoretical orientation of these training programs have their roots primarily in the training and theoretical orientations of their respective CP faculty members. Academic Canadian community psychologists have backgrounds in a range of different subdisciplines including clinical, community, developmental, feminist, critical, and applied social psychology. Promotion/prevention, attention to empowerment, work with public agencies and institutions, and program evaluation are the major theoretical emphases of training at Laval. Since its inception, the program at Laurier has emphasized a value-based framework for understanding and action, systems/ecological analysis of issues in their immediate and larger contexts, and a critical analysis of power and its implications for understanding and overcoming oppression (see Nelson, Poland, Murray, & Maticka-Tyndale, 2004). At UQAM, the concept of behavioural ecology and an interdisciplinary orientation have been the cornerstones of the program. Other sources of theoretical influence at UQAM include empowerment, social epidemiology, community building, and promotion/prevention. Program evaluation is also a major emphasis. The OISE program was known for its strong feminist theoretical basis, emphasizing critical theory and practice with a focus on race, class, gender, and sexual identity (e.g., O'Sullivan, 1990; Wine & Ristock, 1991).

CP training at some Canadian universities is or has been embedded within a training program in clinical psychology (Acadia, Manitoba, Montréal, Ottawa, Université du Québec à Trois-Rivières). This has meant that students typically receive much more emphasis on clinical psychology than CP in their training. The University of Ottawa has a growing emphasis on CP within its clinical psychology program and now has three faculty members with CP interests. Ottawa also provides training opportunities for students through its Centre for Research on Community Services. However, CP training at several universities (e.g., Guelph, Manitoba, Montréal, Simon Fraser, Windsor, Université du Québec à Trois-Rivières) is represented by only one CP faculty member. Aside from the limited breadth of training in CP that this poses, there is the additional problem that when the one CP faculty member retires, that person is not necessarily replaced by another community psychologist at these universities (e.g., Acadia, Brock, Sherbrooke). Perhaps this helps to explain the fact that from the early 1980s (Nelson & Tefft, 1982) to the mid-1990s (Walsh-Bowers, 1998), the number of Canadian universities providing training in CP diminished.

In addition to the CP section of CPA (with 75 members in 2005) and the CJCMH, there is a CP listserv called cp-loop, which was started at Laurier, but which is now open to community psychologists across Canada (there were 185 people on cp-loop in 2005). In 2002, 2004 and 2006 community psychologists at Laval, Laurier, Ottawa and UQAM held CP conferences. Recently, two CP texts have been published by Canadian authors, one in French (Dufort & Guay, 2001) and one in English (Nelson & Prilleltensky, 2005).

What Are the Areas of Research and Action of Community Psychologists in Canada and What Theories Inform That Research and Action?

In this section, we highlight *some* of the principal areas of research and action in CP in Canada and the key theoretical concepts that underlie this work.

Values and Ethics

Values and ethics have always been an important part of CP throughout the world, and a number of Canadian community psychologists have made contributions to the literature on values and ethics in CP. Isaac Prilleltensky, formerly of Canada, articulated a set of values for CP that has been very influential on the field (e.g., see Dalton et al., 2001). These values, which include social justice, self-determination, participation, caring and compassion, health, and human diversity, have served both to critique mainstream psychology, which upholds the societal status quo in the name of value neutrality, and to anchor theory, research, and action in CP (Prilleltensky & Nelson, 1997). For example, Prilleltensky, Peirson, Gould, and Nelson (1997) used these values in their consultation with a children's mental health agency undergoing an organizational renewal process. Similarly, Ed Renner has used social justice as a guiding value in his research and action related to the sexual assault of women (Renner, Alksnis, & Park, 1997), and Yann LeBossé and Francine Dufort (2001) have elaborated an empowerment model of how values and perspectives can guide the practice of CP.

Prilleltensky, Rossiter, and Walsh-Bowers (1996) developed a social-ethical framework to study clinicians' lived experiences of ethics in a qualitative research study in three different Canadian organizations and in Cuba. Similarly, Jean Pettifor (1986) critiqued the usefulness of ethical codes for CP, arguing that existing codes emphasize the relationship between psychologists and individual clients rather than the relationship between psychologists and communities. Revisions to the CPA code of ethics were prompted in part by the problems noted by Pettifor and the desire to have a code of ethics that was "made in Canada."

Pat O'Neill has also contributed to the debate about ethics in CP. O'Neill (1989) argued that community psychologists often face two ethical questions: to whom are they accountable? and for what are they accountable? Through case studies, he illustrated that these two questions are difficult to answer, because in CP it is not always clear who the client is and because there may be unforeseen consequences that arise from the intervention. In his recent 2004 presidential address to CPA, O'Neill (2005) argued ". . . that since our research can provide a justification for either changing or maintaining the status quo, it has ethical implications" (p. 13). Using several examples, he illustrated how CP can be used in the service of social responsibility. In the area of prevention, Camil Bouchard (1994) spurred debate on values, stressing the dilemmas arising from attempts to integrate personal responsibility with programs or prevention policies.

What all of these different inquires into values and applied ethics share in common is an emphasis on the contextual nature of ethical issues through an examination of real-life dilemmas experienced by community psychologists. Moreover, this work has helped to raise the consciousness of the field about the ethical challenges that saturate CP research and action and to elaborate a social-ethical framework for CP.

Community Mental Health

Following in the tradition of early CP pioneers in Canada, Canadian community psychologists have continued to work in the field of mental health. Responding to the problems of deinstitutionalization of people with mental illness in the 1970s, Canadian community psychologists with clinical training have contributed to community mental health programs for people with serious mental illness. As Davidson (1981) noted, the relationship between CP and community mental health in Canada is quite consistent with the roots of CP in the United States.

The contributions of CP to community mental health are many and varied. Richard Walsh-Bowers (Walsh, 1982) developed a psychoeducational approach to community support for people with serious mental illness, while Bruce Tefft (1987) organized a province-wide advocacy coalition to put pressure on the Manitoba government to shift resources from institutions to community supports. Tim Aubry and Heather Smith Fowler have researched homelessness and mental illness, including a controlled, longitudinal evaluation of the effectiveness of case management programs. Céline Mercier has studied the homeless, with an emphasis on subgroups made up of women, adolescents, and so forth (Fournier & Mercier, 1996); advanced quality of life research with people with mental illness (Mercier, 1998); and conducted program evaluation of community services for people with mental illness (Mercier, 1990). Myreille St-Onge has strived to have communities achieve heightened awareness of the needs of the mentally ill (St-Onge & Tessier, 2004), while Geoff Nelson and colleagues have conducted participatory action research with mental health consumer/survivor-run organizations (e.g., Nelson, Ochocka, Janzen, Trainor, & Lauzon, 2004).

Canadian community psychologists have used a number of theoretical concepts to guide this work, including empowerment, community integration, and social justice. Nelson, Lord, and Ochocka (2001) articulated a multilevel empowerment framework that they used to examine shifts in policy, organizational culture, and service delivery for individuals in one Ontario community. Ed Pomeroy and colleagues (Trainor, Pomeroy, & Pape, 1999) developed a "Framework for Support" that was adopted by the Ontario government as the centrepiece of its mental health reform process. This framework emphasizes that the person directs the support, and support is conceived more broadly than professional services and includes family, peer support, generic community services, and basic entitlements (e.g., housing, income). Based on the work of Hadley and collaborators (1987) in Great Britain, Jérôme Guay (2001) has proposed two practice approaches: (a) a client-centered practice targeting the person in need and his or her network and (b) a community-centered practice, in which the person is supported within his or her milieu before a crisis. An ecological model is at the core of both of these approaches to case management.

Health Promotion and Prevention

Like CP in other Western countries, CP in Canada has been rooted in the concept and practice of prevention, dating back to the early work of Bott and Line at the U of T. A major influence on the involvement of Canadian CP in prevention is Canadian health policy. The federal document the Lalonde Report (1974), *A New Perspective on the Health of Canadians*, was one of the first policy documents in the world to underscore the importance of prevention in health policy. Subsequent Canadian policy documents reinforced the need for a shift in Canadian health policy and practice from an exclusively biomedical focus on the treatment of disease to the inclusion of population and community-wide approaches to health promotion and disease prevention (Epp, 1986). Following the paradigm shift called for in the Lalonde report, the federal government convened a Federal-Provincial Mental Health Advisory Committee from 1975 to 1977, which included community psychologist Ed Bennett who introduced a CP way of thinking about mental health (Federal-Provincial Mental Health Advisory Committee, 1977). Contextual factors that have influenced the practice of prevention in Canada are the fact that health care in Canada is universal, publicly funded, and administered by the provinces (Davidson, 1981). This means that each province has both federal and provincial funds for health care and considerable latitude in how they organize and deliver services.

Canadian community psychologists have contributed to the development of health promotion and prevention approaches for a number of psychosocial problems, including violence in dating relations and sexual harassment (Lavoie, Vézina, Piché, & Boivin, 1995;) (http://viraj.psy.ulaval.ca), child maltreatment (Éthier & Lacharité, 2000; Laurendeau, Chamberland, & Lefort, 2002; Prilleltensky, Nelson, & Peirson, 2001), and suicide (Chagnon & Mishara, 2004; Daigle & Gariépy, 2003; Mishara & Tousignant, 2004). Many CP practitioners are employed in public health departments and other health promotion programs and have contributed to the advancement of community-based health promotion and prevention.

Prevention programs in which community psychologists have played a leadership role use a multilevel ecological analysis of risk and protective factors as their theoretical framework. For example, in an analysis of risk factors, Michel Tousignant has promoted an ethnopsychiatric and contextual approach in the epidemiology of mental health problems (Tousignant, 1992; Tousignant & Harris, 2001). As well, some Canadian community psychologists have pioneered a community development approach to prevention, in which programs are more driven by community stakeholders, particularly community residents, than by professionals. There are several examples of this community-driven approach, including Better Beginnings, Better Futures in Ontario (Peters, 1994), 1, 2, 3 GO! in Montréal (Bouchard, 2005), the Communities that Care program in eastern Ontario that is being evaluated by Bob Flynn of the University of Ottawa, the community-based crime prevention programs of the Waterloo Region Community Safety and Crime Prevention Council in Ontario led by Christiane Sadeler, and the work of Laurier's Mark Pancer with the national Centre for Excellence for Youth Engagement on youth-driven approaches to community change. Claire Chamberland and Lucie Fréchette, in a critical account of 307 prevention projects for children in Québec, conclude that interventions should try harder to harmonize services at the social and individual levels and to foster more community involvement (Chamberland et al., 2000). From a conceptual standpoint, another Canadian contribution has been the work of Sylvie Jutras on the definition of health as viewed by children and their perceptions of empowerment and their roles in the promotion of health (Jutras, 1996; Kalnins, Jutras, Normandeau, & Morin, 1998).

Community psychologists have also made contributions to prevention policy. For example, Camil Bouchard, who is now an elected representative in the Québec government, authored an influential report, *Un Québec Fou de ses Enfants* (Bouchard, Côté, Daigle, et al., 1991). This report emphasized the need for a prevention orientation for programs for children and families. In part due to this report and other social influences, Québec has led the way in Canada in progressive prevention policies for children and families, including its $7 per day childcare program (Bouchard, 2005), and in creating an infrastructure for community-based prevention programs (Laurendeau & Perreault, 1997). More recently, the work of several community psychologists, among them Marie-Hélène Gagné and Claire Malo, has brought interest in adding the concept of psychological violence to Québec legislation on child maltreatment and in training workers in child protection agencies (Malo & Gagné, 2002). Relative to the other provinces, Québec has made a more substantial commitment to promotion/prevention in its health care and social policies, and Québec community psychologists have played a leadership role in advancing the prevention agenda in that province.

Social Network Intervention and Mutual Aid

Community psychologists quickly grasped the enormous potential of turning to resources available in the environment. Several government policy documents have emphasized the importance of social networks and community resources (Epp, 1986; Paquet, Lavoie, Harnois, et al., 1985; Trainor et al., 1999). The discourse concerning networks and community resources has evolved to a certain extent from a critical assessment of the hyper-professionalization of care and the negation of the knowledge of the layperson to recognition of the place to be made for community groups contributing to innovation in health care through critiques and alternative interventions. At the same time, the need for a change in professional practice has been advocated.

Notable in Canada is the contribution of Ben Gottlieb who approached networks from a global standpoint, describing their many forms (from the buddy system in mutual aid groups to volunteer work). His main message might be summarized as follows: although researchers have stressed the concrete contribution of support networks to the well-being of various populations or situations (e.g., widowhood, divorce, diseases, etc.), it remains to be proven that professional interventions, the "artificial" creation of various support mechanisms, replicate this helpful connection (Gottlieb, 2000). Gottlieb's recent work delves into social policy related to ageing and volunteer work and the role of family caregivers of the elderly (Gottlieb, 2002; Gottlieb & Johnson, 2000).

Another original contribution dealing with natural helping networks has been advanced by Jérôme Guay. His approach in support of changes in professional practices, mostly regarding mental health problems, favours consultation among teams of professionals within an organization and the implementation of organizational change to revolutionize practice. Respectful recourse to user networks and the community concerned are seen as instrumental in any changes in practice by clinicians (Guay, 1998). Guay (1984) also proposed intervention on the scale of districts and neighbourhoods. One might summarize his thoughts by referring to a replacement of the notion of program per se, by the premise of a client and his or her social environment. Both Gottlieb and Guay have advocated for a shift in clinical–community intervention to include social networks and community support.

Mutual Aid Groups

Other Canadian community psychologists have promoted and shown interest in the potential of alternative groups, in the form of mutual aid groups or networks of alternative groups. Francine Lavoie (1989), for example, has participated in the debate on the recognition of mutual aid groups, emphasizing the presence of therapeutic factors and their crucial role in the critical assessment of traditional institutions. The training of professionals with respect to mutual aid groups has also been the subject of much documentation. Themes have included the need for participatory research (Lavoie, 1984), necessary professional skills, and ethical challenges (Lavoie, Farquharson & Kennedy, 1994; Lavoie & St-Onge, 1988). Canada was also the first country to organize a scientific conference on self-help, in 1992, which was attended by both researchers and self-help advocates (Lavoie, Borkman & Gidron, 1994).

On the other hand, comparing the philosophical stance and practices of two provincial alternative networks of psychiatric survivors, Corin, Del Barrio, and Guay (1996) drew attention to the great versatility and diversity of these alternative resources and their focus on individual special needs. Beaudoin, Duguay and Fréchette (1999) explored a local mutual aid resource in mental health offering various services to its members and highlighted the challenges experienced by this setting. Finally, as shown by Vanier and Fortin (1997), it should be noted that not all community groups share or exercise a community psychology approach.

The debate on the role of the community psychologist as a "militant or consultant" remains an issue of current interest in the context of mutual aid or network intervention (Payette & Guay, 1987). Theoretical sources are inspired by the role chosen, and one finds various forms of influence: theories on coping and social networks, on community organization at the neighbourhood or group level, and on resource mobilization and empowerment. Studies on providers of support also influence practice such as the work of Sylvie Drapeau on sibling relationships and foster care placement or divorce (Drapeau, Simard, Beaudry, & Charbonneau, 2000).

Promotion of Inclusion and Diversity

Canadian CP researchers and practitioners struggle with and for sectors of the population who have been stigmatized and/or denied equal access to rights and resources on the basis of race/culture, gender, dis/ability, or sexual identity. The attention to these issues within CP has grown over time as liberation movements for these disenfranchised groups have become more visible and active in Canada. Feminist community psychologists have advanced "gynocentric" and feminist standpoints in psychology (Caplan, 1985; Wine & Ristock, 1991) and critiqued the development and use of the *Diagnostic and Statistical Manual* as an instrument for pathologizing individuals (Caplan, 1995). June Larkin (e.g., Larkin, Rice, & Russell, 1999) has made significant contributions to the links between sexual harassment of girls, school performance, and eating disorders calling for system-level changes to promote gender equity. Ed Renner has investigated the construction of sexual assault in the Canadian criminal system and its relationship to the societal attitudes to violence against women (Renner et al., 1997). With Christine Alksnis, he is currently conducting a community-based, intersectoral campaign, called the "Making a Difference Project." This project arises out of the National Action Plan Against Sexual Assault and advocates for greater effectiveness in the prosecution of sexual assault cases (http://www.napasa.org/). In Québec, Claire Chamberland (2003) has written about influences of the social environment on both family violence and violence against women.

Marg Schneider (1991) has brought visibility to the psychosocial issues of lesbian, gay, bisexual and transgendered (LGBT) adolescents and young adults, their coming out process and need for services and peer supports. She has also provided training on service provision for transgender clients to APA and community agencies in Canada. Janice Ristock (2002) has also made considerable contributions in the area of lesbian/gay/queer studies with attention to violence within lesbian relationships. Ristock and Julien (2003) recently edited a special issue of the CJCMH entitled "Disrupting Normalcy: Lesbian, Gay, Queer Issues and Mental Health." In her studies of gay and lesbian couples and their children, Julien has focused on conjugal and family communication, conjugal distress, and social support (Julien, Chartrand, Simard, Bouthillier, & Bégin, 2003).

Native and non-Native community psychology researchers have begun to respond to the needs of Aboriginal communities to take control of research processes and to promote access to services and resources that are culturally appropriate. Collin Van Uchelen's work (Van Uchelen, Davidson, Quressette, Brasfield, & Demerais, 1997) contributed to an important shift from a needs/deficit approach to a community assets and strengths focus in working with Aboriginal populations. Van Uchelen's collaborative work with First Nations involved open-ended interviews to gain understanding of indigenous concepts of wellness and strength. After identifying these indigenous concepts, the researchers developed an action plan to support and build upon existing indigenous resources that reflected these concepts. Terry Mitchell's engagement with various Aboriginal communities has resulted in reflections on Canada's failed assimilation project; residential schooling, enforced processes of deculturation, and resultant intergenerational trauma. Mitchell theorizes that a posttraumatic stress response is an explanatory factor for the gross health disparities suffered by Aboriginal peoples and calls for increased awareness, restitution, and cultural healing (Mitchell & Maracle, 2005). Mitchell and Baker provide critical reflections on methodological issues in cross-cultural, participatory action research calling for advocacy research with Aboriginal communities and for research with explicit community building versus career building outcomes (Mitchell & Baker, 2005).

Canadian community psychologists have attended to issues of identity/marginalization and diversity/inclusion from feminist, postmodernist, anticolonial, and social justice perspectives. With increased immigration, particularly in the past 30 years, of people from Asia, Africa, and South America, Canada has become a more multicultural and diverse society. In response to this trend, community psychologists have done important research and advocacy work on the integration of new Canadians. For example, Joanna Ochocka (a part-time faculty member in Laurier's CP program), Rich Janzen, and colleagues at the Centre for Research and Education in Human Services (www.crehs.on.ca), along with academic and community partners have recently obtained a 5-year community–university research alliance grant for research and action on the issue of mental health and cultural diversity. In Québec, Michel Tousignant and colleagues (Beiser, Hou, Hyman, & Tousignant, 2002; Tousignant et al., 1999) have conducted an ecological analysis of the mental health of immigrant and refugee children, examining the impacts of both poverty and family factors.

Social Intervention and Community Economic Development

Canadian community psychologists have recognized the larger, macrodeterminants of health and well-being, including employment and income, and have strived to change social structures and processes toward the goal of social justice. Ed Bennett (2003) has described his work in community economic development in rural communities, particularly with the Old Order

Amish people. The focus of his efforts has been on sustaining their traditional ways of life in the face of increasing economic, political, and bureaucratic obstacles. Jack Quarter (1992) has outlined the role of worker-owned cooperatives as an important social intervention strategy. Danielle Papineau and Margaret Kiely (1996) described a participatory evaluation of an organization that promotes a variety of community economic development initiatives for immigrants and refugees and other economically disadvantaged groups in Montréal. Papineau and Landry (2001) offer a reminder of the large range of groups associated with local economic development and of their challenges. The research of Racine and St-Onge (2000) and work by Lucie Fréchette (2000) has contributed to a better understanding of the potential of community kitchens as important community initiatives. The fate of economically and socially excluded young fathers has been described in the work of Devault, Lacharité, Ouellet, and Forget (2003). Their research should lead to the development of a means to reach out to these individuals. Working for the United Church of Canada, David Hallman (1987) played a leadership role in organizing a successful international boycott of the Nestlé corporation over its practice of marketing infant formula in developing nations that, for many reasons, is associated with infant malnutrition and health problems.

Canadian community psychologists have been influenced by the distinction between first-order (ameliorative) and second-order (transformative) change and the emphasis on "reframing the problem" (Bennett, 1987, 2003; Nelson & Prilleltensky, 2005). Another theoretical perspective on social change is O'Neill's theory of cognitive CP (2000). O'Neill (1981) has linked research from social cognition with the ecological perspective in CP to elaborate on the importance of the person–environment interaction for social change.

Summary and Reflection

Research and practice in CP has been influenced both by trends within the subdiscipline of CP and contextual factors in the Canadian milieu. Like many countries in the Western world, Canadian CP has been firmly rooted in community mental health, health promotion/prevention, and social network intervention and mutual aid. As Prilleltensky and Nelson (1997) pointed out, these areas and related theoretical concepts (e.g., social support, risk, and protection) reflect the values of health, caring, and compassion. During the 1980s, the values of self-determination and participation became more prominent in the work of Canadian community psychologists (Prilleltensky & Nelson, 1997). The concept of empowerment, which is based on the values of self-determination and participation, came into sharper focus in the areas of community mental health and health promotion/prevention. The concepts of consumer choice and control in mental health, and a community-driven approach to prevention, are examples of this shift in focus.

In addition to these disciplinary influences, elements of the larger Canadian context have influenced these traditional areas of practice. Policies that have supported the shift from treatment to prevention and that have emphasized the importance of informal social support and mutual aid have reinforced work in these areas. Moreover, the fact that Canada has government-funded public health care has meant that promotion/prevention and community mental health programs have received some attention in government budgets. With respect to the area of social network intervention and mutual aid, Davidson (1981) noted that increased reliance on social networks and natural helpers is a particularly important consideration for rural and remote communities that have limited access to professional services.

Reflecting the focus on and value of diversity, there was emergence of increased attention to issues of oppression and inclusion in Canadian CP during the 1980s. Work on sexism, homophobia, and related issues was led in English Canada by the OISE/U of T CP program, which had a strong emphasis on feminist theory and critical analysis of race, class, gender, and sexual orientation. Attention to the contemporary challenges faced by First Nations people by CP stems from the historical legacy of systemic oppression of Aboriginal people in Canada and contemporary concerns about how to deal with the consequences of this legacy (Bennett, 1982; Mitchell & Maracle, 2005). As well, more recent pressures from diverse groups and the responses of governments in Canada (e.g., increased immigration and Canada's policy of multiculturalism, pressure from gay rights organizations and the legalization of gay marriage) have created conditions favourable to a more inclusive society.

The CP areas of social intervention and community economic development attend to the value of social justice and the fair and equitable distribution of resources in society. In Québec, the work of community psychologists has been consistent with the aims of the previous provincial government to create more just social policies (e.g., Bouchard, 2005). In English Canada, particularly through the work of Laurier CP faculty, students, and graduates, CP has established a history of concern about social justice and the need to bring about systemic, transformative change through social intervention (Bennett, 1987).

Conclusion: Opportunities and Challenges for the Future of Community Psychology in Canada

Although CP in Canada took root in the period immediately following World War II with its connection to mental health and schools, it was not until the 1980s that it coalesced on a nationwide basis. In its short 25-year history, much has been accomplished in Canadian CP. Canadian community psychologists have built a few graduate training programs, some of which have been sustained or strengthened in the past few years, with more than

300 master's-level graduates and 70 doctoral-level graduates from four of these programs; they have created a bilingual, interdisciplinary journal, the CJCMH, and other vehicles for communication and networking, including three recent conferences; and they have begun to develop a body of research and practice on several different important themes/issues that we touched upon in this chapter. Moreover, the main CP training programs reflect a healthy diversity of theoretical perspectives.

In the future, researchers and practitioners of CP in Canada face specific challenges and exciting opportunities at several different levels. Within the discipline of psychology, CP will continue to face the challenge of being a minority or altogether absent in Canadian psychology departments that have been dominated by experimental and clinical psychology. Competition for resources and legitimacy is difficult when the science and practice of psychology have historically been defined in ways that marginalize or exclude CP and resist its growth. The subdiscipline of CP is seldom mentioned in introductory psychology courses, and many undergraduate psychology majors in Canada can go through their entire 4 years of university without ever hearing of CP. The lack of visibility of CP extends beyond the walls of universities into work settings, professional certification organizations, and the community.

However, there are also opportunities for CP within psychology. The pioneering work of community psychologists in areas such as prevention and social support has been acknowledged within the mainstream of psychology, thus enabling greater collaboration with colleagues in traditional areas, such as clinical, social, and developmental. As well, community psychologists may be able to forge partnerships with other newly emerging areas of psychology, including feminist psychology, cultural diversity, and health psychology. Such partnerships could help to provide community psychologists with enough of a critical mass to advance their work and avoid professional isolation. Opportunities for bridging of CP have also been identified in Latin America where (in this text) they identify the opportunity for the development of community clinical psychology. In Britain, where CP is also viewed as a "minority pursuit," but its principles have been incorporated into the general practice of psychology, they note a parallel opportunity of fostering a "really social psychology" (this volume).

Canadian public policy also offers opportunities and poses challenges for CP. As a country that has historically aspired to be a "just society" with national health care, social welfare programs, an appreciation for cultural diversity, and an emphasis on social solidarity, Canadian public policies have often supported or complemented the goals of CP. Consider, for example, the following definition of mental health from a federal mental health policy document:

Mental health is the capacity of the individual, the group and the environment to interact with one another in ways that promote subjective well-being, the optimal development and use of mental abilities (cognitive, affective, and relational), the achievement of individual and collective goals consistent with justice and the attainment and preservation of conditions of fundamental equality. (Epp, 1988, p. 7)

This definition reads like it was written by a community psychologist, as it embodies several core constructs of community psychology: ecology, strengths orientation, and social justice. Community psychologists are well-suited in terms of their values, theoretical perspectives, and research and action skills to shape public policy and programs and to contribute to their implementation and evaluation. As we have shown in this chapter, there are numerous examples of the contributions of community psychologists to many different areas of public policy. While from an international perspective Canadians enjoy the benefits and relative security of a social democracy, as cherished Canadian public policies are under attack, we must heed the lessons of our Latin American colleagues (this volume) who discuss empowerment in terms of the need "to generate conscious citizens."

Beginning in the 1980s and continuing until today, federal social policies have been eroded, with a reduction of transfer payments to the provinces for health, education, and social services. These shifts in public policy challenge the values and mission of CP, for a just and equitable society, and call for community psychologists to raise their political consciousness and to increase their knowledge of the public policy process in order to resist further dismantling of the welfare state (Nelson & Prilleltensky, 2005).

There are also challenges and opportunities related to the geography, gender politics, languages, and culture of Canada. As we noted, Canada is a very large country in terms of land mass, but training in CP is concentrated in Ontario and Québec. CP training at the doctoral level is needed so that CP scholars can find employment in universities across the country. Gender politics are a continuing concern for CP in Canada. Historically, the majority of faculty members in CP programs have been male, while the majority of graduate students have been female. Although the nature of the faculty complement is changing, we need to remain vigilant about creating and sustaining a more diverse and gender balanced profile and nonracist, nonsexist climates in our training programs.

The bilingual nature of Canada poses a challenge and significant opportunity for CP. The formation of the CJCMH and recent conferences and collaborations between Anglophone and Francophone community psychologists have helped to build links across these two language groups. But there has also been resistance, if not prejudice, to working with the minority population of French Canadian community psychologists, just as there has been conflict between these two groups in the larger historical and political context. Through ongoing links, our hope is that this bilingual, bicultural tradition will continue to be viewed as a source of enrichment.

Likewise, our colonial history also poses a challenge and a focus of resistance and healing. The Aboriginal tradition in Canada should be a source of humility and inspiration to CP, as the values of Aboriginal communities (e.g., holism, cooperation, caring) preceded and are compatible with those of CP (Connors & Maidman, 2001). In Latin America, New Zealand, and Australia, our CP counterparts (this volume) have also identified both a responsibility and an opportunity for CP researchers/theorists/educators/ practitioners to acknowledge the lived values, epistemologies, and practices of the world's indigenous peoples. More efforts are needed to recruit First Nations' faculty and students into our CP programs and to collaborate with First Nations' communities on issues of concern to them. Moreover, as Canada is becoming a more culturally diverse nation, more work in CP will need to be focussed on the development of culturally sensitive interventions and research. Increasingly the work of Canadian community psychologists must address issues of oppression and resilience in relation to the cultural historical and linguistic makeup of our diverse population with attention to the challenges and opportunities of an increasingly diverse community with unresolved colonial roots.

Acknowledgments. The authors thank the editors and the following individuals who provided information for the chapter and/or who read and gave comments on an earlier draft of this chapter: Ed Bennett, Marie-Hélène Gagné, Margaret Kiely, Céline Mercier, Pat O'Neill, Jack Quarter, and Michel Tousignant.

References

Babarik, P. (1979). The buried Canadian roots of community psychology. *Journal of Community Psychology, 7*, 362-367.

Beaudoin, L., Duguay, P., & Fréchette, L. (1999). L'ODEC et la santé mentale: De l'entraide à l'ouverture sur la communauté locale. *Revue Canadienne de Santé Mentale Communautaire, 18(2)*, 73-86.

Beiser, M., Hou, F., Hyman, I., & Tousignant, M. (2002). Poverty, family process, and the mental health of immigrant children in Canada. *American Journal of Public Health, 92*, 220-227.

Bennett, E. M. (1982). Native persons: An assessment of their relationship to the dominant culture and challenges for change. *Canadian Journal of Community Mental Health, 1(2)*, 21-31.

Bennett, E. M. (Ed.). (1987). *Social intervention: Theory and practice*. Lewiston, NY: The Edwin Mellen Press.

Bennett, E. M. (2003). Emancipatory responses to oppression: The template of land-use planning and the Old Order Amish of Ontario. *American Journal of Community Psychology, 31*, 157-171.

Bibeau, G., Sabatier, C., Corin, E., Tousignant, M. & Saucier, J.-F. (1989). La recherche sociale anglo-saxonne en santé mentale: Tendances, limites et impasses. *Santé Mentale au Québec, 14(1)*, 103-120.

Bouchard, C. (1994). Discours et parcours de la prévention de la violence: Une réflexion sur les valeurs en jeu. *Revue Canadienne de Santé Mentale Communautaire, 13(2)*, 37-45.

Bouchard, C. (2005). Commentary - Disadvantaged children and families: The power of a just asymmetry. In G. Nelson & I. Prilleltensky (Eds.), *Community psychology: In pursuit of liberation and well-being* (pp. 464-466). London: Palgrave Macmillan.

Bouchard, C. (2005). Searching for impacts - The case of a community-based initiative: 1, 2, 3 GO! In J. Scott & H. Ward (Eds.), *Safeguarding and promoting the wellbeing of children, families, and their communities* (pp. 228-241). London: Jessica Kingsley Publishers.

Bouchard, C., Bouchard, C., Côté, D., Daigle, A., Désy, J., Duplantie, J.-P., Lavoie-Gauthier, L., Guimont, M., Laforest, B., Lemieux, D., Lemire, S., Manseau, H., Moreau, N., Ouellet, O., Roberge, C., Rouleau, R., Thibaudeau, S., Tremblay, R. E., & Trudel, A. (1991). *Un Québec fou de ses enfants*. Rapport de Groupe de travail pour les jeunes, Québec, Direction de Communications, Ministère de la Santé et des Services Sociaux.

Caplan, P. J. (1985). *The myth of women's masochism*. Toronto: University of Toronto Press.

Caplan, P. J. (1995). *They say you're crazy: How the world's most powerful psychiatrists decide who's normal*. Reading, MA: Addison-Wesley.

Chagnon, F., & Mishara, B.L. (Éds.). (2004). *Évaluation de programmes en prévention du suicide*. Ste-Foy: Presses de l'Université du Québec. Éditions EDK.

Chamberland, C. (2003). *Violence parentale et violence conjugale: Des réalités plurielles, multidimensionelles et interreliées*. Sainte-Foy: Presses de l'Université du Québec.

Chamberland, C., Dallaire, N., Hébert, J., Fréchette, L., Lindsay, J., & Cameron, S. (2000). Are ecological and social models influencing prevention practice? An overview of the state of affairs in Québec for child, youth and family intervention. *Journal of Primary Prevention, 21*, 101-125.

Connors, E., & Maidman, F. (2001). A circle of healing: Family wellness in Aboriginal communities. In I. Prilleltensky, G. Nelson, & L. Peirson (Eds.), *Promoting family wellness and preventing child maltreatment: Fundamentals for thinking and action* (pp. 349-416). Toronto: University of Toronto Press.

Corin, E., Del Barrio, L. R., & Guay, L. (1996). Les figures de l'aliénation: Un regard alternatif sur l'appropriation du pouvoir. *Revue Canadienne de Santé Mentale Communautaire, 15(2)*, 45-67.

Daigle, M., & Gariépy, Y. (2003). Vers une meilleure concertation dans les services offerts aux hommes suicidaires. *Revue Québécoise de Psychologie, 24(1)*, 243-254.

Dalton, J. H., Elias, M. J., & Wandersman, A. (2001). *Community psychology: Linking individuals and communities*. Toronto: Wadsworth/Nelson Thompson Learning.

Davidson, P. O. (1981). Some cultural, political, and professional antecedents of community psychology in Canada. *Canadian Psychology, 22*, 315-320.

Devault, A., Lacharité, C., Ouellet, F., & Forget, G. (2003). Les pères en situation d'exclusion économique et sociale. *Nouvelles Pratiques Sociales, 16(1)*, 45-58.

Drapeau, S., Simard, M., Beaudry, M., & Charbonneau, C. (2000). Siblings in family transitions. *Family Relations, 49(1)*, 77-85.

Dufort, F., & Guay, J. (Eds.). (2001). *Agir au coeur des communautés: La psychologie communautaire et le changement social*. Saint-Nicolas: Les Presses de l'Université Laval.

Epp, J. (1986). Achieving health for all: A framework for health promotion. *Canadian Journal of Public Health, 77*, 393-407.

Epp, J. (1988). *Mental health for Canadians: Striking a balance*. Ottawa, Ontario: Ministry of Supplies and Services.

Éthier, L. S., & Lacharité, C. (2000). Impact of a multidimensional intervention program applied to families at risk for child neglect. *Child Abuse Review, 9(1)*, 19-36.

Federal-Provincial Mental Health Advisory Committee (1977). The mental health aspects of a comprehensive health system. *Canada's Mental Health, 25(1)*, 3-7.

Fournier, L., & Mercier, C. (1996). *Sans domicile fixe: Au delà du stéréotype*. Montréal: Méridien.

Fréchette, L. (2000). *Entraide et services de proximité, l'expérience des cuisines collectives*. Sainte-Foy: Presses de l'Université du Québec.

Gottlieb, B. H. (2000). Selecting and planning support interventions. In S. Cohen, L. G. Underwood, & B. H. Gottlieb (Eds.), *Social support measurement and intervention: A guide for health and social scientists* (pp. 195-220). London: Oxford University Press.

Gottlieb, B. H. (2002). Older volunteers: A precious resource under pressure. *Canadian Journal on Aging, 21(1)*, 5-9.

Gottlieb, B. H., & Johnson, J. (2000). Respite programs for caregivers of persons with dementia: A review with practice implications. *Aging and Mental Health, 4(2)*, 119-129.

Guay, J. (1984). *L'intervenant professionnel face à l'aide naturelle*. Alma: Gaëtan Morin.

Guay, J. (Ed.). (1987). *Manuel de psychologie communautaire*. Boucherville: Gaëtan Morin.

Guay, J. (1998). L'intervention clinique communautaire: Les familles en détresse. Montréal: Les Presses de l'Université de Montréal.

Guay, J. (2001). L'intervention de réseau et l'approche milieu. In F. Dufort & J. Guay (Eds.), *Agir au coeur des communautés: La psychologie communautaire et le changement social* (pp. 249-295). Saint-Nicolas: Les Presses de l'Université Laval.

Hadley, R., Cooper, M., Dale, P., & Stacy, G. (1987). *A community social worker's handbook*. London: Tavistock Publications.

Hallman, D. (1987). The Nestlé boycott: The success of a citizens' coalition in social intervention. In E. M. Bennett (Ed.), *Social intervention: Theory and practice* (pp. 187-229). Lewiston, NY: The Edwin Mellen Press.

Julien, D., Chartrand, E., Simard, M. C., Bouthillier, D., & Bégin, J. (2003). Conflict, social support, and conjugal adjustment: An observational study of heterosexual, gay, and lesbian couples' communication. *Journal of Family Psychology, 17*, 419-428.

Jutras, S. (1996). L'appropriation: Un modèle approprié pour la promotion de la santé mentale des enfants? *Revue Canadienne de Santé Mentale Communautaire, 15(2)*, 123-142.

Kalnins, I., Jutras, S., Normandeau, S., & Morin, P. (1998). Children's health actions within the context of daily living. *American Journal of Health Behavior, 22(6)*, 460-472.

Kiely, M., & Moreau, D. (1975). Psychologie communautaire. Courrier Cours. *Cours par correspondance de la Corporation professionnelle des psychologues du Québec. 2(1)*, février, 1-14.

Lalonde, M. (1974). *A new perspective on the health of Canadians*. Ottawa: National Health and Welfare.

Larkin, J., Rice, C., & Russell, V. (1999). Sexual harassment education and the prevention of disordered eating. In N. Piran, M. Levine, & C. Steiner-Adair (Eds.), *Preventing eating disorders: A handbook of intervention and special challenges* (pp. 194-207). Philadelphia: Brunner/Mazel.

Laurendeau, M.-C., Chamberland, C., & Lefort, L. (2002). Étude pancanadienne sur le bien-être des familles et la prévention des mauvais traitements: La perception des informatrices et informateurs clés québécois. *Nouvelles Pratiques Sociales, 15*, 131-146.

Laurendeau, M.-C., & Perreault, R. (1997). L'amorce du virage préventif en santé mentale au Québec: Enquête sur les politiques, les structures et les programmes de prévention en santé mentale. *Psychologie Canadienne, 38*, 13-24.

Lavoie, F. (1984). Action-research: A new model of interaction between the professional and self-help groups. In A. Gartner & F. Riessman (Eds.), *Mental health and the self-help revolution* (pp. 173-182). New York: Human Science Press.

Lavoie, F. (1989). Évaluation des groupes d'entraide. In J.-M. Romeder et collaborateurs. *Les groupes d'entraide et la santé: Nouvelles solidarités* (pp. 77-98). Ottawa: Conseil canadien de développement social. [In English: The Self-help way]

Lavoie, F., Borkman, T., & Gidron, B. (Eds.). (1994). *Self-help and mutual aid groups: International and multicultural perspectives*. New York: Haworth Press.

Lavoie, F., Farquharson, A., & Kennedy, M. (1994). Workshop on "Good Practice" in the collaboration between professionals and mutual aid groups. *Prevention in Human Services, 11(2)*, 303-313.

Lavoie, F., & St-Onge, M. (1988). Non-ingérence, non-indifférence: l'implication des intervenant-e-s professionnel-le-s auprès de groupes d'entraide en santé mentale. *Santé Mentale au Québec, 13*, 203-207.

Lavoie, F., Vézina, L., Piché, C., & Boivin, M. (1995). Evaluation of a prevention program for violence in teen dating relationships. *Journal of Interpersonal Violence, 10*, 517-525.

LeBossé, Y., & Dufort, F. (2001). Le pouvoir d'agir (empowerment) des personnes et des communautés: une autre façon d'intervenir. In F. Dufort & J. Guay (Eds.), *Agir au coeur des communautés: La psychologie communautaire et le changement social* (pp. 75-115). Saint-Nicolas: Les Presses de l'Université Laval.

Malo, C., & Gagné, M.-H. (2002). Quand c'est à la tête et au coeur que ça frappe! Développement d'un outil de dépistage des mauvais traitements psychologiques envers les enfants. *Défi Jeunesse, 7(2)*, 21-27.

Mercier, C. (1990). L'évaluation des programmes d'intervention en milieu naturel. *Canadian Journal of Program Evaluation, 5(1)*, 1-16.

Mercier, C. (1998). Quality of life evaluation in mental health: The Canadian experience. *Canadian Journal of Community Mental Health, Special supplement No. 3, Winter, 17*, 53-59. Traduction française: 59-66.

Mishara, B. L., & Tousignant, M. (2004). *Comprendre le suicide*. Montréal: Presses de l'Université de Montréal.

Mitchell, T., & Maracle, D. (2005). Healing the generations: Post-traumatic stress and the health status of the Canadian Aboriginal Population *Journal of Aboriginal Health, 1(2)*, 14-23.

Mitchell, T., & Baker, E. (2005). Community building vs career building research: The challenges, risks, and responsibilities of conducting participatory cancer research with Aboriginal communities. *Journal of Cancer Education, Special Supplement, 20* (Spring), 41-46.

Nelson, G., Lord, J., & Ochocka, J. (2001). *Shifting the paradigm in community mental health: Towards empowerment and community*. Toronto: University of Toronto Press.

Nelson, G., Ochocka, J., Janzen, R., Trainor, J., & Lauzon, S. (2004). A comprehensive evaluation approach for mental health consumer-run organizations: Values, conceptualization, design, and action. *Canadian Journal of Program Evaluation, 19(3)*, 29-53.

Nelson, G., Poland, B., Murray, M., & Maticka-Tyndale, E. (2004). Building capacity in community health action research: Towards a framework of training guidelines. *Action Research, 2*, 389-408.

Nelson, G., & Tefft, B. M. (1982). A survey of graduate education in community psychology in Canada. *Canadian Journal of Community Mental Health, 1(2)*, 6-13.

Nelson, G., & Prilleltensky, I. (2005). *Community psychology: In pursuit of liberation and well-being*. London: Palgrave Macmillan.

O'Neill, P. (1981). Cognitive community psychology. *American Psychologist, 36*, 457-469.

O'Neill, P. (1989). Responsible to whom? Responsible for what? Some ethical issues in community intervention. *American Journal of Community Psychology, 17*, 323-341.

O'Neill, P. (2000). Cognition in social context: Contributions to community psychology. In J. Rappaport & E. Seidman (Eds.), *Handbook of community psychology* (pp. 115-132). New York: Kluwer Academic/Plenum.

O'Neill, P. (2005). The ethics of problem definition. *Canadian Psychology, 46*, 13-20.

O'Sullivan, E. (1990). *Critical psychology and critical pedagogy*. New York: Begin and Garvey.

Papineau, D., & Kiely, M. C. (1996). Peer evaluation of an organization involved in community economic development. *Canadian Journal of Community Mental Health, 15(1)*, 83-96.

Papineau, D., & Landry, M. (2001). La contribution du psychologue communautaire aux initiatives de développement économique communautaire. In F. Dufort & J. Guay (Éds.), *Agir au coeur des communautés: La psychologie communautaire et le changement social* (pp. 298-322). Saint-Nicolas: Les Presses de l'Université Laval.

Paquet, R., Lavoie, F., Harnois, G., Fitzgerald, M., Gourgue, C., & Fontaine, N. (1985). *La santé mentale: Rôles et place des ressources alternatives*. Collection: Avis du Comité de la santé mentale du Québec. Québec: Gouvernement du Québec.

Payette, M., & Guay, J. (1987). Tour d'horizon des types d'intervention. In J. Guay (Ed.), *Manuel québécois de psychologie communautaire* (pp. 65-85). Chicoutimi: Gaëtan Morin.

Peters, R. DeV. (1994). Better Beginnings, Better Futures: A community-based approach to primary prevention. *Canadian Journal of Community Mental Health, 13(2)*, 183-188.

Pettifor, J. L. (1986). Ethical standards for community psychology. *Canadian Journal of Community Mental Health, 5(1)*, 39-48.

Pinard, A. (1964). Le modèle scientiste-professionnel: synthèse ou prothèse. *Psychologie canadienne, Canadian Psychology, 5a(4)*, 187-208.

Pols, H. (2000). Between the laboratory, the school, and the community: The psychology of human development, Toronto, 1916-1956. *Canadian Journal of Community Mental Health, 19(2)*, 13-30.

Prilleltensky, I., & Nelson, G. (1997). Community psychology: Reclaiming social justice. In D. Fox & I. Prilleltensky (Eds.), *Critical psychology: An introduction* (pp. 166-184). Thousand Oaks, CA: Sage.

Prilleltensky, I., Nelson, G., & Peirson, L. (Eds.). (2001). *Promoting family wellness and preventing child maltreatment: Fundamentals for thinking and action*. Toronto: University of Toronto Press.

Prilleltensky, I., Peirson, L., Gould, J., & Nelson, G. (1997). Planning mental health services for children and youth: Part I - A value-based approach. *Evaluation and Program Planning, 20*, 163-172.

Prilleltensky, I., Rossiter, A., & Walsh-Bowers, R. (1996). Preventing harm and promoting ethical discourse in the helping professions: Conceptual, research, analytical, and action frameworks. *Ethics and Behaviour, 6*, 287-306.

Quarter, J. (1992). *Canada's social economy: Cooperatives, non-profits, and other community enterprises*. Toronto: Lorimer.

Racine, S., & St-Onge, M. (2000). Les cuisines collectives: Une voie vers la promotion de la santé mentale. *Revue Canadienne de Santé Mentale Communautaire, 19(1)*, 37-62.

Renner, K. E., Alksnis, C., & Park, L. (1997). The standard of social justice as a research process. *Canadian Psychology, 38*, 91-102.

Ristock, J. (2002). *No more secrets: Violence in lesbian relationships*. New York: Routledge.

Ristock, J., & Julien, D. (Eds.). (2003). Disrupting normalcy: Lesbian, gay, queer issues and mental health [Special issue]. *Canadian Journal of Community Mental Health, 22(2)*, 1-139.

Schneider, M. (1991). Developing services for lesbian and gay adolescents. *Canadian Journal of Community Mental Health, 10(1)*, 133-151.

Statistics Canada (2005). *Canadian statistics – Tables by subject: Population and demography*. Available at http://www40.statcan.ca/01/cst01/popula.htm.

St-Onge, M., & Tessier, L. (2004). Les personnes d'âge adulte ayant des troubles mentaux et la diversité de leurs besoins: Des repères pour l'action. In R. Émard & T. Aubry (Éds.), *Suivi communautaire en santé mentale: Une invitation à bâtir sa vie* (pp. 1-29). Ottawa: Presses de l'Université d'Ottawa.

Tefft, B. M. (Ed.). (1982). Community psychology in Canada. *Canadian Journal of Community Mental Health* [special issue], *1(2)*.

Tefft, B. (1987). Advocacy coalitions as a vehicle for mental health system reform: A case study. In E. M. Bennett (Ed.), *Social intervention: Theory and practice* (pp. 155-185). Queenston, ON: The Edwin Mellen Press.

Tefft, B. M., Hamilton, G. K., & Théroux, C. (1982). Community psychology in Canada: Toward developing a national network. *Canadian Journal of Community Mental Health, 1(2)*, 93-103.

Théroux, C., & Tefft, B. M. (1982). Internships in community psychology. *Canadian Journal of Community Mental Health, 1(2)*, 14-19.

Tousignant, M. (1992). *Les origines sociales et culturelles des troubles psychologiques*. Collection Psychiatrie ouverte. Paris: Presses Universitaires de France.

Tousignant, M., Habimana, E., Biron, C., Malo, C., Sidoli-Leblanc, E., & Bendris, N. (1999). The Québec Adolescent Refugee Project: Psychopathology and family variables in a sample from 35 nations. *The American Journal of the Academy of Child and Adolescent Psychiatry, 38*, 1426-1432.

Tousignant, M., & Harris, T. E. (2001). *Événements de vie et psychiatrie*. Collection Références en Psychiatrie. Paris: Doin.

Trainor, J., Pomeroy, E., & Pape, B. (1999). *Building a framework for support: A community development approach to mental health policy*. Toronto: Canadian Mental Health Association/National Office.

Vanier, C., & Fortin, D. (1997). Ressources en santé mentale dans la communauté: Développement d'une typologie. *Revue Canadienne de Santé Mentale Communautaire, 16(1)*, 87-103.

Van Uchelen, C. P., Davidson, S. F., Quressette, S. V., Brasfield, C. R., & Demerais, L. H. (1997). What makes us strong: Urban aboriginal perspectives on wellness and strength. *Canadian Journal of Community Mental Health, 16(2)*, 37-50.

Walsh, R. T. (1982). A psychoeducational approach to community intervention with ex-mental patients. *Canadian Journal of Community Mental Health, 1(2)*, 76-84.

Walsh, R. T. (1988). Current developments in community psychology in Canada. *Journal of Community Psychology, 16*, 296-305.

Walsh-Bowers, R. (1998). Community psychology in the Canadian psychological family. *Canadian Psychology, 37*, 281-287.

Wine, J. D., & Ristock, J. (1991). *Women and social change: Feminist activism in Canada*. Toronto: James Lorimer and Company Publishers.

2
History and Theory of Community Psychology: An International Perspective of Community Psychology in the United States: Returning to Political, Critical, and Ecological Roots

HOLLY L. ANGELIQUE AND MARCI R. CULLEY

Abstract

In this chapter, we explore the historical roots of community psychology in the United States from a critical feminist perspective. We discuss how unique historical and sociopolitical contexts contributed to the development of the field as well as its fundamental theories and concepts. Our feminist critique of the field illustrates how these contexts contributed to what can be described as largely Anglo- and androcentric scholarship, suggesting an ongoing struggle with tensions between stated values and actual research and practice. Despite this, we argue that an organic, ever present tendency to distinguish its identity through critique has allowed the field, and those of us who work within it, to move toward better representation of our stated goals and values. We contend that the field would be well-served by a return to its critical, ecological roots via explicit and intentional analyses of social power at multiple levels. Acknowledging the field's roots in white, male power and privilege is one way to facilitate discourse from the margins and to remain forever critical in our growth and development in ways that honor the community psychology's stated value of social justice.

Introduction

Like all disciplines, community psychology (CP) in the United States reflects its historical and sociopolitical roots. We define CP as a field that engages in research and action to promote individual, relational, and societal well-being while working to reduce suffering and oppression. CP values (a) diversity,

(b) ecological analyses, (c) a critical perspective, (d) methodological pluralism, (e) interdisciplinary collaboration, and (f) social change.

From its inception, CP in the United States was situated to be a politically oriented discipline. It was born in a time of widespread social change and emerging critical consciousness as individuals mobilized to analyze and address societal power differences. As such, the discipline's foundation is rooted in an ecological framework, one that links individual change to environmental contexts. In this chapter, we provide a brief overview of the history of CP in the United States.[1,2] We also present an overview of prominent theories of the field. In addition to describing the history and theories of CP, we offer a feminist critique of the field. Throughout the chapter, we argue that CP has struggled with tensions between its values and its actual research and practice as a social science. Finally, we discuss the future of the field, as we envision CP returning to its political, critical roots.

---

[1] Despite our recognition of ever increasing influence from other scholars in other countries, in this chapter, we review literature that has been published in the United States and contributed by U.S. authors. While works from around the world are published in U.S. journals and influence CP in the United States, we have refrained from discussing them here. We realize that we are artificially decontextualizing the development of U.S. community psychology. However, in an effort to avoid the inappropriate appropriation of the contributions to CP from other areas of the world, we feel that it is important to restrict our discussion to scholars (at least first authors) who have published while working in the United States.

[2] Initially, the editors of this book asked us to contribute a chapter that would be more inclusive of the diversity of theories and practice in CP than most Anglo/androcentric historical accounts. However, as this project took shape, we realized that the history of CP in the United States was indeed overshadowed by a white, male perspective. Reporting differently would create an inaccurate revisionist account. Therefore, we felt obliged to describe the foundation of CP as it was created by our fore-"fathers." However, as feminists, we were also committed to reporting the contributions of scholars from a diversity of backgrounds to illustrate how the field has also been shaped by scholars from the margins (including women, racial and ethnic minorities, members of the GLBT community, and persons with disabilities in particular). We soon realized this project remained overly ambitious. Given the page limitations and the requirement to cover the historical and theoretical development of CP in the United States, any serious feminist engagement would be precluded. From this standpoint, we developed a historical presentation with a critical, feminist eye. We realize the limitations inherent in this plan—a feminist approach would require more in-depth analyses, and a feminist history would require further critique. However, we hope that our chapter succeeds in providing an inclusive description of CP in the United States; one that is accurate in its reporting and remains true to the ongoing critiques of the field. We also hope that our predictions about the future of the field are accurate as we envision a CP that is emerging to better reflect its own value stance.

Historical Roots

In this section, we give an overview of the historical developments that led to the emergence of CP in the United States.[3] We offer a brief time line of events specific to the area of mental health and then embed these events within a sociohistorical context. We focus on national public policy changes prior to the origin of CP and on training guides and outlets for scholars after the discipline was established. We end our time line in 1977, when CP's roots were firmly in place.

1946: President Truman signed the National Mental Health Act: This act gave the U.S. Public Health Service more power, supported increased research and was designed to train clinicians in mental health professions. It also led to the establishment of the National Institute of Mental Health (NIMH), making federal funds available for training in mental health issues.

1949: The U.S. Public Health Service sponsored a conference in Boulder, Colorado which led to the development of The Boulder Model; a model for the education of clinical psychologists that included both research and practice. This set the stage for psychology to separate from psychiatry.

1955: President Eisenhower empaneled The Joint Commission on Mental Illness and Mental Health to evaluate the field.

1961: The Joint Commission on Mental Illness and Mental Health released its final report. NIMH responded by proposing a system of community mental health centers.

1963: President Kennedy signed the Community Mental Health Centers Act of 1963, which authorized federal funds for local mental health centers.

1964: President Johnson declared the War on Poverty through the Economic Opportunity Act of 1964 which released federal funds to develop and evaluate social programs.

1965: At a conference on the training of mental health practitioners in Swampscott, Massachusetts, a group of psychologists called for the creation

---

[3] We restrict our focus to two main areas. First, we describe national public policy that preceded the origin of CP. We do not want to imply that public policy ceased in the shaping of the field after the Swampscott convention. However, in the interest of parsimony, we limit our account to the primary policy changes that shaped CP's historical *roots*.

Second, we focus on developments related to the training of new practitioners and outlets for the work of CP scholars. Once CP emerged as a discipline, a primary concern was how practitioners of the field would be trained. The model of practitioners as "participant conceptualizers," change agents, and consultants with community members rather than professionals represented a paradigm shift within the field of mental health. By 1977, the groundwork for CP was in place, Division 27 of APA existed formally, and the major journals and texts had been established. We end our historical account in 1977, with the publication of a textbook that remains a primary training tool today. By this time, CP had formed its historical *roots*.

of a new field, *community psychology*. This is regarded as the birthplace of CP in the United States.

1965: Sheldon Roen became the first editor of *Community Mental Health Journal*, the initial journal of the field.

1966: The Swampscott conferees released *A Report on the Boston Conference on the Education of Psychologists for Community Mental Health* (Bennett et al., 1966).

1967: Community psychologists established their own division within the American Psychological Association (Division 27: now known as The Society for Community Research and Action).

1970: Ira Iscoe and Charles D. Speilberger published *Community Psychology: Perspectives in Training and Research*.

1972: Stuart E. Golann and Carl Eisdorfer published the *Handbook of Community Mental Health*.

1973: Charles D. Speilberger became the editor of a peer-reviewed journal for the field: *American Journal of Community Psychology*.

1974: Melvin Zax and Gerald A. Specter published *An Introduction to Community Psychology*.

1974: Seymour Sarason published *The Psychological Sense of Community: Prospects for a Community Psychology*.

1977: Ira Iscoe, Bernard L. Bloom, and Charles D. Speilberger edited *Community Psychology in Transition*. This book included a chapter devoted to feminism (Leidig, 1977) and one devoted to racism (Meyers & Pitts, 1977).

1977: Julian Rappaport published *Community Psychology: Values Research and Action*. This is generally considered the first textbook in the field in the United States.

Changes in Mental Health

Perhaps the two most important policy changes to influence the development of CP were the National Mental Health Act and the Community Mental Health Centers Act. The National Mental Health Act and National Institute of Mental Health (NIMH) resulted, in part, from a cultural shift in the government's role in the lives of its citizens. With the advent of the Great Depression, President Roosevelt's New Deal proposed that the federal government sponsor plans to address poverty, such as social security and employment programs (Piven & Cloward, 1971). The New Deal Era shifted attention away from individual culpability to ecological concerns. This represented a revolutionary shift in world views and marked the origination of a tension between competing visions of the relationship between the individual and the sociopolitical environment.

In the early 1960s, the *Joint Commission Report* prompted mass deinstitutionalization of individuals from mental institutions across the country. One of the consequences was the urgent need to care for individuals in new ways. Community mental health centers (CMHCs), operated at the local level, were a major step in that direction. From 1965 to 1971, more than 700 CMHCs were developed (Rappaport, 1977). This prompted many psychologists to begin considering mental health in terms of the *health of communities*. By the U.S. birth of CP in 1965, psychologists working in CMHCs were critical of the limits of traditional psychology and began thinking about community wellness in terms of *prevention*. CP in the United States gained formal recognition in 1967 when Division 27 of the American Psychological Association (APA) was established. It was not until some time later, in 1989, that Division 27 was recognized as an independent society (i.e., Society for Community Research and Action) while it remained a division of APA.

The Sociopolitical Context

In 1965, Swampscott attendees were influenced by more than changes in mental health treatment and research. This was an era of social change on a grand scale. While a fight for civil rights and social justice had been ongoing since the beginning of the century [e.g., Jane Addams and Ida B. Wells' settlement house movement, W.E.B. Dubois' cofounding of the NAACP, Margaret Sanger's birth control and women's health activism, Elizabeth Cady Stanton and Susan B. Anthony's suffrage movement (Mankiller et al., 1998)], organized social change efforts became increasingly visible across the country in the late 1950s, the 1960s and into the 1970s.

For example, in 1954, the U.S. Supreme Court mandated that schools desegregate. By the 1960s, the civil rights movement was in full force and continued after the 1968 assassination of Dr. Martin Luther King Jr. Similarly, the second wave of the women's movement was under way, as women fought for full citizenship via an equal rights amendment (which never passed). However, one significant legislative accomplishment of the time was Title VII of the 1964 Civil Rights Act, which prohibited discrimination in the workplace on the basis of race or sex. Gay rights activists became publicly visible in 1969 when the Stonewall riot between gays and police in New York marked the official beginning of the modern gay rights movement. In 1973, the Supreme Court voted in *Roe vs. Wade* that women had the right to safe, legal abortions. Coupled with the availability of oral contraceptives, women gained more autonomy and control over their own bodies and a "sexual revolution" was under way. Gender roles and norms were called into question. Marriage, maternity, and heterosexuality appeared less compulsory.

While civil rights, women's rights, and gay rights [today, more comprehensively termed gay, lesbian, bisexual, and transgendered (GLBT) rights] were a focus of the 1960s, so was an unjust war in Viet Nam. Across the United States, people protested the war and called for peace and social justice. As a growing distrust for the government developed, an underlying tension began to take hold within the field of CP; one that remains today and continues to affect the politics of the field. Namely, the government that had the power to work for the "social good" through the development of initiatives and provisions of federal funds was the same institution to elicit criticism from organized collectives for its power to wage war without adequate democratic process. In this increasing climate of distrust, this age of social mobilization for change, CP was born. Consequently, it is not surprising that Swampscott conferees called for a psychology of social change, one in which they could conduct research as social change agents, political activists and "participant conceptualizers" (Bennett et al., 1966). It is also not surprising that a field that emerged, in part, as a result of governmental initiatives would remain dependent upon that government for grants, largely depoliticizing it. This tension remains strong in the field today, as CP continues to struggle for an identity that is both political and practical.

Thus, CP developed its own critical strand. While the Swampscott attendees were critical of the community mental health movement (Bennett et al., 1966), these psychologists were now politically and historically well positioned to acknowledge power imbalances when working within communities and when analyzing the sociopolitical context. The field began to move from a sole focus on community mental health to a larger umbrella for social change. Today, this is reflected in work on racial and ethnic emancipation (e.g., Potts, 2003; Watts, 1999), feminist liberation (e.g., Grant, Finkelstein & Lyons, 2003), gay and lesbian issues (e.g., Stanley, 2003), and in work related to other disenfranchised groups, such as research on disability issues (e.g., Nary, 2001) and the intersection of class, race, and gender (e.g., Bond, 1997). It is also reflected within the field as CP continues its political struggle to oppose licensure and other forms of institutional credentialing of community practice and participation (e.g., Newbrough, 1992a).

This critical perspective led to new research methodologies as well. Psychology has a tradition of relegating research to individual-level analyses. Critiques of traditional, "classical" research as reductionist, positivistic, and as academic hegemony led to understanding that how one organizes and conducts research influences how findings are interpreted (Caplan & Nelson, 1973). Researchers came to understand victim blaming (Ryan, 1976) as a potential, unanticipated consequence of conducting research *on* people rather than *with* them. An ecological perspective became valued over individual-level analyses that tend to encourage victim-blaming (Prilleltensky, 2003). This shift led to new ways of considering research and scholarship, including varying forms of participatory research and qualitative research that give voice to people at the margins.

In short, the informal historical roots of the field, deeply embedded in movements for social change and born of a critical perspective and a goal of social justice, helped set the stage for a CP that valued diverse perspectives, multiple levels of analysis, multiple research methods, and practitioner models of participatory action. The formal and informal roots of the field helped to inform the theoretical frameworks that shape the field today and laid the foundation for continued theoretical and sociopolitical development of the field.

Theoretical Roots

Many U.S. scholars involved in the early development of CP were influenced by the work of John Dewey and Thomas Kuhn. In the late 1880s, Dewey posited that the field of psychology should be social (i.e., consider contextual influences) and that it should be connected to philosophy (Dewey, 1891). He was one the first to advocate for a psychology of social change. Later, Kuhn (1962, 1970) brought two important ideas to the development of CP. First, he challenged the cultural wisdom about science and the scientific method. Rather than accepting a linear science that searches for an objective truth, he posited that science develops and changes as a result of crises and revolutions, much like societal changes occur. Second, Kuhn underscored the power of paradigms. In science, as in society, paradigms are the belief systems (concepts and values) shared by a community and provide the foundation for defining problems and solutions. When the belief system becomes outdated and fails to provide an adequate groundwork from which to address new social problems (e.g., nuclear disaster or warfare, global capitalism, etc.), new paradigms must be developed. According to Kuhn, these paradigm "shifts" do not develop in an orderly fashion but are created by revolutionary changes. Whether in science or in society, paradigm shifts are embedded in cultural transformation. As such, science is inherently political, and new paradigms must be ecological in order to address individuals in a larger context. Together, these scholars help to set the stage for a CP that valued both theory and method, was inherently critical, and focused on change at a macrolevel.

In the following section, we begin by describing the development of the ecological foundation that remains a cornerstone of CP's identity as a discipline. We then provide a brief overview of some of the most influential theories in CP. Given that entire textbooks have been dedicated to these theories, it is our purpose here to provide an overarching view from which to begin to understand the complexities inherent within the field to date. First, we provide brief descriptions of (a) stress and coping, (b) prevention, (c) empowerment, and (d) sense of community. Then, we discuss the theoretical development of CP in context.

The Ecological Framework

As early as the 1930s, Kurt Lewin (1935) and Henry Murray and colleagues (1938) considered individual–environment interactions. In 1955, Roger Barker and Herbert Wright considered contextual influences when they studied children's lives. But it was not until the 1960s that the notion of an ecological relationship between individuals and their environments took hold. In the 1960s, Jim Kelly outlined ecological principles in a variety of publications (1966, 1970, 1979). Kelly drew upon the field of biology to define four ecological principles: (1) interdependence, the idea that all systems have multiple, interrelated parts; (2) cycling of resources, the notion that a system is defined by its use of resources, (3) adaptation, or the measure of the person–environment fit, and (4) succession, the idea that patterns of change influence the other three principles. Kelly's use of these principles allowed for eloquent description of the complex relationships and interactions between individuals and the environments in which they are embedded. Similarly, Barker (1968) focused on behavior settings and "standing patterns of behavior" that existed regardless of the individuals within the setting. He proposed that the environment was an entity worthy of study on its own. In the 1970s, Rudolph Moos and his colleagues (1973, 1979) built upon the work of their predecessors to develop Social Climate Scales. These scales were developed to measure environmental settings in various groups and organizations. Additionally, Uri Bronfenbrenner (1979) articulated an ecological framework that could be used to describe how individuals and their environments were related in *transactional* ways. Thus, an ecological foundation of CP was established. This paradigm provided a framework from which many new theories emerged.

Stress and Coping

Perhaps best known for the initial work in stress and coping are Barbara Snell and Bruce P. Dohrenwend. Building upon earlier work (cf., Lazarus, 1966), they contributed a model of psychosocial stress that considered individuals within environmental contexts (B.S. Dohrenwend, 1978; Dohrenwend & Dohrenwend, 1981). This well-known model served as a heuristic for understanding stress and responses to stress and for considering stressful life events, situational and psychological mediators (B.S. Dohrenwend, 1978; Dohrenwend & Dohrenwend, 1981). Also, given an emerging ecological framework, it paved the way for mental health intervention beyond the individual. Early research and practice related to life stressors and coping responses prompted a tremendous amount of literature on stress reduction and social support/competency enhancement throughout the 1980s (e.g., Albee, 1982; Heller & Swindle, 1983; Shure & Spivak, 1987) that profoundly influenced the course of CP in the United States—particularly how the field would come to think about prevention.

Prevention

Gerald Caplan (1964) is credited with bringing the term *prevention* to the mental health profession. He defined three types of prevention: primary (interventions with entire populations before problems arise), secondary (early interventions with at-risk population), and tertiary (interventions with affected population). Among community psychologists, prevention has generally been defined as efforts to increase "protective factors" and decrease "risk factors," while the most comprehensive prevention programs are said to include attention to health promotion and wellness (versus pathology, dysfunction, or risk focus), multilevel analysis and intervention (versus individual level focus), and an empowerment approach (e.g., Albee & Gullotta, 1997; Seidman, 1987; Swift & Levin, 1987). Such orientations contrast with other prevention approaches that tend to be "professionalized" or "medicalized," like those common in the public health sciences or those advocated by the Institute of Medicine (1994).

Empowerment

Julian Rappaport (1987) defined empowerment as "a process, a mechanism by which people, organizations, and communities gain mastery over their affairs" (p. 122). Empowerment has been defined as a multilevel and relational construct (e.g., Peterson & Zimmerman, 2004; Speer & Hughey, 1995, 1996; Zimmerman, 1995, 2000). It incorporates individual rights, "sense of control" and actual influence or control, and has purportedly focused on posing a challenge to the status quo, in word and/or action (Kieffer, 1984; Rappaport, 1977, 1981, 1987; Swift & Levin, 1987). Although as Stephanie Riger (1993) indicated, empowerment rarely leads to the actual redistribution of resources, it can be viewed as both "sense of" and "actual" control. The development of empowerment theory, research, and practice has profoundly shaped the evolution of CP in the United States. A commitment to empowerment implicitly and explicitly blurs the lines between the "expert" and "ordinary" folk. Thus, an empowerment orientation encourages research that is collaborative, participatory, and/or action-oriented.

Sense of Community

In 1974, Seymour Sarason defined sense of community (SOC) as "the perception of similarity to others, an acknowledged interdependence with others, a willingness to maintain this interdependence . . . the feeling that one is part of a larger dependable and stable structure" (p. 157). Generally, the concept refers to feelings of connectedness experienced by individuals with respect to where they live (e.g., block, neighborhood, community levels), where they work, or in terms of belonging in political, professional, religious, or social organizations. Notions of SOC have also been integral to the development of CP in the United States. This is not surprising, given the field's purported goal of maximizing the "fit" between persons and their environments.

However, it was not until the late 1980s that SOC received substantial theoretical and empirical attention in the published literature of the field (e.g., Heller, 1989; McMillan & Chavis, 1986; Newbrough & Chavis, 1986a; 1986b). David McMillan and David Chavis (1986) described SOC in terms of group cohesion, feelings of belonging, and a shared belief that members meet each others' needs (p. 9). Since the 1980s, much has been published in the field to debate the theoretical nuances and measurement of various forms of the concept (e.g., Brodsky & Marx, 2001; Davidson & Cotter, 1991; Hughey, Speer & Peterson, 1999). Community and individuals' experiences of connectedness are fundamental building blocks for the development of theory, research and practice in the field.

Theoretical Development in Context

While many theories have been developed in CP, *empowerment* and *prevention* separate the field into two streams of scholarship. Generally, community psychologists engaged in prevention theory development, research, and practice argue that prevention efforts represent the field's commitment to proactive rather than reactive interventions (Albee & Gullotta, 1997; Seidman, 1987; Swift & Levin, 1987). According to Rappaport (1981, 1987), however, prevention emerged as an extension of a "needs" model, while advocacy similarly evolved from a "rights" model. He argued that both models are limited and fail to view persons in a holistic manner. Instead, Rappaport (1981) maintained that empowerment (versus prevention) would allow us to view persons holistically; as individuals with needs and rights. He argued that empowerment was superior on a number of levels: (a) it suggests collaboration versus expert control; (b) it requires the examination and expansion of existing strengths and competencies versus a focus on competency teaching; and (c) it urges naturalistic, multilevel analysis versus a sterile, "expert-controlled" program. By 1987, Rappaport only partially qualified some of his criticisms and ever since, community psychologists doing prevention work have argued that there is a kinder, gentler prevention approach that mandates attention to collaboration, empowerment, multilevel analysis and strengths and competencies for health promotion and wellness (e.g., Albee & Gullotta, 1997).

Other critiques of CP have surfaced. For example, Marybeth Shinn (1987) pointed out that goals of both empowerment and prevention were inadequate if researchers limited interventions to traditional mental health settings. Also, the word *empowerment* has become so popular that it has been co-opted and overused to a point of rendering the term virtually meaningless. Doug Perkins and Marc Zimmerman (1995) analyzed the term's overuse in White House press releases, speeches, and policy statements. They documented the frequency and variety of ways that some form of the word *empower* was used (see Levine, Perkins & Perkins, 2005 for a full discussion). We also recently observed that the use of this term has gone to the ridiculous extreme in U.S. popular culture, as there is now a lipstick color called "empowerment red" and recently, *Hoover* introduced its new "Empower" vacuum cleaner (see http://www.hoover.com/minisite/empower/). The (over)use of *empower* in these two cases not only contributes to the term being rendered meaningless; it suggests co-optation of the term for the explicit purpose of marketing products that have been associated with the marginalization of women.

The Feminist Critique

While CP has always maintained its value of diversity and has been critical of the white middle-class standard of other psychological disciplines (Rappaport, 1977), the roots of the field are undeniably white and androcentric.

Furthermore, the scholarship of the field has reflected a struggle to transcend its culturally hegemonic pull. In the following section, we describe the Anglo- and androcentric history of CP. We then critique the field with regard to its stated value of diversity. Specifically, we discuss work in the areas of GLBT, disability, and gender issues.

White Leaders and Anglocentric Scholarship

As one examines the history of leadership in CP, a primarily white picture emerges. All editors of the major journals of the field have been white men. The founders of CP graduate programs across the country were all white men. Until very recently, all SCRA presidents have been white. The first two people of color elected as president were Melvin Wilson, a black man (2002–2003), and Ana Marie Cauce, a Latina (2004–2005).

Despite its goals to the contrary, in terms of academic scholarship, the field has a history of Anglocentrism. For example, Chalsa Loo and colleagues (1988) analyzed works published on ethnic and cultural diversity from 1965 to 1985 in the *Journal of Community Psychology* (JCP) and the *American Journal of Community Psychology* (AJCP). They discovered that only 13% of the articles contributed to cultural diversity. More specifically, Guillermo Bernal and Noemi Enchautegui-de-Jesús (1994) critiqued work on Latinos and Latinas in CP. They found very little scholarship on Latin cultures or issues.

Male Leaders and Androcentric Scholarship

The roots of the field are primarily male, as well. Anne Mulvey and Meg Bond (1993) provided a historical analysis of women in CP. Their findings suggested that women were virtually invisible for the first decade. When Division 27 of APA was established, the field was led by all white men, and throughout the 1970s, gender issues remained marginalized within the field. This changed somewhat by the 1980s. For example, in 1983, SCRA's executive committee accepted a proposal to establish a formal Committee on Women. In 1988, Anne Mulvey published a classic article on feminism and CP in JCP, bringing feminism into the mainstream discourse of the field. However, even today, researchers contend that women, women's issues, and feminist goals are still underrepresented in the field (Angelique & Culley, 2000, 2003; Swift, Bond & Serrano-García, 2000).

While the second author of the Swampscott report was a woman (Bennet et al., 1966), most community psychologists would be hard-pressed to name her or provide any information about her connection to the field.[4] Moreover, she was the only woman out of 39 conferees to attend the historic convention

---

[4] Her name is Luleen S. Anderson, and according to Revenson et al. (2002), she is currently in private practice.

(Walsh, 1987). To date, with the exception of few women (Karen Duffy, Stephanie Riger, and Jennifer Kofkin Rudkin), all of the primary textbook authors and editors have been men (see Appendix A). Furthermore, nearly all of the "seminal [sic] works" in the field are attributed to men. For example, in 2002, a diverse group (in terms of gender, ethnicity, and sexual orientation) of editors compiled a selection of articles published in AJCP that they considered the most influential in our field. With the exception of Barbara Dohrenwend's work on stress, all first authors of these works throughout the 1970s and 1980s were men (see Revenson et al., 2002).

The field has been critiqued theoretically, as well. For example, Stephanie Riger (1993) argued that notions of empowerment were fundamentally flawed and androcentric. She argued that the two assumptions about empowerment included an individualistic world view (that would lead to competition) and masculine concepts of mastery, power, and control. She challenged community psychologists to consider a vision of empowerment that included traditionally "feminine" concepts of communion and cooperation. Along with others (e.g., Newbrough, 1973, 1992b, 1995; Prilleltensky, 1997; Serrano-García & Bond, 1994), Riger called for some balance of these seemingly paradoxical values. Rappaport (1995) responded by incorporating feminist principles into his expanded theory of empowerment, including narrative analysis as an attempt to give voice to people of interest.

Where Is the Diversity?

Perhaps CP has struggled most with its stated value of diversity juxtaposed with a history of scholarship that has largely reflected the status quo. For example, it was not until 1973 that the American Psychiatric Association erased homosexuality from its list of mental disorders. So perhaps it is not surprising that CP dealt with GLBT issues by ignoring them for many years. In 2003, Anthony D'Augelli wrote an eye-opening account of the isolation associated with being gay in CP and the further marginalization associated with conducting research on gays and lesbians in rural areas.

GLBT visibility began to increase in 1998 when SCRA's executive committee accepted a proposal to form a special interest group focused on GLBT issues. Specifically, the interest group was developed to heighten awareness via increased conference presentations, mentoring of GLBT students, and a regular column in CP's newsletter, *The Community Psychologist* (TCP). The interest group also published special issues of TCP (Spring, 1999) and AJCP (2003; Gary W. Harper and Margaret Schneider and editors). Harper and Schneider (2003) reported that less than 1% of the published work in the field focused on GLBT issues through 1998, and most focused only on gay males. None focused on lesbians, bisexuals, or transgendered people exclusively. They called for increased attention to GLBT oppression and discrimination.

Similarly, disability issues have long been overlooked in the field. While many community psychologists may engage in research related to physical disabilities, it has not been well reflected in the field's major publications. A recent search for articles on physical disabilities and CP revealed very little. With the exception of very few articles (e.g., Dowrick & Keys, 2001; Nary, 2001), physical disabilities are virtually absent in the literature. Recently, SCRA's executive committee accepted a proposal to establish a disability interest group, and there have been increased efforts to address the needs of those with physical disabilities at the biennial conferences. For example, the executive committee dedicated funds for a disability representative to investigate conference sites and make recommendations for better accessibility than in the past.

To address the issue of diversity, AJCP published a special issue on minorities in 2000. In that same year, it published a double special issue on feminism. Rebecca Campbell and Sharon Wasco (2000) described feminist epistemologies and outlined different feminisms to aid in the utilization of feminist approaches in CP. We also contributed an analysis of the literature on women's issues (Angelique & Culley, 2000). We discovered that only 3% of the published literature in the two major journals in CP was about women's issues *and* could be considered feminist. Wanting more than to simply critique the field, we considered solutions and provided examples of how to incorporate feminism into CP. Subsequently, we published a second article, which highlighted instances where the field had gotten it right (Angelique & Culley, 2003). We identified successful feminist scholarship in CP as work that attended to gender-stratified power imbalances, consciousness of gender issues, and multilevel contextual analyses. In a similar vein, Ed Trickett (1996) discussed the notion of diversity and its importance for the future of CP, outlining important developments, including contextualism as an emerging epistemology and movement toward methodological pluralism. Similarly, we see CP developing as a discipline that values (a) analysis of power, (b) critical consciousness, and (c) an ecological focus. These necessarily related components are important for the theoretical development of a psychology of social change that is true to its political, critical roots.

In short, CP was, and still is, a reflection of the very cultural hegemony it critiqued. Specifically, schisms between a stated value of diversity and Anglo/androcentric scholarship prevail. However, an organic, ever present tendency to distinguish its identity through critique has allowed the field, and those of us who work within it, to move toward better representation of our stated goals and values. In spite of a seemingly bifurcated and contentious foundation (or perhaps because of it), CP has emerged as a discipline that will maintain a separate identity from other related fields such as applied psychology, sociology, public health, and social work. Acknowledging the field's roots in white, male power and privilege is one way to facilitate discourse from the margins and to remain forever critical in our growth and development in ways that honor the field's stated value of social justice.

An Evolving Discipline

As we look toward the future, we are both cautious and hopeful. From the first analytic review of the field, CP was critiqued for its limitations. Raymond Novaco and John Monahan (1980) found that CP's published literature had "little theoretical foundation, lack(ed) methodological sophistication, and g(a)ve considerable attention to the assessment of person variables" (p. 141). We are struck by the fact that CP still has a number of tensions with which to contend. These include (a) individual accountability versus societal impact, (b) distrust of the government versus reliance on government funding, (c) social change goals versus classical scientific inquiry as neutral, (d) nonhierarchical professional relationships versus licensing/credentialing pressure, (e) logical positivist critique versus history of person-centered research, (f) ecological, multilevel framework versus individual-level research, and (g) value of diversity versus andro/Anglocentric history. Many of these schisms can be traced back to the origination of the field when one considers the sociopolitical context from which CP was created.

Despite the many pressures that exist, we remain hopeful that CP will continue to emerge as the psychology of social change that it was designed to be. In this final section, we discuss three areas that are important to the continued development of the field. These include an emerging analysis of power, a strong critical presence, and an ongoing commitment to an ecological perspective.

Analysis of Power

Despite the field's attention to empowerment, little attention has historically been given to its root: power. However, as CP moves into the 21st century, the concept has become part of the lexicon of the field. For example, the terms *feminist power* (Mulvey, 2000), *referent power* and *expert power* (Salem et al., 2000), and *power relations* (Himmelman, 2001) have recently been used. Carolyn Swift (1992) advocated examination of power in terms of a "zero plus" versus "zero sum" commodity that adopts a "synergistic" versus "western, patriarchal" perspective. She underscored the importance of viewing power as "power with" versus "power over." Rappaport (1987) similarly described the related construct of empowerment as an "expanding resource." While we agree that resource-expanding notions of power should not be altogether ignored, much of the published discourse about power in the field is limited, as it tends to ignore the less palatable characteristics of power. There are some exceptions.

For example, Bob Newbrough (1995) warned we should not be "naïve" about conflict and power. Paul Speer and Joe Hughey (1995) explicitly employed 'Stephen Lukes' (1974) three-dimensional theory of social power to illustrate how community organizations and the individuals engaged in them could be empowered with an understanding of how social power manifests at multiple levels. Similarly, Speer and colleagues (2003) documented how such a model of community organizing (one that understands and intentionally uses power) worked for an organization in New Jersey. Moreover, Isaac Prilleltensky (2001, 2003) urged examination of our assumptions about power in social relationships and linked it to our thinking about distributive justice, democratic participation, oppression, liberation, and wellness. Even more recently, Angelique (in press), Culley and Hughey (in press), and Prilleltensky, Doug Perkins, and colleagues (http:// powercommunity.blogspot.com) called for more discussion in the field about how power operates in our lives and our communities.

Discussions about power are essential to a critical CP. We must, however, be thoughtful in our reflections about power. Michael Parenti, who views power as multidimensional and relational, much like Stephen Lukes (1974) and John Gaventa (1980), warned against a sanitized or more palatable view of social power. He persuasively argued: "By underplaying the coercive and exploitative features of social action, and by neutralizing the causes of social problems, we have presumed the existence of neutralized solutions" (1978, p. 25). With a naïve view of power then, one unwittingly limits the possibility of alternative solution(s) and will almost assuredly perpetuate the status quo. This simply will not do if we are to move toward an overtly critical community psychology.

Toward a Critical Community Psychology

From the days of the Swampscott Convention, CP has underscored the importance of a critical stance to the development of the field. Central to critical theory in the United States is the idea that power is masked within our culture through institutional structures, social mores, class, race, gender, and sexuality-based stratification. As such, social power is hidden and legitimized within the status quo (Gaventa, 1980; Lukes, 1974; Parenti, 1978). Furthermore, the mechanisms of power work in insidious ways to prevent conflict from arising. The task of the critical theorist in the United States is to unmask and expose how power operates. As such, critical theory in the United States refers to a wide body of scholarship that includes but is not limited to the classic works from the Frankfurt School in Germany.

The work of exposing power leads to the development of liberatory theories and actions. For example, Roderick Watts and his colleagues (2003) have developed a theory of socio-political development (SPD). According to the theory, SPD has the goal of liberation from oppression. This is accomplished by gaining knowledge, skills, and the competence to actively resist oppression. This work introduces theoretical grounding for concrete social change practices, with a goal of transformation as opposed to amelioration, and a vision of social justice to the CP literature. Transformational change is sought via political action to reduce power asymmetries. The focus is on changing social structures rather than simply helping individuals.

Maintaining a critical stance provides a base from which to evaluate the field and operates as a strategy to ensure that it remains political (Prilleltensky, 1994).

One mechanism by which this critical foundation is taking hold in CP is through the Monterey Declaration of Critical Community Psychology. In 2001, a small group of attendees drafted this declaration at a conference on critical psychology in Monterey, California. It was originally published in TCP (Angelique & Kyle, 2002) with 12 signatories representing four nations (three continents) and three disciplines (see Appendix B). We believe that this document can serve as a strong foundation from which a critical CP can continue to develop.

Forever Ecological

Informed by the early work of Dewey and Kuhn, and later by scholars such as Kelly, Barker, and Bronfenbrenner, CP is rooted in an ecological framework. As researchers discovered ways to measure environments as well as individuals, CP developed as a discipline that included multilevel, contextual analyses and person–environment "fit." By investigating problems at individual, mid (groups, organizations, etc.), and macrolevels (communities, society), victim-blaming may be avoided and holistic solutions can be considered. However, just as CP has struggled with disparities in its lack of diversity and scholarship published in the field, CP has also struggled with its ecological identity and scholarship that continues to favor individual-level analyses. To address the lack of multilevel research designs in much of the CP literature, Marybeth Shinn (1996) edited a special issue of AJCP on "Ecological Assessments." This step demonstrates a commitment to move toward more ecological (i.e., multilevel) research in the field.

An ecological foundation also lends itself to interdisciplinarity and methodological pluralism. To address this, Ken Maton, in his 2000 presidential address, proposed a multidisciplinary, multilevel framework for the goal of social transformation. His framework used a community development approach that included capacity building, group empowerment, opportunity structures, empowering communities, relational community building, and challenges to the culture. As such, he outlined an ecological approach that could have transformative outcomes. He, along with other scholars (e.g., Boyd & Angelique, 2002) also addressed the need for interdisciplinary links. To address this need, the executive committee of SCRA accepted a proposal in 2003 for a new interest group focused on interdisciplinary linkages. One of the goals of this interest group is to foster relationships across disciplinary borders.

An ecological framework also opens up the possibility of multiple epistemologies to assess people within sociopolitical environments. While CP developed as a science in much the same way as other social sciences, adopting the logical positivist perspective of the hard sciences, it was one of the first of the social science disciplines to acknowledge the limits of "true experiments," including this perspective's potential to support the status quo and lead to victim-blaming conclusions. Today, the field has emerged with room for strict empiricists and others to work side by side. For example, George (a.k.a. Bill) Fairweather's ESID model (experimental social innovation with dissemination—the use of random assignment to establish causation and rule out alternative explanations combined with a commitment to disseminate findings widely) is still a primary methodology in CP (see Fairweather, Sanders & Tornatzky, 1974, Fairweather & Tornatzky, 1977). Recently Kelly Hazel and Esther Onaga (2003) edited a special issue of AJCP on the ESID model. Juxtaposed are emerging models of *participatory research* (participation as a means rather than an end), *participatory development, and participatory action research* (people defining their own development), just to name a few. Similarly, Isaac Prilleltensky (2001) recently argued for a value-based praxis in CP, including cycles of reflection, research, and social action to advance social justice and social action in CP. To address some of these changes in the field, Ken Miller and Victoria Banyard (1998) edited a special issue of AJCP on qualitative research.

As such, we see CP developing as a discipline that values multiple ways of knowing and embraces methodological pluralism. As we look ahead toward the future of CP, we envision a CP that truly values diversity, power analyses, a critical perspective, and multilevel contextual analyses as the foundation upon which it is constructed. At its core, CP has been a psychology of social change. Today, it is distinguished by an identity formed by critique. From this base, it is a field that continues to move toward reconciliation of tensions between its values and its scholarship. Despite that there is always some resistance to change from the relatively powerful (in this case, a male, white, heterosexual contingency), the field's basic tenets allow for and encourage critical analysis and change. We believe that CP in the United States will continue to develop and struggle for an identity that is political, critical, and forever ecological.

Conclusion

We conclude by bringing an international focus to our analysis. CP is, and has been, practiced around the world for quite a long time. While the field has developed strands across the globe that are unique to the social, cultural, and political contexts of particular regions, some shared experiences and core values of CP are apparent. For example, CP in Latin America shares many similarities with the United States, including a history that reflects the struggle to move from dissatisfaction with previous psychological frameworks in dealing with problems in living to articulation and implementation of a novel kind of "critical psychology"—one that recognizes the political nature of research and values multiple ways of knowing, participatory methods, and social change (see Montero and Varas Díaz, this volume). Given that much of the work of CP in Latin America was founded on the works of Paulo Freire and Orlando Fals Borda, it has developed in large part as a psychology of liberation that has been both unapologetically political and at the forefront of positivist critiques with its examination of oppression, empowerment, and power. This body of community theory, research, and practice is invaluable to those with similar interests and experiences in the United States and elsewhere.

Like Latin America, Britain has also been a leader in the development of antipositivist scholarship and like the United States, critical feminist analyses have been incorporated into the field (see Burton, Kagan, Boyle, and Harris, this volume). While there are many links to CP in the United States, there has historically been a more overt focus on issues of social justice, especially around indigenous issues in both Australia and New Zealand (see Gridley et al. and Robertson and Masters, this volume). Moreover, while the theoretical roots of CP in the United States are Anglo- and androcentric, New Zealand traces its roots to collaborations with Maori scholars. CP has also existed in practice in parts of Africa for a long time, although the term has only recently gained popularity. As CP emerges professionally in countries such as Cameroon and Ghana, links to the United States and Canada are inevitable in that African scholars have been trained in North America (see Akotia and Barimah, this volume). However, more in line with the Asia-Pacific region, CP in Africa is overtly concerned with indigenous issues.

In sum, while CP has developed strands that are unique to the needs of certain regions across the globe, we argue that many shared experiences and core values of the field provide invaluable opportunities to explore how these unique histories have contributed in diverse ways to our common goal of positive social change—one based on a framework that values social justice, diversity, empowerment, a critical perspective, and ecological analyses. Moreover, recognition that we all engage in an ongoing struggle with the tensions between stated values and actual research and practice, coupled with our tendency to distinguish our common and unique identities through critique, will allow CP, and those of us who work within it across the globe, to move toward better representation of our stated goals and values.

References

Albee, George W. (1982). Preventing psychopathology and promoting human potential. *American Psychologist, 37*, 1043-1050.

Albee, George W. & Gullotta, T.P. (1997). Primary prevention's evolution. In G.W. Albee & T.P. Gullotta (Eds.), *Primary prevention works* (pp. 3-22). Thousand Oaks, CA: Sage.

Angelique, Holly L. (in press). On power, psychopolitical validity and play. *Journal of Community Psychology*.

Angelique, Holly L. & Culley, Marci R. (2000). Searching for feminism: An analysis of community psychology literature relevant to women's concerns. *American Journal of Community Psychology, 28*, 793-813.

Angelique, Holly L. & Culley, Marci R. (2003). Feminism found: An examination of gender consciousness in community psychology. *Journal of Community Psychology, 31*, 189-210.

Angelique, Holly L. & Kyle, Ken. (2002). Monterey declaration of critical community psychology. *The Community Psychologist, 35*, 35-36.

Barker, Roger G. & Wright, Herbert F. (1955). *Midwest and its children: The psychological ecology of an American town.* Evanston, IL: Row, Peterson.

Barker, Roger. (1968). *Ecological psychology.* Stanford, CA: Stanford University Press.

Bennett, Chester C., Anderson, Luleen, Cooper, Saul, Hassol, Leonard, Klein, Donald C., & Rosenblum, Gershen (1966). *Community Psychology: A report of the Boston conference on the education of psychologists for community mental health.* Boston: Department of Psychology. Boston University Press.

Bernal, Guillermo & Enchautegui-de-Jesús, Noemi (1994). Latinos and Latinas in community psychology: A review of the literature. *American Journal of Community Psychology, 22,* 531-558.

Bond, Meg (1997). The multi-textured lives of women of color. *American Journal of Community Psychology, 25,* 733-744.

Boyd, Neil & Angelique, Holly L. (2002). Rekindling the discourse: Organization studies in community psychology. *Journal of Community Psychology, 30,* 325-348.

Brodsky, Anne E. & Marx, Christine M. (2001). Layers of identity: Multiple psychological senses of community within a community setting. *Journal of Community Psychology, 29,* 161-178.

Bronfenbrenner, Uri (1979). *The ecology of human development: Experiments by nature and design.* Cambridge, MA: Harvard University Press.

Campbell, Rebecca & Wasco, Sharon (2000). Feminist approaches to social science: Epistemological and methodological tenets. *American Journal of Community Psychology, 28,* 773-791.

Caplan, Gerald (1964). *Principles of preventive psychiatry.* New York: Basic Books.

Caplan, Nathan & Nelson, Stephen D. (1973). On being useful: The nature and consequences of psychological research on social problems. *American Psychologist, 28,* 199-211.

Culley, Marci R. & Hughey, Joseph (in press). Power and public participation in a hazardous waste dispute: A community case study. *American Journal of Community Psychology.*

D'Augelli, Anthony (2003). Coming out in community psychology: Personal narrative and disciplinary change. *American Journal of Community Psychology, 31,* 343-354.

Davidson, William B. & Cotter, Patrick R. (1991). The relationship between sense of community and subjective well-being: A first look. *Journal of Community Psychology, 19,* 246-253.

Dewey, John (1891). *Psychology.* New York: Harper and Brothers.

Dohrenwend, Barbara S. (1978). Social stress and community psychology. *American Journal of Community Psychology,* 1-14.

Dohrenwend, Barbara S. & Dohrenwend, Bruce P. (1981). Socioenvironmental factors, stress, and psychopathology. *American Journal of Community Psychology, 9,* 128-164.

Dowrick, Peter W. & Keys, Christopher B. (2001). Community Psychology and disability studies. *Journal of Prevention and Intervention in the Community, 21,* 1-14.

Fairweather, George W., Sanders, David H., & Tornatzky, Lou G. (1974). *Creating change in mental health organizations.* New York: Pergamon Press.

Fairweather, George W. & Tornastzky, Lou G. (1977). *Methods for experimental social innovation.* New York: Wiley.

Gaventa, John (1980). *Power and powerlessness: Quiescence and rebellion in an Appalachian valley.* Urbana, IL: University of Illinois Press.

Grant, Kathryn E., Finkelstein, Jo-Ann S., & Lyons, Aoife L. (2003). Integrating psychological research on girls with feminist activism: A model for building a liberation psychology in the United States. *American Journal of Community Psychology, 31,* 143-157.

Golann, Stuart E. & Eisdorfer, Carl (1972). *Handbook of community mental health.* New York: Appleton-Century-Crofts.

Harper, Gary W. & Schneider, Margaret (2003). Oppression and discrimination among lesbian, gay, bisexual, and transgendered people and communities: A challenge for community psychology. *American Journal of Community Psychology, 16,* 243-252.

Hazel, Kelly & Onaga, Esther (2003). Experimental social innovation and dissemination: Its promise and its delivery. *American Journal of Community Psychology, 32,* 285-294.

Heller, Kenneth & Swindle, Ralph W. (1983). Social networks, perceived social support and coping with stress. In R. Felner, L. Jason, J. Moritsugu & S. Farber (Eds.), *Preventive psychology: Theory, research and practice in community intervention.* New York: Pergamon.

Heller, Kenneth (1989). Return to community. *American Journal of Community Psychology, 17,* 1-15.

Himmelman, Arthur T. (2001). On coalitions and the transformation of power relation: Collaborative betterment and collaborative empowerment. *American Journal of Community Psychology, 29,* 277-285.

Hughey, Joseph B., Speer, Paul & Peterson, Andrew (1999). Sense of community in community organizations: Structure and evidence of validity. *Journal of Community Psychology, 27,* 97-113.

Institute of Medicine (1994). *Reducing risks for mental disorders: Frontiers for preventive intervention research.* Washington, DC: National Academy Press.

Iscoe, Ira & Speilberger, Charles D. (1970). *Community psychology: Perspectives in training and research.* New York: Appleton-Century-Crofts.

Iscoe, Ira, Bloom, Bernard L. & Speilberger, Charles D. (Eds.). (1977). *Community psychology in transition: Proceedings of the national conference on training in community psychology.* Washington, DC: Hemisphere Publication Corporation.

Kelly, James G. (1966). Ecological constraints of mental health services. *American Psychologist, 21,* 535-539.

Kelly, James G. (1970). Toward an ecological conception of preventive interventions. In D. Adelson & B. Kalis (Eds.), *Community psychology and mental health* (pp. 126-145), Scranton, PA: Chandler.

Kelly, James G. (1979). T'aint what you do, it's the way you do it. *American Journal of Community Psychology, 7,* 244-258.

Kieffer, Charles R. (1984). Citizen empowerment: A developmental perspective. In J. Rappaport, C. Swift, & R. Hess (Eds.), *Studies in empowerment: Steps toward understanding and action* (pp. 9-36). New York: Haworth.

Kuhn, Thomas (1962/1970). *The structure of scientific revolutions.* Chicago: University of Chicago Press.

Lazarus, Richard S. (1966). *Psychological stress and the coping process.* New York: McGraw-Hill.

Leidig, Margerie Whitaker (1977). Women in community psychology: A feminist perspective. In I. Iscoe, B.L. Bloom, & C.D. Speilberger (Eds.), *Community psychology in transition: Proceedings of the National Conference on Training in Community Psychology,* (pp. 274-277). Washington, DC: Hemisphere Publication Corporation.

Levine, Murray, Perkins, Douglas D. & Perkins, David V. (2005). *Principles of community psychology: Perspectives and applications (third edition).* New York: Oxford University Press.

Lewin, Kurt (1935). *A dynamic theory of personality.* New York: McGraw-Hill.

Loo, Chalsa, Fong, Kenneth T. & Iwamasa, Gayle (1988). Ethnicity and cultural diversity: An analysis of work published in community psychology journal, 1965-1985. *Journal of Community Psychology, 16,* 332-350.

Lukes, Stephen (1974). *Power: A radical view.* London: Macmillan Press, Ltd.

Mankiller, Wilma, Mink, Gwendolyn, Navarro, Marysa, Smith, Barbara & Steinem, Gloria (Eds.). (1998). *The readers companion to US women's history.* New York: Houghton Mifflin Co.

Maton, Kenneth I. (2000). Making a difference: The social ecology of social transformation, *American Journal of Community Psychology, 28,* 25-58.

McMillan, David W. & Chavis, David M. (1986). Sense of Community: Definition and theory. *Journal of Community Psychology, 14,* 6-23.

Meyers, Ernest R. & Pitts, Henry (1977). Community psychology and racism. In I. Iscoe, B.L. Bloom, & C.D. Speilberger (Eds.), *Community psychology in transition: Proceedings of the National Conference on Training in Community Psychology,* (pp. 267-270). Washington, DC: Hemisphere Publication Corporation.

Miller, Kenneth, & Banyard, Victoria (1998). The powerful potential of qualitative research for community psychology. *American Journal of Community Psychology, 26,* 485-505.

Moos, Rudolph (1973). Conceptualizations of human environments. *American Psychologist, 28,* 652-665.

Moos, Rudolph (1979). *Evaluating educational environments: Procedures, measures, findings and policy implications.* San Francisco, CA: Jossey-Bass.

Mulvey, Anne (2000). Stories of relative privilege: Power and social change in feminist community psychology. *American Journal of Community Psychology, 28,* 883-912.

Mulvey, Anne (1988). Community psychology and feminism: Tensions and commonalities. *Journal of Community Psychology, 16,* 70-83.

Mulvey, Anne & Bond, Meg (1993). Finding our own voices: A history of women in community psychology. Unpublished manuscript.

Murray, Henry A., Barrett, William G., Homburger, Erik et al., (1938). *Explorations in personality: A clinical and experimental study of fifty men of college age.* New York: John Wiley & Sons, Inc.

Nary, Dorothy (2001). Consumers as collaborators in research and action. *Journal of Prevention and Intervention in the Community, 21,* 15.

Nelson, Nici & Wright, Sue (1995). Participation and power. In *Power and participatory development: Theory and practice,* N. Nelson & S. Wright (Eds.), London: Intermediate Technology Publications.

Newbrough, Robert J. (1973). Community psychology: A new holism. *American Journal of Community Psychology, 1,* 201-211.

Newbrough, Robert J. (1992a). Community psychology for the 1990s. *Journal of Community Psychology, 20,* 7-9.

Newbrough, Robert J. (1992b). Community psychology in the postmodern world. *Journal of Community psychology, 20,* 10-25.

Newbrough, Robert J. (1995). Toward community: A third position. *American Journal of Community Psychology, 23,* 9-38.

Newbrough, Robert J. & Chavis, David M. (1986a). Psychological sense of community: I. theory and concepts[Special Issue]. *Journal of Community Psychology, 14(1).*

Newbrough, Robert J. & Chavis, David M. (1986b). Psychological sense of community: II. Research and applications. [Special Issue]. *Journal of Community Psychology, 14(4).*

Novaco, Raymond W. & Monahan, John (1980). Research in community psychology: An analysis of work published in the first six years of the *American Journal of Community Psychology*. *American Journal of Community Psychology, 8*, 131-145.

Parenti, Michael (1978). *Power and the powerless*. New York, NY: St. Martin's Press.

Peterson, Andrew & Zimmerman, Marc (2004). Beyond the individual: Toward a nomological network of organizational empowerment. *American Journal of Community Psychology, 34*, 129-143.

Perkins, Douglas D. & Zimmerman, Marc A. (1995). Empowerment theory, research, and application. *American Journal of Community Psychology, 23*, 569-580.

Piven, Frances Fox & Cloward, Richard A. (1971). *Regulating the poor: The functions of public welfare*. New York: Vintage Books.

Potts, Randolph G. (2003). Emancipatory education versus school-based prevention efforts in African American communities. *American Journal of Community Psychology, 31*, 173-185.

Prilleltensky, Isaac (1994). Psychology and social ethics. *American Psychologist, 49*, 966-967.

Prilleltensky, Isaac (1997). Values, assumptions, and practices: Assessing the moral implications of psychological discourse and action. *American Psychologist, 52*, 517-535.

Prilleltensky, Isaac (2001). Value-based praxis in community psychology: Moving toward social justice and social action. *American Journal of Community Psychology, 29*, 747-749.

Prilleltensky, Isaac (2003). Understanding, overcoming and resisting oppression: Toward psychopolitical validity. *American Journal of Community Psychology, 31*, 195-203.

Rappaport, Julian (1977). *Community psychology: Values, research and action*. New York: Holt, Rinehart and Winston.

Rappaport, Julian (1981). In praise of paradox: A social policy of empowerment over prevention. *American Journal of Community Psychology, 9*, 1-25.

Rappaport, Julian (1987). Terms of empowerment/exemplars of prevention: Toward a theory for community psychology. *American Journal of Community Psychology, 15*, 121-144.

Rappaport, Julian (1995). Empowerment meets narrative: Listening to stories and creating settings. *American Journal of Community Psychology, 23*, 795-808.

Revenson, Tracey A., D'Augelli, Anthony R., French, Sabine E., Hughes, Diane L., Livert, David, Seidman, Edward, Shinn, Marybeth & Yoshikawa, Hirokazu (Eds.). (2002). *A quarter century of community psychology: Readings from the American Journal of Community Psychology*. New York: Kluwer Academic/Plenum Publishers.

Riger, Stephanie (1993). What's wrong with empowerment? *American Journal of Community Psychology, 21*, 279-291.

Ryan, William (1976). *Blaming the victim*. New York: Vintage Press.

Salem, Deborah A, Reischl, Thomas, & Gallacher, Fiona (2000). The role of referent and expert power in mutual help. *American Journal of Community Psychology, 28*, 303-325.

Sarason, Seymour P. (1974). *The psychological sense of community: Prospects for a community psychology*. San Francisco, CA: Jossey-Bass.

Seidman, Edward (1987). Toward a framework for primary prevention research. In J.A. Steinberg & M.M. Silverman (Eds.), *Preventing mental disorder: A research perspective*, (pp. 2-19). Washington, DC: Department of Health and Human Services.

Seidman, Edward (1988). Back to the future, community psychology: Unfolding a theory of social intervention. *American Journal of Community Psychology, 16*, 3-24.

Serrano-García, Irma & Bond, Meg (1994). Empowering the silent ranks: Introduction. *American Journal of Community Psychology, 22*, 433-438.

Shinn, Marybeth (1987). Expanding community psychology's domain. *American Journal of Community Psychology, 15*, 555-574.

Shinn, Marybeth (1996). Ecological assessment. *American Journal of Community Psychology, 24*, 1-12.

Shure, Myrna B. & Spivak, George (1987). Competence-building as an approach to prevention of dysfunction: The ICPS model. In J.A. Steinberg & M.M. Silverman (Eds.), *Preventing mental disorder: A research perspective.* (pp. 124-139). Washington, DC: Department of Health and Human Services.

Speer, Paul, Ontkush, Mark, Schmitt, Brian, Raman, Padmasini, Jackson, Courtney, Rengert, Kristopher M., & Peterson, N. Andrew. (2003). The intentional exercise of power: Community organizing in Camden, New Jersey. *Journal of Community & Applied Social Psychology, 13*, 399-408.

Speer, Paul & Hughey, Joseph (1995). Community organizing: An ecological route to empowerment and power. *American Journal of Community Psychology, 23*, 729-748.

Speer, Paul & Hughey, Joseph (1996). Mechanisms of empowerment: Psychological processes for members of power-based community organizations. *Journal of Community & Applied Social Psychology, 6*, 177-187.

Stanley, Jeanne L. (2003). An applied collaborative training program for graduate students in community psychology: A case study of a community psychology project working with lesbian, gay, bisexual, transgender and questioning youth. *American Journal of Community Psychology, 31*, 253-267.

Swift, Carolyn F. (1992). Empowerment: The greening of prevention. In M. Kessler, S.E. Goldston, & J.M. Joffe (Eds.), *The present and future of prevention. In honor of George W. Albee*, (pp. 99-111). Newbury Park, CA: Sage Publications.

Swift, Carolyn F. & Levin, Gloria (1987). Empowerment: An emerging mental health technology. *Journal of Primary Prevention, 8*, 71-94.

Swift, Carolyn, Bond, Meg & Serrano-García, Irma (2000). Women's empowerment: A review of community psychology's first twenty-five years. In Julian Rappaport & Edward Seidman (Eds.), *Handbook of community psychology*. New York: Kluwer Academic/Plenum Publishers.

Trickett, Edward J. (1996). A future for community psychology: The contexts of diversity and the diversity of contexts. *American Journal of Community Psychology, 24*, 209-234.

Walsh, Richard T. (1987). A social historical note on the formal emergence of community psychology. *American Journal of Community Psychology, 15*(5) 523-529.

Watts, Roderick J. (1999). Sociopolitical development as an antidote for oppression—theory and action. *American Journal of Community Psychology, 27*, 255-272.

Watts, Roderick J., Williams, Nat Chioke, & Jagars, Robert J. (2003). Sociopolitical development. *American Journal of Community Psychology, 31*, 185-194.

Zax, Melvin & Spector, Gerald A. (1974). *An introduction to community psychology.* Oxford, England: John Wiley & Sons.

Zimmerman, Marc A. (1995). Psychological empowerment: Issues and illustrations. *American Journal of Community Psychology, 23*, 581-600.

Zimmerman, Marc A. (2000). Empowerment theory: Psychological, organizational, and community levels of analysis. In Julian Rappaport & Edward Seidman (Eds.), *Handbook of community psychology* (pp. 43-63). New York: Plenum.

Appendix A

Following is a list of the primary textbooks published (some out of print) in CP in the United States.

Dalton, James, Elias, Maurice J. & Wandersman, Abraham (2001). *Community psychology: Linking individuals and communities*. Belmont, CA: Wadsworth.

Duffy, Karen & Wong, Frank Y. (1996). *Community psychology*. Needham Heights, MA: Allyn & Bacon.

Golann, Stuart E. & Eisdorfer, Carl (1972). *Handbook of community mental health*. Englewood Cliffs, NJ: Prentice Hall, Inc.

Heller, Kenneth & Monahan, John (1977). *Psychology and community change*. Homewood, IL: Dorsey Press.

Heller, Kenneth, Thompson, Mark G., Reinharz, Shulamit, Riger, Stephanie & Wandersman, Abraham (1984). *Psychology and community change*. Homewood, IL: Dorsey.

Iscoe, Ira & Speilberger, Charles D. (1970). *Community psychology: Perspectives in training and research*. New York: Appleton-Century-Crofts.

Levine, Murray, Perkins, Douglas D. & Perkins, David V. (2005). *Principles of community psychology: Perspectives and applications (third edition)*. New York: Oxford University Press.

Mann, Philip A. (1978). *Community Psychology*. New York: Free Press.

Murrell, Stanley A. (1973). *Community psychology and social systems: A conceptual framework and intervention guide*. New York: Behavioral Publications.

Nietzel, Michael, Winett, Richard A., McDonald, M. L. & Davidson, William S. II (1977). *Behavioral Approaches to Community Psychology*. New York: Pergamon Press.

Rappaport, Julian (1977). *Values, Research and Action*. New York: Holt, Rinehart & Winston.

Rappaport, Julian & Seidman, Edward (Eds.). (2000). *Handbook of community psychology*. New York: Kluwer Academic/Plenum Publishers.

Revenson, Tracey A., D'Augelli, Anthony R., French, Sabine E., Hughes, Diane L., Livert, David, Seidman, Edward, Shinn, Marybeth & Yoshikawa, Hirokazu (Eds.) (2004). *A quarter century of community psychology: Readings from the American Journal of Community Psychology*. New York: Kluwer Academic/Plenum Publishers.

Revenson, Tracey A., D'Augelli, Anthony R., French, Sabine E., Hughes, Diane L., Livert, David, Seidman, Edward, Shinn, Marybeth & Yoshikawa, Hirokazu (Eds.) (2002). *Ecological research to promote social change: Methodological advances from community psychology*. New York: Kluwer Academic/Plenum Publishers.

Rudkin, Jennifer Kofkin (2003). *Community psychology: Guiding principles and orienting concepts*. Upper Saddle River, NJ: Prentice Hall.

Sarason, Seymour (1974). *The psychological sense of community: Prospects for a community psychology*. San Francisco, CA: Jossey-Bass.

Walsh, Richard T. (1987). A social historical note on the formal emergence of community psychology. *American Journal of Community Psychology, 15*, 523-529.

Zax, Melvin & Specter, Gerald A. (1974). *An introduction to community psychology*. New York: Wiley.

Appendix B

Monterey Declaration of Critical Community Psychology

Preamble

Whereas the Swampscott Conferees of 1965 were motivated in part by a desire to prevent or reduce individual suffering, and by a vision of a more just world,

   whereas the Conferees acknowledged that psychological intervention at the individual level was inadequate to address individual suffering,

   whereas the Conferees declared that "community psychology . . . is devoted to the study of general psychological processes that link social systems with individual behavior in complex relations (Bennett et al. 1966, p. 6-7)

   and whereas community psychologists have not adequately developed that linkage thus far

   Now, therefore

We, the undersigned participants of the Monterey Bay Conference on Critical Psychology do declare:

that preventable human suffering is the result not only of individual psychopathology, but also of individual, group, community, and governmental acts, as well as social, cultural and institutional arrangements;

   that much preventable human suffering is, therefore, intrinsically tied to social *in*justice;

   that community psychologists must, therefore, work for social justice by engaging in both ameliorative and transformative acts at multiple levels; and

   that the field of community psychology must adopt a critical theoretical stance and enact policies and practices in keeping with that stance if the Swampscott vision is to be realized.

Critical Theoretical Principles and Policy Guidelines for Community Psychologists

Article 1 - Ethical Obligation to Redress Social Injustice. Community psychologists have an ethical obligation to redress social injustice and to work actively to transform social, cultural and institutional arrangements that foster social injustice.

Article 2 - Utopian Vision. Community psychologists should employ a critical utopian vision of social life; i.e., we should evaluate policies and institutions on the basis of what could be, not on the basis of what is "normally" acceptable.

Article 3 - Understanding Human Behavior in Context. Community psychologists should understand human behavior in context; i.e., we should actively work to develop an understanding of the social institutions and forces in which individual humans are enmeshed, and we should adopt a social-ecological perspective in our work.

Article 4 - Consciousness Raising and Critical Thinking. Community psychologists should actively foster critical thinking among community members, students and colleagues and facilitate consciencization whenever possible.

Policy 1 - Full Collaboration and Partnership Between Community and University. Community psychologists should collaborate with communities to evaluate/assess projects in light of their potential to affect social change and community psychology programs should place greater emphasis on community involvement in graduate practica.

Policy Guideline 2 - Methodological Diversity. Graduate programs in community psychology should reduce their emphasis on quantitative methods to the exclusion of other methodologies, and should expand the role of participatory research methods.

Policy 3 - Development of Theory. Community psychologists should develop theories that include in-depth analyses of human subjectivity, power asymmetries, and social change.

Policy Guideline 4 - Broad Interdisciplinary Training. Graduate programs in community psychology should include interdisciplinary training in both theoretical and substantive areas of inquiry.

Policy 5 - Address Inequalities. Community psychologists should acknowledge the ill affects of ableism, ageism, bigotry, capitalism, homoprejudice, patriarchy, racism, sexism, and white supremacy, and work to undo them in our community interactions and in our scholarly activities.

Signatures, in alphabetical order

Holly Angelique	Community Psychology, Penn State, Capital College, US
Stephanie Austin	York University, Canada
Arlene Edwards	Georgia State University, US
Isidore Flores	Michigan Public Health Institute, US
Shelli Fowler	Washington State University, US
Jorie Henrickson	Vanderbilt University, US
Ken Kyle	Sociology, Penn State, Capital College, US
Ann V. Millard	Anthropology, Michigan State University, US
Isaac Prilleltensky	Psychology, Victoria University, Australia
Manuel Riemer	Vanderbilt Institute for Public Policy Studies, Vanderbilt University, US
Mrinal Sinha	Social Psychology, University of California, Santa Cruz, US
Todd Sloan	Georgetown University, US

3
Latin American Community Psychology: Development, Implications, and Challenges Within a Social Change Agenda

MARITZA MONTERO AND NELSON VARAS DÍAZ

Abstract

A brief history of the development of community psychology (CP) and of its academic evolution in Latin America is presented, highlighting its roots in Paulo Freire's adult education model, in critical sociology, and in social psychology. The main theoretical influences and topics are discussed, showing how CP embraced a line of research and action engaged with social change for Latin American countries. This research and action perspective united theory and practice while incorporating the people's participation and changing the role to be played by psychologists, and it incorporated new social actors. This development also integrated specific ontological, epistemological, political, methodological and ethical considerations, expressed in its work concerning community organization, health, housing, environmental, and educational needs in both urban and rural communities. A description of CP's academic development in most Latin American countries is made. Also, we highlight the emphasis placed on a reconceptualization of the notion of power, and in empowerment, in order to generate conscious citizens able to manage and transform their living conditions, stressing the role played by participatory methods developed simultaneously. Perspectives on the future directions of CP in Latin America and a comparison with the development of the field in some other countries are also addressed.

Some Considerations Regarding This Chapter

Dealing with a plurality of countries covering the better part of a continent is not an easy task. Take Latin America out and only two nations are left: Canada and the United States. Three of the mightiest rivers, the *Amazonas* (largest and widest), the *Orinoco*, and the *Paraná*, would disappear. The Andean mountain range, the largest forest in the world, and two of the largest cities in the world (Mexico City and São Paulo) would also vanish. Then one question remains for our venture in this chapter: how to squeeze the history, development, influences, academic status, practice, theory, and current state of community psychology (CP) in the space of a book chapter? Our answer to that question is, with great difficulty and with even more fear! In order to do so we have done the following: (1) tried first to convey some of the complexity of our subject, in the hope that it will not reach our readers as some large mass of information reducing this rich environment; (2) tried to subsume the marks of distinctiveness of the CP created in this plurality of countries, cultures, and subcultures during the past 40 years and the causes for that phenomenon; (3) present the influences and the antecedents fostering the emergence of CP in the region; (4) describe the academic development by presenting data from different countries; (5) give a brief account of the present status of CP, followed by the main topics and problems being considered in the Latin American CP literature. Finally, we discuss the possibilities for advancement of certain areas and for stagnation or arrest of others. We also do some brief comparison with what we have found similar or contrasting and what we have learned from other chapters in this book. Regarding outcomes, a view of the references can be used as guide for this aspect.

A Latin American Definition of Community Psychology

Probably most people, not only in Latin America, but anywhere else, will agree that CP refers, deals with, and is concerned with the community. On the other hand, some people do not seem to be aware that communities, social entities with a history and a culture, preexist the psychologists' efforts to approach, study, and intervene with them. This means that a dynamic and complex notion of community as CP's object and active subject of research and action is at the basis for the understanding of the field in Latin America.

CP literature is rich in papers, books, and reports stressing the importance of participation. Whose participation? that of stakeholders, organized community groups, and community movements. We agree that CP has as one of its bases *the active conception* of the people integrating the communities; that CP is made with them, not just for them, or carried out in a community environment (many things can happen in a specific environment that may not concern the community).

From the early 1980s on, awareness of the need to work on de-ideologizing and strengthening, or empowering, community groups, movements, and stakeholders in order to foster social change was already considered as one of the main tasks for CP in Latin America (see Montero, 2004, about the development of CP). Transformations are then decided with the community, as well as influenced by the political character of the processes leading to them. Such processes include problematization, conscientization, politicization in the sense of community members being aware of rights and duties, and occupation of the public space in order to make the people within communities' voices heard and their needs attended to.

Therefore, we understand that *CP is a branch of psychology studying and facilitating psychosocial processes generated within a community, taking into account the historic, cultural, and social context of that community; its resources, capacities, strengths, and needs. CP is oriented towards the production of social changes according with those circumstances and involving the stakeholders' participation and commitment, in order to ensure that power and control are in their hands.*

The Emergence of a Community Psychology in Latin America: Its Causes

The creation of a CP in Latin America has had a plurality of causes, as would naturally be expected from a region with so many indigenous pre-Columbian cultures and with such a vast territory. Although Spanish is the official language spoken in most of the countries, more than 150 million Brazilians speak Portuguese; about 15 million people speak Quechua; many others speak Aymara; Paraguay is bilingual (Guaraní–Spanish), and in Mexico alone, nearly 100 languages are spoken together with, or instead of Spanish. Almost every Latin American country is multicultural, multiethnic and multilingual. This diversity tends to be forgotten and with it pass unnoticed cultural traits that influence social behaviour patterns, such as commonality and individuality. In the first case, modes of social behaviour such as collective working for the benefit of the community or for persons in need belonging to the community have been practices deeply rooted in the Andean regions (i.e., *ayni* and *ayllu*), where the influence of cultures such as the Inca, Aymara, Chibcha, and Timoto-Cuica cultures have left their mark In the Caribbean region, the Caribe, Taíno, and Arawac cultures left their impact, as the Maya, Toltec, Zapotec, Aztec, among others did in the central and northern regions. Simultaneously, each country, as well as cultural and geographical zones crossing several nations, has their idiosyncrasies.

Table 1 shows the countries from which we were able to obtain specific data.

TABLE 1. Latin American countries included in this chapter.

Countries in alphabetical order	
Argentina	Haiti
Brazil	Honduras
Chile	Mexico
Colombia	Panamá
Costa Rica	Paraguay
Cuba	Perú
Dominican Republic	Puerto Rico
Ecuador	Uruguay
El Salvador	Venezuela

Note: The authors regret not having obtained data concerning Bolivia, Guatemala, and Nicaragua.

This mixture of common history of colonization, its influence of the culture of a particular European region, and a common history of influence for certain areas of the Latin American territory by certain indigenous cultures (i.e., Inca, Aztec, Caribe, Arawak, Mapuche, Tupi-Guarani, and others before these, like the Mayas), has to be taken into account when trying to summarize the development of CP in this continent. Those historic facts are needed in order to build a platform in which to support the academic and professional development of this discipline. We shall begin by mentioning the main causes for the construction of CP in Latin America.

The Construction of CP in Latin America: Causes and Marks of Distinctiveness

Seven main factors contributed to or influenced the development and construction of CP in Latin America as we know it today. The first one was social psychology. This field had such a lasting impact on CP that today the term *social–community psychology* is dominant in many places (e.g., Puerto Rico). When one looks back to the mid and late 1970s, with the exception of Puerto Rico where the label of CP was already in use, and perhaps also in the ITESO a college in Guadalajara, or the Iztacala section of UNAM, in Mexico, what can be found in countries like Brazil, Chile, Venezuela, Colombia, Costa Rica, Perú, El Salvador, and in other regions of Mexico, were (1) practices carried out by public institutions; (2) practices conducted by other disciplines like anthropology, sociology, psychiatry, or adult education; (3) practices or researches being done by social psychologists who in a very critical way were trying to introduce changes in social psychology, directed to make that discipline socially meaningful, through a closer contact with communities. It is no wonder that "community development" and "community organisation" were the first concepts frequently being mentioned to designate psychological practices related to communities. Hence, social psychology provided, for the better part of the American continent, the fertile ground from where CP stemmed and nourished in its Latin American beginnings.

The *second distinctive factor* for the start of CP is the nonconformist standing and the critical perspective adopted. By this we refer to the dissatisfaction felt by those psychologists wanting to transform reality while researching about it. Not just researching, and then, after a while, trying to introduce changes in it from what Fernández Christlieb (1994) has called the epistemological perspective of distance. That is, keeping a so-called objective separation between subject (the researcher) and object (the researched) of the research. On the contrary, CP in Latin America has had a predominant orientation towards praxis, linking practice and theory, and introducing the participation of new social actors in the processes of intervention and research.

The *third* factor for the development of CP was the necessity to transform dissatisfaction into action. This entailed crossing the road and going further than mainstream social psychology, and further than complaints like, "I do not like this. It stinks," and doing something that could produce changes and would also become the subject to critique. To do this, a new type of practice and new kind of psychologist was needed. So the redefinition of our role as psychologists became a demand.

The challenge was how to go beyond having a nice relationship with some people to construct a science with the aim of changing social life circumstances. That is the *fourth factor*: social change. If one wants to promote social change, one has to develop modes of doing so. Therefore, if the individualistic form of social psychology dominant at the time could not produce the transformations sought, a *science-searching process (fifth factor) was needed*. But something was missing from this process: the subject. A subject that had been left outside of the researching–intervening relationship: the person in the community, that is, the *community as collective group*, as the realm for expressing the interests, expectations, and actions of people united by a common history of constructing that community. The concept of "collective" usually referring to mobs and masses came to mean a different way to study the relationships between individuals and society: the communities as another ambit and level of social life (and this is a *sixth* factor). Therefore, a mode of relationship that could only be constructed within a *dialogue* was developed (*seventh* factor).

Influences Received by Latin American CP

Kurt Lewin's Ideas

Behind these immediate factors of the development of CP, there were also some influences that had been present in the social sciences since the early 1960s. Most remote perhaps is the influence of Lewin, which came to Latin American CP by way of the intermediary effect it had in both the critical or militant sociology and adult education that began developing in the 1960s in places like Colombia and Brazil, respectively. Both practices were engaged in social transformation and had as a main goal the help of the socially disadvantaged, not by welfare but by incorporating them as actors of the change processes. Two researchers have had an outstanding role in the transmission of Lewin's idea of action-research, transformed in Latin America in participatory action-research: Paulo Freire and Orlando Fals Borda, an educator and a sociologist, whose works have set an imprint in community studies throughout the world. Many concepts used by both social psychology of liberation and CP during the 1980s originated from their work.

The Influence of Marxian Theories

Perhaps the more visible and important influence comes from Marx and Engels' theory; specifically, early works such as the economic and philosophic manuscripts of 1844. *Alienated Work* and the *Critique of the Hegelian*

Dialectic and of Hegel's Philosophy in General and, also later works such as *The German Ideology*, were read during the 1970s in Brazil, Colombia, Mexico, Puerto Rico, and Venezuela, in search for more comprehensive explanations for the breach between the poor and the extremely rich, as well as the foggy zone in between. The explanations about the notions of *interiority* and *exteriority* (Marx, 1844/1965) surprised the first author as a better understanding for the causes of social passivity than those given at the time by some popular attribution theories.

Also influential were the works from some of the philosophers and social scientist who extended Marx and Engels' ideas (e.g., G. Lukacs, K. Kosik, A. Gramsci). The Marxian perspective together with the critical proposal of the Frankfurt School was widely discussed. At the same time, Latin American social sciences had already generated notions such as conscientization and de-ideologizing (Freire's adult education, Fals Borda's critical sociology), which also had had the same influence. So, the Marxian presence came not only from the reading of those works, but also through the advances in practice and theory being created by other disciplines in contact with communities, which were already leading the way towards the transformation of Latin American societies.

The Theory of Dependency

At the end of the 1950s and the beginning of the 1960s, there was also the impact of a theory about the interpretation of social dynamics in Latin America: the theory of Dependency (Cardozo & Faletto, 1978, among others). This theory states that national economic underdevelopment is dependent on subordinated links to foreign economic policies generated at centres of power. This dependency happens in such a way that both external variables as well as internal variables originated within those societies coincide in the generation of relationships of dominance–submission. This theory of dependency, developed by economists, political scientists, and sociologists from Argentina, Brazil, Chile, Colombia, Costa Rica, Perú, and Venezuela, had the effect of driving Latin American social scientists to look to their societies from an internal perspective. That is, neither using explanations produced outside their countries nor interpreting the phenomena happening around them with models created for other realms. Rather, Latin American researchers produced categories of analysis and explanations rooted in their countries' realities.

The Critical Stance, the New Role

As a result of a critical dissatisfaction with what was being done and what was still needed, a critical social science was translated into a practice and its interpretation constructed under the name of CP, a term that for quite a few was discovered after some 3 to 4 years of trying to make a dent in reality by working along with people in need and striving to live in different conditions.

Psychologists in Latin America were not only aware of the crisis in social psychology, which coincided with the crisis of the academic system and the critical vision of society (Carranza & Almeida, 1995; Wiesenfeld & Sánchez, 1995), but also a part of them wanted to overcome this crisis by transforming the psychologists' role and the ways of performing that role. Those "coincidences" that had begun to be discussed among Latin American social psychologists amidst the course of becoming community psychologists, during the late 1970s and the beginning of the 1980s, were another transformation-inducing influence.

Antecedents for Community Psychology in Latin America

As it usually happens in the realm of science, CP did not fall from a cloud or step out of the waters, complete and beautifully shaped. Social conditions and scouting ideas advancing modes of perceiving, interpreting, explaining, and doing generated beliefs and disbeliefs and fostered experiences that pointed out weaknesses in the accepted ways of thinking, showed empty spaces, and provided a taste of what could be. This happened in spite of the brief or isolated character initial experiences (research carried out, but which did not lead to papers published) or scattered publications might have had (Escovar, 1979; Irizarry & Serrano-García, 1979; Montero, 1980). Hence, authors writing about the history, evolution, and systematization of CP in our part of the American continent usually are careful and keen about bringing up those previous unpublished experiences and little known papers that were predecessors of this field of psychology (Alfaro, 1993; Asún, Krause, Aceituno, Alfaro & Morales, 1995; Carranza & Almeida, 1995; Chinkes, Lapalma & Nicenboim, 1995; Giorgi, Rodríguez & Rudolf, in press; Granada-Echeverry, 1995; Krause-Jacobs & Jaramillo, 1998; Lane & Sawaia, 1995; López-Sánchez & Serrano-García, 1995; Montero, 1982, 1988, 1995, 1998a; Reid & Aguilar, 1995; Wiesenfeld, Sánchez & Cronick, 1995).

Those antecedents to the development of CP can be summarized as follows:

- Antecedents can be found in private projects and social policies trying to respond with more or less success to the demands and needs of the population, especially concerning mental health. In some cases, like Venezuela (Montero, 1988), the psychological action took place at communities but was designed and directed at governmental institutions created with the objective to help develop and organize low-income communities. Sociologists, anthropologists, social workers, and also psychologists were the agents.
- Those antecedents (projects and policies) were not originated within psychology. Most were produced in the field of medicine (but incorporated

psychologists), especially those concerning prevention. Some were part of the movement to reform psychiatry and psychiatric institutions. Examples can be found in the "intracommunity psychiatry" and "population mental health" created in Chile between 1968 and 1973 (Asun, Krause, Aceituno, Alfaro & Morales, 1995), and in the "community psychiatry" proposed by some projects in Argentina during the 1960s. Actions of this type were influenced in some cases by the anti-psychiatry tendency generated by Basaglia and Basaglia (1977) in Italy, during the sixties. There was also a Latin American movement called "alternatives to psychiatry," which was very active in the 1970s and early 1980s. Community intervention projects developed by social scientists (critical sociology; popular education) also had a major influence. Others happened within the social sciences field.

- Prevention was the main goal of the antecedents. In order to achieve that prevention, in some cases, the incorporation and participation of communities was sought.
- Other antecedents can be found in academic programs produced in Brazil and Chile, as early as the 1950s, but mainly in the 1960s, particularly in social psychology courses or in research centers in Argentina, Brazil, Chile, Colombia, Mexico, Perú, and Venezuela, carrying out projects aiming to deal with and solve social problems of communities in need.

Academic Development of Community Psychology in Latin America

The need to have a socially meaningful practice and at the same time to derive from it knowledge produced academic changes. Some came very fast, some have been very slow. In this section, we describe how and when CP entered academia. The second half of the 1970s was teeming with criticism to social psychology, and although some academic courses began approaching community aspects (see the Colombian information later in this chapter), two countries were almost simultaneous in introducing CP systematic studies: Mexico and Puerto Rico. The latter generated both undergraduate and graduate courses and rapidly began developing methodological and theoretical knowledge. The former had two experiences, quite different, which did not have the influence obtained by the Puerto Rican development.

Puerto Rico as an Academic Cornerstone for Community Psychology

Although the values and ideals of CP roamed the halls of the University of Puerto Rico long before 1975, it was in that year that an official program on the discipline was established. Few published works have addressed its development in detail. Two notable exceptions are the writings of Rivera-Medina (1992) and Serrano-García and Alvarez Hernández (1992). These serve as historical documentation of the program's development and the challenges faced ever since.

The program established in 1975 encompassed a master's degree in social–CP. Later during the same year, the program was expanded to include a Ph.D. degree. Its development is contextualized by Rivera-Medina (1992) in a social sciences department whose professors and students felt the need to establish an academic program within the Department of Psychology that addressed the most common social problems in Puerto Rico differently from traditional clinical psychology. Concerns over quality of life and community health were present during the development of the program, particularly with reference to poor and socially marginalized communities. These concerns fostered a strong support of primary prevention efforts that at the time opposed the traditional medical model as a means to solve social problems. In this sense, the program was a reflection of the dissatisfaction with clinical and social psychology spanning the United States and Latin America.

Although the program objectives have changed over time, a strong interest has always been manifested in the crucial role of research in addressing community needs and the development of intervention skills among students. These objectives have been permeated by the need to develop critical ways of thinking about the Puerto Rican realities. Social change is expressed as the main objective that permeates the ideals of the program. The commitment of the program with the idea of social change was strengthened in 1978 with the recruitment of faculty members with formal education in CP (from the United States), influenced by the ideas of psychologists from the United States and Latin America (Rivera-Medina, 1992).

The emphasis on social change and a critical perspective of social phenomena prompted the program to establish the social constructionist perspective of Berger and Luckman (1967) as a cornerstone of the program's theoretical underpinning. These positions were also manifested in the program's interest in developing psychologists interested and committed to "intervention in research" (different from action-research) promoting interventions developed simultaneously with research projects (Serrano-García, López & Rivera-Medina, 1992).

CP has always faced challenges from mainstream psychology whose purpose and ideals vary greatly from ours. This situation has caused community psychologists to constantly try to answer two questions: Who are we? and What do we do? This Puerto Rican program in CP has been characterized by a constant debate on its identity(ies) within a psychology program and in the academy. The debate as to what social–community psychology is and what it contributes to society and the advancement of scientific knowledge continues to this day. Probably the most evident manifestation is the publication of a paper on the "identity" of social–CP by Mangual Rodríguez (2000) in a local journal explaining to its readers (mainly clinical psychologists) what the discipline is and its philosophical and social dimensions. Although the program has graduated almost 100 students in the past three decades (B. Ortiz, personal communication, November 18, 2004), the debate seems to be a never ending one. In our opinion, this is a sign of strength within the program and the challenges faced when creating a different psychological praxis within an academic setting. After all, a critical praxis requires constant reflection as to one's role within the community, in this case in academia.

This experience of establishing CP in Puerto Rico is better understood in light of the concurrent developments happening throughout other countries in Latin America. Let us explore some of those developments in CP courses and practices.

Mexico: Tradition and Innovation

By 1977, the Instituto Tecnológico y de Estudios Superiores de Occidente (ITESO), in Guadalajara, México, had introduced courses in CP at the undergraduate level and started a master's course in CP with the participation of J.R. Newbrough, a community psychologist from the United States (Gómez del Campo, 1986). At the same time, the unique academic experience and psychology degree offered by the Iztacala Section of the Universidad Nacional Autónoma de México was being developed. This experience ended in 1982, but it deserves special mention, for it presented a program of studies for a career in psychology where all subjects were specifically oriented towards the community and had a behaviorist tendency. The experience ended after Emilio Ribes-Iñesta, its founder, left the program, and it took an approach towards a traditional psychology curriculum.

The ITESO continues offering its courses in CP but has not had much international projection. The Iztacala experience, in spite of its originality and the ambitious goals, produced more curiosity than admirers disposed to try and follow the model. Its short life (5 years) and probably theoretical differences contributed to this situation.

Also during the 1970s, five Mexican universities were simultaneously including CP content in their programs, although not as specific courses with that denomination: Universidad Autónoma del Estado de México, Universidad Autónoma del Estado de Guerrero, Universidad Autónoma de Nuevo León, Universidad Autónoma de Sinaloa, and Universidad de Guadalajara.

The Autonomous University of Morelos State (UAEM) as well as the Autonomous University of Puebla (Almeida, Martínez & Varela, 1995) have developed programs of studies in CP during the past 20 years while at the same time generating active community development practices (CEDeFT, 1986). Valenzuela Cota (1995) mentions that clinical psychology used to have a practice in communities during the 1970s related to mental health programs. She mentions that the Universidad Nacional Autónoma de México (UNAM) created a Community Centre at the Psychology Faculty, which provided clinical services as well as research. Recently, in 2004, at the UNAM a course in CP with a social and educational orientation was created by Dr. María Montero at the Faculty of Psychology. The orientation of this course is the training of practitioners in "Psychology and Community," considering CP as a form of psychology applied to the community. It offers training in five types of competencies: (1) theoretical–methodological; (2) technical; (3) contextual; (4) adaptability, managerial and innovative; and (5) ethics.

Development and Diffusion of Community-Related Specific Courses and Practice in Other Latin American Countries

Because Latin America is such a large region, the speed of creation of an academic niche for CP, and even for general work with communities, has been quite uneven. During the 1970s, some community-related courses were included in academic syllabi. Those subjects were not exactly referring to CP, but certainly they were approaching it and preannouncing systematic studies in the field. They also were fostering a strong support of primary prevention efforts that, at the time, opposed the traditional medical model as a means to solve social problems.

By the 1980s, faculties and schools of psychology in most major universities in Latin American countries included some type of course or subjects in CP, both at the undergraduate and graduate levels. They also started successful programs of community research and intervention. By the early 1980s, not only were there enough experiences to prove the existence of the field, but also methodological and theoretical contributions were creating the scientific space of the discipline. By the 1990s, in most Latin American countries, CP had obtained an academic place.

In many cases, CP entered the academic world through the road opened by social psychology, as an applied form of it (Brazil, Chile, Colombia, Costa Rica, Dominican Republic, México, Perú, and Venezuela have been examples of this approach). Between 1976 and 1979, many psychologists later defining themselves as community psychologists thought they were doing a community type of social psychology. In 1979, at the XVII Interamerican Congress of Psychology, celebrated in Lima, Perú, the CP denomination came to be generalized. There, for the first time, psychologists from different countries in the Americas had the opportunity to meet and discuss their practice, including theoretical and methodological aspects. The latest addition of which we have had information was created in the year 2000 in Ecuador at Universidad Politécnica Salesiana del Ecuador. It is the first undergraduate course including community psychology as part of the psychology syllabus, and they are celebrating in August 2006 the First Ecuadorian Congress of Community Psychology.

Graduate Studies in CP

Until the 1990s, with the exception of the University of Puerto Rico and the ITESO in Mexico, the predominant mode of academic insertion was the inclusion of specific subjects about CP within general undergraduate studies in psychology, followed by postgraduate studies in CP, or by the possibility of obtaining a master's or a Ph.D. degree in social psychology, or more generically, in psychology, with specific CP contents. This last model is predominant, probably because it allows the possibility for students of manifold roads within the same generic program. Most universities leave open the possibility for their students to become specialists according to their specific interests; limited only by the capacity of the programs to provide the right mentors. Some examples include Universidad Central de Venezuela; Pontificia Universidade Católica of São Paulo, Pontificia Universidade Católica de Río Grande do Sul, Universidade Federal de Rio Grande do Sul, and Universidade Federal do Espirito Santo (these four in Brazil); Pontificia Universidad Católica de Chile and Universidad de Chile; Universidad Nacional Autónoma de México; and the Universidad Nacional de Tucumán in Argentina.[1]

The Pioneers and the Dissemination of CP in Latin America

Luis A. Escovar played a linking and disseminating role for CP. During the second part of the 1970s, he carried out important community work with peasants in the Panamanian Tonosí region, employing both attribution and alienation theories in the effort to produce some explanation to the passivity he was trying to fight and to the changes produced during community interventions. He traveled through Latin America observing, lecturing and, diffusing that information, as well as trying to develop a theoretical model to explain and understand the new practice. This model (Escovar called it "Social Psychology for Development") was later published in Venezuela (Escovar, 1979; 1980). Escovar left the scene by the early 1980s, but before that, in 1979, he created a task force for CP, within the Interamerican Society of Psychology (ISP), incorporating a small but enthusiastic group of psychologists.[2] Lively discussions, both face to face and by correspondence; intense exchange of papers, questions, answers, doubts, criticism and jokes, as well as academic exchanges between the countries involved, gave way to strong scientific links and friendships still alive today. The task force met with certain reticence from some people, in some academic ambits, promptly

---

[1] The above-mentioned academic institutions are examples, probably others were simultaneously doing the same, but the authors have not had information about them or could not verify it.

[2] Leonte Brea and Emmanuel Silvestre from Dominican Republic; Luis Correa and Bernardo Jiménez from Colombia; Sylvia Lane and Marilia Graziano from Brazil; Marta Mercedes Morán from El Salvador; Luis Escovar from Panamá; Maritza Montero and Alberto Ocando from Venezuela; and Eduardo Rivera-Medina and Irma Serrano-García, who were the only ones, at that time, with community psychological professional identities.

silenced by the ever increasing production that followed. By the beginning of the 1990s, CP had installed itself as a psychological domain, and the ISP had a CP Commission that began producing proceedings and, later, books. The latest was presented in 2005 (Varas Díaz & Serrano-García, 2005).

The ideas developed in Puerto Rico were among the first to travel to other countries in the region, and for their diffusion, the *Boletín* and other publications of the Venezuelan Association of Social Psychology (AVEPSO) were prominent. Not only Escovar's papers, but also two early and very influential works produced in Puerto Rico (Irizarry & Serrano-García, 1979; Santiago, Serrano-García & Perfecto, 1983), as well as works by other authors emerging during the 1980s and 1990s were also published in the *Boletín*, now called *Revista de AVEPSO*.

In some countries, academic courses in CP coexisted with an important practice carried out by NGOs and other institutions (e.g., churches, health organizations). Sometimes this was a politically oriented community mental health work focused on intervention, such as what happened in Chile during the Pinochet dictatorship, where NGOs were providing clinical assistance to victims of repression and their families. In other countries, the practice, carried out as a state policy, preceded the academic appearance of the field. This was the case of Venezuela, where two governmental foundations (Fundacomun and Fundasocial) were created in the late 1960s and early 1970s for the organization and development of communities. In that same country, along with abundant academic research, the first course in CP was created in 1986 at the School of Psychology of Universidad Central de Venezuela (Montero, 1988).

Brazil: Rapid Growth and Development

Brazil, a country that currently has a wide range of community studies and practice, during the 1970s had begun producing critical views of social psychology that led to the promotion, in the early 1980s, of academic changes in teaching and in the perspectives to study the Brazilian society (Lane & Codo, 1984). Lane (1996), a leading Brazilian social psychologist, placed a preventive approach to mental health, combined with the multidisciplinary approach of "popular education" (the adult education created by Paulo Freire), and its participatory perspective as the main influences propelling the creation of CP in Brazil. Cruz, Quintal de Freitas, and Amoretti (in press) consider that CP, as a systematic field within psychology, received its first impulse from academic programs and, specially, from the support received from Brazilian Social Psychology Society (ABRAPSO).

The works of Lane and Sawaia (1991, 1995) and Sawaia (1994) could be considered as representative of the critical focus and the social change orientation characteristics of much Brazilian community psychological work. Another strong feature of the CP carried out in this country is its search for theoretical explanations and rigorous methodological approach. By the 1980s, CP in Brazil had fully emerged and consolidated itself as an academic practice. This was preceded by a social practice developed since the mid-20th century, when it began to extend through governmental organizations, being included as part of social policies. In the practice that was being developed emerged first the specificity of the new field (CP), and later (towards 1988) with the academic input came the theory–practice systematization. But practice, according to Quintal de Freitas (1998b), has begun to drift towards an ameliorative and demobilizing tendency. Scarparo (2005) also refers to the role played by the concern with mental health as one of the main factors in the beginnings of CP in Rio Grande do Sul, a region in southern Brazil.

Although usually the focus of CP production tends to be placed in the southern (and more industrialized) part of the country (São Paulo, Minas Gerais; Rio Grande do Sul, Paraná), it should be said that in northern areas (Ceará, Paraíba) there are also active centres of CP praxis (dialectic relation between theory and practice) with a defined theoretical profile (Brandão, 1999). An example is the case for the Núcleo de Psicología Comunitária of the Federal University of Ceará (Mendes and Correia, 1999). There, first as a practice that was part of a course in "Psicologia Popular" (1982) and later (1988) as "Psicologia Comunitaria" (CP), a conception of CP was developed, founded upon the relation between consciousness and life, engaged in a Latin American comprehension of community phenomena, intervening while researching, researching during interventions; essentially dynamic, historic, and participatory (Góis, 2003).

Colombia: Practice and Academia

Arango Calad (unpublished manuscript) collected papers covering some 25 years of CP development and reviewing the emergence of CP studies at Universidad del Valle in Cali, Colombia. At this university, a subject called "community problems" was created in 1976, showing the interest felt about the field. From his first course in 1979, when he was appointed as lecturer at a CP undergraduate seminar (also created in 1976), to 1992 when he left in order to do graduate studies in Spain, he describes the development of CP in that university, as a critical line of action, linked to the Network of Alternatives to Psychiatry (a Latin American movement favoring a different treatment for mental patients, inspired by Basaglia's ideas), as well as towards Freire's Popular Education. By the end of the 1990s, CP at Universidad del Valle had left the undergraduate classrooms, becoming part of postgraduate courses in psychology and in popular education and community development.

In Bogotá, Javeriana University offered until 2005 a master's course in CP that was created in the 1980s. Furthermore, the Costa Atlántica Project at Universidad del Norte in Barranquilla, one of the most successful projects in the country, as well as community projects carried out at Universidad del Valle in Cali, illustrate well the expansive and fruitful character of the union between systematic studies and community interventions. Other universities in Manizales, Popayán, and other cities have included CP in the psychological studies curricula. And a master's course in CP is being created at Universidad de Medellín in Colombia.

Chile: From Resistance to Institutionalization

Chile has had an interesting development. Alfaro (2000) says that after the intracommunity psychiatry and population mental health work carried out in the 1950s and early 1960s, a practice generated as a function of social demands was developed, later giving way to academic programs. Asun, Krause-Jacob, Aceituno, Alfaro, and Morales (1995) reiterate this information. CP practiced by nongovernmental institutions such as ILAS,[3] PIDEE, and FASIC[4] and church programs played an important role during the Pinochet dictatorship, allowing a practice directed to help the victims of political repression and aggression; to empower the communities in order to resist these sources of oppression and protect themselves; to keep active the political consciousness of the population; and to defend human rights. At the same time, courses in CP where part of the curricula in many state and private universities in that country (i.e., Universidad de Chile among the former; Universidad Católica de Chile and Universidad Diego Portales, among the latter). It was then a community mental health politically oriented psychology, aware of its social role, incorporating the people's participation, and doing what was most necessary at the moment. It defined its role, as in other Latin American countries, as committed to social change. Krause-Jacob and Jaramillo Torrens (1998) and Krause-Jacob (2002) have described the development of CP in Chile from the 1960s to the late 1990s. Drawing from them, we can outline the main traits characterizing CP in that country: social commitment, quality of life, and parallelism between practice and academia. They also have studied the transformations that have taken place in Santiago de Chile showing the increasing institutionalisation of community psychological programs during the past 15 years; something that has also been studied by Piper (2003). According to those studies, institutionalization has begun to change the orientation of CP, driving it toward a form of assistance controlled by organizations.

The Insular Caribbean: Dominican Republic, Haiti, and Cuba

The role of community psychology within academic settings in the insular Caribbean has been equivocal. On one hand, Puerto Rico is an example of how community psychology made its way into faculties halls early during the

---

[3] ILAS publications (e.g., ILAS: Becker and Lira, 1989; ILAS: Lira, 1994) evidence the intricate interaction between political and community psychology in Chile. ILAS: Institute of Latin American Studies and Human Rights.
[4] PIDEE: Protection for Infants in Emergency State; FASIC: Foundation for Social Aid of Christian Churches.

1970s. On the other hand, the experience in the Dominican Republic, Cuba, and Haiti has been different. Haiti has never had a program on the discipline in any university. In the early 1980s, there was some interest in linking the community to health psychology in the Dominican Republic, and a master's degree was established in the Autonomous University of Santo Domingo. Unfortunately, the demand for training in industrial and organizational psychology has haltered in its development and implementation (B. Ortíz Torres, personal communication, October 22, 2004). These diverse levels of manifestations in academic settings and practice evidence the challenges that the establishment of the discipline has faced in Caribbean scenarios.

In Cuba, health psychology made a fast development and was frequently represented at Interamerican Conferences, and some psychologists working in the field came to be well-known throughout the continent. On the contrary, CP as a specific branch of psychology is rather recent. It was only during the 1990s that community psychologists in other Latin American countries began to have news about some undergraduate courses being created in the island, and contacts about community work and publications began to flow in that direction. After the revolution, the Cuban government concentrated great efforts into the development of both educational and health systems; developing a system of relations and control about educational and health needs in the population functioning through the Committees for the Defense of the Revolution (CDR). Those committees had a political function serving as links between the population and the state.

Carreño (2005) gives two reasons for this late appearance: The "uncritical import of perspectives from Soviet psychology," which generated conditions impeding to understand that community and population are not synonyms, as well as "the diverse subjectivities of their members" (pp. 4–5). The social–historical context: The revolutionary model supposed that the government's policies would cover all of the population needs and did not consider a community approach as a priority.

Community psychology had to wait until the late 1980s and mainly the 1990s to acquire an academic and social place. Probably the first Cuban paper concerning CP known outside the country was published by the *Journal of Community Psychology* (1998) and written by Manuel Calviño. During the past decade, some institutions and groups have begun to carry out community work projects. An example is The Martin Luther King Jr. Memorial Centre, created by the Cuban Presbyterian Church at the beginning of the 1990s. That centre has had the influence of "Liberation Theology" and promotes community participation (Carreño, 2005).

Again Carreño (2005), our main source of information, says that three master's courses in CP have been created at Universidad of Havana; Universidad of Santa Clara (corroborated by B. Ortiz, personal communication, October 22, 2004), and at the National Sexual Education Centre. She also considers that this still is "a modest development in terms of research and publishing," because of the "scarcity of writing, conceptualization and theoretical production" due to the novelty of the field in the country (Carreño, p. 1); although practice is increasing.

Three Central American Countries: Costa Rica, Honduras, and El Salvador

Costa Rica, where academic studies in psychology started in the 1970s, introduced CP from the very beginning at the undergraduate level, giving both theoretical and methodological training in the field and generating a line of research–interventions where political perspective and CP are intertwined (Garita & Vargas, 1991; Cordero, 1995); something characteristic of much of the CP being carried out in Latin America. From Honduras we have only obtained information about a program of childcare (Atención Integral al Niño; AIN) created by the government. This program is focused on health and nutrition for babies and toddlers under 2 years of age, and it incorporates community participation (Suárez-Balcázar, Balcázar & Villalobos, 2001).

Also during the mid-1970s, CP appeared in El Salvador (Moran, 1979), equally marked by that joint action between political- and community-oriented studies and practice. This was an inevitable link in a country that was a battlefield until the early 1990s. Those particular political circumstances gave way to a political psychology, started by Ignacio Martín-Baró, which by 1986 gave way to what this author defined as a possible answer to the unjust and oppressive conditions affecting a vast majority of the Latin American population: the psychology of liberation. This psychology of liberation incorporates elements that were already present in the CP being developed; while at the same time becoming a major current influence in the CP being done in the continent.

Argentina, Uruguay, and Paraguay

The development and current state of CP in Argentina is being addressed by another chapter of this book. We shall only mention that in 1988, the Avellaneda Project was created at the Psychology Faculty of Universidad de Buenos Aires (Chinkes, Lapalma & Nicenboim, 1995; Saforcada, 1992). That project was based on a larger program: the "Social Epidemiology and Community Psychology Program." Saul Fuks created in the mid-1980s a community program at the Extension Secretariat of National University of Rosario, the Centro de Asistencia a la Comunidad (CeAc, Centre for Community Assistance). During the early 1990s, other community intervention and assistance centres were created, among them the UNIR (Una Nueva Iniciativa Rural) Project at San Miguel de Tucumán, integrating community interventions carried out by different disciplines, including community psychological ones. And as this book is being prepared, a graduate program in CP is being created at the National University of Lanús, in the Buenos Aires province.

In Uruguay, in spite of community work carried out by NGOs and by social workers during the 1960s (Carrasco, 1998; Rodríguez, 1998), the Universidad de la República in Uruguay created the first academic course in CP only in 1988, adding another one ("Techniques of Community Assessment") as part of the health field of studies at the Faculty of Psychology in 1994. An interesting practice and research in the field is being carried out by members of the Psychology Faculty (Giorgi, Rodríguez, Rudolf, Netto, personal communications). Paraguay has not had systematic academic programs in CP until very recently. Contacts with communities were focused from a medical perspective directed by psychiatrists or hygienists. Later, CP projects were carried out at Universidad Católica, but the first course in CP at Universidad Nacional was created in the first semester of 2004, at the undergraduate level (Unsain, 2004).

Perú

CP courses exist in several Perúvian universities, and important projects directed to work with communities have been created within and without them. An example of these is the community psychological work carried out in the area of children's mental health by the Program for Attending to Child Mental Health (PASMI), a program created in 1994, whose target is the child victims of political violence, specially those whose families, or what remains of them, have been displaced (Avenzur & Padilla, 2000; Bustamante, 2000). EDAPROSPO is another organization carrying out community work (education and development) at poor suburbs in the outskirts of Lima (Montero López, 1992; Castro, Jerónimo, Pinto & Yarnold, 1992). The Childhood and Family Network (REDINFA) carries out outstanding work with community groups and organizations of displaced people, recovering with them the historic collective memories of those groups (Chauca, Bustamante & Oviedo, 2004a; 2004b).

Venezuela: From Government Programs to Academia

The academic milieu was not the first to introduce the community approach in Venezuela. Community work and interventions in this country began during the late 1960s, blooming in the 1970s. Organizations like CONSALUD (2001), CESAP (Centre for People's Action Services), CEPAP, MIC (Movement for the Integration of the Communities), among others developed an intense and important activity, still in action. Those organizations and programs hired social psychologists, and for a while, in the late 1970s, the transformational efforts carried out by social psychologists in academic centers ran parallel to what those organizations were carrying out.

In Venezuela, CP had its first academic incursions through research carried out in the Social Psychology Department at Universidad Central de Venezuela (UCV) from the mid-1970s on. But CP was only introduced as a formal course in 1986 as part of the social psychology undergraduate studies. Later, during the 1990s, the master's course in social psychology was modified to allow the introduction of CP as a line of studies and research (equivalent to what is called a major), and at the same time a graduate course of three semesters entitled "Resolving Social Problems," focused in communities, was created. It should be said that master's and Ph.D. theses in social psychology have been a very prolific way to carry out CP research. Simón Rodríguez University incorporates in its Education Studies a community orientation, and the School of Psychology, created in May 2004 at Universidad Metropolitana, in Caracas, has directed one of the four main lines chosen as fields to apply psychology to community-oriented studies. In 1999, Universidad Católica "Andrés Bello" introduced a graduate course in community–clinical psychology and almost immediately began to publish an Annual Review (Revista de Psicología Clínica-Comunitaria) about this specific branch of CP, oriented towards the creation of a clinical practice incorporating the community. The students of this course carry out their community projects through the "Parque Social 'Manuel Aguirre, S.J.,'" an institution providing services to communities, in the educational, medical, legal, and psychological fields.

Currently, academic programs, NGO activities, and autonomous communities' and governmental projects make community studies and work a thriving milieu where visiting scholars from Europe and other Latin American countries carry out observations and practices.

What Is Currently Being Done by Community Psychology in Latin America

This brief summary of the academic development of CP in Latin America does not intend to give a complete view of the continent but just a glimpse into the commonalities and some differences in the development of the discipline in this region. It could take another book to develop in detail the network of influences, the tendencies and impacts of the publications made in CP (Venezuela, Brazil, and Puerto Rico produce the larger portion of the Latin American CP books and papers published in and out of the region; followed by Chile, Perú, and Colombia); the complex weave of psychological, sociological, historic, economic, and political factors influencing the development of CP in Latin America. We feel it is only possible to summarize the main characteristics in the community practice, research and teaching in the continent, as well as the contributions to the development of the discipline in this chapter.

It is important to point out that CP has not been conceived as a practice and realm in which only one type of knowledge reigns. If something has characterized the Latin American way to do CP, it is it's opening to other forms of knowledge through a multidisciplinary perspective (e.g., sociology, anthropology, ethnography, philosophy, and several branches of psychology, including social psychology). What is called ordinary or commonsense knowledge and also folk or indigenous ways of knowing have always had a place along with the scientific production. This is expressed in the understanding that people in the communities know things that the psychologists working with them do not; just as we psychologists introduce the community to new information and practices. Therefore, two kinds of agents carry out the tasks necessary to generate changes in communities: external agents, those coming from academic or other type of institutions; and internal agents such as stakeholders from the communities. Both produce knowledge, create practices, and develop explanations and perspectives to interpret what is happening. Moreover, CP values, research techniques, and intervention strategies are being applied to a wide variety of issues including human sexuality (Feliciano, 2004), stigmatization (Varas Díaz, 2002b; Varas Díaz, Serrano-García & Toro Alfonso, 2004), public policy evaluation (Pérez Jiménez, 1995), couples and family dynamics (Cintrón Bou & Walters Pacheco, 2004), among many other subjects.

Current Topics and Problems in Latin American CP

The following topics and problems are currently being addressed by Latin American community psychologists. This is not an exhaustive list, and we do not believe there is such a thing as what usually is called "state-of-the-art." All intents to cover what is happening everywhere at the same time are still utopian. So, surely there are many specific issues or subjects that are the object of research and intervention, but those presented here can be found in recent literature and in reports from the region.

1. Discussion of topics related to *epistemology, ontology, ethics, politics,* and *methodology*. Conceptions and critical discussions about what to do and why and how to do it in CP configure a paradigm and provide definitions of its object–subject of study (Cruz, Quintal de Freitas & Amoretti, in press; Ferullo de Parajón, 1991; Montero, 1999, 2002a, 2002b, 2003a; Moreno, 1999; Ortiz, 2000; Sawaia, 1998; Wiesenfeld, 1998). That paradigm addresses the topics mentioned above and has been called both "the Critical Construction and Transformation Paradigm" (Montero, 1998b) or simply the Latin American CP. Certainly, the generative responses produced within the Latin American part of the continent define the subjects (ontology) of CP research and action. They also have created a mode of producing knowledge (epistemology), incorporating inputs from both scientific and ordinary knowledge. They have developed participatory methods and modes of intervention responding to the needs of the communities while incorporating those communities to the definition, solution of their problems, or satisfaction of their needs (methodology). Awareness and critique of life conditions, as well as empowerment and liberation of

communities' stakeholders and groups, and the development of citizenry show the relationship between CP and politics, understood in its transcendent sense. Ethics are expressed through the episteme of relatedness (Moreno, 1993; Montero, 1998b, 2002b, 2003a, 2003c, 2004) and the introduction of *analectics* (Dussel, 1998). Analectics are understood as an extension of dialectics incorporating a new possibility in the construction of knowledge: otherness (*alterity*), not related to the lifeworld of the I, from which knowledge is constructed.[5] To this is added the demands for respect and inclusion in the construction of knowledge, of the Other in its similarity and in its diversity. These aspects configure a paradigm in construction.

2. The difficulties and ways to define or to conceptualize the *notion of community*, and sense of community, and the consequences of this issue upon practice (Krause-Jacob, 2001; Montero, 1998a, 1998c, 2004). The community has been studied both from the location and the relation perspectives, and its fuzzy character has also being pointed out. After going through many reports, book chapters, articles in journals, and academic papers, we dare to say that the prevailing view is that of considering the community as an expression of social life, not only inevitable because of the gregarious character of human beings, but also one that allows people to thrive, be it by the creation of urban groups or by linking people as a function of common interests. As the experiences gathered in the past 40 years show, community psychologists in Latin America have learned both to put aside romantic views of human solidarity and the consideration of communities as evil pits. Communities are a human phenomenon, with all the assets and difficulties of any other human deed. They have an important role in facilitating the achievement of a better quality of life, as much as they can obstruct that very task. Community psychologists know they have to deal with dichotomy.

3. *Community participation*, its definition, effects, scope, and limitations (Hernández, 1998; Montero, 1996; Sánchez, 2000, 2004). Participation is a main issue in Latin American CP. Although there are a certain number of projects carried out from a traditional-institutional perspective; that is, designed and directed according to goals established at hospitals, schools, and other institutions, there is an ever increasing incorporation of the people's participation in different degrees of engagement. The participatory character of CP is one of its main features in Latin America, lending to it a distinctive character.

4. *Community networks* and their scope and hurdles presented in community practice related to them (Goncalves de Freitas & Montero, 2003; Itriago & Itriago, 2000; Morillo de Hidalgo, 2000). Although it is not the

---

[5] Analectics comes from the Greek word *anas*, meaning what is beyond, in another plane, or another perspective.

most extended field of research, in Colombia, Brazil, and Venezuela, and also from a general perspective transcending the community in Argentina (Dabas, 1993), networks are a developing area of community studies. CP has been studying in the above-mentioned countries, both its positive and its limiting effects in community development.

5. Modes of applying *participatory action-research* (PAR) and its possibilities as a method in the CP field (Rodríguez Gabarron & Hernández-Landa, 1994; Montero, 1994a, 2006, 2000b, 2006; Santiago, Serrano-García & Perfecto, 1992). PAR has been present in the application of CP since its introduction in Latin American countries. Characteristic of its development has been the interaction kept with other social sciences and practices (especially adult education and sociology). In the first papers published and diffused throughout the region, methodological considerations about participatory methods, and specifically to PAR, are frequent (e.g., Serrano-García & Irizarry, 1979).

6. The role of *emotion and affectivity* in community work, and in the transformations expected to happen in the communities is also a line with research and action stemming out of the fact that a lot of community work is the outcome of carefully reasoned, strategically planned, and strong emotional motivation sustaining and driving it. Acknowledging the force of affection has helped both participants and researchers understand what mobilizes and what freezes community participation at certain moments (Lane & Sawaia, 1991; Lane & Camargo, 1994; Galano, 1994; León & Montenegro, 1998; Sawaia, 2003, Varas Díaz & Serrano-García, 2002).

7. *Community health and its promotion* and the *prevention* of psychological and other illnesses (Fernández Alvarez, 1994; Fernández Alvarez & Nicemboim, 1998; Ortiz-Torres, Rosado & Rapkin, 2004; Serrano-García, Bravo-Vick, Rosario-Collazo & Gorrín-Peralta, 1998; Toro Alfonso & Varas Díaz, 2004; Varas Díaz & Toro Alfonso, in press; Samaniego, Antivero, Bártolo, Bonzo, Btesch, Dominguez, Garcia, Labandal, Iurcovich & Villegas, 2005). This is not only a fast-growing field, but also one producing much literature presenting the outcomes of successful projects, showing modes of preventing illnesses, and promoting health practices with the active concourse of community members. The CP perspective has entered the grounds usually covered by health psychology as can be seen in Saforcada (2001). Research and intervention about prevention of illnesses and health promotion in the community have been carried out across Latin America and have been collected and published across the continent. Papers dealing with public and community health from Brazil, Colombia, Honduras, Mexico, Puerto Rico, and Venezuela can be read in Balcázar, Montero, and Newbrough, (2001) and reports about mental health and CP coming from Chile have been presented by Olave and Zambrano in 1993.

8. Critical examination and reflection about main CP *processes and concepts produced in community praxis* (practice producing reflective theory), such as empowerment, community identity, leadership, power, and problematization, de-ideologization and conscientization (Cerullo & Wiesenfeld, 2001; Gonçalves de Freitas, 1997; León, Montenegro, Ramdjan & Villarte, 1997; Montero, 1994b, 2003b, 2004; Serrano-García & López Sánchez, 1994; Vázquez, 2004) taken from the works of Paulo Freire were developed as part of the CP research and intervention, while working on the psychological aspects of those processes. Although introduced first by Paulo Freire, problematization, de-ideologization, de-naturalizing, and conscientization have been adopted by Latin American CP, giving to their definitions a psychological dimension coming out of their being put into community psychological practice through PAR. Many papers and reports coming from research developed in countries like Colombia, Brazil, or Venezuela show the orientation derived from the conceptual framework provided by those notions and phenomena. In the case of concepts that can be found in psychosocial literature, such as empowerment, leadership, power, or identity, the close contact between theory and practice kept by CP in many Latin American countries has provided new perspectives for their understanding and scope.

9. *Power* of, in, and within, the community. Another current topic of research and discussion are the theoretical perspectives of power and of ways to exert that power in the community, by the different agents working within it (Montero, 2003b; Cordero, 1998; Hernández, 1998; Serrano-García & López Sánchez, 1994). This is a topic in which the influences of certain European authors (e.g., Marx, Engels, Gramsci, Foucault) can be seen. Also seen are how those perspectives have taken a different twist when confronted with the community practice carried out in these parts of the world, specifically concerning the weight of the Weberian asymmetry that has marked conceptions of power since the beginning of the 20th century. Considering power as asymmetrical, that is, as present only at one pole of the relation, does not allow liberation, because efforts to subvert the power differentials would lead to a change of oppressors: those before oppressed would become a powerful group relating with others in the same unbalanced way they suffered once. This would leave the inequality intact, because in becoming the new powerful, there would be at the same time new groups dispossessed. Although recognizing the asymmetry in the control of certain resources, what is proposed in this conception is the possibility for all actors in the relationship to display different strategies and different resources in order to obtain their goals (Serrano-García & López Sánchez, 1994; Montero, 2003).

10. *Political effects of psychosocial community work*. The relationship between community and citizenship development, and civil society

development, has been not only explored, but also the object of direct programs of intervention, community education, and the indirect outcome of many community projects throughout Latin America (e.g., Krause-Jacob & Jaramillo, 1998; Quintal de Freitas, 1996; Montero, 1998b, 1998c, 2003a). The liberating character of community work and its awareness and insistence in citizenship education and action respond to this political side of CP.

11. Ways to practice CP and the definition of the *role of community psychologists*. (Krause-Jacob & Jaramillo, 1998; Quintal de Freitas, 1998a, 1998b; Montero & Giuliani, 1999; Roitman & Toledo, 2000; Spink, 2003). In fact, very early in its Latin American development, community psychologists defined themselves as agents of change and catalysers of social transformations. Also, they abandoned the role of experts, preserving at the same time their condition as psychologists and leaving space for ordinary and specific knowledge brought by community members (e.g., stakeholders, participants, members of organised groups within the community). This position allowed for two kinds of agents of change in CP work: external agents (external to the community) and internal agents (belonging to the community).

12. The *liberating and ethical* character that the participatory condition and relatedness oriented CP may have (Quintal de Freitas, 2000; Montero, 2000a, 2003c; Varas Díaz & Serrano-García, 2003). This aspect has been produced by most of the topics previously described, by the exchanges and influence maintained with liberation psychology, and by the development of what has been defined as the episteme of relatedness. This episteme postulates that the relation, and not the isolated individual, is the "primary and ultimate residence of the Being" (Montero, 2003c), for being resides in relatedness; and it happens between elements existing because of the connection established between them. Therefore, subjects are constructed because of and within relations. The ethical consequences of this episteme are the inclusion of diversity and the acknowledgement of the otherness as a condition pertaining to all subjects—essential to their existence.

The initial bases and these 12 topics, as said, do not cover the whole span of Latin American CP. They are just controversial and problematic nodes of study and action. There are more questions than answers, and there is the need to clarify where, in some interventions, psychosocial or health interventions end and CP begins, and why it is so (one of the reasons why CP is considered by many Latin American researchers and authors as a community social psychology). There is, like in other fields of knowledge and science, fuzziness—something that is both puzzling and thought-provoking and, therefore, good ground for research.

Table 2 presents a brief recollection of prominent aspects marking the development of CP in Latin America.

TABLE 2. Dates and prominent aspects in the development of CP in Latin America.*

Dates	Prominent aspects
1955–1974	Social sciences approach to communities: militant (engaged) critical research in sociology; adult education.
	Social policies and government programs sometimes with a populist and politically "clientelist" orientation.
	Introduction of participation within action-research, in social sciences.
	Generation of new concepts: liberation, problematization, conscientization.
1975–1979	First outcomes with community orientation in Latin American social psychology.
	Introduction of academic courses.
	Creation of participatory methods.
	Clinical work with community orientation influenced by the "Alternatives to Psychiatry" movement.
1977	The name of *participatory action research* is definitely linked to the active, participatory research being carried out since the late 1950s.
1980–1983	Definition of community psychology and its object. Construction of a new role for the social psychologists (now community psychologists). (Introduction and reflection about the principles of community psychology. Influence of the *theology of liberation*.
	(Throughout most Latin American countries)
1981–1982	Theoretical discussion of the concept of *need* and development of needs and resources assessment techniques.
1983–1984	Theoretical discussion and practice of the concepts of *strengthening* and *empowerment*, and *de-ideologization*.
From 1983 on	Descriptions of community psychosocial work. Inventory and reflection about the development of CP in each country. Academic courses started in undergraduate and postgraduate programs in a variety of countries.
	(Most Latin American countries)
1985–1995	Analysis and re-conceptualization of the notion of *power*.
1986 on	Interrelation and interinfluence between CP and social psychology of liberation.
1987–1992	Development of theoretical models. Discussion of the *sense of community* concept.
	Critical discussion and theoretical development of concepts tied to the *conscientization* process.
From 1990 on	Theoretical development of the concepts of *habituation, naturalization*, and other concepts linked to them.
1991–2005	Critical revision and definition of the concepts of *participation, community and self-management*, and *participatory-action research* within CP.
1991–2000	Critical revision of the concept of community and the social influence of *active minorities*.
1992	Analysis and critique of the use of medical model in community psychology.
	Defense of the holistic vision developed in Latin America.
	(Most Latin American countries)
1995–1998	Redefinition of the concepts of *familiarization, commitment*, and *systematic restitution* to the community of research findings.
1998	Critical re-conceptualizing of the concept of *social support* and construction of a participative conception of *social community psychology of health*.
1997–2004	Critical construction of the *epistemological bases* of CP.
	Discussion of *ontological bases* of CP.
	Epistemology of relatedness. Elaboration of a paradigm.
1991–1999	Role of *emotion* in community work being discussed. Emotion as an analytical category.

(Continued)

TABLE 2. Dates and prominent aspects in the development of CP
in Latin America*— cont'd.

Dates	Prominent aspects
1998–2004	Critical revision of the concept of systematic restitution of produced knowledge. Re-conceptualization as *evaluative systematic discussion* and *socialized communication of knowledge* produced during community work.
2005	Analysis of the concept of *problematization* as a process leading to transformations and conscientization in community psychological work.

* The aspects highlighted in this table have been mainly produced in those countries where CP has had a more intense development both as a practice and as an academic subject (Brazil, Colombia, Chile, Mexico, Puerto Rico, Venezuela).

What Is Ahead for Community Psychology in Latin America?

Working with communities is like being inside the clockwork of a heart: systolic and diastolic palpitations impel and expel the blood that gives life. Communities also palpitate, contracting and expanding themselves; adding and losing. They are continuously changing. In responding to this community condition, CP has been shaping its own field of work, a task that includes specific subbranches. The first was the line oriented to the *promotion of community health and prevention of illnesses*. This area is solid and will keep growing. Every day, social policies, academic programs, and NGO projects are generated throughout the region in order to deal with the enormous health problems present in our part of the continent. Another subbranch that has been very active in some countries (Venezuela, Brazil, Mexico) is the *environmental–community* line, which could expand and accelerate its growth as the effects of the global warming and the need to protect the natural resources are understood both by governments and population. The impact of studies developed along this line of community work in Venezuela and in Mexico has related the necessities of having a shelter and of preserving the quality of the environment as part of a more general need: that of living in a healthy environment. This has produced successful outcomes in the field of participatory self-managed housing projects for the poor (Jiménez Domínguez, 1994; Sánchez, 2000; Wiesenfeld, 2000).

Community clinical psychology is beginning to develop as a subbranch not only to promote mental health but also to develop and apply forms of psychotherapy carried out *with* communities and accessible to people that have neither the means nor the habit, time and cultural understanding of traditional forms of therapy. We can predict that the field of this new branch of CP will grow and more undergraduate and graduate courses will be created all over Latin America. The social and political role that CP can play for development and for the amelioration of the quality of life for the vast majorities in this part of America has just begun to be understood.

At the same time as new forms of practice are being created, some changes are being experienced in countries like Chile and Brazil (Krause-Jacob, 2002; Quintal de Freitas, 2003), where the type of CP programs centred in the communities and carried out with their full participation are being substituted by traditional ameliorative institutional programs that exclude the people's control. Paternalism prevailing over independence within participatory compromise can paralyze communities, driving them to passivity. As an effect, people can become beggars, depending on overpowering authoritarian governments, distributing aid as payment for fidelity and silence. Countries develop and grow not only by the designs of their governments but by also including in government program the work and opinion of the people. So, in the same measure that Latin America manages to have democratic governments, eradicating corruption, CP will have an emancipatory and empowering role, not only in the satisfaction of needs, but also in the development of citizenry engaged in social transformation. But one should not think that a reasonably good government should be a condition to be obtained before the expansion of CP is produced. CP has to work for the development of conscious citizens. At the same time, citizens have to exert their rights to have honest governments. The movement is dialectic, as is the CP being produced in Latin America.

Latin American CP in a Plural World Perspective

Reading about the development, in many cases, the struggle to develop a CP, in other countries represented in this book has been a learning experience. The first aspect that came into our reflection is that the double origin of CP, one of its sources being social psychology, and the other being clinical psychology, should remind community psychologists of the need to integrate both directions in the search of a more comprehensive, able practice and teaching. Some countries in Latin America and elsewhere have achieved that integration, but there still is much to do, and the subbranches announcing themselves not only in this regions but in some other countries (we found particularly interesting the information coming from India, Aotearoa/New Zealand, and Australia, and the ways they are studying and incorporating indigenous sources of knowledge). One can see how out of the narratives coming from America, Asia, Africa, and Europe, the constitution of CP as a field trying to respond to social conditions and exigencies is being developed. It is very revealing to read about how, in a variety of ways, efforts are been made to respond to each country's peculiarities and culture.

Latin America shares with other countries (e.g., Aotearoa/New Zealand, Canada, Germany, United States) the criticism of the dominance of positivist theories and methods, as well as of the individualistic tendency of mainstream psychology, as one of the motivational forces leading to the production of a CP. But at the same time, conflicts between methods and their validity, about the role played by psychologists and their relations with what used to be "subjects" and now are seen as participants, and about the theories supporting these views are not settled. Reflecting about this, we think that is a good sign, for the contradictions between both paradigms will help to strengthen their best outcomes, thus enriching psychology as a science.

Contrasting Latin American academic inclusion of CP with what has happened in other countries can lead to a view of the model prevalent in most Latin American countries (generic titles for graduate programs, with specific theses in CP included under such "umbrella" courses) in a different way: it can be considered as a useful way for CP to penetrate the academic shield, facilitating the space for teaching and research in the field, without having to go through endless administrative corridors that are usually the domain of very traditional scholars. But it makes one acutely aware that although an academic identity is developing, this very way can be a hurdle for its strengthening, so more specific programs should be created too.

Possible increase of contradictions between community empowerment through self-management, and public policies and specific programs, may be expected. CP as a discipline for social transformation may collide with populist approaches that, while exalting the people's welfare, actually demobilize the people's independent participation and voicing of their opinions, setting back the liberating effect sought by CP. This point highlights the political character of CP. The term *political* is here understood as the democratic occupation and intervention of the public space, to which every citizen is entitled in a democratic political system. Necessarily, the conceptions of power and empowerment must be carefully defined and studied, for as is pointed out in the U.S. chapter, those terms can be easily deprived of their liberating meaning, becoming senseless words.

This book has been conceived as an effort to present the diversity and plurality of CP. Indeed one can see it in the chapters integrating it. Voicing the reflections provoked by the array of experiences, influences, hurdles, achievements, and developments, and in four words, we think that community psychologists should: *Look around, focus inside.*

References

Alfaro, J. (1993). Elementos para una definición de la psicología comunitaria. In R. M. Olave & L. Zambrano (Eds.), *Psicología comunitaria y salud mental en Chile* (pp. 14-31). Santiago, Chile: Universidad Diego Portales.

Alfaro, J. (2000). *Discusiones en Psicología Comunitaria.* Santiago, Chile: Universidad Diego Portales.

Almeida, E., Martínez, M. & Varela, M. (Eds.). (1995). *Psicología Social Comunitaria.* Puebla, México: Universidad Autónoma de Puebla and Universidad Autónoma de Yucatán.

Arango Calad, C. (Unpublished manuscript). *Psicología comunitaria de la convivencia.* Cali, Colombia.

Asún, D., Krause-Jacob, M., Aceituno, R., Alfaro, J. & Morales, G. (1995). La Psicología comunitaria en Chile. Análisis de sus características y perspectivas. In

E. Wiesenfeld & E. Sánchez (Eds.), *Psicología social comunitaria. Contribuciones latinoamericanas* (pp. 151-188). Caracas, Venezuela: UCV-FHE-CEP.

Avenzur, L. & Padilla, D. (2000). *Salud mental y violencia política. Metodología para la formación de formadores.* Lima, Perú: PASMI.

Balcázar, F., Montero, M. & Newbrough, J. R. (2001) (Eds.), *Modelos de psicología comunitaria para la promoción de la salud y prevención de enfermedades en las Américas.* Washington, DC: PAHO-WHO.

Basaglia, F. & Basaglia, F. U. (1977). *La mayoría marginada.* 2nd Edition. Barcelona, Spain: Laie.

Berger, P. & Luckman, T. (1967). *The social construction of reality.* New York: Doubleday.

Brandão, I. R. (1999): As bases epistemológicas da psicologia comunitária. In I. R. Brandão & Z. A. C. Bomfin (Eds.), *Os jardins da psicologia comunitária* (pp. 32-48). Fortaleza, Brazil: UFC-ABRAPSO-Ceará.

Bustamante, M. E. (2000). *Orquídeas y girasoles. Una propuesta de trabajo en salud mental infantil.* Lima, Perú: PASMI.

Calviño, M. (1998). Reflections on community studies. *Journal of Community Psychology, 26(3)*, 253-261.

Cardozo, F. H. & Faletto, E. (1978). *Dependencia y desarrollo en América Latina.* México DF, México: Siglo XXI.

Carranza, M. & Almeida, E. (1995). La psicología comunitaria. In E. Almeida, M. Martínez & M. Varela (Eds.), *Psicología social comunitaria* (pp. 13-130). Puebla, México: Fac. de Psicología BUAP-Facultad de Psicología-UADY.

Carrasco, J. C. (1998). A modo de prólogo. Un entramado de historia y esperanza. In L. Jiménez (Ed.), *Cruzando umbrales. Aportes uruguayos en psicología comunitaria* (pp. 7-14). Montevideo, Uruguay: Lapsus.

Carreño-Fernández, M. (2005). The development of community psychology in Cuba: Community work in La Marina. Unpublished paper written and translated at Manchester Metropolitan University, United Kingdom.

Castro, C., Jerónimo, L., Pinto, L. & Yarnold, R. (1992). *Rol del maestro y su compromiso con la comunidad.* Lima, Perú: EDAPROSPO.

CEDeFT (1986). Encuentro estatal sobre experiencias educativas y desarrollo comunitario bajo enfoques innovadores. Cuernavaca, México: CEDeFT.

Chauca, R. L., Bustamante, E. & Oviedo, V. (2004a). *A pesar de todo estamos todavía para construir un futuro mejor. Propuesta metodológica para la elaboración de memoria histórica en comunidades rurales.* Lima, Perú: Redinfa.

Chauca, R. L., Bustamante, E. & Oviedo, V. (2004b). *A pesar de todo estamos todavía para construir un futuro mejor. Módulo de formación y capacitación. Módulo de intervención.* Lima, Perú: Redinfa.

Cerullo, R. & Wiesenfeld, E. (2001). La concientización en el trabajo psicosocial comunitario desde la perspectiva de sus actores. *Revista de Psicología (Universidad de Chile), 10*, 11-26.

Chinkes, S., Lapalma, A. & Nicenboim, E. (1995). Psicología comunitaria en Argentina. Reconstrucción de redes e información de una práctica psicosocial. *Contextos grupales, 1*, 35-66.

Cintrón Bou, F. & Walter Pacheco, K. (2004). *La familia reconstituida desde las voces de sus integrantes.* Master's degree thesis. University of Puerto Rico, Río Piedras Campus.

CONSALUD (2001). *Participación comunitaria.* Caracas, Venezuela: CONSALUD.

Cordero, T. (1995 July). *Organización, identidad y violencia en la lucha por la tierra en Pavones del Golfito.* Paper presented at the 25th Interamerican Congress of Psychology, San Juan, Puerto Rico.

Cordero, T. (1998). Psicología comunitaria y relaciones de poder. *Actualidades en Psicología, 14 (96).*

Cruz, Quintal de Freitas, M. F. & Amoretti, J. (in press) Psicología Social comunitaria. In J. Sarriera and E. Saforcada (Eds.), *Psicología comunitaria. Aspectos históricos, teóricos, metodológicos y aplicados.* Buenos Aires, Argentina: Paidós.

Dabas, E. N. (1993). *Red de redes.* Buenos Aires, Argentina: Paidós.

Delgado Mercado, N. (2002, November). *Múltiples escenarios para la psicología social comunitaria: Más allá del ámbito académico.* Oral presentation at the 49th Convention of the Puerto Rican Psychological Association, Ponce, Puerto Rico.

Dussel, E. (1998). *Ética de la Liberación.* Madrid, Spain: Trotta.

Escovar, L. A. (1979). Análisis comparado de dos modelos de cambio social en la comunidad. *Boletín de la AVEPSO, 2(3),* 1-6.

Escovar, L. A. (1980). Hacia un modelo psicosocial del desarrollo. *Boletín de la AVEPSO, 3(1),* 1-7.

Estrada Mesa, A. M. (Ed.), *Psicología comunitaria. Investigación, enfoques y perspectivas.* Bogotá, Colombia: Fac. de Psicología, Pontificia Universidad Javeriana.

Feliciano, Y. (2004, July). *HIV prevention: Young women who have sex with women have needs.* Presentation at the XV International AIDS Conference, Bangkok, Thailand.

Fernández Alvarez, H. (1994). Pautas de intervención comunitaria para la prevención de los trastornos mentales. In M. Montero (Ed.), *Psicología social comunitaria. Teoría, método y experiencia* (pp. 259-292). Guadalajara, México: Universidad de Guadalajara.

Fernández Alvarez, H. & Nicemboim, E. (1998). Prevention of mental disorders: steps toward community interventions. *Journal of Community Psychology, 26,* 205-219.

Fernández Christlieb, P. (1994). La lógica epistémica de la invención de la realidad. In M. Montero (coord.) *Conocimiento, realidad e ideología* (pp. 19-36). Caracas, Venezuela: AVEPSO, Fascículo 6.

Ferullo de Parajón, A. G. (1991). Hacia la construcción de un marco teórico en psicología comunitaria. *Boletín de AVEPSO, 14,* 23-29.

Galano, M. H. (1994). As emoções no interjogo grupal. In S. T. M. Lane and B. Sawaia (Eds.), *Novas veredas da Psicología Social* (pp. 147-156). São Paulo, Brasil: Brasiliense.

Giorgi, V., Rodríguez, A. & Rudolf, S. (in press) La psicología comunitaria en Uruguay. Historia de la construcción de una identidad. In J. Sarriera & E. Saforcada (Eds.), *Psicología comunitaria. Aspectos históricos, teórico-metodológicos y aplicados.* Buenos Aires, Argentina: Paidós.

Góis, C. W. de L. (2003). *Psicología Comunitária no Ceará. Uma Caminada.* Fortaleza, Brazil: Instituto Paulo Freire de Estudos Psicossociais.

Gómez del Campo, J. (1986). *A history of community psychology in Mexico.* Unpublished manuscript.

Gonçalves de Freitas, M. (1997). La desprofesionalización, la entrega sistemática del conocimiento popular y la construcción de un nuevo conocimiento. In E. Wiesenfeld (coord.) *El horizonte de la transformación: Acción y reflexión desde la psicología comunitaria* (pp. 55-66). Caracas, Venezuela: AVEPSO, Fascículo 8.

Gonçalves de Freitas, M. & Montero, M. (2003). Las redes comunitarias. In M. Montero (Ed.), *Teoría y práctica de la psicología comunitaria. Tensión entre comunidad y sociedad* (pp. 173-201). Buenos Aires, Argentina: Paidós.

Granada-Echeverry, H. (1995). Intervenciones de la psicología social comunitaria: El caso de Colombia. In E. Wiesenfeld and E. Sánchez (Eds.), *Psicología social comunitaria. Contribuciones latinoamericanas* (pp. 117-150). Caracas, Venezuela: UCV-FHE-CEP.

Hernández, E. (1998). Assets and obstacles in community leadership. *Journal of Community Psychology, 26*, 261-268.

ILAS: Becker, D. & Lira, E. (Eds.). (1989). *Derechos humanos: todo es según el dolor con que se mira.* Santiago de Chile, Chile: ILAS.

ILAS: Lira. E. (Ed.). (1994). *Psicología y violencia política en América Latina.* Santiago de Chile, Chile: IL.

Irizarry, A. & Serrano-García, I. (1979). Intervención en la investigación. Su aplicación al barrio Buen Consejo, Río Piedras, Puerto Rico. *Boletín de AVEPSO, 2(3)*, 6-21.

Jiménez Domínguez, B. (1994). Contexto y significado en el análisis psicosocial de los problemas urbanos. *Revista de la Universidad de Guadalajara. Special Issue.* September-October, pp. 54-64.

Itriago, M. A. & Itriago, A. L. (2000). *Las redes: el cambio social.* Caracas, Venezuela: Sinergia.

Krause-Jacob, M. J. (2001). Hacia una redefinición del concepto de comunidad. *Revista de Psicología (Universidad de Chile), 10*, 49-60.

Krause-Jacob, M. (2002). The institutionalization of community interventions in Chile: Characteristics and contradictions. *American Journal of Community Psychology, 30*, 547-570.

Krause-Jacob, M. & Jaramillo, A. (1998). *Intervenciones psicológico comunitarias en Santiago de Chile.* Santiago, Chile: Pontificia Universidad Católica de Chile.

Lane, S. T. M. (1996). Histórico e fundamentos da psicología comunitária no Brasil. In R. H. Freitas Campos (Ed.), *Psicologia Social Comunitária. Da solidariedades à autonomia* (pp. 17-34). Petrópolis, Brasil: Vozes.

Lane, S. T. M. & Codo, W. (Eds.). (1984). *Psicologia. O homem em movimento.* São Paulo, Brasil: Brasiliense.

Lane, S. T. M. & Camargo, D. de (1994). Contribuição de Vigotski, para o estudo das emoções. In S.T.M. Lane & B. Sawaia (Eds.), *Novas Veredas em Psicología Social* (pp. 115-133). São Paulo: Brasil: Brasiliense.

Lane, S. T. M. & Sawaia, B. (1991). Psicología ¿Ciencia o Política?. In M. Montero (Ed.), *Acción y discurso. Problemas de Psicología Política en América Latina* (pp. 59-85), Caracas, Venezuela: Eduven.

Lane, S.T.M. & Sawaia, B.B. (1995). La psicología social comunitaria en Brasil. In E. Wiesenfeld & E. Sánchez (Eds.), *Psicología social comunitaria. Contribuciones latinoamericanas* (pp. 69-116). Caracas, Venezuela: UCV-FHE-CEP.

León, A., Montenegro, M., Ramdjan, N. & Villarte, I. (1997). Análisis crítico del concepto de autogestión en la psicología social comunitaria. In E. Wiesenfeld (coord.) *El horizonte de transformación. Acción y reflexión desde la psicología social comunitaria* (pp. 67-76). Caracas, Venezuela: AVEPSO, Fascículo No. 8.

León, M. & Montenegro, M. (1998). Return of emotion in psychosocial community research. *Journal of Community Psychology, 26*, 219-227.

López-Sánchez, G. & Serrano-García, I. (1995). Intervenciones de comunidad en Puerto Rico: El impacto de la psicología social-comunitaria. In E. Wiesenfeld and

E. Sánchez (Eds.), *Psicología social comunitaria. Contribuciones latinoamericanas* (pp. 219-248). Caracas, Venezuela: UCV-FHE-CEP.

Mangual Rodríguez, S. (2000). La identidad de la psicología social-comunitaria: Perspectivas filosóficas y sociales. *Ciencias de la Conducta, 15*, 17-37.

Marx, K. (1844/1965). *Escritos de juventud* [Early Writings]. Caracas, Venezuela: Instituto de Estudios Políticos, Facultad de Derecho, Universidad Central de Venezuela.

Mendes, A. R. M. & Correia, S. B. (1999). O núcleo de psicología comunitária à guisa de um breve histórico. In I. R. Brandão and A.A.C. Bomfin (Eds.), *Os jardins da psicologia comunitária* (pp. 21-31). Fortaleza, Brazil: UFC/ABRAPSO-Ceará.

Montero, M. (1982). La Psicología Comunitaria: Orígenes, Principios y Fundamentos teóricos. *Boletín AVEPSO, 5*, 15-22.

Montero, M. (1988). Alcance y roles de la psicología comunitaria en Venezuela. *Boletín de la AVEPSO, 11*, 3-8.

Montero, M. (1994a). La investigación-acción participante. La unión entre conocimiento popular y conocimiento científico. *Revista de psicología. Universidad Ricardo Palma, 6*, 31-45.

Montero, M. (1994b). Consciousness raising, conversion and de-ideologisation in psychosocial community work. *Journal of Community Psychology, 22*, 3-11.

Montero, M. (1995). La psicología social comunitaria en América Latina. In E. Wiesenfeld & E. Sánchez (Eds.), *Psicología social comunitaria. Contribuciones latinoamericanas* (pp. 7-19). Caracas, Venezuela: UCV-FHE-CEP.

Montero, M. (1996). La participación: significado, alcances y límites. In E. Hernández (Ed.) *Participación. Ámbitos, retos y perspectivas* (pp. 7-20). Caracas, Venezuela: CESAP.

Montero, M. (1998a). Introduction: The Latin American approach to community psychology. *Journal of Community Psychology, 26*, 199-204.

Montero, M. (1998b). Psychosocial community work as an alternative mode of political action. (The construction and critical transformation of society). *Community, Work and Family, 1*, 65-78.

Montero, M. (1998c). La comunidad como objetivo y sujeto de acción social. In A. Martín González (Ed.), *Psicología comunitaria. Fundamentos y aplicaciones* (pp. 210-222). Madrid, Spain: Síntesis.

Montero, M. (1999). Los unos y los otros: De la individualidad a la episteme de la relación [The Ones and the Others: From individuality to the episteme of relatedness]. *Revista AVEPSO, XXII (2)*, 67-83.

Montero, M. (2000a). Retos y perspectivas de la psicología de la liberación. In J. Vásquez (Ed.), *Psicología social y liberación en América Latina* (pp. 9-26). México City, México: Universidad Autónoma Metropolitana Iztapalapa.

Montero, M. (2000b). Participation in participatory action-research. *Annual Review of Critical Psychology, 2*, 131-143.

Montero, M. (2002a). On the construction of reality and truth. Towards an epistemology of Community Social Psychology. *American Journal of Community Psychology, 30*, 571-584.

Montero, M. (2002b). Construcción del Otro, liberación de Si Mismo. *Utopía y Praxis Latinoamericana, 7*, 41-52.

Montero, M. (2003a). Ethics and politics in Psychology. *International Journal of Community Psychology, 6*, 81-98.

Montero, M. (2003b). *Teoría y práctica de la psicología social. La tensión entre comunidad y sociedad.* Buenos Aires, Argentina: Paidós.

Montero, M. (2003c). Relatedness as the basis for liberation. *International Journal of Critical Psychology, 9*, 61-74.

Montero, M. (2004). *Introducción a la psicología comunitaria*. Buenos Aires, Argentina: Paidós.

Montero, M. & Giuliani, F. (1999). La docencia en la Psicología Social Comunitaria: Algunos problemas. *Psykhe, 8*, 57-63.

Montero López, V. (1992). Huaycan: Un pueblo que se construye, lucha y celebra. Lima, Perú: EDAPROSPO.

Moran, M. M. (1979, July). *Psicología y comunidad en El Salvador*. Paper presented at the XVI Interamerican Congress of Psychology, Lima, Perú.

Moreno, A. (1993). *El aro y la trama. Episteme, modernity and people*. Caracas, Venezuela: CIP.

Moreno, A. (1999). De la psicología comunitaria a la psicología de comunidades. In *La psicología al fin del siglo. Proceedings of the XXVII Interamerican Psychology Congress* (pp. 209-224). Caracas, Venezuela: Universidad Simón Bolívar-SIP-Fundación Polar.

Morillo de Hidalgo, C. (2000). Las redes sociales: nuevo modelo de organización para el desarrollo humano sostenible. *Puntal, 6*(11), 10-15.

Olave, R. M. & Zambrano, L. (1993) (Eds.), *Psicología comunitaria y salud mental en Chile*. Santiago, Chile: Universidad Diego Portales.

Ortiz, A. M. (2000). Notas sobre algunos cuestionamientos teóricos y epistemológicos en relación a un nuevo paradigma para la psicología social comunitaria. In Ana G. Ferullo de Parajón (Ed.), *Recorridos en Psicología Social Comunitaria. Perspectivas teóricas e intervenciones* (pp. 51-64). Tucumán, Argentina: Universidad Nacional de Tucumán.

Ortiz, B. (2004). Personal communication sent to N. Varas Díaz, on October 24.

Ortiz-Torres, B., Rosado, B. & Rapkin, B. (2004, July). *Normative beliefs and sexual practices in a sample of Haitian heterosexual women*. Presentation at the XV International AIDS Conference, Bangkok, Thailand.

Pérez Jiménez, D. (1995). *Hacia una política pública sobre el VIH/SIDA para Puerto Rico: Aportaciones desde la Psicología Social-Comunitaria*. Unpublished doctoral dissertation. University of Puerto Rico, Río Piedras Campus.

Piper, I. (2003). The blurring of criticism: notes on dissent. *International Journal of Critical Psychology, 9*, 125-142.

Quintal de Freitas. M. F. (1994). Prácticas en comunidad y psicología comunitaria. In M. Montero (Ed.), *Psicología Social Comunitaria. Teoría, método y experiencia* (pp. 139-166). Guadalajara, México: Universidad de Guadalajara.

Quintal de Freitas, M. F. (1996). Contribuições da psicología social e psicología política ao desenvolvimento da psicología social comunitária. *Psicología e Sociedade, 8*, 43-82.

Quintal de Freitas, M. F. (1998a). Models of practice in community in Brazil: possibilities for the psychology-practice relationship. *Journal of Community Psychology, 26*, 261-268.

Quintal de Freitas, M. F. (1998b). Novas práticas e velhos olhares em psicología comunitária. Uma conciliação possível? In L. Souza, M. F. Q. Freitas & M. M. Rodríguez (Eds.), *Psicología: Reflexões (im)pertinentes* (pp. 83-108). São Paulo, Brazil: Casa do Psicólogo.

Quintal de Freitas, M. F. (2000). Voices from the soul: The construction of Brazilian community psychology. *Journal of Community and Applied Social Psychology, 10*, 315-326.

Quintal de Freitas, M. F. (2003). Psychosocial practices and community dynamics. Meanings and possibilities of advance from the perspective of the engaged social actors. *International Journal of Critical Psychology, 9*, 107-124.

Reid, A. & Aguilar, M. A. (1995). México: La construcción de una psicología social comunitaria. In E. Wiesenfeld and E. Sánchez (Eds.), *Psicología social comunitaria. Contribuciones latinoamericanas* (pp. 189-218). Caracas, Venezuela: UCV-FHE-CEP.

Rivas, M. (2002, November). *Una psicología social comunitaria, Inc.* Oral presentation at the 49th Convention of the Puerto Rican Psychological Association, Ponce, Puerto Rico.

Rivera-Medina, E. (1992). La psicología social-comunitaria en la Universidad de Puerto Rico: Desarrollo de una experiencia. In I. Serrano-García & W. Rosario Collazo (Eds.), *Contribuciones Puertorriqueñas a la Psicología Social-Comunitaria* (pp. 3-18). Río Piedras, Puerto Rico: Editorial de la Universidad de Puerto Rico.

Rodríguez, A. (1998). La psicología comunitaria. Un aporte a su construcción y desarrollo. In L. Jiménez (Ed.), *Cruzando umbrales. Aportes uruguayos en psicología comunitaria* (pp. 81-94). Montevideo, Uruguay: Lapsus.

Rodríguez Gabarrón, L. & Hernández-Landa (1994). *Investigación participativa.* Madrid, Spain: Centro de Investigaciones Sociológicas.

Roitman, S. & Toledo, M. D. (2000). El lugar de la coordinación y/o cómo pensar lo grupal. In A. G. Ferullo (Ed.), *Recorridos en Psicología Social Comunitaria. Perspectivas teóricas y metodológicas* (pp. 111-121). San Miguel de Tucumán, Argentina: Universidad Nacional de Tucumán.

Saforcada, E. (1992). Introducción. In E. Saforcada (Ed.), *La psicología comunitaria. El enfoque ecológico-contextualista de James G. Kelly y otros* (pp. 7-34). Buenos Aires, Argentina: Centro Editor de América Latina.

Saforcada, E. (2001) (Ed.), *El factor humano en la salud pública.* Buenos Aires, Argentina: Proa XXI.

Samaniego, C.V., Antivero, N., Bártolo, M., Bonzo, C., Btesch, E., Domínguez, C., García Labandal, L., Iurcovich, S. & Villegas, A. (2005): Evaluación de una estrategia comunitaria de promoción del abandono del consumo de tabaco [Evaluation of a community strategy for promoting of stopping smoking tobacco]. En I. Serrano-García & N. Varas Díaz (Eds.), *Psicología comunitaria: Reflexiones, implicaciones y nuevos rumbos* (pp. 217-244). San Juan, Puerto Rico: Publicaciones Puertorriqueñas.

Sánchez, E. (2000). *Todos con la "Esperanza." Continuidad de la participación comunitaria.* Caracas, Venezuela: Comisión de Postgrado, Facultad de Humanidades y Educación, Universidad Central de Venezuela.

Sánchez, E. (2004). Organization and leadership in the participatory community. *Journal of Prevention and Intervention in the Community, 27*, 7-24.

Santiago, L., Serrano-García, I. & Perfecto, G. (1983), La Psicología-social comunitaria y la teología de la liberación. *Boletín de la AVEPSO, 6(1)*, 15-21.

Santiago, L., Serrano-García, I. & Perfecto, R. G. (1992). Metodología partícipe: Una experiencia puertorriqueña. In I. Serrano-García and W. Rosario C. (Eds.), *Contribuciones puertorriqueñas a la Psicología Social Comunitaria* (pp. 283-304). San Juan: EDUPR.

Sawaia, B. (1994). Psicología Social: Aspectos epistemológicos e éticos. En S.T.M. Lane & B. Sawaia (Eds.), *Novas Veredas da Psicologia Social* (pp. 45-54). São Paulo, Brasil: EDUC-Brasiliense.

Sawaia, B. B. (1998). Psicología comunitaria: Un área paradigmática de conocimiento científico comprometido. In A. Martín González (Ed.), *Psicología Comunitaria: Fundamentos y aplicaciones* (pp. 173-192). Madrid, Spain: Visor.

Sawaia, B. B. (2003). Affectivity as an ethical-political phenomenon and locus for critical epistemological reflection in Social Psychology. *International Journal of Critical Psychology, 9*, 13-30.

Scarparo, H. B. K. (2005). *Psicología Comunitária no Rio Grande do Sul. Registros da construção de um saber-agir.* Porto Alegre, Brazil: Pontificia Universidade Católica de Rio Grande do Sul.

Serrano-García, I. & Alvarez Hernández, S. (1992). Análisis comparativo de marcos conceptuales de la psicología de comunidad en Estados Unidos y América Latina. In I. Serrano-García & W. Rosario Collazo (Eds.), *Contribuciones Puertorriqueñas a la Psicología Social-Comunitaria* (pp. 19-74). Río Piedras, Puerto Rico: Editorial de la Universidad de Puerto Rico.

Serrano-García, I., Bravo-Vick, M., Rosario-Collazo, W. & Gorrín-Peralta, J. (1998). *La psicología social-comunitaria y la salud.* San Juan, Puerto Rico: Publicaciones puertorriqueñas.

Serrano-García, I. & Irizarry, A. (1979). Intervención en la investigación. *Boletín de la AVEPSO, 2(3)*, 6-21.

Serrano-García, I. & López-Sánchez, G. (1994). Una perspectiva diferente del poder y el cambio social para la psicología comunitaria. In M. Montero (Ed.), *Psicología social comunitaria. Teoría, método y experiencia* (pp. 167-210). Guadalajara, México: Universidad de Guadalajara.

Serrano-García, I., López, M. M. & Rivera-Medina, E. (1992). Hacia una psicología social-comunitaria. In I. Serrano-García & W. Rosario Collazo (Eds.), *Contribuciones Puertorriqueñas a la Psicología Social-Comunitaria* (pp. 75-106). Río Piedras, Puerto Rico: Editorial de la Universidad de Puerto Rico.

Spink, M. J. P. (2003). O trabalho do psicólogo na comunidade. A identidade socioprofissional na berlinda. In M. J. P. Spink (Ed.), *Psicología social e saúde. Práticas, saberes e sentidos* (pp. 122-131). Petrópolis, Brazil: Vozes.

Suárez-Balcázar, Y., Balcázar, F. & Villalobos, C. (2001). Participación de la comunidad en un programa de vigilancia del crecimiento. In F. Balcázar, M. Montero & J. R. Newbrough (Eds.), *Modelos de Psicología comunitaria para la promoción de la salud y prevención de enfermedades en las Américas* (pp. 49-64). Washington, DC: Organización Panamericana de la Salud and Organización Mundial de la Salud.

Toro-Alfonso, J. & Varas-Díaz, N. (2004). The development of social support networks for men who have sex with men and live with HIV/AIDS: Alternative for public policy interventions. In C. Cáceres, J. Fesca, M. Pecheny & V. Terto (Eds.), *Sexual citizenship in Latin America: Opening the debate* (pp. 79-90). Lima, Perú: Cayetano Heredia University.

Unsaín, A. (2004). *Propuesta: Curso pre-grado Psicología comunitaria año 2004.* Asunción, Paraguay: Universidad Nacional.

Valenzuela Cota, M. A. (1995). Retrospectiva y prospectiva de la Psicología comunitaria en México. In E. Almeida; M. Martínez & M. Varela (Eds.), *Psicología Social Comunitaria* (pp. 131-145). Puebla, México: Universidad Autónoma de Puebla and Universidad Autónoma de Yucatán.

Varas Díaz, N. (2002a, November). *Retos y trampas de la hibridez: Reflexiones en torno a la Psicología Social-Comunitaria.* Oral presentation at the 49th Convention of the Puerto Rican Psychological Association, Ponce, Puerto Rico.

Varas-Días, N. (2002b). *Peligrosidad encarnada: Estigma y VIH/SIDA en Puerto Rico.* Doctoral dissertation. University of Puerto Rico, Río Piedras Campus.

Varas-Díaz, N. & Serrano-García, I. (2002). Did you think getting emotional was simple?: Emotions as biological, cognitive, and social phenomenon. *Revista Puertorriqueña de Psicología, 13*, 9-28.

Varas-Díaz, N. & Serrano-García, I. (2003). The challenge of a positive self-image in a colonial context: A psychology of liberation for the Puerto Rican experience. *American Journal of Community Psychology, 31*, 103-115.

Varas-Díaz, N. & Serrano-García, I. (2005). *Psicología comunitaria: Reflexiones, implicaciones y nuevos rumbos.* San Juan, Puerto Rico: Publicaciones Puertorriqueñas.

Varas-Díaz, N., Serrano-García, I. & Toro-Alfonso, J. (2004). *Diferencia Social y Estigma: VIH/SIDA en Puerto Rico.* Río Piedras, Puerto Rico: Ediciones Huracán.

Varas-Díaz, N. & Toro-Alfonso, J. (In press). The stigmatization of HIV/AIDS and gregarious life: Contradictions in the development of social support networks for people living with HIV/AIDS in Puerto Rico. *Revista Ciencias de la Conducta.*

Vázquez, C. (2004). Refortalecimiento: Un debate con el empowerment. *Revista Interamericana de Psicología, 38*, 41-52.

Vázquez, C. (2002). *Refortalecimiento: Una propuesta de trabajo para la Psicología Social Comunitaria.* Oral presentation at the 49th Convention of the Puerto Rican Psychological Association, Ponce, Puerto Rico.

Wiesenfeld, E. (1998). Paradigms of Community Social Psychology in Six Latin American countries. *Journal of Community Psychology, 26*, 229-242.

Wiesenfeld, E. (2000). *La autoconstrucción. Un estudio psicosocial del significado de la vivienda.* Caracas, Venezuela: Consejo Nacional de la Vivienda.

Wiesenfeld, E. & Sánchez, E. (Eds.). (1995). *Psicología social comunitaria. Contribuciones latinoamericanas.* Caracas, Venezuela: CEP-FHE-UCV-Tropykos.

Wiesenfeld, E., Sánchez, E. & Cronick, K. (1995). La psicología social comunitaria en Venezuela. In E. Wiesenfeld & E. Sánchez (Eds.), *Psicología social comunitaria. Contribuciones latinoamericanas* (pp. 249-282). Caracas, Venezuela: UCV-FHE-CEP.

4
Community Psychology in the River Plate Region (Argentina–Uruguay)

ENRIQUE SAFORCADA, VÍCTOR GIORGI, ANTONIO LAPALMA,
ALICIA RODRÍGUEZ, ANA GLORIA FERULLO, SUSANA RUDOLF,
AND SAÚL FUKS

Abstract

This chapter describes the historical, sociocultural, economic, and political drivers that set the scene for the emergence of psychology in general, and, more specifically, of community psychology (CP), in the River Plate region. CP began to develop in Uruguay and Argentina through professional field practice, which was chiefly based on common sense, social awareness, and/or political conceptions. Then, a number of psychologists who used to work and are currently working with communities started to conceptualize and search for theoretical references, more particularly with regard to CP development in Latin America and Spain. The cultural power of the clinical model together with its unsuitability as a tool for the effective exercise of community psychology or for the creation of a theoretical framework for such a discipline may have prevented it from fully developing in these two countries, in contrast with what occurred in the rest of Latin America. However, in the foreseeable future, CP is expected to expand in both theoretical and practical terms, given the sociocultural, economic, and political crisis that hit both countries following the recipes of the Washington Consensus.

Introduction

As stated in its title, this chapter deals with community psychology (CP) development in the so-called River Plate region, which, from a geopolitical point of view, is composed of two countries: Uruguay and Argentina. This chapter includes four sections: the historical, political, and cultural drivers; the role of public universities and psychology-related drivers; CP development in the past 20 years; and the current status of CP in the region and its future prospects.

Definition of Community Psychology

In the River Plate region, CP is defined as the set of middle-range theories and conceptualizations that support the development of ethically grounded objectives and professional practices; intervention strategies; technologies aimed at research and/or action; and ways of professional subordination to the common good and to the demands of comprehensive human development, with due respect for the determining factors and peculiarities inherent to all cultures, and, more particularly, to the one that is the target for action.

This entire set of components, which might apply to any field of specialization in psychology, shares, in the case of CP, the objectives or aspirations of the rest of Latin America with regard to contributing to the awareness and distortion of the factors and processes that lead to and/or perpetuate poor living conditions, as well as those hampering the process of the integrated human development of family environments, while fostering, by the same token, the empowerment of the community, its self-determination processes, and health care and promotion for all its members. These goals are also focused on enabling communities to evaluate and control the mechanisms of the State in the areas of disease treatment, health care and the promotion of education—ranging from child care centers to higher education—by developing in citizens the skills for political action that are needed to demand, before the relevant governmental organizations, a solution to the problems of a public nature where they may have a stake.

More recently, some professional groups have started to think of a new objective in CP: achieving peace and putting an end to community manipulation, exploitation, and/or damage by national or multinational corporations in their quest for profit. In this regard, the thoughts of Eduardo Subirats (2006), theory of culture professor, New York University, are extremely noteworthy when he reflects upon the devastation inflicted ". . . on the mountain ranges and Amazon rainforests of Colombia, Ecuador and Peru . . ." by both the military and financial power exercised by a number of corporations from developed countries. A local and very topical example is that of the settlement in Uruguay of two huge plants (together, they will make up the world's largest undertaking of its kind) for the exclusive manufacturing of paper pulp—one of the most highly contaminating industries, with the lowest value-added in production, and the lowest use of labor. Among other environmental damages, this industry is expected to pollute the Uruguay River, as one-fourth of a ton of organochlorinated substances will be dumped into the river per year. Such substances are carcinogenic and affect the immune system. Botnia and Ence, the two paper pulp companies, are Finnish and Spanish, respectively, and would never be allowed to open these very same plants in Europe because the technologies involved are banned by European Community legislation on account of environmental impact concerns. By way of example, Ence was forced to dismantle its Pontevedra plant when Spain joined the EU.

Historical and Sociocultural Drivers in the Emergence of Community Psychology in the River Plate Region

The development and practice of psychology, in general, and of CP, in particular, in Argentina and Uruguay cannot be analyzed without reference to the social and cultural backgrounds of both societies and the ways in which their citizens have adopted their civic responsibilities. Therefore, before addressing the issue at hand, it is necessary to provide a historical background pointing out differences as well as similarities.

Even though the countries on both sides of the River Plate have undoubtedly been part of a regional sociocultural unit, each has its own particularities and its political, economic, cultural, and social reality. Similarities and differences are intertwined in their national histories.

The history of Argentina and Uruguay starts with the two nations as a single political unit belonging to the River Plate Viceroyalty. The process of independence from Spain started in May 1810 and concluded in 1816 for Argentina and in 1825 for Uruguay, at which point both states became sovereign nations.

After reaching full sovereign status, both nations went through a lengthy period of civil wars, which lasted longer in Argentina than in Uruguay. At the turn of the 20th century, they were both prosperous nations. Compared with Uruguay, Argentina boasted a huge geography and bountiful natural resources, turning it into one of the emerging nations with the greatest chances of joining a path of development that would earn it a position among the most developed nations.

Against all forecasts, after the Second World War, Argentina entered a period of steady decline, which accelerated from 1955 onwards. This process, marked by frequent coups d'état by the armed forces, designed to overthrow democratically elected governments and replace them with military dictatorships, created a chain of frustrated hopes and unfulfilled expectations in the population, affecting the middle and working classes in different ways. The *clientelistic* policies used by various governments—above and beyond the rhetoric used to justify them—and by the two majority parties (Peronism and Radicalism) gradually destroyed the culture of work as a social value and produced generations of individuals that cannot imagine a future without the aid of the state (in food and money) or without the support of local political leaders. Likewise, most of the middle class was overcome by a crisis regarding its own identity as the *social stratum* that bore the *national identity*. This progressively led the middle class to reconsider its civil identity and its relationship with the State and its representatives. While the structurally poor preserved their networks and survival strategies on the basis of internal solidarity within their social conglomerates and a parasitical relationship with both officials and politicians, the impoverished middle class got into a state of shock and disorientation. This, added to its deeply rooted individualism, prevented it from creating an organized and sustained political response to the traditional political parties that it so heatedly repudiated.

From the 1980s onwards, strife intensified as a result of a succession of democratically elected presidents, a number of constitutional processes, and a series of resignations caused by civil uprisings or palace intrigues— Argentina saw six presidents take office between December 1999 and May 2003.

In certain respects, the political history of Uruguay in the 20th century was markedly different from Argentina's. The dawn of the 20th century saw the creation of the fundamentals of the modern Uruguayan state, a welfare state that was protective and concerned with providing equal access to social and educational services for all sectors of the population. A profuse, cultivated, and liberal middle class developed and served as a model for the emergence of a European, white, and urban cultural hegemony that denied any differences. Thus, the various immigration streams, the culture of Afro-descendants, and the 19th century rural cultural legacy were all assimilated into one blend, bringing to life the myth of a country free from social, cultural, or ethnic disparities. A favorable trade balance and the encouragement of industrial development paved the way for a relatively prosperous future. However, by the mid-20th century, Uruguay was hit by crisis. Thus, a period marked by inflation and social strife began: with growing repression and rampant social conflict, the country's democratic structures progressively deteriorated until, on June 27, 1973, the president in office staged a coup d'état in combination with the armed forces.

From the mid-1970s onwards, the histories of these two countries began to move along similar tracks. Authoritarian systems that systematically exercised state sponsored terrorism as a means of controlling the population became prevalent, using torture, abduction, and incarceration to enforce a heavily regressive political program.

In both countries, the military governments faithfully adhered to a neoliberal and monetarist doctrine, fostering fiscal balance and neglecting the role of the state with the goal of facilitating the entry of foreign capital. As a result, progressive factory shutdowns, production stagnation, and rampant unemployment ensued. In 1980, the Uruguayans demonstrated to express their disagreement over a constitutional reform intended to perpetuate the military rule. The latter, haunted by economic deterioration and estranged from part of the civil population, embarked on a period of negotiations that concluded with the 1984 national elections. In Argentina, the military dictatorship collapsed in 1983 in the wake of the nation's defeat in the Malvinas/Falklands Islands War.

Although liberties were gradually restored in both countries, the issue of human rights remained at the center of the so-called democratic reconstruction. In both Uruguay and Argentina, large sectors of the citizenry continued to press governments for light to be shed and justice to be served on many cases of human rights violations and crimes against humanity perpetrated by the military dictatorships, either separately or as part of joint endeavors in what was known as the "Condor Plan." This led to considerable transformations in social subjectivity and in the social fabric itself as a result of the emergence of impunity: the population lost its trust in the exercise of its rights and the efficacy of the judiciary, and the values that had once formed a robust foundation in the societies of both nations were violently shaken.

On the economic side, the democratic governments that succeeded both dictatorships maintained and intensified the neoliberal model, leading to impositions by those in control of the products and services market, deregulating the labor market, and privatizing (in Argentina) or attempting to privatize (in Uruguay) state-owned companies.

This model left profound scars in both countries. The acute effects of the strengthening of the model promoted by the Washington Consensus were reflected in soaring poverty and indigence rates, rampant social exclusion, weakened labor unions and social organizations and networks, and the encroachment of individualism, crime, and violence.

During 2001 and 2002, the model began to fall apart in the River Plate, dragging both countries into a profound financial crisis with serious social ramifications leaving their inhabitants in a state of unprecedented decay.

Poverty affects a higher proportion of children than adults: this has led to the debate on the "childlike face of poverty," which is most acutely found in the younger age groups. In 2003/2004, 31% (Uruguay) and 44% (Argentina) of the population was poor, with the following averages: 50% and 60% of children under 12; 43% and 54% of children in the 14 to 22 age range; 28% and 38% of adults, and 10% and 23% of people aged 65 and older. This means that more than 50% of children under 6 years of age were at a high risk of being deprived of proper development as human beings. This is coupled with unemployment rates approaching 20%, as part of the general decline facing the labor market both in Argentina and Uruguay.

Such was the state of affairs on the agenda of the current presidents when they took office (on May 25, 2003, in Argentina and on March 1, 2005, in Uruguay). Both administrations stand out as being the first progressive governments—in Uruguay's case, it was the first time that the country saw a left-wing politician take office as chief of state. Faced with profound social and economic deterioration, the new governments have undertaken to invest heavily in public policies, attempting to gradually restore social and economic rights to the more underprivileged sectors.

The Role of Public Universities and Psychology-Related Drivers

Both Uruguayan and Argentinian universities strongly adhere to the Latin American model based on the Córdoba University Reform. Such reform was born in the National University of Cordoba, Argentina, in 1918 and expanded to all universities across Latin America. One of its most outstanding components is the struggle for freedom on the basis of civic responsibility. The reform led to the amendment of university bylaws and to the creation of the university outreach service, through which reformers argued that, because the public university existed as a result of the citizens' efforts, it would give back part of what it received by striving to solve the problems of society. This became the engine that has been motivating university students and teachers to share their knowledge for the benefit of their fellow citizens, with a specific emphasis on the more underprivileged sectors in terms of economic well-being, health, education, culture, housing conditions, and so forth.

Currently, university outreach is a critical pillar of public universities in Argentina and Uruguay. Besides its inherent ethical and ideological commitment, it is grounded on the idea that professional training must be closely linked to the real problems of society, which in turn are a privileged source for the production of knowledge. The initial conception of the university graduate indebted to society evolved towards a dialectic model where academic knowledge interacts with popular knowledge in a process of mutual enhancement. However, in general, such activities still fail to progress from working *for the community* to working *with the community*.

Influences in Education

A significant element that serves to explain the development of social organizations in the River Plate is the emergence of anarchism and early workers organizations towards the end of the 19th century. One of its lasting results was a certain connection between the workers' movement and university student movements. Even though only a few vestiges of anarchism have remained in Argentina, its legacy can still be seen in Uruguay in some forms of unionist, community, and university action and organization. This ideology has had remarkable influence on large sectors of the professional and intellectual milieu on both sides of the River Plate.

Finally, the most remarkable aspect of anarchism and utopian socialism in the region is the social dimension brought in by European immigrants—Italians, Germans, Russians, Spaniards, and so forth—which boasts two essential components: *cooperation* and *mutual help*.

Psychological Interventions

Arguably, in both Uruguay and Argentina, training at psychology schools has been mainly focused on a clinical approach of mental disease, both within the theoretical psychoanalytical framework and within the model of private practice. However, from the 1950s and 1960s onwards, Uruguayan universities started to undertake psychology projects at rural and urban communities, in connection not only with health but also with education and social organizations. Towards 1969, Professor Juan Carlos Carrasco, a

Uruguayan psychologist, suggested developing a *psychology of everyday life*, which was to be community-oriented and firmly committed to the needs of the actual human being (Carrasco, 1991). This landmark may be viewed as the founding of CP in Uruguay (Aguerre & Rudolf, 1998; Rodríguez, 1998). Unfortunately, the academic and professional agenda entailed in this proposal was aborted by the disruption of democracy in the country.

In Argentina, the creation of the Psychopathology Service at the Gregorio Aráoz Alfaro Hospital in 1956 in Lanús (Province of Buenos Aires), then led by Dr. Mauricio Goldenberg, was a milestone in the field of community health. The services of this department could be accessed freely by the entire community and were streamlined as a result of Goldenberg's innovative ideas. Services were enhanced by Gerald Caplan and the Dohrenwends' principles of dynamic psychiatry and community mental health, so that the institutional model was transformed into an interdisciplinary and community-oriented approach. This was possible, among other reasons, because Goldenberg had created the Social Psychiatry Department as part of the service (Lubchansky, 1972), and had appointed Isaac L. Lubchansky (now Itzhac Levav) to run it in 1969.

Around the same time, José Bleger, a doctor, psychoanalyst, and professor at the School of Psychology of the University of Buenos Aires, pointed to the legitimacy of the psychologist's role within communities. At a seminar for graduates on mental hygiene, held in 1962 at the Psychology Department of the School of Philosophy and Literature, Bleger argued that "the social role of the clinical psychologist should not be that of a mere therapist, but should rather cover public health in general, and mental hygiene in particular. Psychologists must involve themselves intensively in all the aspects concerning psychological hygiene and avoid intervening only when people get sick. [. . .] We must embrace a social dimension of the psychologist's profession, and with that, gain awareness of its role in public health and towards society at large [. . .], so that we may take its fundamental concerns from the field of disease and therapy to the area of community health . . ." (Bleger, 1962, p. 355–361).

This historical background calls for immediate reflection: if in the 1960s a social approach to psychology was a matter of questioning and discussion, what happened afterwards that prevented CP from developing fully, allowing just a few fragmented experiences to emerge?

Essentially, to understand this phenomenon two concurrent situations must be considered (Chinkes, Lapalma & Nicemboin, 1995):

1. The repeated interruptions of democracy and the ensuing military governments, for which a community approach was basically suspicious and frequently regarded as subversive or terrorist;
2. The strong influence of the clinical assistance model, fostered by most faculty members at psychology schools.

These concurrent factors may serve to explain the delay in the emergence of CP in the River Plate and the path that was then taken, characterized by a move from practical experience to conceptual development and by the limited dissemination and systematization of CP in both countries.

Psychology and the Community

At the beginning of the 1970s, in the Province of Córdoba, a number of projects involving psychological work at the community and with the community were undertaken by the Department of Social Psychology II and the Centro de Investigaciones en Psicología Social (CIPS; The Center for Social Psychology Research) of the School of Philosophy and Humanities of the National University of Córdoba. CIPS activity is based on three areas: community health, organizational issues, and criminal behavior. In 1974, Dr. Juan Marconi, who had implemented a Comprehensive Mental Health Program in the southern portion of Santiago, Chile, in the 1960s, was hired for a period of 9 months (Marconi, 1969, 1971, 1973; Marconi & Ifland, 1973). In partnership with the CIPS team, Marconi designed and implemented the Comprehensive Alcoholism Program of Córdoba City (Marconi, 1974a, 1974b; Marconi & Saforcada, 1974a, 1974b). Like its Chilean counterpart, this program involved strong community participation and turned out to be a true CP project, even when this discipline was not yet known by that name.

In 1974 and 1975, the above-mentioned Social Psychology Department focused on social psychology as applied to public health, giving rise to sanitary psychology, a discipline created in Argentina and to which CP is explicitly inherent.

In Uruguay, as a consequence of the repression exerted on political and unionist activities, all available energy concentrated on social work. A significant number of community programs developed during this decade, but psychologists were involved only to a minor extent. *Community development, popular education*, and *social promotion* were some of the self-defining terms used to designate these experiences in an environment of censorship and in the absence of a clear theoretical background. Neither psychology nor psychologists were altogether accepted by these collectives, as they were identified with the traditional clinical model aimed at the middle and upper classes. However, in some scientific papers of the period, significant changes are described on a subjective level in local neighbors, health promotion workers, and external players. The reports documenting such experiences refer to such things as changes in the beneficiaries' self-esteem, the assignment of new meaning to their personal and collective histories, the unblocking of their creative abilities, and the restoration of cultural belongings and social identities that influence their bonds, feelings, thoughts, and actions. Likewise, contact with other cultures and lifestyles gave rise to a critical attitude, led to the introduction of new models, and set in motion a process of self-criticism and transformation of attitudes, values, and life plans.

Psychologists had a major role to play in the "popular polyclinics movement," though they were chiefly motivated by a drive to expand clinical assistance to all sectors of society rather than by the determination to take the community itself and its social networks as their field of intervention. It might be claimed that work was performed *at* the community, rather than *with* it. On the other hand, the style that was implemented in practice tended to reproduce the clinical model of private practice, which is predominately individual in nature (Giménez, 1998; Giorgi, 1998).

Community Psychology Development in the Past 20 Years

The past 20 years of CP development in the River Plate roughly coincided with the return of democracy to the region. The approval of the Declaration of Alma-Ata and the seeming incongruity of both governments subscribing to it in 1978—in the middle of their dictatorships—laid the foundations for the conceptualizations relating to the primary health care (PHC) strategy to spread through the discourse and interventions of psychologists in the community field. The emphasis placed on health promotion and disease prevention activities is linked with the progress made in health sciences in countries such as Canada (PAHO, 1996) and the positioning of psychology as a driver for the implementation of many such changes in the region.

These new approaches mixed fairly quickly with the stream of those whose practice had involved community intervention since much earlier, as they had been strongly oriented to the health field.

Peculiarities of the Uruguayan Case

In Uruguay, training in CP was included in the University of the Republic's new Psychology Studies Curriculum in 1988. In 1993, it was set up as a department, articulating its practices through university outreach activities. Thus, in the last year of undergraduate education within the health area, a theoretical–practical course called "Community Care Techniques" is taught. This is a mandatory course that spans a full year. Also, during the last 2 years of their studies, undergraduate students must enroll for an annual traineeship at some of the psychological care services for the population offered by the university, several of which are defined as community services.

Only when CP was included in the academic world did it start to articulate a theoretical body of its own and to generate instruments different from those employed by other players that share the same field of action.

At the intersection of the streams—those arising from their own unique roots and those arising from their contact with contributions from the international sphere—a kind of CP has been developed that preserves a solid ideological and ethical position as its starting point, that has also incorporated the psychoanalytical imprint and inherited elements of clinical psychology as well as popular education, and that has used the public university arena as its main setting for production and formation. This is where strife for academic consolidation takes place, and where new knowledge is generated aimed at transforming reality—which is the ultimate goal of all socially useful knowledge.

A significant number of psychologists define themselves as "community" psychologists; however, the elements they consider in doing so are quite variable, such as working in popular environments and with poor sectors of society, serving at health centers located in the city outskirts, practicing outside institutional walls, and so forth. Definition may also be based on opposition: the activity inherent to CP is considered to comprise any efforts other than the clinical ones developed in private practice. In any case, it is important to highlight the steady increase in the number of psychologists who gear their practice towards the community and use it as reference to build their professional identity, though it may be somewhat detached from the academic developments of the discipline as it does not necessarily observe the hierarchy of the defining and essential components of CP (Rodriguez 1998, 2000). These components involve a special approach to psychology where (a) individuals are viewed as active beings, with the potential to transform themselves and their environment; (b) individuals are considered as developers of meaning and knowledge about reality, as valid as those coming from the academic field; and (c) community participation acquires an ethical, technical, and political sense. It could be claimed that community practices respond to social demands, and that they gradually start being developed by Uruguayan psychologists even without a theoretical or technical articulation of the discipline or an acknowledgement of its academic uniqueness.

It is worth noting here that, within the State sphere, since 1990 the Municipality of Montevideo (IMM), along the lines of its PHC strategy, has promoted community orientation among the psychologists who work for its Health Service System units, which are located in areas with fewer resources. The decentralization process on which the IMM has since been embarked highlights some of the key issues inherent to CP, such as community organization and involvement, the sense of belonging to local spaces, the concept of community itself, the construction of social identity, leadership and the issue of power, among others. On the other hand, within the framework of social policies resulting from a State reform strategy, a diversity of programs has been developed in recent years that are comanaged by the state and society at large. Psychologists have joined these programs, seeking to develop a community perspective.

It is important to highlight a major university outreach experience conducted in Montevideo by the University of the Republic since 1991: the Learning-Outreach Program at the Cerro district (Programa APEX-Cerro). Originally financed by the Kellogg Foundation, this is a multiprofessional community program in which psychologists have had a constant, sustained participation. It is mainly, though not exclusively, community focused.

Peculiarities of the Argentine Case

In general, no Argentine universities have yet included CP as a mandatory subject in the undergraduate curriculum for psychology studies. The closest attempt is a course called "Community Intervention Strategies" offered by the Schools of Psychology of the National Universities of Córdoba, Buenos Aires, and Tucumán (at the latter two as an optional subject). At postgraduate level, between 1992 and 1995 the National University of Tucumán offered the first four CP courses ever organized in the country. They were taught by Argentine, Latin American, and Spanish professors. This university currently offers a 120-hour Graduate Curriculum Segment (Tramo Curricular de Posgrado) in CP, opened in August 2004.

In 1997, the School of Psychology, University of Mar del Plata (Province of Buenos Aires), created the first Master's Program in Social-Community Psychology in the country, with local professors and lecturers from the Central University of Venezuela, Autonomous University of Madrid, Autonomous University of Barcelona, and University of Chile. The master's program was discontinued after 4 years of being active.

Since 1999, CP has been one of the subjects taught in the Specialization Program in Institutional and Community Clinical Psychology at the National University of Rosario. As for university outreach experiences, significant activity has been conducted at the Schools of Psychology of the National Universities of Buenos Aires, Tucumán, and Rosario.

In March 1988, in response to a proposal made by Itzhac Levav—then regional advisor in mental health at the Division of Health Promotion and Protection of the Pan American Health Organization (PAHO)—the School of Psychology, University of Buenos Aires, created an orientation to community approaches in public health care through its Department of Public/Mental Health I, to be included in undergraduate training and outreach activities. In the same year, the Inter-American Network for the Development of Psychology in Community Health Care was created in the United States of America. The above-mentioned School of Psychology, together with other universities in the Americas, the PAHO, the Inter-American Society of Psychology (ISP), and the American Psychological Association (APA), all became members of the Network. The Network's Steering Committee designated the School of Psychology of the University of Buenos Aires as ". . . the pilot center to develop an early experience of reorientation of psychology training towards the community domain" (Saforcada, 2001).

With support from the PAHO and the network, and taking the Department of Public/Mental Health I as the theoretical–technical and operative focal point, in late 1988/early 1989 the Social Epidemiology and Community Psychology Program called Programa Avellaneda was created (Saforcada, 2001). Its policies, principles and objectives explicitly laid down its marked social orientation, revolving around community participation and having health promotion and protection as its primary goal. The program, launched within the framework of an agreement between the above-mentioned school and the Municipality of Avellaneda, a district in the Province of Buenos Aires, was wide-ranging and involved many diverse sub-programs and projects geared towards a participatory community solution for problems including nutrition, cholera and TB prevention, among others. It also included a variety of research efforts in the field of psychosocial epidemiology and sanitary psychology.

The program was strongly supported by the network and the PAHO in areas such as bibliography, technical advice, and other aspects. Mention is due to the seminars organized in Buenos Aires by J.R. Newbrough (Vanderbilt University), James Kelly (University of Illinois, Chicago), Jaime Arroyo Sucre (health psychiatrist from Panama, and PAHO and WHO consultant), and Francisco Morales Calatayud (psychologist; vice president at the Higher Institute of Medical Sciences in La Habana, Cuba), and attended by the program's work teams as part of their professional development plan.

In November 2002, the School of Psychology, University of Buenos Aires, signed another framework agreement with the Municipality of San Isidro—another district in the Province of Buenos Aires—which provided legal grounds for the creation of the Psychosocial Epidemiology and Sanitary, Community and Environmental Psychology Program, or Programa San Isidro. This initiative started off as an immediate heir of Programa Avellaneda but has a more comprehensive perspective, as it integrates the approaches provided by sanitary and environmental psychology.

In the Province of Tucumán, Argentina, a project was developed in 1987: the University Project of Community Promotion (Proyecto Universitario de Promoción Comunitaria, or PUPC). Partly funded by the Kellogg Foundation, it was an innovative proposal to modify the process of human resource formation in higher education. It sought to encourage cross-disciplinary interaction both within the university and between this institution and the inhabitants in marginal rural areas, with the aim to spur sustained change in both. Thus, through the creation of multidisciplinary teams of professionals who spent some time living at six marginal rural communities in the province, the role that the university plays in society—in this case, in relation to the most deprived sectors—among other aspects, became redefined.

The project's general objectives are linked with three domains, as follows:

(a) University: promote cross-disciplinary human resources development, by means of participation in a work plan oriented to the integrated development of communities.
(b) Community: provide support to enable communities—through an assessment of their needs, and the definition and implementation of an action plan to meet those needs—to develop their own potential throughout a process aimed at achieving higher levels of training, organization, and self-management.
(c) Services: contribute to the provision, adjustment, and improvement of services required to meet the basic needs of the population—health, education, production, housing, and recreation.

As it gained experience and in view of the changing realities in the region and the country, the project changed its name and adjusted its objectives and strategies (Proyecto UNIR, 1999). Undoubtedly, the experience of psychology as part of this initiative has greatly affected the profession and the society in the region, as it has created and strengthened the role of the psychologist as a member of interdisciplinary teams involved in community work, in sharp contrast with the widespread conception that psychologists restrict their work to the clinical area, with an individual approach.

Since 1984, the University Outreach Bureau reporting to the President's Office of the National University of Rosario has been behind a Community Assistance Project implemented specifically in that city (Province of Santa Fe). Its activity is carried out via the Community Assistance Center (CeAC), launched at a Primary Mental Health Care Center which already existed in the area. From early on, the project was linked to the Higher School of Psychology, School of Humanities and Arts (nowadays, School of Psychology), National University of Rosario. Its goals are to

(a) Develop a community program focused on health issues, using a prevention model and a participative methodology, seeking community integration;
(b) Contribute knowledge and techniques to recover and create the appropriate resources that enable the community to solve its problems;
(c) Foster scientific production where health, education, and social policy planning converge, and
(d) Generate scientific proposals in areas that have little or no space in the traditional academic curriculum.

The 20 years in which this program has been running have witnessed the transformation of the Primary Mental Health Care Center, thanks to the involvement of local neighbors, into a Community Health Program (which includes the health element, together with community participation, and both undergraduate and graduate psychology training). It has ultimately become a program whose underpinnings have been and still are a cross-disciplinary approach, coupled with community participation.

The catalyst for such transformation was the active inclusion of community members as experience builders, gradually transforming the usual struggles for power into a dialogue on the conditions and possibilities to establish relationships of cooperation.

Current Status of Community Psychology in the Region and Future Prospects

So far, CP activities have mostly taken place based on common sense, social sensitivity, and, in some cases, political positioning. Nonetheless, some community psychologists have been developing concepts and searching, yet partially, for theoretical referents directly from the progress made by CP in Latin America and Spain.

It is important to point out that this discipline has not yet been acknowledged as such in the region, nor does it have its own specific professional organization. In neither country is there a specialized CP journal.

In Argentina, CP has not been included among the institutionalized specialties considered by provincial psychologist associations. Nor does it have formal recognition from the Federation of Psychologists of the Argentine Republic (Federación de Psicólogos de la República Argentina; http://www.fepra.org.ar/espec.htm), which acknowledges only six specialties: clinical, occupational, legal, social, sanitary, and educational psychology.

Uruguay, in turn, has not yet institutionalized specialties in the field of psychology. The graduate courses and master's degrees offered by the School of Psychology at the University of the Republic are still at a budding stage, and no proposals concerning the CP field are found at this university or in private higher education.

However, in the River Plate region, the cradle of university reform, public education at all levels has played a key role in defining the position of professionals and academics regarding social issues.

The social commitment dimension that has characterized most CP in Latin America has also been a major factor in both countries, which is illustrated by the fact that the most acclaimed contributions of CP in the River Plate have arisen in the public health area. This is due to the adoption of a PHC strategy in both countries, as has already been mentioned. Such strategy is founded upon community participation, the structuring of multidisciplinary *health teams*, and community awareness building; lacking such components, PHC loses its essential traits and becomes useless and ineffective.

Although much of the CP effort is focused on health, it does not mean that CP in this region involves health psychology. This latter specialty does not exist in the River Plate as a body of knowledge and practice or as a concept of its own right.

Most CP activity has been conducted within the PHC and public health spheres, which may have determined the fact that the richness of practice did not usually extend to theoretical production. It did not inhibit, however, the emergence of an interesting field for reflection, in which the epistemological fractures of the 1990s made themselves felt (Fuks, 1992).

One of the factors that have triggered the conditions for greater CP visibility was the commotion stemming from the ethical, theoretical, and epistemological questioning of the traditional, realistic, and positivist models, as well as the *community enlighteners*. This process of critical conceptual change became increasingly evident after constructivist/constructionist epistemologies were incorporated, which shifted the centers of observation, and thus the observer. Following this shift in attention, from *what happens to others* to *areas of possible liaison and networking*, a process was started to reframe work teams from an epistemological and operational perspective.

This process became apparent in the transformation of the way work teams saw themselves, their social spaces, and their function. From this standpoint, cross-relationships and networking between teams and the community started to be considered emerging constructions in the *social nodes*, understood as the conceptual, emotional, and action structures concerning both the community and the professional teams themselves.

These differences in perspective gradually awakened a growing interest in the emerging processes found in the complex community-team interconnections, focusing concerns and research on the conditions under which such intersections yielded shared (*co-built*) projects.

As part of the same process, self-criticism and reflection brought about by the return of democracy and its political processes also entailed the revision of the *messianic* thesis posed by social scientists in the 1970s, a decisive factor in this profound reflection upon the identity and the function of social scientists. This process was enhanced by a context where, as the paradigms of modernity associated with postmodernism fell apart, many assumptions have been challenged.

The social sciences have received this as a direct impact, as it affected the methodologies used by its practitioners. However, this turbulence has had a positive aspect, shown in the new productions that integrated Morin's complex thinking (1976, 1990, 1994, 2004), Gergen's social constructionism (1988, 1989, 1992; Gergen & Gergen, 1988), Pearce's coordinated management of meaning, or CMM (1989, 1994), the transdisciplinary, systemic approach (Fried Schnitman & Fuks, 1993, 1994; Fuks, 1992), and the social network perspective (Dabas, 1998; Elkäim, 1987) with the developments of CP in the region. While the conceptual and methodological production resulting from this convergence was nowhere to be seen in the usual CP forums, in Argentina and Uruguay it made a strong impact on the cross-disciplinary fields of community health, citizenship building, or means of alternative dispute resolution, and mediation/intermediation.

Over the past 20 years, these regional peculiarities have paved the way for interesting opportunities to link some public health and education projects, programs, and policies with CP-based experiences.

Regarding the events in the region, a comment arises as to the advantages and disadvantages for CP development entailed by the lack of a wide-ranging, well-structured academic body that facilitates processing, systematizing, publicizing, and confronting community experiences. Such lack of a structure faces practice with the false dilemma to choose between generating low-complexity theories, only to validate or feed action strategies, or having to resort to an inter- or transdisciplinary level as a possible space for reflection. In the light of the political processes prevailing in the region over the past 3 years, there is a possibility for this false dilemma to wither away and leave in its stand an enriched process of reflection, systematization, and theoretical construction within CP. Should this come to happen, as the current state of affairs would suggest, there should be a renewed wealth of work with communities and research to assess results. Not only that, but also solid, stable academic spaces are bound to open up in order to provide adequate training for professionals in this specialty, thus granting it proper acknowledgement, efficiency, and effectiveness.

Taking a closer look—a reflection that could apply to the River Plate region as well as elsewhere in the world under the influence of the European academic and scientific subculture—a major hindrance that prevents CP from becoming fully developed, epistemologically solid, and fruitful in its applications is the current prevalence of the Cartesian and mechanistic conceptions of the human being and their social organizations. Due to the very nature of its object of study and its practice, CP seems to demand the advent of a new paradigm of life sciences (Capra, 1998, 2003)—one based on a holistic, systemic and ecological conception of the human factor as a nonessential part of the biosphere, and thus forced to maintain peace, in the face of the full power of destruction of the nuclear weapons it has created.

Acknowledgements. This chapter was translated to English by Mariana Saforcada.

References

Aguerre, L & Rudolf, S. (1998). El Psicólogo trabajando en comunidad. Características del proceso en el Uruguay. Historiando un poco. In L. Giménez (comp.). Cruzando Umbrales. Aportes uruguayos en Psicología Comunitaria. Editorial Roca Viva, Montevideo.

Bleger, J. (1962). El psicólogo clínico y la higiene mental. ACTA Psiquiátrica y Psicológica de América Latina, Vol. VIII, N° 4.

Carrasco, J. C. (1991). Rol del psicólogo en el mundo contemporáneo. In: V. Giorgi y col. El Psicólogo: Roles, escenarios y quehaceres. Editorial Roca Viva, Montevideo.

Capra, F. (1998). La trama de la vida. Una nueva perspectiva de los sistemas vivos. Anagrama, Barcelona.

Capra, F. (2003). Las conexiones ocultas. Implicaciones sociales, medioambientales, económicas y biológicas de una nueva visión del mundo. Anagrama, Barcelona.

Cole, M. (1999). Psicología cultural. Una disciplina del pasado y del futuro. Madrid, Ediciones Morata.

Chinkes, S., Lapalma, A. & Nicemboin, E. (1995). Psicología Comunitaria en Argentina. Reconstrucción de una práctica psicosocial en Argentina. In: E. Wiesenfeld & E. Sánchez (comp.). Psicología Social Comunitaria. Contribuciones Latinoamericanas. Tropycos, Caracas, Venezuela.

Dabas, E. (1998). Redes Sociales, familias y escuela. Buenos Aires, Paidós.

Elkäim, M. (1987). Les Practiques de Réseau. Santé Mentale et Contexte Social. Paris, ESF.

Fried Schnitman, D. & Fuks, S. (1993). Paradigma y Crisis: Entre el Riesgo y la Posibilidad. *Psykhe*, 2(1), 33-42.

Fried Schnitman, D. & Fuks, S. (1994). Modelo Sistémico y Psicología Comunitaria. *Psykhe*, 3(1), 65-71.

Fuks, S. (1992). La Psicología Comunitaria y el enfoque transdisciplinario en salud. Presentation at the Laboratoire de Medecine Preventive et Social, Saint Antoine, Universite Pierre et Marie Curie, Paris, Francia.

Gergen, K. J. & Gergen, M. M. (1988). Narrative and the self as relationship. In L. Berkowitz (Ed.). *Advances in experimental social psychology*. New York: Academic Press.

Gergen, K. J. (1988). If persons are texts. In: S. B. Messer, L. A. Sass y R. L. Wollfolk (Eds.), Hermeneutics & psychological theory. New Jersey: Rutgers University Press.

Gergen, K. J. (1989). La Psicología posmoderna y la retórica de la realidad. In: T. Ibañez-Gracia (coord.). El Conocimiento de la Realidad Social. Barcelona, Sendai Ediciones.

Gergen, K. J. (1992). El Yo Saturado. Buenos Aires, Paidós.

Giménez, L. (comp.). (1998). Cruzando umbrales. Montevideo, Roca Viva.

Giorgi, V. (1998). Soportes teóricos de la Psicología Comunitaria. In: L. Giménez (comp.). Cruzando umbrales. Aportes uruguayos a la Psicología Comunitaria. Editorial Roca Viva, Montevideo.

Lubchansky, I. L. (1972). Psiquiatría social. Contenido y forma de una experiencia. ACTA Psiquiátrica y Psicológica de América Latina, Vol. XVIII, N° 3.

Morin, E. (1976). Para una crisiología. In: R. Stara, E. Le Roy Ladurie, R. Thom, A. Béjim, H. Breochier, J. Attali, J. Freund, H. Stourdzé, J. Schlanger & E. Morin. El Concepto de Crisis. Buenos Aires, Asociación Ediciones La Aurora.

Morin, E. (1990). Introduction à la Pensée Complexe. Paris, ESF Editeur.

Morin, E. (1994). La noción de sujeto. In: D. Fried Schnitman (Ed.). Nuevos Paradigmas, Cultura y Subjetividad. Buenos Aires, Paidós.

Morin, E. (2004). Introducción al pensamiento complejo. México, Gedisa.

Marconi, J. (1969). Barreras culturales en la comunicación que afectan el desarrollo de programas de control y prevención en alcoholismo. ACTA Psiquiátrica y Psicológica de América Latina, Vol. XV, N° 4.

Marconi, J. (1971). Asistencia psiquiátrica intracomunitaria en el área sur de Santiago. Bases teóricas y operativas para su implementación (1968/1970). ACTA Psiquiátrica y Psicológica de América Latina, Vol. XVII, N° 4.

Marconi, J. (1973). La revolución cultural chilena en programas de salud mental. ACTA Psiquiátrica y Psicológica de América Latina, Vol. XIX, N° 1.

Marconi, J. & Ifland, S. (1973). Aplicación del enfoque intracomunitario de neurosis a la consulta externa ACTA Psiquiátrica y Psicológica de América Latina, Vol. XIX, N° 9.

Marconi, J. (1974a). Análisis de la situación de la salud mental en la ciudad de Córdoba. ACTA Psiquiátrica y Psicológica de América Latina, Vol. XX, N° 4.

Marconi, J. (1974b). Diseño de un programa integral de salud mental para la ciudad de Córdoba. ACTA Psiquiátrica y Psicológica de América Latina, Vol. XX, N° 4.

Marconi, J. & Saforcada, E. (1974a). "Diseño y estudio de factibilidad psicosocial de un Programa Integral de Salud Mental (alcoholismo y neurosis), variantes Institucional e Intracomunitaria, para los afiliados al Instituto Provincial de Atención Médica." Instituto Provincial de Atención Médica (Internal Publication), Córdoba.

Marconi, J. & Saforcada, E. (1974b). Formación de personal para un programa integral de Salud Mental en Córdoba. ACTA Psiquiátrica y Psicológica de América Latina, Vol. XX, N° 6.

Pan-American Health Organization (PAHO). (1996). Health Promotion: An Anthology Collection. Washington, DC, OPS Scientific Publication No. 557.

Pearce, W. B. (1989). Communication and the Human Condition. Carbondale and Edwardsville, Southern Illinois University Press.

Pearce, W. B. (1994). Nuevos modelos y metáforas comunicacionales: el pasaje de la teoría a la praxis, del objetivismo al construccionismo social y de la representación a la reflexividad. In: D. Fried Schnitman (Ed.). Nuevos Paradigmas, Cultura y Subjetividad. Buenos Aires, Paidós.

Proyecto UNIR. (1999). UNA NUEVA INICIATIVA RURAL. Universidad Nacional de Tucumán; Gobierno de la Provincia; Comunidades del Valle Calchaquí, Valle de Trancas y estribaciones del Aconquija. Tucumán, Argentina, Top Graph.

Rodríguez, A. (1998). La Psicología Comunitaria. Un aporte a su construcción y desarrollo. In: L. Giménez (comp.). Cruzando Umbrales. Aportes uruguayos a la Psicología Comunitaria. Editorial Roca Viva, Montevideo.

Saforcada, E. (2001). "El programa Avellaneda de la Facultad de Psicología de la Universidad de Buenos Aire". In: E. Saforcada (comp.). El factor humano en la salud pública. Una mirada psicológica dirigida hacia la salud colectiva. Proa XXI, Buenos Aires.

Subirats, E. (2006). "Bajo la bandera del socialismo." Newspaper Página 12, martes 13 de junio de 2006. http://www.pagina12.com.ar/diario/contratapa/13-68270-2006-06-13.html.

ASIA-PACIFIC

5
So Far and Yet So Near? Community Psychology in Australia

HEATHER GRIDLEY AND LAUREN J. BREEN

Abstract

Australian community psychology (CP) has a shared history as well as regional variations, resulting in an eclectic mix of ideas, methodologies, and practices. In this chapter, we review the emergence of CP in Australia from within the dominant paradigm to its official recognition as a subdiscipline of psychology and the development of postgraduate programs. CP's formal history in Australia has links with the parallel, recent history of the subdiscipline elsewhere, particularly in the United States; informally, the climate in which it was born was distinctly Australian, resonating with the cultural pluralism and emergent debates around decolonisation and political realignment within the Asia-Pacific region that characterised the 1970s in this country. In this chapter, we critically examine a number of aspects of that history: the impact of the decision to locate the subdiscipline as a professional specialisation; the role of community psychologists in consciousness–raising around social justice within psychology and society; and the importance of geography in determining the nature of CP theorising and applications in this part of the world. We draw on the responses from a survey of 25 CP academics, practitioners, and students in order to personalise the emergence and subsequent development of CP in Australia.

So Far and Yet So Near? Community Psychology in Australia

. . . Mexico's problem was that it was so far from God and so close to the United States. Perhaps our problem is that our orientation is so close to America and Britain, but that we are so far away. (O'Neil, 1987, p. 142)

The formal history of community psychology (CP) in Australia has clear links with the parallel, recent history of the subdiscipline elsewhere, particularly in the United States. Informally, the climate in which it was born was distinctly Australian, resonating with the cultural pluralism and emergent debates around decolonisation and political realignment within the Asia-Pacific region that characterised the 1970s in this country.

The invitation to write this chapter coincided with the 21st anniversary of the establishment in 1983 of the Australian Psychological Society (APS) Board (now College) of Community Psychologists, the formal birth date of the discipline in Australia. To mark the occasion, the group's Victorian Section hosted a 'history dinner' in June 2004, which was attended by around 30 current and past members and students. We took the opportunity to distribute a brief questionnaire on the night of the dinner and afterwards via e-mail to others who had been involved with the development of the field here. We also printed it in the December 2004 issue of the college's journal, *Network*. We were interested in tracing some of the key developments of CP in Australia and particularly wanted to gather insights from those who were among the founders of the field. The four questions concerned the history and development, formal recognition and professionalisation, contributions, and future of CP in Australia.

Some of the 25 respondents were current students, others were long-standing members of the college, and some were 'fellow travellers' who were not APS members but shared a commitment to CP principles and approaches. With permission, and acknowledgement where possible, a selection of responses are included to personalise the events surrounding the emergence and subsequent development of CP in Australia.[1]

In this chapter, we critically examine the history of CP in Australia, from its emergence from within the dominant paradigm of psychology to its formal recognition as a subdiscipline of psychology and the development of postgraduate programs. Specifically, we focus on the impact of the decision to locate the subdiscipline alongside professional specialisations such as clinical and counselling psychology; the role of CP in consciousness-raising around social justice within psychology and society; and the importance of geography in determining the eclectic nature of CP in this part of the world. We begin by providing an overview of the history of psychology in Australia, in order to set the scene for the emergence of CP.

For the purposes of this chapter, we define CP by drawing on the description in the APS College of Community Psychologists' brochure (Figure 1).

---

[1] For the most part, the only identifiable responses were from questionnaires that had been distributed to potentially information-rich informants with a long history of association with community psychology, and some responses from current students. All survey responses have been italicised in the text to distinguish them from quotes drawn from other sources.

The APS College of Community Psychologists

Who are Community Psychologists?

Community psychologists, while being trained as psychologists in every sense of the word, have advanced training in understanding the needs of people in their communities. They focus less on 'problems' and more on the strengths and competencies of community members. The aim of community psychologists is to work in partnership with people to achieve the goals and aspirations of their community or social groups.

Philosophy and Values

Community Psychologists value human differences, and are thus committed to core principles of flexibility, equity and respect for cultural diversity in meeting the needs of different populations.

Community Psychologists:

- recognise people's strengths and resources
- work to break down existing social barriers
- emphasise empowerment and collaboration rather than dictating readymade solutions
- promote the sharing of skills and knowledge
- recognise that all research is value-based
- use qualitative and quantitative methods of investigation.

FIGURE 1. APS College of Community Psychologists' brochure (excerpt).

Psychology in Australia: The Dominant Paradigm

Psychology has been taught in most Australian universities virtually since their inception. In the 19th and early 20th centuries, it was treated as a sub-discipline of philosophy, with a strong Scottish influence. Its passage was probably made easier by the fact that these new colonial universities were being established just as the 'new' discipline of psychology was celebrating its 'birth' in Wundt's Leipzig laboratory. The rise of modern science also provided a convenient justification for colonialism's 'civilising mission.' The currency of social Darwinism contributed to the *zeitgeist* that saw psychology's founding fathers in Australia gathering and measuring the skulls of Indigenous people (Davidson, Sanson & Gridley, 2000). Even today, much of Australian cross-cultural psychological research is focused on comparing and contrasting different ethnic/cultural groups, primarily from the unacknowledged perspective of the dominant culture.

The application of psychology to practical problems is a feature of the discipline in Australia, according to most commentators (e.g., National Committee for Psychology of the Australian Academy of Science, 1996; Taylor & Taft, 1977). Taft and Day (1988) described the nature of Australian psychology as eclectic, pragmatic, and applied—but not particularly innovative, taking its cue largely from developments in the Northern Hemisphere. Even now, Australian psychology textbooks are virtually indistinguishable from the standard mass-produced North American texts. Most commonly, we use North American textbooks that say nothing specific about Australia. Furthermore, most psychology academics adopt such texts without taking their potential (ir)relevance to the local context and cultures into account. It remains all too easy to download an entire lecture series, complete with back-up activities and examination questions— along with North American norms, colloquialisms, examples, and style conventions.[2]

The Beginnings of CP in Australia

In the 1960s and early 1970s, several factors converged to lay the ground for the emergence of CP as a fresh, and at times radical, approach to psychology's relationship with the societies in which it was embedded. First, the sociopolitical context of 1970s Australia saw the election (and dismissal 3 years later) of a reformist Labor government at the national (federal) level after more than 20 years of conservative leadership. A dramatic series of legislative changes marked the introduction of a universal health insurance scheme, free tertiary education, an expanded national community health program, and no-fault divorce. Indigenous activism was bearing fruit in the legitimation of the notion of Aboriginal land rights and the replacement of assimilationist policies with a commitment to Aboriginal self-determination. In addition, moves toward de-institutionalisation in the mental health and disability fields gathered momentum.

Second, matters such as social responsibility, Indigenous issues, and the treatment of those with mental illness were being increasingly debated within psychology (Cooke, 2000). Primarily as a result of such discussion, the APS formed the Committee on Social Issues in 1974. However, no names associated with the early days of CP appear as drivers in Cooke's account of the establishment of this committee. Instead, it emerged from initiatives led by feminist psychologist Una Gault, urging the APS to contribute to public debate on issues as diverse as discrimination against homosexuals, Aboriginal land rights, and the Vietnam War.

Third, the expansion of tertiary education provision beyond the 'sandstone' universities[3] opened up new territory for the teaching of social and behavioural sciences. After 1980, the continuing expansion of higher

---

[2] In this chapter, we have chosen to use Australian spelling and minor stylistic departures from standard APA format, in the belief that to do otherwise would be to comply with the cultural homogenising of CP and to negate any notion of global diversity in our field.

[3] More or less equivalent to Ivy League in the US, or Oxbridge in the UK.

education into suburban and regional areas where educational opportunities had previously been very limited was marked by paradoxes, with some identifying their mission firmly within their local community, and others seeking to replicate and compete with 'the sandstones.' It is no coincidence that all three universities that have offered accredited postgraduate programs in CP are products of post-1990 mergers of former colleges of advanced education, teachers' colleges, and technical colleges.

Fourth, as in North America, Australian CP's 'parents' were social and clinical psychology. In the post–Vietnam War era, many who had taken literally the antiprotest bumper sticker 'America – love it or leave it!' found themselves in Australia, often employed as educators during the post-war expansion in secondary and tertiary education. Furthermore, the first people to introduce aspects of CP into university psychology courses were North American: activist social psychologists James Gardner and Arthur Veno in Queensland and Syd Engleberg in New South Wales (NSW) in the mid-1970s. Around the same time, clinical psychologist and social activist Robin Winkler reoriented the clinical program at the University of Western Australia to be more evidence-based and community-focussed (Gridley, Fisher, Thomas, & Bishop, 2007). Soon after, a small number of clinical psychologists within the APS Victorian Branch formed a CP group to explore Winkler's ideas, reports of which were beginning to filter across the country from Western Australia.

Finally, the developments described above created demands for a suitably trained (or retrained) workforce able to adapt to community approaches rather than institutional settings. Respondents to our survey shared their recollections of how these factors affected their work and outlook. Some respondents referred to connections with organisational psychology, criminology, the public sector and local communities, dating back as far as *"1962 when it was called social psychology,"* with one recalling how they had to *"battle [the] perception that CP was not 'real' psychology but sociology."* Others made reference to their involvement as clinicians and change agents in the *"Community Health and Mental Health movements in the 1970s . . .,"* and their growing awareness of the inadequacy of individual, treatment-based approaches. Neil Drew, who began his career as a practitioner in Queensland before moving to academic positions in Western Australia, described how he became disenchanted with mainstream, institutional approaches to intervention:

I found that it was very easy to apply standard interventions with a captive audience. The problems emerged when we returned [abused and detained youth] to an essentially unchanged environment. I was very clear that much of the time, not only were we doing no good – we were in fact doing harm . . . [Later] I was a live-in supervisor of a psychiatric halfway house . . .. Again, I became aware of the shortcomings of the system. People were released to the community with very little support and certainly a manifestly inadequate sharing of the resources.

Formal Recognition of CP in Australia

After the APS was formed in its own right in 1966, its membership grew rapidly from fewer than 1,000 to nearly 4,000 by the early 1980s.[4] This growth, and an ongoing debate as to whether the APS should be "a learned society, a professional society, or both" (Cooke, 2000, p. 127) led to the formation of subdivisions, the first being the Division of Clinical Psychology. Eventually in 1981, the APS set up two overarching divisions—Scientific Affairs and Professional Affairs—with the existing divisions coming under the umbrella of Professional Affairs, as 'Boards.'

A 1982 position paper (Hill, unpublished) canvassing support for the emerging area of CP drew almost entirely on U.S. sources, and the accompanying proposal for the creation of an APS Board of Community Psychologists mentioned potential links with APA Division 27 (now SCRA). The CP Board's establishment (Armstrong, 1982) marked the formal recognition of CP in Australia. The report of its inaugural meeting (Fyson, 1984) noted that "by far, the thing most people wanted to get out of the Board was an exchange of ideas (applied)," and that a key founding principle was "open systems and participation" (p. 13).

Interest in the new board was strong through the 1980s. The first issue of the board's newsletter, *Network*, appeared in 1984 (becoming a refereed journal in 2001, currently published online as *The Australian Community Psychologist*). CP gained significant influence quickly; in fact, CP formed part of the undergraduate curriculum in almost 50% of all Australian tertiary institutions where psychology was taught at that time (Farhall & Love, 1987).

Attracting some 4,000 psychologists from around the world, the 1988 International Congress in Psychology marked the 'coming of age' of Australian psychology in general, and of CP in particular. Links were cemented with neighbouring colleagues in Aotearoa/New Zealand, as well as in the Asia-Pacific region and North America. The board hosted four symposia and an invited address by Julian Rappaport. Rappaport explored mutual help and community care and highlighted one of the few cases when an Australian innovation has been successfully exported to the United States—the mutual help organisation GROW (formerly Recovery), founded in the late 1950s by a Sydney Catholic priest. The titles of the symposia provide a snapshot of the range of CP perspectives at that time: psychology of oppression and empowerment; the community emphasis in mental health policy and practice; preventative psychology in applied settings; and cultural contexts: the development of localised patterns for CP.

The congress also marked the beginnings of Australian community psychologists' collective conscientisation and mobilisation around social justice. At subsequent APS conferences, loose alliances began forming between

---

[4] APS Membership is now more than 15,000 (APS Annual Report, 2005).

community psychologists, critics of the invoking of science as a justification for psychological practice (e.g., John, 1984, 1988; McGartland & Polgar, 1994), peace psychologists (Sanson, 1989), feminists (Gridley & Turner, 2005), and APS members concerned about psychology's treatment of Indigenous issues (Gridley, Dudgeon, Pickett, Davidson & Sanson, 2000). There was thus some overlap in membership of/association with such groups.

Another direct sequel to the congress was the establishment of a series of gatherings/small conferences alternating between Australia and Aotearoa/ New Zealand, which came to be known as the Trans-Tasman conferences.[5] The strength of commitment to bicultural psychology and the related processes of decolonisation and depowerment of dominant culture groups within Aotearoa/New Zealand acted as a catalyst for consciousness-raising and considerable soul-searching amongst Australian community psychologists, emboldening us to articulate social change as a core activity for CP. In 1992, Thomas and Veno edited a joint CP textbook that foregrounded social change agendas reflecting local and regional priorities in both countries (Thomas & Veno, 1992). Personal links were later established with critical/ community psychology colleagues in South Africa, enabling a wider exchange of ideas and an expansion in our shared understandings of what characterises CP in the Southern Hemisphere.

Membership of the CP board rose again in the early 1990s, with the separate establishment of postgraduate programs in community psychology in three states, but this growth was dramatically curtailed in 1995 with the imposition of uniform postgraduate entry requirements for all APS boards, renamed colleges. This and related changes undermined the inclusive values inherent in community psychology, with the result that it is now one of the smallest of the nine APS colleges. Further, attempts by the college to attract or involve interested people unable to fulfil college membership criteria, via a 'Friends of the College' category, were blocked by the APS, and so it has not been possible to broaden the membership base as SCRA has done in the United States. There is however an active e-mail discussion list operating out of Curtin University that has close to 200 subscribers, of whom only 25% are college members.

The CP board's decision to pursue specialist status as a college was a largely defensive move to protect the capacity of universities to offer CP training at postgraduate level. Thus, the relationship between the college and the small number of accredited programs is symbiotic—because without college status, the APS would not accredit the programs, and they would likely die; and without accredited programs, the college would lose both legitimacy

---

[5] The sites and dates of the 10 Trans-Tasman conferences held to date are as follows: Pakatoa (1989), Maralinga (1990), Rotorua (1992), Yarrabah (1993), Toodyay (1996), Hamilton (1998), Melbourne (2001), Perth, (2002), Tauranga (2004), and Sydney (2006).

and its primary sources of new members, and would also die. Either of these outcomes is an ever-imminent possibility, but so far, we have survived.

When we celebrated the college's 21st birthday (and survival) in 2004, respondents to our survey gave us their assessment of the college's achievements to date. They focussed on its influence on the psychology discipline/profession, especially within APS itself. The establishment of the board/college provided opportunities for *"support and stimulation for those whose interest is in community action/change,"* said one older member. A younger member commented, *"despite being a small College, members have had an influence on a number of discussion papers, directorates, etc. within the APS."* Foundation member Anthony Love described the college's major contribution as *"helping change a very entrenched, conservative culture within psychology to one that is generally speaking far more inclusive/pluralistic and proactive."*

Social Responsibility and Social Justice: The Nexus with CP in Australia

Parallel to the emergence and formal recognition of CP within the APS, a growing interest on the part of many psychologists in social justice issues forced the APS to establish 'Interest Groups' in 1984, amid vigorous debates about the place of sociopolitical concerns within a discipline staking claims to scientific objectivity (Cooke, 2000). However, this move did not entirely resolve the question of how to locate social issues within the discipline and its organisational/professional structures. To individual psychologists with specific social justice concerns, the synergies between social welfare concerns and the emergent subdiscipline of CP began to become apparent towards the end of the 1980s. In Australia, the relationship between CP and social justice has evolved differently in three areas: feminism, peace psychology, and Indigenous issues.

CP Discovers Feminism

The 1970s feminist slogan 'the personal is political' meant that psychology was (and still is) fertile ground for feminist action, and that political questions came to be seen as psychology's business. Feminist consciousness-raising groups resonated with community psychologists' support for self-help groups and consumer-based movements. As Mulvey (1988) observed, both feminism and CP focused on social policy, advocacy, empowerment, the demystification of experts, and prevention ahead of cure. But shared values and goals, and the common experience of 'swimming against the tide' of mainstream psychology did not lead to much integration between the two emergent subdisciplines, and in Australia it was some years before there was a critical mass of feminist women in CP ranks making connections between the burgeoning social movement and the self-styled radical subdiscipline within psychology.

In Australia, most psychologists associated with the early days of the APS Women and Psychology Interest Group, (W & P, formed in 1984) were either academics or counselling/clinical practitioners (Cooke, 2000). Many community psychologists distanced themselves from 'the personal' as reflecting psychology's traditional victim-blaming stance, and tended to take up 'public' ahead of 'private' causes as their intervention targets—which might explain why they paid very little attention to women (Gridley & Turner, 2005). In Australia, Judith Cougle, Heather Gridley, and Colleen Turner were the first community psychologists to be equally involved in W & P, and their collaboration bore fruit in the early 1990s, particularly as the links with feminist colleagues in Aotearoa/New Zealand supported their analysis of the overlap between their shared interests.

Australian community psychologists were challenged by the work of feminists like New Zealander Ingrid Huygens (1988), the U.K.'s Celia Kitzinger (1991), and the U.S.A.'s Laura Brown (1997) to unpack taken-for-granted notions of empowerment and to focus instead on power, privilege, and control. CP practitioners in direct service settings were excited by synergies between CP principles and the feminist-infused social constructionist narrative therapy approaches of Michael White (Shopland, 2000). The collaboration between feminist and community psychologists remains mainly confined to Victoria, where joint activities and research projects have eventuated in areas such as family violence and women's mental health.

All Aboard the Peace Psychology Train

The formation in 1984 of the APS Interest Group on Psychologists for the Prevention of War (PPOWP, now Psychologists for the Promotion of World Peace) emerged alongside responses from psychologists elsewhere in the Western world to nuclear proliferation and the widespread fear of war (Cooke, 2000). PPOWP's founder, Connie Peck, was keen to forge links with the community board as a natural ally for the fledgling interest group, and urged her members to affiliate with the board as well. In the absence of restrictive entry requirements, membership of the interest group rapidly exceeded that of the board. The alliance remained strong, with joint activities, a special issue of *Network* devoted to peace psychology (Sanson, 1989), and co-sponsorship of several Trans-Tasman conferences, including a mobile workshop/journey in 1993 from Brisbane to the Aboriginal community at Yarrabah, North Queensland, that was dubbed 'the peace train.'

Engagement with Indigenous Issues

Community psychologists were galvanised to engage with Indigenous issues by events at the International Congress in Psychology in Sydney in 1988 (Gridley et al., 2000). As the bicentennial anniversary of British settlement, 1988 was a year of widespread debate within the Australian community about whether colonisation was a cause for celebration or regret, particularly in terms of its impact on the Indigenous inhabitants. The congress's complete lack of attention to such questions, alongside the absence of any Indigenous content in the conference's scientific or even social program, acted as a trigger point for the community psychologists in attendance to reflect on their social responsibility. As Davidson et al. (2000) observed in reviewing a century of psychological research with Australia's Indigenous people, the challenge was then, and continues to be today:

> . . . knowing what to do with a century of research that Indigenous scholars have viewed as an integral part of colonialism and cultural suppression . . . . It is about reconciling the scientific majority with an important scientific and moral minority of psychologists and Indigenous professionals who are building post-colonial models of psychology in Indigenous communities. (p. 92)

Connections were initially made with a small number of Indigenous psychologists and educators, with a view to developing a symposium on issues of race and power, which eventuated at the 1990 APS Conference in Melbourne. Immediately afterwards, the first Trans-Tasman conference held in Australia got under way, designed to raise participants' awareness of social (in)justice issues and their effects on Indigenous people. This 'social change workshop,' organised by Veno, involved a 7-day journey to meet with elders of the *Maralinga Tjarutja* community in the South Australian desert, on the site of British atomic bomb tests in the 1950s.

The APS Interest Group on Aboriginal Issues, Aboriginal People, and Psychology was formed at the 1991 APS conference in Adelaide and gradually replaced the community board as the society's principal advocate on Indigenous issues. The driving force behind the Interest Group's development was Patricia Dudgeon (then head of Curtin University's Centre for Aboriginal Studies), one of just a handful of Indigenous psychologists in the country. A strong partnership between the centre and Curtin's community psychologists enabled the interest group to maintain its commitment to Indigenous leadership with the support of the more numerous non-Indigenous psychologists working for change within psychology and beyond.

Throughout the 1990s, the partnership between the interest group and the board/college remained strong and productive. Some of the achievements include the development of APS ethical guidelines for research and practice with Indigenous people (Davidson, Dudgeon, Garton, Garvey & Kidd, 1995), a special issue of the APS journal *Australian Psychologist* on Indigenous psychologies in Australia (Sanson & Dudgeon, 2000), the *Handbook for Psychologists Working with Aboriginal People* (Dudgeon, Garvey & Pickett, 2001), and regular programs of Indigenous content at APS conferences, with a substantial proportion of Indigenous people presenting papers. When the rise of Pauline Hanson's *One Nation* party in the mid-1990s signalled a public backlash against reforms in areas such as Native Title, Indigenous self-determination, and the national process of reconciliation, several community psychologists contributed to the APS position paper on racism and prejudice (Sanson et al., 1998).

The involvement of CP in Indigenous issues needs to be contextualised as a relatively limited supporting contribution to the efforts of Indigenous peoples themselves to reclaim direction and control of their destinies. Like the reconciliation process itself, what these 'achievements' mean in practice will never be settled once and for all but will be a matter for ongoing monitoring, reflection, and truth-telling. However, community psychologists can legitimately claim to have played a key role in consciousness-raising within Australian psychology around racism and Indigenous issues, whereas theoretical and organisational links with activist psychologists in areas such as peace psychology and feminism were forged after some years of relatively separate development.

Contributions to Other Domains of Social Justice

In recent years, the college has continued to act as an umbrella group for other politically oriented APS Interest Groups (e.g., Gay and Lesbian Issues in Psychology, Psychology and Cultures, and Psychology and the Environment) by lobbying for the limited space in APS conference programs, or arguing the case for more socially and culturally responsive policies.[6] The current APS executive director, Lyn Littlefield, a member of the CP college, is working hard to give meaning to the reference in the society's mission statement to "improving community wellbeing" (APS, 2005, p. 1) by influencing government policy in areas such as health, ageing, and family and community services.

A Wide Brown Land: Regional Differences in CP

The overview we have provided of the development of CP in Australia might give the appearance of a relatively unified past. However, CP developed distinct flavours within different regions of Australia. The fact that the two major 'enclaves' are situated on the west and east coasts, some 4,000 kilometres apart, might explain why their respective histories and orientations differ from one another. During the 1990s, postgraduate programs in CP were developed in Western Australia, Victoria, and Queensland. All three are strongly identified with their region—Edith Cowan University (ECU) in rapidly developing outer suburban Perth, Victoria University (VU) in Melbourne's industrialised, multicultural west, and the University of Southern Queensland (USQ) in rural/regional Toowoomba. In addition to the focus on CP, the willingness of each program to embrace innovative pedagogies,

---

[6] It is worth noting that four of the five APS Directors of Social Issues to date have been members of the CP college: Ann Sanson, Heather Gridley, Colleen Turner, and Prasuna Reddy.

diverse research methodologies, and critical reflective practice, has distinguished them from more traditional offerings in psychology.

Victoria

Whether due to the APS national office's location in Melbourne or the relative ease of organisation with greater resources across shorter distances, Victoria provided the base for CP during its formative years, particularly within the APS via the board. At that stage, the majority of psychologists were employed in the public sector, and this was reflected in the eclectic concerns listed in the report of the first meeting of the board (APS Bulletin, 1983). Indeed, much of the CP activity in Victoria has been practitioner-led, reflecting the need for supportive community models of practice (Gridley et al., 2007). Some of the earliest applications were in the newly established community mental health clinics and by organisational psychologists conducting program evaluation in the public sector. At present, there is a significant core of members and graduates working in local government, education, counselling, community health, and social policy and planning.

The applied focus of CP in Victoria has a long history. One of the most innovative early applications of CP theory to an Australian community context was Arthur Veno's work with motorcycle gangs. Veno and his colleagues utilised principles of prevention, conflict resolution, and collaborative decision-making in working with all parties towards a model of consensus-based crowd control at motorcycle Grand Prix meetings at Bathurst (NSW) and Phillip Island (Victoria) in the 1980s (Veno & Veno, 1992). More recently, the career journeys in applied research and community-based practice of CPs like Colleen Turner, who has worked in areas as diverse as early intervention, aged and disability services, local government, migrant women's health, the Victorian AIDS Council, and the trade union sector, illustrate the 'grassroots' nature of much CP activity in the state. Practitioners continue to drive Victorian CP, and their numbers are increasing as new graduates begin to shape the field's direction in this state.

Within tertiary education in Victoria, elements of CP have been offered within applied social and organisational psychology at Melbourne University (by Anona Armstrong), and at what are now Monash University's regional campuses (by Arthur Veno and later, Rob Curnow), and within clinical psychology at La Trobe (by Anthony Love, Lyn Littlefield, and John Farhall). The establishment in 1990 of a Graduate Diploma in CP at Victoria University marked the first stand-alone CP course in the state. It evolved into the current master's/doctoral program coordinated by Heather Gridley and Adrian Fisher. In 2001, Isaac Prilleltensky established a Wellness Promotion Unit underpinned by a critical CP framework. The unit undertakes collaborative, community-based projects and hosts practicum placements for CP students.

The VU CP program has developed a strongly integrated research and practice ethos, with students gaining exposure to a range of theoretical and skill bases required for work within the community sector. Students can be found doorknocking for a neighbourhood renewal project, evaluating a 'walking school bus' program, facilitating community engagement in an environmental precinct, or assisting a feminist women's service to embed family violence awareness guidelines within mainstream health services. But they are equally likely to be found offering counselling, advocacy, and outreach services in community settings, thus reflecting the twin emphases on applied social research and community-based practice that have historically marked CP in Victoria. VU master's student Kathryn Magor reflected:

The past 18 months of community psychology has been an amazing and inspirational adventure. After four years of mainstream psychology, I felt like I had been 'freed', and that finally I was in a space that allowed me to explore and challenge much of what I had been taught so far . . . However, this course has given me more than just ideals and dreams for the future of our communities. It has provided me with the practical skills and knowledge to transfer my visions/dreams into a 'reality'.

Western Australia

In contrast with Victoria's predominantly practitioner base, CP in Western Australia (WA) emerged primarily from applied social psychology and CP. Winkler's early efforts to infuse the clinical program at the University of Western Australia (a 'sandstone' university) with a community mental health approach were cut short by his premature death in 1988.[7] Meanwhile, Americans Paul Jennings, Robert Reiff, and Arthur Veno introduced social and early CP theories that influenced the development in the late 1970s of the postgraduate program at the WA Institute of Technology (now Curtin University). The CP stream did not survive an amalgamation with an organisational psychology program, but Brian Bishop continues to mentor a generation of doctoral students attracted to his singular brand of CP research.

With Geoff Syme, Bishop established an enduring relationship with the Commonwealth Scientific and Industrial Research Organisation (CSIRO) that saw the pair undertaking community and industry consultation and problem-solving in a period of rapid urban and regional development that was placing great strain on the state's fragile environment and scarce water resources. Bishop and Syme (1992) proceeded to develop models for community psychologists as participant-conceptualisers and social change agents, in contexts as diverse as forestry and land use, urban development on the rural fringe, and the impact of the mining industry on Indigenous communities. Taking necessity as the mother of invention, their work demanded a willingness to take risks and tolerate ambiguity beyond the parameters of scientist-practitioner or even applied psychology models, toward the development of iterative-generative reflective practice (Bishop, Sonn, Drew & Contos, 2002).

---

[7] The Community College has since established an award in Winkler's memory "to encourage and recognise excellence in a project in the field of applied community psychology" (Terms of Reference, Robin Winkler Award).

CP, Curtin-style, formed the basis for a new postgraduate coursework program in the early 1990s at the fledgling Edith Cowan University (formerly the Western Australian College of Advanced Education). The two founders of that program, Noel Howieson and John Carroll, were (are) psychoanalytically oriented psychologists *"with a deep and wonderful humanity,"* according to Neil Drew, who joined the team in 1989, quickly followed by Moira O'Connor (from the United Kingdom) and Adele Hills:

They said they had been looking into a sub-discipline called community psychology and would I be interested in that. I began reading and was astonished and delighted to find the intellectual, emotional, and spiritual home I had been looking for! Everything that I read about community psychology resonated with the journey I had been on for the previous 10 years.

The ECU program initially emphasised community environmental psychology, with a focus on practical skills relating to community engagement and social impact assessment, in keeping with the issues of the day around population expansion within a fragile natural environment. The term *community environmental psychology* was thoroughly debated—it was not community 'and' environmental, nor was it community 'dash' environmental—but rather a hybrid form that capitalised on the principles and values of CP, especially relating to person-environment fit.

Over the years, the course was influenced by and drew from aspects of primarily American critical perspectives and theorists, as well as the employment of people such as Chris Sonn (via Curtin University). Sonn almost single-handedly put issues of social justice—Aboriginal People and reconciliation, refugees and asylum seekers—firmly in the sights of CP students. The increased awareness of and commitment to issues of social justice has also led many students down the path of liberation psychology and to the work of some key South American community psychologists. Since the departure of both Drew, now at University of Notre Dame in Fremantle (UNDA), and Sonn (now at VU), students continue to embrace critical perspectives and alternative methodologies. In recent years, the stream has offered a CP doctoral program.

A recent and unexpected development is the establishment of an undergraduate behavioural science program taught solely by community psychologists at the private and Catholic UNDA. The bold decision not to seek APS accreditation means that the course has the potential to have *"all the good things without APS interference"* according to an envious colleague from another WA university. Because the APS controls almost every aspect of Australian psychology, and given that an independent critical psychology research unit in NSW floundered after less than 5 years in operation, UNDA's decision to 'go it alone' was not taken lightly.

Other States

Outside Victoria and Western Australia, CP has struggled to establish a firm base, despite the fact that there was nationwide interest in the early days of the new field. Today, the college has members in every state, but they do not gather in the numbers needed to form a readily identifiable presence, and so do not have the capacity to lobby for locally based programs and activities. Only in NSW and Queensland has there been any form of CP training, collective activity, or identifiable practice beyond a few individuals.

New South Wales

New South Wales (NSW) is Australia's most populous state, with the second largest number of CP college members. A number of these are practitioners in community settings who are also members of other APS colleges, specialising in counselling, clinical, or educational psychology, and based at some distance from one another in sprawling Sydney and throughout the state. Despite a lengthy CP presence stemming from the work of Syd Engelberg (from the United States) and others, with no APS-accredited postgraduate program in CP, it has proved very difficult to maintain. Yet core CP values such as community collaboration, social change, and empowerment are reflected in domains such as education (e.g., Stephen Fyson, a former student of Engelberg, now principal of a regional Christian-based school), the family-community nexus (e.g., the Family Action Centre, University of Newcastle), and community mental health (e.g., Meg Smith, University of Western Sydney). Smith's involvement with mental health service consumers living with bipolar affective disorder stemmed from her own experience and led to a sustained engagement with teaching, public policy, and grassroots community activism (Smith, 2002).

Queensland

CP has had a chequered history in Queensland. Gardner and Veno's radical experiment with a multidisciplinary CP program at University of Queensland lasted from 1973 until 1978 (Gardner & Veno, 1979). It was considered too radical for the traditionally conservative state at the time. Ten years later, the regional Darling Downs Institute of Advanced Education (now University of Southern Queensland) adopted a community/health psychology orientation under Andrew Ellerman that eventually led to the appointment in 1995 of Grace Pretty from Canada and Mark Rapley (now at ECU) from the United Kingdom. However, their postgraduate stream in community and health psychology did not survive the APS accreditation ruling that streams could only be identified with one specialist field.

Pretty has nonetheless continued to apply her extensive knowledge base in adolescent sense of community to a wide range of contexts within Australia and abroad, particularly with a view to enhancing the well-being, resilience, and civic participation of young people—another example of the creative adaptation and localised application of CP theories originating elsewhere. With Bishop, Fisher, and Sonn (2005), she produced a paper for the APS on the potential contribution of sense of community theory and research to understandings of everyday life in Australia, alongside currently popular concepts such as social capital, community engagement, and capacity building.

In Queensland, CP principles, values, and theories have been incorporated into non-CP domains and programs. However, while these vibrant new developments in the field are occurring outside the APS web, in schools of community studies, public health and even criminology, their advantages in encompassing knowledge beyond one academic discipline tend to be offset by the consequence that they do not 'fit' anywhere. Thus, they face difficulties in establishing a core identity and gathering a critical mass of like-minded colleagues.

Australian CP's regional variations have resulted in a truly eclectic mix of ideas and methodologies. Perhaps the very existence of CP, Australian-style, provides a counterpoint to 'one size fits all' answers to the perennial question 'What is community psychology?' The key unifying agent across such distance and diversity has been CP's organisational home, the APS College of Community Psychologists. Yet relationships between the society, the college and the field at large have not always been smooth or straightforward.

CP and the APS: A Contentious Issue

CP in Australia has been formalised to a greater degree than anywhere else in the world, not only within the APS but, for a short time, to the extent of state registration (licensing) as a field of specialist practice. In 1992, a case was made by the CP board for the creation of the specialist title 'community psychologist' alongside the other six specialisations that were proposed as part of the new Victorian Psychologists Registration Act. Although the case was successful, another Act in 2000 abandoned specialist titles altogether. Other states, notably WA, have persisted with registering specialisations, but 'community psychologist' is not listed as one.

The ongoing tension between our often uncomfortable fit with bodies such as APS and registration boards and our dependence on APS structures for survival is apparent in the comments of respondents to our survey. The positive aspects of formalisation were identified by clinical community psychologist John Farhall as having been initially *"to support identity around being a 'community psychologist'; to learn from what others were doing; to enable a critical mass to form enabling training to emerge."* For other respondents, there was ambivalence about *"dangers in a 'College' approach to areas of psychology."* One respondent rejected specialisation altogether: *"I think psychology has too many 'specialisations.' We could do with a bit more humility I reckon."* Unlike other specialisations, there is generally no particular career advantage in joining the CP college. People join, or stay, simply *"because it is my philosophy"*—at a cost that is often too high for beginning practitioners as well as for those nearing the end of their working life. Foundation member Stephen Fyson summed up the dilemma in compromising the original vision for the sake of professional/organisational survival:

When we started the Board, we hoped the emphasis would be on interdisciplinary exchange, as well as a common meeting ground for psychologists who wanted to think more broadly – it was thus a tension when it became 'professionalised' (in the Sarason sense of limiting access to knowledge and recognition) as a College. . . .. The 'professional' recognition is important, but it has greatly limited the original attempts at the broader aims (in contrast to the Interest Groups).

Meanwhile the people with whom we like to think we have most in common—community development workers, social planners, Indigenous mental health workers, political activists, epidemiologists, community artists, and so on—are excluded from 'the club' and/or are mostly unaware of our existence. Crucial questions regarding the role of the APS remain to be answered: Is the APS the most appropriate vehicle to promote the college/CP into the future? How can we foster a true sense of collaboration with like-minded people from other disciplines? The energy expended in responding to and complying with all the APS administrative demands and regulatory practices has often restricted the field to an inward 'maintenance' focus instead of a more transformative, outward engagement with Australian society at large.

Visions for the Future

When we asked our survey respondents about their visions for the future of CP, they appeared to be looking both inwards and outwards. Some focussed on CP's potential contribution to psychology itself, to *"keep yapping and nipping at the heels of the profession to help it to think more critically about how humans can change"* (John Farhall, clinical/community psychologist and foundation college member), to *"influence 'mainstream' psychology more"* (Christine McKersie, master's student and rural high school teacher), and *"keep the forces of cultural change and renewal within the organisation (APS) alive and kicking"* (Anthony Love, clinical/community psychologist and foundation college member). As Neil Drew put it, *"community psychology is the burr in the butt that reminds psychologists that we have an obligation to work towards a better world."*

Others looked more to what community psychology might have to offer the Australian community at large, whereby it could *"be much more involved as leaders of community capacity; research into community issues; training community leaders"* (Anona Armstrong, foundation college member); *"progress community capacity and wellbeing";* give *"a voice to the marginalised,"* and develop *"policy/program/knowledge/strategies that can be imparted to numerous areas of the Australian community – education, environment, [and] health."* And finally,

GROW. . . .. I am looking forward to the future, as my CP history is still in its youth (Tamara White, VU masters student and youth counsellor).

Discussion and Conclusions

As with psychology in general, CP in Australia has predominantly relied on developments in the Northern Hemisphere, although the Australian versions of core concepts such as sense of community, mutual help, and reflective-generative practice have a vitality and a political edge that is not always apparent (or possible?) in larger-scale contexts. The influences of critical and feminist theories, albeit derived in part from our British colonial roots, are also more in evidence here than in most CP publications and programs from the United States.

As we compare our history with accounts of CP's development in other parts of the world, we find many resonances as well as a number of points of departure. Not surprisingly, our history comes closest to that of Aotearoa/New Zealand and Canada. The observation by Nelson, Lavoie, and Mitchell (2007) that "Canadian community psychologists must address issues of oppression and resilience in relation to the cultural historical and linguistic make-up . . . of an increasingly diverse community with unresolved colonial roots" (p. 30) could be equally applied here, with the possible exception of language. All chapters make reference to the sociopolitical context in which CP emerged and is practised in each country. But there are differences in the degree to which critical, political activism is foregrounded as 'core business' or seen more as a backdrop to an essentially professional or academic enterprise. Words like liberation, participation, and social change can sound hollow in Euro-Western contexts; but they are intensely meaningful in places where there are long histories of oppression/struggle/revolution (Latin America) and "liberatory models of community praxis" (Africa). CP's professed values resonate readily with the roots of Indigenous cultural traditions such as the Maori "profoundly ecological view of life" or the Cameroon "communitarian practice." Australian community psychology cannot claim to have been influenced to the same extent by Indigenous precursors to its formal emergence.

Another issue raised by a number of contributors concerns the relative constraints and advantages of professional affiliation/accreditation/formalisation; the desire for professional identification and an administrative homeplace is offset by trends in places such as India, Hong Kong, and the United States towards interdisciplinary collaborations with action-oriented social scientists—a goal made more difficult in Australia by our location within the APS. Such tensions between the individualistic, positivist, territorial nature of mainstream psychology and its professional bodies and community psychology's more collectivist, outward looking standpoint seem particularly strong in the United Kingdom, New Zealand, and Australian accounts. Who 'does' CP? Is it a 'really social psychology' (U.K.), 'everyday life psychology' (Argentina/Uruguay), 'anthropoanalytical practice' (Portugal)? Does it matter?? We find ourselves concurring with our U.K. colleagues:

With . . . a permeating notion of liberatory practice, any debate about who is really doing community psychology, and about how to organise to do it, perhaps fades away as only of interest to careerist professionals. (Burton, Boyle, Harris & Kagan, 2007, p. 234)

Australia is indeed 'so far away' from North America and Britain, but how much does it matter if our orientation is as close to theirs as this chapter implies, albeit with a local flavour? Perhaps true maturity lies in owning, rather than apologising for, those gifts of our forebears and mentors that prove useful for our particular journey while always working towards a more culturally inclusive, postcolonial critical praxis. It is our belief that by now Australian community psychology's relationships with the subdiscipline elsewhere are fully reciprocal.

Acknowledgements. The authors wish to thank the many people who have provided helpful comments on drafts of this account of the historical development of community psychology in our country, particularly Neil Drew, Colleen Turner, Christopher Sonn, Adrian Fisher, Emma Sampson, and Stephen Fyson, as well as the 25 respondents to our 'history survey.'

References

APS Bulletin (1983). Report from the Board of Community Psychologists. *Bulletin of the Australian Psychological Society, December,* 23.

Armstrong, A. (1982). *Community Psychology.* Proposal to establish a Board of Community Psychologists, presented to APS Annual Conference, Melbourne, August 1982.

Australian Psychological Society. (2005). *Annual Report.* Melbourne: Author.

Bishop, B. J., Sonn, C. C., Drew, N. M., & Contos, N. E. (2002). The evolution of epistemology and concepts in an iterative-generative reflective practice: The importance of small differences. *American Journal of Community Psychology, 30,* 493-510.

Bishop, B. & Syme, G. (1992). Social change in rural settings: Lessons for community change agents. In D. R. Thomas & A. Veno (Eds.), *Community psychology and social change: Australian and New Zealand perspectives* (Ch. 5, pp. 93-111). Palmerston North, NZ: Dunmore Press.

Brown, L. (1997). Ethics in Psychology: *Cui bono?* In D. Fox & I. Prilleltensky (Eds.), *Critical psychology: An introduction,* (p. 51-67). London: Sage.

Burton, M., Boyle, S., Harris, C., & Kagan, C. (2007). Community Psychology in Britain. In S. M. Reich, M. Riemer, I. Prilleltensky, & M. Montero (Eds.), International Community Psychology: History and Theories (Ch. 10 pp. 219-237), NY: Springer.

Cooke, S. (2000). *A meeting of minds: The Australian Psychological Society and Australian Psychologists 1944-1994.* Melbourne: The Australian Psychological Society.

Davidson, G., Dudgeon, P., Garton, A., Garvey, D., & Kidd, G. (1995). *Guidelines for the provision of psychological services for and the conduct of psychological research with Aboriginal and Torres Strait Islander people.* Melbourne: Australian Psychological Society.

Davidson, G., Sanson, A., & Gridley, H. (2000). Australian psychology and Australia's Indigenous people: Existing and emerging narratives. *Australian Psychologist, 35,* 92-99.

Dudgeon, P., Garvey, D., & Pickett, H. (Eds.). (2001). *Handbook for psychologists working with Indigenous Australians*. Perth: Gunada Press.

Farhall, J. & Love, A. (1987). A survey of community psychology teaching in tertiary institutions in Australia. *Network, 3(2)*, 7-19.

Fyson, S. (1984). Board of Community Psychologists – Update. *Bulletin of the Australian Psychological Society, February,* 13.

Gardner, J. & Veno, A. (1979). An interdisciplinary, multilevel, university-based training program in community psychology. *American Journal of Community Psychology, 7*, 605-620.

Gridley, H., Fisher, A., Thomas, D., & Bishop, B. (2007). Development of community psychology in Australia and Aotearoa/New Zealand, *Australian Psychologist, 42(1)*, 15-22.

Gridley, H. & Turner, C. (2005). Gender, power and community psychology. In G. Nelson & I. Prilleltensky (Eds.), *Community psychology: In pursuit of liberation and well-being*. Basingstoke UK: Palgrave MacMillan.

Gridley, H., Dudgeon, P., Pickett, H., Davidson, G., & Sanson, A. (2000). The Australian Psychological Society and Australia's Indigenous people: A decade of action. *Australian Psychologist, 35*, 88-91.

Hill, M. (unpublished). *Community Psychology: A science, a profession, a means of promoting human welfare*. Position paper prepared to accompany the proposal to establish the APS Board of Community Psychologists at the APS Annual Conference, August 1982.

Huygens, I. (1988). *Empowering our natural communities: An alternative to prevention*. Paper presented at the 24th International Congress of Psychology, Sydney, Australia.

John, I. D. (1984). Science as a justification for psychology as a social institution. *Australian Psychologist, 19*, 29-37.

John, I. D. (1988). The theory of the relationship between theory and practice in psychology as an impediment to its understanding. *Australian Psychologist, 23*, 289-304.

Kitzinger, C. (1991). Feminism, psychology and the paradox of power. *Feminism and Psychology 1*, 111-129.

McGartland, M. & Polgar, S. (1994). Paradigm collapse in psychology: The necessity for a 'two methods' approach. *Australian Psychologist, 29*, 21-28.

Mulvey, A. (1988). Community psychology and feminism: Tensions and commonalities. *Journal of Community Psychology, 17*, 70-83.

National Committee for Psychology of the Australian Academy of Science (1996). *Psychological science in Australia*. Canberra: Australian Government Publishing Service.

Nelson, G., Lavoie, F., & Mitchell, T. (2007). The history and theories of community psychology in Canada. In S. M. Reich, M. Riemer, I. Prilleltensky, & M. Montero (Eds.), International Community Psychology: History and Theories (Ch. 1 pp. 13-36), NY: Springer.

O'Neil, W. (1987). *A century of psychology in Australia*. Sydney: Sydney University Press.

Pretty, G., Bishop, B., Fisher, A., & Sonn, C. (2005). What research and practice have told us about our sense of the Australian community. Paper presented at *the 40th APS Annual Conference, Melbourne*.

Sanson, A. (Ed.). (1989). Peace psychology – Special issue. *Network, 5 (2)*.

Sanson, A. & Dudgeon, P. (2000). Special Issue on Australian Indigenous psychologies. *Australian Psychologist, 35*.

Sanson, A., Augoustinos, M., Gridley, H., Kyrios, M., Reser, J., & Turner, C. (1998). Racism and Prejudice: An Australian Psychological Society Position Paper. *Australian Psychologist 33*, 161-182.

Shopland, J. (2000). Women and counselling: A feminist perspective. *Healthsharing Women, 11(2)*, 7-11.

Smith, M. (2002). Morning teas and mailouts: Practising community psychology in the areas of mental health and people with disabilities. Special guest editorial. *Network, 13, 1*, 5-6.

Taft, R. & Day, R. (1988). Psychology in Australia. *Annual Review of Psychology, 39*, 375-400.

Taylor, K. F. & Taft, R. (1977). Psychology and the Australian zeitgeist. In M. Nixon & R. Taft (Eds.), *Psychology in Australia: Achievements and prospects* (pp. 35-51), Rushcutters Bay, NSW: Pergamon Press.

Thomas, D. R. & Veno, A. (Eds.). (1992). *Psychology and social change: Creating an international agenda*. Palmerston North, NZ: Dunmore.

Veno, A. & Veno, E. (1992). Managing public order at the Australian Motor Cycle Grand Prix. In D. R. Thomas & A. Veno (Eds.), *Psychology and social change: Creating an international agenda* (Ch. 4, pp. 74-92). Palmerston North, NZ: Dunmore.

6
Community Psychology in Aotearoa/New Zealand: Me Tiro Whakamuri ā Kiā Hangai Whakamua*

NEVILLE ROBERTSON AND BRIDGETTE MASTERS-AWATERE

Abstract

Aotearoa/New Zealand has been forged in the interaction between indigenous (Māori) and settler peoples within the context of colonisation and resistance. A treaty signed in 1840 continues to play a central, if contested, role in mediating a bicultural relationship. Community psychology concepts are reflective of Māori world views, which emphasise the interrelationship of people, land, sea, and the elements; the importance of placing people within their historical, social, and geographic context; and a strong preference for collectivist arrangements over individualism. Collectivist traditions can also be found within (mainly British) settler society. Within the academy, these local traditions have been attenuated by imported scholarship, primarily British and American. Feminist and culturally anchored critiques of mainstream psychology have been particularly influential, and, in recent years, Kaupapa Māori approaches to research and action. Values, especially social justice, collaboration, and diversity, are central to teaching and practice. Practitioners work in a wide range of settings and roles, mostly outside what is commonly regarded as the province of psychologists. They typically work at the macro and meso levels, fulfilling roles such as policy analyst, planner, health promoter, advocate, community developer, researcher, and evaluator.

Our Definition of Community Psychology

Community psychology is a context-sensitive, applied social science that attempts to promote social justice and enhance the life circumstances of groups of people, especially those who are oppressed, stigmatised, or marginalised. Although its origins lie in psychology, community psychology

---

* "Look backwards in order to move forward with purpose."

favours interdisciplinary approaches. It has permeable boundaries, owing as much to sociology, community development, education, and the policy sciences as it does to the "parent" discipline.

Community psychology favours critical perspectives on knowledge creation and truth claims, recognising that what is regarded as legitimate knowledge is often context-specific and inevitably coloured by the social and cultural position of the "knower." Experiential knowledge is valued, along with knowledge derived from empirical studies. Thus, community psychology research employs a wide range of methodologies, the choice of method being determined by the particular context and issue being addressed.

Community psychology is multilevel in that it recognises the limitations and potentially victim-blaming nature of individually focused interventions, favouring instead group, community, and societal interventions which address the structural factors maintaining oppression and suboptimal health.

Community psychology pays particular attention to process, valuing bottom-up, inclusive, and collaborative ways of working over top-down solutions to problems imposed by political elites.

Introduction

Being a New Zealander comes with an acute sense of there being a big world out there. Aotearoa/New Zealand lies in the southwest corner of the Pacific. Vast stretches of ocean separate us from our neighbours; Australia to the west and the Pacific Islands of New Caledonia, Fiji, Samoa, Tonga, and the Cook Islands to the north and east. There are fewer of us (4.1 million) than in many of the cities of the world.

We are a relatively young country. Geologically, you can see that in our land-forms, dominated by rugged mountains and steep-sided valleys. Our human history goes back not much more than 1,000 years with the arrival of Māori. Waves of immigrants came much later, initially from Europe, but increasingly from the Pacific and Asia. The interaction of indigenous and settler peoples has shaped our history and continues to do so.

This is as true of community psychology (CP) as other aspects of our life. Although we adopted the term from the United States, the way CP has developed in Aotearoa/New Zealand owes much to our history. In the following section, we provide an overview of this history, emphasising certain aspects of Māori and settler societies that provided fertile ground for CP. We follow this with an account of some of the scholars whose work was influential. CP in this country is very practice-oriented, and in the third section we describe aspects of this practice and the institutional and organisational arrangements that govern it. In the final section, we set out some the major theories and frameworks that characterise CP in Aotearoa/ New Zealand.

Informal Historical Roots of Community Psychology

As we argue below, the scholarly origins of CP in Aotearoa/New Zealand[1] can be traced to the middle of the 20th century, particularly to the work of Ernest Beaglehole. That scholarship owes much to the interaction between two bodies of knowledge: that of the indigenous Māori[2] and that of the primarily British settlers. Remediation of the impact of colonisation and the search for cultural justice are central concerns of contemporary CP. Thus, understanding the development of the discipline requires an understanding of the history of Aotearoa/New Zealand, particularly the history of colonisation.

Māori, who arrived in several waves of migration from East Polynesia, enjoyed largely undisturbed occupation of the islands from around AD 900 to 1800. Society was organised around the whānau, hapu, and iwi (extended family, subtribe and tribe) with each unit being essentially self-governing within the context of the larger unit. Social bonds were cemented through shared whakapapa (genealogy) and utu (reciprocity). In what might, from the perspective of the 21st century, be termed a profoundly ecological view of life, people's connection to the land was a vital part of their identity, and the status of tangata whenua (local people) was a prerequisite for holding political authority. Concepts such as kaitiakitanga (guardianship of natural resources) and mechanisms such as tapu (set apart) and rāhui (conserve, protect) reflected a deep spiritual connection between people and the natural environment.

While never extinguished, these values and many other features of Māori life were severely undermined by the process of colonisation. Initially, Māori dealt with the new (mainly British) settlers from a position of strength. Indeed, early Pākehā (white, European) settlement happened only with the consent and protection of tangata whenua. But things began to change, at least in the northern parts of the country, as more and more settlers arrived, bringing with them alcohol, muskets, and venereal diseases and engaging in unscrupulous land dealing (King, 2003). Partly in response to such problems and in the face of a threat of annexation by France, northern leaders gathered at Waitangi in 1835 and signed a declaration of independence, affirming the country as an "Independent State under the designation of the United Tribes of New Zealand," and seeking recognition of a Māori flag and the protection of the King of England (King, 2003, p. 154). On February 6, 1840, a larger gathering saw the signing of Te Tiriti o Waitangi (Treaty of Waitangi) by

---

[1] Although *New Zealand* is the officially sanctioned name for our country, we prefer to use *Aotearoa/New Zealand* in recognition of our bicultural heritage.
[2] Indigeneity is more correctly covered by the term *tangata whenua* (people of the land), which is typically applied to people of a specific region. The use of the term *Māori* as an ethnic label is taken from its literal meaning: "ordinary." It was used in response to the arrival of European settlers who were not ordinary.

William Hobson on behalf of the British government and by the assembled chiefs on behalf of their respective iwi. Over the following months, representatives of most iwi signed, notable exceptions being the paramount chiefs Te Heuheu of Tūwharetoa and Te Wherowhero of Tainui (Walker, 1990).

Te Tiriti o Waitangi

The treaty was drafted, in English, under the supervision of Hobson, and then translated into Māori (Te Tiriti). It comprises three written articles.[3] In Article I, often cited as the kawanatanga article, the chiefs ceded to the British Crown the right to establish a government in Aotearoa. In Article II, often cited as the tino rangatiratanga article, the Crown undertook to protect the chiefs and "all the people of New Zealand in the unqualified exercise of their chieftainship over their lands, villages and all their treasures" (Kawharu, 2005). At the same time, where land was to be disposed of, it was to be sold to the Crown at a mutually agreed price. Article III extended to Māori the rights and duties of British citizenship.

Although the British subsequently dishonoured Te Tiriti in many ways, it never lost its importance to Māori and today provides a focus for achieving cultural justice. Its meaning and role has been much debated. Of crucial important, there has been much contestation over the meaning and relative weighting of kāwanatanga (Article I) and tino rangatiratanga (Article II). Part of the contestation relates to differences between Hobson's English draft and the Māori version that was presented for signing. In the English draft approved by Hobson, Article I had Māori leaders ceding to Queen Victoria "absolutely and without reservation all the rights and powers of Sovereignty" (State Services Commission, 2005). Given the numerical and military superiority of tangata whenua (there were only about 2,000 European settlers at the time), it is extremely unlikely that Māori leaders would have willingly ceded sovereignty (Orange, 1987; Walker, 1990). Nor would they have signed away mana (integrity, prestige, jurisdiction), the Māori word most closely resembling the English concept of sovereignty. Instead, in the Māori translation prepared by the Protestant missionaries Henry and Edward Williams, the signatories accepted the right of the British Crown to exercise kawanatanga. With the use of this term, derived from kawana, a transliteration of *governor* (Walker, 1990), Article I was likely to be thought of as allowing for a limited system of self-government among the settlers (Orange, 1987). This reading is consistent with the wording used in Article II, which clearly guaranteed to

---

[3] A verbal promise by Hobson that the British government would protect religious freedom (both the various Christian denominations represented in Aotearoa at the time and traditional Māori religious practices) is sometimes referred to as a fourth article.

Māori tino rangatiratanga,[4] a word much closer in meaning to sovereignty than kawanatanga. Moreover, in resolving the different readings of the treaty, it should be recalled that it was the Māori text to which nearly all the signatures were affixed and it is the Māori text that takes precedence under the principle of contra proferentem (that is, any discrepancies in the interpretation of a treaty should be resolved in favour of the party that did not draft it) (Te Puni Kōkiri, 2005). Te Tiriti protects both kāwanatanga and tino rangatiratanga. The exercise of the former must not infringe upon the later.

In fact, from the beginning, the colonial administration governed largely as if it had absolute sovereignty. For example, through the 1852 Constitution Act, it established a franchise based on land held in individual title, effectively denying the vote to almost all Māori, for whom land was held collectively. While constituting only a third of the population at the time, Pākehā were able to exercise almost total power at the ballot box (Walker, 1990). Later governments were influenced by Chief Justice Prendergast's ruling in 1877 that "the whole treaty was worthless – a simple nullity (which) pretended to be an agreement between two nations but (in reality) was between a civilised nation and a group of savages" (cited in King, 2003, p. 325).

That is, despite Te Tiriti, colonisation proceeded in Aotearoa/New Zealand in much the same way as it did in other parts of the world colonised by European powers. Immigration proceeded rapidly. By 1858, just 18 years after Te Tiriti was signed, the population of Pākehā surpassed that of Māori (Walker, 1990). During the 1860s, the settler-dominated government "deliberately used armed force to drive through land purchases, crush Māori autonomy movements and confiscate land" (State Services Commission, 2005). The individualisation of land title by the Native Land Court undermined tribal authority and made land easier to "buy." The government was implicated in numerous dubious land purchases, and certain cultural practices were suppressed. Other patent abridgements of the human rights of Māori included the 1880 Māori Prisoners Act, which provided for indefinite detention without trial of Māori arrested while resisting land surveying in Taranaki and the exclusion of Māori from land allocations given to Pakeha soldiers returning from the First World War. Even as late as the 1930s, Māori were entitled to only half the unemployment benefit available to out-of-work non-Māori. Such blatant abrogation of the individual and collective rights of Māori, together with more subtle, but equally powerful monocultural processes, have consistently produced more negative outcomes for Māori compared with Pākehā, as evidenced in statistics relating to health, life expectancy, educational achievement, employment, income, and imprisonment (Te Puni Kōkiri, 2000).

---

[4] It is also worth noting that the term rangatiratanga was used in the 1835 Declaration of Independence.

Although Māori continued to resist, both from outside the parliamentary system (e.g. the Kingitanga movement) and from within (the first Māori entered Parliament in 1868 when just four seats were reserved for them), by the last two decades of the 19th century, economic and political power had swung decisively in favour of the settler government. Pākehā dominance was particularly evident in the cities and in most farming areas, whereas the Māori communities that survived best were often those in remote mountainous areas. (Some communities were relocated in such areas designated by the government as less desirable.)

However much abused, Te Tiriti has consistently been the focus of Māori efforts to achieve justice. For example, during the 1920s, the Ratana Church campaigned for Te Tiriti to be ratified (King, 2003), and during the 1970s and 1980s, Nga Tamatoa and other groups revitalised Māori resistance with calls to "Honour the treaty." During the last quarter of the 20th century, governments, in response to growing Māori anger, enacted legislation that referred to the treaty, most notably in the establishment of the Waitangi Tribunal[5] to hear claims against the Crown in respect of breaches of Te Tiriti. Other references to the treaty appear in recent legislation and other government policy documents relating to planning; the protection and utilisation of natural resources; health; and social services. Typically, these provisions avoid references to tino rangatiratanga. Instead, they require only that state agencies "consult" with Māori and/or that consideration be given to the "principles" of the treaty.[6] Such provisions have been useful. For example, they have enabled the establishment of Māori-driven health, education, and social services. However, the initiatives that have been established remain beholden to the power of the state. They are, at best, a diluted and limited statement of tino rangatiratanga.

Imported Socialist Traditions

Within settler society, the last part of the 19th century saw the emergence of a more socially just tradition, albeit it one that often excluded Māori. From 1891 to 1912, successive Liberal Party governments laid down the basis of the welfare state (King, 2003). Women gained the vote in 1893. An old age pension was introduced, as were labour laws that improved conditions for workers. Although only in a limited way, government built houses to be let to workers for affordable rents. Large estates were bought up and through a ballot system made available to would-be farmers to take advantage of

---

[5] The tribunal has recommendatory power only.
[6] Various principles have been defined by the courts, the Waitangi Tribunal (Te Puni Kōkiri, 2005), and the Royal Commission on Social Policy (1988). The most commonly cited are partnership (between the Crown and Māori), protection (of Māori interests), and participation (of Māori in general society).

buoyant conditions for agricultural trade. The Liberal era also saw significant advancements in public health.

Like many countries, Aotearoa/New Zealand was badly affected by the depression of the early 1930s. As the depression waned, voters elected the first Labour government, which true to its socialist roots, immediately reversed cuts to the old age pension made by its predecessor, nationalised the Reserve Bank, extended free education to secondary schooling, introduced a minimum wage, and made union membership compulsory for workers (Belich, 2001; King, 2003). But its crowning achievement was social security "from the cradle to the grave" (King, 2003, p. 357). The phrase, used by Prime Minister Michael Savage, referred to a comprehensive package of measures including (mostly) free health care, a universal pension for people over the age of 65, and unemployment and disability benefits. Later, income grants to families with dependent children were added.

The socialist agenda upon which the Labour Party had been founded was never fully implemented. Land was not nationalised. Most of the economy remained in private hands, albeit subject to a high level of regulation. But for much of the 20th century, there was a strong consensus that the state should provide basic health, education, and social services and actively work to reduce inequalities in society.[7] While its basis was the state and not the whānau, in this limited way, settler society had developed some collectivist ways of organising social life, not altogether dissimilar to that of Māori.

Urbanisation

The mid-20th century saw a significant change in Māori society. Previously a largely rural population, Māori began to migrate to the cities in large numbers as industrialisation created an unprecedented demand for workers. This did not mean the abandonment of traditional communities. Typically, Māori families returned home for summer holidays and important community events. But it did mean that many of those traditional communities faced significant challenges in maintaining important aspects of community life. Moreover, the migration meant that in the cities, Māori and Pākehā were interacting—and intermarrying—to an extent not seen outside rural areas since the early days of colonisation. This and a renaissance in Māori culture, together with significant immigration from the Pacific (and later South and East Asia), meant that "race relations," as they were typically called, were firmly on the political and social agenda. However, as the term suggests, the focus was on maintaining cordial relationships, not on cultural justice.

---

[7] This consensus was somewhat undermined during the 1980s and 1990s, which saw successive neo-liberal governments deregulate much of the economy, sell government-owned businesses, cut social welfare benefits, and introduce competitive market models into health and education.

The 1960s and 1970s saw a significant shift in the way many New Zealanders viewed their relationship with the rest of the world. With Britain's entry into the European Union (as it later became known), the focus of foreign relations swung perceptibly away from the "mother" country of the British settlers towards the United States. Its dominance of English language media, especially popular music, film, and television, resulted in many young New Zealanders looking towards the United States for their cultural prototypes. A parallel process occurred in academia, particularly in psychology, where U.S. texts dominated reading lists.

Thus, the context in which community psychology was developed in Aotearoa/New Zealand in the 1970s had the following characteristics. Colonisation by Pākehā and resistance by Māori. A contested tradition of socialist measures in national politics and a strong tradition of collectivist arrangements among Māori. An increase in the cultural diversity among settler peoples and a renewed energy in Māori society. For all New Zealanders, a growing influence of the United States in popular culture, with this influence clearly reflected in the discipline of psychology. But while the term *community psychology* was imported directly from the United States, to a large extent, the theoretical roots of the field in Aotearoa/New Zealand lie closer to home.

Theoretical Roots

If there is one person whose work provided the earliest models for the establishment of community psychology in Aotearoa/New Zealand, it would be Ernest Beaglehole, although Ivan Sutherland also deserves mention. Both were students of Thomas Hunter (1876–1953), sometimes referred to as "the father of psychology in New Zealand" (Shouksmith, 1990, p. 433), and both, interestingly, formed strong friendships with eminent Māori scholars; Beaglehole with the noted anthropologist Te Rangi Hiroa (at one time, Professor of Anthropology at Yale) and Sutherland with political leader and scholar Apirana Ngata (Ritchie, 2003; Ritchie & Ritchie, 1999). According to Ritchie and Ritchie, Sutherland "picked up the challenge of Māori psychology and saw the contribution New Zealand might make to the rather blatant but hitherto unquestioned assumption that Western psychology was universal and pre-eminent" (1999, p. 106). Thus, the notion that psychology was not some culture-free endeavour was planted in some of the early psychological writing in the country (see Sutherland, 1940).

Although Beaglehole was a student of Sutherland, it is to Beaglehole that CP in Aotearoa/New Zealand owes the most, partly because of his role as a teacher of another generation of psychologists, some of whom played key roles in the establishment of CP. Beaglehole, who became Professor of Psychology at Victoria University of Wellington, has been described as an ethnopsychologist (Ritchie & Ritchie, 1999), influenced by the founders of psychological anthropology, Edward Sapir, Ruth Benedict, and Margaret Mead among them (Ritchie & Ritchie, 2003). He published various studies of Pacific Island and Māori communities. But his contribution to CP is perhaps most evident in his 1950 book, *Mental Health in New Zealand*. If the language were updated, it could easily pass as a contemporary manifesto for community psychology.

Predating Swampscott by 15 years, *Mental Health in New Zealand* (Beaglehole, 1950) is explicitly concerned with the prevention, as well as the treatment, of psychological disorders. In discussing the causation of psychological problems, Beaglehole emphasised environmental factors and emotional stressors, including "strained personal, social and economic conditions, together with unsuitable or unsatisfactory employment" (p. 47). He argued that enhancing health required improvements in housing, participation in social networks, feelings of security and belonging, and being part of a cooperative common life. He drew a connection between culture and mental health, citing aggressive competition and consumerism as being implicated in mental disorder. Critiquing approaches to the study of personality which ignore the social context, Beaglehole called for the scientific study of "personality-in-culture" (p. 126). Treatment, he argued, should include manipulation of environmental factors, not just the individual, although he limited such intervention to the immediate setting (workplace, family, and school) rather than wider social systems such as the economy.

Although he did not use these terms, in Beaglehole's work it is possible to see fundamental principles and concepts of CP: the stress-coping paradigm; a multilevel systems approach; social support and social capital; sense of community; and a concern for the prevention of psychological problems. And throughout the text, an acknowledgement that human life can only be understood within a context and that culture is a major feature of that context.

Beaglehole's pioneering work in ethnopsychology was continued by his student (and later, son-in-law) James Ritchie, who, in 1964 became the foundation Professor of Psychology[8] at the newly established University of Waikato. In his inaugural address, Ritchie (1967) set out three objectives, each of which can be seen as contributing to the theoretical building blocks of CP in Aotearoa. Firstly, he argued for a trans-disciplinary approach to research, bringing together psychology, sociology, and anthropology. Secondly, he called for an emphasis on applications in the real world and advocated the use of action research. A third objective was the establishment of a "Centre for the Study of Māori Contemporary Social Life and Culture . . . (which) . . . will not do research on people but for people" (p. 51). Indeed, the Centre for Māori Studies and Research, as the centre was eventually named, played an important

---

[8] In Aotearoa/New Zealand, the term *professor* is reserved for the top rank (of four) of academic appointments.

role in carrying out much of the research that underpinned an historic settlement reached between Tainui (the local tribal confederation) and the government in respect of the confiscation of land and other breaches of Te Tiriti o Waitangi. The Centre was also the site of another example of collaboration between Māori and Pākehā scholars. For many years, the director of the Centre was Robert Mahuta, who later led Tainui's negotiations with the government, while James Ritchie combined his role as Professor of Psychology with the role of Deputy Director of the Centre.

Early Courses

Under Ritchie's leadership, the Department of Psychology at Waikato established undergraduate and graduate courses[9] in applied social psychology. These were the responsibility of David Thomas, who joined the department in 1973 and subsequently became its second professor. Like Ritchie, Thomas was a graduate of Victoria University (master's in social psychology), although he completed his Ph.D. in cross-cultural psychology at the University of Queensland (Australia). Following the publication of Julian Rappaport's 1977 text, Thomas renamed the courses he taught "Community Psychology" and in 1980, a full graduate programme in community psychology was launched. During the first 2 years of this 3-year programme, students took core courses in CP, evaluation research and the professional practice of psychology, along with optional courses in related areas. They also completed a research thesis and project work in the community. In their third year, they completed a full-time 12-month internship. Graduates could become registered as psychologists.

Indigenous Epistemologies

Thus, in terms of Western traditions, the theoretical roots of CP in Aotearoa/New Zealand can be found in cross-cultural psychology, ethnopsychology, and applied social psychology. However, this is an incomplete account for at least two reasons. Firstly, it leaves out the influence that Māori scholars such as Te Rangi Hīroa, Apirana Ngata, and Robert Mahuta had on the key Pākehā scholars mentioned above. Secondly, it fails to acknowledge that many of the "new" ideas to emerge from Swampscott (Bennett et al., 1966) and subsequent CP scholarship were hardly new to Māori. Take for example the ecological perspective (e.g., Kelly, 1966) and systems theory (e.g., Rappaport, 1977). An underlying value of Māoridom is that everything is connected to everything else. Ranginui (sky father) and Papatūānuku (earth

---

[9] Here we use "course" (otherwise known as a "paper," "module," or "seminar") to describe the basic component of a degree. Depending on its weighting, a course typically constitutes between one-half and one-quarter of a year of full-time study.

mother) provide us with sustenance. People are descended from one of their sons, Tānemahuta, the god of the forest and the father of humankind. Through him we are related to all the other gods and their children (e.g., birds, fish, and all other living entities). In this context, two of Tanemahuta's brothers are particularly significant, Tangaroa (the god of the sea) and Rongo mā Tāne (agriculture) (Hīroa, 1949). Māori cosmology and epistemology determine a relationship between individuals, their families, and their environment, through an intricate web of interrelationships. The central role of whakapapa (genealogy) in establishing links between people is an example of interrelationships between humans. Conservation practices governing fishing, agriculture, and the use of forest resources (Barlow, 1991; Orbell, 1985) attest to Māori understandings of the interrelatedness of people and their natural environments.

As a second example, it can be noted that Māori history includes many narratives of empowerment and social justice. Leadership is ascribed to those who are born into the role (leaders through whakapapa such as Te Atairangikahu, the Māori Queen, 1966-2006) and to those who earn it through their actions and deeds (recent examples include land rights campaigners Whina Cooper and Eva Rickard). That is, leaders are followed by those who consider them to be worthy: leadership is not bestowed on people who are cruel and selfish. The most revered leaders are those who care a great deal for the people. Examples are Tohu Kakahi (Smith, 2003) and Te Whiti-o-Rongomai, leaders of Māori passive resistance to colonisation in Taranaki (Keenan, 2003), and Te Kooti Arikirangi, military and religious leader in the eastern and central parts of the North Island (Binney, 2003). These leaders fought against colonial oppression in a manner that has brought about change for their people even beyond their deaths.

While a complete discussion of the theoretical roots of CP in Aotearoa/New Zealand must include reference to the contribution of Māori epistemology, it is also important to recognise that this contribution has often been ignored or marginalised within CP writing, in much the same way as it has in other areas of psychology (Older, 1978; Nairn, 2004). Laura Whangapiritia's (2003) study of the use of Rongoa Māori (traditional healing remedies) is a notable exception. More positively, CP has provided fertile ground for Māori to address issues of cultural justice, as well as for both Māori and non-Māori psychologists to address the ethnocentrism and monoculturalism of the parent discipline (e.g., Black, Goodwin & Smith, 1994; Levy, 2003), a theme we return to below.

Recognition, Professionalisation, and Certification

As noted above, CP has been recognised as a distinct area of the psychology curriculum in Aotearoa/New Zealand since David Thomas applied the term, first to two courses he taught at the University of Waikato, and then to a full graduate programme he subsequently developed. If the seeds of CP in this country can be found in Beaglehole's work, it took Thomas's arrival at Waikato to ensure their germination.

As we write, the Waikato programme is enjoying its 25th year of operation. To use North American terminology, it can be described as a free-standing community psychology programme. A different approach was adopted at Victoria University in Wellington. Under the leadership of Professor Tony Taylor, an applied M.A. degree in community and clinical psychology was established in 1975. Interdisciplinarity and an applied, practical focus were distinguishing features of this programme. However, the CP component did not survive a reorganisation of clinical training carried out after Taylor's retirement in 1992.

At the University of Auckland, CP was initially identified with the work of John Raeburn, a psychologist teaching within the Department of Psychiatry. Raeburn and his doctoral student, Fred Seymour, pioneered a CP approach to well-being based on community houses in several Auckland suburbs. Describing themselves as "behaviourally trained clinical psychologists who became self-educated community psychologists" (Raeburn, 1986, p. 391), they acted as consultants to grassroots community groups in underserviced areas who lobbied and raised funds to establish community houses. The houses were run by local residents and provided the venue for a variety of programmes to address lifestyle issues such as weight loss and stress reduction and were a focus for neighbourhood interactions and community-building (Raeburn, 1996). More recently, courses in CP have been established within Auckland's Department of Psychology by Niki Harré. As is the case with Waikato, these have developed from an applied social psychology perspective.

An anthropological perspective is evident at one other university to formally teach community psychology. For many years, American-born Bob Gregory taught a course at Massey University in Palmerston North. Offered both on campus and via distance learning, this course has reached a large number of undergraduate students. (Thus, currently, three of the seven university psychology departments include CP in their coursework).

Practice

Since its inception, CP within Aotearoa/New Zealand has always had a strong focus on professional practice. That practice is characterised by its diversity in at least three ways. Firstly, practitioners can be found in a wide range of sectors. They work in health services, health promotion, social and welfare services, education, criminal justice, community development, environmental protection, domestic violence, injury prevention, disability services, housing, town planning, child protection, and addictions. Many work across several such fields as researchers, evaluators, or consultants. Secondly, practitioners can be found in a range of organisational contexts. They are employed by government (national, regional, and local), by health services, by iwi (tribal) organisations, by not-for-profit social services, and by research companies. Some are self-employed. Thirdly, practitioners can be found in a range of roles. That is, few have *community psychologist* as their job title. Instead, they carry diverse job titles such as *policy analyst, community development officer, planner, adviser, coordinator, manager, consultant, trainer, researcher, evaluator,* and *advocate,* bringing to such roles community psychology concepts, values, and ways of working (Huygens, Nemec, Hungerford & Hutchings, 2002). To adopt the framework proposed by Prilleltensky and his colleagues (Prilleltensky, Nelson & Peirson, 2001), most practitioners of CP in Aotearoa/New Zealand work at the macro (collective) and meso (relational) levels, although some work at the micro (personal) level, typically as counsellors or advocates.

In most respects, this diversity is a positive feature of practice in this country. Community psychologists have been influential in many areas of society. Less positively, because they commonly work in fields and roles outside those traditionally associated with psychologists, community psychologists have not had a high profile within the parent discipline. For many, professional identity is focused on their field and role rather than their disciplinary training. They think of themselves primarily as *health policy analysts* or *injury prevention consultants,* for example, rather than as *psychologists.* Indeed, many report a somewhat ambivalent relationship to the parent discipline. A reflection of this is that relatively few community psychologists belong to the main professional organisation for psychologists, the New Zealand Psychological Society.

Professional Organisation

However, it would be wrong to assume that community psychologists have not been active within the Society. For example, it was community psychologists who, in 1987, promoted a constitutional change requiring the Society "To promote the development and use of psychological knowledge for the alleviation of social problems and reduction of social inequalities, consistent with the principle of empowerment" (New Zealand Psychological Society, 2005a). Community psychologists have also been heavily involved in the adoption of Rule 3, which requires the Society to "encourage policies and practices that reflect New Zealand's cultural diversity and . . . (to) have due regard to the provisions of, and to the spirit and intent of, the Treaty of Waitangi" (New Zealand Psychological Society, 2005a). They are strongly represented on the National Standing Committee of Bicultural Issues, which oversees the implementation of Rule 3.

Recent years have seen the development of formal subdisciplinary groupings, generally called *institutes,* within the New Zealand Psychological Society. The Institute of Community Psychology Aotearoa was launched in 2004. Its mission statement is to "promote the application of psychology and related knowledge to enhancing social and cultural justice within Aotearoa"

(New Zealand Psychological Society, 2005b). It is expected that the establishment of the Institute will make membership of the Society more attractive to CP practitioners.

Licensing

Although the New Zealand Psychological Society is the peak professional organisation for psychology in Aotearoa/New Zealand, licensing is the responsibility of the New Zealand Psychologists' Board. Under recently revised regulations, the board has established a two-tier approach to the registration of psychologists. The first tier comprises a generic registration of "psychologist." Community psychologists with relevant training are eligible for this registration, as are psychologists of other specialisations. The second tier comprises specialist registrations. Currently, specialist registration is available for clinical psychology and educational psychology only. Other specialist registrations are likely to be established. As we write, an application for the establishment of a specialist registration in community psychology is being prepared.

Although community psychologists have had an impact on the wider discipline and their training is recognised for registration, in other ways, the field remains marginal. There are still relatively few people who identify strongly as community psychologists. Waikato, the only formal programme, has just 75 graduates. (Currently, there are 1,584 registered psychologists in the country [New Zealand Psychologists Board, 2005]). The diversity of their work and its often explicitly political nature tends to make it easier for some to portray it as not "real" psychology. As in some other parts of the world, psychology in this country continues to be dominated by positivist, quantitative, and individual-treatment oriented models. The survival of CP can never be taken for granted.

Theories and Frameworks

Early teaching and writing in CP in Aotearoa/New Zealand were heavily influenced by North American scholarship. Course reading lists in the early days of the graduate programme at Waikato consisted almost entirely of material published in the United States. Localisation, defined as "the process of evolving social change strategies from within the social and cultural environment where they will be used and . . . the adaptation of change strategies, used elsewhere, to suit local conditions" (Veno & Thomas, 1992, p. 31), became an explicit agenda of the programme during the 1980s. There was, at the time, relatively little suitable local psychological writing on which to draw. Instead, teachers of CP drew heavily on local writing in education, health, sociology, political science, and social work. Localisation thus served to increase the interdisciplinary nature of CP in Aotearoa/New Zealand.

Interdisciplinarity continues to be a major characteristic today. One consequence of this is that most of the theories and frameworks that have influenced CP in Aotearoa/New Zealand are not unique to the field but are shared with allied disciplines. What has emerged can fairly be described as a style of CP that is anchored on a set of values, shaped by critiques of mainstream psychology (particularly cultural and feminist critiques) and employing a range of methods.

As is the case elsewhere in the world, CP in Aotearoa/New Zealand has taken a particular stance in relation to values. That is, the notion of value-free science is rejected. Instead, values such as social justice, collaboration, diversity, empowerment, and competence enhancement are frequently cited as foundational values for community psychologists (e.g., Department of Psychology, 2005; Hamerton, Nikora, Robertson & Thomas, 1995; Robertson, Thomas, Dehar & Blaxall, 1989; Thomas & Veno, 1992). As Huygens and colleagues (2002) found, it is the values underlying practice that unify CP in Aotearoa/New Zealand. Indeed, given the diversity of endeavours in which community psychologists engage, CP in this country can be described as an approach ("working community psychologically") as much as a field.

Cultural Perspectives

As might be expected given its antecedents in ethnopsychology and cross-cultural psychology, CP here has paid more attention to culture than has been the case in most other branches of psychology. However, cross-cultural comparative studies are rare. Culture has generally not been studied as just another variable as if there is some culture-free point from which to view diverse cultures. Instead, the inherently (mono) cultural nature of psychology itself has been exposed (Black, Goodwin & Smith, 1994; Hunt, Morgan & Teddy, 2001; Lawson-Te Aho, 1994; Waldegrave, 1993). An important stream of local community psychology research comprised studies of the experiences of Māori within psychology training programmes (e.g., Masters & Levy, 1995; Masters, Levy, Thompson, Donnelly & Rawiri, 2005; Hunt, Morgan & Teddy, 2001) and within professional work settings (e.g. Levy, 2002; Masters, 1999), including the evaluation of efforts to support the development of a Māori workforce within psychology (Nikora, Levy, Henry & Whangapiritia, 2002). A related stream of research has examined the experience of Māori in the context of a wide range of issues including epilepsy (Hills, Nikora & Morrison, 2001), sexual health (Nikora, Tamatea, Fairbrother & Te Awekotuku, 2001), youth offending (Spee, 1998), gambling (Morrison 1999), recovery from mental illness (Lapsley, Nikora & Black, 2002), and secondary schooling (J.M. Robertson, 2004).

While the majority of the authors cited above are Māori, non-Māori community psychologists have also made a contribution. One of the outcomes of CP's focus on culture has been the elaboration of models for non-Māori researchers and other professionals to work in ways that do not reproduce the privilege of Pākehā and the silencing of Māori. Ingrid Huygens has developed *An accountability model for Pākehā practitioners*, which "reverses the usual flow of power by making the Pākehā practitioner accountable to relevant Māori authority" (1999, p. 17). Similarly, Nikora and Robertson (1995) have described a treaty-based model for structuring the relationship between Māori and non-Māori social service workers and ensuring the delivery of culturally appropriate services. Although less well developed, a related strand of work turns the gaze on the dominant group and the privileges it enjoys (Black, 1997, 2004; N.R. Robertson, 2004.) Such work can expose the taken-for-grantedness of dominant group realities, ensuring, in this context, that Pākehā are "marked" (Black, 2004) as possessors of culture rather than being the unmarked norm against which Māori, Pasifika,[10] and other ethnic groups are judged.

Feminism

As Oliver and Hamerton (1992) pointed out, for the first decade of CP in this country the dominance of men and the marginalisation of women were fundamentally undisturbed. Largely because of their work and the work of their students, this changed quite rapidly. Among CP practitioners, women now outnumber men by 4 to 1, and while numerical superiority does not equate with a shift in power, the influence of feminism can be seen in local community psychology research. For example, topics that have a particular salience for women appear frequently among CP theses, including attempted suicide and other forms of self-harm among women (Curtis, 2003; Greenwood, 1996), location choices made by elder women (Hungerford, 1994), Pakeha women's memories of adolescence (Hamerton, 2000), Māori women's experiences of health (Huijbers, 1996), and a number of studies relating to violence against women (Corbett, 1999; Flaherty, 1996; Furness, 1993; Pratt, 1997; Robertson, 2000). Equally important, feminist epistemology is evident in the approach of such work, reflecting such things as valuing subjectivity, connecting women though the use of groups, working out ways of reducing the power differential between researcher and participants, preserving women's voices (e.g., through the use of narratives and case studies), and recognizing the emotionality of science (cf. Campbell & Wasco, 2000).

Methodological Pluralism

As is perhaps evident in the above, CP in Aotearoa/New Zealand has been hugely influenced by critiques of positivist science. Qualitative research is common. However, CP research cannot be pigeonholed into a neat

---

[10] *Pasifika* is a term increasingly used to refer to people who have settled in Aotearoa/ New Zealand from other Pacific nations, primarily Samoa, the Cook Islands, Tonga, and Niue.

epistemological or methodological category. Rather, it is characterised by its diversity of methods, the choice of method being primarily driven by the purpose and context of the investigation. Thus, as well as examples of life histories, case studies, focus groups, and memory work, one can find structured interviews and surveys. In addition, programme evaluation is a core part of the Waikato programme: graduates frequently find it to be one of their most marketable skills (Huygens et al., 2002). Evaluation can be thought of as a reformist social change strategy (Thomas & Robertson, 1992) especially when applied to programmes or policies that attempt to empower disenfranchised groups (Toki, Robertson & Pfeiffenberger, 2002), address the effects of colonisation and racism (Moeke-Pickering, 1998), provide appropriate services to marginalised groups (Ansley et al., 1998), promote cultural justice (Glover & Sutton, 1991) or support the development of indigenous models of human services (Moeke-Pickering, 1994).

Kaupapa Māori Research

Indigenous models of research are beginning to influence CP. As Linda Tuhiwai Smith has noted, "'research' is probably one of the dirtiest words in the indigenous world's vocabulary" (1999, p. 1). Despite being possibly the most researched people in the world, there is little evidence that the bulk of such research has benefited Māori (Glover, 2002). Instead, "Research was a small but important part of the colonisation process because it concerned defining knowledge. To be colonised is to be defined by someone else and to believe it even though you are confronted daily by evidence to the contrary" (Smith, 1986, p. 8).

Kaupapa[11] Māori research, on the other hand, is based on Māori epistemologies and processes. Although there are various statements of what constitutes Kaupapa Māori research, according to Bishop, it is "the operationalisation of self-determination (tino rangatiratanga) by Māori people" (1999, p. 2). That is, control over the initiation, planning, conduct, legitimisation, and use of research rests in the hands of tangata whenua (Bishop, 1999; Powick, 2002). It takes for granted "the social, political, historical, intellectual and cultural legitimacy of Māori people" (Bishop, 1999, p. 2). Kaupapa Māori research processes are participatory and guided by principles of whakapapa (genealogy), te reo (language), tikanga (custom), rangatiratanga (governance and control), and whanau (familial relationships) (Powick, 2002). Whakawhanaungatanga plays a central role. That is, participants and researchers comprise a literal or metaphoric whānau in which relationships are established, participants exercise control over the processes, and researchers are expected to fully participate in the context (Bishop, 1999;

---

[11] Roughly translates as philosophy, way of doing things.

Powick, 2002). Such an approach stands in sharp contrast to positivist ideas of distance and objectivity as prerequisites for supposedly valid and reliable research. Instead, the quality of research is ensured by closeness and continued involvement. A researcher who is whānau is likely to be held accountable for his or her work in a way that is unlikely to be achieved with researchers from outside the setting.

Comparison with Other Countries

In reviewing other contributions to this book, it becomes evident that it is Australia with whom we have most in common. This is hardly surprising. We are close neighbours. We share a similar history of British colonisation and the attempted subjugation (and subsequent renaissance) of indigenous peoples. Our political systems share a common British heritage. On both sides of the Tasman, the development of psychology has been hugely influenced by British and American (U.S.A.) models and theories. Like the Australian Psychological Society, the New Zealand Psychological Society began life as a branch of the British Psychological Society. And as Heather Gridley and colleagues note, there has been a high level of interaction between community psychologists in the two countries, including biennial conferences.

Although there has not been the same level of interaction, there is much in the Canadian chapter we recognise as familiar: a broadly similar history of colonisation, a concern with values and ethics, involvement in health promotion, and the pursuit of inclusion and diversity. Like our Canadian colleagues, we have faced the rollback of state provision of health and social services. Such is the "fit" between Canadian and New Zealand CP that the University of Waikato CP programme has recently adopted a Canadian-edited book (Nelson & Prilleltensky, 2005) as a text in foundational courses.

As previously indicated, the United States of America and Britain have been important influences on CP in Aotearoa/New Zealand. Both are major net exporters of psychological knowledge (Moghaddam, 1987), and we have imported as much as anyone from these sources. Socially, culturally, and politically, we have more in common with Britain than the United States, and it was certainly British influences that shaped early psychology here. But such has been the nature of United States hegemony over the past three decades—coinciding with the development of CP—that it is American, not British, writers who have dominated our reference lists. Only in relatively recent times has British writing become an important source for community psychologists in Aotearoa/New Zealand, the *Journal of Community and Applied Social Psychology* playing an important role in this regard. The journal's title echoes CP's local origins in applied social psychology. We share with Mark Burton and his colleagues an interest in developing a "really social psychology."

To a large extent, the above comments reflect language as much as history. That is, it has been almost exclusively the English-speaking world that has influenced us here. This is a serious limitation, for the accounts of CP from other parts of the world suggest that we have much to learn. For example, Indian work in developing indigenous theories and explanations could well help inform similar challenges here. The struggle for human rights and social justice described in Latin American contributions resonate with local issues such as the pursuit of cultural justice. Tools for community profiling and network building developed in Italy may have applicability here.

Conclusion

This is the fourth occasion on which one of us (N.R.) has been part of writing an overview of community psychology in this country (for earlier articles, see Hamerton, Nikora, Robertson & Thomas, 1995; Nikora, Oliver, Robertson & Thomas, 1993; Robertson, Thomas, Dehar & Blaxall, 1989). It is humbling to review those earlier efforts and realise how one's view of past events changes with the benefit of greater hindsight. Of necessity, we leave it to future writers to provide a more rounded description of CP in Aotearoa/New Zealand at the dawn of the 21st century.

In the meantime, our snapshot of CP in Aotearoa/New Zealand will need to suffice. Like all snapshots, it is incomplete. It focuses on some things while others remain fuzzy in the background. It is not a movie: it distorts by appearing to fix in time things that are in fact constantly changing. Our account emphasises the importance of history. Too often, in our view, psychology has been a-historical, as if human behaviour can be explained entirely by contemporary events. Yet history is fundamental. It shapes the way we see the world. It helps to determine what we consider to be important. Historic processes such as colonisation, war, economic exploitation, and oppression continue to structure the relationships between groups and between individuals. Without a thorough understanding of our past, our efforts to improve the future will at best be limited. *Me tiro whakamuri ā kia hāngai whakamua.* ("Look backwards in order to move forward with purpose.")

References

Ansley, A., Faull, K., Haereroa, M., Morrison, L., Parata, K., Rua, M. & Wihongi, H. (1998). *An Evaluation of Māori access to Disability Support Services.* Hamilton: Department of Psychology, University of Waikato.
Barlow, C. (1991). *Tikanga whakaaro: Key concepts in Māori Culture.* Auckland: Oxford University Press.
Beaglehole, E. (1950). *Mental health in New Zealand.* Wellington, New Zealand: University Press.
Belich, J. (2001). *Paradise reforged: a history of the New Zealanders: From the 1880s to the Year 2000.* Auckland: Allen Lane/Penguin Press.
Bennett. C.C., Anderson, L.S., Cooper, S., Hassol, L., Klein, D.C. & Rosenblum, G. (Eds). (1966). *Community psychology: A report of the Boston conference on*

the education of psychologists for community mental health. Boston: Boston University Press.

Binney, J. (2003). Te Kooti Arikirangi Te Turuki? - 1893. *Dictionary of New Zealand biography*, updated 16 December 2003. Available at http://www.dnzb.govt.nz/. Retrieved 14 June 2005.

Bishop, R. (1999). Kaupapa Māori Research: An indigenous approach to creating knowledge. In N.R. Robertson (Ed.), *Māori and Psychology: research and practice*. The proceedings of a symposium sponsored by the Māori and Psychology Research Unit. Hamilton: Māori and Psychology Research Unit, University of Waikato. pp. 1-6.

Black, R. (1997). *Beyond the pale: An exploration of Pākehā cultural awareness.* Unpublished master's thesis. Hamilton: University of Waikato.

Black, R. (2004). *Marking Pākehā discourse in the race debate.* Paper presented to the 9th Biennial Australia-Aotearoa (New Zealand) Community Psychology Conference: Community narratives and praxis: sharing stories of social action and change. Tauranga, 5-7 July 2004.

Black, R., Goodwin, L. & Smith, J. (1994). *The report of an evaluation of the bicultural development of the New Zealand Psychological Society Annual Conference 1994.* Unpublished research report available from the Department of Psychology, University of Waikato.

Campbell, R. & Wasco, S.M. (2000). Feminist approaches to social science: Epistemological and methodological tenets. *American Journal of Community Psychology, 28*, 773-791.

Consedine, R. & Consedine, J. (2005). *Healing our history: the challenge of the Treaty of Waitangi.* Auckland: Penguin.

Corbett, L.A. (1999). *Child protection workers' interactions with women abused by their male partners: Five women's stories.* Unpublished master's thesis. Hamilton: University of Waikato.

Curtis, C. (2003). *Female suicidal behaviour: Initiation, cessation and prevention.* Unpublished doctoral thesis. Hamilton: University of Waikato.

Department of Psychology. (2005). *Community Psychology Graduate Handbook.* Available at www.waikato.ac.nz/commpsych. Retrieved 19 June 2005.

Flaherty, E. (1996). *Pills, platitudes and positive practice: Health workers responses to women abused by their male partners.* Unpublished master's thesis. Hamilton: University of Waikato.

Furness, J.A. (1993). *From a victim's perspective: A multiple case study evaluation of an education programme for abusers.* Unpublished master's thesis. Hamilton: University of Waikato.

Glover, M. & Sutton, D. (1991) *". . . side by side?" An evaluation of parallel development in the Te Awamutu women's Refuge and Rape Crisis Inc.* Hamilton: Department of Psychology, University of Waikato.

Glover, M. (2002). *Kaupapa Māori health research methodology: A literature review and commentary on the use of a kaupapa Māori approach within a doctoral study of Māori smoking cessation.* Auckland: University of Auckland, Department of Applied Behavioural Science.

Greenwood, S. (1996). *"I can't work this out . . . I'm at a dead end:" Women discuss their experiences of attempted suicide as young women.* Unpublished master's thesis. Hamilton: University of Waikato.

Hamerton, H., Nikora, L.W., Robertson, N.R. & Thomas, D.R. (1995). Community psychology in Aotearoa/New Zealand. *The Community Psychologist, 28(3)*, 21-23.

Hamerton, H.R. (2000). *Growing up or growing down: Pakeha women's memories of adolescence*. Unpublished doctoral thesis. Hamilton: University of Waikato.

Hills, M., Nikora, L.W. & Morrison, L. (2001). *Kia Whiria: Understanding and supporting Māori with epilepsy*. Hamilton: Māori and Psychology Research Unit, University of Waikato. Available at http://wfass-trinity.fass.waikato.ac.nz/docush are/dsweb/Get/ Document-991/NZPsS+paper.pdf. Retrieved 21 June 2005.

Hīroa, Te R. (1949). *The coming of the Māori*. Christchurch: Māori Purposes Fund Board and Whitcoulls.

Huijbers, K. (1996). *Māori women in Taranaki and their experiences in health*. Unpublished master's thesis. Hamilton: University of Waikato.

Hungerford, R. (1994). *Elder women, identity, and location choice: An interview study with elder women in Te Aroha*. Unpublished master's thesis. Hamilton: University of Waikato.

Hunt, H., Morgan, N., & Teddy, L. (2001). *Barriers to and supports for success for Māori students in the Psychology Department at the University of Waikato*. Unpublished report. Hamilton: Department of Psychology, University of Waikato.

Huygens, I. (1999). *An accountability model for Pākehā practitioners*. In N.R. Robertson (Ed.), *Māori and Psychology: research and practice*. The proceedings of a symposium sponsored by the Māori and Psychology Research Unit. Hamilton: Māori and Psychology Research Unit, University of Waikato.

Huygens, I., Nemec, K., Hungerford, R. & Hutchings, L. (2002). Community psychology graduate employment in Aotearoa New Zealand. *Bulletin of the New Zealand Psychological Society, 100*, 34-38.

Jackson, K. & McRobie, A. (1996). *Historical dictionary of New Zealand*. Auckland: Longman.

Kawharu, H. (2005). *Modern English translation of the Māori text of the Treaty of Waitangi*. Available at http://treatyofwaitangi.govt.nz/treaty/. Retrieved 10 February 2005.

Keenan, D. (2003) Te Whiti-o-Rongomai III, Erueti? - 1907. *Dictionary of New Zealand biography*, updated 16 December 2003. Available at http://www.dnzb.govt. nz/ Retrieved 14 June 2005.

Kelly, J.G. (1966). Ecological constraints on mental health services. *American Psychologist, 21*, 535-539.

King, M. (2003). *The Penguin history of New Zealand*. Auckland: Penguin Books.

Lapsley, H., Nikora, L.W. & Black, R. (2002). *"Kia Mauri Tau!" Narratives of recovery from disabling mental health problems*. Wellington: Mental Health Commission.

Lawson-Te Aho, K. (1994). *The Master's tools . . . Māori development inside Pakeha psychology*. Unpublished master's thesis: University of Waikato.

Levy, M. (2002). *Barriers and incentives to Māori participation in the profession of psychology*. Report for the New Zealand Psychologists' Board. Hamilton: Māori and Psychology Research Unit, University of Waikato. Available at http://wfass-trinity.fass.waikato.ac.nz/docushare/dsweb/Get/Document-1357/New+Zealand+ Psychologists%27+Board +Full+Report.pdf. Retrieved 21 June 2005.

Masters, B. & Levy, M. (1995). *An evaluation of Kaupapa Māori within the Psychology Department at the University of Waikato*. Unpublished report. Hamilton: Department of Psychology, University of Waikato.

Masters, B. (1999). Nga kanohi hou – identifying and exploring the issues: Experiences of an intern. In N.R. Robertson (Ed.), *Māori and Psychology: research and practice*. The proceedings of a symposium sponsored by the Māori and

Psychology Research Unit, University of Waikato. Available at http://wfass-trinity.fass.waikato.ac.nz/docushare/dsweb/Get/Document-998/masters.pdf. Retrieved 21 June 2005.

Masters, B., Levy, M., Thompson, K., Donnelly, A. & Rawiri, C. (2005). *Creating a sense of community: Kaupapa Māori support in the Psychology Department at the University of Waikato.* Hamilton: Māori and Psychology Research Unit, University of Waikato. Available at http://wfass-trinity.fass.waikato.ac.nz/docushare/dsweb/Get/Document-4148/Masters+et+al+submission.pdf. Retrieved 21 June 2005.

Moeke-Pickering, T. (1994). *Evaluation of the Te Whiuwhiu o Te Hau Māori Counselling Programme Practicum Placements.* Hamilton: Department of Psychology, University of Waikato.

Moeke-Pickering, T. (1998). *Evaluation of the effectiveness of a decolonisation/anti and liberation workshop as an intervention strategy.* Hamilton: Department of Psychology, University of Waikato.

Moghaddam, F.M. (1987). Psychology in the three worlds as reflected by the crisis of social psychology and the move towards indigenous third-world psychology. *American Psychologist, 42,* 912-920.

Morrison, L. (1999). *The good and the bad times: Māori women's experience of gambling.* Unpublished master's thesis. Hamilton: University of Waikato.

Nairn, R. (2004). Psychology becoming bi-cultural – Māori keynote addresses; was there something we missed? *Bulletin of the New Zealand Psychological Society,* No. 103, 24-28.

Nelson, G. & Prilleltensky, I. (2005). *Community psychology: In pursuit of liberation and well-being.* New York: Palgrave MacMillan.

New Zealand Psychological Society. (2005a). *Rules.* Available at http://www.psychology.org.nz./about/rules.html. Retrieved 16 February 2005.

New Zealand Psychological Society. (2005b). *Institute of Community Psychology Aotearoa.* Available at http://www.psychology.org.nz/about/Community_Psyc_Inst.html. Retrieved 29 August 2005.

New Zealand Psychologists Board. (2005). *Psychologists Board Newsletter, December.* Wellington: Author.

Nikora, L.W. & Robertson, N.R. (1995). *Parallel development: A model for the delivery of culturally safe social services.* Paper presented to the 5th Biennial Conference on Community Research and Action (Division 27 of the American Psychological Association) Chicago, June 15-17.

Nikora, L.W. Tamatea, A., Fairbrother, V. & Te Awekotuku, N. (2001). *Te Ahurei a Rangatahi Sexual Health Programme: An evaluation.* Hamilton: Māori and Psychology Research Unit, University of Waikato. Available at http://wfass-trinity.fass.waikato.ac.nz/docushare/dsweb/Get/Document-972/2001ahureifinal.pdf. Retrieved 21 June 2005.

Nikora, L.W., Levy, M., Henry, J. & Whangapiritia, L. (2002). *Te Rau Puawai evaluation overview.* Hamilton: Māori and Psychology Research Unit, University of Waikato. Available at http://wfass-trinity.fass.waikato.ac.nz/docushare/dsweb/Get/Document-966/1.+final-overview++report.pdf. Retrieved 21 June 2005.

Nikora, L.W., Oliver, P., Robertson, N.R. & Thomas, D.R. (1993). *Community psychology in Aotearoa/New Zealand.* Paper presented to the Fourth Biennial Conference on Community Research and Action (Division 27 of the American Psychological Association), Williamsburg, Virginia, June.

Older, J. (1978). *The Pākehā papers.* Dunedin: John McIndoe.

Oliver, P. & Hamerton, H.R. (1992). Women, peace, and community psychology: A common agenda for social change. In D.R. Thomas & A. Veno (Eds.), *Psychology and social change: Creating an international agenda.* Palmerston North: Dunmore. pp. 55-73.

Orange, C. (1987). *The Treaty of Waitangi.* Wellington: Allen & Unwin.

Orbell, M. (1985). *The natural world of the Māori.* Dobbs Ferry, NY: Sheridan House.

Powick, K. (2002). *Māori research ethics: A literature review of the ethical issues and implications of kaupapa Māori research involving Māori for researchers, supervisors and ethics committees.* Hamilton: Wilf Malcolm Institute of Educational Research, University of Waikato.

Pratt, R.J. (1997). *Mutual help groups for battered women.* Unpublished master's thesis. Hamilton: University of Waikato.

Prilleltensky, I., Nelson, G. & Peirson, L. (Eds). (2001). *Promoting family well-being and preventing child maltreatment: Fundamentals for thinking and action.* Toronto: University of Toronto Press.

Raeburn, J. (1986). Toward a sense of community: Comprehensive community projects and community houses. *Journal of Community Psychology, 14,* 391-398.

Raeburn, J. (1996). The PEOPLE system: Towards a community-led process of social change. In D.R. Thomas & A. Veno (Eds.), *Community psychology and social change: Australian & New Zealand perspectives.* 2nd ed. Palmerston North: Dunmore. pp. 36-57.

Rappaport, J. (1977). *Community psychology: Values research, and action.* New York: Holt, Rinehart & Winston.

Ritchie, J.E. (1967). The challenge to psychology. In University of Waikato, *Seven inaugural lectures by the foundation professors of the University, 1965-1966.* Hamilton: University of Waikato.

Ritchie, J.E. (2003). Sutherland, Ivan Lorin George, 1897-1952. *Dictionary of New Zealand biography,* updated 16 December, 2003. Available at http://dnzb.govt.nz/. Retrieved 15 February 2005.

Ritchie, J.E. & Ritchie, J. (2003). 'Beaglehole, Ernest 1906-1965'. *Dictionary of New Zealand biography,* updated 16 December 2003. Available at http://www.dnzb.govt. nz/. Retrieved 23 March 2005.

Ritchie, J.E. & Ritchie, J. (1999). Seventy-five years of cross-cultural psychology in New Zealand. *Merging past, present and future in cross-cultural psychology.* Proceedings of the 14th International Congress of the International Association for Cross-Cultural Psychology, Lisse, Netherlands. pp. 105-115.

Robertson, J.M. (2004). *Experiences of Māori students in mainstream secondary school; what helped and what didn't.* Unpublished master's thesis. Hamilton: University of Waikato.

Robertson, N.R. (2000). *Reforming institutional responses to violence against women.* Unpublished doctoral thesis. Hamilton: University of Waikato.

Robertson, N.R. (2004). *Examining white privilege.* Paper presented to 5th European Community Psychology Conference, Berlin, September 16-19.

Robertson, N.R., Thomas, D.R., Dehar, M.A. & Blaxall, M.C.B. (1989). The development of community psychology in New Zealand: A Waikato perspective. *New Zealand Journal of Psychology, 18,* 13-24.

Royal Commission on Social Policy. (1988). *Future directions.* Vol 2 of the Report of the Royal Commission on Social Policy. Wellington: Author.

Shouksmith, G. (1990). New Zealand. In G. Shouksmith & E. Shouksmith (Eds), *Psychology in Asia and the Pacific,* Bangkok: UNESCO. pp. 433-458.

Smith, A. (2003). Tohu Kakahi 1828-1907. *Dictionary of New Zealand biography*, updated 16 December 2003. Available at http://www.dnzb.govt.nz/. Retrieved 14 June 2005.

Smith, L.T. (1986). *Te Rapunga i te Ao Marama: The search for the world of light.* Discussion paper. Auckland: University of Auckland.

Smith, L.T. (1999). *Decolonising methodologies: Research and indigenous peoples.* London: Zed Books.

Spee, K. (1998). *The voice of youth: Young people share their experiences of being involved in the youth justice system.* Unpublished master's thesis. Hamilton: University of Waikato.

State Services Commission. (2005). *The Treaty of Waitangi/Te Tiriti.* Available at http://www.treatyofwaitangi.govt.nz/index.php. Retrieved 22 February 2005.

Sutherland, I.L.G. (Ed.). (1940). *The Māori people today: a general survey.* Christchurch: Whitcombe & Tombs/Oxford University Press.

Te Puni Kōkiri. (2000). *Progress towards closing the gaps between Māori and Māori.* Wellington: Author.

Te Puni Kōkiri. (2005). *Treaty Overview.* Available at http://www.tpk.govt.nz/publications/docs/tpk_treaty/treaty_overview.pdf. Retrieved 10 February 2005.

Thomas, D.R. & Robertson, N.R. (1992). Evaluation of human services: Conceptualisation and planning. In D.R. Thomas & A. Veno (Eds.), *Psychology and social change*. Palmerston North: Dunmore. pp. 191-207.

Toki, E., Robertson, J.M. & Pfeiffenberger, A. (2002). *Evaluation of the Hamilton City Council youth policy.* Hamilton: Department of Psychology, University of Waikato.

Veno, A. & Thomas, D.R. (1992). Psychology and the process of social change. In D.R. Thomas & A. Veno (Eds.), *Psychology and social change: Creating an international agenda*. Palmerston North: Dunmore. pp. 15-36.

Waldegrave, C. (1993). *The challenges of culture to psychology and post-modern thinking.* Address to the Annual Conference of the New Zealand Psychological Society. Available at http://wfass-trinity.fass.waikato.ac.nz/docushare/dsweb/Get/Document-1044/Waldegrave.pdf. Retrieved 21 June 2005.

Walker, R. (1990). *Ka whawhai tonu matou: struggle without end.* Auckland: Penguin.

Whangapiritia, L. (2003). *Tuku Manawa: Patterns of alternative health care practices in Aotearoa/New Zealand.* Unpublished master's thesis, University of Waikato.

7

Historical and Theoretical Orientations of Community Psychology Practice and Research in Japan

TOSHIAKI SASAO AND TOMOYUKI YASUDA

Abstract

This chapter discusses historical roots and theoretical orientations of community psychology (CP) in Japan. The history of Japan's CP has been strongly influenced by the U.S. model at its initial stage. Only a few years after the Swampscott conference, CP was introduced in Japan, followed by a series of community psychology symposia (1975–1998) and the launching of Japanese Society of Community Psychology (1998–2003), and several translated textbooks and active research helped establish the field. An analytic review of research studies in the *Japanese Journal of Community Psychology* (1997–2003), in comparison with several U.S.-based reviews, shows that the U.S. model has influenced all aspects of the Japanese community research and practice. Even though community-oriented research and action is well appreciated among those Japanese researchers and practitioners who identify themselves with CP, our analyses show that most research has been conducted at the *individual* level or *school* settings focusing particularly on personal adjustment. We also highlight the importance of formulating adequate training programs that can work effectively with school systems and other community settings in which most research and intervention or actions would take place. Finally, a cross-cultural model is proposed to enhance the understanding and promotion of CP seeking to be a more distinctive field in Japan.

Introduction

Only a few years after the United States officially launched community psychology (CP) at Swampscott in 1965, this new field of psychology was already being introduced in Japan, just as the field of clinical psychology began receiving attention from mental health professions there (Ando, Hoshino, & Sasao, in press; Shimoyama, 2004; Yamamoto, 1986). Oftentimes, CP in Japan is regarded, implicitly or explicitly, as an "imported" subdiscipline of clinical psychology from the United States. For example, the visions and missions shared at the Swampscott conference (Bennet, Anderson, Cooper, Hassol, Klein, & Rosenblum, 1966) were highly valued by the Japanese psychologists who had to deal with problems and promotions of individual and societal well-being in the Japanese context. Those who embraced the emerging ideas of CP were viewed as the new type of clinical and social psychologists. These psychologists saw the limitations of the individualistic approaches to psychopathology and realized that many mental health problems were partly rooted in communities, neighborhoods, schools, and/or organizations. As such, the early models of community mental health (CMH) were appealing to a growing number of psychologists and have been one of the most influential frameworks on the historical and current development of CP in Japan. Many other professionals in the neighboring disciplines (e.g., sociology, social work, nursing, and education) had joined this small yet growing trend of CP in Japan. After some 30 years, the field of community psychology is diversified and moving along with many changes in social structures and systems in Japan. However, its own indigenous theories or formulations of research and action in CP that are unique to the Japanese society have yet to be explored vis-à-vis the CP models in the United States and other countries.

The major purpose of this chapter is to trace and discuss the historical and theoretical orientations of CP research and practice in Japan. To this end, we examined how CP in Japan formally or informally has developed as an academic discipline. Historical roots were traced by identifying and discussing several events that particularly contributed to the development and promotion of CP in Japan. To further facilitate the discussion, an analytic review of the *Japanese Journal of Community Psychology* (JJCP), the only professional journal dedicated to research and action in community psychology, was conducted in light of the past reviews of the *American Journal of Community Psychology* and the *Journal of Community Psychology* by Lounsbury, Leader, Meares, and Cook (1980), Novaco and Monahan (1980), Speer, Dey, Griggs, Gibson, Lubin, and Hughey (1992), and Martin, Lounsbury, and Davidson II (2004). Finally, we discussed some implications for the current status and future directions of CP in Japan.

Historical and Theoretical Roots

The Beginnings

The history of CP in Japan dates back to 1969 when a symposium entitled "Issues in Community Psychology" was held at the 33rd annual convention of the Japanese Psychological Association (Ando, 1989). It was at this symposium that the term *community psychology* was first introduced to clinical psychologists and other mental health professionals in Japan. Although similar ideas or concepts of CP had already existed in the neighboring disciplines (e.g., social work, sociology, nursing, and public health), it was at this symposium that CP was officially recognized as an academic discipline in Japan. However, not only were the concepts and theories inherent in CP initially difficult to understand or accept among Japanese psychologists at that time, but also the translation of words such as *community* was deemed difficult, if not impossible. For the purpose of retaining the original meaning to be used in community psychology (i.e., geographical and relational components of a community), the term *community* was preserved for translation (i.e., a katakana word[1]: *komuniti* コミュニティ). Adopting a Japanese-translated word such as *chi'iki shakai* 地域社会 could potentially limit the meaning and use of the term only in a geographical sense.

When CP was introduced in Japan, many ideas and theories underlying CP were also imported from the United States. For example, the 1963 Community Mental Health Centers (CMHC) Act, enacted to improve the lives of psychologically maladjusted or impaired citizens and community members, strongly influenced the initial formalization of CP in the United States. Shortly after the introduction of the CMHC policy in the United States, a similar mental health policy was implemented in Japan as well (e.g., Yamamoto, 1986). Similarly, the *zeitgeist* of the 1960s in the United States was also "imported" into the Japanese context when CP was brought to the fore in the Japanese academe.

Development of Community Psychology in Japan

Several factors can be identified that greatly affected the development of CP in Japan. After his sojourner experience with the Wellesley Human Relations Services at Harvard University and Massachusetts General Hospital, Kazuo Yamamoto, a Japanese clinical psychologist at the Japanese National Institute of Mental Health, introduced CP by first translating *An Approach to Community Mental Health* (Caplan, 1961) and then attempting to apply the concepts and techniques of community mental health (CMH) in the Japanese mental health system. At that time, most of the psychological services were primarily based on the traditional clinical treatment services including individually focused therapies and institution-based care. Yamamoto was fascinated by the ideas of building a new system of professional care for individuals with mental disorders based on CP principles so that they could lead meaningful lives in their own communities or neighborhoods rather than in the mental institution. Consequently, he was met with the opposition from many traditional "armchair" clinicians in Japan.

However, the Japanese Mental Health Act of 1965 played a significant role in developing the system of CMH in terms of staffing mental health workers, especially those working with people who have severe mental disorders in the

---

[1] The *katakana* is one of the three Japanese orthographic systems used for transcribing foreign or imported words.

communities (Yamamoto, 1986). Called the "Quickening Period" by Ando (1989), the late 1960s to early 1970s were considered as the era when clinical psychologists and other mental health professionals in Japan started recognizing the importance of human behaviors and problems embedded within socially diverse contexts and environments. This was also a period during which the Japanese society witnessed the revitalization of neighborhood associations, which were banned after World War II mainly because they were feared as promoting Japanese militaristic forces. Furthermore, the traditional function of families was gradually disappearing because of the trend toward nuclear family units amid the rapid economic growth from the 1950s to 1970s.

As a result, the importance of restructuring old resources (e.g., families and neighborhoods) was keenly felt by psychologists to maximize the person–environment fit for the well-being of individuals, because CP studies "the transactions between social systems networks, populations, and individuals; that develops and evaluates intervention methods which improve person-environment fits; that designs and evaluates new social systems, and from such knowledge and changes seems to enhance the psychosocial opportunities of the individual" (Murrell, 1973, p. 23). However, identifying and implementing new resources (e.g., self-help groups) proved to be challenging because clinical psychologists and other mental health professionals, though now exposed to the ideas of community psychology, lacked the knowledge and skills to initiate systems-based interventions.

Community Psychology Symposia

Community psychology continued to develop and evolve in the mid-1970s and now reached the period of what Ando (1989) called the "Birth to Toddling Period." During this period, the field began to underscore the significance of social problems in Japan (e.g., juvenile delinquency, family problems), while toddling around outside the field of mainstream psychology (e.g., Hoshino, 1980, 2005). A relatively narrow and limited focus of CP research and practice based on the CMH model gradually became diversified during this period.

More recent developments started with the annual "Community Psychology Symposium" (nostalgically known as *Shimpo* シンポ). This was initially held in 1975 and continued yearly for more than two decades. Attended each time by a group of 20 to 30 clinical psychologists, social psychologists, and graduate students across the country, the purpose of the annual symposium was to examine how the CP ideas and methods developed in the United States (Bennett et al., 1966) could be adapted appropriately in the Japanese context. These symposia attracted a host of psychologists and other professionals from social work, nursing, and sociology, with a range of topics from theories and foci of CP, community-based approaches to assisting autistic children in schools and families, consultation methods in school, and delivery of mental health services in the university settings (Ando, 1989; Ando, Hoshino, & Sasao, in press).

These annual symposia served specific purposes (Yamamoto, 1986): (a) to facilitate communication among community-based practitioners and researchers; (b) to organize programs that address significant issues related to the work based on community-based research; and (c) to examine deficiencies and problems in approaches to understanding social problems and effective solutions to these problems rather than attempt to expedite the process of formulating the theories of social interventions in the Japanese context.

Additionally, one unique function of these symposia was to serve as opportunities for mentoring individuals who were new to the field but interested in community-oriented practice and research and needed their clinical skills honed based on the CP approaches (Ando, 1989; Ando, Hoshino, & Sasao, in press). Because no formal graduate training or university courses in CP were offered in any Japanese academic setting at that time, the symposia played an important role in maintaining the cohesiveness of community-oriented practitioners and researchers. It was also around this time that the new resources in CP, such as the Japanese translation of S. A. Murrell's (1973) *Community Psychology and Social Systems*, began appearing in the professional literature.

Cross-Disciplinary Orientation of Community Psychology in Japan

The progress of CP continued throughout the period of "Development and Independence" (Ando, 1989) in the 1980s. Some attempts to establish indigenous approaches to CP appeared at that time, and new knowledge accumulated as the translations of the CP writings from the United States became more frequent and available. Also, the field benefited from methodological and conceptual developments in other social and health science fields within Japan. Yet, many "movers and shakers" of the field were clinical and social psychologists who mainly organized and advanced the field through the symposia.

Even though the focus of CP during this period tended to be clinical in that the issues such as interpersonal relations between helping professionals and the clients with severe mental illness were most commonly discussed, other topics (e.g., the systems-based or ecological perspectives as applied to school consultation, methods of social and community intervention) were also explored during this period. Simultaneously, the definitions of CP were being challenged in reference to social problems and issues within the Japanese context, and the characteristics and levels of interventions underwent reexamination as well. As a result, topics such as community structures as well as theoretical development based on the U.S. model vis-à-vis the Japanese culture invited lively discussions in the CP literature (see Yamamoto, 1986).

During this period, many Japanese psychologists subscribed to what they called the "community approach" (e.g., Yamamoto, 1986) in reference to CP. The approach is essentially synonymous in terms of definitions and levels of interventions that CP proclaims in the U.S. model. Particularly, it posits that individual maladjustment does not necessarily originate from intrapersonal factors. Instead, maladjustment often comes from adverse social systems that surround an individual (i.e., individuals in ecological contexts) and from the misfit between person and environment. Communities are seen not as the experimental field that provides us with empirical data, but as the field that psychologists need to participate in, so that they understand the problems and engage in action when needed (i.e., advocacy and social action).

These theoretical developments led to the guiding framework for working with various Japanese communities in need of psychological and often medical interventions. The individuals or groups who often benefit from the community approaches were the children with autism, people with HIV/AIDS, and victims of domestic violence (e.g., Yamamoto, 2001; Yamamoto, Hara, Miguchi, & Hisata, 1995). Also, a variety of CP practices in dealing with problems that plague the Japanese society (e.g., the care for the elderly, support for the victims of the Great *Hanshin* earthquake in western Japan, social and educational support services for the children of illegal aliens, youth violence and bullying) have been documented (e.g., Yamamoto, 2001).

Provision of support and services for some culture-specific issues, such as suicide problems and social withdrawal, or *hikikomori*, has also become salient among Japanese psychologists in general and community-oriented practitioners in particular. Thus, the methods of delivering services to these people were explored. Other topics such as community development in rural Japanese villages, environmental effects on psychological well-being, and quality of life among ethnic minorities in Japan were also included in a series of symposia and workshops that ensued (e.g., Yamamoto, 1986).

Searching for New Roles and Identities

The field of CP in Japan gradually experienced the search for new roles and identities that were potentially associated with clinical psychology. Yamamoto (1986) argued that the traditional role of a clinical psychologist, such as psychological assessment and psychotherapy, should be expanded by incorporating broadly defined clinical or nonclinical services. These new roles included being a change facilitator, consultant, evaluator, system organizer, participant conceptualizer, among other things (e.g., Bennett et al., 1966). In a similar vein, an attempt was made by Ando (1989) and Yamamoto (1986) to categorize a group of community-oriented practitioners and researchers in Japan, per Scribner (1970) who defined a community psychologist as a social movement psychologist, social action psychologist, new clinical psychologist, and social engineer. The Japanese psychologists with a community orientation struggled to wear these multiple hats and integrate them into a cohesive set of frameworks while doing community work.

As described earlier, the CP symposium was first held in 1975. It continued until March 1998, when it was replaced by a large-scale professional organization called the Japanese Society of Community Psychology (JSCP). This was the period when CP in Japan really "took off" after 20 years or more of building foundations. Many individual members were recruited from a variety of social and behavioral science fields, and the membership now reaches about 450. Concurrently, the first issue of the *Japanese Journal of Community Psychology (JJCP)* was published in 1997, attempting to gain more professional recognition in psychology and related disciplines in Japan.

An Analytic Review of the Articles Published in the *Japanese Journal of Community Psychology* (1997–2003)

The above discussion expounds how CP has been formalized as an academic and professional discipline in Japan. Many CP models originated in the United States, most notably the CMH model, adapted by the early clinical psychologists and mental health professionals in Japan. As a result, theoretical orientations of the U.S. model of CP had a significant influence on the development of CP in Japan.

There are several reviews of the literature that comprehensively cover CP research in the United States (e.g., Lounsbury, Leader, Meares, & Cook 1980). Similarly, in an effort to provide further discussion about theories and research in Japan, a critical review of the published work in JJCP, the only professional journal in community psychology in Japan, should be useful in evaluating the nature of contemporary CP work in Japan.

The current review was conducted in the manner of past reviews including Lounsbury et al. (1980), Speer et al. (1992), and Martin et al. (2004). In doing so, the coding system developed by Lounsbury et al. (1980), adapted later by Speer et al. (1992) and Martin et al. (2004) in the subsequent reviews, was used here as well. We wanted to examine the similarities and differences of the U.S. and Japanese research databases in CP with respect to some methodological and contextual factors (i.e., research designs, setting categories, and dependent/outcome variable categories).

The current review began by first locating the research articles published in JJCP between 1997 and 2003. Of all the published papers in JJCP, including nonempirical articles (e.g., position papers, theoretical/conceptual reviews, and "academic essays") and book reviews, a total of 36 research articles were included. The total number was considerably fewer than those of the U.S. counterpart, which totals 478 research articles in the *American Journal of Community Psychology* (AJCP) and *Journal of Community Psychology* (JCP) (1973–1978), 235 in AJCP and JCP (1984–1988), and a random sample of 132 research articles from a total of 244 articles (54%) in AJCP (1993–1998).

Research Designs

We first examined the similarities and differences of the research designs used in relation to the Cronbach's (1957) classic design framework (e.g., Speer

TABLE 1. Percentages of research designs in *Japanese Journal of Community Psychology* articles (1997–2003) per Cronbach's (1957) criteria.

	United States			Japan
Research design	1973–1978 (N = 478)	1984–1988 (N = 166)	1993–1998 (N = 66)	1997–2003 (N = 20)
Experimental	60.0	20.0	14.7	25.0
Correlational	19.0	68.0	25.0	48.0
Mixed method/other	21.0	12.0	60.3	15.0
Total	100.0	100.0	100.0	100.0

Note: Mixed-method studies included both experimental and correlational approaches.

et al., 1992). As seen in Table 1, about half of the articles published in JJCP (48%) were classified as *correlational* research, whereas one-fourth used an *experimental* approach. The overall patterns of the distribution were somewhat comparable with those of Speer et al. (1992) whose review identified 68% of the articles were in the *correlational* research category, while relatively lower numbers of the articles were categorized as experimental (20%) or mixed (12%) research, between 1984 and 1988 in the United States. Although there was a growing trend for using mixed methodology in the U.S. literature between 1993 and 1998, the percentage of articles that fit this category in the Japanese publications were only 15.0% between 1997 and 2003.

Although many community-based practices were documented in other forms of publications in Japan (e.g., book chapters, conference proceedings), the research database has been primarily based on the *correlational* or sometimes *case study* method with small samples. Community-based research, at least in the field of psychology, is yet to be widely established.

Setting Categories

Table 2 shows the findings from comparing different setting categories or affiliations where research participants were recruited. In contrast with a decreasing trend of research conducted in academic settings in the United States, about 30% of the research articles in JJCP were conducted in university or academic settings. Indeed, more than half (51.5%) of them dealt with issues originated at university or public school settings. School-based research is most often concerned with how school-based mental health professionals (e.g., school psychologists and school counselors) serve better the needs of at-risk students and their families. Only a few studies (6.1%) were conducted in the community settings. Interestingly, notwithstanding the enduring interest in clinically oriented community psychology and community mental health issues in particular, no study was identified where participants were drawn from local community mental health centers. A total of 18.2% of the JJCP articles was categorized as "other settings"

TABLE 2. Percentages of studies in setting categories for research in *Japanese Journal of Community Psychology* articles (1997–2003).

Setting category	United States			Japan
	1973–1978 (N = 453)	1984–1988 (N = 235)	1993–1998 (N = 80)	1997–2003 (N = 33)
Mental health centers or clinics	19.0	5.6	5.0	—
Colleges or universities	17.0	13.0	6.3	30.3
Local community (no organizational affiliation)	15.0	35.0	36.3	6.1
Private or public schools	14.0	15.0	13.8	21.2
Mental hospitals or residential facilities	13.0	6.4	1.3	—
Criminal justice or law enforcement agencies	13.0	6.0	1.3	—
Social service organizations	11.0	0.4	31.3	15.2
Hospital settings	4.0	4.0	1.3	9.1
Defense (armed) forces	2.0	0.4	—	—
Conferences or workshops	1.0	2.4	—	—
APA division	1.0	0.8	—	—
Other[a]	1.0	11.0	6.0	18.2
Total	111.0[b]	100.0	100.0	100.0

[a] This category also includes activity settings, mutual self-help groups, and places of worship (e.g., Martin et al., 2004).
[b] Columns do not necessarily add up to 100% due to multiple coding of some articles.

that involved those research studies conducted in private sectors or business settings.

Topical Areas

Following Lounsbury et al. (1980) and Speer et al. (1992), the JCCP articles were categorized into four major topics: (1) mental health services and programs; (2) specific problem areas and issues; (3) provision of human resources, and (4) issues in measurement and research methods. Akin to the findings by Speer et al. (1992) that 71% of the AJCP and JCP articles were classified as the specific problem areas and issues, the current analysis also revealed that 69% of the JJCP articles belonged to this category. In contrast, mental health services and programs, such as therapy and clinical intervention, comprised 27.1% of the total JJCP articles. Moreover, only 1.7% of the research examined the issues related to the provision of human resources, or issues in measurement and research methodologies.

Table 3 displays the subtopical categories that were subsumed under the specific problem areas and issues. In particular, one topic that concerned *individual-level* psychological adjustment was found to be most frequently studied in Japan, just like the U.S. counterpart. Issues related to personal adjustment in work settings was commonly investigated in Japan as well followed by social support issues. On the other hand, research studies dealing

TABLE 3. Percentages of subtopic categories (specific problem areas and issues) in *Japanese Journal of Community Psychology* articles (1997–2003).

Subtopic category	United States		Japan
	1973–1978 (N = 211)	1984–1988 (N = 166)	1997–2003 (N = 41)
Social support	—[a]	22.0	19.5
Individual adjustment	17.0	21.0	24.3
Prevention	7.0	18.0	—
Person–environment relations or fit	7.0	8.0	12.2
Minority problems and concerns	9.0	8.0	12.2
Work adjustment	8.0	7.0	22.0
Health or medical problems and issues	3.0	6.0	—
Suicide issues	2.0	4.0	—
Parental training	2.0	2.0	2.4
Drugs and alcohol problems	11.0	2.0	—
Epidemiology	1.0	1.0	—
Attitudes and beliefs about mental illness	12.0	—[a]	4.9
Community planning and development	4.0	—[a]	—
Ethical concerns and legal issues	3.0	—[a]	—
Other (poverty, death and dying, etc.)	13.0	—[a]	2.4

[a]Category not used for this time period (e.g., Speer et al., 1992).
Note: An article can be classified in multiple categories; however, this category was not used by Martin et al. (2004).

with prevention, one of the core values in CP (e.g., Dalton, Wandersman, & Elias, 2001), were not found in the Japanese literature, although there is a great deal of prevention research in the United States (e.g., Speer et al., 1992).

Person–environment relations or fit also seemed to serve as one guiding research framework in Japan, constituting a total of 12.2% of the articles published by JJCP. Furthermore, a higher percentage of work adjustment (22%) in JJCP seems to reflect a culture-specific issue in the Japanese CP research and actions that are mostly conducted in business settings.

Dependent/Outcome Variable Categories

The final set of analyses was concerned with the types of outcome or dependent variables used in the JJCP articles. As seen in Table 4, 26.9% of the studies involved the assessment and measurement of psychological, social, or mental health outcomes. This finding was in line with the U.S. research literature even though the declining trend has been witnessed over time. Affective and attitudinal variables (e.g., attitudes toward persons with mental illness) were also investigated frequently in Japan, comprising 19.2% of the research studies in JJCP. Investigations concerning quality of life or life satisfaction were also of particular interest to the Japanese community psychologists (11.5%).

TABLE 4. Percentages of dependent/outcome variable categories used in *Japanese Journal of Community Psychology* articles (1997–2003).

	United States			Japan
Outcome/dependent variable	1973–1978 (N = 478)	1984–1988 (N = 166)	1993–1998 (N = 86)	1997–2003 (N = 26)
Personality, adjustment, mental health, stress, anxiety, coping	44.0	34.0	20.2	26.9
Specific actions, behaviors, activities, events, prevention	60.0	24.0	18.5	7.8
Social support, social networks, social interactions	14.0	17.0	16.1	3.8
Achievement, learning, knowledge, skills, empowerment	11.0	7.0	15.3	3.8
Sentiment, attitudes, interests, opinions, values	38.0	14.0	8.1	19.2
Cognitions, beliefs, self-perception	18.0	7.0	4.8	11.5
Specific attitudes (e.g., attitudes towards programs)	7.0	1.0	3.2	—
Physical, motor, sensory functions, health outcomes	8.0	5.0	2.4	3.8
Other (e.g., motivation, resource allocation, risk indices)	—	9.0	2.4	—
Demographic data	38.0	3.0	1.6	—
Work-related constructs, job placement, occupational stress	2.0	6.0	0.8	7.8
Quality of life, life satisfaction	—	3.0	0.8	11.5
Mental abilities (e.g., IQ)	8.0	0.0	0.0	—
Sociological constructs	3.0	7.0	3.2	3.8
Organizational constructs, structures, person–environment fit	4.0	3.0	2.4	—

Note: Total percentages do not add up to 100% because some of the studies used multiple categories for dependent/outcome variables.

Toward a Distinctive Community Psychology in Japan

The U.S.–Japan comparison of CP research above showed overall similarities and differences in the methods employed, topics studied, and targets of intervention. Most notably, however, many research and action studies in Japan have been conducted at the *individual* level (e.g., personal adjustment and stress) or *micro*-level (e.g., social support) in community settings. There appears very little or almost no research and action that may be unique to the Japanese context and beyond the practice of clinical psychology in real-world settings. It may be argued that Japan's CP may have emerged as such, or in the ways that the United States or other countries have embraced CP. This section will provide somewhat speculative discussion on why there is very little community-oriented research in CP in Japan, while some indigenous approaches in CP appear to exist in other countries as seen in other chapters of this volume.

One possible reason for the scarcity of community-oriented research can be attributed to the lack of adequate professional CP training in Japanese graduate and professional schools. There are no free-standing CP graduate programs that offer comprehensive training in community-based research and action. Rather, CP has been taught or introduced as part of other fields of psychology (e.g., developmental, social, educational, industrial, clinical) or through related disciplines (e.g., communication studies, educational policy studies, public administration, sociology, public health, social work). Many CP researchers and practitioners in Japan receive "unofficial" training through these disciplines mostly at domestic institutions. Fortunately, in some good or unintended ways, Japanese CP has become multidisciplinary or cross-disciplinary in its tradition over 30 years, accommodating diverse thoughts and approaches with "a little bit of everything" that may or may not be akin to the CP known in the United States or other countries. Interestingly, the U.S. community psychologists have been trying to be more interdisciplinary in their approaches by developing partnerships with other disciplines in the past several years, whereas Japanese CP could be interdisciplinary by birth or by default.

Another possible reason for the lack of community-oriented research and practice in Japan is the nature of different social and service structures and systems in which Japanese researchers and practitioners find themselves. While the core concepts and principles of CP in the U.S. model, such as empowerment and sense of community (e.g., Dalton et al., 2001), are shared sufficiently among Japanese researchers, the translation of these ideas into culturally appropriate services or research may be a difficult task for Japanese researchers and practitioners. Just like individual psychotherapy techniques developed in the Western tradition do not necessarily work in other cultures, relevant CP theories and models from the United States may not be adapted or integrated adequately in serving various Japanese communities.

For example, Japanese schools are often unwilling to establish collaborative relationships with university-based researchers and practitioners. This is mainly because teachers and students are *not* accustomed to being "studied" by outside researchers. Moreover, even though individual schools or school districts show interest in developing partnership with university researchers and practitioners, the level of administrative autonomy within schools is not as high as that of other countries including the United States. As a result, most of the middle- or large-scale school-based interventions are implemented under the direction of the Japanese government. Furthermore, because there is no formal or recognized system of ethical standards for psychology research and practice (e.g., institutional review boards, informed consent procedures), the values of psychology research or social science research in general are often misperceived and underappreciated in many Japanese schools. Thus, how the Japanese social systems operate would make it difficult to establish a long-term committed relationship with Japanese school systems. This is especially true given that the idea of evidence-based program evaluation including program development has just been introduced by the Japanese Ministry of Education, Culture, Sports, Science, & Technology several years ago. In order to successfully promote community research and action with more robust research designs with more diverse targets in various settings, it is important to establish relevant training programs at the undergraduate, graduate, and/or professional levels.

So, given the foregoing discussion, would Japan develop its own distinctive CP, separate from the U.S. model? To answer this question on any future development of CP in Japan, a framework or model is needed to assess cross-cultural validity of CP research and action beyond a single culture. Taking cues from Kuhn's (1971) model of scientific progress, Sasao and Yasuda (2004, 2005a, 2005b) argued that an understanding of CP in one culture from another requires both an intellectual choice to adopt a view of CP, that is, "persuasion," and an act to translate this view into action by internalizing it, that is, "conversion" (cf. Trickett, 1984). The significance of this viewpoint is applicable not only in light of the U.S.-based CP but also in light of a cross-cultural or international CP developed in cultures other than the United States. The ideas inherent in conversion could potentially be branched into "disciplinary conversion" (i.e., to what extent CP is internalized and how it is manifest in Japan's community psychology research and action) and "cultural conversion" (i.e., to what extent we convert to the cultural baggage or hideously complex cultural inferences that come with our persuasion in the research and practice of CP) (Sasao & Yasuda, 2004). In order to examine cross-cultural validity of CP between the two cultures (e.g., the United States and Japan), we have proposed a conceptual framework elsewhere (Figure 1) (Sasao & Yasuda, 2004, 2005a, 2005b).

In this model, there could be at least three aspects of CP in which cross-cultural validity should be examined and established, that is, theory, research, and practice/action across cultures. We argue that in order for the U.S. model of CP to be incorporated appropriately into the Japanese context or vice versa, cross-cultural validity needs to be established with respect to each component as well as interactions between these components.

Several important issues can be considered for the exploration and establishment of the links between the concepts. For instance, any link between theories across cultures should be explored in order to confirm similarities and potential differences between the definition and its use of the core CP concepts (e.g., psychological sense of community and empowerment). Adequate knowledge transformation, exchange, and dissemination between cultures also seem necessary, and that some theories may or may not be adapted without modification and adjustment when they are transformed into different cultural contexts.

Similarly, a *within-culture* research itself involves a multilevel unit of analysis (i.e., individual, group, organizational, institutional, community, and societal), and a *between-culture* research further requires us to apply cross-cultural multilevels of analysis, pointing to the significance of and need for investigating any "cultural amplifier or modifier" as described in Figure 1. For example, cross-cultural validity of the U.S. model of practice must be ideally

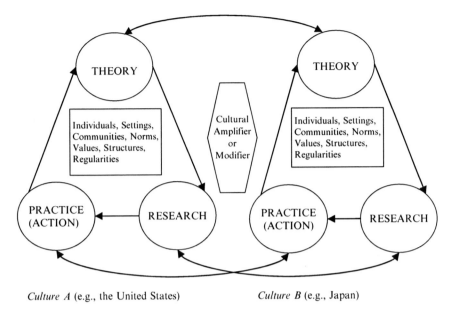

Culture A (e.g., the United States)   Culture B (e.g., Japan)

FIGURE 1. Toward a comparative framework for understanding the progress of community psychology research and action across cultures.

established before proper interventions are implemented and actions occur in the Japanese context. It is possible that ecological constraints (Kelly, 1986) may be different from one culture to another.

Concluding Remarks

The purpose of this chapter was to trace the historical roots and theoretical orientations of CP research and practice in Japan. The chapter first identified relevant events that helped gain recognition of the field and contributed to the development of CP in Japan. The U.S. model of CP, particularly its early CMH movement, had a significant influence on CP in Japan especially at its initial stage. The analytic review of published work in the JJCP included in this chapter unambiguously informed how comparable or different the CP research databases are between the United States and Japan. Given the findings of this analytic review, two major reasons for the lack of culturally unique perspectives on CP in Japan were proposed: (a) insufficient and inadequate training opportunities for CP in Japan and (b) the effects of culturally unique social structures and systems on designing and evaluating culturally appropriate intervention strategies. Finally, it was argued that the future development of a distinctive CP in Japan depends largely on how we pay closer attention to the interplay of theory, research, and practice across cultures, thereby encouraging further collaboration domestically and internationally, and the rigor of our graduate and professional training program that would emphasize research conducted with more methodologically sound and stronger theoretical orientation in real-world, community-based settings.

References

Ando, N. (1989). Community psychology in Japan: A historical review. *Applied Psychology: An International Review, 38*, 397-408.

Ando, N., Hoshino, A., & Sasao, T. (in press). Community psychology in Japan. In Japanese Society of Community Psychology (Ed.), *Handbook of community psychology*. Tokyo: University of Tokyo Press. [in Japanese]

Bennett, C. C., Anderson, L. S., Cooper, S., Hassol, L., Klein, D. C., & Rosenblum, G. (1966). *Community psychology: A report of the Boston conference on the education of psychologists for community mental health*. Boston: Boston University Press.

Caplan, G. (1961). *An approach to community mental health*. New York: Grune and Stratton.

Cronbach, L. (1957). The two disciplines of scientific psychology. *American Psychologist, 12*, 671-684.

Dalton, J., Elias, M., & Wandersman, A. (2001). *Community psychology: Linking individuals and communities*. Belmont, CA: Wadsworth.

Hoshino, A. (1980). Japan's Community Psychology: Its brief history and direction for future work. *Japanese Journal of Social Psychiatry, 3*, 185-193. [in Japanese].

Hoshino, A. (2005). The psychology goes beyond the borders: Community psychology's beginnings, progress and the directions in the future. *Japanese Journal of Community Psychology, 9*, 41-59.

Kelly, J. (1986). Context and process: An ecological view of the interdependence of practice and research. *American Journal of Community Psychology, 14*, 581-589.

Kuhn, T. (1971). *The structure of scientific revolutions*. Chicago: University of Chicago Press.

Lounsbury, J. W., Leader, D. S., Meares, E. P., & Cook, M. P. (1980). An analytic review of research in community psychology. *American Journal of Community Psychology, 8*, 415-441.

Martin, P. P., Lounsbury, D. W., & Davidson II, W. S. (2004). *AJCP* as a vehicle for improving community life: An historic-analytic review of the Journal's contents. *American Journal of Community Psychology, 34*, 163-173.

Murrell, S. A. (1973). *Community psychology and social systems: A conceptual framework and intervention guide*. New York: Behavioral Publications.

Novaco, R. W., & Monahan, J. (1980). Research in community psychology: An analysis of work published in the first six years of the *American Journal of Community Psychology*. *American Journal of Community Psychology, 8*, 131-145.

Sasao, T., & Yasuda, T. (2004). Historical and theoretical orientations of community psychology in Japan: Toward a culturally indigenous community psychology in the globalizing world. Paper presented at the 1st Japan-Korea Seminar in Community Psychology, Seoul, Korea.

Sasao, T., & Yasuda, T. (2005a). Prevention research in Japan: Findings from an Analytical Review of the *Japanese Journal of Community Psychology*. Paper presented at the 2nd Japan-Korea Seminar in Community Psychology, Tokyo, Japan.

Sasao, T., & Yasuda, T. (2005b). The intellectual development of community psychology in four areas of the world: Japan. Paper presented at the 10th Biennial Conference of the Society for Community Research & Action, University of Illinois at Urbana-Champaign, USA.

Shimoyama, H. (2004). *Toward contemporary clinical psychology.* Tokyo: Seishin Shobo Books. [in Japanese]

Scribner, S. (1970). What is community psychology made of? In P. E. Cook (Ed.), *Community psychology and community mental health: Introductory readings.* San Francisco: Holden-Day.

Speer, P., Dey, A., Griggs, P., Gibson, C., Lubin, B., & Hughey, J. (1992). In search of community: An analysis of community psychology research from 1984-1988. *American Journal of Community Psychology, 20,* 195-209.

Trickett, E. (1984). Toward a distinctive community psychology: An ecological metaphor for the conduct of community research and the nature of training. *American Journal of Community Psychology, 12,* 261-279.

Yamamoto, K. (1986). *Community Psychology: Theory and practice in social intervention.* Tokyo: The University of Tokyo Press [in Japanese].

Yamamoto, K. (2001). *The evolution of community approaches in clinical psychology practice.* Tokyo: Baifukan Books [in Japanese].

Yamamoto, K., Hara, H., Miguchi, M., & Hisata, M. (1995). *Clinical-community psychology: Foundations of community approaches in clinical psychology.* Kyoto: Minerva Books.

8
History and Theory of Community Psychology in India: An International Perspective

Sangeeta Bhatia and Nandini Sethi

Abstract

The term *community psychology* is very new to India. To describe the field, it is helpful to examine the historical developments that preceded the existence of community psychology. A history of psychology in India shows a movement from intrapsychic emphasis to experimental, and more recently to a contextual approach in understanding behavior. The mental health movement is shown to be independent of and a parallel discipline of psychology, as psychology in India has largely remained an academic discipline with its research conducted within the four walls of the laboratory. The efforts by a few psychologists to have an independent subfield of community psychology have shown fruition only in the past decade but have remained largely overshadowed by work done in community development by departments of social work in universities. This chapter highlights the aims of psychologists in India to use a culturally relevant methodology that identifies the needs and resources of a community. The context is important in defining the goals of a people, who should be encouraged to participate in planning and implementation of programs. The authors envisage an ideal 'organization' where the national policymakers while formulating interventions for optimizing mental health share the conceptualization of a community's needs jointly with psychologists.

Introduction

The study of a community implies looking at the characteristics that distinguish it as an interdependent group with opportunities for close social interactions among the members. Communities are social systems that serve to meet human needs. Therefore, community psychology (CP) can be defined as understanding the needs of a people and the resources available to meet those needs. Understanding a community helps CP to focus on formulating interventions that provide opportunities for optimum growth of its people, because a lack of resources (individual, organizational, and community level) can have negative impacts on their mental health. For example, social conditions of poverty, alienation, isolation, and, in general, a lack of social resources are clearly seen to contribute to mental health problems, a domain of CP. Trying to summarize the field in such a large country is daunting, especially in such a small amount of space. In order to help this process, we have divided our introduction into topical areas to better frame the context of this chapter.

Beginnings of a Psychology

In India, we assume that the terms *community psychology* and *community mental health* have been used synonymously. Social workers from the field of psychiatry since the early 20th century have been involved in the implementation of policies, implicating a 'disease' model in diagnosis and treatment of mental illness, rather than a 'contextual' approach. The chapter begins with a brief description of events in pre- and post-independence India (from the 1940s) that helped define the mental health policies, some programs, and their implementation.

Issues for Present-Day Psychology

The main focus of Indian psychologists up to the 1970s and early 1980s remained confined to the personality characteristics of the individual rather than the context in understanding processes involving social change. However, there has been a change in the past two decades in the assumptions used by Indian psychologists to explain factors that determine behavior. That is, a contextual study of behavior is expected to better explain the issue of Indian philosophical thought and traditions that contribute to well-being. We examine the efforts of psychologists to arrive at an indigenous psychology and exemplars of research conducted using culturally appropriate variables.

Community-Based Practice

For a developing country with a huge population that lives below the poverty line with dismal levels of literacy, the efforts of the national government toward improvement of the status of people have been supplemented by community development projects by non-governmental organizations (NGOs) and social workers affiliated with political parties and from academia. For this chapter, we describe the efforts of a few NGOs and other researchers in carrying out action-based research with successful results. We also include examples of the work undertaken by mental health professionals in disaster management to help communities cope with psychosocial problems. Even though most work in India is not based on a conscious use of principles of CP, these examples will nevertheless demonstrate that there has been definitive work in community development that reflects these principles.

Concept of Mental Health in India

In India, there was a sort of 'birth' of an indigenous psychology in the 1980s, however, the effectiveness of the discipline as an applied field hinges on operationalization of the term *health* by psychologists wanting to use CP principles. The strategies to bring about any change in a behavior would have to incorporate the belief systems of a community to be effective in their implementation. We therefore attempt to highlight that for any work in a community in India that is based on CP principles, an insight in the philosophical system of a community is of paramount significance to obtain effective change. We include briefly the meaning of health and conceptualization of the term in the Indian context so as to highlight the uniqueness that a community brings forth and the commonality it has with the definition given by the World Health Organization (WHO).

With this in place, we are now able to examine the psychology in India that is of a more contextual and applied nature. However, before we begin describing the development of psychology in general and CP specifically, we would like to conclude this introduction with a comment regarding the goals of CP in India.

Goals of CP in India

The Community Psychology Association of India (CPAI) was founded in 1987 at Lucknow University with the aim of serving the communities. The *Indian Journal of Community Psychology*, started in 2004, is an official journal of CPAI, which is a significant step towards documenting research in this area. We feel this is an extremely healthy sign as there is a strong need for action research and community participation in defining development, identifying its indicators, and defining relationships between institutions and individuals with the aim to plan strategies for national development. Finally, to fulfill any goal meaningfully, sound and relevant methodologies are required. Because CP in India is in its nascent stage, we also discuss the methodological issues for CP so as to be a viable option.

Beginnings of a Psychology

India, having obtained independence from colonial rule as recently as 1947, is a young country with a rich, ancient culture. India is the second country in the world to cross the 1 billion mark (Census of India, 2001) for residents with 26% of the population living below the poverty line and 74% living in rural areas (NPP, Government of India, 2000). Nearly 30 million people in India are in need of mental health services (NHRC, 1999) with comparable prevalence rates in rural and urban areas.

Psychology in India was introduced at Calcutta University in 1915 while India was under British rule. The Western models of psychological thinking, thus, were prevalent. Dr. G. Bose joined the Department of Psychology in Calcutta as a lecturer in 1917 and founded the Indian Psychoanalytical Association in 1922. However, he attempted to place a focus on psychology that was different from Freudian thought and made contributions in the theory of mental life and the 'gunas' (temperament). He emphasized the cultural, religious, and psychological contexts of the Indian culture, suggesting a guru-shishya paradigm in therapy. The word *guru* is used to depict a teacher, and the *shishya* denotes a disciple. The disciple is the recipient of knowledge from his teacher, who by all means is an expert with vested authority to impart information. Traditionally, the Indian form of schooling has been focused on this dualistic relationship between a student and a teacher, where the latter is responsible for bringing any change in the pupil. The pupil is totally dependent on what the teacher thinks as appropriate to impart by way of knowledge or skills.

Bose initiated training programs at the Calcutta University to advance clinical psychology and established a journal to document ongoing research. Even though psychology with its strong clinical orientation was thriving in the academic milieu, the provision for care for the mentally ill in the community was grossly inadequate. There were few institutes to provide training to mental health professionals. The existing Custodial Institutions, mainly in major cities of Bombay, Madras, Calcutta, and Ranchi, were overcrowded with extremely poor hygienic conditions. Families were not involved in the care or recovery of patients. This was against the very ethos of the Indian culture, where families look after the ill and frail within their homes and also exhibit strong feelings of stigma towards the mentally ill. They would prefer to have an ill member confined within the boundaries of the household so as to safeguard their status in the community. The custodial approach therefore impeded the patient's effective rehabilitation and integration back into the community.

An increase of public pressure and a rise in numbers of individuals suffering from a mental illness as a result of multiple wars and political strife in the subcontinent in the early 20th century forced the Indian government to establish a committee headed by Joseph Bhore to look into the existing facilities for the mentally ill so as to reformulate policies. The Bhore committee report (1946) brought into focus the plight of people affected with mental illness and referred to the extremely unsatisfactory conditions of existing hospitals. This report led to a major shift in the national health policy with a movement away from custody, care, and cure, to prevention, education, and community integration. The committee emphasized a strong need for trained professionals and greater manpower, better hospitals and rehabilitation strategies to improve health services. Dr. Vidya Sagar (1971), for example, involved families in the treatment of patients during the 1950s. In implementing mental health services, the approach used was the comprehensive involvement of families in the care, recovery, and aftercare of psychotic patients and facilitation of acceptance and return of patients to their own homes in the community. However, it was not until the 1970s that centers at Bangalore and Chandigarh took up community mental health with the goal of incorporating mental health care into general health care.

Starting in 1975 and continuing to this day, the Neurological Institute of Mental Health and Sciences (NIMHANS) Bangalore has carried out training programs in community mental health care with the aim of developing manpower in the field of mental health. Primary health centers in the rural sectors have also been running programs both for training personnel as well as for identifying and managing patients with acute disorders. The aim of such centers was to enhance the capacity of the mental health infrastructure to serve a greater number of service seekers. Another goal was to initiate research that would provide information on planning and implementing appropriate services.

The establishment of the centers has improved the accessibility to at least basic psychiatric facilities within the community for as large a section of the population as possible in all parts of the country. Also, due to the limited resources and low income levels of the consumer population, services have been made more affordable. Additionally, increasing acceptance of mental health care by the target population has helped, especially in the context of low levels of literacy, ignorance, superstition, and lack of empowerment of women and children. These positive changes can be attributed to greater access to services by all segments of the population.

The breadth of these changes, however, were slow and limited in scope because the dominant view of the community towards mental illness evoked stigma and prejudice towards the patients as well as their families. There was little research into the needs of affected families and their experiences. The overriding themes of research articles were psychological interpretations that focused on individual dysfunction (Pareek, 1981). The literature on phenomenology and epidemiology was conspicuous by its absence, and this was a major handicap in the planning of effective services. Currently, comprehensive surveys of psychology research initiated by the Indian Council of Social Science Research present critical reviews and reflect major changes and shifts in psychological research in India in the past 50 years. A review of studies included in the three surveys compiled in 1971, 1980–1981, and in 1988 reveal a wide area of topics covered, spanning social, organizational, physiological, and personality psychology. However, CP as an independent subarea does not find a place in any of the volumes. One chapter in volume 2 of the 1988 edition (J. Pandey) covers mental health, illness and therapy. The chapter gives epidemiological findings, concepts on mental illness in the cultural context, treatment, and some findings related to outcome research.

As India was signatory to 'the Alma Ata Declaration (1978),' to set the goal of an acceptable level for providing "health for all" by 2000 through a primary health care approach, this declaration resulted in accelerated services in the area of mental health. But it was only as recent as 1987 that the Mental Health Act was passed with a focus on promotion of health and prevention of illness as well as rehabilitation of patients. More importantly, de-stigmatization of mental illness through education became the major thrust of the national program. However, most of the services are located predominately in urban areas even though the majority of the population lives in rural settings. Evaluations of the effectiveness of these programs is done by the national government from time to time.

Issues for Present-Day Psychology

In order to understand properly the issues confronted by developing countries, theories and principles should articulate the relationship between the sociopsychological processes and particular kinds of social systems, preferably taking into account social change.

As such, India has witnessed a variety of both planned and unplanned changes in every aspect of social life since its independence 50 years ago. Traditionally, the values of affiliation, dependency, collectivism, and tolerance have been fostered in the individual. However, these were incongruent with the changing of an agrarian community to an industrialized one, which required different attributes in inculcating achievement. These industrial-age sets of values such as individuation and economic independence isolated individuals from social relationships and weakened their social moorings. Hence, with an increase in wealth due to employment, there came an increase in social pathology.

It must be noted, however, that not all sections of the population have benefited equally from these societal changes because the Indian social structure includes a hierarchical classification based on class and caste. Those who were in advantageous positions, such as those living in urban areas having obtained greater economic self-sufficiency and higher levels of education, derived maximum benefits from various provisions and facilities. Disadvantaged groups, such as those belonging to backward caste and tribe, who are deprived of economic sufficiency, cultural sophistication, and social advantages, continue to suffer from malnutrition, lack of provisions for health and sanitation, and poor or nonexistent educational facilities. This is a plurality that is inherent in our culture, which provides challenges for creating uniform policies to benefit the majority of people utilizing services. Unless the methodology to understand concepts and application of tools is contextualized, psychology in India will largely remain 'textbookish.'

So far, there has been significant borrowing of theories from the West. People in India face uncertainties constantly and instabilities that are the core characteristics of the rapid socioeconomic changes taking place. Misra (1990) points out that the rural and urban constitute two largely independent subsystems that require separate tools for data collection and separate parameters for analysis and understanding in their own right. One cannot understand the rural by applying the parameters and principles derived from urban samples. However, since psychology in India has its roots in the Western traditions, such as experimentation to isolate cause and effect relationships, the focus of studying behaviors has been based on tools and methods developed in the West. This imported approach, however, has ignored the social realities by yielding research that is based on the use of verbal techniques, Western personality inventories and scales without bothering to find out whether the items are even comprehended or if the concepts are present in the minds of the respondents (Sinha, 1986).

Towards an Indigenous Psychology

The appeal to students, teachers, and practitioners towards developing a psychology that is more relevant to Indian culture was initiated by Professor Durganand Sinha (1922–1998). Prof. Sinha is the most well-known psychologist of the Indian continent and internationally renowned for contributions to the advancement of cross-cultural psychology. He founded the Department of Psychology at Allahabad University, which is now a Center for Advanced Study in Psychology. He related psychology to social change through analysis of value orientation across generations and emphasized indigenization and development of a problem-oriented psychology. Sinha incorporated the framework of research by advocating a dialogue between text and context, theory and practice, and culture and psychology.

The importance of contextualized research did not start to be realized until the late 1970s and 1980s when attention was paid to the problems of poverty, illiteracy, population growth, deprivation, disadvantage, rural development, and educational innovations (Misra, 1990). This reorientation of contextualization has been visible towards indigenization when research focused on discrimination and prejudice (Singh, 1981), deprivation (Misra & Tripathi, 1980), and family influences (Sinha, 1986, 1988). According to a survey of research in psychology in India by Pandey (1988), research in India is gradually orienting towards assessment in a subcultural context. Researchers are recognizing Indian philosophical thought and tradition as the roots of psychology and attempting to shape psychology for a socioeconomic change and national development.

This reorientation of psychology in India from a Western paradigm to culturally relevant context has largely been due to the tireless efforts of Durganand Sinha and Gireshwar Misra. Their research has advocated for contextual interpretation of social issues and succeeded in according an independent status to applied social psychology in India. A significant historical milestone in the area of psychology was the recognition of the indigenous theories by the West, which has helped Indian research to find its way into handbooks of cross-cultural psychology and gain international attention. The focus of studying social change to account for behavior outcomes became the mainstay of social psychology in the 1980s and 1990s.

Psychologists in India now realize the need to understand the etiology of community issues and to focus on the forces acting upon and within a community. This shift in thinking was needed to better understand the sources of community problems and find sustainable solutions, which might come from a concomitant change in the social system itself (Asthana, 2004). As such, Asthana proposes that in most instances, people are likely to find the actual network of relations between members of a community as stressful. Their effort, therefore, should be directed towards maneuvering with the required psychological skill and insight of the situation for substituting a network of healthier interpersonal relations that are rewarding and satisfying in place of the older network. And in doing this, they should largely make use of the resources available within the community. Hence, there is a need to understand the etiology of community issues and to focus on the forces acting upon and within a community (Asthana, 2004). The psychology of a community would be expected to identify the needs of a community, as defined by locale, caste, socioeconomic status, or a common experience, such as a disaster or illness.

Community-Based Practice: Useful Examples

Writings on Community-Based Work

There has been a dearth of books written by Indian authors on the subject of community organization theory and practice. A few books such as *Working with Communities: An Introduction to Community Work* written by H. Y. Siddiqui (1997), who has been part of professional social work academia, focus on concepts such as community work and organization. The book traces the history of community work in India and focuses on the necessity for theoretical underpinnings of social work practice. The author provides useful tips on the process of community work and describes case studies in the field of community work. The role of professionals from various disciplines, such as sociology, social work, economics, psychology, and psychiatry, is seen as important to working in communities. The community is projected as being in total control and, thus, able to initiate change on its own. To understand the extent of community participation, the National Institute of Educational Planning and Administration, New Delhi, organized a seminar on the theme of "Community Participation and Empowerment in Primary Education in India." The proceedings of the seminar (edited by Govinda & Diwan, 2003) highlight the attempts of states and their experiences in incorporating participation in education. Articles within this text exemplify these experiences. For instance, an article by Tharakan talks about school education in Kerala and claims that decentralization has resulted in greater community participation. Govinda reiterates that informal participation in rural life in framing policies has unleashed a new dynamics of power equation in the states of Rajasthan and Madhya Pradesh.

Community-Based Programs

An illustration of a successful program based on community participation was documented by Moni Nag (2002), wherein a STD/HIV Intervention Program in a red-light area of Kolkatta became a catalyst for the formation of an association of sex workers. The association of sex workers became a vehicle for the poor and the powerless and helped the disadvantaged to gain some control over their own lives and environment. The training and recruitment of a few select sex workers as peer educators at the beginning of the project was the first step. The novel experience of working together with the project physicians and college graduate women supervisors for the welfare of the community gave the peer educators a new sense of pride and self-confidence. They became increasingly convinced that in order to protect their health and fight against the injustices they suffered from, sex workers had to mobilize themselves and demand their legitimate rights through an association of their own. The activities of the facilitators and participants showed that active participation of sex workers in all aspects of the HIV/AIDS intervention project was essential for the project's success and also contributed towards an overall betterment of their life.

NGO Work and Other Research

Along with the work of researchers and academicians, contributions to community-based work in India have involved both governmental and nongovernmental organizations. The period since India gained independence has seen a mushrooming of voluntary agencies labeled nongovernmental organizations (NGOs) that took up the task of community welfare programs aimed at the underprivileged sections of society such as the urban poor, the rural poor, and the tribes.

The NGOs have accepted the challenge of translating the concepts of equity, social justice, and community participation into the participatory development approach. Pachauri (1994) documents the work based on a qualitative narrative in a book titled *Reaching India's Poor: Non Governmental approaches to Community Health*. Dr. Coyaji reiterates in the book that if practitioners can motivate families to participate in identifying problems, defining solutions, and implementing programs, the aim of improving their quality of life will be successful. The book also documents a program in Uttar Pradesh, a state in northern India, where a rural development program is run on the strategy of self-reliance rather than economic well-being. Its model of village development today offers a vision of the potential for self-help that can be mobilized in Indian villages. Among the important themes tackled in this volume are health care financing, maternal and child health, community participation, indigenous health systems, and the role of community health workers.

Other significant contributions to community-based work in India are seen in a review of the research documented in the *Indian Journal of Social Work*.

Dubey and Tyagi's (1996) article on the involvement of the community in rural development in the South Asian Association of Regional Cooperation (SAARC) argues that the role of the community could be more complimentary by the creation of awareness, selection of schemes, and also in the process of decision making and feedback.

Mental Health Work

Community-based research has the ability to change policy and resources. For example, Murthy's (2000) work describes the responses of mental health professionals in disasters. From India, the major disaster of importance and a reference point is the Bhopal gas tragedy. Mental health professionals, psychiatrists, clinical psychologists, and social workers have contributed to the current high awareness of the psychological aspects of disasters for the affected population. Their work encouraged a change in the attitude of the administrators by presenting video recording of the interviews of psychological distress. Specifically, the prevalence of a cluster of symptoms like panic attacks in the general population helped to convince the authorities and the population of the real nature of the complaints. Recognizing the psychological reactions as understandable, normal, and requiring specific help and support was the result of this process of sensitization.

Murthy's (2000) research proved that the role of mental health professionals is going to be a constant factor for many years to come, due to the lack of existing mental health infrastructure in most parts of the country. The mobilization of mental health professionals from different parts of the country to the disaster-affected populations is generally not a desirable approach to mental health care for the reason that in a country as diverse as India, the affected population may speak a different language, have different cultural beliefs and practices, and the visiting teams may not be sensitive to these aspects. However, this is a viable option in situations of need after disasters affecting large populations. Mental health professionals in India have recognized the need to share their skills with health workers, volunteers, and doctors for managing the psychological impact of disaster, and they have also gone on to prepare information booklets and manuals in a user-friendly manner (Murthy et al., 1987; Srikala et al., 2000).

Further Evidence of the Impact of Community Health Research and Intervention

With respect to gender discrimination, a project with women in a rural community used participatory research to help better understand the culture, power, structure, problems, and priorities of felt needs with the help of case study and interview methods (Singh, 1998). While providing social casework services, methods of counseling, manipulations in social milieu, and administration of practical services have generally been used to help people understand

and tackle their psychosocial problems. This intervention provided a wide variety of programs organized for women such as female adult education, sanction of old age and widows pension, establishment of a reading room and recreation center equipped with books, installation of hand-pumps for drinking water, and arrangement of institutional credit. An evaluation of the program by Singh (1998), after a few months of implementation, showed significant improvements in women's health, better awareness of legal rights, and increased level of social awareness.

Psychologists in India have now taken it upon themselves to redirect therapeutic efforts for mental health problems towards mobilizing community resources such as involving the family and participation of the affected in the planning of the rehabilitation process. The focus of research is not only on those with mental illness but also on the problems of physical challenges, poverty, population increase, and discrimination. The paradigm for conducting research is now based on action-research and community participation, because it is recognized that the Indian village community has different norms, obligations, and institutions, and, thus, the problems are of a different kind from those living in affluent urban settings. There are problems of poverty, health, superstition, economic exploitation, discrimination, and now increasing violence and sectarianism. Therefore, community psychologists, who have sought to establish an independent identity in the past decade, need to have a multidisciplinary approach and be able to work hand in hand with sociologists, social workers, legal, educational, and clinical psychologists, which, so far, has not been commonly seen.

The field of psychology in the 1990s was, thus, attempting to break from its three decade old mold of catering to only the mentally ill and starting to include in its purview the relevance of indigenous theories, socially embedded contexts, qualitative inquiry, and usage of both inductive and deductive methods in the analysis of social problems. The aim was to restore optimum functioning and health to the afflicted person and empower the unafflicted by raising their awareness and sensitizing them to issues that may undermine their well-being. The implication is that enhanced awareness of needs will motivate a community to participate in decision-making processes that will ultimately improve their lot by necessitating collective action. Henceforth, community work is seen not only as treatment of the mentally ill but also includes the participation of the community in facilitating their own growth based on a realization of their potential and creation and utilization of relevant resources that are required for optimization of mental health.

Conceptualization of Health: Indian Perspective

It is pertinent to look at the question of operationalizing mental health by community psychologists so as to have a uniform perspective in approaching this concept. Health systems and practices in all societies are based on certain shared beliefs about the world, self and human existence. These cultural beliefs provide the necessary framework for defining health, understanding the causes of illness, and deciding the modes of treatment. In the Indian cultural tradition, no sharp boundaries are drawn between individuals and the environment they live in (Pandey, 2001). A healthy individual is one who has a harmonious relationship with the community, surroundings, and the supernatural world. *Health, in this sense, is considered to be integral to the general well-being of the person, where no clear-cut distinction is made between physical, mental, and spiritual health* (Paranjpe, 1984). Thus, to obtain an understanding of the causes of an illness, attention should be focused on the subjective experiences of the individual, as well as on the conditions of the external world. Based on variant causal beliefs about illness, a wide array of treatment options were developed in India over time, ranging from the highly professional Ayurvedic practitioner to the local shaman as part of the healing tradition. These health care providers offer not only different modes of treatment but also different ways of understanding the illness. As these traditional health practitioners have continued to be the primary source of information for many people, they help structure these people's beliefs about health and diseases. The commonsense beliefs influence health practices, in terms of diet, hygiene, preventive measures, and treatment choices.

The theoretical roots of a psychology that is based on understanding stress and well-being can be traced to ancient Indian scriptures where the Indian conceptualization of ill health and well-being are understood at different levels of an individual's mental, physical, and spiritual life with forces from the environment interacting with the individual to produce good or ill health. Conversely, Western methods tend to be anchored exclusively on one aspect or another in a simplistic fashion in search of scientific respectability. The Eastern holistic approach requires far more complex ways of evaluation (Balodhi, 1991). Sinha (1990) noted that the Indian conceptualization of health is broad based and affirmative. He quoted Sushrat, the ancient proponent of the traditional system of medicine and surgery, who defined health as 'prasannanmendriyamanah swastha,' that is, a state of delight, or a feeling of spiritual, physical, and mental well-being. The essential features of a healthy person are possessing in right quantities of (sama) the defects or weaknesses (samadosah), digestive quality (samaagni), semen (samadhatu), and normal bodily functions (malakriya). In this sense, health of both men and women is perceived as total well-being and feeling of happiness. Meditation and exercise through yoga are described as two significant pathways to wellness! This definition is similar to the WHO definition, which views health as a state of complete physical, mental, and social well-being and is not merely the absence of disease or infirmity.

Also prevalent in India are the belief systems based on 'karma,' one's work and duty towards the social world. This theory states that good and bad deeds accumulate over previous lives, and if a person is suffering, he or she must have done some bad deeds in this or previous lives. As most of the diseases were believed to be due to sins, crimes, and nonobservance of natural and religious laws, the cure prescribed was to appease the gods with prayers, vows, holy baths, and sacrifices. Tripathi (1993) concluded from an empirical study of the meaning of health and sickness in the rural areas that the meaning was commonly shared by the respondents who were from different demographic backgrounds. Omprakash (1989) posited that belief in the theory of karma has many psychological consequences, including an uncritical acceptance of misery and inequality and hope for a better future through "right" actions. This theory is the most potent explanatory model for a large number of physical and mental diseases in India. Joshi (1988) demonstrated in a study in the central Himalayas that the ill and their families made a clear distinction between 'bis,' a primary, supernatural, and actual cause, and 'bimari,' a secondary physical effect for which one sought medical treatment. Thus, they discussed their emotional problems with faith healers to get rid of the primary cause of the illness. They consulted the medical doctor only when they sought treatment for physical symptoms. Temple healers, shamans, yoga practitioners, folk doctors, and ojhas are not only a part of the pluralistic health care system but also of the psychosocial support system.

Given these traditional and deep rooted beliefs of 'karma' in a majority of people, the desire to intervene and provide solutions for problems that cause poor quality of life is the initiative of government agencies or social workers. For instance, there is strong resistance by many communities for immunization, birth control, and education of the girl child. Needless to say, these factors contribute to higher incidence of illness and mortality, increasing population, and few opportunities for women to have productive employment. The approach undertaken by practitioners to bring about change is through contacting intermediaries, such as the village elders, known as 'Panchayat.' Panchayats comprise roughly five (panch) male members of a village community who are selected by its members to resolve disputes. Decisions taken by a Panchayat are final and have nothing to do with legal or judiciary issues at the national level. Any interaction with a community will be most meaningful when routed through the Panchayat. For example, to attain immunization or educational goals, the justification must be presented to the elders of the community. People of the community will be open to change when the rationale for a program is presented to them by the Panchayat. Therefore, to target a change in behavior, which implies shedding of an age old belief system, community work needs to be started at a meso-level (community representatives) and gradually widen to the macro-level (residents of a community).

Goals of Community Psychology

To be viable, CP has to understand the social realities and belief systems of our country. It needs to work in partnership with existing mental health programs to ensure application of mental health knowledge, promote community participation, and to encourage self-help. The work done in community-based settings have so far been within the domain of social work departments of academia as well as the government. There is not much attempt in the literature of any discipline to integrate the findings of policymakers, NGOs, and social workers.

To overcome this shortcoming, the Community Psychology Association of India (CPAI) was established in 1987 at Lucknow University with the aim to serve the communities by using CP-based values. The objective of the association is to bring together professionals for meaningful interchange and document their work. The members are academicians and researchers from varied fields such as psychology, sociology and social work. Because CP is not taught as an independent subject at the undergraduate level of psychology course, students who work at the doctoral level in the area of community development are more likely to seek affiliation to CPAI. Students at the undergraduate and postgraduate level are familiar with the concept of community mental health and community development, which are discussed as a part of curriculum of clinical psychology. However, the theories taught are based on Western thought and an inclusion of field-based work is largely insulated from any linkages with theoretical principles underlying CP.

CP Publications

The *Indian Journal of Community Psychology*, which started in 2004 with S. N. Dubey as the editor, is a serious effort in coordinating and presenting research from a multidimensional perspective. The journal seeks to publish articles related to community problems, theory, research, and practice. Articles that advance our understanding of community problems, community mental health, and intervention technique stimulating debate and discussion are encouraged. Dubey reiterates in the inaugural issue that psychology is one of the most practical disciplines and one that needs to dispel the lay notion in the common man's mind that it is a discipline of insane people. The focus of CP is not only on mental health but also on a community's identification of needs and empowerment through participatory research. He emphasizes the need to practice psychology beyond the closed walls of laboratories. Because CP is a public enterprise, one must communicate with the public. To be effective, psychologists must adopt scientific methodology in its structure, strategies, and planning so that psychology in India can become more effective and productive. Dubey (2004) appeals to psychologists in India to keep in mind that it is imperative that one makes efforts to develop theories and principles relevant to the Indian culture and society. Some examples of titles of articles published in the recent edition of the journal are 'Health competence and capacity building,' 'Consequences of socio-cultural deprivation on mental health of Indian adolescents,' and 'Life stress and social support.'

Methodological Issues

According to Nagpal (2004), qualitative experimentalism in CP is required. This takes an individual's lived experience as the beginning and end points of the researcher's inquiries. Because self-realization is the goal of human life, our psychological life needs profound and deep study for the enfoldment of our consciousness. Nagpal stresses the need for holistic methodological approaches so as to revive ancient wisdom of the Indian culture along with knowledge. Thus, CP's formalization as an organization should help integrate the ongoing mental health services as envisioned by the National Mental Health Program (NMHP; 1982) with principles of psychological theory. This program proposes to use the primary health care structure to provide basic mental health services. This means that at least at the grassroots level of health care, mental health will be totally integrated into the general health care delivery system. The close cooperation of mental health professionals with other providers of care is thus imperative. In fact, it is hoped that mental health consciousness will become an integral part of all health and welfare endeavors in India. A strong linkage of the program should be with social welfare and education sectors. The status of mental health efforts by government policies must be evaluated before articulating and implementing the goals of mental health promotion (Singh, 2004). Psychological studies to augment community participation need innovative methodologies. This movement focuses on the need for a method that provides the people of a community with a voice. Sharma, Burdhan, and Dube (1987) suggested methodologies for participatory and action research to understand the community's perspective and to promote self-reliance.

Licensing

Finally, there is no statutory body in India that regulates the standards of competence that govern practice. The question of monitoring, evaluating, and accrediting training programs requires conclusive attention. These programs may equip successful candidates to provide services at different levels of functioning in a country as large as India and with a dearth of trained professionals (Aggarwal, 2004). However, The Rehabilitation Council of India has a prescribed code of conduct and also has the power to inspect, evaluate, and accredit training programs in the nation's interest. There is a need to focus on mental health aspects of the community with special focus on rehabilitation psychology, health psychology, community psychology, and counseling psychology rather than focus only on clinical psychology. This is because prevention of illness and enhancement of health requires a more multidisciplinary approach based on awareness of issues, belief systems, relevant therapies, and a qualitative method to assess experiences of people.

Conclusions

The emergence of CP in India is seen as the need felt by a certain segment of psychologists to apply the principles of psychology to resolve community problems. The main interest of community psychologists is in a more 'practical' and utility-oriented research paradigm (Asthana, 2004). According to the editor of the *Indian Journal of Community Psychology*, S. N. Dubey, community psychology is an upcoming branch that stands between clinical and social psychology. The publication of utility research was the catalyst for the publication of the journal, and the editors note that it took their efforts 17 years for the first issue to materialize! Efforts that were directed towards molding psychologists with a clinical and social orientation to look again at their fields with a greater applied focus. The collection of funds to initiate a formal association (Community Psychology Association of India) has been recorded as a challenge by the founding members. The journal is composed of members from countries such as Iran, United Kingdom, Japan, and Sharjah. The editors reiterate that unless psychologists engage in useful research, the basis for a CP, the discipline of psychology will remain largely theoretical. According to Dubey, "Psychologists should not hesitate to face the people and their issues. Rather than only producing students and teachers of psychology by training them in theory, there should be a focus on training students of psychology as practitioners. Unlike students from other disciplines, such as medicine and engineering, who can practice their profession after five years of study, psychology students are not skilled in applying the principles to real settings after completion of graduate studies" (Dubey, 2004).

CP is a young discipline in India. It is indeed difficult at this initial stage to provide a comprehensive review of the literature or a review of the principles of community that are put to practice. The chronological events in the development of psychology in India are given in the chapter to develop an insight into the discipline and to think critically about whether the processes are taking us towards our goal; that is, the goal to help people solve their problems and to improve their quality of life. Even though CP in India is in its infancy, it may be emphasized that there is a strong need for a deeper and continued interest in the field so as to make psychology applicable to a wider diversity of people as well as a wider variety of settings and issues. The varied problems in India such as poverty, deprivation, caste and class discrimination, population growth, illiteracy, disease, and lack of infrastructure need solutions that cannot be arrived at from a psychology of the individual. Theories based on collective groups must be tested and interventions designed. It is believed that one must continue with the new directions and challenges as defined by the community psychologists so as to guide prevention, treatment, and policy in an era of rapid socioeconomic and technological changes.

There are several things community psychology needs to do to develop legitimacy in India. First, theories in psychology, yet underdeveloped in the Indian context, suggest ways of understanding situations/behaviors even if their proponents do not point specifically or directly to forms of practice. Choices about how to intervene still need to be articulated by the Indian community psychologist. Second, because community-based practice is largely followed by the departments of social work and NGOs, community psychologists can coordinate their activities with the aim of helping people and promote positive social change. The purpose for sharing psychology is based on the belief that psychological expertise resides principally among the people of a community themselves and among the social workers who have helping roles within the community but have little training in psychology. This view of CP differentiates it from other branches of psychology, which take a more patronizing view. Activities such as prevention and consultation should be accorded a high priority. In a country as diverse as India in terms of religion, caste, class, socioeconomic status, and education level, community mental health cannot be equated with community psychology. CP must deal with organizational systems and the difficulty of changing them. As depicted in the chapter, psychology in India has largely followed a clinical orientation with holding individual treatment as a method of choice for change. The emergence of applied social psychology, which has emphasized the culture as context in studying behavior, has not focused on social change or participation as its aim. It uses the context to describe and explain behaviors but leaves the issue unresolved as to whether the context needs to be modified to promote well-being in its people. Also, the branch does not delineate the need of a practitioner or a social change activist. The community psychologist seems to be a natural choice to expand on the paradigm set by social psychologists and implement change.

Substantial amounts of research conducted by departments of social work have been documented in the *Indian Journal of Social Work* and journals published by the Tata Institute of Social Science Research. The discipline of social work is offered at the graduate level in Indian universities with a view to impart training to students to develop skills in community-based practice. This is not a part of psychology curriculum. Hence, a modified academic curriculum is a requisite for students of psychology, who are currently not offered training in community-based principles, so that they can identify issues of significance for a 'specific' community, examine the underlying assumptions, and relate them to theory. Finally, the students should be allowed to design interventions and apply them in real-life settings. Evaluation research should then follow to conclude the initial goal of study; that is, to determine whether the desired behavior occurred, changed or was modified. Hypotheses must be picked from real-life settings, with people from the setting defining their needs and practitioners working as facilitators in helping people meet their needs. This can be attained by university departments of psychology working with a local community to develop new theories and effective style of practice that then support this work.

The underlying assumption is that people have the resources to realize their potential; what they require are conditions under which to fulfill their needs.

The goal should be empowerment of the community through participation and action research. CP is expected to take the form of a multidisciplinary subject linking psychology with community mental health, health promotion, organizational change, and community development. A 'hands on' (practice-based) approach to psychology is expected to help attain the goals of CP and make the field of psychology more meaningful and applicable in India.

Compare and Contrast Conclusion

Development of CP in India finds many commonalities with the development of CP in countries included in this book. The roots of CP are universally seen in the fields of social and clinical psychology. The 1970s and 1980s have been dominated by the field of clinical psychiatry with an emphasis on custodial care of the mentally ill. It was only in the late-1980s and 1990s that the term *mental health* found a place in psychology, with CP paving the way for action-based research and participatory methods to evaluate and improve the mental health of people. In contrast with India, an explosion is seen in the West of interest in programs of community development and social change. Prevention of illness and social problems has become the mainstay of CP worldwide, and there are encouraging reports of integrated research with multidisciplinary fields to have greater impact on communities seeking change. Meanwhile in India, there is an ongoing struggle by psychologists to establish an indigenous psychology that uses its own tools and theories for understanding its people. Few students of psychology are taught community-based practice, unlike in the universities of the Americas and Australia. Fewer are exposed to the myriad complexities of a pluralist culture of India. Unless this improves, the initiatives of the CP association may remain slow to be implemented for want of culturally sensitive members and practitioners! Countries such as Canada, Australia, and those in Latin America have attempted to integrate their indigenous people successfully by acknowledging their unique lifestyle. Indian CP faces the challenge of learning to understand a new language and culture every few hundred miles in the same country if a program needs to be implemented. Those who have access to higher education are an urban minority and insulated from the traditions and thoughts of the vast rural and illiterate majority. Thus, there remains a gap between people who have the knowledge of their native culture and those who are professionally trained to help resolve problems. This slows the development of a coherent and comprehensive CP that can be universally represented as 'Indian.' On the brighter side, because CP is about improving availability of resources, solving problems, and in effect an empowerment of a community, it is a universal theme that has a utility to people who may belong to any culture. Given the hugely large population of India, and a limitation of available resources, 'prevention' should become the core theme of CP here, and a greater number of programs can develop strategies for prevention and promotion of mental health. The research outlined in all the other chapters in this book indicates that though the degree of work done by professionals in the field of CP may vary, the message we get is that by making concerted efforts, CP can significantly contribute to national development by utilizing the principles of 'prevention' and 'empowerment.'

References

Aggarwal, S.P. (2004). *Mental Health: An Indian Perspective-1946-2003.* Directorate General of Health Services, Ministry of Health and Family Welfare: New Delhi.

Asthana, H.S. (2004). Community psychology: Issues, relevance and directions. *Indian Journal of Community Psychology, 1(1),* 1-10.

Balodhi, J.P. (1991). The psychological significance of Hindu myths. *The Vedic Path, 54,* 74-80.

Bhore, J. (1946). *Health Survey and Planning Committee.* New Delhi: Government of India.

Census of India (2001). *Provisional Population Totals: India.* New Delhi: Office of Registrar General.

Dubey, S.N. (2004). Editorial. *Indian Journal of Community Psychology, 1(1),* 1-3.

Dubey, A.K. & Tyagi, A. (1996). Involvement of community in rural development: Experience in SAARC countries. *Indian Journal of Social Work, 57(3),* 429-441.

Government of India (2000). *National Population Policy (NPP).* MoHFW, Department of Family Welfare, Nirman Bhavan, New Delhi.

Govinda, R. & Diwan, R. (2003). *Community participation and empowerment in primary education.* New Delhi: Sage Publications.

Joshi, P.C. (1988). Traditional medical system in the Central Himalayas. *The Eastern Anthroplogist, 41,* 77-83.

Misra, G. (1990). *Applied Social Psychology in India.* New Delhi: Sage Publications.

Misra, G. & Tripathi, L.B. (1980). *Psychological consequences of prolonged deprivation.* Agra: National Psychological Corporation.

Murthy, R.S. (2000). Disaster and mental health: Responses of mental health professionals. *Indian Journal of Social Work, 61(4),* 675-692.

Murthy, S., Isaac, M.K., Chandrashekhar, C.R. & Bhide, A.V. (1987). *Bhopal disaster manual of mental health care for medical officers.* Bangalore: ICMR Centre for Advanced Research in Community Mental Health, NIMHANS.

Nag, M. (2002). Empowering female sex workers for AIDS prevention and far beyond: Sonagachi shows the way. *Indian Journal of Social Work, 63(3),* 473-501.

Nagpal, S. (2004). Editorial. *Indian Journal of Community Psychology, 1(1),* i-iii.

NHRC, Government of India (1999). *Quality assurance in mental health.* New Delhi: National Human Rights Commission.

Omprakash, S. (1989). The doctrine of karma: Its psychological consequences. *Journal of Community Psychology, 17,* 133-145.

Pachauri, S. (1994). *Reaching India's Poor: Non-Governmental approaches to Community Health.* New Delhi: Sage publications.

Pandey, J. (Ed.). (2001). *Psychology in India: The state-of-the-art* (Vol. 2). New Delhi: Sage.

Pandey, J. (Ed.). (1988). *Psychology in India: The state-of-the-art* (Vol. 2 & 3). New Delhi: Sage.

Paranjpe, A.C. (1984). *Theoretical psychology: Meeting of east and west*. New York: Plenum Press.

Pareek, U. (1981). *A survey of research in psychology, 1971-76, Part 2*. Bombay: Popular Prakashan.

Sagar, V. (1971). *Innovations in Psychiatric Treatment at Amritsar Hospital - Report on a seminar on the Organization and Future Needs of Mental Health Services*. New Delhi: World Health House.

Sharma, B.B.L., Burdhan, A. & Dube, D.C. (1987). People's participation in health care. *Social Change, 17*, 34-52.

Siddiqui, H.Y. (1997). *Working with communities: An introduction to community work*. New Delhi: Hira Publications.

Singh, A.K. (1981). Development of religious identity and prejudice in Indian children. In D. Sinha (Ed.), *Socialization of the Indian child*. New Delhi: Concept, 17-25.

Singh, S. (1998). Social work project with women in a rural community. *The Indian Journal of Social Work, 59(4)*, 1032-1051.

Singh, S. (2004). Community Mental Health in India: A WHO Perspective. *Indian Journal of Community Psychology, 1(1)*, 46-62.

Sinha, D. (1986). *Psychology in a third world country: The Indian experience*. New Delhi: Sage.

Sinha, J.B.P. (1988). Developing psychology as a policy science: prospects and problems. Paper presented at the Symposium on Psychology, National Development and Social Policy, Allahabad University, Allahabad.

Sinha, D. (1990). Concept of psycho-social well-being: Western and Indian perspectives. *NIMHANS Journal, 8*, 1-11.

Srikala, B., Chandrashekhar, C.R., Kishore Kumar, K.V., Choudhury, P., Parthasarthy, R., Girimaji, S., Sekar, K. & Srinivasa, M.R. (2000). *Psychosocial care for individuals after the Orissa super cyclone*. Bangalore: Books for Change.

Tripathi, R. (1993). *Psychosocial factors in health behavior*. Doctoral dissertation, University of Allahabad, Allahabad.

9
Community Psychology in a Borrowed Place with Borrowed Time: The Case of Hong Kong

SHEUNG-TAK CHENG AND WINNIE W.S. MAK

Abstract

The development of community psychology takes on a unique, nontraditional course in Hong Kong. Rather than being an organized field, community psychology remains to be practiced in an idiosyncratic manner by a few psychologists who are trained with a community orientation. Concepts such as sense of community, empowerment, mutual help, and prevention take on different meanings and forms within a mobile population in a densely packed society that values economic stability over social progression. Due to a lack of infrastructure and funding resources, services to disadvantaged individuals (e.g., individuals in poverty, with chronic illnesses, socially marginalized groups) are limited by international standards. It is argued that community psychology has a long way to go in contributing to community and social development in Hong Kong. Conceptualization, research, and implementation of community psychology must be done in a culturally sensitive way to imprint a lasting effect on the changing society. Using examples from community mental health and other social developments, this chapter analyzes the sociocultural backgrounds upon which community psychology must be built and discusses the challenges that lie ahead for the continued development of community psychology in Hong Kong.

It is difficult to write about the history of a "field" when there was no event(s) that marked the birth of the field. Hong Kong has neither a program nor a professional body associated with community psychology (CP). The senior author teaches the only undergraduate course that is focused entirely on CP (there used to be a course at the Chinese University of Hong Kong from which he obtained his enlightenment years ago). By necessity or by choice, concepts in CP are covered together with health psychology in a single course at the only two master's level clinical psychology programs. Hence, although graduates of such programs have heard of CP, or some fragmented ideas of it, they are not meant to think in "community" ways. Thus, CP develops in sort of an ad hoc and sometimes unintentional fashion, most typically in the work of specific individuals/groups that seized the opportunity to do something for the community, part of which can be proactively or retrospectively framed in CP terms. For the large part, CP is understood as community mental health, perhaps also prevention, by most psychologists here. Nonetheless, ideas of social justice, empowerment, human diversity, wellness promotion, community building (e.g., sense of community, mutual help, volunteering), and ecology are rooted in the minds of a few psychologists trained with a community orientation in the United States. This being the case, the perspectives of CP are far from being integrated into the mainstream in practice and research (especially the spirit of collaborative inquiry; cf. Cheng & Chan, 2003; Cheng, Chan, & Phillips, 2004). In this chapter, we try to highlight the idiosyncratic development of CP in Hong Kong by (1) laying out the sociopolitical and cultural contexts that shape the community, (2) introducing the background of community mental health, (3) covering briefly other developments in CP, and (4) discussing the future directions of CP.[1]

Sense of Community from a Historical Perspective

Hong Kong had been a British colony for more than 150 years prior to the handover of sovereignty to the People's Republic of China on July 1, 1997. As a time-limited polity, Hong Kong has been frequently referred to as a "borrowed place, borrowed time." Within this 1,102 km^2 of land, the population was very mobile. Before World War II, Hong Kong was a trade port where many came to make a living and then returned to their homeland in Mainland China. It was after World War II and the establishment of the Communist government in China in 1949 that its population experienced a sharp increase with exodus of refugees from China and a postwar baby-boom. At that time, many families lived in self-erected temporary structures in hazardous and dilapidated conditions. On the Christmas Eve of 1953, a fire broke out in one of the squat areas at Shek Kip Mei, a place near the now City University campus, which left 53,000

---

[1] It should be emphasized that given our linkage with Mainland China, Hong Kong is by no means the only geopolitical entity in which community psychologists based in Hong Kong practice. For example, the senior author used to belong to the Nurturing the Young Association, which aims at improving educational opportunities for children in poverty by rebuilding schools in rural China. Another psychologist, Fanny Cheung, has been a delegate to the National Congress of Women of the All-China Women's Federation. Through her work, the Standing Committee of the National People's Congress is considering legislating against sexual harassment in China. Nonetheless, this chapter will focus on CP in Hong Kong.

people homeless and a staggering death toll. A year later, as many as 100,000 people, or 5% of the urban population, were left homeless due to a series of squat fires.

In reaction to these disasters, the government started to build low-cost public housing. The estates were built to house some 2,200 persons on just 1 acre of land, with hundreds of families in just one *block* (a term actually meaning a building here), or more than 60 families (roughly 400 persons) on just one *floor*. Families considered themselves as lucky to be chosen to live in these resettlement estates, where the entire family was squeezed into a compact unit with a standard provision of 2.2 m² of space per person and communal toilets. By 1972, the largest estate had 29 blocks housing 67,000 people—the size of a town in many countries. Living in such spatially constrained residences might change the meaning of privacy and crowdedness among Hong Kong people and impact their patterns of social interactions and well-being in ways that might be different from other regions of the world (Chan, 1999).

Despite such resettlement housing development, the number of squatters doubled from 300,000 (or ~13% of the population) in 1953 to 600,000 (17% of the population) in 1964 and remained at 477,000 (9% of the population) by 1985. By the early 2000s, the size of the squatter population dropped substantially due to housing programs, but some 20,000 squatters continued to exist in central urban areas and another 200,000 in the rural or less urban areas in the New Territories (totaling 3% of the population; see Census and Statistics Department, 2002; Lim & Nutt, 2003; Yeung, 2003). Since the 1970s, more spacious and better equipped public housing estates were built, and land development has spread to the New Territories (then rural areas, now suburbs). Eventually, many families were relocated over the years to the newly developed towns in the New Territories and were removed from the community they were once used to, if not attached to. One wonders what sense of community meant to such a mobile and dense population. Yet empirical research on this issue was lacking.

When Britain and China signed the Joint Declaration in 1984 to return Hong Kong to China in 13 years' time, waves of emigration and different forms of migratory style flourished (Cheng, 1993). Some families chose to have the wife and children stay in a foreign country to fulfill the residency requirement while the husband kept working in Hong Kong to support the family (a phenomenon nicknamed "astronauts," meaning "wife absent"), others moved together but returned to Hong Kong upon obtaining citizenship, and still others uprooted themselves only to find their adult children returning to Hong Kong looking for job opportunities after finishing their education. After the handover in 1997, the Hong Kong government was given 50 years of autonomy. With this special arrangement expiring in 2047, Hong Kong people are reminded of how transient their lives and their communities are, on this borrowed place with borrowed time. Once again, how sense of belonging and attachment develops in such a changing society is another empirical question that awaits to be answered.[2]

The time-limited colonial sovereignty saw little sense to commit to welfare development for the constant influx of refugees and immigrants. It had therefore favored a small government and a "positive noninterventionist" approach. As a general rule, public spending grew only in proportion to GDP growth, and dependence on the state was to be discouraged. Welfare was fundamentally the responsibility of the individual and his or her family. Social stability was the prime concern of the government, and social policies were generally limited to dealing with issues/crises that had a potential of disrupting the social order or that dovetailed with economic development. Democracy was to be avoided, because public/political pressures would put demand on the government to provide more services and welfare and consequently increase public spending.[3] In a land with little self-supply of food and materials, the economy was highly dependent on foreign investment. To attract foreign investment and to commensurate with the philosophy of a small government, corporate income tax has been set at approximately 16%.

---

[2] The foregoing discussion by no means implies that developing a sense of belonging to the new neighborhood/community is not possible. Moreover, an experimental project by Aberdeen Kaifong Association (a nongovernmental organization) is trying to rebuild the sense of belonging by mobilizing support for disadvantaged groups within an old community. Many young adults have left the public housing estates in which they grew up and moved to private or subsidized housing to improve their living condition, often leaving their parents or grandparents behind. While they often return to visit their seniors, they can be mobilized to provide assistance to those in need in the community—a resource yet to be tapped.

[3] At its extreme, the government sought a legal interpretation of Hong Kong's Basic Law by the Standing Committee of the National People's Congress in Beijing over the right of abode by children born to Hong Kong parents. These are typically cases in which the child was born in China and one of the parents is a Hongkonger (usually the father) and the other is a Mainland Chinese (usually the mother). Prior to 1997 only 150 persons, including spouse and children, can emigrate from China to Hong Kong on a daily basis. Article 24 of Hong Kong's Basic Law, the constitution that took effect on July 1, 1997, says that children born to Hong Kong permanent citizens have the right of abode in Hong Kong. After some legal disputes, Hong Kong's Court of Final Appeal affirmed in early 1999 the right of abode of such children. The government then sought an interpretation of Article 24 of the Basic Law by the National People's Congress Standing Committee in Beijing, which overturned the Court of Final Appeal decision, thus preventing an alleged number of 1.67 million children from reuniting with their parents in Hong Kong. Their coming was thought to overwhelm Hong Kong's expenditure in educational, welfare, and health services. The Standing Committee said that Article 24 was to be implemented together with the 150 quota a day, thus effectively rendering that article invalid. Many are concerned about the loss of judicial autonomy of Hong Kong as a result of this and similar incidents to come. At the same time, we like to note that children born in countries outside of our own motherland, China, are not subject to similar restrictions—an example of value contradictions that permeate our society.

Ruling was mainly in the hands of a small group of elite bureaucrats and business leaders who were regularly appointed to the highest-level policy-making bodies (Chow, 1985; Miners, 1995; Wilding, 1997). Little changed after 1997, and the government's main duty is to maintain order and stability while creating an economic environment for sustaining prosperity.

We are not here to give an overall history of the territory's housing development, nor do we want to give a thorough analysis of the political situation in Hong Kong; both are much beyond the scope of this chapter. Rather, we want to use this brief introduction to illustrate a fundamentally limited time perspective on the part of both the people and the government, and consequently, its effects on government's commitment to social welfare and the shaping of mental health and community services.

Social Welfare in the Hong Kong Communities

The foregoing discussion illustrates the fundamentally conservative political and social climates in Hong Kong, which according to Levine and Levine (1992) is not conducive to seeing human suffering as rooted in structural problems in the society and environmental factors—a basic tenet in CP.

A few examples would suffice to illustrate what this "small government and noninterventionist" philosophy means to the everyday person in need. Because the business sector has been so influential in cutting down on operational costs, one of the things that Hong Kong people have been deprived of until recently is retirement fund contributions (an exception is the government, which provides pension to its employees). Yet, up to this day, an elderly person has to bring children to the Social Welfare Department, who all have to declare their unwillingness or inability to support the parent in order to apply for Comprehensive Social Security Assistance, which provides cash benefits at subsistence levels. This system discourages many elders to apply for public assistance due to family disgrace in the Chinese context of filial piety, keeping them in poverty (Cheng & Chan, 2006). As for medical care, the average waiting time is approximately 3 months for specialist appointments and 9 months for nonemergency surgical operations (Chan & Phillips, 2002). The waiting time for residential care for frail elders in a publicly funded facility is even more ridiculous—almost 3 years! Many die before a vacancy becomes available (Chan & Phillips, 2002; Cheng, 1993; Cheng & Chan, 2003). If anything has changed since 1997, spending has been cut back further due to a budget deficit after the Asian financial crisis and the necessity for redistributing resources into epidemic control and related research after the SARS epidemic in 2003. It is the individual's lot or responsibility if he or she wants anything better than these treatments.

Hong Kong people, however, appear to be quite content with the way they have been governed as long as there is prosperity and stability. Political scientists have attributed this to the Chinese culture of conflict avoidance, apolitical orientation, and submission to authorities (Lau, 1982; Miners, 1995; Wilding, 1997). The Hong Kong society is generally described as a very pragmatic one. Awareness of humanitarian values and human rights has increased, but economic interests often come first. In a classic study on the Hong Kong society (Lau, 1982), it was suggested that the people embraced "utilitarian familism"; that is, the interest of the family was placed above the society and other groups/individuals, with an emphasis on mutual aid within the family. Although utilitarian familism is not specific to the Chinese in Hong Kong, its significance in Hong Kong can be understood from the historical background of Hong Kong people having to survive through war and very harsh conditions.

The crowded living condition has had a two-sided effect on the people. On the one hand, it may enhance interaction and networking among people; on the other, it brings immense stress on a day-to-day basis and serves as a constant reminder of how little social resources are up for competition by the massive number of people. Issues related to urban living are further compounded by outgroup hostility in the formation of community relations. Subgroups based on ethnicities, dialects, ancestral roots, among others, are formed within the community to fight for their ingroup interests, often at the expense of others. Such antagonism towards outgroups and favoritism towards ingroups are particularly pronounced in some villages, where the men of the clan take the lead (Watson & Watson, 2003). Unfortunately, relatively little research has been conducted on the effect of this amalgam of sociocultural values and community relations on people's psychological sense of community and neighborhood in Hong Kong (Forrest, La Grange, & Yip, 2002).

Development of Community Mental Health Services

The prevalence of mental illness in the adult population is generally estimated to be about 10% (World Health Organization, 2001), among which only a small fraction ever seek professional services (Regier et al., 1993). If we use this figure to estimate the scope of mental health problems within the densely packed communities in Hong Kong, a potentially large number of individuals with diagnosable mental disorders may be living within a block without receiving any form of services. Furthermore, the afflicted and their families are likely to experience stigma that prevent them from participating fully in vocational and social spheres.

Similar to the stigma of mental illness observed in other parts of the world (World Health Organization, 2001), substantial stigma has been evident in the Hong Kong general public. Despite public education efforts in the 1980s (e.g., Cheung, 1990), 40% of the respondents in three large-scale telephone surveys conducted in the 1990s did not want to be neighbors of people with mental illness and did not endorse the establishment of rehabilitation facilities in their community (Chou & Mak, 1998; Lau & Cheung, 1999; see also Cheung, 1988, 1990; Tsang, Tam, Chan, & Cheung, 2003). Those with mental illness are likely to be aware of such public sentiment and conceal their status lest they be discriminated against. Besides the afflicted, their close affiliates may be similarly stigmatized. Not only do the family members have to carry the responsibility of taking care of their relatives with mental illness in an unsupportive society (Wong, 2000; Wong, Tsui, Pearson, Chen, & Chiu, 2004), they also need to face the misunderstanding and discrimination that abound in the community. Such compound of multiple stressors may adversely affect their well-being and quality of life.

From the late 19th century to the 1950s, few services were provided to individuals with mental illness. Patients were housed in the one and only psychiatric hospital and were treated with physical restraint or custodial care. It was not until the 1960s that the development of mental health services began to accelerate, with the establishment of the Castle Peak Hospital and four community clinics. The main reason for building these facilities was overcrowding due to the closure of the one and only mental hospital. In the 1970s, more community clinics and psychiatric wards within general hospitals were established. The second mental hospital, Kwai Chung Hospital, was opened 20 years after Castle Peak (crowding eventually became a perennial issue in the two hospitals). Community psychiatric nursing, with the primary responsibility of facilitating patients' return to community living, became available in 1982. Specialty clinics for children were also founded a few years later. Enlightened by services elsewhere, nongovernmental organizations (NGOs), namely the New Life Psychiatric Rehabilitation Association (the forerunner being a mutual aid group of ex-mental patients) and the Mental Health Association of Hong Kong, started to open up halfway houses and other community rehabilitation services in the late 1960s (Lo, 2003).

Psychology played a very minor role in the development of community mental health. By 1984, there were only nine clinical psychologists employed by the then Medical and Health Department, which operated the services (Lo, 2003). The mainstay of mental health care in Hong Kong had taken little advice from the wisdom of community mental health developed elsewhere (Yip, 2000). Although there was a certain degree of parallel between Hong Kong and the United States in terms of crowding in mental hospitals at the start of the 1960s, deinstitutionalization was not an option for Hong Kong due to the lack of community facilities to take care of the patients. Massive discharge of patients would arouse social unrest as the public had not developed an accepting attitude toward persons with mental illness (Yip, 2000). The colonial government, as we have argued, had placed a premium on maintaining the social order in the most efficient and cost-effective way, and so the newer mental health facilities, be they community clinics or hospitals, were meant to provide the most basic forms of care and treatment to the growing number of mentally ill patients secondary to population growth. Moreover, professional orientations were not compatible with the ideologies inherent in the concept of community care (Heller, Jenkins, Steffen, & Swindle, 2000). From a different angle, local psychiatric authorities had not been enthusiastic about deinstitutionalization in light of the downside of the deinstitutionalization movement in the United States (see Levine, 1981).

Let us pause for a moment and read a passage from the government's consultation paper in 1976, a precursor to the first-ever policy on rehabilitation:

In Hong Kong, as in most territories, reliable statistics on the size of the disabled [all disabilities included] population are not available. It is estimated conservatively that the figure is at least 8% of the total population. Unless these people are restored to maximum working capacity and economic independence, the economic and social *waste* [italics added] generated by this large number of people becomes an *intolerable burden* [italics added] on the community and economy as a whole . . .. The disabled, given the treatment, services, opportunities and encouragement that they require, can provide a useful and productive source of manpower. The community must be prepared to lend a helping hand not out of a sense of charity but because it must be the *basic human right* [italics added] of every individual to make his life as useful and satisfying as possible. (Secretary for Social Services, 1976, p. 1)

It should be fair to say that the development of community-based mental health services was, at least initially, driven more by economic than humanitarian reasons or therapeutic effectiveness.

Although the establishment of community psychiatric clinics had made services more accessible to the public, as scholars have well-argued (Prilleltensky, 1997; Sarason, 1972), services of a similar form can vary dramatically in operation and purpose, depending on the supporting values. As mentioned, the motivation for expanding mental health services was to ease the problem of overcrowding in mental hospitals, not a desire to support patients to stay close to their family and the community. Outpatient clinics and halfway houses were welcomed by the government as inexpensive alternatives to hospitalization (Lo, 2003), although support for the effectiveness of community-based psychiatric rehabilitation services was equivocal (Chan, Ungvari, & Leung, 2001; Lai, Li, & So, 1988). Nonetheless, the community-based services provide an alternative practice venue for professionals who might otherwise become dissatisfied with hospital responsibilities (Lam & Ho, 1989).

Scholars have argued that Hong Kong's policies are often developed in an ad hoc fashion, without any guiding philosophies (Chow, 1985; Miners, 1995; Wilding, 1997). This being the case, it should not be surprising to find that the law has not been in favor of protecting the rights of citizens and patients. The Mental Health Ordinance (Chapter 136 of *Laws of Hong Kong*), originally started in 1960, has gone through major revisions in 1988 and in 1996–1997 (Cheung, 2000; Lo, 1990). In our view, the 1996–1997 Mental Health Ordinance amendment has made a significant stride. After years of community discontent, mental handicap (retardation) was finally separated from the legal definition of mental illness, and mentally handicapped persons can no longer be involuntarily admitted to a mental hospital unless the person is abnormally aggressive or seriously irresponsible in conduct. Nonetheless, the comment from a senior official of Castle Peak Hospital was revealing, "for even in the old MHO [1988 Mental Health Ordinance] a mentally handicapped person (MHP) could not be . . . compulsorily detained for longer than 28 days . . . the impact of this new distinction . . . will therefore be extremely minimal. Its real meaning is therefore more political, to apparently appease certain community groups" (Cheung, 2000, p. 4–5). Human rights are human rights, period. To justify the brutal removal of civil rights because it is temporary is another testimony to how so-called community mental health in Hong Kong has developed without the supporting values.

A summary of some of the salient features of the ordinance will illustrate our point. Only recommendation from *one general practitioner* is required for the magistrate or district judge to commit a person to a mental hospital for 7 days (prior to 1988, such a medical certificate was required *only* if the detention period was more than 7 days). Detention beyond the seventh day and up to 28 days can be made with the recommendations of two medical doctors, at least *one* being a psychiatrist. Detention beyond the 28th day can be made on the ground of danger to self or others, certified by *one* psychiatrist and one other medical doctor. No hearing is provided *throughout*, although a hearing can be granted on request before the initial detention order is made. Once a person is committed, he or she can only appeal to the Mental Health Review Tribunal formed in 1988, which only meets once every 2–3 months. If the appeal is denied, another one cannot be made within *12 months* of the last unsuccessful appeal.

In what sense does the law serve to prevent patients from the adverse effects of unnecessary hospitalization? In what sense was the law drafted on the spirit that patients should be returned to the community as quickly as possible to minimize disruption to occupation, social life, and status? The possibility that a person can be committed on the opinion of a general practitioner is astounding. Although this might have served a historical purpose when psychiatrists were few in number (Lo, 2003), we can no longer understand its necessity given Hong Kong's development in psychiatric training in the past 20 years.[4] It is therefore no wonder that the average length of stay at the two major psychiatric hospitals is around 6 months long (Hospital Authority, 2004).

Just as hospital treatments are not necessarily set up in a way to enable patients to quickly return to their community, community clinics are not set up in a way to prevent minor problems from deteriorating into major ones. In 2004–2005, the average waiting time was 5 weeks for adult psychiatric outpatient services (that for children's services was even longer, around 6 months), 6 months for halfway houses, and 6.3 years for long-stay care homes

[4] According to the statistics from the Hong Kong College of Psychiatrists, as of January 2004, there are 263 medical doctors with recognized psychiatric qualifications practicing in both public and private sectors in Hong Kong.

(Legislative Council, 2005; Social Welfare Department, 2005). Given the inadequacies of the system, many have turned to self-help groups for mutual support and care.

Self-Help or Mutual Help Groups

Since the 1980s, self-help groups have begun to be organized by professionals in NGOs. With the support from the 1990 Social Welfare White Paper and the 1992 Green Paper on Rehabilitation Policies and Services, its development was further accelerated in the 1990s. Most of these groups were formed by social workers or medical personnel. Psychologists have not played much role in the self-help movement, although there are notable exceptions (e.g., the Women's Centre founded by Cheung (1989) and a mutual help group for parents of preemies founded by the senior author). Whereas self-help groups in Western countries vary substantially in the degree of professional involvement (Shepherd et al., 1999), those in Hong Kong are almost invariably professionally led, operating within the service units of NGOs and financially dependent on them (Mok, 2001). Some even characterize this form of service as "formalized informal care" (Yip, Lee, & Law, 2004). It appears that professional leadership is vital to the survival of self-help groups due to the traditional passivity in Chinese behaviors (Yip, 2004), although empirical data on this issue is lacking.

Recently, a total of 211 self-help groups were identified (Mok, 2001), and a surprising majority are related to medical conditions. Based on the limited number of studies done on self-help groups in Hong Kong, these groups were found to serve the functions of promoting personal well-being and social support, although their utility as a vehicle for advocacy is limited (Cheung, Mok, & Cheung, 2005; Mok, 2001, 2004). Thus, although members felt psychologically empowered with opportunities to understand more about their conditions and to establish social networks, collectively they still have not gained momentum in affecting social policies and in fighting for their needs and rights. However, studies conducted so far have been based on volunteer samples that typically consist of active members within the groups. A more complete picture on the impact of such groups on the average member remains to be investigated.

Given the fact that self-help group development is still in its infancy, there is still a long road towards empowerment, and empowerment in Hong Kong may take on a culturally distinct form. With families being the bedrock of societies, empowerment may start from the families rather than focused on the individual (Yip, 2004). Where possible, self-help groups may incorporate family involvement or form a coalition with families and caregivers in advocating for more resources and communal services. With the Chinese value emphasizing harmony, rather than aiming for radical changes and reform, clients, families, government, and the society may welcome gradual changes and reserved forms of plea. How CP can mix with Chinese ideologies and the social milieu of Hong Kong in addressing community services reform is an interesting issue that needs to be further explored and evaluated.

Prevention

As alluded to before, the limited mental health resources are concentrated on the treatment of the more severe cases, and prevention is rather peripheral in the mental health scene. As a result, the practice of prevention tends to be small-scale and short-lived and typically takes the form of mental health education, crisis hotlines, outreach, and early case finding. The body of established knowledge on prevention (e.g., the need for booster programs; Felner, Felner, & Silverman, 2000) is rarely referred to in the design of such programs. Primary prevention, which often requires challenging social values and norms and developing broad-based societal support (Levine, 1998), is slow to develop in this highly conservative society. Perhaps the nature of primary prevention is antagonistic to the dominant orientation toward efficiency and quick results.

One of the most well-known contributions to secondary prevention by local psychologists was started in 1993 after a stampede in a popular bar and dining area on New Year's Eve. It involves active outreach to primary and secondary victims of disasters and debriefing of posttraumatic stress reactions to reduce the chance that problems develop into clinical proportions (Leung, Wong, Li, Lau-Yu, & Wu, 1993). Another notable example is the recent initiative by the Hospital Authority to prevent elderly suicide through early identification in social service and medical settings and referral to so-called fast-track clinics. A decided shortcoming in the practice of prevention in Hong Kong is the lack of empirical support for their short- and long-term effectiveness, which justifies their importance and propagation in the community.

Advocacy and Social Actions

Besides self-help groups, some NGOs and non-psychology academics (typically social workers and sociologists) have strived to advocate for the needs of marginalized groups, including children and elderly in poverty, homeless people, ethnic minorities, and new immigrants (for examples, see Wong, 2001; Wong & Lee, 2002). Some of them act as social activists, a role that psychologists in Hong Kong are generally uncomfortable with. Although it is not mandatory for community psychologists to be actively involved in all social movements, they need to take up some of the social responsibility in providing sound research data to inform and steer social actions in an interdisciplinary fashion. However, such a collaborative relationship has yet to emerge.

Policy Development

Nowadays, a good number of psychologists would identify themselves as clinicians with a community orientation (i.e., community mental health) but do not see social change as relevant for their professional role. A few individuals who are more identified with the field of CP have, however, sought to influence the larger systems using public policy as a platform. Psychologist Fanny Cheung at the Chinese University of Hong Kong was the founding chairperson of the Equal Opportunities Commission, which has taken the lead in formulating and implementing antidiscriminatory legislation in Hong Kong. She continues to be actively involved in advocating the rights of oppressed groups, in particular women (e.g., Cheung, Karlekar, De Dios, Vichit-Vadakan, & Quisumbing, 1999). She was pivotal in the establishment of the Women's Commission in 2001, which advises the government on policy directions concerning women. The senior author of this chapter (S.-T. Cheng) has advised the government and NGOs on elderly services and policies concerning the regulation of nursing homes (Chan & Cheng, 2005; Cheng & Chan, 2003). His recent appointment to the government's Working Group on Active Aging mentioned his expertise in, specifically, "community psychology." The committee advises the government on ways to promote active and productive aging and to remove social barriers (e.g., ageism) against participation by older people. The citation of CP in his committee appointment is an illustration of the gradual penetration of CP perspectives into government decision-making.

Although the influence is relatively limited in scope, fundamental to the work of Cheung and Cheng is the use of policy to address problems in the larger society that affect the individual, and this is an important counterforce to the prevailing social norm of blaming the victim. Besides local policy involvement, linkage with or representation at high-level policy bodies internationally (e.g., Cheng, 2005; Cheng, Chan, & Phillips, in press; Cheung, 1998) can sometimes function as effective leverage in pushing for social change in one's own region. Nevertheless, to engage more local psychologists in policy development, psychologists-in-training need to be taught to think in both "macro" and "micro" ways and to be involved in community efforts to promote social justice and well-being for all. This entails readiness from both the profession and the society at large.

Conclusion and Future Directions

In summary, the influence of CP in the development of social and community programs and in our understanding of social psychological phenomena in Hong Kong has been subtle and amorphous. With the exception of a few individuals, little concerted efforts have been given in incorporating CP principles in research and practice. In recent decades, the development of professional psychology and rehabilitation services in Hong Kong has grown. One way for psychologists to participate more actively in community change is to collaborate with action-oriented social scientists. More importantly, the society needs to change its entrenched way of thinking about human problems, and it will need a lot more pressure before doing so.

We believe that the aging population will present such an opportunity, because the society (not just Hong Kong) will have to cater to the needs of a rapidly increasing elderly (and caregiver) population with proportionally fewer resources. Hence, concepts like prevention, wellness promotion, productive aging, mutual help, and even social change are increasingly being discussed among professionals and policymakers (Chan & Cheng, 2005; Cheng, 2005). CP has a lot to contribute to the conceptualization, research, and implementation of these ideas in the aging world. Hopefully it will not be too long before CP is more widely recognized and its wisdom more broadly diffused into different sectors of the society.

Having discussed the sociopolitical climate and the prevailing community issues that may influence the development of CP in Hong Kong, we take a moment to compare CP in Hong Kong with that existing in various countries around the world. As it is evident in the aforementioned sections, the development of CP is still at a nascent stage that is struggling with a range of training, research, and practice issues. Its growth and development in Hong Kong suffered on several fronts. Unlike other regions (i.e., Canada, Italy, Latin America, United States) where CP was developed as an extension of the social movements that had been going on and later served as an active component in social change, community psychology never picks up speed locally due to the lack of massive consciousness in social issues (i.e., contextualism, diversity, social oppression, minority rights) and the overshadowing of social justice by interests towards economic growth. Given its priority on social stability and economic prosperity, the society is not ripe to appreciate and embrace CP values that focus on prevention of human suffering, the reduction of oppression, and the promotion of individual, relational, and societal well-being.

Not only is the zeitgeist not conducive to the development of CP, as an academic discipline, it lacks the organization and visibility that is enjoyed by related disciplines such as clinical psychology and social work. Lagging behind other regions (e.g., Australia, Britain, Canada, Japan, Italy, New Zealand, United States), where CP is professionally organized with its own training programs, professional identity, research outlets, and a body of scholars, CP does not have a distinct footing in Hong Kong in terms of training and professional organization. Its situation is quite akin to that discussed by Bergold and Seckinger for Germany. Not only is there a lack of training programs in CP and the lack of awareness of CP among psychology students, the identity of CP is also eroding as a result of the adoption of CP concepts (e.g., empowerment, prevention, mutual aid) by social work and public health. This dwindling of influence in psychology and the society at large is also lamented by authors of many other regions. Combined with the increasing competition for resources among various psychology subfields and blending of related CP concepts by neighboring disciplines, CP across the globe is battling with the issue of academic survival and the revival of psychology students' interest. Although interdisciplinary collaboration and contribution to community projects and research are certainly a practice that we support and believe can best serve the communities, many CP researchers and scholars share the concern that CP may not be recognized and its values may not be upheld down the road.

As long as CP is considered a subfield of psychology, and as long as psychology does not mingle well with other social science disciplines concerned with the broader social context of human suffering, the degree to which CP can thrive as an intellectual and professional discipline will continue to be limited. Countries where CP has thrived well have invariably a vision for psychology that is closely tied to entrenched social issues (e.g., Australia, New Zealand, Italy, Latin America, United States). When that vision is tainted, the status of CP also declines. Hence much of CP's future in Hong Kong depends also on the role defined for psychology, our mother discipline, in academia and the society at large. This will depend on our persistent efforts in generating knowledge relevant for addressing social problems and in changing society's image of what psychology can offer within the broader context of the social sciences. With globalization and internationalization, the time is ripe to learn from each other about the challenges that are shared by CP across the world. Through cross-cultural collaboration and local adaptation, scholars and practitioners of CP can ally together to propagate CP values through innovative and culturally sensitive means and to overcome professional and practical challenges that the discipline is facing in the 21st century.

References

Census and Statistics Department. (2002). *Hong Kong 2001 population census main report, Vols. I & II*. Hong Kong: Author.

Chan, Y. K. (1999). Density, crowding, and factors intervening in their relationship: Evidence from a hyper-dense metropolis. *Social Indicators Research, 48*, 103-124.

Chan, A. C. M., & Cheng, S.-T. (2005). *Impacts of an ageing population on government policies*. Report submitted to Central Policy Unit, Hong Kong SAR Government.

Chan, A. C. M., & Phillips, D. R. (2002). Policies in ageing and long-term care in Hong Kong. In D. R. Phillips & A. C. M. Chan (Eds.), *Ageing and long-term care: National policies in the Asia-Pacific*. Singapore: Institute of Southeast Asian Studies.

Chan, G. W. L., Ungvari, G. S., & Leung, J. P. (2001). Residential services for psychiatric patients in Hong Kong. *Hong Kong Journal of Psychiatry, 11*, 13-17.

Cheng, S.-T. (1993). The social context of Hong Kong's booming elderly home industry. *American Journal of Community Psychology, 21*, 449-467.

Cheng, S.-T. (2005). *A proposal for a worldwide age integration index*. Invited address to Expert Group Meeting of the Division of Emerging Social Issues, United

Nations Economic and Social Commission for Asian and the Pacific, March 24-25, Bangkok, Thailand.

Cheng, S.-T., & Chan, A. C. M. (2003). Regulating quality of care in nursing homes in Hong Kong: A social-ecological analysis. *Law & Policy, 25*, 403-423.

Cheng, S.-T., & Chan, A. C. M. (2006). Filial piety and psychological well-being in well older Chinese. *Journal of Gerontology: Psychological Sciences, 61B*, P262-P269.

Cheng, S.-T., Chan, A. C. M., & Phillips, D. R. (2004). Quality of life in old age: An investigation of well older persons in Hong Kong. *Journal of Community Psychology, 32*, 309-326.

Cheng, S.-T., Chan, A. C. M., & Phillips, D. R. (in press). Ageing situation in Asia and the Pacific: Trends and priorities. In United Nations, *World Ageing Situation Report 2007*. New York: Author.

Cheung, F. M. (1988). Surveys of community attitudes toward mental health facilities: Reflections or provocations? *American Journal of Community Psychology, 16*, 877-882.

Cheung, F. M. (1989). The Women's Center: A community approach to feminism in Hong Kong. *American Journal of Community Psychology, 17*, 99-107.

Cheung, F. M. (1990). People against the mentally ill: Community opposition to residential treatment facilities. *Community Mental Health Journal, 26*, 205-212.

Cheung, F. M. (1998). *Implementing the CEDAW Convention: The need for a central mechanism in Hong Kong*. Paper presented to a seminar organized by the Centre for Comparative and Public Law and the Women's Studies Research Centre, University of Hong Kong, November 28, 1998, Hong Kong.

Cheung, F. M., Karlekar, M., De Dios, A., Vichit-Vadakan, J., & Quisumbing, L. R. (Eds.). (1999). *Breaking the silence: Violence against women in Asian*. Hong Kong: Equal Opportunities Commission.

Cheung, H. K. (2000). The new Mental Health Ordinance 1996 to 1997 – A reference guide for physicians and mental health workers. *Hong Kong Journal of Psychiatry, 10*, 3-13.

Cheung, Y. W., Mok, B. H., & Cheung, T. S. (2005). Personal empowerment and life satisfaction among self-help group members in Hong Kong. *Small Group Research, 36*, 354-377.

Chou, K. L., & Mak, K. Y. (1998). Attitudes to mental patients in Hong Kong Chinese: A trend study over two years. *International Journal of Social Psychiatry, 44*, 215-224.

Chow, N. (1985). Welfare development in Hong Kong: The politics of social choice. In Y. C. Jao et al. (Eds.), *Hong Kong and 1997: Strategies for the future*. Hong Kong: Centre for Asian Studies, University of Hong Kong.

Felner, R. D., Felner, T. Y., & Silverman, M. M. (2000). Prevention in mental health and social intervention: Conceptual and methodological issues in the evolution of the science and practice of prevention. In J. Rappaport & E. Seidman (Eds.), *Handbook of community psychology* (pp. 9-42). New York: Kluwer.

Forrest, R., La Grange, A., & Yip, N. M. (2002). Neighbourhood in a high rise, high density city: Some observations on contemporary Hong Kong. *Sociological Review, 50*, 215-240.

Heller, K., Jenkins, R. A., Steffen, A. M., & Swindle, R. W. (2000). Prospects for a viable community mental health system: Reconciling ideology, professional traditions, and political reality. In J. Rappaport & E. Seidman (Eds.), *Handbook of community psychology* (pp. 445-470). New York: Kluwer.

Hospital Authority. (2004). *Hospital Authority statistical report 2002-2003*. Hong Kong: Author.

Lai, B., Li, E. W. F., & So, A. W. K. (1988). A follow-up study of social adjustment of halfway house residents I: Outcome of social adjustment in one year. *Hong Kong Journal of Mental Health, 17*, 67-73.

Lam, D. J., & Ho, D. Y. F. (1989). Community psychology in Hong Kong: Past, present, and future. *American Journal of Community Psychology, 17*, 83-97.

Lau, J. T. F. & Cheung, C. K. (1999). Discriminatory attitudes to people with intellectual disability or mental health difficulty. *International Social Work, 42*, 431-444.

Lau, S. K. (1982). *Society and politics in Hong Kong*. Hong Kong: Chinese University Press.

Legislative Council (2005). Agenda for May 25, 2005. Available at http://www.legco.gov.hk/yr04-05/english/counmtg/agenda/cmtg0525.htm. Retrieved September 12, 2005.

Leung, E. Y., Wong, C., Li, E. K. W., Lau-Yu, P., & Wu, K. K. (1993). What can clinical psychologists contribute after a disaster? Post-disaster intervention model in the local context. *Bulletin of the Hong Kong Psychological Society, 30/31*: 93-103.

Levine, M. (1981). *The history and politics of community mental health*. New York: Oxford University Press.

Levine, M. (1998). Prevention and community. *American Journal of Community Psychology, 26*, 189-206.

Levine, M., & Levine, A. (1992). *Helping children: A social history*. New York: Oxford University Press.

Lim, B., & Nutt, T. (2003). Planning and locational aspects. In Y. M. Yeung & T. K. Y. Wong (Eds.), *Fifty years of public housing in Hong Kong: A golden jubilee review and appraisal* (pp. 45-62). Hong Kong: Chinese University Press.

Lo, W. H. (1990). Development of legislation for the mentally ill in Hong Kong. *Hong Kong Journal of Mental Health, 19*, 50-53.

Lo, W. H. (2003). A century (1885 to 1985) of development of psychiatric services in Hong Kong – With special reference to personal experience. *Hong Kong Journal of Psychiatry, 13*, 21-29.

Miners, N. (1995). *The government and politics of Hong Kong*. Hong Kong: Oxford University Press.

Mok, B. H. (2001). The effectiveness of self-help groups in a Chinese context. *Social Work with Groups, 24*, 69-89.

Mok, B. H. (2004). Self-help group participation and empowerment in Hong Kong. *Journal of Sociology and Social Welfare, 31*, 153-168.

Prilleltensky, I. (1997). Values, assumptions, and practices: Assessing the moral implications of psychological discourse and action. *American Psychologist, 47*, 517-535.

Regier, D. A., Narrow, W. E., Rae, D. S., Manderscheid, R. W., Locke, B. Z., & Goodwin, F. K. (1993). The de facto U.S. mental and addictive disorders service system: Epidemiologic Catchment Area prospective 1-year prevalence rates of disorders and services. *Archives of General Psychiatry, 50*, 85-94.

Sarason, S. B. (1972). *The creation of settings and the future societies*. San Francisco: Jossey-Bass.

Shepherd, M. D., Schoenberg, M., Slavich, S., Wituk, S., Warren, M., & Meissen, G. (1999). Continuum of professional involvement in self-help groups. *Journal of Community Psychology, 27*, 39-53.

Secretary for Social Services. (1976). *The further development of rehabilitation services in Hong Kong*. Hong Kong: Author.

Social Welfare Department. (2005). *Stocktaking on residential services for people with disabilities.* Hong Kong: Author. Available at http://www.legco.gov.hk/yr04-05/english/counmtg/agenda/cmtg0525.htm. Retrieved August 31, 2005.

Tsang, H. W. H., Tam, P. K. C., Chan, F., & Cheung, W. M. (2003). Stigmatizing attitudes towards individuals with mental illness in Hong Kong: Implications for their recovery. *Journal of Community Psychology, 31*, 383-396.

Watson, J. L., & Watson, R. S. (2003). *Village life in Hong Kong: Politics, gender, and ritual in the New Territories.* Hong Kong: The Chinese University Press.

Wilding, P. (1997). Social policy and social development in Hong Kong. *Asian Journal of Public Administration, 19*, 244-275.

Wong, D. F. K. (2000). Stress factors and mental health of carers with relatives suffering from schizophrenia in Hong Kong: Implications for culturally sensitive practices. *British Journal of Social Work, 30*, 365-382.

Wong, D. F. K., Tsui, H. K. P., Pearson, V., Chen, E. Y. H., & Chiu, S. N. (2004). Family burdens, Chinese health beliefs, and the mental health of Chinese caregivers in Hong Kong. *Transcultural Psychiatry, 41*, 497-513.

Wong, H. (2001). *Concern streetsleepers 2000: Study of late night streetsleepers.* Hong Kong: St. James' Settlement and Christian Concern for the Homeless. [In Chinese]

Wong, H., & Lee, K. M. (2002). *The Hong Kong poverty line study.* Unpublished manuscript, Division of Social Studies, City University of Hong Kong. [In Chinese]

World Health Organization. (2001). *The World health report—Mental health: New understanding, new hope.* Geneva, Switzerland: Author.

Yeung, Y. M. (2003). Milestones in development. In Y. M. Yeung & T. K. Y. Wong (Eds.), *Fifty years of public housing in Hong Kong: A golden jubilee review and appraisal* (pp. 19-43). Hong Kong: Chinese University Press.

Yip, K. S. (2000). Have psychiatric services in Hong Kong been impacted by the deinstitutionalization and community care movements? *Administration and Policy in Mental Health, 27*, 443-449.

Yip, K. S. (2004). The empowerment model: A critical reflection of empowerment in Chinese culture. *Social Work, 49*, 479-487.

Yip, K. S., Lee, L. F., & Law, S. O. (2004). Self-help groups in Hong Kong. *Administration and Policy in Mental Health, 31*, 351-360.

EUROPE AND MIDDLE EAST

10
Community Psychology in Britain

MARK BURTON, STEPHANIE BOYLE, CARL HARRIS,
AND CAROLYN KAGAN

Abstract

This chapter describes and analyses the evolution of community psychology in the United Kingdom. The British welfare state and its contradictions, the nature of British psychology and international developments in theory and practice have all been influential in shaping the relatively small field of community psychology in Britain. The contributions of clinical, educational, and social psychologists are highlighted, together with the largely informal networks that have developed for mutual support of psychologists who want to work in a community-orientated way.

Definitions of Community Psychology

Two of the authors (C.K. and M.B.) define community psychology (CP) in the following terms:

Community psychology offers a framework for working with those marginalised by the social system that leads to self-aware social change with an emphasis on value-based, participatory work and the forging of alliances. It is a way of working that is pragmatic and reflexive, whilst not wedded to any particular orthodoxy of method. As such, community psychology is one alternative to the dominant individualistic psychology typically taught and practised in the high income countries. It is *community* psychology because it emphasises a level of analysis and intervention other than the individual and their immediate interpersonal context. It is community *psychology* because it is nevertheless concerned with how people feel, think, experience, and act as they work together, resisting oppression and struggling to create a better world.

However, this definition, essentially that of a community *social* psychology, would not necessarily be shared with all the protagonists in British CP. Although many would have similar definitions, some would emphasise promotion of good mental health or the empirical basis of psychological knowledge. The chapter takes a broadly inclusive approach to the relatively small field in

Britain, where CP is characterised by people working towards a nonindividual-istic community-based, and community-oriented alternative to dominant applied psychology. CP considered here is therefore largely that which is self-defined by its practitioners, and we have only excluded those approaches that we see as being solely traditional psychological practice in community contexts.

Introduction

Community psychology in Britain can appear to be relatively underdeveloped in comparison with that in other regions. Some reasons for this have been examined elsewhere in an article subtitled "Why this gap in Britain?" (Burton & Kagan, 2003), but in this chapter our focus is more on the description of what CP there is in the country and how it developed. Despite the absence of a highly organised and numerically strong discipline, there are some distinct centres and approaches that suggest that it is meaningful to talk, if not about a British CP, at least of a family of approaches developed in the societal, academic, professional, and lay contexts here. Indeed that relative lack of an organised presence (especially a professional organisation and training courses) does not mean that community psychological work is not going on here. A theme that has emerged repeatedly in the research we have carried out for this chapter has been that a lot of work that would elsewhere be branded as CP is not called that here nor seen primarily in these terms at all.

As there is a dearth of historical material available about the development of CP in the United Kingdom, we undertook some empirical work in prepa-ration for this chapter. This included an e-mail questionnaire posted on a U.K. CP website and listserve along with open invitations for views and comments; targeted interviews with people who have played key roles in developments, as identified through discussion between authors and sugges-tions from others in the field; and documentary analysis of archive material. Quotations from personal communications throughout the article are from these interviews, questionnaire responses, or subsequent e-mails. A number of facts were checked with key actors. As actors in the field, the authors also added their own knowledge and perspectives. Chapter drafts were posted on the website and comments and reflections invited. Different sources of infor-mation were combined through discussion amongst the authors, and various chronological phases of development were identified.

Waves of Community Psychology

Pre–Community Psychology, Pre-1970

There have been a number of precursors to CP in Britain, and it is beyond the scope of this chapter to identify and delineate them all. Psychology in the United Kingdom before the Second World War was often characterised as interdisciplinary and sought to develop innovative methodological approaches to understanding social issues, as, for example in St Andrews (Oeser, 1937). The Mass Observation movement, which involved lay people in producing rich descriptions of ordinary life in a northern mill town (Roiser, 1998), grew in part from methodological innovations at St Andrews.

Marie Jahoda, who became professor of social psychology at the then new University of Sussex in the 1960s was one of a group of social scientists who had previously worked as engaged and committed community activists in Austria prior to the nightmare of fascism. She utilised a similar, interdisciplinary approach to deep fieldwork when working with mining communities in Wales (Bellin, 2002; Fryer, 1999).

Later on, in the intellectual disability field the work of the 'psychologists' group' which included Jack Tizard, Herbert Gunzburg, Elizabeth and John Newson, Norman O'Connor, Beate Hermelin, Alan and Ann Clarke, and Peter Mittler, for example (along with psychiatrist Albert Kushlick) could be characterised as a broadly social and contextualist approach that challenged 'therapeutic pessimism' and paved the way for the more radical approaches that combined service development, policy development, and social change by later workers in the field (including Chris Gathercole, Paul Williams, Jim Mansell, David Felce), recognising intellectually disabled people as citizens for whom it was necessary to both open up and make competent their community.

Psychodynamic psychologists at the Tavistock Institute developed a practice as organisational change agents. Others explored ideas like that of the therapeutic community (which originated in the United Kingdom—Claybury, Paddington, Henderson hospitals—also Richmond Fellowship) as alternatives to medicalised hospitalisation, creating social settings that facilitated healing and growth. Other psychologists worked with families and other allies to support the rights and citizenship of vulnerable children, within the child guidance services that were established before the 1939–1945 war (Aiyegbayo, 2005).

However, none of these diverse and informal roots led into a coherent and self-defined 'CP,' and it was not until the term began to be used in North America that it began to appear in Britain. One reason for the limited development of community-oriented applied psychology was the very individualistic approach of British academic psychology, dominated by a few institutions, such as the University of Cambridge. Despite the work of the socially inclined Frederick Bartlett in the 1930s (Bartlett, Ginsberg, Lindgren, & Thouless, 1939), by the post-war period the university had promoted a very narrow idea of the discipline, albeit with a strong applied focus adopted by psychologists who went on to work elsewhere (such as Argyle and Broadbent). Moreover, the control of university curricula by the British Psychological Society (BPS) constrained the possibility of the exploration of alternative approaches to psychology. In most places, applied psychology was largely oriented to psychometric testing.

1970 to 1980

The 1970s in Britain as elsewhere opened with the questioning of the dominant approaches to psychology. Although in mainstream academia this was often no more than the replacement of one positivist paradigm, behaviourism, by another, the cognitivist/information processing one, more fundamental critiques especially in social psychology were emerging (Armistead, 1974; Harré & Secord, 1972; Israel & Tajfel, 1972). In Britain this led not to a community practice (Burton, 2004a) but rather to a distinctly European genre of experimental social psychology (Graumann, 1995), as well as increasingly academic and theoretical work in critical psychology (Parker, 1999). There was also an emphasis on social constructionism, the role of language and poststructuralist critiques of the discipline, as reflected through the short-lived journal *Ideology and Consciousness* and subsequent writings (Adlam et al., 1977; Henriques, Hollway, Urwin, Venn, & Walkerdine, 1984). Paradoxically, just as the academics were abandoning behavioural approaches, their applied colleagues were getting excited by them because they offered a technology of therapeutic change that would also help psychologists break out of the psychometric straightjacket that constrained their role as technical support to psychiatrists.

However, by the 1970s the term 'CP' was appearing with some regularity in the *Bulletin of the British Psychological Society*, and some psychologists, for example Mike Bender (in Newham, London, since 1968) and Brian Tully were exploring a recognisable CP (Bender, 1972, 1976, 1979; Tully, Doyle, Cahill, Bayles, & Graham, 1978). These developments would appear to be a product of the opening of a space for community work in the United Kingdom (Burton & Kagan, 2003) along with awareness of developments in North America. In Bender's case, a whole department of mostly clinically trained psychologists was established in the alternative (to the Health Service) institutional home of the London borough of Newham's Social Services Department.

Newham was innovative. It worked across all client areas, except Child Guidance; it had many assistant (graduate) psychologists (which traditional clinical psychologists disliked) but also a team of clinical psychologists/psychotherapists. So through the seventies and into the mid-eighties, it was showing how psychology could be delivered; and the concept of intensive, researched input ("the project" approach) had some influence.

(M. Bender, correspondence with the authors, January 14, 2005)

Bender's book in 1976 became the first introduction to the ideas of CP for a subsequent generation. The series in which his book appeared (*Essential Psychology*, Methuen) also contained other challenges to the mainstream (Heather, 1976; Stacey, 1976). Another influential book series was the radical education initiative of Penguin, which brought Freire and his work to an English-speaking readership (Freire, 1972a, 1972b).

At the same time, educational psychologists were also developing community psychological work. As Peter Jones puts it:

There was little in the way of literature that specifically named Community Psychology, but I certainly see the struggles between educational psychology and clinical psychology for ownership of child psychology and working in schools in the community to directly reflect what had happened in the USA during the 60s. The Court and the Trethowan reports [on disabled children and the role of clinical psychologists respectively], the role of the British Psychological Society during that period and the relationships between Clinical Psychologists and Educational Psychologists, were happening in the context of Educational Psychologists having already shed the shackles of medical domination and many of them moving to more systemic practice in schools in the community, rather than being constrained as psychometricians/para-therapists in child guidance clinics. The radicalisation of much practice for Educational Psychologists during the 70s and 80s reflected and extended some of that thinking. For example, Sheffield had a community educational psychology service in the 70s.

(P. Jones, correspondence with the authors, February 24, 2005)

Elsewhere, both educational and clinical psychologists established community-based interventions oriented to working with a variety of mainly marginalised populations in more ecologically appropriate locations (McPherson and Sutton, 1981). Thirty years later, this work may now seem dated with much seeming to have been concerned with rolling out the new behavioural technology to non-psychologists. The location of much of this work was in the first generation of compromised community-based service settings such as hostels and day centres for intellectually disabled people or those with mental health problems. Compared with developments elsewhere, these developments were small in scale. As we have argued before (Burton & Kagan, 2003), all this work was dependent on the availability of niches that could be occupied by psychologists and on the preparation of psychologists to work in this more socially oriented way. However, in the event, the gaps in state-promoted collectivist practices were filled, in the main, by other professionals, such as community workers.

1980 to 1990

The domination of the institutions of the British national and local state continued to exert an influence. In the universities, the turn to social constructionism continued while work was done in broadening the paradigms for both thinking about and researching in psychology, through what became known as new paradigm, anti-positivist research (Reason & Rowan, 1981). However, it was not until 1994 that the first compendium of qualitative methods in psychology in the United Kingdom was produced (Banister, Burman, Parker, Taylor, & Tindall, 1994). In a similar vein, there was an interest in feminist analyses and influence on research practice at this time (Burman, 1990; Wilkinson, 1986).

In psychological practice, other developments occurred. A loosely organised group of people, mostly but not all professional psychologists, came together in 1983 to form the group Psychologists in Community Settings (PICS). Core to the objectives of PICS was the crossing of the intraprofessional divisions and uniting different kinds of psychologists in an area of common interest. For several years, PICS remained determined to remain outside the structures of the BPS, deciding not to become a division, section or special interest group, in order to represent members *outside* the traditional categories of the BPS (Barlow, 1987), whilst retaining an interest in influencing various BPS committees.

By 1987, there were 100 members of PICS and some further 90 people interested in its activities. (This is similar to the number of people who are currently signed up to the U.K. national CP e-mail list,[1] although now the pool of psychologists is larger. (See the section on Scotland below for details of this list.)

PICS held seminars, residential courses, and circulated discussion papers. Some of these contained discussion of the nature of community, the possibilities of a CP (different from existing clinical or educational psychology practised in community settings), and sharing information about working as community psychologists. A 3-day conference entitled "Community Psychology in the late 1980s" was held in 1986, aimed at clinical psychologists.

The concern of PICS had initially been to develop a different form of practice, but in the end the workplace pressures led to an emphasis on protecting the interests of psychologists working in a specific setting—social service departments. The contemporary special group of Psychologists and Social Services within the British Psychological Society has its roots in the PICS initiative. This group acts as a forum for exploring the common issues arising from and for psychologists working in social service settings.

Reviewing the possibilities for transforming psychological practice, at this time, McPherson and Sutton (1981) called for a psychological practice that went beyond the individual. They recognised that practice would remain predominantly in public welfare services, paid for by the NHS and local authorities. Importantly, the tension between the niche advantages of individual work, providing good careers, and expanding professions was acknowledged. Perhaps this was why a genuine CP did not take root at this stage.

However, the period of the 1980s was also a time of more fundamental changes in British government and society and its welfare systems. In 1979, the Conservative (or Tory) Party was elected under Margaret Thatcher, and it began a transformation (inspired both by the Chicago neoliberal economists and the experiment of the Pinochet dictatorship in Chile [Becket, 2002]) that prefigured the current neoliberal 'consensus.' The collective influence of the working class was directly attacked and weakened, and the institutions of

---

[1] See http://www.jiscmail.ac.uk/lists/COMMUNITYPSYCHUK.HTML

the welfare state subjected to an incessant regime of budgetary cuts, strengthened general management, and subsequently (from the mid-1980s) to the 'discipline of the market' with swathes of provision being cut or out-sourced. The very notion of 'the social' became disreputable, as manifest in Thatcher's famous emblematic statement: '. . . who is society? There is no such thing! There are individual men and women and there are families' (Thatcher, 1987, p. 8).

These developments made the 'really social psychology' of CP a difficult case to argue, at least in terms of the ideal of radical transformative practice. For those influenced by Marxism and feminism and by what had been the growing attempts to apply these approaches to practice (e.g., through the new journal, Critical Social Policy, founded in 1981, or texts such as Corrigan & Leonard, 1978), this could be a disorienting period.

Nevertheless, the Thatcher years (the regime was to last for four parliamentary terms up until 1997) did offer some opportunities for community psychological practice, but throughout the 1980s there was little talk of CP as such. Opportunities for community psychological work were provided by the policy initiatives of Care in the Community. These led to the resettlement of people from long-stay institutions, and the development of new more flexible support systems in, if not usually of, the community. There was a new North American influence, that of normalisation or social role valorisation (Wolfensberger, 1992), promoted in the United Kingdom by Paul Williams (who had also convened the community psychology conference for PICS) that provided a vision of inclusive community living for the most impaired. However, other ideas, such as the Latin American notion of conscientisation and more traditionally British notions of social responsibility and public service were also influential. A large variety of developments took place, some with and some without the involvement of psychologists. Clinical psychologists took a leading role in some of these. The work of Chris Gathercole in the northwest of England is particularly notable, exemplifying the ethos of CP—interdisciplinary, transformative, preventative, value based, emphasising evaluation, making alliances with family carers and disabled people—yet never referred to as CP. The remnants of a decimated community development sector provided a home for other radical psychologists (Gilchrist, 2004), and yet others were active in the disability movement, promulgating the social model of disability as a challenge to medical, deficit models (Finkelstein & French, 1998). These developments opened the way for new forms of evaluation and for reframing individual interventions in community psychological ways (Burton and Kagan, 1995; Kagan and Burton, 2000).

At the time that de-institutionalisation took off in the southwest of England, the clinical psychology training course headed by Jim Orford took the opportunity to rebrand itself as the Exeter Community and Clinical Psychology training course in 1983, although Orford had been teaching about CP since the late 1970s (Orford, 1979). This however, was rather exceptional. Although Exeter provided a nucleus for a self-aware variant of (clinical) CP, in the main the term had little currency in the 1980s.

A rather different process affected educational psychology (dicussed above, 1970 to 1980). In 1981, a new Education Act was passed that established a new approach to the specification of children's special educational needs. While before, children were assigned to special education on the basis of a broadly medical definition of their disabling condition, the new act required a statement of special education needs, based on a multidisciplinary assessment. This was an attempt to individualise provision. Although it did enable many children's difficulties to be recognised and addressed in mainstream educational provision, it did little to change the segregation of children with more substantial disabling conditions. However, it was the educational psychologists who were in charge of the 'statementing' process. As a result, at least in England and Wales (the situation in Scotland has always been rather different), the role of educational psychologists became much more tied to the bureaucratic operation of the system. As such, the scope for intervention in systems and in community contexts was significantly reduced.

In the late 1980s, Sue Holland, a feminist psychotherapist with roots in community action, was working with a group of women on the White City Estate in London. She developed an approach that began with individual psychotherapy, progressed to involvement in groups and then to collective social action. In this process, mental health was reframed: instead of being seen as private individual distress in mainly biomedical terms, it was seen more in a societal context (Holland, 1988). Her work, which is frequently cited as influential by clinically oriented community psychologists in Britain, drew on both psychoanalytic theory and on the idea of conscientisation from Freire (Freire, 1972b). Her work appeared in a collection (Ramon & Giannichedda, 1988) that also included work from Psiciatrica Democratica in Italy, which also influenced some community-oriented psychologists. During the 1980s, another international influence resulted from the personal involvement of some psychologists in the solidarity movement with the Sandinista revolution in Nicaragua, where a more social model of mental health was being articulated (Sveaass, 2000; Steve Melluish, correspondence with the authors 2005).

1990 Onwards

It was in the 1990s that interest in an explicitly *community* psychology re-emerged or consolidated itself in several locations. In describing what happened in these places, we can also identify the main currents of British CP and some of their interconnections.

The following categorisation is necessarily approximate. It risks marginalising developments outside the boundaries of these centres of gravity, for example the community educational psychology practised by Peter Jones and others, as described in Box 1.

Box 1. Community educational psychology.
- Understands education as a model of social change or stability for individuals, communities, and cultures;
- Works directly to enable individual and community development, learning, and well-being in schools and other agency settings;
- Recognises how the reality of social power and values shapes not only disadvantaged groups but the role of applied psychology;
- Builds on the experience of school psychologists working in the interests of all populations in schools, not only those with disabilities, difficulties, or illness;
- Sees learning as a person–environment interaction shaped by the historical narratives of each side for the pattern of events arising;
- Offers a preventative, reflexive application of psychology and collaborative research to individuals, communities, and strategic policymakers;
- Uses understandings from community development and alliance building to increase social inclusion and empowerment of service users;
- Promotes and sustains multiagency partnerships and networking;
- Rigorously examines narratives for psychological development, learning, and well-being and is well-placed to understand and inform the agendas that constitute children's, young people's, and family services.

(Peter Jones, January 2005, DECP conference, London)

There is also the danger of prematurely freezing understanding of history and therefore of reducing the likelihood of other characterisations of this period up to the present. With these risks in mind, the following is offered as a loose organising framework for diverse information.

London

In London, the work of the Newham department led to a continued interest and production of community psychological work. After Bender left in 1988, there was a move of people from the local authority into the health service (especially in the London boroughs of Newham, Tower Hamlets, Hackney, and Haringey) where in many cases the community emphasis continued (Kagan, 2000; Phillips, Hughes, & Bell, 1998). In the Newham health service's psychology department, for example, it was a contractual obligation of all staff that they spent a half day session per week on CP. The influence seems to have reached the clinical psychology training course at North East London Polytechnic (now the University of East London), regarded as one of the more socially critical and progressive training programs.

Meanwhile, at University College London, Chris Barker and colleagues, from within a clinical psychology teaching programme, have maintained a programme of work on informal social support (e.g., Solomon, Pistrang, & Barker, 2001) A similar emphasis is adopted by Derek Milne in Northumberland (Milne, 1999).

More recently, a new master's level course in health, community and development—with an explicit CP focus—was established in 2005 at the London School of Economics by a group with roots elsewhere (social and health psychology in the United Kingdom, South Africa and Latin America) (Campbell & Murray, 2004). It builds on the long-standing interest of the department in a macro social psychology, one that studies social phenomena and cultural forces that both shape, and in turn are shaped by, people's outlooks and actions (Gaskell & Himmelweit, 1990).

Exeter

The origins of community psychology in Exeter were mentioned above. Orford's work (e.g., Feldman & Orford, 1980; Orford, 1976, 1979, 1992) has consistently provided a conduit for CP concepts in the British context, and his 1992 textbook remains the only U.K. produced textbook of CP. His own work has been largely from a clinical base with an emphasis on mental health and addictions. However, his role in stimulating and developing U.K. CP has been considerable. Not only has he provided inspiration through his own writings, he has also opened possibilities for a community clinical practice. He has promoted community psychological work through his role as a founding editor of the *Journal of Community and Applied Social Psychology* and has offered encouragement advice, support, and legitimation for many of those trying to work community psychologically in often isolated settings. In addition, Jim Orford, along with David Fryer and Mark Wilson, both from Scotland, was an active member of the European Community Psychology network and was prominent in the working group that oversaw its transformation into a European Community Psychology Association, which launched in Naples in September 2005 (Fryer, 2005; Orford, Duckett, & McKenna, 2003).

Birmingham

Orford moved to Birmingham in 1993 but the emphasis of the Exeter course has been maintained (through the work of Louise Goodbody [now in Kent], Annie Mitchell, and others), and a variety of community-based projects are in existence. The 2004 Community Psychology conference was held in Exeter. In Birmingham, a group of professionals with an interest in critical and community approaches to mental health established the West Midlands Community and Critical Psychology group in 2002 (which includes two of the authors of this chapter). Some clinical psychologists are beginning to undertake some explicitly community psychological projects as part of their roles.

Nottingham

The other location where CP has emerged from within clinical psychology has been Nottingham. As with Jim Orford, several of the people we interviewed or who wrote to us in preparation for this chapter mentioned

David Smail, who was the psychology services manager for the Nottingham health service department of clinical psychology. His own work (e.g., Smail, 2001, 2005) has explored the power and the limitations of psychotherapy, in its most recent form setting out an account of psychological/emotional distress which places the embodied subject in a social environment in a real, material world (Smail, 2005). His other influence has been through the encouragement (and permission) for others to explore community psychological approaches. A good example is Melluish's work with unemployed men (Melluish & Bulmer, 1999). Another example would be the community psychological project, *Building Bridges* in Liverpool (Fatimilehin & Coleman, 1998, 1999). A group of clinical psychologists in Nottingham established the U.K. Community Psychology Network, following a meeting in 1993 with George Albee, which was arranged by Richard Marshall and Bob Diamond, attended by people from across the country, and at which the political nature of CP and the importance of solidarity in taking the activity forward was stressed. Following a further meeting the next year, Steve Melluish compiled a list of interested people who became the network for CP in the United Kingdom. This network has held conferences with increasing frequency, and for the past 3 years there have been annual events. Jan Bostock was an influential member of this group prior to her move to Northumberland, publishing her practical and theoretical work with communities (Bostock & Beck, 1993; Bostock & Smail, 1999; Sharpe & Bostock, 2002) and holding an editorial position with *Journal of Community and Applied Social Psychology* (JCASP).

The network remains informal, with individual members taking on responsibilities on an ad hoc basis. Some discussion has taken place about a possible evolution into something more formal inside or outside the BPS, but nothing has been agreed at the time of writing (summer 2005).

Manchester

In Manchester, around the Manchester Metropolitan University, there is another grouping of community psychologists and associated people, but unlike the previous groupings its roots are not in clinical psychology (although there is some mutual influence). Work began in the early 1980s with both value-based community projects and theoretical analysis (the 'Trafford School'). The roots are more in social and environmental psychology and there is a strong influence from disciplines outside psychology itself (ecology, political theory, liberation studies, systems methodologies) (e.g., Kagan, 2002). The first and to date the only master's programme in CP was developed at MMU. Most of the work is participatory and emphases include disability (Duckett & Pratt, 2001; Goodley & Lawthom, 2005; Moore, Beazley, & Maelzer, 1998); marginalisation (Kagan & Burton, 2004); health and well-being (Sixsmith & Boneham, 2002; Sixsmith, Kagan and Duckett, 2004); crime in the community (Kagan, Caton, & Amin, 2001); and regeneration (Edge, Kagan and Stewart, 2004). The journal *Community Work and Family* is edited from Manchester by Carolyn Kagan and Sue Lewis and has community psychologists from around the world on the editorial board. In addition, some Manchester people are on the editorial board of JCASP. From Manchester, Mark Burton manages the Community Psychology U.K. website, unofficial, but used as a gateway to CP in the United Kingdom (www.compsy.org.uk); and Paul Duckett and Rebecca Lawthom manage the national website drawing together learning and teaching strategies and materials in CP in higher education (http://cphe.org.uk/). The strong CP group at MMU links closely with the Discourse Unit, a centre for critical and feminist psychology (Burman, 1998; Parker, 2005; Parker & Spears, 1996). It is from this base that the *Annual Review of Critical Psychology* is published, and that networking and campaigning organisations, including the Hearing Voices Network, Psychology, Politics and Resistance, and the Paranoia Network have been supported (Parker, 1994). See Burton (2004a) for a discussion of the relationships between critical academic psychology and CP.

Scotland

CP in Scotland is based primarily at Stirling University where David Fryer heads the critical CP group. Inspired by Mark Wilson's work in Easterhouse on the fringes of Glasgow, David and his colleagues have developed a CP praxis that is in partnership with community groups. The focus of their work is largely in the area of mental health and (un)employment, but recently they have diversified to work with community groups on a number of other change issues. The Stirling group (in particular Mark Wilson, David Fryer, and Steve McKenna) has been part of the European Network for Community Psychology since its inception and has hosted a number of visits by community psychologists from elsewhere. David Fryer was a member of the editorial committee of the *Journal of Community and Applied Social Psychology* for a number of years, developing both the book review and Praxis sections. Stirling University has recognised the importance of CP by awarding honorary doctorates to both George Albee and Marie Jahoda. Writings from the Stirling group (e.g., Fryer, 1986; Fryer, 1999; Fryer & Fagan, 2003) have influenced practitioners elsewhere in the United Kingdom. In 2001, Rebekkah Pratt, a New Zealand–trained community psychologist who had spent some time in Stirling, began the U.K. community psychology e-mail listserve, which is now moderated by her and David Fryer. However, the tensions created by the British Psychological Society's hold over curriculum issues puts strain on small university-based groups of community psychologists like the Stirling group (Fryer, 2000). Similarly the Research Assessment Exercise that evaluates British universities' strengths in research and development also impacts negatively on CP academics who work in unconventional research paradigms and who tend not to publish in those outlets (e.g., APA and medical journals) that the psychological establishment rates most highly (Annie Mitchell, personal communication, May 28, 2005).

Recent and Current Context

In 1997, the period of Tory rule came to an end with the election of the 'New Labour' government of Tony Blair. Labour has not proved to be any less committed to policies that favour the market over the state and civil society than were the Tories (Watkins, 2004), but they have had an explicit agenda about reducing what they call social exclusion (what we used to call poverty), and about promoting partnerships between the agencies of the local and national state, voluntary organisations, and the private sector. This has opened up some spaces for community psychologists. For example, the Health Action Zones of the first labour term created opportunities for community psychological work on the prevention of poor health (e.g., Sharpe & Bostock, 2002), capacity building for programme evaluation (Boyd et al., 2001), and self-harm (Chantler, Burman, & Batsleer, 2003). Other (mostly urban) regeneration projects have supported action research projects such as Carl Harris's work in Birmingham (Harris, 2005) and Kagan, Caton, and Amin's (2001) work in Greater Manchester.

Formal Organisation

The role of the British Psychological society is paradoxical (Burton & Kagan, 2003). On the one hand it has supported community psychological developments by, for example, funding visits under the Visiting Fellow and Visiting Psychologist schemes to community psychologists from Australia, Canada, Cuba, Italy, Mexico and the United States. It has provided financial support for the development of an international conference in CP. Sue Holland (discussed above) was the first recipient in 1994 of the British Psychological Society's award, by the Standing Committee for the Promotion of Equal Opportunities, for members who have challenged inequalities or promoted equal opportunities in their work, and Carolyn Kagan is the most recent recipient of the award. The society is currently providing encouragement to interested parties to establish formally a Community Psychology Section.[2] On the other hand, it retains tight control of and scrutiny of the undergraduate and postgraduate curricula. There is no mention in the nine pages of the benchmarking statement for psychology, produced by members of BPS committees, of CP theory, applications, or perspectives (QAA, 2004).

In 1991, the first European journal to include CP, the *Journal of Community and Applied Social Psychology*, was founded through development from its antecedent, the *Journal of Social Behaviour*. The founding editorial declares

---

[2] Sections are subject-related interest groups. They sometimes develop subsequently into divisions, which are subprofession based (clinical, educational, counselling, forensic, occupational, etc.), with powers of accreditation.

a commitment to stimulating the growth of CP alongside clinical psychology, applied behaviour analysis, and social psychology(Mansell, Orford, Reicher, & Stephenson, 1991). Jim Orford, as one of the founding editors of the journal, has continued to strongly influence the presence of CP in the United Kingdom.

Conclusions

Despite the developments described above and an increasing degree of coordinating of effort, British CP remains a minority pursuit. In part, this seems to have something to do with the institutional pressures that define what psychology is. These include the positivist emphasis of 'evidence-based practice' and the continuing fascination with therapy in clinical psychology; the administrative burden in educational psychology; and the constraining influence of the Research Assessment Exercise as well as the BPS control of the undergraduate curriculum in the universities. These dominant understandings of what is proper for psychologists to do continue to exert a bias against the alternative and nonindividualistic psychology that is aspired to by community psychologists. Yet meanwhile, a growing number (if not a growing proportion) of psychologists do practice what would elsewhere be termed CP, often without ever thinking of applying that term. Perhaps that situation also hints at a problem with the very notion of 'CP,' which has been dependent on a particular conjuncture of psychological ideas, unoccupied niches in which to work, and legitimation from professional and other bodies. Should we be thinking more in terms of 'really social psychology,' that is nonindividualist in its understanding of the societal construction and place of people, realist in its understanding of people's embodied and contextualised subjectivity, and social in its programme of action, irrespective of what subdiscipline the psychologist belongs to? With such a permeating notion of liberatory practice, any debate about who is really doing CP, and about how to organise to do it, perhaps fades away as only of interest to careerist professionals.

Finally, comparing the development of CP in Britain with that in other places (after revising this chapter and reading others), we make the following comments. CP in Britain has developed in the context of a core capitalist country with a welfare state and public services. It thereby presents a contrast with much of the African, Asian, and Latin American experience. The social history surrounding our CP is more postindustrial (as opposed to postcolonial in Africa and Latin America). However, there are differences with other wealthy countries: there is less emphasis on cultural difference or diversity in ours (as opposed to the Aotearoa/New Zealand chapter). Related to that point, we are located in a culture that has significant individualistic discourses (a feature we share with the United States illustrated by Thatcher's comment above), but which also has a more social approach to welfare as in other European countries, Canada, and Australasia (while all being subject to neoliberal policies of privatisation and state residualism). An issue that we have not covered above is the repressive policies of the British state as a context for CP (for example, in relation to people fleeing the economic and political consequences of Anglo-American neo-imperialism): we do think that this is a critical issue for an engaged CP, and we are perhaps not alone among the authors of this book in failing to situate the CP of our country in a properly articulated analysis of the social, political, and economic construction and destruction of community.

We seem to share with other chapters an academic and professional higher education element to the development of CP, and we also share with others the experience that not all CP is being done by those who take the label of community psychologist. This would present a problem for a historian who wished to focus on "approved CP" without wishing to "colonise" or rather "appropriate" others' activities (with or without their consent).

Acknowledgements. We are grateful to the following people who took part in interviews or submitted their thoughts on the history of community psychology in Britain: Chris Barker, Mike Bender, Jan Bostock, Bob Diamond, Peter Jones, Steve Melluish, Annie Mitchell, Jim Orford, John Puddifoot, David Smail, Frederic Stansfield, and Mark Wilson. The first draft of the chapter was written by M.B., who also obtained information from a number of informants by means of an e-mail questionnaire devised by the authors. S.B. and C.H. provided information from interviews and data gathering from a number of informants, with a focus on the relationship between community and clinical psychology. Following comments on the draft, C.K. revised it and provided additional archive material. Bibliographic work was by M.B. and C.K.

References

Adlam, D., Henriques, J., Rose, N., Salfield, A., Venn, C., & Walkerdine, V. (1977). Psychology, ideology and the human subject. *Ideology and Consciousness*, 1, 15-56.

Aiyegbayo, O. (2005). Waveney Bushell: a pioneering black educational psychologist. *History and Philosophy of Psychology*, 7(1), 36-44.

Armistead, N. (Ed.). (1974). *Reconstructing Social Psychology*. Harmondsworth: Penguin.

Banister, P., Burman, E., Parker, I., Taylor, M., & Tindall, C. (1994). *Qualitative Methods in Psychology: A research guide*. Milton Keynes: Open University Press.

Barlow, N. (1987). Letter from Chairperson. *PICS Letter*, issue 4, pp. 1-2.

Bartlett, F. C., Ginsberg, M., Lindgren, E. J., & Thouless, R. H. (1939). *The Study of Society*. London: Kegan Paul.

Becket, A. (2002). *Pinochet in Piccadilly; Britain and Chile's Hidden History*. London: Faber and Faber.

Bellin, W. (2002). Marie Jahoda and Wales/Marie Jahoda a Chymru. *The Psychologist in Wales*, 13, 14-15.

Bender, M. P. (1972). The role of the community psychologist. *Bulletin of the British Psychological Society*, 27, 211-218.

Bender, M. P. (1976). *Community Psychology*. London: Methuen.

Bender, M. P. (1979). Community psychology: When? *Bulletin of the British Psychological Society*, 32, 6-9.

Bostock, J., & Beck, D. (1993). Participating in social enquiry and action. *Journal of Community & Applied Social Psychology*, 3, 213-224.

Bostock, J., & Smail, D. (1999). Special Issue: Power, the Environment and Community Psychology. Issue Edited by Janet Bostock, David Smail. *Journal of Community & Applied Social Psychology*, 9(2), 75-78.

Boyd, A., Geerling, T., Gregory, W., Midgley, G., Murray, P., Walsh, M., et al. (2001). *Capacity Building for Evaluation: A Report on the HAZE Project for Manchester, Salford and Trafford health Action Zone*. Hull: Centre for Systems Studies.

Burman, E. (Ed.). (1990). *Feminists and Psychological Practice*. London: Sage.

Burman, E. (Ed.). (1998). *Deconstructing Feminist Psychology*. London: Sage.

Burton, M. (2004a). Radical psychology networks: a review and guide. *Journal of Community & Applied Social Psychology*, 14, 119-130.

Burton, M., & Kagan, C. (1995). *Social Skills for People with Learning Disabilities: A Social Capability Approach*. London: Chapman and Hall.

Burton, M., & Kagan, C. (2003). Community psychology: why this gap in Britain? *History and Philosophy of Psychology*, 4(2), 10-23.

Campbell, C., & Murray, M. (2004). Community health psychology: promoting analysis and action for social change. *Journal of Health Psychology*, 9(2), 187-196.

Chantler, K., Burman, E., & Batsleer, J. (2003). South Asian women: systematic inequalities in services around attempted suicide and self harm. *European Journal of Social Work*, 6(2), 34-48.

Corrigan, P., & Leonard, P. (1978). *Social work practice under capitalism: a Marxist approach*. London: MacMillan.

Duckett, P. S., & Pratt, R. (2001). The researched opinions on research: visually impaired people and visual impairment research. *Disability and Society*, 16(6), 815-835.

Edge, I., Kagan, C and Stewart, A. (2004). Living Poverty: surviving on the edge. *Clinical Psychology*, 38, 28-31.

Fatimilehin, I. A., & Coleman, P. G. (1998). Appropriate services for African-Caribbean families: views from one community. *Clinical Psychology Forum,* 111, 6-11.

Fatimilehin, I. A., & Coleman, P. G. (1999). 'You've got to have a Chinese chef to cook chinese food!' Issues of power and control in the provision of mental health services. *Journal of Community & Applied Social Psychology,* 9(2), 101-117.

Feldman, P., & Orford, J. (1980). *Psychological Problems: The social context*. Chichester: Wiley.

Finkelstein, V., & French, S. (1998). Towards a Psychology of Disability. In J. Swain, V. Finkelstein & M. Oliver (Eds.), *Disabling Barriers: Enabling Environments* (pp. 26-332). London: Sage.

Freire, P. (1972a). *Cultural Action for Freedom*. Harmondsworth: Penguin.

Freire, P. (1972b). *Pedagogy of the Oppressed*. Harmondsworth: Penguin.

Fryer, D. (1986). The Social Psychology of the invisible: An interview with Marie Jahoda. *New Ideas in Psychology*, 4(11), 107-118.

Fryer, D. (1999). Marie Jahoda: A social psychologist for and in the real world. In K. Isaksson, L. Hogestadt, C. Eriksson & T. Theorell (Eds.), *Health Effects of the New labour Market*. New York: Kluwer Academic/Plenum Press.

Fryer, D. (2000). The Primary Prevention of Community Psychology. In C. Kagan (Ed.), *Collective Action and Social Change*. Manchester: IOD Research Group.

Fryer, D. (2005) Community psychology news from Europe. *The Community Psychologist*, 38(4), 17-18.

Fryer, D., & Fagan, R. (2003). Towards a critical community psychological research perspective on unemployment and mental health research. *American Journal of Community Psychology*, 32(1/2), 89-96.

Gaskell, G., & Himmelweit, H. (Eds.). (1990). Societal Psychology. Newbury Park, CA: Sage.

Gilchrist, A. (2004). *The well-connected community. A networking approach to community development*. Bristol: Policy Press.

Goodley, D., & Lawthom, R. (2005). *Disability and Psychology. Critical Introductions and Reflections*. London: Palgrave.

Graumann, C. F. (1995, January 14 2005). *History*. Available at http://www.eaesp.org/about/history.htm. Retrieved January 24, 2005.

Harré, R., & Secord, P. F. (1972). *The Explanation of Social Behaviour*. Oxford: Blackwell.

Harris, C. (2005). The Family Well-being Project: Providing psychology services for children and families in a community regeneration context. In C. Newnes & N. Radcliffe (Eds.), *Making and Breaking Children's Lives*. Ross-on-Wye: PCCS Books.

Heather, N. (1976). *Radical Perspecticves in Psychology*. London: Methuen.

Henriques, J., Hollway, W., Urwin, C., Venn, C., & Walkerdine, V. (1984). *Changing the Subject: Psychology, social relations and subjectivity*. London: Methuen.

Holland, S. (1988). Defining and experimenting with prevention. In S. Ramon & M. Giannichedda (Eds.), *Psychiatry in Transition: The British and Italian experiences*. London: Pluto.

Israel, J., & Tajfel, H. (Eds.). (1972). *The Context of Social Psychology: A critical assessment*. London: Academic Press.

Kagan, C. (Ed.). (2000). *Collective Action and Social Change: Report of the National Community Psychology Conference, 7 & 8 January 1999*. (Vol. 1/00). Manchester: Manchester Metropolitan University: IOD Research Group.

Kagan, C. (2002). *Making the Road by Walking It . . . some possibilities for a community social psychology, Inaugural professorial lecture*. Manchester: Manchester Metropolitan University.

Kagan, C., & Burton, M. (2000). Prefigurative Action Research: an alternative basis for critical psychology? *Annual Review of Critical Psychology*, 2, 73-87.

Kagan, C., & Burton, M. (2004). Marginalization. In G. Nelson & I. Prilleltensky (Eds.), *Community Psychology: In pursuit of liberation and wellness*. (pp. 293-308). London: MacMillan/Palgrave.

Kagan, C., Caton, S., & Amin, A. (2001a). *Report of Feasibility Study of a Community Witness Support Scheme for Heartlands, North Town: The need for witness support*. Manchester: IOD Research Group.

Mansell, J., Orford, J., Reicher, S., & Stephenson, G. (1991). Editorial. *Journal of Community & Applied Social Psychology*, 1(1), 1-4.

McPherson, I., & Sutton, A. (Eds.). (1981). *Deconstructing Psychological Practice*. London: Croom Helm.

Melluish, S., & Bulmer, D. (1999). Rebuilding solidarity: an account of a men's health action project. *Journal of Community and Applied Social Psychology*, 9, 93-100.

Milne, D. (1999). Social Therapy: A guide to Social Support Interventions for Mental Health Practitioners. London: Wiley.

Moore, M., Beazley, S., & Maelzer, J. (1998). *Researching Disability Issues.* Buckingham: Open University Press.

Oeser, O. A. (1937). The methods and assumptions of field-work in social psychology. *British Journal of Psychology*, XXVII(4), 343-363.

Orford, J. (1976). *The Social Psychology of Mental Disorder.* Harmondsworth: Penguin.

Orford, J. (1979). Teaching community psychology to undergraduate and postgraduate psychology students. *Bulletin of the British Psychological Society*, 32, 75-78.

Orford, J. (1992). *Community Psychology: Theory and Practice.* Chichester: Wiley.

Orford, J., Duckett, P., & McKenna, S. (2003). European Community psychology in theory, practice and praxis? - The European Network of Community Psychology (ENCP) fourth European congress of community psychology and business meeting, Barcelona, 2002 - three contrasting views. *Journal of Community & Applied Social Psychology*, 13(3), 258-265.

Parker, I. (1994). Psychology, Politics and Resistance in the UK. *RadPsy News: Newsletter of the Radical Psychology Network*, 5 (August 1994).

Parker, I. (1999). Critical psychology: critical links. *Annual Review of Critical Psychology*, 1, 3-18.

Parker, I. (2005). *Qualitative Psychology. Introducing Radical Research.* Buckingham: Open University Press.

Parker, I., & Spears, R. (1996). *Psychology and Society.* London: Pluto Press.

Phillips, L., Hughes, G., & Bell, L. (1998). Special Issue: Community Psychology. *Clinical Psychology Forum*, 122, 4-50.

QAA. (2004). *Subject Benchmarking Statement: Psychology.* London: Quality Assurance Agency for Higher Education. Available at http://www.qaa.ac.uk/crntwork/benchmark/phase2/psychology.pdf. Retrieved January 12, 2005.

Ramon, S., & Giannichedda, M. (Eds.). (1988). *Psychiatry in Transition: The British and Italian experiences.* London: Pluto.

Reason, P., & Rowan, J. (Eds.). (1981). *Human Inquiry: A Sourcebook of New Paradigm Research.* Chichester: Wiley.

Roiser, M. (1998). The Democratic Social Science of Mass-Observation. In M. Cheun Chung (Ed.), *Current Trends in History and Philosophy of Psychology* (Vol. 1, pp. 21-27). Leicester: British Psychological Society.

Sharpe, J., & Bostock, J. (2002). *Supporting People with Debt and Mental Health Problems: Research with Psychological Therapists in Northumberland.* Newcastle: Northumberland Health Action Zone / Action Against Poverty, Northumberland.

Sixsmith, J., & Boneham, M. (2002). Men and masculinities: Stories of health and social capital. In C. Swann & A. Morgan (Eds.), *Social Capital for health: Insights from qualitative research.* London: Health Development Agency.

Sixsmith, J., Kagan, C. & Duckett, P. (2004). *Pupils' Emotional Well-Being in School.* Research Institute for Health and Social Change, Manchester Metropolitan University, May 2004. Available at http://homepages.poptel.org.uk/mark.burton/PUPILS%92_EMOTIONAL.pdf. Retrieved January 21, 2006.

Smail, D. (2001). *Why Therapy Doesn't Work and What We Should Do About It, and The Nature of Un-happiness.* London: Robinson.

Smail, D. (2005) *Power, Interest and Psychology Elements of a Social Materialist Understanding of Distress.* Ross on Wye: PCCS Books.

Solomon, M., Pistrang, N., & Barker, C. (2001). The benefits of mutual support groups for parents of children with disabilities. *American Journal of Community Psychology*, 29, 113-132.

Stacey, B. (1976). *Psychology and Social Structure*. London: Methuen.

Sveaass, N. (2000). Psychological work in a post-war context: experiences from Nicaragua. *Community Work and Family*, 3(1), 37-64.

Thatcher, M. (1987). Interview. In article, D. Keay, AIDS, Education and the Year 2000! *Women's Own Magazine,* October 3, pp. 8-10.

Tully, B., Doyle, M., Cahill, D., Bayles, T., & Graham, D. (1978). Psychology and community work in mental health. *Bulletin of the British Psychological Society*, 31, 115-119.

Watkins, S. (2004). A Weightless Hegemony. *New Left Review* (second series) 25, 5-33.

Wilkinson, S. (1986). Introduction. In S. Wilkinson (Ed.), *Feminist Social Psychology.* Milton Keynes: Open University Press.

Wolfensberger, W. (1992). *A brief introduction to social role valorization as a high-order concept for structuring human services* (2nd ed.). Syracuse, NY: Training Institute for Human Service Planning, Leadership and Change Agentry, Syracuse University.

11
Community Psychology Between Attitude and Clinical Practice: The German Way

Jarg Bergold and Mike Seckinger

Abstract

The development of community psychology (CP) in Germany is described in four steps: (1) the politicalization of psychology in the 1970s by the student movement, (2) the critical theory, (3) the social psychiatry movement, and (4) a favorable economy for the context of development. The introduction of CP was stimulated by the CP development in the United States, the discussions about psychiatric illness, and the critical analysis of psychiatric institutions. Although CP is currently taught in several German universities, full academic institutionalization has never been achieved. CP research is closely connected to practice with a strong emphasis on community mental health. CP-oriented research can be found in the fields of psychiatry, prevention, self and mutual help, social networks and social support, counseling, and neighborhood and city quarter development. This chapter describes how the mental health system and psychiatric and psychosocial institutions and their cooperation have been analyzed for their influence on professional work and well-being of clients. Finally, some of the contradictions between CP principles and professionalisation of CP are shown. They lead to problems of professional and academic identity. The consequences for the development in Germany are discussed.

Introduction

In this chapter, we are going to portray the development of German community psychology as a path through a social, political, and economical landscape. It has been influenced greatly by the economic conditions and accompanying political climate, from financial stability in the 1950s to current-day unemployment and increased poverty. CP is understood in accordance with Orford (1992) as the study of the person in contexts ranging from the proximate social setting of the couple or the family to higher-order systems like neighbourhood, social-cultural groups, institutions, or society. CP actions are oriented towards the well-being of individuals, groups, and special populations such as minorities. These actions are based on values, decisions, and critical reflection on social and societal conditions of power and inequality. In Germany, research and practice are conceptualized as closely interconnected. CP is seen on the one hand as a psychological discipline and on the other hand as a basic attitude in professional work that can be extended to other areas like social work, self-help, and so forth.

This chapter shows that CP in Germany developed primarily in discussions within the fields of clinical psychology and psychiatry, describes the main events that led to the establishment of CP in Germany, including the mental health/psychiatry movement, identifies some of the barriers to formalization of CP, provides examples of the main areas of CP-driven work, and lists some of the inherent contradictions of CP as a profession in Germany. We conclude the chapter by illuminating some of the main problems Germany faces today and our ideas about CP's future direction in our country.

The Context of the Development

In Germany, the development of CP started during a period of radical societal change resulting from many different but interconnected factors. What follows is a short description of some of these factors that are important in understanding the development of CP in Germany.

The Student Protests

The German economy flourished after World War II. Monetary reform and the social market economy provided security to the majority of the population and produced a stable political system with three major parties. For the younger generation, however, this societal status was connected with feelings of stagnation and restriction. The majority of people in Germany avoided looking back to what had happened in Germany during the Nazi regime and left many of the old structures in economy, politics, and education unchanged. During the second half of the 1960s, frustration with these conditions led to student protests targeted at the antiquated and hierarchical structure of the universities and the degree to which Germany had not dealt sufficiently with its past, as exemplified by the employment of former representatives of the Nazi regime for political and administrative positions. The Vietnam War was also a popular target of these student protests.

Concurrent with the political developments described above, an intellectual discussion developed in the universities, providing new theoretical means to criticize the social, political, and economic development in post-war Germany. Several well-known sociologists who had emigrated during the

Nazi regime returned to Germany. They advocated a theoretical thinking that was very critical of the governmental structure in Germany and the existing society. Particularly, the critical theory of the "Frankfurt School," initiated by Max Horkheimer and Theodor W. Adorno, had a strong effect on the new generation of sociologists and later on the student movement. This school of thought provided a critical potential for the analysis of many different fields. Quite a number of students in psychology applied these concepts and analytical tools to criticize academic psychology, clinical psychology, and more specifically behavior therapy and modification.

Development of Psychology in Germany During and After World War II

The politicalization of psychology also had its roots in the development of academic psychology during the Nazi regime and after World War II. During the Nazi regime, famous Jewish psychologists (e.g., Kurt Lewin) were forced to leave Germany. Many of the academic psychologists either aligned themselves with the Nazis or became convinced members of the Nazi party. During this time, psychology developed in a way very much in-line with the Nazi ideology. After the defeat of the Nazis, some of these Nazi-era psychologists remained in their positions and kept teaching their ideology-tainted theories at German universities. When alternative approaches like statistics, learning theory, experimental research, and particularly behavior therapy were introduced in Germany, they were well reviewed by the generation that had grown up after the fall of the Nazi regime.

The Psychiatry Movement

Some years later, the field of psychiatry experienced changes as well. In August 1971, the German government called together an expert commission to analyze the status of psychiatry in Germany. The report of this commission triggered many professional and scientific activities, which were in part stimulated by the ideas of social psychiatry in the United States and partially by more radical ideas like "anti-psychiatry" (e.g., Laing, 1960) in England and "democratic psychiatry" in Italy (e.g., Basaglia et al., 1987).

A rather strong community psychiatry movement developed in Hamburg at the end of the 1960s. The German Association for Social Psychiatry (DGSP) became a melting pot for professionals (nurses, psychologists, doctors, social workers, etc.) working in mental health, motivated by social inequalities in mental health treatments, and who were looking for an alternative to traditional psychiatry. These professionals experimented with new forms of professional–patient relationships, outpatient treatments, and concepts of de-institutionalization and tried to change the situation for their patients by influencing politicians to introduce new policies in the field of mental health.

The Development of German CP

These developments in the political, intellectual, and professional fields influenced those clinical psychologists who were discontent with the individual-centered clinical approach. They were influenced by behavior therapy and modification and simultaneously by the student movement. They were fascinated by the idea that by changing the social conditions of people, even psychiatric illness could be influenced.

Gert Sommer and Heiko Ernst started the first course on CP at the University of Heidelberg in 1973 (Sommer, personal communication[1]). In 1977, Sommer and Ernst edited the first reader in German with the word *Gemeindepsychologie* (community psychology) in its title. A year after this edited volume, Sommer and his co-workers published an article in the *German Handbook of Clinical Psychology* (Sommer, Kommer, Kommer, Malchow & Quack, 1978). This paper described the main characteristics of CP with topics on maximal degree of psychosocial health as the main aim, focusing on primary prevention, actively reaching out to people in need, sharing psychology with other professionals and nonprofessionals, supporting mutual-help, emphasizing epidemiology and more specifically on epidemiology of competences, and using program evaluation. The authors discussed the shortcomings of the German psychiatric system and proposed alternatives such as community mental health centres and stressed the necessity of prevention.

These first publications on CP in Germany were written by psychologists with strong social involvement and interest in psychiatric epidemiology, who wanted to promote change particularly in the area of psychiatry. These psychologists wanted to use all the knowledge and techniques of psychology and other neighboring disciplines to change the living conditions of people in a way that would maximize psychosocial health.

A Critical View on Clinical Psychology

A major contribution to the development of CP in Germany was a new sociological approach to the problem of "psychiatric illness." Heiner Keupp introduced the topic of "labeling theory" in Germany, starting in 1972 with a book entitled *Psychological Disorders as Deviant Behaviour*. He drew his theoretical arguments from the debates in sociology of medicine in the United States and the analyses of the Frankfurt School of sociology in Germany.

An edited volume by Keupp and Zaumseil (1978) entitled *The Social Organisation of Mental Distress: On the Work of Clinical Psychologists* documented the next step in the development of CP in Germany. The authors

---

[1] E-mail answer to a short questionnaire of the authors, 27 January 2005.

argued that, while clinical psychologists had gained much acceptance for their competencies in therapeutic techniques, during the past few years the condition of Germany's public mental health service system was still very poor. Consequently, Keupp and Zaumseil argued that these therapeutic competencies were not sufficient if psychologists really wanted to contribute to an improvement of the system. What was needed, they argued, was a different kind of reflective professional identity. They argued that psychologists ought to know more about the institutional context of their activities at different levels, reaching from the therapeutic setting to the institution in which they work, all the way up to the institutional politics and finance. Encouraged by the results of the "sociology of medicine" (e.g., Goffman, 1961), most authors tried to introduce a "sociology of psychology" to show that social conditions play an important role in clinical work.

CP as a permanent critical reflection of the professional self was further elaborated by Keupp who argued against new psychosocial experts and against "hyphen psychology." Instead he postulated that "we [psychologists] need much more a radical perspective on the continuously expanding area of psychosocial work" (Keupp, 1982a, p. 11, translation by J.B.). In his opinion, CP could become a radical perspective which "can be characterized as a specific attitude . . .." (p. 11). Keupp argued against the transfer of concepts and technologies from the Anglo-American CP. Instead, he requested a reflection on the beginning economic crisis in Germany and its consequences for the reforms in the field of mental health. To him, the existing scientific approaches to handle mental illness by individualizing these problems seemed inadequate under the social and economic conditions of capitalism.

Keupp's position was obviously influenced by the Frankfurt School of critical thought. The main task of CP, as defined by Keupp, was to critically reflect on the current state of practice and theory of psychiatry, psychology, and other disciplines in the psychosocial field and to engage in social change (Keupp, 1987, p. 193) in the tradition of Murrell and Bennett. Keupp's position, from these seminal pieces, has been very influential in the further development of CP in Germany.

The Institutional Organization of German CP

During the 1970s, many of the clinical psychologists and students of psychology were organized in the German Association for Behavior Therapy (DGVT), which played an important role in the development of German CP. Originally founded to promote behavior therapy and modification, the DGVT became a melting pot for clinical psychologists' discontent with the traditional individualistic approach. This organization galvanized psychologists' willingness to change the mental health system on the basis of new, "progressive" ideas in politics, sociology, community psychiatry, and so forth. CP was widely welcomed as an approach that could help to change the situation for underprivileged people (Daiminger, 2004).

In 1982, the congress of the DGVT had as its motto "Community Psychology Perspectives." The aims of the congress were summarized in a commentary given by members of the CP group: "The demands of the congress aimed on establishing a political awareness (*Politisierung*) of a profession not in the sense of a ritualised declaration of programmatic progressiveness but in the sense of 'inner political awareness,' which aims at professional self-understanding" (Keupp et al., 1983, p. 265). It was hoped that clinical psychologists would break their habit of looking only for efficient therapeutic techniques and begin to see the link between individual crisis and suffering and societal conditions. This aim could not be achieved. The authors noticed that the congress actually had been split in half with one group focusing on the subject of social politics and worlds of living and the other on the subject of clinical and therapeutic developments in a narrow, more traditional sense. The schism, first seen at the congress, never changed in Germany.

At the same time, there was a conflict among community psychologists. One group demanded the incorporation of the results of critical analysis of societal processes in everyday work and critical reflection on the psychological techniques of diagnosis and intervention with the help of this knowledge. The other group wanted to develop existing psychological techniques further in order to help underprivileged people to change their life conditions and promote their well-being. Clearly, these two positions were not completely incompatible. However, the very high moral and political expectations for community psychologists complicated the further development of CP in Germany.

As a step towards more formalization, an annual open forum (Thurnauer Kreis) was founded in 1987. The informal exchange at the forum stimulated the development of CP in Germany to a great extent.[2] In 1995, the members of the forum decided to establish a formal organization, the Gesellschaft für Gemeindepsychologische Forschung und Praxis[3] (GGFP), and to publish a newsletter. At present, the GGFP is a small association with a stable number of members (65). Annual conferences on special topics are organized following the tradition of the forum.

The State of German CP Today

This section will describe the current state of German CP in academia and practice. CP's development has been and continues to be shaped by the changes in the German economy. For instance, the diminishment of the welfare state reduced the possibilities of implementing new CP-oriented

---

[2] Topics at the annual meetings, for example, were neighbourhood development, improvement of practice, CP in Germany.
[3] Society of Research and Practice in Community Psychology.

services on the one hand and on the other hand led to an increasing interest for self-help and citizen engagement.

Teaching CP

CP is taught in different settings (universities and Fachhochschulen[4]) and to different types of students (psychology and social work). At the universities, most of the exponents of CP were appointed as professors of clinical psychology (e.g., Bergold and Legewie in Berlin, Gottwald and Belschner in Oldenburg, Sommer and Roehrle in Marburg). These individuals adopted a CP approach to their practice and redefined their clinical teaching with a CP orientation. In addition, in Munich social psychology was taught with a CP orientation by Keupp. At the Psychological Institute of the University of Flensburg, a department of health psychology and health education with a CP orientation was initiated in 1999 by Faltermaier. In some other German universities like Augsburg, Bamberg, Dresden, and Essen, CP was taught in some courses but did not play an important role in the teaching of psychology overall.

Although CP courses are taught in some universities, formal training in CP does not exist. What is available is teaching that includes practical training in CP-oriented institutions. In two of the three universities in Berlin (Freie Universität and Technische Universität), students doing their diploma in psychology participate, under supervision, in the daily work of CP-oriented staff members in different institutions in the psychosocial and psychiatric field.

Unfortunately, during the past few years, the presence of CP in traditional universities decreased because of this lack of formalization. The CP-focused scientists retired and their chairs were filled by clinical psychologists of different orientations—currently most probably with a neuropsychological orientation. The situation is a bit different in the universities of applied science where social workers and social educators are trained. In about 12 to 15 of these universities throughout Germany, psychologists have been appointed to teach psychology with a CP orientation in social work/education programs. For these professions, CP is attractive because it provides concepts and methods for the analysis of institutional and social contexts as well as knowledge about the functioning of the service institutions and their counseling techniques.

Research and Practice

One of the core characteristics of CP is its linking of practice and research. Therefore, research and practice of CP are presented jointly. When trying to review the literature, some questions immediately arise: Which publications

---

[4] *Fachhochschulen* can be seen equivalent to universities of applied science or professional schools.

can be subsumed under the heading of CP? Should every publication that includes principles and concepts discussed in CP be included or only publications that clearly reference CP? These problems arise because CP can be considered more of a general attitude to look at psychology and psychological practice than as a subdiscipline of psychology. People who define themselves as community psychologists today work on a variety of topics such as health promotion, community mental health services, counseling, youth welfare services, mutual help groups, prevention, health psychology, neighborhood development, and city quarter development that use CP concepts without referring directly to CP. In this paper, we, therefore, decided to show the main issues of research and practice by giving examples that we consider as important points in the development of CP in Germany.

An analysis of the empirical studies during the period between 1977 and 1992 was published in 1995 by Roehrle and colleagues. In this study, the authors searched the German psychological databank PSYNDEX for different types of keywords relevant to CP. Roughly speaking, they found an increase in CP publication rate in relation to the above-mentioned conference for clinical psychology and psychotherapy in 1982 and a decrease in the following years. This may reflect a basic problem for the scientific development of CP in Germany. CP is elicited by two dominant orientations, the stress on critical reflection and the importance of practice. The stress on critical reflection hinders academic psychologists to do empirical studies without having thought through all social and societal implications. Practitioners on the other hand are so busy with their daily work and with inducing change in institutions that they simply do not have the time to do research.

In the following subsections, we describe the main fields of CP-oriented research and practice in Germany. These are (a) psychiatry, (b) prevention in the field of health, (c) self and mutual help, (d) social networks and social support, (e) life environment, (f) counseling, (g) structural aspects of the health system, and (h) methodological developments.

Psychiatry

Psychiatry has been one of the most important areas of conceptual thought, research, and practice in Germany during the 1970s and 1980's. In the big cities of Berlin, Hamburg, and Munich CP has influenced the networks of psychosocial and psychiatric services to a great extent. In collaboration with other professionals, social psychiatric outpatient services and rehabilitation and crisis intervention centers have been developed, which are focused on CP principles like community orientation, low threshold accessibility, participation, deinstitutionalization, and multidisciplinarity. In Munich, these research activities have led to an anchoring of community psychological and community psychiatry ideas and terms in the field of mental health at the local and regional political levels (Cramer, Hochreiter, & Kraus 2003). As a consequence, the local government has provided more money for the development of outpatient services.

All over Germany, CP-oriented research in psychiatry emphasized evaluation, analysis of the functioning of institutions including the mental health system, analysis of subjective theories of professionals, and the daily life and subjective knowledge of people affected by psychiatry and its systems of help. Particularly, the personal perspectives of people in various everyday life situations were scrutinized with qualitative methods.

Since the second half of the 1980s there has been a general change in health politics in Germany. Cost reduction and individualization of health risks have become important issues. As an answer to this development, community psychologists have worked to promote consumer rights and participation of patients in institutional decisions (Achberger, 2000). Additionally, an attempt to democratize the relationship between patients, relatives, and professionals started in Hamburg (Bock, 1994) and is now used in various places. In so-called "psychosis seminars", members of the three stakeholder groups (client, family, and professional) meet on an equal level, trying to develop a shared language and learning from each other about the experiences, concepts, and strategies in handling psychoses.

Prevention and the Field of Health

Health promotion and illness prevention have also been central areas of action and research in German CP. Concepts of professional action were developed out of social analyses of the conviction that there is a close connection between psychic troubles and social conditions, and therefore psychological interventions always have a society-influencing function.

Generally, it can be stated that CP in Germany, aimed at the origination and organization of prevention programs, not only stressed individual responsibility for healthy ways of living but also attempted to change living conditions and to make resources in the community more accessible. These prevention efforts were apparent in the early writings (e.g., Sommer & Ernst, 1977) and later in a book series with the title *Progress in Community Psychology and Health Promotion* (published by DGVT-Verlag). While a multitude of topics concerning the field of prevention have been discussed, we will summarize only the most important clusters. The first cluster of topics is more theory oriented. Among others, Antonovsky's (1979, in German 1997) concept of salutogenesis[5] was discussed and led to a wider understanding of prevention. Along this line of thought, Belschner (1995) and Faltermaier (1999) proposed that quality of life research in health promotion and prevention might be a productive CP approach for the future. Faltermaier further argued for a health promotion on the basis of four elements: integral and positive conception of health, orientation towards the subject and his or her everyday competencies,

---

[5] Antonovsky developed a salutogenetic approach in contrast with the pathogenetic approach in mental health.

promotion of resources and consideration of the life-world (*Lebenswelt*),[6] and the social context. The second cluster focuses on reforms of the public health services (e.g., Trojan et al., 1999) and health promotion and illness prevention at the local or community level in accordance with the "Healthier City" program of the World Health Organization (WHO) (e.g., Trojan & Hildebrandt, 1989). New integrated models of preventive and health-promoting action (e.g., Roehrle, 1999) in the area of community-oriented health promotion were discussed. The third important area has been prevention work with children in families and schools. Concepts and investigations have been presented about such topics as health-promoting schools (Paulus, 1999), violence prevention (Hanewinkel, 1999), and development of competencies (Sommer et al., 1983). A fourth cluster of studies can be identified as including studies on stress and coping with chronic illness and prevention efforts to decrease disorders like depression, anxiety, or addiction (see Manz, 2001). The next subsections will take up some of these topics but will not focus particularly on the area of health promotion.

Self and Mutual Help

The area of self and mutual help relates closely to questions about how to promote individuals' competencies so that they can change their conditions themselves. Self-help centers were founded by professionals with diverse disciplinary background. Community psychologists participated in this development by pointing at the necessity of independence of self-help, its role as an equal partner of a professional supply system, and its contribution to the empowerment of its members. This self/mutual-help agenda triggered a variety of activities at the practical level (e.g., supervision for self-help groups, advice and further education), at the political level (e.g., foundation of a self-help advisory board at a municipal level, demands of public subsidies, organization of public events), and at the research level (e.g., counseling through clients, Büchner et al., 1996; cooperation between mutual-help groups and health services, Bobzien, 2003).

Social Networks and Social Support

The question about the type of consequences the individualization processes have on the individual in collective relationships has led to an intensive discussion in the field of CP about the importance of social networks, their functions for the individual and the society, and the processes of change to which they are subject.

---

[6] The term *life-world* (*Lebenswelt*) was coined by the phenomenological philosopher Husserl and later adopted by Habermas. It denotes the world of the person as seen and experienced by her or him.

The importance of the topics of "social networks" and "social support" in research and practice were first identified in a review by Keupp (1982b). In particular, research groups in Munich (e.g., Straus, 2002) and Marburg (Roehrle et al., 1998) conducted studies on these concepts and promoted their use in the practice of CP and health promotion. Their CP-oriented network research included the study of emotional support as well as other forms of support. Nestmann (1988) studied the helping potential of "everyday helpers" from different professions such as taxi drivers, hairdressers, and bartenders.

On a societal level, it has been questioned how societies must organize themselves when faced with the fact that many people who lose their traditional income and live on unemployment benefit are in danger of solitude and despair. This questioning has led to an intensive discussion of communitarianism and citizen engagement. The latter has become an important topic in the field of CP in Germany.

Life Environment

The influence of the environment on individual and social well-being has been another important area of conceptual thinking and research in German CP. Two triggers for this development can be identified. First, at the end of the 1980s, people became more aware of health risks of environmental threats like the disaster at Chernobyl. Wars and dictatorships all over the world produced awareness of poverty, violence, and injustice in other countries and of the relationship between the so-called developed and underdeveloped countries. The influence of these changes on the development of CP in Germany was discussed in the edited volume by Böhm and colleagues in 1992. In this text, a new stream of thought can be seen. A small group of authors like Cramer and Legewie advocated for a more global understanding of "environment" in CP research and practice, as exemplified in their investigation of the awareness of people involved in environmental crisis (Cramer, 1991), particularly Chernobyl (Legewie, 1990), and their psychological consequences.

Second, during the past decade, neoliberal and globalizing strategies have led to booming new city areas and, simultaneously, to city quarters with bad living conditions, high rates of poverty (including low incomes among immigrants), unemployment, violence, crime, and drugs. To counter this development, German community psychologists have tried to secure the influence of citizens through increased participation and empowerment, which is in opposition to the logic of the traditional German administration. Examples of participation and empowerment include Legewie and Janssen's (1997) study of health promotion in cities via citizen initiatives, Trojan and Hildebrandt's (1989) consideration of health-related network promotion at the local level, and Belschner et al.'s (1998) development of interventional methods to improve housing conditions in big apartment buildings. Trojan and Legewie (2001a) presented an expert report for the German parliament on "Goals, policy, and practice of the design of health-promoting environmental and life conditions" and discussed in a paper city quarter development as a future working field for community psychologists (Trojan & Legewie, 2001b).

Counseling

In educational counseling, CP concepts have been very well received. The concepts of "community orientation," "low threshold accessibility," and "multiprofessionalism" have changed child guidance clinics in city districts (e.g., Rudeck, 1983; Chow, 1985) and rural areas (Lenz, 1990). For example, a survey by Roth (1994) found that all of the 474 participating child guidance clinics used a community-oriented approach to some extent but insufficient capacity of staff members limited its use.

The development of counseling concepts has also contributed to the acceptance of CP in educational counseling. A socioecological perspective, introduced by Lenz (1997), argues that the concepts of "life-world (Lebenswelt)," "orientation towards the social space," "promotion of social networks," and "empowerment" must be included into counseling in order to help families deal with their own and their children's problems in today's difficult economic situation.

With adults, resource-oriented counseling has also been developed (for a survey see: Nestmann, Engel, & Sickendiek, 2004). It is conceptualized as an alternative to the problem orientation of traditional clinical psychology and psychotherapy by focusing on resources as life-world and social networks. Along these lines, a community-oriented crisis intervention service has been developed in Berlin. This program is strongly influenced by CP concepts. It offers resource-oriented, anonymous counseling 24 hours a day by phone, in person, and by mobile teams. The program is organized regionally, can be utilized anonymously, and is free of charge. It is closely connected with other service institutions in the particular region (Bergold & Zimmermann 2003).[7]

Structural Aspects of the Health System

The structural analysis of the health system and of the psychosocial and psychiatric institutions has been another important field of research and reflection in German CP. This analysis has been stimulated by the work of Goffman, Foucault, and Castells and by Dörner (1975) in Germany, just to name a few. Under this perspective, social justice is closely connected to individuals' adequate access to health facilities and services. Therefore, the health system as a whole as well as the construction of particular institutions and their interrelations have been studied with regard to their exclusive function for certain populations.

---

[7] See http://www.krisendienstforschung.de

A starting point for the analysis of the health system has been the crisis of the welfare state. Wolff (1983) proposed an explanation for this crisis and put forward some potential measures for handling this situation such as increasing transparency for the consumers and better consumer protection. The unification of the two German states in 1990 opened up the possibility of comparing the two basically different constructed psychiatric systems in East and West Germany. Bergold and his colleagues (e.g., Bergold, 1996) analyzed the mental health service systems in the two states and described the main characteristics. Zaumseil and Leferink (1997) studied the everyday life, identity, and social relationships of chronic schizophrenics under different political and cultural conditions after the fall of the wall in East and West Berlin and the changes due to the adaptation of the Eastern to the Western system.

The function of professionalisation in the area of psychosocial help has been analyzed, too (Enzmann & Kleiber, 1989). Wolff (1981) stressed the idea that, basically, the helping relationship is a societal not a personal relationship. It was shown that certain groups of the population were excluded by producing an expert-dominated relationship. As a result, German community psychologists became very conscious of the problems of expert dominance.

The structure of institutions, too, can exclude parts of the population with low income and poor education—even without the conscious knowledge of the professionals. The institutions establish criteria for services such as appropriateness, legality, thoroughness, and understandability. In this way, institutions have a kind of self-preservation tendency; they select clients who justify their existence and simultaneously restrict the access to the institution particularly for the underprivileged part of the population (e.g., Breuer 1979).

A stronger cooperation between the different types of help offered by professional services and nonprofessional institutions is required by the increasing differentiation of life-worlds, the complexity of problem situations, and the unintended consequences of a continuously increasing specialization of psychosocial services. The cooperation between psychosocial and psychiatric health services in crisis intervention has been studied by Filsinger and Bergold (1993) and Bergold (1992). Santen and Seckinger (2003) have investigated networks and cooperation between different youth welfare institutions, and Lenz (2005) showed the necessity of institutional cooperation to help children with mentally ill parents. These authors also discuss the risks of extensive control of users when cooperation between institutions is very high. It is proposed that the disadvantages for the users of these services can be limited by models of user control, which may provide a counterbalance against the possibility of institutions to accomplish their own aims (Seckinger, 2006).

Methodological Development

In conducting research within the field of CP, researchers are confronted with topics of high complexity like empowerment and social networks and characteristic features of CP like participation of the research partners, closeness to everyday life, multiple perspectives, partiality, and process orientation (Bergold, 2003).

CP research is very often intimately connected with the everyday life of people and with projects that aim at inducing change to their situations. Traditionally, there has been a wide gap between researchers, their institutions (universities), and practice. The relevance of the research results for practitioners and their clients is, at times, very limited. This problem was discussed in Germany under the topic of "practice research" starting with a reader published by Beerlage and Fehre in 1989. Practice research proposes to formulate research questions and to do research jointly with professionals working in practice institutions (Bergold & Zaumseil, 1989). In this way, the transfer of results between research and practice might be achieved in a way that avoids colonization of the practice (Straus, 1992).

Bergold (2003) has argued that there is a certain affinity between qualitative methods and community psychology. For many research questions in CP, qualitative methods or the combination of qualitative and quantitative methods seem to be the most appropriate methodology. Consequently, Leferink and Bergold (1996) have argued that for the evaluation of complex systems like a crisis intervention center, a social ecological evaluation concept has to be developed that takes into account the institutional context and their effects by using qualitative and quantitative methods. Also, some new methodological approaches have been developed. For example, Straus (2002) has proposed methods for network analysis, and Brueninghaus et al. (1991) have developed a "Contact Analysis Interview Scheme" for community psychology field research.[8]

Final View on German CP Development

Altogether, CP in Germany has inspired research and practice in clinical and social psychology and diverse neighboring disciplines. Ideas, concepts, and action strategies that are of high importance to CP can be found in different areas even if their relatedness to CP is not explicitly mentioned. However, the history and particularly the current state of CP cannot be presented as a history of success. Despite some institutionalization, German CP today is neither academically nor practically accepted as a subdiscipline of psychology on a broad scale. We will try to sketch some of the possible arguments for the lack of success of CP in Germany.

---

[8] "Contact Analysis Interview Scheme" is a structured interview system for describing interpersonal transactions. Target groups in particular are individuals threatened by social isolation.

Characteristics of CP

CP requires high professional and personal standards. We will present some of those that have been important for the development of CP in Germany. Nearly all of them contradict the "normal" role of professionals.

- *Empowerment and participation* demand an acceptance of competencies and skills of individuals, groups, and communities. Professionals, therefore, cannot define themselves as experts in the field. On the contrary, they should strengthen people in their competence for action, perpetually question their own role as an expert, and critically consider the interrelation between the living conditions of the individual and the institutional and societal context.
- The demand of community psychologists to "give psychology away" questions the expert status because the community members become "psychology" experts themselves who no longer need psychologists in the particular problem area.
- Community psychologists should strive for *societal change,* which leads to more social justice. Among others, this may arouse conflicts with basic beliefs of their employer as representatives of societal norms.
- *Multidisciplinary* research and practice is not only an important aim of CP but also a necessity when working in real-life situations where psychological knowledge and know-how is not enough to understand processes or develop useful strategies to handle situations. Community psychologists have to be able to work with theories and concepts of other disciplines thereby questioning their status as experts.
- *Critical reflection of power* is one of the necessities when working with underprivileged groups. Community psychologists have to consider the power structure in the field in which they work in order to help their clients to achieve their aims. Simultaneously, they have to reflect on the relationship of power between themselves and their partners to avoid colonizing the world of their partners.
- Community psychologists strive to help their partners to find *their own solution* to problems. They define themselves more as a midwife than a builder. They do not offer techniques for change to people like behavior modification, for example.

Consequences for Community Psychologists in Germany

We think that all these points have consequences for the development of CP and its professionalisation. What happens in a particular country depends on the context in which this development (e.g., Burton & Kagan, 2003) takes place. Here, we will consider the situation in Germany and try to figure out what are consequences of the contradictions in this context.

Problems of Identity

We would like to put forward the thesis that the above-exposed characteristics produce problems of identity for community psychologists and problems of identification for CP. We further believe that this might be one of the reasons why today so many psychologists in Germany and in other countries no longer define themselves as community psychologists.

The development of professional identity—particularly for beginners—is made very difficult by the demand for reflexivity and the acceptance of the other as expert of his own world. The idea that the status of an expert could be defined by his ability of helping others to regain the power to organize their lives by themselves without secure tracks seems to be a paradox. Therefore, German community psychologists hesitated to develop clearly defined professional tools despite a long discussion in the German association. On the other hand, many of the CP practitioners feel that a reflexive attitude is not enough in a situation in which financial and personal resources are reduced and efficiency is demanded.

In the academic field, the requested interdisciplinarity does have a detrimental effect on the institutionalization of a psychological subdiscipline CP—even though today interdisciplinarity is demanded everywhere. The academic system functions accordingly to the principles of demarcation. Successful scientists have to make their own mark. Being able to work interdisciplinary and in cooperation with other disciplines hinders the possibility of defining a distinct academic field for one's own career. Furthermore, having a critical background, many German academic community psychologists are very suspicious of power. This is an advantage in CP work but it may hinder those in the academic game. Therefore, community psychologists have not conquered academic power positions that would enable them to institutionalize CP in the universities.

Competition with Social Work

A number of important CP concepts like empowerment and participation were developed in other disciplines long before CP started. In Germany, CP is in competition with the widespread concepts of social work, which habitually stresses the importance of social and societal factors for understanding and intervention in problems like poverty or social deviances. Important aspects of these approaches can be characterized by the terms "life-world" and "community work." Social workers are a well-established profession in the German health system and at present preferred by employers because they are paid less than psychologists.

Change of the Political Situation

The political situation in Germany has changed since the first half of the 1980s when CP started. Neoliberal concepts have become very influential.

254 Europe and Middle East

Because of financial problems, many of the achievements of the welfare state have been withdrawn. The causes attributed to illness and failing social integration are more and more individualized. In psychology, biological concepts play an increasingly important role—particularly at the universities. In this situation, theoretical and practical concepts, which stress the connection between individual and societal responsibility, lose their attractiveness.

Strategies for Survival

In the face of this situation, community psychologists in Germany will have to contemplate surviving the future. At the moment, the situation is not as bad as it seems. There are many practitioners in varied fields who are open to CP and work with its basic concepts. The future may be worse. CP is not established in any of the universities. There are no programs on any level. In the long run, this may lead to reduction of knowledge about CP in Germany because CP will no longer be taught in regular university courses. To deal with this situation, the German association (GGFP) started to develop guidelines in which the basic values of CP are formulated. Focusing on cooperation with other initiatives and on certain issues and activities is another strategy to strengthen CP in Germany.

A close cooperation with other European countries and their associations is another strategy. In 2005, the new European Community Psychology Association (ECPA) was founded as a successor of the European Network of Community Psychology (ENCP). Hopefully, this cooperation will strengthen the position of CP in Europe and in Germany, too, for example, by developing a European master's program in CP, which should result in a European degree in CP that would be accepted in all European countries.

Comparison of Worldwide Developments from a German Perspective

In looking over the developments in the different countries, we were able to find many similarities and differences to the German development that are thought-provoking. Because space is restricted, we decided to concentrate on one aspect only. It is an aspect that momentarily bothers German community psychologists particularly: the increasing marginalization of CP in the academic field and the lack of visibility in practice.

We have the impression that problems with integration and connection are not only German problems but can be recognized in many different countries. Therefore, we used the chapters of this volume as texts that we analyzed in the way of "Grounded Theory" with the help of the computer program Atlas.ti to learn something about structural similarities. The scheme of Figure 1 was developed from the emerging categories.

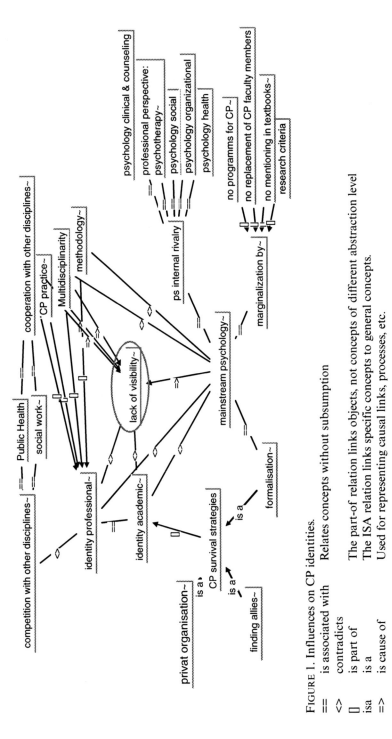

FIGURE 1. Influences on CP identities.

=	is associated with	Relates concepts without subsumption
<>	contradicts	
□	is part of	The part-of relation links objects, not concepts of different abstraction level
isa	is a	The ISA relation links specific concepts to general concepts.
=>	is cause of	Used for representing causal links, processes, etc.

We learned from our analysis that we had to differentiate between the academic and the professional field in terms of acceptance and impact of CP, but "lack of visibility" has resulted as the central category in both fields. Nelson et al. from Canada (this volume) state this very clearly: "The lack of visibility of CP extends beyond the walls of universities into work settings, professional certification organizations, and the community."

Because a discipline needs new blood, we will start our discussion with the situation in the universities. This area is controlled by the so-called mainstream psychology, which dominates the academic boards and associations. It can be characterized by adhering to a nomothetic epistemiological position and an individualistic approach. Important subdisciplines are experimental psychology, latterly neurocognitive psychology, and in the applied field clinical psychology with a strong orientation towards psychotherapy.

In our analysis of the problems of the establishment of CP in German universities, we highlighted the fact that CP does not have a clear-cut "psychology" identity. It incorporates theories and concepts from different sciences like anthropology, sociology, education, health, political science, social work, philosophy and so forth. The following statement from Australia seems to be rather typical for the situation in many countries: "Some respondents referred to connections with organizational psychology, criminology, the public sector, and local communities, recalling how they had to "battle perception that CP was not 'real' psychology but sociology." The epistemiological and methodological approaches in CP are another aspect that makes it difficult for mainstream psychology to accept CP. Using qualitative methods, hermeneutic and discursive approaches, structural analysis, and so forth, is contrary to the nomothetic, quantitative approach of mainstream psychology. A third aspect can be seen in a certain rivalry between CP and established psychological subdisciplines like social, organizational, and health psychology and particularly clinical psychology.

All these aspects result in marginalization of CP by different strategies. First of all, at many universities, graduate-level training programs in CP were not established. Therefore, there are only few appointments, and an academic career is difficult in this field (e.g., Australia, Canada, Germany, and United Kingdom). Similarly, CP is not mentioned in many introductory textbooks. Not replacing CP faculty members when retiring seems to be another strategy in countries where CP had been able to establish itself in some universities (e.g., Canada, Germany).

Today, academic community psychologists have started to think about survival strategies. The traditional way of establishing a scientific discipline would be a formal recognition in the universities and the academic associations. As we have already pointed out, this has been only practically successful in the past. However, the conditions imposed on CP by the academic associations also can restrict the development of CP enormously because such formalization always needs negotiations with mainstream psychology. In some countries, therefore, community psychologists seek allies (e.g., health psychology) to develop training programs that adhere to CP's values and basic scientific positions. Because traditional forms of formalization can be a dubious gift, a tendency to private organization of training can be recognized.

If we turn to the practice side of CP, we can recognize that CP is in a strange situation. On one side, CP concepts and theories seem to be broadly accepted and used in practice. Authors from many countries report that these concepts are used by many practitioners. Israel might be seen as an extreme example of this state. Raviv et al. (this volume) state ". . . that despite the small number of publications using the specific term, Israeli psychologists are familiar with the principles of community psychology and apply them extensively."

On the other hand, community psychologists do not have a clear professional identity in most of the countries. Different points can be made responsible for this phenomenon.

- Psychologists with other academic specializations often use CP concepts. They do not need a formal CP training. It does not help their career.
- The demand of CP to cooperate with other disciplines and to work in multidisciplinary teams to solve complex problems obscures often the peculiarity of the psychological subdiscipline "community psychology."
- Other disciplines like social work, public health, anthropology, and so forth, work in the same field and in part with the same concepts as CP. Before and parallel to the development of CP, there has been a development of community actions. Therefore, a legitimate question could be asked: Why should these activities and ideas now be called CP? Only because some psychologists have become aware of them? We assume that there is also some rivalry between CP and these neighbor disciplines—despite all cooperation. Several countries point at the fact that in many professional areas, CP concepts are used in practice but not attributed to or associated with CP (e.g., Israel, India).

We as community psychologists should accept the fact that reasonable and open professionals develop strategies that also could be called CP when confronted with certain problematic situations. But, what does that mean for our professional and academic life and the possibility to make our living? Under this perspective, the following sentence from the U.S. chapter of this volume sounds like whistling in the dark: "CP has emerged as a discipline that will maintain a separate identity from other related fields such as applied psychology, sociology, public health and social work."

After the analysis of the chapters, we think that community psychologists still have to work hard to establish this identity and make it visible to others. Doubtlessly, the power of CP theory and practice can be seen in this book, but this is probably not enough. To our opinion, it is still necessary to show the advantages of a particular psychological perspective to all the other professions when working together with others in community research and action. The psychological perspective has to be interconnected with other academic, professional, and everyday knowledge. CP identity under this perspective, therefore, could be called a "participative identity."

References

Achberger, C. (2000). Verbindliches Handeln im Fachbereich Psychiatrie des PARITÄTISCHEN Schleswig-Holstein und den Leitsätzen "Qualität sichern" und "NutzerInnen stärken". In M. Seckinger & S. Stiemert-Strecker & K. Teuber (Eds.), *Qualität durch Partizipation und Empowerment. Einmischungen in die Qualitätsdebatte* (pp. 77-84). Tübingen: Deutsche Gesellschaft fuer Verhaltenstherapie.

Antonovsky, A. (1979). *Health, stress, and coping.* San Francisco: Jossey-Bass.

Basaglia, F., Scheper-Hughes, N., Lovell, A. M., & Shtob, T. (1987). *Psychiatry inside out: Selected writings of Franco Basaglia.* New York, NY: Columbia University Press.

Beerlage, I., & Fehre, E.-M. (1989). *Praxisforschung zwischen Intuition und Institution.* Tübingen: Deutsche Gesellschaft fuer Verhaltenstherapie.

Belschner, W. (1995). Aufbruch zu einem neuen Gesundheitsverstaendnis in Gemeinde- und Gesundheitspsychologie. Eine Collage von Fragen und tastenden Antworten. In B. Roehrle & G. Sommer (Eds.), *Gemeindepsychologie: Bestandsaufnahmen und Perspektiven* (Vol. 1, pp. 160-176). Tuebingen: Deutsche Gesellschaft fuer Verhaltenstherapie.

Belschner, W., Graeser, S., & Mastall, E. (1998). Wohnen - Gesundheitsfoerderung im Alltag ermoeglichen. In G. Amann & R. Wipplinger (Eds.), *Gesundheitsfoerderung. Ein multidimensionales Taetigkeitsfeld* (pp. 307-327). Tuebingen: Deutsche Gesellschaft fuer Verhaltenstherapie.

Bergold, J. B. & Zaumseil, M. (1989). Forschungsdienst Wedding: Versuch der Entwicklung eines gemeindepsychologischen Forschungszugangs. In I. Beerlage & E. M. Fehre (Eds.), *Praxisforschung zwischen Intuition und Institution* (pp. 137-150). Tübingen: Deutsche Gesellschaft fuer Verhaltenstherapie.

Bergold, J. B. (1992). The systemic character of the psychosocial and psychiatric health services. In W. Tschacher & E. J. Schiepek & E. J. Brunner (Eds.), *Self-organization and clinical psychology. Empirical approaches to synergetic in psychology* (pp. 416-433). Berlin: Springer.

Bergold, J. B. (1996). A dimensional analysis of mental health service systems. Comparing East- and West-Germany. In M. Montero (Ed.), *Memorias de Psicología Comunitaria del XXV Congreso Interamericano de Psicología.* Caracas.

Bergold, J. B. (2003). The Affinity between Qualitative Methods and Community Psychology. *Forum Qualitative Sozialforschung / Forum: Qualitative Social Research,* 1. Available at: http://www.qualitative-research.net/fqs-texte/2-00/2-00bergold-e.htm.

Bergold, J. B., & Zimmermann, R. B. (2003). Wie arbeitet ein Krisendienst? Bericht ueber die Evaluation des Berliner Krisendienstes? Report on the evaluation of the Berlin Crisis Intervention Service. *Psychotherapie im Dialog,* 4(4), 382-388.

Bobzien, M. (2003). Kooperation von Selbsthilfekontaktstellen mit dem professionellen Versorgungssystem - den Wandel mit den Akteuren initiieren Selbsthilfeunterstützung in der Integrierten Versorgung am Beispiel der Entwicklung eines Kooperationsprojektes "dialog - Münchner Ärzte und Selbsthilfegruppen."

Bock, T. (1994). Sprachbilder vom Erleben einer Psychose Versuche der Verstaendigung von Psychose-Erfahrenen, Angehoerigen und Therapeuten in einem gemeinsamen Seminar. In F. Rotter (Ed.), *Psychiatrie, Psychotherapie und Recht. Diskurse und vergleichende Perspektiven* (pp. 77-94). Frankfurt a. M.: Lang.

Böhm, I., Faltermaier, T., Flick, U., & Krause Jacob, M. (1992). *Gemeindepsychologisches Handeln: Ein Werkstattbuch.* Freiburg i. Br.: Lambertus.

Breuer, F. (1979). *Psychologische Beratung und Therapie in der Praxis.* Heidelberg: Quelle & Meyer.

Brueninghaus, T., Petermann, F., & Riepe, J. (1991). Entwicklung eines Verfahrens zur Gemeindepsychologischen Feldforschung: Der Kontaktanalysebogen. *Zeitschrift fuer Klinische Psychologie, Psychopathologie und Psychotherapie, 39*(2), 158-172.

Büchner, B., Stark, W., & Bachl, A. (1996). Beratung durch Betroffene. Verbindung von sozialer Unterstützung und Dienstleistung. In U. Walter & W. Paris (Eds.), *Public Health - Gesundheit im Mittelpunkt.* Meran: Alfred & Söhne.

Burton, M., & Kagan, C. (2003). Community psychology: why this gap in Britain? *History and Philosophy of Psychology, 4*(2), 10-23.

Chow, S. (1985). Vier Jahre offene Arbeit – einige persönliche Gedanken. In R. Anneken & T. Heyden (Eds.), *Wege zur Veraenderung: Beratung und Selbsthilfe. Deutsche Gesellschaft fuer Verhaltenstherapie.* Tuebingen, 1985.

Cramer, M. (1991). *Unser Doppelleben. Neue Studien zur Umweltbetroffenheit.* Muenchen: Fachhochschule, Fachbereich Sozialwesen.

Cramer, M., Hochreiter, S., & Kraus, E. (2003). *Sachstandsbericht über Aktivitäten und Entwicklungen im gemeindepsychiatrischen Verbund München-Süd.* (manuscript). Muenchen.

Daiminger, C. (2004). WWW - Eine Erfolgsgeschichte mit Differenzen. Ein Beitrag zur Geschichte der Professionalisierung der Verhaltenstherapie und der DGVT in der BRD. Available at: http://www.diss.fu-berlin.de/2005/64/.

Dörner, K. (1975). *Diagnose der Psychiatrie.* Frankfurt: Campus.

Enzmann, D., & Kleiber, D. (1989). *Helfer-Leiden. Streß und Burnout in psychosozialen Berufen.* Heidelberg: Asanger.

Faltermaier, T. (1999). Subjektorientierte Gesundheitsfoerderung: Zur Konzeption einer salutogenetischen Praxis. In B. Roehrle & G. Sommer (Eds.), *Praevention und Gesundheitsfoerderung* (Vol. 4, pp. 27-52). Tuebingen: Deutsche Gesellschaft fuer Verhaltenstherapie.

Filsinger, D., & Bergold, J. (1993). Entwicklungsmuster und Entwicklungsdynamik psychosozialer Dienste: Probleme und Perspektiven der Vernetzung. In J. Bergold & D. Filsinger (Eds.), *Vernetzung psychosozialer Dienste. Theoretische Reflexionen und empirische Fallstudien über stadtteilbezogene Krisenintervention und ambulante Psychiatrie* (pp. 11-47). Weinheim: Juventa.

Goffman, I. (1961). *Asylums. Essays on the social situation of mental patients and other inmates.* New York: Praeger.

Hanewinkel, R. (1999). Praevention von Gewalt an Schulen. In B. Roehrle & G. Sommer (Eds.), *Praevention und Gesundheitsfoerderung,* Deutsche Gesellschaft fuer Verhaltenstherapie. Tuebingen, 1999, (pp. 135-159). Series: Fortschritte der Gemeindepsychologie und Gesundheitsfoerderung, Band 4.

Keupp, H. (1972). *Psychische Störungen als abweichendes Verhalten. Zur Soziogenese psychischer Stoerungen.* München: Urban & Schwarzenberg.

Keupp, H. (1982a). Einleitende Thesen zu einer radikalen gemeinde-psychologischen Perspektive psychosozialer Arbeit. In H. Keupp & D. Rerrich (Eds.), *Psychosoziale Praxis - gemeindepsychologische Perspektiven* (pp. 11-20). Muenchen: Urban & Schwarzenberg.

Keupp, H. (1982b). Soziale Netzwerke. In H. Keupp & D. Rerrich (Eds.), *Psychosoziale Praxis - gemeindepsychologische Perspektiven. Ein Handbuch in Schluesselbegriffen* (pp. 43-53). Muenchen: Urban & Schwarzenberg.

Keupp, H. (1987). Psychosoziale Praxis in einer sich spaltenden Gesellschaft - das "psychosoziale Projekt" im Umbruch. In J. Bergold et al. (Eds.), *Veraenderter Alltag und Klinische Psychologie* (pp. 89-109). Tuebingen: Deutsche Gesellschaft fuer Verhaltenstherapie. Series: Forum fuer Verhaltenstherapie und psychosoziale Praxis, Nr. 12.

Keupp, H., Cramer, M., Giese, E., Stark, W., & Wolff, S. (1983). Psychologen auf der Suche nach einer neuen politischen Identitaet. In M. Cramer & E. Giese & M. Koeppelmann-Baillieu & R. Rudeck (Eds.), *Gemeindepsychologische Perspektiven. Band 4: Orientierungshilfen zu einem beruflichen Selbstverstaendnis* (pp. 265-271). Tuebingen: Deutsche Gesellschaft fuer Verhaltenstherapie.

Keupp, H., & Zaumseil, M. (Eds.). (1978). *Die gesellschaftliche Organisation psychischen Leidens. Zum Arbeitsfeld klinischer Psychologen.* Frankfurt: Suhrkamp Taschenbuch Verlag.

Laing, R. D. (1960). *The Divided Self.* London: Tavistock Publications.

Leferink, K., & Bergold, J., B. (1996). Integration neuer psychosozialer Einrichtungen ins Versorgungssystem: Überlegungen zu einem sozialoekologischen Evaluationskonzept am Beispiel einer Krisenambulanz. *Psychiatrische Praxis, 23,* 270-274.

Legewie, H. (1990). Zwischen Resignation und Engagement Zur Psychologie des Risikobewusstseins nach Tschernobyl. *Psychosozial, 41,* 59-68.

Legewie, H., & Janssen, M. (1997). Buergerinitiativen foerdern Gesundheit in der Stadt. In C. Klotter (Ed.), *Praevention im Gesundheitswesen* (pp. 326-356). Goettingen: Verlag fuer Angewandte Psychologie.

Lenz, A. (1990). *Laendlicher Alltag und familiaere Probleme Eine qualitative Studie ueber Bewaeltigungsstrategien bei Erziehungs- und Familienproblemen auf dem Land.* Muenchen: Profil Verlag.

Lenz, A. (1997). Gemeindepsychologisches Handeln in der Beratung - eine sozialoekologische Perspektive. *Gemeindepsychologie-Rundbrief, 3*(1), 25-39.

Lenz, A. (2005). *Kinder psychisch kranker Eltern. Goettingen:* Hogrefe Verlag.

Manz, R. (2001). *Praevention und Gesundheitsfoerderung Band III Psychologische Programme fuer die Praxis* (Vol. 9). Tuebingen: Deutsche Gesellschaft fuer Verhaltenstherapie.

Nestmann, F. (1988). *Die alltaeglichen Helfer.* Berlin/New York: Walter de Gruyter.

Nestmann, F., Engel, F., & Sickendiek, U. (Eds.) (2004). *Das Handbuch der Beratung. Band 2: Ansaetze, Methoden und Felder.* Tuebingen: Deutsche Gesellschaft fuer Verhaltenstherapie.

Paulus, P. (1999). Die Gesundheitsfoerdernde Schule als paedagogischer Schulentwicklungsansatz. In B. Roehrle & G. Sommer (Eds.), *Praevention und Gesundheitsfoerderung* (pp. 117-134). Tuebingen: Deutsche Gesellschaft fuer Verhaltenstherapie.

Orford, J. (1992). *Community psychology. Theory and practice.* Chichester: Wiley.

Roehrle, B. (1999). Ein Modell praeventiven und gesundheitsfoerderlichen Handelns. In B. Roehrle & G. Sommer (Eds.), *Praevention und Gesundheitsfoerderung* (Vol. 4, pp. 53-68). Tuebingen: Deutsche Gesellschaft fuer Verhaltenstherapie.

Roehrle, B., Glueer, S., & Sommer, G. (1995). Die Entwicklung der gemeindepsychologischen Forschung im deutschsprachigen Bereich (1977-1993). In B. Roehrle & G. Sommer (Eds.), *Gemeindepsychologie: Bestandsaufnahmen und Perspektiven* (pp. 25-54). Tuebingen: Deutsche Gesellschaft fuer Verhaltenstherapie.

Roehrle, B., Sommer, G., & Nestmann, F. (Eds.). (1998). *Netzwerkintervention.* Tuebingen: Deutsche Gesellschaft fuer Verhaltenstherapie.

Roth, M. (1994). Gemeindenahe Arbeitsweisen an Erziehungsberatungsstellen Ergebnisse einer Befragung der Bundeskonferenz fuer Erziehungsberatung. In H. Cremer & A. Hundsalz & K. Menne (Eds.), *Jahrbuch fuer Erziehungsberatung. Band 1* (pp. 239-252). Weinheim: Juventa.

Rudeck, R. (1983). Beratungs - und Kontaktarbeit im Stadtteil. Eine "gemeindepsychologische" Perspektive? In W. Belschner & H. Ernst & P. Kaiser & M. Koeppelmann-Baillieu & R. Rudeck & G. Sommer (Eds.), *Gemeindepsychologische Perspektiven. Band 1: Grundlagen und Anwendungsfelder* (pp. 170-175). Tuebingen: Deutsche Gesellschaft fuer Verhaltenstherapie.

Santen, E. V., & Seckinger, M. (2003). *Kooperation: Mythos und Realität einer Praxis. Eine empirische Studie zur interinstitutionellen Zusammenarbeit am Beispiel der Kinder- und Jugendhilfe.* München: Verlag Deutsches Jugendinstitut.

Seckinger, M. (Ed.). (2006). *Partizipation – ein zentrales Paradigma. Analysen und Berichte aus psychosozialen und medizinischen Handlungsfeldern.* Tübingen: Deutsche Gesellschaft fuer Verhaltenstherapie.

Sommer, G., & Ernst, H. (Eds.). (1977). *Gemeindepsychologie. Therapie und Prävention in der sozialen Umwelt.* München: Urban & Schwarzenberg.

Sommer, G., Kommer, B., Kommer, D., Malchow, C., & Quack, L. (1978). Gemeindepsychologie. In L. Pongratz, J. (Ed.), *Handbuch der Psychologie. Klinische Psychologie. 2. Halbband* (pp. 2913-2979). Göttingen: Hogrefe.

Sommer, G., Korn, R., Ruecker, G., & Steinhauer, A. (1983). Kompetenzepidemiologie: Einige theoretische Ueberlegungen und eine empirische Untersuchung zur Praevalenz von Kompetenzen. In D. Kommer & B. Roehrle (Eds.), *Gemeindepsychologische Perspektiven. Band 3: Oekologie und Lebenslagen* (pp. 186-195). Tuebingen: Deutsche Gesellschaft fuer Verhaltenstherapie.

Straus, F. (1992). Und die Praxis? - Transformationsprobleme gemeindepsychologischer Forschungsergebnisse. In I. Boehm & T. Faltermaier & U. Flick & M. Krause-Jacob (Eds.), *Gemeindepsychologisches Handeln. Ein Werkstattbuch* (pp. 234-247). Freiburg i. Br.: Lambertus.

Straus, F. (2002). *Netzwerkanalysen: Gemeindepsychologische Perspektiven fuer Forschung und Praxis.* Wiesbaden: Deutscher Universitaets-Verlag.

Trojan, A., & Hildebrandt, H. (1989). Konzeptionelle Ueberlegungen zu gesundheitsbezogener Netzwerkfoerderung auf lokaler Ebene. In W. Stark (Ed.), *Lebensweltbezogene Praevention und Gesundheitsfoerderung. Konzepte und Strategien fuer die psychosoziale Praxis* (pp. 97-116). Freiburg: Lambertus.

Trojan, A., & Legewie, H. (2001a). *Nachhaltige Gesundheit und Entwicklung Leitbilder, Politik und Praxis der Gestaltung gesundheitsfoerderlicher Umwelt- und Lebensbedingungen.* Frankfurt a. M.: VAS Verlag fuer Akademische Schriften.

Trojan, A., & Legewie, H. (2001b). Quartiersmanagement - Ein Arbeitsfeld für Gemeindepsychologie? *Gemeindepsychologie-Rundbrief,* 7, 5-11.

Trojan, A., Stumm, B., Suess, W., & Zimmermann, I. (1999). Kommunale Gesundheitsfoerderung. In B. Roehrle & G. Sommer (Eds.), *Praevention und Gesundheitsfoerderung* (pp. 69-101). Tuebingen: Deutsche Gesellschaft fuer Verhaltenstherapie.

Wolff, S. (1981). Grenzen der helfenden Beziehung. Zur Entmythologisierung des Helfens. In E. v. Kardorff & E. Koenen, K. (Eds.), *Psyche in schlechter Gesellschaft* (pp. 211-238). München: Urban & Schwarzenberg.

Wolff, S. (1983). Zur Organisation von Fuersorglichkeit. In M. Cramer & E. Giese & M. Koeppelmann-Baillieu & R. Rudeck (Eds.), *Gemeindepsychologische Perspektiven. Band 4: Orientierungshilfen zu einem beruflichen Selbstverstaendnis* (pp. 107-113). Tuebingen: Deutsche Gesellschaft fuer Verhaltenstherapie.

Zaumseil, M., & Leferink, K. (1997). *Schizophrenie der Moderne - Modernisierung der Schizophrenie Lebensalltag, Identitaet und soziale Beziehungen von psychisch Kranken in der Grossstadt.* Bonn: Psychiatrie-Verlag.

12
Community Psychology in Italy: Past Developments and Future Perspectives

Donata Francescato, Caterina Arcidiacono, Cinzia Albanesi, and Terri Mannarini

Abstract

The aim of this paper is to review the history of community psychology in Italy. We begin by illustrating the early developments of community psychology in the 1970s, which was a period of strong social change. The main part of the chapter is focused on the contribution of Italian scholars to the development of European perspectives in the field and to the elaboration of theoretical principles that should guide community psychology interventions. Taking into account the construct of social representation, Italian community psychologists view the connections between psychological and social determinants of personal action and between individual and collective processes as the core features of the discipline. They have, therefore, given much attention to exploring the historical link between the process of valorisation of individual freedoms and collective struggle; to promoting sociopolitical empowerment and social capital; and to examining the multiple meanings of community and sense of community. In the last part of the chapter, we outline the theoretical principles that guide some community psychology interventions such as community profiling, multidimensional organisational analysis, affective education and empowerment training, which have been developed by Italian community psychologists. We conclude by focusing on future opportunities and challenges.

Introduction

Italian community psychologists have promoted a rich debate on community psychology (CP) theories referring to the interaction between individuals and contexts. They have also privileged the development of research and intervention methodologies closely related to theoretical principles. Our primary aim in this paper is to illustrate some of the unique features of Italian CP, starting with a brief description of the historical context in which it was born. The reasons why both some Italian academic and professional psychologists in the late 1970s showed interest in CP can be easily understood only by keeping in mind the reciprocal interaction between the sociopolitical culture of a country at a given time and the diffusion of specific disciplines. In Italy, the 1970s were a time of innovative collective struggles, which engaged students, women, mental health patients, and health professionals in powerful political movements to obtain new rights. In this period, many mental health professionals joined "Psichiatria Democratica" (the movement for the closure of mental hospitals led by Franco Basaglia). Furthermore, a series of laws were passed aimed at moving educational, social, and health services interventions from secondary and tertiary prevention to primary prevention, encouraging citizen participation, networking among the services, and, above all, promoting health and quality of life. Several professionals had been experimenting with intervention strategies, which moved beyond the individual level, stressing the interaction between people and social contexts. Thus, some CP methodologies such as action research, community development, and mental health consultation appeared particularly appealing.

Informal Historical Roots and Early Beginnings

In this context of strong social change, CP in Italy informally began with the scientific and political activity of Donata Francescato, who received her Ph.D. in clinical psychology from the University of Houston and studied CP during her internship at Southshore Mental Health Centre, in Quincy, where Saul Cooper had worked. While in the United States, Francescato also attended a CP course held by Ira Goldenberg at Harvard in the early 1970s. In 1973, she returned to Italy and became an assistant professor at the University of Rome, which 3 years earlier had just begun to offer the first university degrees in psychology. In the context of several academic seminars and professional meetings, Donata Francescato brought a CP perspective to this dialogue, in which she talked about the strengths and limitations of the moderate and radical wings of CP as it had developed in the United States. She also published the first book about possible applications of this approach in the changing Italian context (Francescato, 1977a; 1977b).

Akin to the writing of Francescato in the late 1970s, practitioners who wanted to give more autonomy to local services and to promote participation of customers in the running of the territorial services were beginning to become more interested in CP and promoted its development in Italy. These professionals (social psychologists, clinical psychologists, psychotherapists, psychiatrists, and social workers) shared the belief that individual problems have social roots and could be better faced through collective struggles. They saw a local community as a complex system in which each component is connected to the others; and that above all, problems should be handled at multiple levels with customers, professionals, and administrators using multidimensional strategies. CP methodologies appeared to them particularly suitable to translate these views and principles into action and were experimentally used as bases to introduce innovations in professional practice.

The growing interest on CP methodologies and principles as well as the need to share and discuss them led practitioners and academics to meet at the first CP conference organized in 1979 by Guido Contessa and Margherita Sberna, who after reading Donata Francescato's book invited her and Mike Bender to illustrate some community experiences from the United States and Great Britain.

In 1980, in order to illustrate what was happening in Italy in the field, Augusto Palmonari and Bruna Zani published a book that focused primarily on the new role community psychologists could play in the development of decentralized social and health services. Three more books on CP's Italian pioneer experiences also appeared in the early 1980s (Contessa & Sberna, 1981; Francescato, Contesini & Dini, 1983; Garofalo, 1981).

Community psychologists in the 1980s made many contributions in defining the new roles psychologists could play in the renovated public social and health services. Some community psychologists started to promote the diffusion of self-help groups and to encourage networking among public services and volunteer groups. In this climate of strong social change, community psychologists started the first steps toward the formalisation and professionalisation of the discipline.

The Formalisation and Professionalisation of Community Psychology in the 1980s and 1990s: Advantages and Drawbacks

In the 1970s, innovative laws concerning individual health rights, abortion, contraception, and divorce were passed thanks to the effort of the Italian Women's Movement and of several leftist party supporters. However, these laws sharply divided public opinion, and many professionals who were supporters of the medical model opposed the new changes. Therefore, professionals who wanted to support the new changes felt the need to form new professional organisations. In 1980, the Division of Community Psychology was created within the Italian Psychological Society (SIPS). Donata Francescato was elected national coordinator, followed for two terms by a psychologist working in a Mental Health Centre, Marco Traversi, who died prematurely after doing a wonderful job of spreading community psychology among professionals.

In the early 1980s, there was still no public university training program in community psychology. However, the new division did promote theoretical seminars, training sessions, debates, and annual conferences. In this period, people could learn CP principles and methodologies only in two master's programs, offered by private institutes: ARIPS and ECOPOIESIS. These master's programs attracted mostly professionals who already worked in the field and wanted to further their education.

CP Role in Italian Universities

The mid 1980s and 1990s were a period of significant change for Italian universities. In 1985, CP was formally introduced as a fundamental discipline and began to be taught in all major Italian universities offering a new degree in clinical and community psychology. In the late 1990s, another major legal reform took place in the Italian universities, granting them much more autonomy than in the past. This led to CP being taught in several universities, as part of different kinds of psychology programs, focused not only on clinical psychology but also social, educational, and work psychology. The drawback was that, while CP had been a compulsory subject for many clinical and community psychology degrees, now each university was free to decide whether to offer CP as a subject or not. Because most Italian psychologists are psychotherapists and most college professors are also primarily psychodynamically oriented, it is unlikely that CP will be taught as widely in the future as it is now. However, not all hope is lost; because a 3-year doctoral program in community psychology and training processes promoted by the Universities of Lecce, Torino, and Rome was established in 1998. Additionally, the University of Padua offers a master's in community development, and there are several privately organised master's in Rome, Pisa, and Naples as well as a 4-year specialization school (ASPIC) in Rome, which offers the opportunity to learn both psychotherapy and CP.

The First National Association: SIPCO

While there has been a professionalisation of psychology, thanks to the establishment of a professional organization as part of the Italian Psychological Society (SIPS) in 1994 in Italy, there is no clearly defined certification for community psychologists. That is, the title of community psychologist is not protected or certified by any law. In 1994, SIPS obtained the passage of a law that certified the profession of "psychologist" and created a professional society (Ordine degli Psicologi) to which all psychologists have to belong. Not long after, the Italian Psychological Society decided to terminate its existence. In its place, different psychological associations were born, according to academic and professional interests. In the same year, the Italian Society of Community Psychology (SIPCO) was founded. The new CP society promoted yearly seminars and conferences on empowerment and self-help, community psychology and politics, adolescents' needs and social services, intercultural issues and empowerment, Euro-Mediterranean Intercultural dialogue, strong and weak points of CP in Italy, and prevention in schools and communities.

Both the Division of Community Psychology until its dissolution in 1994 and SIPCO since its birth in 1994 published periodical newsletters. Only in 2005, however, did SIPCO sponsor the birth of the first Italian community psychology scientific journal, entitled *Psicologia di Comunità. Gruppi, ricerca-azione e modelli formativi* ("Community Psychology Groups, action research and training models").

Among the most important achievements of SIPCO was the organisation of the first European Congress of Community Psychology in Rome in 1995, where the European Network of Community Psychologists (ENCP) was created and a European perspective to community psychology began to emerge.

The European Perspective of Italian Community Psychologists

The idea of promoting more exchanges among European community psychologists was first formulated at the CP conference in Lisbon in 1992 by Donata Francescato, Jose Ornelas (from Portugal), and Wolfgang Stark (from Germany). These community psychologists hoped to develop what could be a more "European approach" to CP and were among the founders of ENCP (European Network of Community Psychologists), which organised yearly international meetings and biennial European Community Psychology Congresses in Lisbon (1998), Bergen (2000), Barcelona (2002), and Berlin (2004).

These meetings were very fruitful for Italian community psychologists, who shared both the new theoretical frameworks and intervention strategies that had been developed in Italy and took advantage of many opportunities to learn what had been elaborated in other European contexts (Orford, 1992; Ornelas, 2000; Sánchez Vidal, Zambrano Constanzo & Palacín, 2004). The exchange among community psychologists, coming from several different European countries, favoured the integration of key ideas and intervention strategies into what Francescato and Tomai (2001) have called "A European Approach to Community Psychology" (p. 371).

Italian Contributions to Ground Community Psychology on Stronger Theoretical Underpinnings

Theories and ideas from many countries have framed the development of CP in Italy. While all Italian community psychologists recognize the debt owned to U.S. community psychology, several Italian authors, such as Zani and Palmonari (1996), Amerio (2000; 2004), and Francescato, Tomai, and Ghirelli (2002), have especially felt the need to underline differences between the U.S. and European approaches to CP. These authors maintain that certain European countries share broad cultural values as well as historical and political experiences, which are different from those of the United States. These differences emerge in their social representation of the world, which influences the formulation and diffusion of particular theories. Zani and Palmonari (1996) and Amerio (2000) have utilized the work of European social psychologists on social representations and emphasized how much the contribution of the social-constructivist viewpoint can add to the theoretical underpinnings of CP.

According to Francescato and Tomai (2001), community psychologists living in Germany, Italy, Spain, and Portugal (who experienced fascist dictatorships in the past century) do not believe, for instance, in the myth of the self-made man that, as Julian Rappaport (2000) brilliantly showed, is prevalent in U.S. culture and language. For Francescato et al. (2005), the psychological "equivalent" of the self-made man myth can perhaps be seen in the importance given by U.S. authors to the concept of self-efficacy.

Beyond Self-Efficacy: Stressing the Historical Link Between the Process of Valorisation of Individual Freedoms and Collective Struggles

Several Italian community psychologists have tried to distinguish among self-efficacy and empowerment, arguing that we need more sociopolitical empowerment. Self-efficacy implies that a person believes in his or her ability to perform well in some particular domain. But, whether a person can have social access to a specific domain and develop a self-efficacy belief depends also on environmental settings that give or deny that access according to gender, skin colour, age, socioeconomic status, and so forth. Moreover, increasing people's self-efficacy does not automatically grant improvement in their quality of life, at least until access to resources is limited by social inequalities. Different authors (e.g., Amerio, 2000, 2004; Lavanco, 2001; Migliorini & Venini, 2001; Zani & Palmonari, 1996) have underlined how in certain historical periods some political elites have tried to pursue public policies that foster both the protection and widening of individual rights and the increase of the "social capital"—the trust and bonds between people. In a global culture dominated by American individualistic values, Italian community psychologists feel it is crucial to underline the historical link between the process of valorisation of individual freedom and collective struggles that have given many Europeans more social rights, including wide access to health care, education, and unemployment protection.

Along these lines, Amerio (2000, 2004) argues that the link between the concern for individual well-being and the political struggles, which promote the human well-being, is one of main theoretical foundations of CP. As such, Amerio has integrated the individualistic and social-constructionist viewpoints, placing CP at the interface between individual and collective domains. Responsibility for solving problems is plural; it rests both on individuals and on social systems. For Amerio, the identity of CP resides, therefore, in the study and intervention on human and social problems. CP is seen in the interface between the individual and the collective, the psychic and the social, as integrating a clinical concern for the welfare of the single person with a political vision.

Collective struggles require active citizenship, political involvement, and social capital, which are all based on participation at different local, national, and international levels. Recently, several Italian psychologists have examined which forms of participation are declining and increasing in the era of globalisation and have explored the meanings of concepts such as participation, community, and social capital (Amerio, 2004; Arcidiacono, 2004a; Francescato, Tomai & Mebane, 2004; Gelli, 2002; Lavanco & Novara, 2002; Mannarini, 2004). Briefly it can be said that for Italian CP, the aim is to work for individual rights—but not at an individual level. Italian community psychologists look at collective empowerment and the social capital that bridges people within communities as strategic resources to improve individual's life, with some important limitations.

Promoting More Sociopolitical Empowerment and Bridging Social Capital

Italian theorists view bonding and bridging social capital (Flap, 1994; Coleman, 1990) as vital for community building. Some Italian authors, however (Arcidiacono, 2004a, 2004b; Francescato, Tomai, & Ghirelli, 2002), stress that sense of community and social capital have also a "dark side." People can have a strong sense of community and be hostile to newcomers or they can have strong sense of belonging to a community and still have negative emotions toward their community (Arcidiacono & Procentese, 2005). Personal and collective outcomes made possible through bonding and bridging social capital may have negative or positive ethical effects depending on which values are pursued. Also, another limit of social capital and sense of community theoretical approaches is that they do not focus on the unequal distribution of resources and power. Paradoxically, one can have a local community with lots of social capital and strong sense of community, which is still disempowered, that is, deprived of structural socioeconomic and cultural opportunities like many of the ethnic ghettos that exist in several large metropolitan areas.

The concept of empowerment should have a sociopolitical side and redirect attention to socioeconomic resources and power unequally available in different networks and communities. Empowerment processes for Italian community psychologists should strongly emphasize that we have to pay attention to both psychological and sociopolitical aspects. As such, it is necessary to promote (1) self-efficacy and psychological awareness of power dynamics in one's settings; (2) participatory competence in personal networks (bonding social capital); and (3) active participation in civic and political organisations or movements (bridging social capital) to obtain legal, economic, and cultural changes.

Community psychologists need to study the influence of the global culture, dominated by commercial mass media, in promoting moral disengagement and individualistic values and behaviours. This is especially crucial in a historical period when the world faces many complex economic, environmental, and cultural challenges in work, educational, and family settings that require collective collaborative problem solving (Amerio, 2004; Francescato, 1998) and stronger sense of community. Therefore, some Italian community psychologists have focused on exploring the various historical meanings of community and sense of community.

Re-examining Various Historical Meanings of "Community"

Several Italian community psychologists (Amerio 2004; Arcidiacono & Procentese, 2005; Gelli, 2002; Mannarini, 2004) accept the idea that in post-modern society, communities can take multiple forms and different characteristics. Nevertheless, they argue that, whatever shape a community takes, it still fulfils unique needs of membership, and therefore the concept of a community of relationships stands out as the core meaning.

In some recent Italian works (e.g. De Piccoli & Lavanco, 2003), the term *community* is also used to define the setting of the intervention. From this point of view, community indicates any social context placed at a micro-, meso-, and exo-level (according to the hierarchy of social systems proposed by Bronfenbrenner). It includes small groups, organizations, and local communities. In both these meanings, the community is the link that bridges individuals and society. Because of its relational nature, great attention is paid to the community's internal differences, its dynamics, and its conflicts.

Despite the widespread acknowledgement of the polymorphism of the community, most Italian community psychologists focus mainly on the community rooted in a geographical territory, on the ties that link people to places, and on the internalisation of the physical features in their identity structure (Mannarini, 2004; Prezza & Santinello, 2002). The environmental dimension has then acquired an increasing relevance in CP's design and evaluation of community-based interventions, especially for the role it plays in fostering or restraining the processes of collective actions and, by consequence, community empowerment. Participation, seen as the essence of the community itself, is therefore considered one of the main means and goals for promoting development at the local level. Community is seen also as a metaphor, an ideal to which one can aspire: it refers to ways of living together, which can help people improve their life conditions, cope with stressful events, strengthen their resources, and lead them to a higher level of personal and collective empowerment. Therefore, several Italian community psychologists have made special efforts to measure how different groups of people do or do not feel their sense of community.

Sense of Community: Italian Contributions to Its Definition and Measurement

Research on sense of community in Italy has mainly been devoted to understanding its relationships with perception of quality of life in various groups of adults and to capture the relevance and the peculiarities of sense of community in adolescent populations. Concerning adult population, the only instrument validated in Italy to measure sense of community (SOC) is the Italian Sense of Community Scale (Prezza et al. 1999).

Many studies have been implemented using Prezza et al.'s (1999) scale, exploring the connections of SOC with different aspects of quality of life in different kinds of territorial communities and pointing out that:

- SOC and life satisfaction are lower in larger communities compared with smaller ones (Prezza & Costantini, 1998);
- SOC is related to life satisfaction and loneliness both in large and small towns and it can be predicted from neighbourhood relations (Prezza et al., 2001);
- SOC has strong correlations with perceived social support, and both SOC and life satisfaction increase social well-being (Cicognani et al., 2001);
- Members of volunteers and civic organizations have higher levels of SOC compared with nonmembers (De Piccoli et al., 2003b; Zani, Cicognani & Albanesi, 2004).

Italian community psychologists have dedicated a significant amount of research to analyze the relationships between SOC and fear of crime. Globally considered, these studies emphasised the buffering effect of SOC on fear of crime (Albanesi, 2003; Santinello, Gonzi & Scacchi, 1998; Zani, 2003).

The Italian SOC Scale has been applied in many other studies involving adults and adolescents (e.g., Albanesi, Cicognani & Zani, 2004; Prezza & Pacilli, 2002) and has been a very powerful instrument for collecting comparable data sets and allowing Italian community psychologists to discuss the applicability and relevance of McMillan and Chavis' model in different kinds of communities (relational vs. geographical) or in different evolutionary phases (childhood, preadolescence, adolescence, adulthood). Also in view of the critical approach developed in Italy on the multiple meanings of community, this debate has produced new efforts dedicated to the revision of SOC measurements (Prezza et al. 2004). For instance, Albanesi, Cicognani, and Zani (2005) used focus group discussions with adolescents in order to verify how community and community relationships are perceived in that developmental stage.

Theoretical Principles That Guide Community Psychology Interventions: Toward a Unifying Theory

Francescato and Tomai (2001) and Francescato, Tomai, and Ghirelli (2002), building both on theoretical and empirical contributions described so far, have tried to formulate a series of principles that describe what they call a European Community perspective and guide its intervention strategies. These guiding principles are summarized in Table 1. Based on these principles, CP interventions should:

- *Encourage pluralistic interpretations of social problems that integrate objective and subjective knowledge, and broaden the viewpoints from which a given situation can be considered.* Pluralistic interpretations should promote

TABLE 1. Guiding principles for 'a theory of practice' in community psychology.

1. Problems attribution	Human problems always have an individual side, because it is a person who suffers from and must cope with them, and a social side because most problems are born in social contexts and in them one can find the psychological and material tools to solve them.
2. Vision of the individual	The individual is viewed as an active subject, socially, culturally, and historically situated, whose potentialities can be activated in a specific environmental context, which offers opportunities and limits in an unequal manner for different individuals. Human beings are seen as social agents who build meanings in their interactions with others.
3. Vision of the social context	The social environment is a hierarchical context, historically created, and the inequalities of power and access to resources among individuals are not "natural" but historical and modifiable.
4. Interaction between person and context	The hierarchical social context can facilitate or hinder the individual who can, in turn, influence social settings with which she or he interacts according to the position she or he occupies in them and according to the available interpretations on the origin and legitimisation of existing social stratifications.
5. Complexity of the social system	The transactions among individuals and the hierarchical social context are multidirectional and occur at multiple levels (other individuals, small groups, organisations, local communities, macro communities, and virtual communities).
6. Levels of interventions	Problems have to be faced not only in their subjective personal dimensions as traditionally done in psychology but also in the "material" and objective dimensions, in the different levels of social contexts where resources and obstacles are to be found.
7. Link between individual empowerment and collective political struggle	CP stresses the historical link between the processes of expansion of individual empowerment and the political struggles that have been necessary to obtain human, civic, and social rights.
8. Narratives' role in empowerment processes	Group, communal, cultural, and political narratives connect the individual and collective realms; the psychological and the social aspects. The narratives furnish both traditional and innovative interpretations of social hierarchies that influence the identity, self-esteem, and status of individuals' socially valued roles and the visions of possible futures.
9. Integration between positivist and constructivist models	CP integrates different kinds of knowledge, deriving both from the traditional positivist scientific approach and the modern theories of social constructionism. CP can use a traditional positivist approach when looking for regularities in the interactions between individuals and their social settings and employ postmodern paradigms when trying to promote personal and social change.
10. Focus both on meliors and stressors	CP looks at each level of intervention (individual, group, organisation, community, etc.) both at the *meliors* (strong points, positive experiences) and at the *stressors* (problems, handicaps, structural limits).

Table 1. Guiding principles for 'a theory of practice' in community psychology—cont'd.

11. Constructive role of active participation as a tool to both adapt to and change contexts	CP underlines the constructive meaning of active participation, because acting links mental and practical processes, individual and social domains, giving the individual the possibility not only to adapt to the social contexts but to contribute to change them.

Source: From Francescato, Tomai, & Ghirelli, 2002, pp. 96-97.

interventions and combine tools coming from different disciplines and activate forms of participation that acknowledge the importance of "local knowledge" (that is, knowledge owned by people involved in social problems).

- *Examine the historical roots of social problems and the unequal distribution of power and access to resources in the social context.* CP should stimulate shared reflections on how dominant narratives legitimate this unequal distribution of resources.
- *Give voice to minority narratives, which break the silent consensus with which social actors legitimate the conventional interpretations of power inequalities.* CP should promote the production of new metaphors or new narratives that help "imagine" new scripts and roles for individuals and social groups and create the symbolic base that legitimates change.
- *Create ties among people who share a problem.* The goal of CP is to increase people's social capital, because changing narratives is only the first step for overcoming the economical, legal, cultural, and social barriers.
- *Identify the points of strengths to obtain a change.* CP should identify the problems that can be resolved at the level of the target group and the problems that require different levels of interventions (e.g., organisations or community networks).
- *Spread psychological knowledge and competencies.* CP should put into practice the principle of "giving psychology away," that is, CP should give attention to the psychological training of professionals of any field.

From Principles to Action: Empowering Tools Developed by Italian Community Psychologists

Using the theoretical viewpoints outlined above as guidelines, several methodologies of interventions have been developed. We will briefly describe three such intervention methodologies: (1) community profiling and network building; (2) multidimensional organisational analysis; and (3) socioaffective education and empowerment training strategies. These three intervention methods operate at different levels (community, organisations, and groups).

Their common goal is to increase psychological awareness of power dynamics in one's local settings and to increase participatory competence, social capital, and sociopolitical empowerment.

Community Profiling and Network Building

Community profiling and network building, initially developed in Italy by Martini and Sequi (1988), then modified by Francescato, Traversi, and Leone (1993) and Francescato, Tomai and Ghirelli (2002), and further redefined in Austria (Ehmayer, Reinfeldt & Gtotter, 2000), have been used to enhance participation in local programs sponsored by the European Union to promote better health (Healthy Cities), protect the environment (Agenda 21), or help local municipal officials assess the needs and wishes of community residents (De Piccoli & Lavanco, 2003; Mannarini 2004; Prezza & Santinello, 2002).

Community profiling allows the users to find out what particular problems and strengths characterize a local community. Eight profiles (territorial, demographic, economic, service, institutional, anthropological, psychological, and future) are drawn through a variety of data-gathering techniques. Profiles are examined by a core research group made up of residents and community psychologists. This core group, helped by key experts, identifies the strong points and the problems areas, using "hard data" such as rates of unemployment, demographic changes, measured levels of air pollution, and number and types of services.

To explore the affective components of community belonging (i.e., shared values, feelings about living in certain neighbourhoods, fears and hopes for the future), analysis of the psychological, anthropological, and perception of future profiles is performed. To take emotional snapshots of how residents feel, Italian community researchers use storytelling and narratives of all types and a group movie script technique. During a final meeting, in which all people who participated in the research are urged to attend, main strengths and weak points emerging in all eight profiles are discussed as well as priorities for change. Goals and activities to strive towards are also formulated.

Multidimensional Organisational Analysis

Professionals, teachers, and parents often find obstacles in the organisational rules that dominate schools, organisations, or services. Frequently, one has to promote organisational as well as personal or group changes in order to implement durable modifications. Therefore, several European community psychologists have attempted to develop strategies to promote organisational empowerment.

One of these tools is called multidimensional organisational analysis and involves people on all hierarchical levels in a specific organisation. For instance, in a school, students, parents, teachers, janitors, and office staff together will analyse their organisation across four dimensions (structural-strategic, functional, psycho-environmental, and cultural). These four dimensions follow a continuum that varies from dealing with "hard" objective variables (market share, increase or decrease of number of students, legal forms, age and educational level of staff, etc.) to "soft" subjective perceptions (unconscious representations of work settings, attitudes toward power, intergroup conflicts, level of satisfaction, etc.). Each dimension is analysed with methodologies appropriate for the level of data being considered. After weaknesses and strengths have been identified by the various organisational actors, they formulate different narratives and preferred visions of the future.

At the end of the analysis, participants formulate plans for desired changes that can be achieved through the resources available within the organisation and outline the problems or solutions that cannot be tackled without intervention at some different level. Focusing on feasible change necessarily favours empowerment and increases the capacity of organisations to foster creative change. The strongly participatory nature of this methodology makes it unsuitable for highly hierarchical organisations, unless top managers allow workers at all levels to participate. However, in the Italian experience it is a very appropriate tool for all organisations where members elect their leaders such as unions, volunteer organisations, professional groups, and cooperatives. Evaluation of the efficacy of this tool has been carried out on more than 60 organisations ranging from unions to schools, from volunteer organisations to hospitals (e.g., Francescato, Traversi & Leone, 1993; Francescato, Tomai & Ghirelli, 2002).

Affective Education and Empowering Training

This intervention strategy integrates concepts and tools from the affective education movement and CP. From affective education, Italian CP borrowed the idea that the learning process can best take place in a context of positive interpersonal relations. Francescato and Putton (1995) modified the technique of circle time, which favors affective sharing, by using group observers and facilitators to help group members learn about their functioning as a group and become a more empowered and empowering group. Francescato and Putton have applied this technique to different kinds of groups: from elementary classrooms to high schools, to teams of workers, to self-help organizations, and to volunteer and political groups. When these different tools—community profiles, multidimensional organizational analysis, and affective education empowerment training—are used together, they can promote self-efficacy, participatory competence, and sociopolitical empowerment (Francescato et al. 2004b).

Looking Toward the Future

In this section, we would like to outline what we think are some promising new trends and possible problems that we foresee in the future of community psychology in Italy.

The Opportunities Provided by Virtual Communities: Teaching Community Psychology Online to Promote Social Capital and Sociopolitical Empowerment in Educational and Professional Settings

The growing role of virtual communities for an increasing number of people forces CP to consider new forms of social capital that can be built online. Computer supported collaborative learning (CSCL), based both on the theoretical contributions of cooperative learning models and new technologies that offer multiple communication modalities for interaction, can be a great tool for disseminating CP principles and intervention strategies, as well as creating new social capital.

Because CP intervention strategies promote sociopolitical empowerment (Francescato et al. 2004a), integrating CSCL and CP intervention strategies can create social capital at universities. A series of studies at the University of Rome (Francescato et al., 2006; Mebane et al., in press) have found face-to-face and online seminars equally effective in (a) developing professional skills such as action research, community profiling, multidimensional organisational analysis, small group and affective education, (b) increasing social efficacy, problem-solving efficacy, and sociopolitical empowerment, and (c) increasing social capital. Another action research study (Francescato et al., 2005) found that integrating CSCL and CP intervention strategies could create social capital among professionals operating in high-risk local communities.

We need, as community psychologists, to conduct more research to understand what kind of social capital can be built and maintained in online learning and professional communities and networks. The possibilities are manifold. The integration of CP intervention strategies and CSCL could also be used in settings where members of teams live in different countries, such as in international nonprofit organizations. Training programs could be set up for virtual teams using CSCL to foster the growth of social as well as professional skills in people belonging to the same organization but living in different areas or countries, or in people belonging to different organizations who need to network for a particular project, or for creating bridges among students of different universities or different ethnic groups.

We need to introduce more collaborative learning in our school and university settings and create more opportunities for civic and political participation for our students, especially because in Italy psychology attracts primarily female students, and females in Italy have traditionally been less interested in political participation and in political issues.

Psychology Becoming a Mostly Female Profession: A Gender Problem or an Asset for Italian Community Psychology?

Community psychology unites clinical psychology's traditional concern with the welfare of the individual with an interest in the legislative and political processes that create the conditions in which individuals live. However, in Italy, we are having problems getting female students interested in CP, perhaps because while women's cultural heritage pulls them toward the "caring professions," the same cultural heritage pushes them toward the "privatization" of social problems. In spite of the changes promoted by feminism, Italian women are still less likely than men to be politically interested, informed, or be activists in political parties and movements (Caciagli & Corbetta, 2002). This attitudinal deficit contributes substantially to the gender gap in political activity. University training is an adult socialisation process that can change attitudes: we can and should provide in our university and professional training more opportunities for young women to understand the relevance of politics to their professional careers and their personal lives and help ensure that an adequate number of female students will choose community psychology as their specialty field.

In Italy, while our current psychology university majors offer dozens of subjects related to clinical topics, very few require students to take subjects such as contemporary history, sociology, political psychology, and health psychology, which deal with social issues. We know that learning CP skills such as multidimensional organisational analysis or community profiles, which focus on the interplay among structural economic, demographic, and political variables and interpersonal and intrapersonal dimensions, help young women widen their viewpoints. Our research has shown significant increases in social political empowerment in male and female students exposed to community psychology training (Francescato, Tomai & Mebane, 2004).

Looking Through International Lenses: Future Challenges for Italian Community Psychology

Looking at the chapters of this book, one can see that there are many common threads in the development of community psychology in various countries and that much work that has been done in distant regions of the world can be a source of inspiration for Italian community psychologists.

One common feature stands out: although CP has been growing in the past decades both in the academic and in the professional field, this branch of psychology still has a minority status among psychological disciplines in all countries represented in this book. Nevertheless, the scanty acknowledge-ment provided by the academy has not prevented CP practices and tools from being disseminated in many countries and a variety of fields, often even outside psychology (e.g., health and social services, education, social policy).

Another common trend in all countries is that everywhere the onset of community psychology has been more or less strongly influenced by the United States, but in many countries local community psychologists have made original contributions developing new theoretical concepts, creating new intervention strategies, or applying U.S.-born concepts and tools to different issues.

Several countries (United States, Italy, Australia, for instance) gave birth to community psychology in a period of strong social change, in the 1960s and 1970s. In various countries (e.g., Great Britain, United States, Italy), when governments shifted in more conservative directions, the changed *Zeitgeist* offered fewer opportunities for community psychologists' ideas, values, and projects. The ebbs and flows of CP fortunes in several countries documents how the development of a social science is always partially dependent on the sociopolical conditions of a particular country in a given historical period. In general, community psychologists seemed to have fared better when progres-sive governments were in power and provided the financial, legislative, and cultural support for community programs.

The development of CP in Italy shares some features with Latin America. In Italy as in Latin America for instance, particular importance has been given to theoretical issues, linking practice and theory, and, therefore, impor-tant theoretical contributions have been made by community psychologists in both regions. Both Latin American and Italian community psychologists have developed innovative tools that link theory to practice, but we think we have much to learn from the work of our Latin American colleagues especially in promoting participation in deprived neighbourhood settings.

Compared with the orientation characterising CP in countries such as Canada, United States, Australia, and New Zealand, Italian CP looks some-how "more traditional" in its theoretical underpinnings. The main evidence of that is provided by the lack of debate on postcolonial and feminist theories, which have proved less influential. Italian CP needs to update the internal theoretical debate and deal with the critiques posed by feminist, cultural, and postcolonial perspective.

It seems that Italian CP has, so far, dedicated little attention to different aspects of diversity, for instance, cultural, ethnic, and sexual diversity, dis-ability, and therefore to the issues of racism and prejudice. We have also worked comparatively less on women and gay communities and here we can learn a lot from the United States, Canada, and other countries that have explored these issues more thoroughly. Several community psychologists are feminists and have written extensively on women (e.g., Arcidiacono, Francescato, Gelli), nevertheless community psychologists as a group have not dealt so far with gender issues. In the last seminar in Naples (September

2005), a women and politics interest group was formed, so hopefully CP in Italy will give more attention to this issue.

In Italy, we have focused on marginalized groups (dropouts, unemployed, residents of troubled neighbourhoods, disadvantaged children and families, volunteer organisations, self-help groups), but we have dealt much less than other countries with problems of colonisation and racism. We are only now facing the challenges of cultural diversity that countries with longer history of immigration and indigenous population minorities have already encountered. We think that the latest book by Nelson and Prilleltensky (2005), which addresses all these issues, can be extremely stimulating and useful.

References

Albanesi, C. (2003). Legami sociali e insicurezza in ambiente urbano: uno studio empirico. *Bollettino di Psicologia Applicata, 240*, 15-25.

Albanesi, C., Cicognani, E., & Zani, B. (2004). Adolescents' sense of community: Which measures for which communities? In A. Sánchez Vidal, A. Zambrano Constanzo, & M. Palacín (Eds.), *European Community Psychology: Community, ethics, and values* (pp. 288-293). Barcelona: Publicacions Universitat de Barcelona.

Albanesi, C., Cicognani, E., & Zani, B. (2005). L'uso dei focus group per la costruzione di una scala di misurazione del senso di comunità in adolescenza. *Sociologia e ricerca sociale, 76/77*, 159-171.

Amerio, P. (2000). *Psicologia di comunità*. Bologna: Il Mulino.

Amerio, P. (2004). *Problemi umani in comunità di massa: una psicologia tra clinica e politica*. Torino: Einaudi.

Arcidiacono, C. (2004a). *Toward a commo future: hope, social responsability and sense of community*. In A. Sánchez Vidal, A. Zambrano Constanzo, & M. Palacín (Eds.), *European Community Psychology: Community, ethics, and values* (pp. 218-228). Barcelona: Publicacions Universitat de Barcelona.

Arcidiacono, C. (2004b), *Volontariato e legami collettivi*. Milano: Franco Angeli.

Arcidiacono, C., & Procentese, F. (2005). Distinctiveness and sense of community in the historical center of Naples: A piece of participatory action-research. *Journal of Community Psychology, 5*, 1-8.

Caciagli, M., & Corbetta, P. (Eds.). (2002). *Le ragioni dell'elettore*. Bologna: Il Mulino.

Cicognani, E., Albanesi, C., & Berti, P. (2001). Dimensioni del benessere sociale: applicazione di uno strumento di misurazione. *Psicologia della Salute, 1*, 105-122.

Coleman, J. S. (1990). *Foundations of social theory*. Cambridge (Mass.): Harvard University Press.

Contessa, G., & Sberna, M. (Eds.). (1981). *Per una psicologia di comunità*. Milano: CLUED.

De Piccoli, N., & Lavanco, G. (Eds.). (2003). *Setting di comunità. Gli interventi psicologici nel sociale*. Milano: Unicopli.

De Piccoli, N. Tartaglia, S., Greganti, K., & Ceccarini L. (2003, September 26). *La gestione della cosa pubblica. Atteggiamenti e comportamenti della partecipazione sociale e politica*. Paper presented at V AIP National Congress–Social Psychology Division, Bari.

Ehmayer, C., Reinfeldt, S., & Gtotter, S. (2000, May 12). *Agenda 21 as a concept for sustainable development*. Paper presented at III Panel of Experts, Vienna.

Flap, H.D. (1994, July 20). *No man is an Island: the research program of a Social Capital Theory*. Paper presented at the XIII World Congress of Sociology, Bielefeld.

Francescato, D. (1977a). Psicologia di Comunità: un nuovo ruolo per lo psicologo?. *Giornale Italiano di Psicologia, 1*, 11-63.

Francescato, D. (1977b). *Psicologia di comunità*. Milano: Feltrinelli.

Francescato, D. (1998). *Amore e potere*. Milano: Mondadori.

Francescato, D., Contesini, A., & Dini, S. (Eds.). (1983). *Psicologia di comunità. Esperienze a confronto*. Roma: Il Pensiero Scientifico.

Francescato, D., Traversi, M., & Leone, L. (Eds.). (1993). *Oltre la psicoterapia. Percorsi innovativi di psicologia di comunità*. Roma: Carocci.

Francescato, D., & Putton, A. (1995). *Star meglio insieme*. Milano: Mondadori.

Francescato, D., & Tomai, M. (2001). Community Psychology: should there be a European perspective? *Journal of Community and Applied Social Psychology, 11*, 371-380.

Francescato, D., Tomai, M., & Ghirelli, G. (2002). *Fondamenti di psicologia di comunità*. Roma: Carocci.

Francescato, D., Gelli, B.R., Mannarini, T., & Taurino, A. (2004a). Community development: action-research through community profiles. In A. Sánchez-Vidal, A. Zambiano Constanzo, & M. Palacín (Eds.), *European community psychology: community, power, ethics and values* (pp. 247-261). Barcelona: Publicacions Universitat de Barcelona.

Francescato, D., Tomai, M., Porcelli, R., Mebane, M., Andò, M., Benedetti, M., & Foddis, A. (2004b). Computer supported collaborative learning as a tool to modify teaching methods and promote self-efficacy and social empowerment of university students. In *TEL 03 Proceedings: International Conference on Technology-Enhanced Learning* (pp. 109-114). Milano: IS.

Francescato, D., Tomai, M., & Mebane, M. (2004). *Psicologia di comunità per la scuola, l'orientamento e la formazione. Esperienze faccia a faccia e online*. Bologna: Il Mulino.

Francescato, D., Mebane, M., Sorace, R., Andò, M., & Porcelli, R. (2005, September 18). *Integrating community psychology intervention strategies and computer supported collaborative learning to build empowering communities and increase social capital*. Paper presented at the 5th European Congress in Community Psychology, Berlin.

Francescato, D., Porcelli, R., Mebane, M., Cuddetta, M., Klobas, J., & Renzi, P. (2006). Evaluation of the efficacy of collaborative learning in face to face and computer supported university contexts. *Computers in Human Behavior, 22*, 163-176.

Francescato, D., Porcelli, R., Mebane, M.E., Attanasio, C., & Pulino, M. (2007). Developing professional skills and social capital through computer supported collaborative learning in university contexts. *International Journal of Human-Computer Studies, 65(2)*, 140-152.

Garofalo, D. (1981). *Prevenzione, scuola e territorio*. Bulzoni: Roma.

Gelli, B.R. (2002). *Comunità, rete, arcipelago. Metafore del vivere sociale*. Carocci: Roma.

Lavanco, G. (2001). *Oltre la politica. Psicologia di comunità, giovani e partecipazione*. Milano: Franco Angeli.

Lavanco, G., & Novara, C. (2002). *Elementi di psicologia di comunità*. Milano: McGraw-Hill.

Mannarini, T. (2004). *Comunità e partecipazione*. Milano: Franco Angeli.
Martini, E.R., & Sequi, R. (1988). *Il lavoro nella comunità*. Roma: NIS.
Mebane, M., Porcelli, R., Iannone, A., Attanasio, C., & Francescato, D. (in press). Evaluation of the efficacy of affective education online training in promoting academic and professional learning and social capital. *International Journal of Human-Computer Interaction*.
Migliorini, L., & Venini, L. (2001). *Città e legami sociali*. Roma: Carocci.
Nelson, G., & Prilleltensky, I. (Eds.). (2005). *Community Psychology in Pursuit of Liberation and Wellbeing*. New York: Palgrave MacMillan.
Orford, J. (1992). *Community psychology. Theory and Practice*. Chichester: Wiley & Sons.
Ornelas, J. (Ed.). (2000). *Actas do II Congresso Europeu de Psicologia Comunitaria*. Lisboa: Instituto Superior de Psicologia Aplicada.
Palmonari, A., & Zani, B. (1980). *Psicologia sociale di comunità*. Bologna: Il Mulino.
Prezza, M., & Santinello, M. (2002). *Conoscere la comunità*. Bologna: Il Mulino.
Prezza, M., & Pacilli, M.G. (2002). Il senso di comunità, in M. Prezza, & M. Santinello *Conoscere la comunità* (pp. 161-192). Bologna: Il Mulino.
Prezza, M., Pacilli, M.G., Alparone, F.R., Paoliello, A., & Ruggeri, M.R. (2004, June 5). *Verso la costruzione di una scala multidimensionale del senso di comunità: tappe e principali risultati*. Paper presented at the 5th National Congress of Community Psychology, Palermo.
Prezza, M., Amici, M., Roberti, T., & Tedeschi, G. (2001). Sense of Community referred to the whole town: its relations with neighboring, loneliness, life satisfaction and area of residence. *Journal of Community Psychology, 1*, 29-52.
Prezza, M., & Costantini, C. (1998). Sense of community and life satisfaction: Investigation in three different territorial contexts. *Journal of Community and Applied Social Psychology, 3*, 181-194.
Prezza, M., Costantini, S., Chiarolanza, V., & Di Marco, S. (1999). La Scala Italiana del Senso di Comunità. *Psicologia della Salute, 3-4*, 135-159.
Rappaport, J. (2000). Commentaries on Prilleltensky and Nelson. *Journal of Community and Applied Social Psychology, 10*, 107-122.
Sánchez Vidal, A., Zambrano Constanzo, A., & Palacín, M. (Eds.), *European Community Psychology: Community, ethics, and values*. Barcelona: Publicacions Universitat de Barcelona.
Santinello, M., Gonzi, P., & Scacchi, L. (1998). *Le paure della criminalità. Aspetti psicosociali di comunità*. Milano: Giuffrè.
Zani, B., & Palmonari, A. (1996). *Manuale di psicologia di comunità*. Bologna: Il Mulino.
Zani, B. Cicognani, E., & Albanesi, C. (2004). Quale comunità per adolescenti e giovani: linee di ricerca su partecipazione, appartenenza e benessere sociale. In N. De Piccoli, & G. Quaglino (Eds.), *Psicologia sociale in dialogo* (pp. 247-263). Milano: Unicopli.
Zani, B. (2003). (Ed.), *Sentirsi in/sicuri in città*. Bologna: Il Mulino.

13
Community Psychology in a Scandinavian Welfare Society: The Case of Norway

ERIK CARLQUIST, HILDE EILEEN NAFSTAD,
AND ROLV MIKKEL BLAKAR

Abstract

In the current review of CP in Norway, it is concluded that little CP is being undertaken, according to a stringent definition of CP work. However, many Norwegian psychologists across a wide scope of fields integrate and adopt CP principles in their work. Yet, the critical and political nature of CP has been absent. This situation is explained on the basis of sociocultural and political conditions. The ideals of social justice and security, empowerment, and community participation have been cornerstones in the development of the Norwegian welfare state. CP-oriented psychologists in Norway have more or less tacitly taken for grated that they are part of a larger system or process—the welfare society—characterized by fairness and social justice. As it is argued in the current review, the recognition of these values is diminishing, due to globalization and the gradually stronger influence of neoliberalism (cf. Nafstad, Carlquist & Blakar, in press). Therefore, in the years to come, CP in Norway should render itself into a more prominent and critical discipline within Norwegian psychology, explicitly focusing on and arguing for alternative values based on solidarity and social equality.

Introduction

In describing community psychology (CP) in Norway, we have faced two related problems. First, in the Norwegian language, there exists no direct translation of 'community psychology.' This is due to the fact that the English concept of 'community' falls somewhere between the Norwegian terms of 'nærmiljø' (local community in a geographical sense) and 'samfunn' (society). Second, there is no easily identifiable branch of psychology in Norway for which 'community psychology' would be a suitable term. One reason for this is that many of the aims of CP have in fact been ensured or at least aspired towards by the comprehensive Norwegian state welfare system, which has been crucial to the development of Norwegian society at least since

World War II. The welfare system has involved a high level of social security, free education, and redistribution of wealth between regions. Psychology in Norway has up to now largely taken this background for granted, and psychologists are working mainly within the conventional service production of the public mental health and educational sectors. Most Norwegian psychologists, moreover, identify themselves as clinicians. To some extent, the welfare state may thus have served as a justification for not taking the comprehensive task of developing a full-fledged CP.

We shall begin this chapter by defining CP. Thereafter, we will trace the historical, academic, and value roots of current Norwegian CP. We will provide a review of how CP is practiced, including research and other projects, with a more or less clear CP profile. Moreover, we will document the formal status of CP at the universities. Finally, we will compare CP in Norway with CP in other regions.

Brief General Background

Norway has a population of 4.6 million and is divided into 19 counties and more than 400 municipalities (communes). As mentioned, the Norwegian society has, to a large extent, been characterized by an equitable distribution of wealth, and stable, transparent, small-scale communities. The development of CP, including the lack of CP as a clearly defined field, naturally reflects this historical and cultural context.

It has been estimated that 80% of Norwegian psychologists who identify themselves with the 'samfunnspsykologi' ('societal psychology') discipline label in practice, in fact, attend mostly to the problems of individuals and families, rather than larger-scale systems or communities (Grinde, 2002). The levels of analysis as well as the interventions that are taught and practiced are mainly concerned with the individual and the individual's immediate interpersonal context. Despite the absence of a formally organized discipline of CP taught at universities, and the existence of very few municipal psychologists in the 400 municipalities, there are approaches that may be described or classified as CP. Thus, work that by a more stringent definition is not CP may in our review be labeled as CP.[1] As we will show in this review, it is particularly within clinical and social psychology that such work can be found.

Although there is no Norwegian equivalent to the term 'community psychologist,' the Norwegian term 'kommunepsykolog' (municipal psychologist) carries similar connotations to those of CP. There is an increasing tendency

---

[1] In referring to work and institutions in Norway that carry more or less resemblance to community work proper, it is unavoidable that some who feel that they should have been included are not, and others who do not conceive of their work as community psychology at all may be included in our review.

for local councils to employ municipal psychologists (SHD, 1998a), although this development has been slow (cf. Knoff, Bogen, Austlid & Isdahl, 1983; Skuterud, 2000).

Community Psychology: Our Definition

In our view, CP is on a par with sociology and social psychology taking a systems or group perspective to behavior and human well-being. However, CP is more applied than those academic disciplines in adopting psychological knowledge to promote individual, relational, and societal well-being. Theoretically and conceptually, CP is rooted in an ecological theoretical framework. Moreover, adhering to the predominant U.S. terminology of the field, we also conceive of CP as an intrinsically critical discipline focusing on the prevention of human suffering, therefore having to critically analyze and take into consideration how historical, cultural, social, economic, and political contexts contribute to oppression and suffering. CP has, therefore, an ethical obligation to fight against macro arrangements that foster human indignity and injustice. We do not claim that all the psychological work reviewed in this chapter meets these criteria. In particular, critical perspectives are lacking in contemporary Norwegian psychology (cf. Blakar & Nafstad, 2006). It should be mentioned, however, that the feminist contributors have provided critical, important, and necessary voices about gender oppression in the Norwegian society (Aas, 1975; Holter, 1970; Haavind, 1998, 2002).

Historical Roots: Sociocultural, Political, and Ideological

One of the central functions of the welfare state is to provide comprehensive physical and mental health care services for all citizens, largely financed by public budgets. As Grinde (1977) concludes, the various roles of community psychologists must be understood in this general context. The role of Norwegian psychologists engaged in community issues has therefore largely been one of involvement in the preexisting structures of the welfare state, participating in conventional state and communal services. Consequently, Norwegian community-oriented psychologists have been closely connected to clinical psychology, and with a few exceptions (e.g., Axelsen, 1976) less engaged in politics, activism, and planning.

What then about the overarching frameworks for general health care and clinical psychology? Since the 1970s, the mental health sector in Norway, as in most of the Western world, has been characterized by deinstitutionalization and decentralization. In Norway, the number of long-term hospital beds has been reduced by two-thirds from 1970 to 1999 (Kringlen, 2004; Romøren, 2001). In principle, this development has enabled patients to receive treatment to a larger extent in their local communities. However, the motives behind these developments can also be traced back to economic considerations (Grinde, 1977). Moreover, the downscaling of long-term institutional care was not met by an adequate expansion of community-based services (Romøren, 2001) and may thus have involved short-term savings for government.

The National Mental Health Program, running from 1999 to 2008, however, aims at improving accessibility, quality, and organization of mental health services and treatment on all levels (SHD, 1998b). This governmental program involves a significant increase of funding for mental health care. A central component of the program is to expand community-based mental health services. Recently, community-based services known as district psychiatric centers (DPS) have been developed in many of the Norwegian counties. Psychologists play a central role within these centers as services include multidisciplinary treatment and teamwork, in addition to programs for increasing living skills as well as occupational and social support.

However, as Knoff, Bogen, Austlid, and Isdahl (1983) pointed out more than 20 years ago, the conventional health care system is not sufficiently oriented towards prevention. The need for easily available, broadly scoped service, particularly aimed at at-risk groups, is still large. Arguing for the development of low-threshold services has, therefore, been an important task for Norwegian psychologists with a CP-oriented approach.

Historical Roots: Academic

In the decades after World War II, psychology in general and social psychology in particular were established in Norway as critical disciplines aiming at resolving societal problems, many of them of the type that CP has traditionally embarked on. With funding from the so-called Marshall Fund, various social science disciplines—among them social psychology—were established as modern research-oriented disciplines at the Institutt for Samfunnsforskning (Institute of Social Research). Resolution of real societal problems in the post–World War II Norwegian society set the agenda for research. Pioneers in this clear community psychology orientation at that time included Harriet Holter, Per Olav Tiller, and Einar Thorsrud. Holter (1966, 1984) undertook societal level research of the oppression of women in the post–World War II Norwegian society. Tiller (1969, 1973) adopted the ecological metaphor and demonstrated how macro factors such as working life and gender roles strongly influenced children's social and personality development. In the organizational field, action research and employee participation in the workplace was advocated by Thorsrud (see, e.g., Thorsrud & Emery, 1970). For a review of this embryonic period of Norwegian social psychology, see Nafstad and Blakar (1982).

Particularly from the 1970s, the scientific fields of sociology and social psychiatry became important for the development of CP in Norway. These fields have stressed the social roots of individual problems. Similarly, in the 1970s clinical psychology was characterized by the emergence of a systemic and ecological approach to mental health. This trend provided an invigorating alternative to the more individualizing paradigms of psychoanalysis and behaviorism (Tjersland & Eriksen, 1994). In clinical training programs and practice today, these diverse approaches are rather integrated (Reichelt, 1987). However, the systemic and ecological approaches within clinical psychology still tend to focus on illness rather than well-being, depicting mental health and coping as operating merely within micro systems of families, schools and workplaces, rather than being strongly shaped by the wider communities and larger political and ideological frameworks in which these micro systems are embedded (Bronfenbrenner, 1979; Nelson & Prilleltensky, 2005).

Social psychology in Norway from the 1970s until now has concentrated on applied social psychology and health psychology rather than on experimental approaches (Nafstad & Blakar, 1982; Ommundsen & Teigen, 2005). These approaches are compatible with CP. Explicit political, value-oriented approaches of academic social psychology have been lacking, however (cf. Blakar & Nafstad, 2006). On the other hand, studies in social and health psychology have contributed to the development of interventions and policies under the framework of the welfare state. Largely based on the bio-psycho-social model (Engel, 1977), Norwegian health psychology has conducted considerable research in the field of prevention (Schjødt, 2002).

As is the case for the other countries represented, Norwegian CP is based substantially on the ecological metaphor (Bronfenbrenner, 1979). Norwegian CP is directly inspired by Urie Bronfenbrenner who visited Norway several times on invitations from different ministries. However, except for the decades after World War II, as described above, there has been little original theoretical development of the ecological model in the field of CP in Norway. In her account of possible roles of community psychologists in Norway, Grinde (1977), however, draws on the conceptual framework of Sarason (1974) in addition to ecological and system theoretical approaches.

CP at Norwegian Universities and in the Norwegian Psychological Association

Formal Training

The universities of Bergen, Oslo, Tromsø, and Trondheim offer some training in 'samfunnspsykologi'/CP primarily as part of their 6-year clinical psychology programs. For example, in Oslo, the largest of the universities, there exist no specific courses in CP as part of the clinical psychology program, but systemic and ecological perspectives are given weight. Overall, there is currently no comprehensive, formal educational program in CP offered at any of the universities.

Research

The different universities are all undertaking research relevant to CP.

University of Bergen

The Research Center for Health Promotion (HEMIL) at the University of Bergen is a leading interdisciplinary research institution in the field of health promotion. The center, founded in 1988, employs a number of psychologists. The center engages in both "traditional" health psychology research and more action-oriented approaches. Several strands of research at HEMIL have a strong local community approach, such as the development and use of the Bergen Social Relationships Scale (BSRS), a six-item self-report scale intended for use in community research (Mittelmark, Aarø, Henriksen, Siqveland & Torsheim, 2004). The Olweus Bullying Prevention Program was developed at the University of Bergen and is offered to a large number of schools in Norway as well as internationally (Olweus, 2004). It involves interventions at three levels: the school, classroom, and individual level. The program has been evaluated a number of times and shows substantial reductions in bullying problems (Olweus, 2004). Another area of research adopting critical and discourse analytical approaches is the study of children growing up with lesbian or gay parents. Anderssen (2001) has exposed the regulatory causes and effects of sexual categories and sexual citizenship in the Norwegian society.

University of Oslo

Social psychologists at the Institute of Psychology conduct research within health psychology and the psychology of attitudes, findings from which have relevance for preventive work. For instance, Ommundsen, Hak, Mørch, Larsen, and Van der Veer (2002) have conducted research on attitudes towards illegal immigration. Wold and her collaborators (Wold, 2004; Bezemer, Kroon, Pastoor, Ryen, & Wold 2004) have studied language learning in multicultural contexts. Nafstad, Carlquist, and Blakar (in press) have analyzed ideological changes as reflected in media language and discourse. They have identified shifts from communal values towards individualist consumer values. Such changes are largely due to the increasingly global ideology of neoliberalism and represent severe challenges to CP and the values underpinning it.

University of Tromsø

The social psychology group at the University of Tromsø consists of a diverse and international group studying among other issues multiculturalism in communities (see, e.g., Javo, Rønning, Heyerdahl & Rudmin, 2004).

University of Trondheim

Research in the field of risk attitudes and behavior is a central area at this university of relevance to CP (e.g., Iversen, Rundmo & Klempe, 2005).

At present, cultural and cross-cultural research in psychology is undertaken at all our universities. From the perspective of CP, however, it is thought-provoking that very little community relevant research has been conducted within psychology on our oppressed, indigenous national minority, the Sami people. A notable exception to this is the work of social psychiatrist Javo and her collaborators in mental health care in Sami communities (see, e.g., Javo, Rønning & Heyerdahl, 2004).

Professional Organization

The Norwegian Psychological Association offers postgraduate programs leading to official accreditation as a specialist in clinical psychology. Among these is a program in 'samfunnspsykologi' (societal psychology), which draws on systemic approaches and clinical aspects of CP. But only about 100 psychologists, of which 50 are specialists, have followed this program since its establishment in 1990. Recruitment areas include municipal services, including the recent 'kommunepsykolog' role (municipal psychologist) and within health stations or ambulant services, school psychology services, public sector planning, evaluation, consulting, and more conventional individual clinical work. Psychologists with this specialization will fill a special function with regard to designing preventive interventions and to cooperate with and disseminate psychological knowledge to other professional groups. However, about half of the psychologists from this program work in conventional treatment services such as hospitals or district psychiatric centers (DPS). Only around one in ten are involved in planning of mental health or educational services (www.samfunnspsykologi.info; Alseth & Andreassen, 2004). In conclusion, these observations indicate that Norwegian community psychologists currently endorse a more clinical orientation.

Programs, Strategies, and the Role of the Municipalities: Examples of Community-Oriented Work

In this section, we will give examples of how CP principles are more or less subtly integrated in different applied research and community programs and strategies in Norway. The municipal structure and organization, with as noted more than 400 local councils, provides an advantageous institutional foundation for community approaches. Local community approaches and strategies of empowerment are mentioned by government (SHD, 1998a) as two mutually strengthening approaches for enhancing public health. Empowerment-oriented strategies aim at increasing involvement and participation. Empowerment can be obtained more easily in local contexts, where people interact frequently and with a high degree of continuity (Mittelmark

& Hauge, 2003). It is an explicit political aim to stimulate the development of local and regional partnerships for public health (HD, 2003). These public health strategies have many components in common with a CP orientation. The sector of children and youth will first be reviewed.

Health Stations for Infants, Children, and Adolescents

The health stations are part of the municipal health system and aim to reach all preschool children and their families. Almost all families with young children use the services of the health station (Mathiesen, 1995; Sommerschild & Moe, 2005). More generally, these services are central to preventive work. Particular emphasis is placed on identifying at-risk groups, developing support programs and interventions, and informing and referring clients to other services. They have been obliged by law since 1974 to engage in work to prevent mental health problems. Many health stations also play an instrumental role in improving and expanding networks of mothers with little social support (Mathiesen, 1995). Generally, increasing the number of psychologists at health stations would be fruitful as this would strengthen the role of CP in prevention (Borge, 2001).

Certain municipalities, moreover, have established more comprehensive "low-threshold" services aiming at early intervention for children and adolescents. The service is free, and—contrary to practice elsewhere—a referral from first-line general medical practitioner is not required. The service seeks to be just as easily available as somatic health services are. Psychologists are involved in prevention, consultation, supervision, and short-term therapy. Furthermore, psychologists organize courses for health station staff for prevalent problems, for example, sleep disruptions for toddlers. Discussion groups, some of which have developed into informal self-help groups, have been important in the development of such services. The "municipal diagnosis," which is an assessment of the specific structure and prevalence of mental problems and at-risk groups in the local community, is a valuable planning tool that is actively applied in designing the low-threshold schemes. The services cooperate closely with school psychology service, health stations, and the specialist mental health service (Alseth & Andreassen, 2004; Austlid, personal communication). A large number of local councils have also established separate health clinics for adolescents. These clinics aim to reduce physical and psychological problems among youth.

The establishment of dialogue groups (Bogen, 1977) has been one of the strategies employed by health stations to ensure dissemination of information and increasing community awareness. Child-rearing and family issues have been central topics of these groups, which may be led by a professional or a community member. Since 1995, many municipalities offer parental guidance schemes, often provided by local health stations. The aim of the schemes is to prevent psychosocial difficulties among children and interactional difficulties between parents and children. Informative leaflets and discussion material are available in several languages, thus reflecting that the formerly culturally homogenous Norway is moving towards a multicultural society. This approach is similar to that of the International Child Development Programmes, a competence-building nongovernmental organization in the field of psychosocial and educational care of children at high risk, working with caregivers and families (Hundeide, 1996).

School Psychology Service

The school psychology service has its origins in the post–World War II years. The Special Schools Act of 1951 created a need for differentiating pupils. This requirement increased when a law in 1955 opened up for supportive teaching for pupils with special needs within the regular school system. In this period, a number of local advisory offices were established (Læringssenteret, 2001). The school psychology service in this period was oriented towards psychological testing, a trend that can still be observed. The school psychology service was reformed in 1975, when a new primary school law stated that every municipality in Norway should provide a school psychology service ('Pedagogisk-psykologisk tjeneste'; PPT). The reformed service was a means to ensure equal educational rights for all, which meant adapting to the needs, well-being, and situation of each individual pupil (Læringssenteret, 2001).

The main functions of PPTs include the provision of counseling and interventions for children with special needs, in cooperation with parents, as well as competence building and organizational development, the primary users of which are the schools themselves. Recently, a move towards more systemic interventions, rather than focusing attention on the individual child, could, in principle, improve the importance of PPT for prevention (SHD 1998a; Anthun, 2000; Borge, 2001). However, the emphasis of this approach is limited largely to the school system in isolation, whereas PPT historically has given attention to the wider psychosocial situation of the child. The future role for PPT as a first-line provider of services to children and adolescents is therefore unclear. However, the role of the PPT psychologist, both in the past as well as for the future, draws implicitly on CP principles to guide school psychology work.

Substance Abuse and Metal Health

There have been substantial efforts on substance abuse issues in Norway. Historically, the field of substance abuse prevention and treatment has been organizationally fragmented. After a major organizational reform took place in 2004, treatment has become a specialist health service similar to somatic and mental health care. Service users now have status as patients and consequently enjoy rights on the basis of the Patient Rights Act (www.rustiltak.no). This reform has led to an increasing number of psychologists becoming involved with substance abuse–oriented interventions.

On request from the Norwegian National Directorate for the Prevention of Alcohol and Drug Problems, researchers with a community approach have recently developed a plan for a community-based substance abuse prevention project among older adolescents and young adults (Skutle, Iversen & Bergan, 2002).

Adults and Environment: Work Life

The Work Research Institute (WRI) in Oslo has been instrumental in action research in work psychology, advocating employee participation in the workplace (e.g., Thorsrud & Emery, 1970). This empowerment-oriented research was crucial to the development of the Working Environment act of 1977 (Hem, 2003). Currently, central perspectives of the WRI include occupational health, job mastery, absenteeism due to illness, exclusion, employability, and measures to promote life-long learning. The WRI emphasizes bringing about a collaborative approach in order to prevent exclusion from the workforce and promote permanent work and secure development (www.afi-wri.no).

New Policy on Problem Solving in the Municipalities: Conferencing

The Mediation and Reconciliation Service in a municipality can be used in both criminal cases and in matters not reported to the police. All age groups may use the Mediation and Reconciliation Service including those under the age of criminal responsibility (www.konfliktraadet.no). Often considered as an alternative to conventional retributive legal action or clinical therapy, community conferencing and network mediation have preventive effects. This tradition is based on the concept of restorative justice (McCold & Wachtel, 2003), with roots in the Maori culture. Central to this approach is to counteract what Christie (1977) calls "conflict theft," that is, the tendency of the professionals to take control of the conflict, thus depriving the initial parties of the conflict an active role in resolving it and benefiting from this healing experience (Tschudi & Reichelt, 2004).

Strategies in Local Communities Characterized by Declining Population

The population in Norway is concentrated in the southeastern part of the country. Due to increasing requirements of financial efficiency, most new workplaces have been established in this region. The north of Norway, in particular, has been under continual threat of falling population numbers. An important task for CP in Norway would therefore be to contribute to community well-being in these areas. However, as pointed out earlier, clinical, social, health, and community psychology in Norway have not been characterized by adopting explicitly critical stances to societal development. With few exceptions, it is the disciplines of sociology and social psychiatry that have undertaken such more critical research, which is beyond the scope of this chapter.

Future Challenges for Norwegian Community Psychology: Towards a Critical Psychology

The Norwegian welfare state is currently facing increasing pressure to limit the nature and extent of its services. This pressure stems from economic globalization, an ageing population, and rapidly increasing health budgets. The Scandinavian welfare model is becoming dysfunctional as a consequence of its success: Expectations of what it can provide is financially suffocating the major producers of welfare, that is, the 400 local municipalities, and professional "helpers" report increasing disempowerment due to rapidly increasing complexity of service provision (Hem, 2003). This situation of the welfare state, operating at its limits, poses huge new challenges for psychologists engaged with community issues.

There is little doubt that during the past years in Norwegian society, the relationships between the state, organizational actors, and individuals has been substantially influenced by a neoliberalist ideology, in particular the principles of New Public Management (NPM) (Nafstad, Carlquist & Blakar, in press). This is an organizational model aiming to improve the efficiency and effectiveness of service production and provision in the public sector. It involves an increasing emphasis on contractual relationships between government institutions and market actors, as well as the introduction of market mechanisms to management of the public sector itself (Pollitt & Bouckaert, 2000). Deregulation, competitive tendering, transfer of decision-making power to producers in the market, and quantitative monitoring of goal attainment are key elements of NPM.

Deregulation within the NPM ideology does not necessarily entail outright privatization as the final responsibility for public service provision is usually retained at the governmental level. NPM is, therefore, compatible with a "third way" policy that seeks to balance the needs for an effective economy with demand for social welfare (Giddens, 1998). Despite the claims of "third way" policies to ensure social, mental, and physical welfare, public sector service providers in this model are often forced to compete with private-sector actors and may be discontinued if they do not win contracts. Furthermore, privatization policies may accompany NPM.

Therefore, NPM reflects and contributes to other values, that is, competition, short-term economic efficiency, and profit maximization, than those originally endorsed by the Norwegian welfare society, that is, empowerment, participation, and social justice. Christensen (2003) argues that the "supermarket state" undermines some of the integrative and collective features of

Norway's political culture. The Norwegian social philosopher Vetlesen (2004) characterizes current society as 'opsjonssamfunnet' (a society of options). As we see it, this shift of societal values has potentially negative effects on social bonds, communal obligations, and individual motivations.

Analyses of ideological changes in the Norwegian society as reflected in the language in public discourse (Nafstad, Carlquist & Blakar, in press) suggest that neoliberalist values are rapidly permeating both the individual citizens as well as a number of sectors of society that so far have been protected from the logic of short-term financial efficiency and profit maximization. Although controversial, competition is increasingly accepted not only as a regulatory mechanism but a value in its own right. However, as Deutsch (1990) has argued, the commonly assumed trade-off between efficiency and equality has meager evidence in psychological literature. Therefore, the neoliberalist emphasis on competition as a means of individual and societal-level efficiency and effectiveness might be misguided.

In sum, neoliberalist, competition-oriented, and consumerist values are being infused into more and more layers and sectors of society, including those of social security, health care, and education (Nafstad, Carlquist & Blakar, in press). Changing values and representations contribute to a climate of legitimacy for social inequalities that has so far been unfamiliar to the Norwegian mindset. Our stance is that these ideological changes provide an equally great—if not even larger—challenge to the future of Norwegian communities than the increasing financial pressures on the welfare state per se. The role of CP and psychologists as agents of the well-being of the individual and microsystems such as family, school, and workplace is thus likely to change from largely working within the boundaries of a well-functioning welfare state to providing critical and research-based arguments against the ongoing changes in society increasingly inspired by neoliberalism.

To conclude, the ideals of social justice and security, empowerment, and community participation have been cornerstones in the development of the Norwegian welfare state. A particular consequence of this sociocultural situation is that within Norwegian CP there has been an absence of critical analyses of value and political issues. CP-oriented psychologists in Norway have, thus, more or less tacitly taken for granted that they are part of a larger system or process—the welfare society—characterized by fairness and social justice. As shown, the validity of this assumption should now be questioned (Nafstad, Carlquist & Blakar, in press).

Concluding Remarks: Comparisons with Other Regions

This book illustrates the many similarities between CP in Norway and in other regions. As in many other countries, the development of CP in Norway is influenced by theories and models developed in the United States. In the same way as in most other countries, Norwegian CP also integrates social and clinical psychology in search for a CP identity. Moreover, CP in Norway still represents a rather weak and vague professional identity; a situation for CP also reported in the chapters from a variety of other countries, among others Germany, Great Britain, Italy, and Ghana. Norwegian CP is neither an organized field, nor a formally established (sub-)discipline. It is better understood as a minority voice within psychology at large. However, as in the other countries, concepts and approaches from CP can be found both in research and practice. Nevertheless, similar to the situation for example in Germany, Great Britain, and Canada, CP in Norway has never become an integral part of university curricula or of mainstream psychological research and practice.

There are also striking differences between CP in Norway and that of other countries. Until now there has been a broad consensus in Norwegian society regarding fundamental values underpinning the welfare state, such as social equality, social security, and equitable distribution of wealth. Therefore, CP-oriented psychologists in Norway have not systematically articulated political and action oriented visions and values. As mentioned, a notable exception to this has been feminist psychology. In sum, compared with CP in for example Latin America and the United States, Norwegian CP has until now hardly recognized and practiced the political nature of CP.

The Norwegian society, like the rest of the world, is undergoing substantial ideological changes due to globalization. The ideology underpinning current globalization is first and foremost that of the free market and neoliberalism (Bauman, 2000; Bourdieu, 1998; Stiglitz, 2002; Thurow, 1996), a late modern form of capitalism (Giddens, 1991; Nafstad, 2003).[2] This ideology is redefining previously noncommercial spheres such as health and care systems. Broadly stated, the neoliberal ideology emphasizes the values of individualism, consumerism, competition, and materialism, thus legitimizing or even promoting social and economic inequalities. One of the consequences of globalization and neoliberalism is an increasing gap between those who have and those who do not have—within countries as well as between countries and regions. After decades of reducing the gaps between people (SHD, 1998a), social inequality is again increasing in the Norwegian society (Underlid, 2005). An increasing minority, comparing themselves with the living standards of the majority, is therefore experiencing social injustice, dissatisfaction, and materially frustrating lives. Furthermore, the hitherto taken-for-granted status of the welfare state may itself contribute to a denial among decision makers to recognize that poverty exists in this generally wealthy country (Andenæs, 2004). In our opinion, ideological awareness, critical analyses, and concepts such as solidarity, equality, and concern for communality should therefore constitute central issues of CP in Norway the future.

---

[2] Together with Albert Botchway, a Ph.D. student at the University of Oslo and citizen of Ghana, we are currently studying and comparing the impact of globalization and neoliberalism on Norway and Ghana.

In our view, CP in Norway must aspire toward a more prominent and critical discipline within Norwegian psychology in the years to come; explicitly focusing on and arguing for alternative values based on solidarity and social equality. Inspired by CP in for example Latin America and the United States, CP in Norway will now face the challenge of becoming a critical discipline and no longer take values such as solidarity and social equality for granted as integral parts of the Scandinavian welfare society.

References

Aas, B. (1975). On female culture: An attempt to formulate a theory of women's solidarity and action. *Acta Sociologica, 18,* 142-161.

Alseth, Ø. & Andreassen, B.A. (2004). *Kraftsenterundersøkelsen. Psykisk helsearbeid for barn og unge i kommunene. Rapport.* Oslo: Norsk Psykologforening.

Andenæs, A. (2004). Hvorfor ser vi ikke fattigdommen? Fra en undersøkelse om barn som blir plassert utenfor hjemmet. *Nordisk sosialt arbeid, 24,* 1, 19-33.

Anderssen, N. (2001). A critical look at psychological research on the children of lesbian or gay parents. *International Journal of Critical Psychology, 1,* 173-181.

Anthun, R. (2000). Quality dimensions for school psychology services. *Scandinavian Journal of Psychology, 41,* 181-187.

Axelsen, T. (1976). *Det tause sykehuset.* Oslo: Universitetsforlaget.

Bauman, Z. (2000). *Liquid modernity,* Polity Press, Cambridge.

Bezemer, J., Kroon, S., Pastoor, L d.W., Ryen, E., & Wold, A.H. (2004). *Language teaching and learning in a multicultural context. Case studies from elementary education in the Netherlands and Norway.* Oslo: Novus Forlag.

Blakar, R.M. & Nafstad, H.E. (2006). Critical Psychology in Norway: A brief review commenting on why critical psychology is currently virtually absent. *Annual Review of Critical Psychology 5,* 1-6.

Bogen, B. (1977). Erfaringer fra en psykologrolle i forebyggende arbeid innen primærhelsetjenesten. *Tidsskrift for Norsk Psykologforening, 14(5),* 10-22.

Borge, A.I.H. (2001). *Psykologer i folkehelsearbeid.* Working report. Oslo: University of Oslo.

Bourdieu, P. (1998). *Acts of resistance. Against the new myths of our time.* Oxford: Blackwell.

Bronfenbrenner, U. (1979). *The ecology of human development. Experiments by nature and design.* Cambridge, MA: Harvard University Press.

Christensen, T. (2003). Narratives of Norwegian governance: Elaborating the strong state tradition. *Public Administration, 81,* 163-190.

Christie, N. (1977). Conflict as property. *British Journal of Criminology, 17,* 1-15.

Deutsch, M. (1990). Forms of social organization: Psychological consequences. In H. Himmelweit & G. Gaskell (Eds.), *Societal psychology* (pp. 157-176). Newbury Park: Sage.

Engel, G.L. (1977). The need for a new medical model: A challenge for biomedicine. *Science, 196,* 129-136.

Giddens, A. (1991). *Modernity and self-identity: Self and society in the late modern age.* Cambridge: Polity Press.

Giddens, A. (1998): *The third way. The renewal of social democracy.* Cambridge: Polity Press.

Grinde, T. (1977). New roles of the community psychologists in Norway. *Tidsskrift for Norsk Psykologforening, 14,* 4, 1-27.

Grinde, T. (2002). Noen utfordringer for samfunnspsykologene. *Tidsskrift for Norsk Psykologforening, 39*, 218-221.

Haavind, H. (1998). Understanding women in the psychological mode. In D. von der Fehr, A.G. Jonasdottir & B. Rosenbeck (Eds.), *Is there a Nordic feminism?* (pp. 243-271). London: UCL Press.

Haavind, H. (2002). What is gender about – when women are no longer and not yet? In C. Hofsten & L. Backman (Eds.), *Psychology at the turn of the millenium, Vol 2: Social and clinical issues* (pp. 472-497). London: Psychology Press.

HD (2003). *St.meld. nr. 16. Resept for et sunnere Norge. Folkehelsepolitikken*: Oslo: Ministry of Health.

Hem, H.E. (2003). Aksjonsforskning. Forskning til nytte i møtet med velferdssamfunnets hovedutfordringer. In H.A. Hauge & M.B. Mittelmark (Eds.), *Helsefremmende arbeid i en brytningstid. Fra monolog til dialog?* (pp. 74-100). Bergen: Fagbokforlaget.

Holter, H. (1966). Women's occupational situation in Scandinavia. *International Labour Review, 93(4)*.

Holter, H. (1970). *Sex roles and social structure*. Oslo: Norwegian University Press.

Holter, H. (Ed.). (1984). *Patriarchy in a welfare society*. Oslo: Universitetsforlaget.

Hundeide, K. (1996). *Ledet samspill. Håndbok til ICDP's sensitivitetsprogram*. Asker: Vett og Viten.

Iversen, H., Rundmo, T., & Klempe, H. (2005). Risk attitudes and behavior among Norwegian adolescents: The effects of a behavior modification program and a traffic safety campaign. *European Psychologist, 10(1)*, 25-38.

Javo, C., Rønning, J.A., Heyerdahl, S. (2004). Child-rearing in an indigenous Sami population in Norway: A cross-cultural comparison of parental attitudes and expectations. *Scandinavian Journal of Psychology, 45(1)*, 67-78.

Javo, C., Rønning, J.A., Heyerdahl, S., Rudmin, F.W. (2004). Parenting correlates of child behavior problems in a multiethnic community sample of preschool children in northern Norway. *European Child and Adolescent Psychiatry, 13(1)*, 8-18.

Knoff, R.H., Bogen, B., Austlid, E., & Isdahl, P.J. (1983). *Psykologiske almentjenester., Psykologarbeid i helsestasjon, skole og sosialkontor*. Oslo: Universitetsforlaget.

Kringlen, E. (2004). A history of Norwegian psychiatry. *History of Psychiatry, 15*, 259-283.

Læringssenteret (2001). Håndbok for PP-tjenesten. Oslo: Læringssenteret.

Mathiesen, K.S. (1995). Helsestasjonen og de utsatte småbarnsmødrene. In O.S. Dalgard, E. Døhlie & M. Ystgaard (Eds.), *Sosialt nettverk: Helse og samfunn.* (pp. 108-125). Oslo: Universitetsforlaget.

McCold, P. & Wachtel, T. (2003). *In Pursuit of Paradigm: A Theory of Restorative Justice*. Paper presented at the XIII World Congress of Criminology, Rio de Janeiro.

Mittelmark, M.B., Aarø, L.E., Henriksen, S.G., Siqveland, J., & Torsheim, T. (2004). Chronic social stress in the community and associations with psychological distress: A social psychological perspective. *International Journal of Mental Health Promotion, 6*, 5-17.

Mittelmark, M.B. & Hauge, H.A. (2003). Helsefremmende politikk for vurdering av helsekonsekvenser. In H.A. Hauge & M.B. Mittelmark (Eds.), *Helsefremmende arbeid i en brytningstid. Fra monolog til dialog?* (pp. 39-51). Bergen: Fagbokforlaget.

Nafstad, H.E. (2003). The neo-liberal ideology and the self-interest paradigm as resistance to change. *Journal of Radical Psychology, 3*, 3-21.

Nafstad, H.E. & Blakar, R.M. (1982). Current trends in Norwegian social psychology: A brief review. *European Journal of Social Psychology, 12*, 195-212.

Nafstad, H.E., Carlquist, E. & Blakar, R.M. (in press). Community and care work in a world of changing ideologies. *Community, Work and Family*.

Nelson, G. & Prilleltensky, I. (2005). *Community psychology: In pursuit of liberation and wellbeing*. Houndmills: Palgrave Macmillan.

Olweus, D. (2004). The Olweus Bullying Prevention Programme: Design and implementation issues and a new national initiative in Norway. In D. Pepler, K. Rigby, & P.K. Smith (Eds.), *Bullying in schools: How successful can interventions be?* (pp. 13-36). New York, NY: Cambridge University Press.

Ommundsen, R. Hak, T., Mørch, S. Larsen, K.S., Van der Veer, K. (2002). Attitudes toward illegal immigration: A cross-national methodological comparison. *Journal of Psychology: Interdisciplinary and Applied, 136*, 103-110.

Ommundsen, R. & Teigen, K.H. (2005). Social psychology in Norway. *European Bulletin of Social Psychology, 17*, 31-38.

Pollitt, C. & Bouckaert, G. (2000). *Public management reform: A comparative analysis*. Oxford: Oxford University Press.

Reichelt, S. (1987). Utviklingstendenser i klinisk psykologi: Henimot integrasjon? In J.P. Myklebust & R. Ommundsen (Eds.), *Psykologprofesjonen mot år 2000* (pp. 53-65). Oslo: Universitetsforlaget.

Romøren, T.I. (2001). Helsetjenesten. In A. Hatland, S. Kuhnle & T.I. Romøren (Eds.), *Den norske velferdsstaten* (pp. 133-159). Oslo: Gyldendal.

Sarason, S.B. (1974). *The psychological sense of community: Prospects for a community psychology*. Oxford: Jossey-Bass.

Schjødt, B. (2002). Helsepsykologi - døren åpen. *Tidsskrift for Norsk Psykologforening, 39*, 401-402.

SHD (1998a): NOU 1998:18 *Det er bruk for alle. Styrking av folkehelsearbeidet i kommunene*. Oslo: Ministry of Health and Social Affairs.

SHD (1998b): St prp nr 63. *Om opptrappingsplan for psykisk helse 1999-2006*. Oslo: Ministry of Health and Social Affairs.

Skuterud, A. (2000). Psykologen i kommunene. *Tidsskrift for Norsk Psykologforening, 37*, 156.

Skutle, A., Iversen, E., Bergan, T. (2002). A community-based prevention program in western Norway: Organisation and progression model. *Addictive Behaviors, 27*, 977-988.

Sommerschild, H. & Moe, E. (2005). *Da barnepsykiatrien kom til Norge: Beretninger ved noen som var med*. Oslo: Universitetsforlaget.

Stiglitz, J.E. (2002). *Globalization and its discontents*. New York: W.W. Norton.

Thorsrud, E. & Emery, F. (1970). *Towards a new company organisation* (Mot en ny bedriftsorganisasjon). Oslo: Universitetsforlaget.

Thurow, L. (1996). *The future of capitalism. How today's economic forces shape tomorrow's world*. London: Nicholas Brealey Publishing.

Tiller, P.O. (1969). Verdiorientering og fremtidsdrømmer hos tre grupper av norske skolebarn. *Tidsskrift for Samfunnsforskning, 10*, 175-191.

Tiller, P.O. (1973). Barns vilkår i Norge. *INAS-report 73:4*, 1-330.

Tjersland, O.A. & Eriksen, P. (1994). Fra karaktertrekk til relasjoner og språk. In S. Reichelt, (Ed.). *Psykologi i forandring: Jubileumsbok, Norsk psykologforening 60 år* (pp. 125-144). Oslo: Norsk psykologforening.

Tschudi, F. & Reichelt, S. (2004). Conferencing when therapy is stuck. *Journal of Systemic Therapies 23*, 38-52.

Underlid, K. (2005). *Fattigdommens psykologi*. Oslo: Det Norske Samlaget.
Vetlesen, A.J. (2004). Det frie mennesket? Et sosialfilosofisk blikk på patologiene i opsjonssamfunnet. In Nafstad, H.E. (Ed.), *Det omsorgsfulle mennesket*. (pp. 17-54). Oslo: Gyldendal Akademisk.
Wold, A.H. (2004). Utvikling av ordforråd med fokus på norsk som andrespråk. In E. Selj, E. Ryen & I. Lindberg (Eds.), *Med språklige minoriteter i klassen* (pp. 97-124). Oslo: Cappelen Akademiske Forlag.

14
Community Psychology in Spain: Realities, Expectations, and Desires

ANTONIO MARTÍN AND JORGE S. LÓPEZ

Abstract

In recent times, community action found space for its development in Spain only after the transition to democracy in the late 1970s. Academics and professionals committed to social transformation encountered in the proposals of community psychology (CP) from the English-speaking world a powerful tool for conceptualization and intervention, combining these with the influences of critical Latin American and European currents. However, in the institutional context, social action was diverted into a markedly assistance-based structure, neglecting community action. The activity of the so-called Third Sector has followed a similar pattern, with a predominance of top-down processes in the determination of goals and priorities and actions of a palliative nature. In the academic environment, CP is now present in numerous universities at the undergraduate level, while several postgraduate programs include content related to it. Nevertheless, there is no universally accepted qualification for professional practice in this field. Spanish CP has become stronger over the past decade, through both the integration of different theoretical and methodological perspectives and the development of its own proposals. Even so, it faces the challenge of penetrating the society of our times, characterized, beneath its apparent opulence, by growing apathy and by new forms of alienation and exclusion.

Introduction

It is with great enthusiasm that we approach the complex task of giving an account of the foundations and development of community psychology (CP) in Spain, and we are grateful for the privilege offered by the cross-cultural perspective of this volume. In undertaking our task, we acknowledge from the outset that community action aimed at social change and well-being has roots in different disciplines and that we owe a debt to every one of them. However, we are also aware that our aim here is essentially to focus on the

299

conceptions and practice of those who have labelled themselves as community psychologists.

In the Spanish context, although there is no formal, consensual definition that precisely delimits the principles, goals, and practices of CP, some elements can be identified that are common to the conceptions of CP endorsed by different authors, and which will serve as the basis for our analysis (Chacón & García, 1998; Hombrados, 1996; Martín & López, 1998; Musitu, Herrero, Cantera & Montenegro, 2004; Sánchez, 1991). In this regard, CP is conceived as a discipline that falls mainly within the field of applied social psychology, sharing with other disciplines an ecological-systemic view of social phenomena, with special emphasis on the conception of social reality as the result of a process of intersubjective construction. On this basis, some of the most important distinguishing principles of CP would be explicit ethical commitment to social change oriented to welfare and equality; emphasis on strategies of promotion and prevention rather than palliative strategies; opting for a commitment to catalysis and social dynamization, as opposed to adopting the professional role of manager; emphasis on empowerment of community and group resources as intervention strategies and, especially, on forms of action aimed at the development of collective awareness, the promotion of participation, and the recovery of citizens' power and responsibility.

Having established this starting point, in describing the main achievements of the discipline we shall try to remain faithful to its spirit and avoid restricting our account to a self-congratulatory list of success stories. On the contrary, we shall try to present a critical but measured summary taking into account both what many of us would like CP to be—an eminently social, proactive, committed, and transformative psychology—and an awareness of the limits imposed on our real activity, threatened by reductionism, the primacy of palliative assistance, and the oscillations of political power. Likewise, so as to avoid a mere retrospective analysis, we shall attempt to systematize the new trends and set out proposals for the future to complement the contributions of other academics and professionals.

Some Peculiarities of the Spanish Historical Context

Geographical spaces shape certain regularities of thought and action in populations throughout history. It is almost unnecessary here to stress that this phenomenon by no means reflects the existence of any kind of national "essence" but constitutes rather the cultural crystallization of events and structural conditions that have shown a relative degree of persistence over time. With this in mind, we believe it makes sense to analyze the ways in which a discipline develops in different contexts and therefore to devote some space here to an historical contextualization of community action in our country.

We consider one of the crucial elements of Spanish history to be a convulsive character that has brought about the juxtaposition of heroic deeds and barbarism, rapid development and sharp decline into decadence, and intellectual or artistic lucidity and cultural drought. Our passage through history has seen successive cycles of confrontation between different perspectives on society, manifested in different variants of the conservatism–progressivism binomial, with none of the conflicting factions being able to avoid involvement in the defence of specific economic or corporate interests. In contrast with the case of numerous European societies in which the dynamic of social conflict has eventually led to a reinforcement of the organizational structures of the middle classes, Spanish society has experienced successive periods of destruction of civil society (Rubinstein, 1994). These periods have taken the form of the expulsion or persecution of certain groups or faiths, the bloody suppression of civil uprisings, the mass exile of intellectuals of one political hue or the other in times of internal strife, and, in our recent history, almost four decades of dictatorial rule with a marked doctrinal and pseudo-ideological character. The transition to democracy that began 30 years ago clearly brought about a spectacular transformation of freedoms and possibilities, but paternalism in the development of social policies in the early phases and an excessive preoccupation with macroeconomic targets in later years have held back the reconstruction of the social structures of participation. From this perspective it is easy to see how, in the field of community action, the Spanish context has on the one hand produced pioneering experiences of great interest, but on the other, has hindered the development over time of active, solid, and consistent civil participation.

The Historical Background of Community Psychology in Spain

Remote Antecedents of Community Action

Although we are conscious of the fact that all historical reviews involve bias in their selection of personalities and traditions, we nevertheless feel it appropriate to mention some of the trends in Spanish thought that took root from the 12th century onwards and flourished in the 16th century, to form the indigenous basis of some of the most characteristic principles of the community perspective. From such trends grew a tradition of thought aptly defined (despite his intentions) by traditionalist historian Menéndez Pelayo as *heterodox*, and whose principal figures range from Ramón Llull to Francisco de Vitoria, by way of Juan Ruiz (Arcipreste de Hita), Juan Luis Vives, and Juan Huarte de San Juan.

This tradition, humanist, optimistic, and tolerant, reached its zenith during the reign of Charles V (1516–1556), flourishing thanks to the influences of Arab and Jewish thought and from Europe, the ideas of Erasmus. These influences generated, first of all, a specific style of realism or "nearness of things" that emphasized the importance of experience (see, for example, the sensualism of Ramón Llull, aka Raymond Lully); secondly, they focused attention on subjectivity and interior awareness, in other words, the idea of the subject making sense of his or her experience and surroundings (see, in an example from literature, *La Celestina*, by Fernando de Rojas); and thirdly, they placed human beings at the centre of the cosmological view, thus setting the scene for greater openness to pluralism and individual liberty (Abellán, 1996; Rodríguez, 1962). Juan Luis Vives (1492–1540) was an eminent representative of this tradition, leaving contributions to the field of psychology that have lost none of their validity or lucidity. For Vives, humans depended not on their *substance*, but on their circumstances, and could improve their environment by virtue of their capacity for intervening in the world and changing aspects of it. He argued that the natural context of human beings is the historical society in which they live, and within which they make sense of reality and orient their behaviour through language, which, as a human construction, makes possible the achievement of social cohesion, harmony, equality, and peace (Grassi, 1993; Quintana, 1996). Vives, commonly considered as one of the originators of social action (Kisnerman, 1990), was the author of the work *On Assistance to the Poor*, which he wrote in the Belgian city of Bruges after studying the needs of its most destitute inhabitants and the causes of their poverty through house-to-house visits. It was also in Bruges that Vives managed to set up the first administrative agency whose purpose was to provide assistance to the needy.

Some continuity of such humanist principles can be found in the *novatorista* movement, which emerged in Spain in the late 18th and early 19th centuries thanks to the incorporation of the Enlightenment spirit, which brought confidence in the capacity of humans to intervene in nature and modify it, and conceived knowledge as based on reason and experience (Abellán, 1996; Rodríguez, 1962). The novatoristas brought about important innovations in the fields of politics (drafting of the radically progressivist 1812 Constitution), economics, education (establishment of nationwide public schooling), health and urban planning. Among its most significant figures was Melchor Gaspar de Jovellanos (1744–1811), who thought progress should begin with education (understood in its widest sense) and should lead to well-being via the improvement of living conditions. This movement was abruptly truncated when its major representatives were exiled (charged with being *afrancesados*, or "Frenchified") upon the accession to the throne of Fernando VII in 1814.

The 19th century, thanks to the synthesis of currents such as Krausism and Positivism, saw renewed development of the pedagogic and social sciences, the fruits of which included the foundation, at the beginning of the 20th century, of the Institución Libre de Enseñanza, an educational institution independent of the state with an agenda based on secular principles and active, comprehensive education. Among the most important initiatives undertaken in the 1930s were the Popular Universities and the Pedagogic Missions, itinerant projects for promoting art and culture among rural populations organized by artists and writers, such as the renowned poet and playwright Federico García Lorca. After the Spanish Civil War (1936–1939), Spain spent 36 years under the dictatorship of General Franco, until his death in 1975. This regime saw a drastic reduction in civil liberties, as well as the suppression of forms of thinking or action of a progressive nature and the persecution of those responsible, leading to the exile of the majority of Spanish intellectuals who survived the Civil War. In the area of social action, as in other philo-fascist regimes, Franco's dictatorship was characterized by a strategy of charity and beneficence (Casado & Guillem, 1986), as well as by policies involving the imposition of juvenile and civil associationism of a vertical nature, which encouraged assimilation of the regime's values through collaboration in social and charitable activities with strong symbolic and ritualistic connotations.

The Transformation of Community Action in Spain During the Transition to Democracy

By the early 1970s, the restrictions imposed on Spanish society by the Franco dictatorship were slackening as a consequence of the weakening of the regime itself and the strong economic, cultural, and political influences from abroad, facilitating the development of the ideas and practices that would lay the foundations for the future transition to democracy. It was in this period that numerous professionals and academics from different disciplines began taking steps to establish new forms of community action.

Social pedagogy and *sociocultural community development* were, as in other countries, pioneers of community development in the Spanish context, combining experience and theory with influences from Latin America in the work of Freire, Fals Borda, Ander-Egg, or Kisnerman, and from the French tradition of Besnard, Moulinier, Labourie, or Pujol (Marchioni, 1989; Quintana, 1986). The professionals in this field, who were also in the vanguard with regard to the establishment of transnational cooperation networks, developed a set of models with a substantial operative and prag-matic component in areas such as participatory action research (López de Ceballos, 1989), sociocultural community development (Cembranos, Montesinos & Bustelo, 1988) and socioeducational intervention (Colom, 1987), which would involve less of the theoretical retrospect and empirical support required in the academic context.

There is a great deal of overlap in the perspectives and activity of those mentioned above with those of professionals involved in the field of *social work*, who in the early 1970s were immersed in a process of re-conceptualizing their positions and practices, with the goal of making the transition from the inherited models of social work to more systematic and transformational models (Barbero, 2002). These professionals were influenced by new forms of community action proposed by Latin American authors, the currents of thought deriving from the movements of May 1968 and Marxist perspectives (Colomer, 1990). Particularly relevant for the specific field of community social work would be the influence of pioneers—such as Marchioni, Colomer or Hytte—many of whom came from abroad (Lillo & Roselló, 2001). The efforts of transformation and systematization in this field led in 1976 to professionals deciding to change its name, from "social assistance" to "social work," and to include training in this area as part of medium-level university courses by the early 1980s (Red & Brezmes, 2003).

In the field of *community mental health*, a group of professionals coming mainly from psychiatry tried in the early 1970s to make progress towards deinstitutionalization and psychiatric reform, having absorbed influences that included anti-psychiatric currents based on the ideas of Cooper, Laing, Foucault, and Basaglia, the proposals arising from the Swampscott Conference and the approaches of authors such as Caplan (Salvador-Carulla, Bulbena, Vázquez-Barquero, Muñoz, Gómez-Beneyto & Torres, 2003). The first steps towards reform were taken in Spain at this time through the improvement of conditions in psychiatric hospitals and the beginning of deinstitutionalization of chronic patients—thanks to the individual efforts of certain professionals. By the early 1980s, marked progress had been made in some institutions, but the formal initiation of the de-institutionalization process dates from 1985, with the publication of the *Report of the Ministerial Commission for Psychiatric Reform*, which finally opened the way for the official incorporation of psychologists in public mental health institutions. Attempts at reform would, however, encounter serious difficulties and yield disappointing results, as was also the case in other countries (Costa & López, 1986).

As regards *psychology* itself, it was in 1969 that it was first included as a university area as part of the degree course in philosophy and arts at the universities of Madrid and Barcelona. It would not be until 1978 that the first departments of psychology *per se* were set up (Musitu, 1998). The need to differentiate the practice and discourse of the newly approved discipline from those of philosophy gave rise to a strong critical dimension. In the field of community intervention, this led to a confrontation of perspectives with those advocating a cognitive-behavioural approach on the one hand, and, on the other, those who combined the contributions of psychoanalysis and Marxist thought (Duro, 2001), though there were also other influences from diverse sources, such as the humanist psychology of Rogers and Maslow or European sociology (Martín, 1986). Not without conflict, and given the need to furnish a differentiated space with operative proposals, the result was that in institutions the cognitive-behavioural perspective and the neopositivist approach prevailed in the design and evaluation of intervention. Meanwhile, the contributions of a critical and dialogical nature were largely shelved and forced to wait until postmodernism was in full swing to return with greater operative strength and formalization. In any case, the cognitive-behavioural perspective was adopted among community action professionals with a clear influence from the models of *empowerment* generated within the 'Anglo-Saxon' tradition. At the same time, action strategies were characterized by a marked social commitment in the delimitation of the aims and strategies of action—a reflection also of their clear progressivist tendencies, and of the influences of other theoretical currents (Costa & López, 1986; Martín, Chacón & Martínez, 1988). The proposals derived from the re-conceptualization of Latin American community action would gradually become apparent in professional approaches but would have to wait some time before emerging more explicitly.

The Development of Community Psychology in Spain

In analyzing the development of CP in Spain, we shall consider it with regard to two areas that, despite being linked in many respects, have developed in different ways: the professional context, closer to the ground, and more subject to the demands of social and political reality; and the academic context, more formalized and more concerned with tasks of conceptualization. In either case, it can be stated that CP emerges in a progressive manner, through the combination of praxis and theoretical reflection, without a specific, single point in time that clearly signifies the starting point of the discipline in the Spanish context.

The Development of CP in Spain in the Professional Context

By the late 1970s, developments were taking place that can be considered as CP in the true sense. Such is the case of the setting up of the Neighbourhood Psychology Commission in Madrid (Duro, 2001), or the psycho-pedagogical surgeries in Valencia and Barcelona (Musitu, 1998). With the enactment of the 1978 Constitution, Spain became a democratic state with a regionally devolved structure and began implementing active social policies. The so-called Autonomous Regions (*Comunidades Autónomas*) were given responsibility in the area of "Social Assistance," "Social Services," or "Social Welfare," terms used by the legislators as synonymous (López-Cabanas & Chacón, 1997), as well as in the field of "Health," which already appeared as symbolically and operatively dissociated from the other fields. From this point on, spaces were potentially opened up for the incorporation of community psychologists in the professional context.

As far as *institutional social action* is concerned, the early 1980s saw the creation in different locations of the *Equipos de Base de los Servicios Sociales* (Basic Social Service Teams), in which the presence of psychology professionals soon began to grow. The significant efforts of reflection and conceptualization, together with the enthusiasm with which those involved set about the creation of a new system of social action, was clearly conditioned by obstacles hinted at in the very label "Social Services" given to the structure of the program. The actual political entities close to the social action were unable in practice to shrug off the old, profoundly palliative air. Professionals accepted a pragmatic commitment between their desires and the restrictions of reality. In consequence, social services grew in a somewhat unbalanced fashion, and the structure contented itself with being a system of service provision, prioritizing individual subsidization strategies to the great detriment of actions aimed at community dynamization and participation (Sáez, 2003). Nevertheless, in recent decades, the system has incorporated more and more psychologists who, despite the clear and manifest restrictions present in its structure, have attempted to develop community work projects (Musitu & Arango, 1995).

As regards intervention within the *institutional health system*, it was also after 1980 when the municipal health centres were created in different parts of Spain, representing an important transformation towards a health care framework more alert to psychosocial aspects and closer to an interdisciplinary perspective, favouring the inclusion of psychologists in the system (Costa & López, 1986; Duro, 1991). These reforms, as we have mentioned, also facilitated the incorporation of psychologists in the mental health centres and hospital psychiatric attention services. However, the psychology professionals working in this context, with very few exceptions, found themselves largely restricted to adopting roles close to the traditional one of the clinical psychologist, obliged by a structure whose fundamental *raison d'être* was palliative care for individual health problems (Musitu & Arango, 1995). Contributing to this has been society's perception, which persists today, of psychology as principally and even exclusively clinical, the intensely clinical dimension attributed to psychology in the majority of university environments, and the near absence of social components, in general, within the concept of health itself in many institutional settings.

In the context of *institutional community development*, it should be stressed that Spain's entry into the European Union resulted in a substantial flow of structural funds aimed at promoting, among other things, the creation of new forms of sustainable economic development in the least favoured geographical areas. The European Regional Development Fund (ERDF) and the European Social Fund (ESF) stimulated the generation of an extensive set of development and training programs in which community psychologists have been accommodated. Even so, the effectiveness of such actions has been reduced by a lack of appropriate attention to the social and human dimensions of development from supranational agencies, which have prioritized purely economic aspects to the detriment of the reinforcement of community networks. Furthermore, the promotion of effective community action has been hampered by the system for fixing priorities and allocating resources, with decisions made at the top by authorities far removed from the destinations of the resources.

The so-called Third Sector, comprising a heterogeneous set of private non-profit organizations, has grown spectacularly in Spain in the past decade (Ruiz-Olabuénaga, 2000), becoming, with all its potential and all its contradictions, one of the most relevant professional niches for community psychologists. Public funding from various sources has been supplemented, paradoxically, by contributions from large financial corporations, which have promoted—as they themselves have expanded—the setting up of foundations and awards supported on the basis of priorities distinct from those of the population by some of the profits of their economic activities. Community action professionals of different types have been involved in these kinds of projects, which are usually aimed at specific sectors, such as the family and children, the elderly, or the disabled (Fundación Tomillo, 2000). These professionals have found clear advantages of the flexibility allowed by extrainstitutional work, but also significant disadvantages as a result of job instability and difficulties for carrying out long-term work. Special mention should be reserved for the area of *cooperation for development*, which has represented for many young professionals an opportunity to channel their interest and concern that is unlikely to be afforded elsewhere in the Spanish context. For those working in this area, the absence of care structures in the target societies has often permitted the development of professional skills and the application of projects that are orthodoxly communitarian, even though the career of such professionals is often beset by the difficulties of subsequent readjustment to their original environment.

Summarizing, it can be said that in the professional context, certain conditions in Spain have favoured the development of CP and of professionals equipped to implement CP projects and programs. However, neither social policy nor the institutional structures generated in the area of social action (in either the public or the private sectors) have favoured the appropriate development of the role assigned to the community psychologist insofar as they have prioritized more individualist and top-down approaches.

The Development of CP in the Academic Context

Early community work activity and the proposals framed within CP from other areas were accompanied by growing interest on the part of academics from the field of psychology in different Spanish universities with close links initially between professionals and institutions on the one hand and academics interested in social action on the other. This interest made its presence felt in the 1980s through a series of meetings which began taking on more and more importance and in various other efforts to promote the incorporation of CP in the academic context basically under the aegis of social psychology. These initiatives culminated in the inclusion of CP principles and practices in different forms and different levels of academic activity.

As far as *teaching* is concerned, the content of CP was incorporated in the 1980s in the different strata of formal education. Psychology degree and diploma in social work courses at numerous universities included, and still include today, subjects that either specifically mention CP in their title or cover content associated with it, although there is no common institutional credential that qualifies the holder to work in CP. In postgraduate education, many institutions teach units related to CP as an option within Ph.D. courses, and there are also several universities offering specific postgraduate and masters' courses leading to professional qualifications in the field. However, despite this presence, the psychosocial approach, in courses in general and in CP in particular, represents minority content in study programs still dominated by the clinical perspective based on the individual, and by content remote from the applicability required for fulfilling social needs.

In the area of *research*, teams formed in different institutions have been active in areas commonly linked to the field of CP such as social support, volunteer work, youth programs, rural development, social services, programs for the elderly, program assessment, risk behaviours, family intervention, health promotion and preventative health, children's services, and ethical and conceptual aspects (Musitu & Cava, 2000). Although many of these teams have frequently been involved in intervention programs with public and private institutions, the dynamic of assessment of scientific activity in the academic system—more concerned with the product generated in a given time according to external standards than with the effectiveness and applicability of the action—has obliged them to focus their attention on research of a more atomized nature, often to the detriment of community research-action.

As far as *publications* are concerned, academics committed to CP in Spain made substantial early efforts to define a conceptual and operative framework for CP, stressing its social and committed nature with a view to avoiding its being reduced to a mere dimension of clinical intervention. In this regard, the works by Costa and López (1986), Barriga, León, and Martínez (1987), Martín, Chacón, and Martínez (1988), and Sánchez (1988, 1991) can be considered to represent the foundations of the literature in this aspect. These works served as the first reference books for Spanish students and professionals, though today there are numerous texts articulating the basic principles of different aspects of the discipline (Hombrados, 1996; López-Cabanas & Chacón, 1997; Martín, 1998; Musitu, Herrero, Cantera & Montenegro, 2004; Sánchez & Musitu, 1996). A further result of attempts to spread information on CP in Spain was the creation in 1992 of the journal *Intervención Psico-social: Revista sobre igualdad y calidad de vida* ("Psychosocial Intervention: Journal on Equality and Quality of Life"), published by the Spanish Psychological Association and the National Coordinating Agency of Social Services. Also worthy of note is the *Revista de Psicología Social Aplicada* ("Journal of Applied Social Psychology"), first published in 1991 by the Social Psychology Society of Valencia, which includes content related to CP and social services. In the area of conferences, Spanish CP has been featured at generalist events, but there are, as yet, no regular national meetings of a more specific nature.

On the whole, it can be said that in the Spanish academic context, CP maintains a presence in close association with the field of social psychology, supported by a clear demand for training derived from the growth of the Third Sector, and favoured by freedom in the generation and expression of ideas in the university environment. Nevertheless, it is obliged to operate within a context largely marked by a clinical conception of psychology, and one that is out of touch (by no means a new problem in the academic environment) with reality and social needs.

Theoretical Referents of Community Psychology in Spain: Beginnings and Evolution

As mentioned above, professionals and academics working in CP in Spain initially based their approach on models of a cognitive-behavioural nature. The neopositivist perspective was their guide in developing strategies of intervention, evaluation, and research, though their vocation was clearly one of social commitment and participatory action, influenced by less formalized currents from the Latin American and European traditions, as well as humanist psychology. In the first Spanish texts that can be considered to fall within the category of CP, such as those of Costa and López (1986), Martín, Chacón, and Martínez (1988), or Sánchez (1988, 1991), the authors, in outlining their theoretical frameworks, made repeated allusions to the proposals of the Swampscott Conference and models of *empowerment*, also referring to ecological-environmental models, cognitive-behavioural models related mainly to stress and social support, and to a lesser extent frameworks of collective action and social change. Albee, Dohrenwend, Caplan, Rappaport, and Sarason are among the authors most frequently mentioned in these early texts, but there are also widely diverse references to different traditions in psychology, philosophy, and the social sciences.

The years since then have seen some important developments that are reflected in the most recent works (Hombrados, 1996; López-Cabanas & Chacón, 1997; Martín, 1998; Musitu, Herrero, Cantera & Montenegro, 2004; Sánchez & Musitu, 1996; San Juan, 1996). *First*, there has been a considerable increase in the number of references to Spanish authors, thanks in turn to a rise in the volume of work published, reflecting the current professional and research activity in this country. A great deal of the work of Spanish community psychologists has been devoted to critical reflection on the responsibilities of the discipline, arguing strongly in favour of its social, committed, and transformative tradition, given the dangers involved in converting it into a sophisticated tool of state paternalism or despotism, or in the tendency to reduce its approach to that of the individualist perspective of clinical practice (Martín & López, 1998; Musitu & Cava, 2000; Musitu, Herrero, Cantera & Montenegro, 2004; Sánchez & Musitu, 1996; 1999). The areas covered have also been diverse. The most significant among them being the systematization of concepts and action strategies in the contexts of social services (López-Cabanas & Chacón, 1997; Medina, 1996), social support (Barrón, 1996; Gracia, 1997; Gracia, Herrero & Musitu, 2002), social participation (García, 2004), volunteerism (Chacón & Vecina, 2002), welfare in general (Casas, 1996), or the empirical study and design of action strategies from ecological perspectives on social problems such as social exclusion (Bueno, 1998), drug addiction (Barriga, 1997; Becoña & Martín, 2004), risk behaviours (Martín, Martínez, López, Martín & Martín, 1998), child abuse and marginalization (Casas, 1998), and the reporting of different experiences of community intervention (Sánchez, 1993).

Second, there has been a greater influence of Latin American CP, whose critical analysis of reality and emphasis on action aimed at social change and the transformation of power structures has struck a chord with Spanish community psychologists. Of great importance for this interchange have been the exchange forums for Latin American and Spanish professionals and academics as well as the setting up of interinstitutional collaboration conventions. University exchange programs, despite their design by Spanish ministerial agencies being more motivated by criteria of political visibility than of efficient use of resources, have eventually also contributed to facilitating the flow of ideas and initiatives. Special mention—apart from the influences of now-classic authors in the field of social pedagogy and community action, such as Freire or Fals Borda—should be reserved for the work of Ignacio Martín-Baró, now re-published in Spain (1998). The ideas of Martín-Baró have had considerable impact on the new generations of community psychologists and continue to grow in importance as an ethical and intellectual reference. Also worthy of note (without resorting to flattery) is the growing relevance of the efforts of Maritza Montero (1994, 2003) to systematize and theoretically underpin the proposals of CP (so often justified in a purely circular manner), articulating them as operative epistemological and psychosocial referents. Finally (and with apologies to those we have omitted, in a list that is inevitably unjust and incomplete), we should like to acknowledge the presence in Spanish CP of the contributions of community psychologists from Puerto Rico (Serrano-García), Venezuela (Cronick, Sánchez, Wiesenfeld), Brazil (Freitas, Lane, Sawaia, Sarriera), and Argentina (Álvarez, Diéguez, Fuks, Saforcada). This influence is clearly reflected, in formal terms, in the frequent mention of some of these authors in Spanish texts, and in terms of content, in the fact that aspects such as participatory action research (PAR) have become a part of the "spinal cord" of Spanish CP (López & Martín, 1998, López-Cabanas & Chacón, 1997; Musitu, Herrero, Cantera & Montenegro, 2004).

Third, in addition to incorporating the diverse influences from abroad, Spanish CP, academically linked to social psychology, has also taken aboard and developed the influences generated from both classic Anglo-American referents and those of today's burgeoning European social psychology. Thus, in the analysis of social problems, CP has incorporated the theoretical framework provided by theories on attribution, aggressive and altruistic behaviour, the structure of attitudes and processes of persuasion, among others (see Gilbert & Fiske [1998] for an overview). As regards European influences, among the most important are the consideration of social representations, the study of social influence and research on collective movements (see Hewstone & Stroebe [2001] for an overview). Such influences have helped to facilitate and consolidate the move from the individual perspective to the analysis of meso- and macro-social levels, with the goal of increasing awareness of the social dynamics underlying people's living conditions. The proposals derived from social identity theory (Tajfel, 1982) and theories on social categorization (Turner, Hogg, Oakes, Reicher & Wetherell, 1987), still making their way within CP, already constitute fundamental reference points for analysis and intervention in the field of intergroup relations and processes of stereotyping, prejudice, and discrimination, which are emerging as elements of enormous relevance in multicultural societies.

And finally, *fourthly*, as far as epistemological and methodological aspects are concerned, CP, fundamentally academic, has incorporated on the one hand advances (more technical than conceptual) in the practice of neopositivist research related basically to greater sophistication in strategies of data collection and analysis. On the other hand, in accordance with trends in other European countries, Spanish CP has begun to incorporate the epistemological conceptions and methodological tools generated from what have been labelled as the critical, hermeneutic, and constructivist paradigms. With a nod to the classic authors associated with such proposals, we highlight the contribution to the resurgence of the poorly-titled "qualitative methodology" of the sustained work of systematization by authors such as Denzin, Guba, Schwandt, and Lincoln, the operative formulas of Glaser, Corbin, Strauss, Miles, and Huberman, and the influence of Spanish sociologists and anthropologists, such as Ibáñez, Ruiz-Olabuénaga, Vallés, and Villasante (López, 2003; López & Scandroglio, 2007).

New Proposals in an International Context

In this final section, having attempted so far to restrict our account to what CP *is*, we would like to reflect on what it could or should be within in an increasingly internationalized context. CP still faces the traditional problems, but on top of these, new challenges are emerging. The so-called welfare societies (often constructed at the cost of "poorfare" for the rest) have failed even in their own internal scope in attempts to reduce social exclusion. Instead they maintain a series of now chronically marginalized sectors and add to these new groups of excluded people, such as those of thinly populated rural areas, immigrants working in the black economy and neglected older people, in an atomized social context (European Communities, 2004; UNICEF, 2005). Furthermore, these societies have contributed to creating large sectors of the population that, cushioned and anaesthetized by the provisions of the welfare state and 21st-century versions of *bread and circuses*, are actually in a genuine state of alienation, given their alarming ignorance of the structural and political dynamics that define their lifestyle and their feelings of apathy and impotence with regard to civil participation. In such a situation, the system of democratic representation ends up camouflaging strategies that are basically imposed by political or economic lobbies, but which present themselves in the public sphere as options freely chosen by the population. The frequent reduction of political participation mechanisms to a periodic vote on a limited set of programs or candidates contributes to shaping this process, granting elected representatives a blank cheque for the development of countless aspects of economic and social policy.

In this context, psychosocial intervention of a reductionist nature, in which the participation of the population is considered as an instrument for achieving objectives more or less preordained by government or supranational agencies, runs the risk of turning into a sophisticated and highly perverse version of despotism. Governments of all kinds have learned to make a great show of applying urgent emergency and palliative measures to social problems that are actually derived from the structural dynamics maintained by the social system itself. We might well ask ourselves whether or not many of the practices typical in the area of psychosocial intervention in the Western world are actually genuine examples of "type 1 change" (Watzlawick, Weakland & Fiske, 1976)—changing something so that everything stays the same. The strategies of subsidization and support that consume the majority of social service resources serve to reduce the visibility of structural inequalities without acting on them. Actions aimed at increasing the capacity to cope with stress at an individual level contribute to perpetuating a context in which stress, unhealthy environment, and negative lifestyle habits are structurally promoted. At another level of activity, the impressive and outwardly philanthropic donations to nonprofit organizations by financial corporations serve to cushion situations of marginalization derived from the economic dynamic these companies tend to sustain for their own benefit. Likewise, the abusive employment of civil volunteers exploiting the promotion of altruistic values conceals a lack of professional resources devoted to social transformation: individual generosity is called upon to deal with what is the responsibility of society as a whole. A parallel case is that of the allocation of funds to "developing countries," making up through external resources for the obligations persistently unfulfilled by local power elites, which the economic interests of the "first world" help to support.

We believe that some of the solutions to these problems could lie in the integration of contributions to the CP field in different geographical and cultural contexts. It therefore seems to us essential to adopt the critical, consciousness-raising, and transformative approach of Latin American psychology and to integrate it with the substantial set of conceptual and operative tools developed from the Anglo-American and European traditions.

The combination of the backbone of PAR with strategies of empowerment can come to constitute a highly powerful tool that should be adapted to new forms of alienation, suffered not only by marginalized and geographically defined populational groups, but also by large sectors of citizens dispersed within the urban environment. Work can thus be based on a broader concept of community, in which, as in the dynamics of new social movements, feelings of belonging derive not necessarily from direct contact or cultural or territorial proximity, but rather from a set of shared needs, values or categorizations, which—as shown by the study of identitary processes (Klandermans, 1997; Kriesi, della Porta & Rucht, 1999)—permits and consolidates solidary collective action. In turn, research–action strategies should complement the direct and sustained work advocated in the classical proposals with strategies that use, both sequentially and in parallel, different media for gaining knowledge, informing, sharing, analyzing, and generating decisions in more extensive and heterogeneous populational groups. In such a framework, community psychologists, through their own training and through their involvement in interdisciplinary teams, should provide themselves with the theoretical and operative tools that allow them to tackle macro-social dynamics.

In our experience, one of the most powerful recipes for social transformation would derive from the union of this critical perspective with the operative tools of research and action developed from other traditions. The demonization of neopositive approaches, whose essence has been confused with their circumstances, has in many contexts made community work inoperative, producing a perverse effect whereby after lucid exercises of deconstruction and problematization, communities are condemned by absolute relativism, impotence, or refuge in a sterile intellectualism due to a lack of operative instruments of action. Thus, on the basis of shared reflection, the tools provided by the extensive work carried out within the behavioural science and social cognition traditions can constitute powerful instruments for the achievement of human welfare and social transformation. These should be complemented, avoiding a duality that seems to be more and more a thing of the past, by the tools from related perspectives of a more qualitative nature, derived from the critical and hermeneutic tradition.

In concluding, we should like to stress our firm conviction that CP is just as pertinent and relevant today—if not more so—as it was at its origins. Nevertheless, the new demands of our societies and the experience acquired with regard to the obstacles encountered in its application make necessary a reflection and creative re-conceptualization that will enable it to rise to the challenges it faces.

Acknowledgments. We are greatly indebted to our dear colleague Gonzalo Musitu, lucid and systematic analyst of the course of community psychology in Spain, and whose work has provided a crucial reference for the reflections presented here. We should also like to thank Bárbara Scandroglio for her invaluable help in documenting the historical and philosophical tradition of community action in Spain.

References

Abellán, J.L. (1996). *Historia del pensamiento español. De Séneca a nuestros días.* Madrid: Espasa-Calpe.

Barbero, J.M. (2002). *El Trabajo Social en España.* Zaragoza: Mira Editores.

Barriga, S. (1997). *Drogas. Fundamentos para la prevención de las drogodependencias.* Ed. Sevilla Kronos.

Barriga, S., León, J.M. & Martínez, M.F. (1987). *Intervención Psicosocial.* Barcelona: Hora.

Barrón, A. (1996). *Apoyo social.* Madrid: Siglo XXI.

Becoña, E. & Martín, E. (2004). *Manual de intervención en drogodependencias.* Madrid: Síntesis.

Bueno, J.R. (1998). *Exclusión e intervención social.* Valencia: Nau Llibres.

Casado, D. & Guillem, E. (1986). Los Servicios Sociales en Perspectiva Histórica, *Documentación Social,* 64, 9-22.

Casas, F. (1996). *Bienestar Social: Una introducción psicosociológica.* Barcelona: PPU.

Casas, F. (1998). *Infancia: perspectivas psicosociales.* Barcelona: Paidós.

Cembranos, F., Montesinos, D. & Bustelo, M. (1988). *La animación sociocultural: una propuesta metodológica.* Madrid: Popular.

Chacón, F. & García, J. (1998). Modelos teóricos en Psicología Comunitaria. In A. Martín González (Ed.), *Psicología Comunitaria. Fundamentos y Aplicaciones* (pp. 31-47). Madrid: Ed. Síntesis.

Chacón, F. & Vecina, M.L. (2002). *Gestión del voluntariado.* Madrid: Síntesis.

Colom, A.J. (1987). *Modelos de intervención socioeducativa.* Madrid: Narcea.

Colomer, M. (1990). Trabajo social en España en la década de los setenta. *Revista de Servicios Sociales y Política Social, núm. 20.* Madrid: Consejo General de Colegios Oficiales de Diplomados en Trabajo Social y Asistentes Sociales.

Costa, M. & López, E. (1986). *Salud Comunitaria.* Barcelona: Martínez Roca.

Duro, J.C. (2001). *Psicología y salud comunitaria durante la transición democrática.* Monografías profesionales de Clínica y Salud. Madrid: Colegio Oficial de Psicólogos.

European Communities (2004). *Poverty and social exclusión in the UE. Statistics in focus. Population and social conditions.* 16/2004.

Fundación Tomillo. Centro de Estudios Económicos (2000). *Empleo y trabajo voluntario en las ONGs de Acción Social.* Madrid: Ministerio de Trabajo y Asuntos sociales.

Gilbert, D.T. & Fiske, S.T. (1998). *The Handbook of Social Psychology.* Boston: McGraw-Hill.

García, J. (2004). *Políticas y programas de participación social.* Madrid: Síntesis.

Gracia, E. (1997). *El apoyo social en la intervención comunitaria.* Barcelona: Paidós.

Gracia, E., Herrero, J. & Musitu, G. (2002). *Evaluación de recursos y estresores psicosociales en la comunidad.* Madrid: Síntesis.

Grassi, E. (1993). *La filosofía del humanismo. Preeminencia de la palabra.* Barcelona: Anthropos.

Hewstone, M. & Stroebe, W. (2001). *Introduction to Social Psychology. An European Perspective*. Oxford: Blackwell.

Hombrados, M.I. (1996). *Introducción a la psicología comunitaria*. Málaga: Aljibe.

Kisnerman, N. (1990). *Teoría y práctica del Trabajo Social*. Buenos Aires: Humanitas.

Klandermans, B. (1997). *The Social Psychology of Protest*. Oxford: Blackwell.

Kriesi, H., della Porta, D. & Rucht, D. (Eds.). (1999). *Social Movements in a Globalizing World*. London: Macmillan.

Lillo, N. & Roselló, E. (2001). *Manual para el Trabajo Social Comunitario*. Madrid: Narcea.

López de Ceballos, P. (1989). *Un Método para la Investigación-acción participativa*. Popular: Madrid.

López, J.S. (2003). Teoría y práctica de la investigación en Psicología: desafíos actuales. *PSICO*, 34, 2, 219-237.

López-Cabanas, M. & Chacón, F. (1997). *Intervención Psicosocial y Servicios Sociales*. Madrid: Síntesis.

López, J.S. & Scandroglio, B. (2007). De la investigación a la intervención; La metodología cualitative y su integración con la metodología cuantitativa. In A. Bianco & J. Rodríguez-Marin: Interrención Psicosocial (pp. 555-609).

Marchioni, M. (1989). *Planificación social y organización de la comunidad. Alternativas avanzadas a la crisis*. Popular: Madrid.

Martín, A. (1986). *Psicología Humanística, Animación Sociocultural y Problemas Sociales*. Madrid: Popular.

Martín, A. (Ed.). (1998). *Psicología Comunitaria. Fundamentos y aplicaciones*. Madrid: Síntesis.

Martín, A. & López, J.S. (1998). De aquí y de allá. Hacia una psicología social comunitaria plural e integradora. In A. Martín González (Ed.). *Psicología Comunitaria. Fundamentos y Aplicaciones* (pp. 193-210). Madrid: Ed. Síntesis.

Martín, A. Martínez, J.M., López, J.S., Martín, M.J. & Martín, J.M. (1998). *Comportamientos de riesgo: violencia, prácticas sexuales de riesgo y consumo de drogas ilegales en la juventud*. Madrid: Entinema.

Martín, A., Chacón, F. & Martínez, M.F. (Eds.). (1988). *Psicología Comunitaria*. Madrid: Visor.

Martín-Baró, I. (1998). *Psicología de la Liberación*. Madrid: Trotta.

Medina Tornero, M.E. (1996). *Gestión de Servicios Sociales*. Murcia: DM/PPU.

Montero, M. (1994). *Psicología Social Comunitaria. Teoría, método y experiencia*. México: Universidad de Guadalajara.

Montero, M. (2003). *Teoría y práctica de la Psicología Comunitaria. La tensión entre comunidad y sociedad*. Buenos Aires: Paidós.

Musitu, G. (1998). La psicología comunitaria en España. En A. Martín (Ed.), *Psicología Comunitaria. Fundamentos y aplicaciones* (pp. 141-158). Madrid: Síntesis.

Musitu, G. & Arango, C. (1995). La psicología comunitaria en España: Pasado y presente. In J.A. Conde & A.I. Isidro (Comps.). *Psicología Comunitaria, Salud y Calidad de Vida*. Salamanca: Eudema.

Musitu, G. & Cava (2000). La Psicología comunitaria en España: relaciones con los contextos anglosajón y latinoamericano. In A. Ovejero Bernal (Ed.). *La psicología social en España al filo del 2000: balance y perspectivas* (pp. 161-182). Madrid: Biblioteca Nueva.

Musitu, G., Herrero, J., Cantera, L.M. & Montenegro, M. (2004). *Introducción a la psicología comunitaria*. Barcelona: Editorial UOC.

Quintana, J. (1986). *Investigación Participativa. Educación de Adultos*. Madrid: Narcea-SC.

Quintana, J. (1996). J.L. Vives. Educación y psicología. En: M. Sáiz y D. Sáiz (Eds.), *Personajes para una historia de la psicología en España* (pp. 63-79). Barcelona: Pirámide.

Red, N. de la & Brezmes, M. (2003). Trabajo Social en España. In T. Fernández & C. Alemán (coord.), *Introducción al Trabajo Social* (pp. 131-152). Madrid: Alianza Editorial.

Rodríguez, L. (1962). *El desarrollo de la razón en la cultura española*. Madrid: Aguilar.

Rubinstein, J.C. (1994). *Sociedad Civil y participación ciudadana*. Madrid: Fundación Pablo Iglesias.

Ruiz-Olabuénaga, J.I. (dir) (2000). *El Sector No Lucrativo en España*. Madrid: Fundación BBV. Documenta.

Sáez, A. (2003). Acción social y trabajo social en España. Una revisión histórica. *Acciones e Investigaciones Sociales*, 13, 5-42.

Salvador-Carulla, L., Bulbena, A., Vázquez-Barquero, J.L.,. Muñoz, P.E., Gómez-Beneyto, M. & Torres, F. (2002). La salud mental en España: Cenicienta en El País de las Maravillas In. J.M. Cabasés, J.R. Villalba & Carlos Aibar (Eds.), *Invertir para la salud. Prioridades en salud pública. Informe Sespas 2002* (pp. 301-26). Valencia: EVES.

San Juan, C. (1996). *Intervención psicosocial*. Barcelona: Anthropos.

Sánchez, A. (1988). *Psicología Comunitaria. Bases conceptuales y métodos de intervención*. Barcelona: PPU.

Sánchez, A. (1991). *Psicología Comunitaria*. Barcelona: PPU.

Sánchez, A. (1993). *Programas de prevención e intervención comunitaria*. Valencia: PPU.

Sánchez, A. (1999). *Etica de la Intervención social*. Barcelona: Paidós.

Sánchez, A. & Musitu, G. (1996). *Intervención comunitaria: Aspectos científicos, técnicos y valorativos*. Barcelona: EUB.

Tajfel, H. (1982). *Social identity and intergroup relations*. Cambridge: Cambridge University Press.

Turner, J.C., Hogg, M.A., Oakes, P.J., Reicher, S.D. & Wetherell, M.S. (1987). *Rediscovering the Social Group: A Self-Categorization Theory*. Oxford: Blackwell.

UNICEF (2005). Pobreza infantil en países ricos 2005. *Innocenti Report card N. 6*. Florencia: Centro de investigaciones innocenti de UNICEF.

Watzlawick, P., Weakland, J.H. & Fiske, R. (1976). Cambio. Formación y resolución de problemas humanos. Barcelona: Herder.

15
Community Psychology in Portugal: From "Revolution" to Empowered Citizenship

Isabel Menezes, Pedro M. Teixeira, and Mariana Fidalgo

Abstract

In this chapter, we discuss the evolution of CP in Portugal by demonstrating its connections with the historical and political developments in the past four decades, particularly the dictatorship that ruled the country from 1928 to 1974, the democratic revolution of April 1974, and the entrance into the European Community in 1985. This has been a period for the successful institution of psychology both as a theoretical domain, a research field, and a profession, and, particularly since the mid-1980s, for the expansion of CP-oriented values and practice. Examples of intervention projects and research reveal that although it is probably too soon to speak of a uniquely Portuguese theoretical contribution to the field of CP, the influence of North American and European authors are combined to assert the need for a more political community psychology.

Introduction

In a recent discussion of a European approach to community psychology (CP), Donata Francescato and Manuela Tomai (2001) consider that one of its distinctive traits is the belief that "it is crucial to help people become more aware of the historical link between the process of valorization of individual freedoms and collective struggles, which have given the European more social rights" (p. 373), and in this sense, the political and historical emphasis of this chapter is in line with a European perspective of CP. However, the political contents make this clearly a Southern narrative: Southern European, as we share important commonalties with other Southern European countries such as Spain, Greece, and Italy; but also, and mainly for cultural and political factors, South America.

In this chapter, we will begin by characterizing the political and historical background with an emphasis on the dictatorship that ruled the country until 1974 and the subsequent revolutionary period. From the mid-1970s to the

317

mid-1980s, psychology was in an initial stage of development, but it is possible to trace two community intervention projects that would be influential in the development of the field and in the combination of European and North American references. An intense expansion of psychology is clear from the mid-1980s to the 1990s particularly in terms of training and public recognition. And even if CP could be more systematically emphasized in pre- and post-graduation, CP-oriented values and practice, reinforced by regulations and funds from the European Union, have flourished—as demonstrated by two existing projects in the field of mental heath and family development. We will conclude by discussing the contribution of research in the development of a creative synthesis between empowerment, citizenship, and politics that implies advocating—as others from this and the other side of the Atlantic, from the North and from the South—for a more political CP.

Political and Historical Background

Portugal was under a dictatorial regime of fascist inspiration from 1926 to 1974, when a military revolution restored democracy. The regime assumed a 'proudly alone' philosophy that excluded the country from the international community. Portugal was ruled by the same dictator from 1928 to 1968; maintained overseas colonies from as long as the 15th century; had insidious signs of underdevelopment in terms of infant mortality, illiteracy, and income per inhabitant; and experienced in late 1970s the "the last 'socialist revolution' in Europe" (Barreto, 2002, p. 28).

As a consequence of this political situation, until 1974 individual rights were minimal and social and political rights severely limited. Even if the violence of the regime cannot be compared with the military dictatorships in South America, the goals of maintaining a poor educational and cultural level of the population and of restraining any initiatives for the development of a civil society were similar and effectively accomplished. Additionally, the country was involved from 1961 in a colonial war that implied severe losses both for Portugal and for Angola, Mozambique, and Guinea-Bissau. As Gil puts it, the public space was "reduced, mutilated, until it finally disappeared under the strokes of censorship and the prohibitions of freedom of speech and association" (p. 24). Civic involvement was limited to local recreational, cultural, or neighborhood associations that were quite vivid until the 1970s, but were not by themselves capable of creating a civic culture.

With the revolution, an intense period of social conflict and change emerged with a rapid and intense evolution in terms of citizens' participation and involvement as "the 25 of April is a definite turning-point regarding the openness of the civil society and the exercise of citizenship" (Martins, 2003, p. 113). This involvement had also relevant implications in the field of community intervention initiatives, particularly in the area of alphabetization campaigns inspired by the work of Paulo Freire (Stoer & Dale, 1999) that constituted one of the few examples of popular education in Portugal. One important consequence of the fascist regime was the extremely low level of education (until the 1960s, Portugal was the European country with the lowest mandatory education: four years!) and quite a high percentage of the population never attended school and was illiterate. Alphabetization campaigns involved a coalition between civilians, mainly university students, and the military, inspired by the Cuban alphabetization campaigns, with the goal to promote cultural development in a broad sense, across the country, and generating some resistance particularly in the most conservative regions. Freire was an inspiration for these initiatives for several reasons: he wrote in Portuguese, lived in exile (as many of the intellectual elite that returned after the revolution), and had ideological and political proximity with the goals of the Portuguese socialist revolution. Stoer and Dale point out, however, that alphabetization campaigns based on Freire's critical literacy were of a para-doxical nature: aiming to promote the visibility of the "true" culture (i.e., the genuine expression of the people) through a top-down process that simulta-neously "requested the 'imposition' of certain ideas and a method based on the 'dialogical pedagogue'—central in the process of 'conscientization'" (p. 75). It is curious to note, as Stoer and Dale underline, that these initiatives were in those same days criticized by others who advocated a bottom-up approach also inspired by Freire's libertary pedagogy. Therefore, Freire was an explicit reference for state-based initiatives for community development during the revolutionary period.

The involvement of psychologists as such in this process was nonexistent. Psychology was, since 1962, an unofficial degree conferred by a private school—the Instituto Superior de Psicologia Aplicada (ISPA). However, until 1976/1977, there was no official degree of psychology, which was only taught as a course within the philosophy departments of public universities since the early 20th century; in the 1960s, medical psychology was also introduced in medicine degrees (Milheiro, 2003). The creation of the uni-versity degree in psychology (a 5-year-long 'licenciatura') in 1977 was the result of a typical process of that period, involving students' demonstra-tions and vivid social conflict. It was only in 1980 that the Ministry of Education created the Faculties of Psychology and Education Sciences in the three major state universities—Porto, Coimbra, and Lisboa—with a staff that had been to a certain extent graduated or post-graduated in European universities. Therefore, it was only in the late 1970s that Portugal defined an academic accreditation for psychology, but this did not imply any professional regulation or the definition of an ethical and deontological code of conduct.

It is possible that the concurrence of the two former events—the associa-tion of Freire with the revolutionary period and the quest for legitimacy of the "new" Portuguese psychologists—explains the late development of CP in Portugal and the fact that North American authors would become the core theoretical background. In fact, during the 1970s in most European countries, a psychologist was a well-recognized and respected professional. It was only during the 1980s that psychologists with a university degree began to practice in Portugal, and during that initial stage the fields of education, rehabilitation, organizational and clinical psychologies were prevalent. However, the involvement of psychologists in community interventions, although less frequent, deserves attention because it illuminates the theoretical underpinnings of CP in Portugal. In the following section, we will refer to some early projects that were influential in the development of the field of CP in Portugal.

Major Community Intervention Projects in the 1980s

Even though psychology as a practice was at a very initial stage during the 1980s, two projects were clearly inspired by CP values and concepts: the antropoanalytical community of Boavista and the Alcácer Project. The two projects are quite distinctive in terms of intervention contexts (urban vs. rural) and scope (mental health vs. education), and while the former was led by the psychiatrist Carlos Caldeira from the University of Lisbon, the latter was initiated by Bártolo Campos, a professor from the Faculty of Psychology and Education Sciences of Porto University. However, both projects reveal how CP was emerging in Portugal under a strong influence of North American authors, even if combined with European references.

Caldeira was inspired by the client centered therapy of Carl Rogers and the anti-psychiatry movements—which were intense in Europe particularly after May 1968 and the work of Foucault (1972) and Deleuze and Guattari (1972). He proposes anthropoanalysis as a perspective that seeks to understand the human being in his or her community assuming a balanced view of human existence:

it is not a matter of ignoring and denying that we cry, but to affirm that we also laugh; that, in the conflict between Eros and Death we stand, determined, by choice, before everything, beside the forces of life. And, therefore, that sociality, libido, pleasure – the construction of the fraternity – are chosen as pillars of every intervention. (Caldeira, 1982, p. 80)

Therefore, the emphasis on communion is central to the intervention process. However, the distinctive trait of anthropoanalysis is that it combines the Rogerian principles with Sartre's existentialism and Freire's conscientization. Anthropoanalytical practice, in line with existentialism, advocates "the construction of autonomous communities made by people committed to a freeing dialectic, cooperating in participation without identification, in communication without rupture" (Campiche, Hyppolite & Hipólito, 1992, p. 39). Additionally, it follows Freire's assumption that the oppressed, instead of being conceived as objects to be freed, should be regarded as co-authors of their own liberation.

The *anthropoanalytical community of Boavista* (1974–1979), an impoverish neighborhood near Lisbon, was the context for the implementation of these ideas. The project was initiated by a team of a psychiatric hospital with the goal of promoting the autonomous capacity of the community to be actively involved in the discussion and resolution of its problems. The team involved six doctors, two nurses, two psychologists, one social worker, one economist, one sociotherapist, and a secretary. The project began with a series of socio-metric and sociomedical studies that identified the community's major complaints (Campiche, Hyppolite & Hipólito, 1992), and the creation of a local mental health service (Caldeira, 1982), with the waiting room serving as a nuclear space to promote discussions "of the relational problems experienced between families and in the community" (p. 86) and as a catalyst for community assemblies. Formal meetings began in January 1976 and occurred every month until July 1979, during which community members addressed their common problems. The idea was, in the long run, to train local people as community animators who would assume the leadership of the project, allowing "the team to retreat, leaving the community to itself, free" (p. 85). Despite the positive results in terms of the active involvement of community members, changes in hospital policies resulted in the termination of the project in 1979; however, by proposal of a local participant, a community association of mental health was created, whose main objectives were to defend the rights of people with mental health problems and to promote the mental health of the community (Campiche, Hyppolite & Hipólito, 1992).

The second example, the *Alcácer Project*, was developed during the early 1980s by a group of researchers supported by the Gulbenkian and the Bernard Van Leer Foundations under the leadership of Bártolo Campos from Porto University. The team initiated a community action-research project to be implemented in seven daycare centers, serving children from 3 to 6 years, of the rural community of Alcácer do Sal, in southern Portugal. A special feature of the Alcácer Project was that the daycare centers were created by popular initiative after April 1974, run by parents and with a staff composed mainly by mothers recruited from the local community with no academic or professional training. The goal of the project was "to offer staff training in order to promote the development of the children, guaranteeing that besides a caring function the centers would also assume an educational role" (Campos, 1990, p. v). A multiprofessional team offered support to the various centers and established "a collaboration contract to analyze together and locally" the current situation of each center and to "elaborate, implement and evaluate action plans, inside the centers and in their relationships with the surrounding community" (pp. v–vi). The operationalization on the centers' quality of life was based on Bronfenbrenner's (1979) ecological perspective of human development, particularly on his definition of microsystem and mesosystem. Bronfenbrenner emphasized the notion of the daycare center as a context for child development and proposed that differential developmental effects could be the result of differences at the microsystem level conceived as "a pattern of activities, roles and interpersonal relations experienced by the developing person in a given setting with particular physical and material characteristics" (p. 22). This notion was essential for the Alcácer Project and served as a guiding framework for analyzing and transforming daily activities, roles, and relations within the daycare centers. Additionally, Bronfenbrenner's proposition that "the developmental potential of a mesosystem is enhanced to the extent that there exist indirect linkages between settings that encourage the growth of mutual trust, positive orientation, goal consensus, and a balance of power responsive to action in behalf of the developing person" (p. 216) justified a proactive involvement of families and the larger community as partners in the education and development of children.

Several initiatives aimed at fostering this partnership. For instance, children and staff initiated regular visits to local craft workers in the community (e.g., bakers, boat constructors, fishermen), observed their daily activities, and used the knowledge thus acquired as a basis for their work in the daycare center, such as drawings and storytelling and cooking. Then, the craft workers were invited to come to the center to see and discuss with the children what they had done. In another project, children collected local riddles, wrote and illustrated them, created new ones, and then edited a riddle book presented at a party in which the local community was invited. With these initiatives, the project assumed a broad vision of "adult training (be it directors, staff, parents, etc.) and teacher training as a means to ecological transformation" (Campos, 1989, p. 138); considering that the project resulted from the reciprocal collaboration between all participations, it is "a collective production in which all are authors, each according to his/her own possibilities in that particular moment" (p. 148). The project was implemented for 5 years and various evaluations showed the progressive emergence of positive results in terms of the quality of the activities, roles and relations that foster the development of children, as well as a more autonomous capacity of local actors to change their own life contexts.

The Inclusion in the European Space at the Level of Accreditation and Training

The inclusion of Portugal in the European space, with the full integration in the European Economic Community (now European Union) in 1985, has had significant implications for the country in various domains, bringing about important evolutions in economic, scientific, and social areas, and even some prosperity, especially during the late 1980s and early 1990s (Almeida, 1994; Barreto, 1994). Europe was a metaphor for democracy that simultaneously worked, as Barreto states, as a "buffer of losses and grieves (. . .) [such as] the shortening of the fatherland and the loss of its historical sense" (Barreto, 1994, p. 1060). The positive attitudes towards Europe and European Union institutions can be detected in different studies with various age groups (Figueiredo, 1988; França, 1993; Menezes, Afonso, Gião & Amaro, 2005), reinforcing the notion that Europe has been a context for "expectations and confidence rather than of rejection and distrust" (Almeida, 1994, p. 63). And, as we shall see, the Portuguese development of psychology, in general, and of community psychology, in particular, are undoubtedly related to the challenges and prospects brought about by the European Union, both in terms of professional accreditation and training and in terms of opportunities for practice.

Recognition

In terms of public recognition, the late 1980s and 1990s were essential for psychology and psychologists, which are now a respected and well-regarded professional group. This very positive image has, nevertheless, a negative side: psychologists are frequently used under compensatory legitimation strategies (Weiler, 1990) whenever a social crisis or a harmful event occurs, that is, it looks like a positive sign of concern to assert that "a psychologist is on the way" even if the problem is not going to be (or cannot be) solved.

Training

In terms of training, with the expansion of the private sector in higher education during the nineties, the offer of psychology degrees was extended to now being offered at 33 institutions with an attendance of about 10,000 students. It is estimated by the European Federation of Psychologists' Associations (EFPA) that by the year 2010, Portugal will reach the goal of having a ratio of 1 psychologist per every 1,000 inhabitants.

Currently, most public universities (Açores Algarve, Aveiro, Beira Interior, Coimbra, Évora, Lisboa, Madeira, Minho, Trás-os-Montes e Alto Douro and Porto) and some of the private universities offer some training in CP during pre-graduation. Therefore, the majority of psychology students do attend some classes on CP, either for one or two semesters. Optional or mandatory, the contents of these classes are varied but tend to include some reference to the major North American theories in this domain and also contributions from Spain (e.g., Gonzalo Musitu, Sanchez Vidal) and Italy (e.g., Donata Francescato). As an area of specialization in itself, CP is only offered in ISPA. At post-graduation level, both ISPA and the University of Coimbra offer a master's in community intervention, but references to the field are common in other master's courses in psychology. Therefore, it can be said that even if training in CP is relatively limited, interest in the field both by graduate students and professionals is clearly growing and, as we shall see, opportunities for practice are intense.

In March 2002, the European Commission issued a directive proposal concerning the recognition of professional qualifications. In this context, the European Federation of Psychologists Associations (EFPA) developed a project on a European diploma in psychology (EFPA, 2001). This project is even more relevant because many European countries are implicated in the reorganization of higher education curricula at the national level following the Bologna process that aims to homogenize higher education across the European Union. The EFPA proposal for a common curriculum framework for education and training for psychologists in Europe considers CP as one of the many and more common areas of applied psychology in Europe but does not consider it as a major area of initial training. The major areas of initial training are traditional areas: work and organizational psychology, educational psychology and clinical psychology. In Portugal, the document has been frequently referred to in the context of the implementation of the Bologna process and if the need for a more intense training in CP is recognized by some universities—thus allowing for an optimistic expectation regarding the intensification of training in the field in the near future—this might also imply that the current situation of CP as a minor area in pre-graduation will be maintained.

Professionalism

In terms of professional accreditation, several scientific and professional associations were created in Portugal since the 1970s, both generic ones like the Portuguese Psychologists' Union and more specific ones such as the Portuguese Society for Community Psychology in 1987, lead by José Ornelas from the ISPA. However, affiliation with these organizations is strictly voluntary and they do not have any accreditation competencies—their role has been more to organize training initiatives (such as scientific meetings) and advocate for psychologists and/or for specific psychological problems or groups (such as victims of child abuse). The union grants a professional certification license that depends solely on academic certification (i.e., to get a license it is only necessary to have a 4- or 5-year academic degree in psychology) and that is not mandatory—therefore, having no practical relevance for employment. However, on September 15, 2005, the Portuguese Parliament approved the legal constitution of the Portuguese Psychologists Association (Ordem dos Psicólogos), which is a registered professional association, independent of the state, which will have professional accreditation competencies.

A major contribution of professional associations and also of training institutions to the development of the field of CP in Portugal has been the organization of scientific meetings that allowed Portuguese psychologists to confront their practice with the experience of other countries. Three major events were very influential: the International Conference on Human Development organized by the Faculty of Psychology and Education Sciences from Porto University in 1988, the International Congress of Community Mental Health organized by ISPA also in 1988, and the European Congress of Community Psychology, also organized by ISPA, under the auspices of the European Network of Community Psychology, in 1998. Other meetings and seminars have also allowed for important both North American and European CP authors to visit the country and express their visions and projects; to name only a few examples, Marianne Farkas, Julian Rappaport, Marc Zimmerman, Donata Francescato, Gozalo Musitu, and Jim Orford. These meetings made it possible to establish direct contacts with the state of the art in CP and constituted a stimulus for the development of the field in Portugal. The opportunities to generate knowledge in the field were also reinforced by European policies and funding which supported the development of intervention projects inspired by CP oriented values and practices—and both were instrumental to the flourishing of CP in Portugal.

The Influence of European Policies in Community Intervention Projects

The influence of the European Union in the development of CP in Portugal is not limited to academic training or accreditation. On the contrary, its major role has been through the European Social Fund (ESF), which is one of four structural funds designed to strengthen economic and social cohesion in the European Union (EU). The ESF has launched, in the past two decades, different support programs that have given various social institutions in Portugal (and elsewhere) opportunities to develop intervention projects in various domains. These projects are influenced by European guidelines and have assumed and disseminated CP values and strategies, such as empowerment, involvement, and cooperation at the intervention and policy levels, on the following main policy fields: active labor market policies, equal opportunities for all, promoting social inclusion, lifelong learning, adaptability and entrepreneurship, and improving the role of women in the labor market. Several community initiatives have been launched to support innovative projects (e.g., POEFDS), particularly in the area of training and transition for active life, targeting disempowered groups such as women (e.g., NOW), unqualified youngsters (e.g., YOUTHSTART), socially excluded populations, such as ethnic minorities, former prostitutes, homeless people (e.g., INTEGRA), and people with mental, physical, and sensory disabilities or with mental health problems (e.g., HORIZON).

For example, URBAN aims to address "the problems of isolation, poverty and exclusion of their inhabitants through interventions that improve the ensemble of their physical and social entourage" using a combination of measures in the area of urban rehabilitation, social exclusion, and environmental quality; specific projects might target disadvantaged groups, such as drug-users or ethnic minorities. In Portugal, the goal was to intervene in disenfranchised communities within the two largest cities: Lisbon and Porto. The initiative has an "explicit commitment in embracing local citizens in the development and implementation of the programmes. Thus, the citizens affected by the interventions are participating in the decision making process and the problems of urban deprivation are being solved at a grass root level" (European Union, 1999).

Another initiative is EQUAL that aims to fight discrimination in the labor market via transnational cooperation. *Partnership* is a key principle for EQUAL, which hopes "to bring together key actors (local and regional authorities, training bodies, public employment services, NGOs, enterprises, social partners) in Development Partnerships (DPs) on a geographical or sectoral level to tackle discrimination and inequality." *Empowerment* is considered another building block defined as "to strengthen capacity building by making all relevant actors, including beneficiaries, work together on an equal footing" (European Union, *n.d.*a).

It is interesting to stress that in the EU site for EQUAL, there is a concern with the definition of the concepts in a multilingual glossary (European Union, *n.d.*b). Portugal is involved in thematic networks dealing with training pathways for disadvantaged groups, social and vocational integration of migrants, refugees and ethnic minorities, local entrepreneurship, organizational development, partnership, reconciling work with family and social life, and rural development—these thematic networks are conceived as "a 'community of practice' that shares information, experiences and work tools" (European Union, 2005).

The Establishment and Expansion of Community Psychology

Obviously, the theoretical perspectives that underlie these EU initiatives have been influential in the development of practice of CP. Psychologists in the field now have to conceive, propose, and implement projects that relate to guiding principles directly connected with CP assumptions and strategies. This directive was furthered in the 1990s with the emergence and dissemination of community centers, strongly supported by EU funds (e.g., see the 1994 report published by the Comissão das Comunidades Europeias), which "have the advantage of enjoying a genuine community integration and, therefore, a larger capacity to work in unison with community problems and resources, becoming integrated projects in the social development of a given community" (Costa & Menezes, 1991, p. 79).

Again, CP-oriented values and developmental-ecological perspectives of life-span development were a key theoretical foundation, and concepts such as sense of community (Orford, 1992; Saranson, 1974), social support (Gottlieb, 1988; Vaux, 1988), and empowerment (Conyne, 1987; Rappaport, 1977; Zimmerman, 1995) entered the professional discourse and practice. Additionally, the involvement in multiprofessional teams and the need to construct a collaborative relation with others—professionals and nonprofessionals—brought consultation to the forefront of professional exercise (Blocher, 1987; Gallessich, 1982; Hansen, Himes & Meyer, 1990; Kelly, 1987; Orford, 1992). This implied a major challenge for psychologists and was even discussed in terms of the threats and potentials for the development of a professional identity. As Duarte (1994) stated, "to work **in, with** and **for** a community implies being open to diverse problems . . ., explicitly clarifying our role, frequently perceived through myths and stereotypes . . . specially since other professionals see us as experts who should stay inside the office . . . with a focus on diagnostic and reactive interventions" (pp. 145–146).

Given the strong emphasis of EU initiatives in the areas of training and employment, Law's theory of community interaction (1981, 1991) is also a relevant influence. Community interaction refers to the relations between the individual and the groups to which she or he belongs (namely within family, neighborhood, peer groups, etc.), standing in the interface between self-concept and opportunity-structure theories. Law advocates networking as a strategy to overcome "the narrow networks of community encounters – that is to say 'ghettos' – [that] have the effect of narrowing and impoverishing conceptions of selves in futures. (There are – of course – white, middle class, affluent ghettos as well as black, working class and poor ghettos. There are also equality-limiting age-ghettos – populated by people of not more than a year-or-so older and younger than self.) The converse implication is that contact beyond the ghetto widens conceptions" (1991, p. 159).

Even if this expansion occurred as a result of the creation of institutions and projects by initiative of the civil society, these efforts were noticeably supported by universities that offered consultation and viewed these projects as both an opportunity for students' training (generally, students in their last year of studies have to do a practicum of around 300 hours in an institution) and for research. People such as Bártolo Campos, Joaquim Bairrão, and Emília Costa, at Porto University, José Ornelas at ISPA, and Pina Prata, Isabel Narciso, Teresa Ribeiro, Luís Miguel Neto, and Worlfgang Lind from Lisbon University gave an important contribution to support the emergence and sustentation of many of these projects. However, the Portuguese history of CP, both in terms of research and action, needs to diversify and develop further to make a difference in theoretical terms—even if some of the existing current research is, as we will refer later, pursuing a creative synthesis between developmental and ecological perspectives, empowerment, citizenship theories, and political participation.

Obviously, these community intervention projects are not exclusively led by psychologists but involve many other professionals such as social workers, educators, sociologists, and mediators that have also training in the field of community intervention. As a result, particularly in the field of education sciences and social work, there are many projects that assume community intervention as a foundation. Many of the assumptions and practices of CP (Nelson & Prilletensky, 2005) are explicitly defended (even if seldom acknowledged, probably because the common linkage with critical sociology is more prevalent) by some of the theorists in these fields. These assumptions and practices also permeate these projects, particularly the ecological focus, the significance of partnership with local actors and communities, the importance of cultural diversity, and the prominence of emancipatory values and social change (e.g., Correia & Caramelo, 2003; D'Epiney & Canário, 1994; Matos, 2005; Stoer & Rodrigues, 1998).

Community Psychology in Context: Two Examples of Community Centers

With the goal to illustrate the expansion and changing nature of community psychology in Portugal, we again turn to practice. Once more, the two projects are distinctive in terms of location (large city vs. medium-size city; South vs. North) and scope (mental health vs. social exclusion). However, both were initiated by associations from the civil society—even if with the support of two community psychologists, José Ornelas from ISPA for the AEIPS and Carlos Gonçalves from Porto University for the GAF—and assume citizenship promotion as a central goal, thus also revealing how politics enters the discourse and practice in Portuguese CP.

Residência Comunitária dos Olivais

The Associação para o Estudo e Integração Psicossocial (AEIPS: http://www.aeips.pt/) is an association created in 1987 by professionals, families, and people with mental illness, aiming "to support the community integration of people with mental illness, particularly in the areas of accommodation and employment" (Moniz, 1999a, p. 1). Its first major initiative was the creation of a residence for people with severe and extended mental health problems (Residência Comunitária dos Olivais, in 1989), where residents could share the responsibility for common tasks, based on Stein and Test's training in community living program (now called assertive community treatment program) developed in Wisconsin during the 1970s (Dixon, 2000; Ornelas, 2000). According to the original program, clients are assisted to relate with their community and use its resources for work, leisure, and so forth, and live in a residence with a low staff-to-client ratio, 24-hour availability, and flexible and individualized services (Tibbo, Joffe, Chue, Metelitsa & Wright, 2001). Every week a community meeting conducted by the coordinator provides the context for "distributing tasks [e.g., cleaning, meals, shopping], discussing what happened, solving problems and/or difficulties, and organizing leisure activities" (Moniz, 1999a, p. 4).

AEIPS also runs a community center to support people with mental health problems using strategies such as empowerment and recovery (Moniz, 1999b). In addition, it provides a variety of services such as individual counseling, self-help groups, sport, cultural, and leisure activities, family groups, and professional training and integration involving specific training courses, internship experiences, and support of work maintenance through individual and group intervention.

Finally, the association has been active in organizing or co-organizing publications and scientific meetings such as the 2004 international conference "Participation and empowerment of people with mental illness and their families: A new vision for community integration." As Ornelas states in the abstract booklet of the conference (2004), the AEIPS model emphasizes the active role of people with mental illness in controlling their own lives by ensuring their participation in their life contexts.

Gabinete de Apoio à Família

Gabinete de Apoio à Família (GAF; http://www.gaf.pt/) is another community center, situated in Viana do Castelo, a city in the north of the country, that was created in 1994 by the religious order of Carmelitas Descalços, with the activities clearly aimed at promoting family development and giving a coordinated response to problems related to family life, namely family disruption and social exclusion. GAF's major priority is to develop partnerships between local institutions and, thus, promote institutional networks (Pontes, 1998), with a strong emphasis on inclusion. During the past 10 years, GAF has diversified its structure to include a variety of projects that target homeless people, families, abused women, children, and low-qualified adults using a combination of methods that include individual counseling, support groups, advocacy, and training. GAF also runs two safe houses for battered women and homeless people.

One of the most innovative features of this project is that concerns with the social insertion of people in risk of exclusion have been translated into the creation of several small businesses: Wash-Gaf is a small car-washing company, Gas-Gaf ensures gas distribution, and an art craft store, "Oficinas," works under the principles of just trade. These small companies have evolved from the occupational ateliers for homeless people and now constitute sites where former homeless people can get a job and simultaneously supply funds for other GAF projects. Another important concern of GAF was to establish a positive relation with the city inhabitants by creating a "GAF friends' club" with associates and volunteers who might contribute in various ways to the project.

Finally, GAF also provides consultation services to other community centers that want to develop community intervention initiatives. The emphasis on networking and partnership with other community institutions and individuals is a distinctive trait of GAF, as is the creation of small businesses that serve both as a work context and as a service provider for the community—thus contributing to "make citizenship a reality" (Vieira, 2005, p. 1).

Empowerment and Citizenship or the Need
for a Political Community Psychology

The emphasis on empowerment and citizenship as central goals of community psychology is undoubtedly a trend in Portugal as in other European countries (see Sánchez-Vidal, Zambrano-Constanzo & Palacín-Lois, 2004). However, we should be aware of Prado's (2002) cautionary note regarding CP in the Americas: "By embracing, respectively, more individualistic positions in the northern hemisphere and more communitarian postures in the southern hemisphere, both [perspectives] point out towards the end of the political, and therefore have a weak commitment to the radicalization of plural and multicultural democratic values" (p. 202).

The emphasis on citizenship and empowerment might clearly assume that risk, particularly as these frequently appear as "consensual" goals. On the contrary, we must recognize that citizenship, although being a contemporary "myth that appeals to our political imagination" (Ignatieff, 1995, p. 53), is an exclusionary category that justifies inclusion on the basis of agreements and conventions, which might collide with basic human rights (Benhabib, 1999; Santos, 1998; van Steenbergen, 1994). Moreover, citizenship is a polysemic concept, and multiple and possibly conflicting visions of 'citizenship' are at stake within the communities we work with, which should be acknowledged and expressed for benefit of pluralism. The political involvement of people in these communities in the discussion of what is citizenship is essential if we want to promote the "development of local communities that truly empower individuals" (Francescato & Tomai, 2001, p. 373); assuming, as we have stated elsewhere, "that no area of collective life (including the economy) should be outside the range of citizens' public deliberation and control—as the experience of the participatory budget of Porto Alegre reveals (see Santos, 2002)" (Menezes, Ferreira, Carneiro & Cruz, 2004, p. 306).

Currently, we are trying to expand these issues departing from a developmental and ecological perspective, explore the meaning and significance of concepts such as empowerment, citizenship, participation, and sense of community in diverse groups (adolescents and adults, men and women, immigrants, gypsies, gays and lesbians, etc.), and discuss the implications of these diverse meanings for the construction, implementation, and evaluation of CP intervention projects (Carneiro & Menezes, 2006; Ferreira & Menezes, 2005; Nata & Menezes, submitted). Our concern is to emphasize a political perspective that departs from Hanna Arendt's (2001) recognition of the eminently (and inevitable) relational and plural nature of politics. However, inspired by the cognitive-developmental perspective of Jean Piaget (1965, 1977) and its applications to the field of intervention by Norman Sprinthall (1991), we assumed that political action—as other broadly defined political experience of participation—is not inherently positive or negative in what concerns its consequences for personal development, social pluralism, and social change. In fact, political participation could result in reinforcing bias or prejudice (see De Piccoli, Colombo & Mosso, 2004). This is why we advocate for the need to consider the quality of participation experience and to design projects where this quality is deliberately ensured. Quality implies time (because no change can be expected from episodic projects), interaction with different others that permits the pursuit of significant projects in an environment that supports the expression of dissent and disagreement and the construction of new and more integrated perspectives.

This emphasis in the political dimension is not uniquely Portuguese, and be it for political reasons (the experience of fascism) or cultural motives (the South), it is shared with other South European countries, as it is evident in the chapters on Italy and Spain. But we do believe that only a political community psychology can live up to the challenge of not "assuming a privileged position of knowledge" (Montenegro, 2002, p. 521) and guaranteeing that, far from diluting social conflicts, our role is to recognize that "the 'other' no longer is able to tolerate even the tolerance and generosity of which he or she is the object, precisely because the 'other' refuses to be an object and aims at claiming its own voice as subject of itself" (Stoer & Magalhães, 2002, p. 700).

References

Comissão das Comunidades Europeias. (1994). *Pobreza é com todos. Mudanças possíveis.* Lisboa: Author.

AIEPS. (2004). *Participation and Empowerment of people with mental illness and their families: A new vision for community integration. Abstracts.* Lisbon: Author.

Almeida, J. F. (1994). Evoluções recentes e valores na sociedade. In E. Ferreira & H. Rato (Eds.), *Portugal hoje* (pp. 55-70). Lisboa: I.N.A.

Arendt, H. (2001). *Qu'est-ce que la politique?* Paris: Seuil.

Barreto, A. (2002). *Mudança social em Portugal, 1960/2000.* Working paper, Instituto de Ciências Sociais. Available at http://www.ics.ul.pt/publicacoes/workingpapers/wp2002/WP6-2002.pdf. Retrieved September 30, 2005.

Barreto, A. (1994). Portugal, a Europa e a democracia. *Análise Social, XXIX*(129), 1051-1069.

Benhabib, S. (1999). Citizens, residents and aliens in a changing world: Political membership in the global era. *Social Research, 22*, 1-24.

Blocher, D. (1987). *The professional counsellor.* New York: MacMillan.

Bronfenbrenner, U. (1979). *The ecology and human development.* Cambridge, MA: Harvard Press.

Caldeira, C. (1982). O sentido de uma comunidade de saúde mental. *Psicologia, III*, 1/2, 79-90, 1982.

Campiche, C., Hyppolyte, J. C. & Hipólito, J. (1992). *A comunidade como centro.* Lisboa: Fundação Calouste Gulbenkian.

Campos, B. P. (1989). Formação de professores centrada na escola e inovação pedagógica. In *Questões de Política Educativa* (pp. 135-153). Porto: Asa.

Campos, B. P. (1990). Prefácio: Intervenção ecológica para o desenvolvimento da criança. In *Projecto Alcácer* (pp. v-ix). Lisboa: Fundação Calouste Gulbenkian.

Carneiro, N. S. & Menezes, I. (2006). La construction de l'identité des juines homo-sexuels au Portugal. *L'Orientation Scolaire et Professionnelle, 35, 2*, 225-249.

Conyne, R. K. (1987). *Primary preventive counseling: Empowering people and systems.* Muncie: Accelerated Development Inc.

Correia, J. A. & Caramelo, J. (2003). Da mediação local ao local de mediação: Figuras e políticas. *Educação, Sociedade & Culturas, 20*, 167-191.

Costa, M. E. & Menezes, I. (1991). Consulta psicológica de adultos em centros comunitários. *Cadernos de Consulta Psicológica, 7*, 77-82.

D'Épiney, R. & Canário, R. (Eds.). (1994). *Uma escola em mudança com a comunidade. Projecto ECO, 1986-1992. Experiências e reflexões.* Lisboa: IIE.

De Piccoli, N., Colombo, M. & Mosso, C. (2004). Active participation as an expression of the sense of community. In A. Sánchez.Vidal, A. Zambrano Constanzo & M. Palacín Lois (Eds.), *Psicologia comunitaria europea: Comunidad, ética y valores* (pp. 262-271). Barcelona: Publicacions Universitat de Barcelona.

Deleuze, G. & Guattari, F. (1972). *L'Anti-Œdipe - Capitalisme et schizophrénie.* Paris: Les Éditions de Minuit.

Dixon, L. (2000). Assertive community treatment: Twenty-five years of gold. *Psychiatric Services, 51*, 6, 759-765.

Duarte, C. (1994). Intervenção psicológica comunitária junto de jovens de uma comunidade do centro histórico do Porto. *Cadernos de Consulta Psicológica, 10/11*, 141-147.

EFPA. (2001). A European Framework for Psychologists' Training. Available at http://www.europsych.org/framework/v5/. Retrieved November 15, 2005.

European Union. (1999). Urban Community Initiative. Available at http://europa.eu.int/comm/regional_policy/urban2/urban/initiative/src/frame1.htm. Retrieved January 2, 2006.

European Union. (2005). Mainstreaming activities in Portugal. Available at http://europa.eu.int/comm/employment_social/equal/mainstreaming/maportugal_en.cfm. Retrieved January 2, 2006.

European Union. (*n.d.*a). How does EQUAL work?. Available at http://europa.eu.int/comm/employment_social/equal/about/index_en.cfm. Retrieved January 2, 2006.

European Union. (*n.d.*b). Glossary. Available at http://europa.eu.int/comm/employment_social/equal/about/glossary-en_en.cfm. Retrieved January 2, 2006.

Ferreira, P. D. & Menezes, I. (2005). The relevance of the quality of life-experiences for citizenship development: An inter-domain developmental study. In I. Menezes, J. L. Coimbra & B. P. Campos (Eds.), *The affective dimension of education: European perspectives* (pp. 185-202). Porto: Centro de Psicologia.

Figueiredo, E. (1988). *Conflito de gerações. Conflito de valores.* Lisboa: Fundação Calouste Gulbenkian.

Foucault, M. (1972). *Histoire de la folie à l'âge classique*, Paris: Gallimard.

França, L. (Ed.). (1993). *Portugal, valores europeus, identidade cultural.* Lisboa: I.E.D.

Francescato, D. & Tomai, M. (2001). Community psychology: Should there be a European perspective? *Journal of Community and Applied Social Psychology, 11*, 371-380.

Gallessich, J. (1982). *The profession and practice of consultation: A handbook for consultants, trainers of consultants, and consumers of consultation services.* San Francisco: Jossey-Bass.

Gottlieb, B. H. (1988). *Marshaling social support: Formats, processes, and effects.* Newbury Park, CA: Sage.

Hansen, J. C., Himes, B. S. & Meier, S. (1990). *Consultation. Concepts and practices.* Englewood Cliffs, NJ: Prentice Hall.

Ignatieff, M. (1995). The myth of citizenship. In R. Beiner (Ed.), *Theorizing citizenship* (pp. 53-77). Albany: State University of New York Press.

Kelly, J. G. (1987). *The ecology of prevention: Illustrating mental health consultation.* New York: Haworth Press.

Law, B. (1981). Community interaction: A "mid-range" focus for theories of career development in young adults. *British Journal of Guidance and Counselling, 9,* 2, 142-158.

Law, B. (1991). Community interaction in the theory and practice of careers work. In B. P. Campos (Ed.), *Psychological intervention and human development* (pp. 151-162). Porto & Louvain-la-Neuve: ICPFD & Academia.

Martins, S. C. (2003). Novos associativismos e tematizações na sociedade portuguesa. *Sociologia, Problemas e Práticas, 43,* 103-132.

Matos, M. (2005). Desenvolvimento e cidadania: Intervenção associativa e acção comunitária. *Cadernos do ICE,* 135-149.

Menezes, I., Afonso, R., Gião, J. & Amaro, G. (2005). *Conhecimentos, concepções atitudes e práticas de cidadania dos jovens portugueses.* Lisboa: DGIDC.

Menezes, I., Ferreira, P. D., Carneiro, N. S. & Cruz, J. B. (2004). Citizenship, empowerment and participation: Implications for community interventions. In A. Sánchez.Vidal, A. Zambrano Constanzo & M. Palacín Lois (Eds.), *Psicologia comunitaria europea: Comunidad, ética y valores* (pp. 301-308). Barcelona: Publicacions Universitat de Barcelona.

Milheiro, J. (2003). *Adão e Eva no deserto . . . Um olhar psicanalítico.* Lisboa: Climepsi Editores.

Moniz, M. J. (1999a). 10° aniversario da residência comunitária dos Olivais. *Comunidade, 1,* 1 and 4.

Moniz, M. J. (1999b). Centro comunitário. *Comunidade, 1,* 2-3.

Montenegro, M. (2002). Ideology and community social psychology: Theoretical considerations and practical implications. *American Journal of Community Psychology, 30,* 4, 511-527.

Nata, G. & Menezes, I. (submitted). Minorities and citizenship: Gypsies and immigrants' associations in the Portuguese context.

Orford, J. (1992). *Community psychology. Theory and practice.* Chichester: Wiley.

Ornelas, J. (2000). Centro comunitário de apoio a doentes mentais. In J. Ornelas (Ed.), Actas do II Congresso Europeu de Psicologia Comunitária (pp. 143-153). Lisboa: ISPA.

Piaget, J. (1965). *Etudes sociologiques.* Geneva: Librairie Droz.

Piaget, J. (1977). *Problemas de psicologia genética.* 4th ed. Lisboa: Publicações D. Quixote.

Ponte, A. F. (1998). *Relatório de estágio.* Unpublished report, Faculty of Psychology and Education Sciences, Porto University.

Prado, M. A. M. (2002). A psicologia comunitária nas Américas: O individualismo, o comunitarismo e a exclusão do político. *Psicologia: Reflexão e Crítica, 15(1),* 201-210.

Rappaport, J. (1977). *Community psychology: Values research and action.* New York: Holt, Rinehart & Winston.

Sánchez-Vidal, A., Zambrano-Constanzo, A. & Palacín-Lois, A. (Eds.). (2004). *Psicologia comunitaria europea: Comunidad, ética y valores.* Barcelona: Publicacions Universitat de Barcelona.

Santos, B. S. (1998). *Reinventar a democracia.* Lisboa: Fundação Mário Soares e Gradiva.

Santos, B. S. (2002). *Democracia e participação: O caso do orçamento participativo de Porto Alegre*. Porto: Afrontamento.

Saranson, S. (1974). *The psychological sense of community: Prospects for a community psychology*. San Francisco: Jossey-Bass.

Sprinthall, N. A. (1991). Role taking programs for high school students: New methods to promote psychological development. In B. P. Campos (Ed.), *Psychological intervention and human development* (pp. 33-38). Porto: ICPFD e Louvain-La-Neuve: Academia.

Stoer, S. R. & Magalhães, A. M. (2002). The reconfiguration of the modern social contract: New forms of citizenship and education. *European Educational Research Journal, 1,* 4, 692-704.

Stoer, S. R. & Rodrigues, F. (1998). *Entre parceria e partenariado: Amigos, amigos, negócios à parte*. Lisboa: Celta Editora.

Stoer, S. R. & Dale, R. (1999). Apropriações políticas de Paulo Freire: um exemplo da revolução portuguesa. *Educação, Sociedade & Culturas, 11, 67-82*.

Tibbo, P., Joffe, K., Chue, P., Metelitsa, A. & Wright, E. (2001). Global assessment of functioning following assertive community treatment in Edmonton, Alberta: A longitudinal study. *Canadian Journal of Psychiatry, 46*, 131-137.

van Steenbergen, B. (1994). The condition of citizenship: An introduction. In B. van Steenbergen (Ed.), *The condition of citizenship* (pp. 1-9). London: Sage.

Vaux, A. (1988). *Social support: Theory, research and intervention*. New York: Praeger.

Vieira, J. (2005). Editorial. *Boletim GAF, 9*, 1, 1.

Weiler, H. N. (1990). Curriculum reform and the legitimation of educational objectives: The case of the Federal Republic of Germany. *Oxford Review of Education, 16*, 1, 15-29.

Zimmerman, M. A. (1995). Psychological empowerment: Issues and illustrations. *American Journal of Community Psychology, 23*, 5, 581-599.

16
Community Psychology in Israel

AMIRAM RAVIV, MIRA ZEIRA, AND KEREN SHARVIT

Abstract

The chapter reviews activities by Israeli psychologists in which community psychology principles are applied. It is argued that despite the small number of publications using the term *community psychology* and the absence of formal specialization and training in community psychology, many Israeli psychologists have internalized the principles of community psychology and implement them in their work. Specifically, we suggest that the application of community psychology principles, such as early detection, prevention, mental health consultation, crisis intervention, and the use of community resources and strengths, is most apparent in two areas of Israeli psychology: school psychology and crisis intervention in the context of Israel's complex security situation. In the main sections of the chapter, we review and present examples for community-oriented activities in these areas.

Introduction

When asked to review community psychology activities in Israel, we began by asking whether community psychology (CP) exists in Israel at all. This is a question of central importance because the concept of CP is rarely found in publications by Israeli writers, which might lead to the conclusion that CP barely exists in Israel. However, at the beginning of this chapter, we shall argue that despite the small number of publications using the specific term, Israeli psychologists are familiar with the principles of CP and apply them extensively. The principles of community psychology, to which we shall refer throughout the chapter, are based on the principles delineated by Levine and Perkins (1997) and mainly include early identification, prevention, mental health consultation, crisis intervention, and the use of community resources and strengths. We will suggest that the application of CP principles in Israel is most apparent in two areas: school psychology and crisis intervention in the context of the security section. Therefore, in the main sections of the chapter, we will review and present examples of community-oriented activities in these areas.

In Israel, there is no official specialization in CP, no specific training program, and the psychologists' law does not recognize a specialization in CP (unlike Division 27 of the American Psychological Association). Further-more, a search for the term *community psychology* in the Szold Institute data-base of publications by Israeli authors yielded only three publications (Zaki, 1987, 1990, 2000). These publications refer to school psychology in Israel and the change it went through as it moved towards models of prevention and consultation. It may therefore seem that CP is almost nonexistent in Israel. However, according to Wingenfeld and Newbrough (2000), authors of a chapter on CP in an international perspective in the *Handbook of Community Psychology*, Israel has a strong affinity to community approaches, beginning in the early days of statehood and grounded in the socialist and humanist principles upon which the state was founded. Nevertheless, these authors argue that because of the fact that CP has never been formalized in Israel, it only provides a general perspective, and its principles can be found in various areas under different names.

In order to best represent activities conducted in Israel based on CP principles, we carried out a literature search of multiple databases, in both English and Hebrew (this enables research to be more available to readers who cannot read Hebrew). We began by searching the Szold Institute database for such search words as "therapy and community" (yielding 32 publications), "educational psychology" (73 publications), "community psychiatry" (40 publi-cations), and "community social work" (24 publications). Next, we searched the Web of Science, Psycinfo, and ERIC databases for the combination "Community and Psychology and Israel" and retrieved 103 additional publica-tions. All publications were then screened for relevance. Our search of the liter-ature supported our view that CP and its conceptual components, which we see as early detection, prevention, mental health consultation, crisis intervention, and the use of community resources and strengths, are most apparent in Israel in the areas of school psychology and interventions related to the security situ-ation, many of which also take place within school settings. The main sections of our chapter will therefore review community-oriented activities in these areas. We also came across some publications that referred to the application of CP principles in the areas of community mental health and interventions with poor or underprivileged populations in Israel. However, we chose not to elabo-rate on these activities in this chapter, because of the limited involvement of Israeli psychologists in them and their marginal relevance to CP.

School Psychology

The broadest application of the central aspects of CP can be found in the operation of school psychology services in Israel. School psychologists in Israel are subjected to three authorities. The school psychology services are provided by municipal authorities, which are the psychologists' direct employers. The supervision and professional development of the psychologists are the responsibility of Shefi, the psychology and counseling unit of the Ministry of Education, and issues of licensing and approval of ranks and specializations are handled by the Ministry of Health (Raviv, Marshak-Pedhatzur, Raviv, & Erhard, 2002).

Shefi was established in the late 1960s and is currently responsible for approximately 2,100 psychologists. Shefi sees school psychology as located at the intersection between the education system, the parents, and the municipal community system, thus enabling the provision of services to children, parents, professional education teams, and the municipal system (see cms.education.gov.il/educationCMS/units/shefi/gapim/psychology). In line with this view, school psychology services in Israel emphasize community-oriented approaches of early detection, primary and secondary prevention, consultation on mental health issues, and system-oriented approaches. The application of these principles is apparent in the definitions of Shefi's mission and areas of responsibility. Thus, the list of mandatory services provided by Shefi, as determined by the Ministry of Education General Manager's Notice (Ministry of Education, Culture and Sport, 2003), includes the provision of consultation and follow-up services to educational teams and parents regarding treatment of students, in order to ensure students' well-being and mental health through detection and prevention, as well as crisis intervention at the system and individual levels within educational institutions and in the community. Additional responsibilities listed by Shefi include, among other things, shaping the community's policy of individual treatment in the education system through local School Psychology Service stations and planning committees in the local municipalities and school psychology counseling for educational institutions and municipal authorities (see cms.education.gov.il/educationCMS/units/shefi/gapim/psychology). A manager of the education department of the city of Tel Aviv reflects the community-oriented approach of school psychologists well, "Psychologists . . . operate in two occasionally related spheres: On the one hand they . . . help individuals in various ways. On the other hand, they represent 'society,' and through this role they assist the development and improvement of educational and social systems" (Levin, 1993, p. 7).

We shall attempt to present a summary of school psychology activities in Israel, with an emphasis on the application of the above-mentioned principles of CP.

Early research on the activities of school psychologists in Israel revealed little relationship between these activities and the above-mentioned principles of CP (Raviv et al., 2002). In the early 1980s, school psychologists devoted most of their time to individual diagnoses but expressed dissatisfaction with the amount of time devoted to this task (Ziv, 1980). Within a few years, there was a movement toward greater application of CP principles with a decrease in the amount of time devoted to diagnoses and an increase in time spent on primary and secondary interventions, as well as assistance of students through work with parents and teachers (Raviv, 1984). Yet this change was slow, and in 1984 school psychologists still devoted most of their time to diagnoses and referrals to special education.

The last two decades of the 20th century brought significant social changes, which influenced schools in general, and school psychologists in particular. Especially salient among these changes was the change in family structure (higher divorce rate and rising numbers of single-parent families) and the privatization of psychology, which resulted in a greater number of psychologists who offered individual therapy. At the same time, schools became more autonomous and began searching for more effective methods of teaching. Education for excellence and parental involvement in schools were emphasized more than ever before. The central change made in Israeli school psychology during these years was an orientation towards a community worldview and community work, which included a greater tendency to assist students through work with parents and teachers. This orientation was based on the systems approach to education, which emphasizes understanding the behavior of children in relation to the larger systems (e.g. family, school, community) of which they are part, and the systems in relation to their contexts (Pianta, 1999). According to the systems approach, children's behavior is influenced by multiple factors such as their families, communities, social processes, cognitive development, schools, teachers, peers, and poverty. All of these factors must be taken into account if children's well-being is to be efficiently promoted. The adoption of the systems approach led to a greater emphasis on psychological work with parents, with the child at the center, as a potential way to assist children. Interventions with parents were based on their importance as agents of childcare and change. The view that the child exists in two educational systems, the family and the school, which interact with each other, became prevalent. Thus, it seemed that through the parents, there is a possibility to promote the mental health of both typically developing and exceptional children and reduce difficulties and abnormalities. Therefore, these activities involved a powerful preventive influence, both at the school level and at the family level (Tatur, 1993).

In general, these changes in perspective led to a decrease in the amount of time psychologists devoted to individual diagnoses and an increase in the amount of time dedicated to primary and secondary prevention. In addition, school psychologists gained new clients—the regular students (rather than solely those with special needs). It is at this point that we can observe a growing emphasis on principles of community work, such as prevention, mental health consultation, and crisis intervention.

School Psychology as Community Work

A relatively new survey of school psychologists (Raviv et al., 2002) reveals a continuing trend toward community work in school psychology. The survey found that psychologists devote about three fifths of their time to system-oriented activities, such as consulting with other professionals like principals and teachers, meetings, observations, and administrative work. The other two fifths of the time are devoted to more clinical activities such as therapy with individual children, counseling parents, and diagnoses. Below are descriptions of some of these system-oriented activities.

One representative example of community fieldwork by school psychologists is a project of psychological and educational work with groups of preschool parents (Tatur, 1993). This intervention, which was the first of its kind with Arab parents in Jaffa, promoted greater involvement of parents in their children's preschools and direct communication with them, which continued even after the group work ended. The intervention, which started a process of greater parental involvement in decisions regarding their children, led parents of children with special needs to be more receptive to guidance and helped them with finding a support system. It also helped parents feel empowered, all of which reflect principles of empowerment and use of community resources, which are central to CP.

Other examples of work with parents include programs that assist parents in developing skills of effective communication with their children. These include parenting schools operated by an organization with branches throughout the country, which provide group and individual guidance to parents and train nonprofessionals to assist parents with child-rearing problems (Abramson, 1982). Additional programs specialize in enrichment for children of low socioeconomic status. One such program is "the challenge" (Lombard, 1981), which combines guidance at home by semiprofessional tutors and group work with mothers and parents.

An example for the application of another central principle of CP, the primary prevention principle, can be found in a study by Klingman (1985). This study found that groups of normal children that were provided with information regarding the treatment they were about to receive and taught techniques for coping with stress experienced less fear and coped more effectively with the stress caused by the medical procedure.

Another principle of CP is an ecological approach, which involves communication with multiple systems with which the person interacts. This principle is applied in school psychology through consultation with teachers and school staff, with an emphasis on achieving optimal classroom climate (Erhard, 2001; Raviv, Raviv, & Reisel, 1990, 1993). A good example of this principle's application can be found in a program implemented in Jerusalem (Benur, 1993), in which teachers were trained to conduct structured simulation activities in the classrooms (6th grade), intended to improve self-esteem and interpersonal relations among children. It was shown that within a short period of time, the program led to improved interpersonal relations among the children and with their teachers, decreased need for defensiveness, and increased openness. Furthermore, the program stimulated multidirectional communication in the classroom and improved children's attention in class. Another conclusion was that teachers' activities could be expanded to include direct and intentional coping with social and emotional problems, so that teachers could operate as agents and mediators of change.

Community Approaches to Child and Adolescent Violence

One of the greatest concerns in Israeli society in general, and the education system in particular, is the prevalence of violent behaviors among children and adolescents. Violence has been a central concern of the education system for many years, but in recent years interest in this issue has grown and become more consistent (Benbenishty & Astor, 2005). Several studies have been conducted in order to assess the extent of youth violence and the factors that may contribute to it (Khoury-Kassabri, Benbenishty, Astor, & Zeira, 2004; Laufer & Harel, 2003). The studies have found that child and adolescent violence is related to family, school, and community factors. Accordingly, many interventions aimed at coping with violence and reducing it have taken a community-oriented approach that includes working with parents and other agents in the community. In addition, interventions aimed at improving classroom climate, which also apply CP principles, contribute to violence reduction indirectly (Erhard, 2001). However, research and publications regarding the effectiveness of these interventions are still unavailable (Benbenishty & Astor, 2005).

Psychological Interventions in the Context of the Security Situation

Crisis intervention is considered a prominent aspect of CP. People who are involved in crises become vulnerable to prolonged psychopathology if they are left untreated (Caplan, 1964; Lindemann, 1944). This highlights the importance of early detection and intervention, as well as the identification and development of support systems. The history of the state of Israel, as a country involved in a protracted conflict, contributes to the salience of this issue. Milgram (1978) even claimed that Israel could be thought of as a natural laboratory for the study of stress induced by external factors such as war. In this section, we shall attempt to briefly review the research and practice activities of Israeli psychologists in the area of crisis intervention in the context of the security situation, with an emphasis on community aspects. We shall begin by presenting activities conducted within the educational system, mainly by school psychologists, and then present different community and military organizations, which are also involved in crisis interventions in communities. We will not be able to address all of the abundant and diverse activities conducted in this area. Therefore, we will only present some of the most salient and typical activities in order to illustrate the processes and developments in the field.

Early Developments in War-Related Crisis Intervention

It should first be pointed out that until 1974, only very little fieldwork and research on war-related stress were conducted in Israel, mainly due to the shortage of human resources and the fact that most of the state's efforts in its early years were devoted to the integration of immigrants from various countries and the rehabilitation of holocaust survivors (Milgram, 1978). One of the few studies conducted after the 1967 Six Day War examined children's reactions to the war and concluded that on first impression, most of them seem to have adapted to the state of war with no unusual difficulties or traumas (De Shalit, 1970).

The positive results of the Six Day War for the Israeli side and the economic prosperity in its aftermath enabled allocation of resources to the rehabilitation of those harmed by the war: the physically and mentally wounded, their families, and the families of those who lost their lives: widows, orphans, and bereaved parents. Although there was some awareness of the fate of psychological casualties of war in these early years, it was not until the Yom Kipur War in 1973 that the severity of the problem was fully recognized. The suddenness of the attack, the initial success of the Syrian and Egyptian armies, the large numbers of casualties, and the conclusions drawn regarding the future of the Middle East led to the attribution of higher importance to war-related stress and effective coping with it (Milgram, 1978). One of the first studies on this issue (Teichman, Spiegel, & Teichman, 1978) examined crisis intervention conducted by volunteers with the families of soldiers who were missing in action. The intervention was organized by the Israeli psychologists, and the guiding principles were mainly of passive intervention, which included listening and showing interest and empathy, without offering advice. The study found that reactions to crisis did not vary with cultural or age differences. The most frequent reaction was a search for information, which was interpreted as a manifestation of the need for social affiliation. With regard to the intervention, the findings showed that the volunteers were well accepted by the families and became involved in emotional interactions with them. Both the families and the volunteers were satisfied with the intervention. However, the authors do not report whether the intervention led to reduced stress and improved coping.

The Center of Community Work in Crisis Intervention: School Psychologists and the Education System

Shortly after the Yom Kipur War, the education system and the school psychology services discovered that they lacked a theoretical doctrine, knowledge, and organized procedures for crisis intervention. Initial attempts by school psychologists to provide the education system with opportunities to study and practice crisis intervention were met with avoidance and denial (Raviv, 2003). Based on the work of American psychiatrists Caplan (1964) and Lindemann (1944), the Psychology and Counseling Service at the Ministry of Education (Shefi) created programs for raising teachers' and parents' awareness of the importance of early intervention in crises. These interventions were meant to prevent the development of psychopathology in response to crises. Later, primary prevention methods were developed, with the intention of providing the education system with the means to prepare for crises before they occur (Raviv, 2003). As a part of Shefi's efforts to promote the development of intervention programs, an anthology was published in 1980, which provided professionals with up-to-date information on crisis intervention (Raviv, Klingman, & Horowitz, 1980). In order to circumvent the resistance to the issue of war among the educational community, the anthology emphasized everyday stress and crisis situations unrelated to the security situation, such as diseases, accidents, and the like (Raviv, 2003).

This anthology already gave much emphasis to the importance of preventive work. Israeli authors Klingman and Ayalon (1980) wrote about the importance of preparation in advance and of teachers' involvement. They listed several key characteristics of preventive work in the community, which included teachers' knowledge of various intervention techniques and proficiency with their implementation, as well as a preference for the use of internal school-based resources rather than external clinical resources.

Unfortunately, the security situation remained unstable after the publication of this initial anthology (Raviv et al., 1980). Therefore, during the years after its publication, further knowledge was been attained, new techniques developed, more books written, and additional fieldwork conducted (Raviv, 2003). During this time, intervention programs were developed based on the assumption that it is important to "vent" feelings related to traumatic events and prepare teachers to deal with such issues in the classroom, with the assistance of mental health professionals. Over time it also became apparent that crisis situations should be addressed from a broad community approach, which would enable coordination between various community services, such as health and welfare, utilization of the available resources of the community, and the creation of an increased sense of security (Klingman, Raviv, & Stein, 2000).

Klingman (2000) developed a typological model of crisis intervention. This model gives special emphasis to antecedent preparations, which are an integral part of the crisis intervention process. Antecedent preparations take place in calm times, before the occurrence of a crisis, when planning and simulations of crisis situations may be conducted without time pressure. Preparations include training in crisis interventions, setting up crisis intervention networks, and planning emergency procedures. The model also takes a community approach to intervention, which argues that appropriate and efficient organization, along with the use of a systems model, allows for an effective, multidimensional, and synchronous preventive intervention. Intervention at the level of the organization or group enables the location of major stress factors, systematic early identification of extreme and unusual responses of individuals and/or groups, and rapid mobilization of support resources and community reservoirs at a time of crisis. Furthermore, the model uses the continuity principle (Omer & Alon, 1994) as a theoretical base. According to this principle, trauma and disaster lead to an acute interruption of the functional continuity in the lives of individuals and communities. Therefore, crisis intervention is geared towards maintaining functional, historical, and interpersonal continuities, at the levels of the individual, family, organization, and community. The continuity principle relates to Salmon's (1919) known principles for the treatment of combat stress reactions—proximity, immediacy, and expectation—and makes them clearly relevant to civilian populations during disasters. Immediacy prevents the interruption of life's continuity and deepening of the disturbance created by the disaster. Proximity maintains individuals' connections to the place where they ordinarily live and function and to their interpersonal networks. Expectation preserves the victims' social roles and prevents them from assuming the role of "patient," which may lead to chronic disorders. These principles are also strongly related to the ideas of CP, which refer to the utilization of existing individual and community resources.

Klingman's (1988) model consists of four stages: the anticipatory preparation stage, the impact stage, the short-term adaptation stage, and the long-term adaptation stage (see also Klingman, 1989). Thus, many schools have taken on the responsibility for crisis intervention, and especially preventive intervention. Emergency teams have been formed, emergency plans prepared, and many counselors and psychologists have expanded their skills in this area.

In summary, it may be argued that the importance of proper organization and leadership at a time of crisis has led many communities to establish emergency teams that come into action as soon as a crisis occurs. This development reflects a gradual transition in the definition of the school psychologist's role. From the traditional role of focusing on "problematic" children, evaluating students for placement purposes, and consultation with the educational system, school psychologists turned to the role of community psychologists, in the broad sense of the term. In times of crisis, their guidance is sought by school personnel as well as the political and professional leadership of the community (Klingman et al., 2000).

Examples of Preventive Interventions in the Context of the Security Situation

The first example to illustrate the preventive approach to intervention in the context of the security situation is a program that addressed Katyusha missile attacks on Israel's northern border and Kiryat Shmona in particular before and after the 1982 war in Lebanon (Ayalon & Lahad, 1990). Since 1979, several projects have been operating in these communities, with the purpose of dealing with the situation by means of primary and secondary prevention. Among other things, these projects include programs for emergency action, such as the formation of emergency teams, bomb shelter entrance drills, and stress inoculation activities in schools during calm times as primary prevention. The assumption underlying these activities is that with adequate preparation and acquisition of coping skills, people would know what to expect and how to act in times of emergency, and as a result, anxiety and panic would be reduced and long-term pathology prevented. Studies by Ayalon and Lahad (1990) on the reactions of children in places being bombed reveal the effectiveness of stress inoculation programs. The studies found a decrease in anxiety and an increase in social cohesiveness and organization after a therapeutic–educational intervention among participants who spent extended periods of time in bomb shelters.

Population-Based Prevention and Intervention Programs

Klingman (1992) lists several other ways in which psychologists, mainly school psychologists, have conducted primary prevention interventions targeted at the entire population. These include the writing and distribution of self-help materials, translated into different languages and adapted to different ages (e.g., written materials on coping skills practice) and appearances by psychologists on radio and television (Raviv, 1993).

Another example of community intervention in crisis, which reflects developments in the area, is the crisis readiness program by the Tel Aviv–Jaffa municipality (Spearman, Buchner, & Friedman, 1997). Unlike the clear frontlines and combat along the borders, which characterized Israel's past wars, the Gulf War and second Intifadah have led to a blurring of the distinction between frontlines and the homefront. This blurring required the municipalities to make special preparations for emergencies. We describe the program enacted by the Tel Aviv–Jaffa municipality in order to illustrate preparation activities. A central feature of this program was the assembly of all relevant units and resources while coordinating efforts and appropriately allocating tasks. The program operates on two levels: the policymaking level and the field intervention level. Both levels involve professionals from various disciplines. The field intervention units include teams that provide immediate physical and mental assistance at the scene of an attack, a hospital connection unit, a unit of teams that inform the victims' families, an emergency public information unit, which includes information centers and a telephone hotline for psychological assistance, and more. The program was formed at a time of relative calm, which allowed the professionals involved to receive support, backing, and resources from the city management and enabled the systematic formation of a multiprofessional organization. These early preparations proved efficient when the program was activated during several emergencies such as terror attacks and enabled the mobilization of professionals, who were available, motivated, prepared in advance, acquainted with each other, and had the appropriate knowledge and skills to give an integrative response to citizens' needs. School psychologists have been involved both in the initiation of this program and its operation.

A final example, which demonstrates the use of CP principles such as primary and secondary prevention, crisis intervention, and empowerment, is the activity of the Israel trauma center for victims of terror and war, called Natal. Terror attacks against civilians have led to the establishment of Natal as a nonprofit organization, with the realization that victims of political terror are distinct from other trauma victims. The purposes of the organization are to provide multiprofessional treatment to victims of trauma resulting from politically motivated violence, to provide training and preventive interventions for professionals and endangered populations, and to promote knowledge and awareness with regards to trauma resulting from politically motivated violence in the entire Israeli society. The clinical division of Natal provides various treatment services including several types of psychotherapy, while the community division provides preventive services. In addition, Natal operates a social club, which emphasizes activities that facilitate empowerment of victims and interactions among them, and a telephone hotline, which provides assistance to victims (www.natal.org.il).

Other Applications of Community Psychology Principles in Israel

We have described the two main areas where community-oriented activities by Israeli psychologists are most frequently observed: school psychology and crisis interventions in the context of the security situation. It should be pointed out that in addition, Israeli psychologists perform community-oriented activities in areas related to community mental health. Examples of such activities include the operation of day centers, counseling and psychiatric outpatient care for children and adults through family and community services, therapeutic clubs, hostels, social clubs, and self-help groups (Elitzur, 1998; Farbstein & Hidesh, 1997). Given the narrow scope of the current chapter and the relatively less dominant involvement of psychologists in such activities compared with psychiatrists and social workers, we chose not to elaborate on them further.

Another area where CP principles are applied in Israel is interventions with poor and underprivileged populations, which emphasize principles of empowerment and social change (Aram, 1999; Kaufman & Mensbach, 2002; Pecker, 2000). However, Israeli psychologists are rarely involved in these activities, and research into their efficiency is scarce. We therefore chose not to include these activities in our review.

A relatively new development in Israel and in the world is the use of the Internet for psychological counseling and operation of self-help groups (Barak & Fisher, 2001; Chen-Gal & Raviv, 2001). The recent growth in Internet use has extended the concept of community to include virtual communities. Psychological counseling and self-help through the Internet often apply principles of CP such as community support and empowerment.

It therefore appears that extended use of the Internet as a source of advice and support may be a new frontier for future developments in CP applications, in Israel and the world at large.

Conclusion

In sum, it appears that CP in Israel did not prosper or receive a special standing as much as was expected when Israeli psychology began to develop. Yet like Moliere's hero who was not aware that he was speaking prose, when we examine the work of all school psychologists and many other mental health professionals in Israel, it becomes apparent that they have internalized and extensively apply many principles of CP. We can only hope that in the future, more attention will be given to the community approach in the academic socialization process of new professionals and that basic and applied research in the area will expand.

This chapter's analysis of the application of community-psychology principles in Israel is based on the definition of these principles as developed by various scholars, mainly in the United States (see Angelique & Culley, this volume). These principles were imported to Israel and adapted to the local needs and to the knowledge and skills of local professionals. Yet as mentioned above, CP has never been officially formalized in Israel, and in this sense its standing is more similar to that of CP in Britain (see Burton, Boyle, Harris, & Kagan, this volume).

Unlike the political orientation of CP in the United States, in Israel political involvement as part of the role of school and other psychologists is rare. Some school psychologists are involved in activities related to the Arab–Israeli conflict, but this is usually done on voluntary basis and in a rather sporadic fashion. Due to the political schism that exists in Israel between hawks and doves with regards to the views of the Arab–Israeli conflict, many psychologists are politically active according to their views, but these activities are usually unrelated to their work as psychologists. More official political involvement of Israeli psychologists has recently been observed in relation to the execution of the "disengagement," which involved the evacuation of Israeli settlements from the Gaza strip and the northern West Bank. Many of the psychological interventions in this context were based on CP principles. Specifically, the early preparation of military personnel for the task of evacuation and the recruiting of professionals to assist the evacuees reflected principles of prevention (Galili, 2005). In addition, attempts were made to keep communities of evacuees together, in order to maintain community support systems.

It should be noted that this chapter focused on the activities of psychologists, not those of social workers and psychiatrists, who also frequently apply principles of CP in areas of mental health, psychiatric hospitalization and rehabilitation, and work with arriving immigrants and marginal populations.

If we go back to the introduction of this chapter, we may consider the state of CP in Israel, reflected by the literature review, as one of failure. But as optimistic community psychologists (and we believe that CP cannot exist without optimism), we can find the internalization and use of CP principles in almost every intervention by mental health professionals in Israel.

References

Abramson, Z. (1982). Parent guidance in the Adler institute. *Ashiot, 4*, 59-72 [in Hebrew].

Aram, E. (1999). The "Dror" program for breaking the chain of deprivation. *Society and Welfare, 19*, 521-543 [in Hebrew].

Ayalon, O., & Lahad, M. (1990). *Living on the border: Inoculation and coping in stressful situations of violence and security risks*. Haifa: Nord [in Hebrew].

Barak, A., & Fisher, W. A. (2001). Internet-assisted sexuality education: Critical evaluation and suggestions for improvement. *School Counseling, 10*, 39-58.

Benbenishty, R., & Astor, R. A. (2005). *School violence in context: Culture, neighborhood, family, school, and gender*. New York: Oxford University Press.

Benur, I. (1993). A self-enrichment program for the class and for the improvement of interpersonal relations. In S. Levinson (Ed.), *Psychology in the schools and in the community* (pp. 199-216). Tel Aviv: Hadar publishing house [in Hebrew].

Caplan, G. (1964). *Principles of preventive psychiatry*. New York: Basic Books.

Chen-Gal, S., & Raviv, A. (2001). Net psychology: Counseling and therapy in the internet. *School Counseling, 10*, 59-76.

De Shalit, N. (1970). Children in war. In A. Jarus, J. Marcus, J. Oren & C. Rapaport (Eds.), *Children and families in Israel: Some mental health perspectives* (pp. 151-182). New York: Gordon & Breach.

Elitzur, A. (1998). Institutionalization and de-institutionalization of a regional mental health service as an alternative. *Society and Welfare, 18*, 13-32 [in Hebrew].

Erhard, R. (2001). *Optimal educational climate: A guide for diagnosis and intervention*. Israel: Ministry of Education, Psychology and Counseling Unit, Department of Research and Development [in Hebrew].

Farbstein, M., & Hidesh, G. (1997). *Rehabilitation of mental patients in the community: Theory and practice*. Tivon: Nord publication [in Hebrew].

Galili, L. (2005, August 24). South Command psychologist: "The soldiers are not in a state of crisis". *Haaretz*.

Kaufman, R., & Mensbach, A. (2002). On the context of value decisions in social work: A case study of advanced warning by a community social worker. *Society and Welfare, 22*, 185-197 [in Hebrew].

Khoury-Kassabri, M., Benbenishty, R., Astor, R. A., & Zeira, A. (2004). The contributions of community, family, and school variables to student victimization. *American Journal of Community Psychology, 34*, 187-204.

Klingman, A. (1985). Mass inoculation in a community: The effect of primary prevention of stress reaction. *American Journal of Community Psychology, 13*, 323-332.

Klingman, A. (1988). School community in disaster: Planning for intervention. *Journal of Community Psychology, 16*, 205-215.

Klingman, A. (1989). A five level intervention model: Division of professional labor and implication for school counseling. *International Journal for the Advancement Counseling, 12*, 59-69.

Klingman, A. (1992). Stress reaction of Israeli youth during the Gulf War: A quantitative study. *Professional Psychology: Research and Practice, 23*, 521-527.

Klingman, A. (2000). Systemic preventive intervention in times of disaster and trauma. In A. Klingman, A. Raviv & B. Stein (Eds.), *Children in stress and in emergencies: Characteristics and psychological interventions*. Jerusalem: Ministry of Education, Psychology and Counseling Service [in Hebrew].

Klingman, A., & Ayalon, O. (1980). Preemptive intervention: A model for coping with stressful situations in schools. In A. Raviv, A. Klingman & M. Horowitz (Eds.), *Children under stress and in crisis*. Tel Aviv: Otsar Hamoreh [in Hebrew].

Klingman, A., Raviv, A., & Stein, B. (Eds.). (2000). *Children in stress and in emergencies: Characteristics and psychological interventions*. Jerusalem: Ministry of Education, Psychology and Counseling Service [in Hebrew].

Laufer, A., & Harel, Y. (2003). The role of family, peers, and school perceptions in predicting involvement in youth violence. *International Journal of Adolescent Medicine and Health, 15*, 235-244.

Levin, Y. (1993). Opening remarks. In S. Levinson (Ed.), *Psychology in the schools and in the community*. Tel Aviv: Hadar publishing house [in Hebrew].

Levine, M., & Perkins, D. V. (1997). *Principles of community psychology: Perspectives and applications* (2nd ed.). New York: Oxford University Press.

Lindemann, E. (1944). Symptomatology and management of acute grief. *American Journal of Psychiatry, 101*, 141-148.

Lombard, A. (1981). *Success begins at home: Educational foundation for preschoolers*. Lexinton, MA: Lexinton books.

Milgram, N. A. (1978). Psychological stress and adjustment in time of war and peace: The Israeli experience as presented in two conferences. *The Israel Annals of Psychiatry Related Disciplines, 16*, 327-338.

Omer, H., & Alon, N. (1994). The continuity principle: A unified approach to disaster and trauma. *American Journal of Community Psychology, 22*, 273-287.

Pecker, P. (2000). *Allocation of funds to social services*. Jerusalem: Center for the study of social policy in Israel [in Hebrew].

Pianta, R. C. (1999). *Enhancing relationships between children and teachers*. Washington, DC: American Psychological Association.

Raviv, A. (1984). Psychology in Israel. In R. J. Corsini (Ed.), *Wiley Encyclopedia of psychology* (Vol. 3, pp. 135-138). New York: Wiley.

Raviv, A. (1993). The use of hotline and media interventions in Israel during the Gulf War. In L. A. Leavitt & N. A. Fox (Eds.), *The psychological effects of war and violence on children*. Hillsdale, NJ: Lawrence Erlbaum Associates.

Raviv, A. (2003). *Between "children under stress and in crisis" and "children in stress and emergencies": Characteristics and psychological interventions*. Paper presented at the 'Born into Conflict' international conference, Vienna.

Raviv, A., Klingman, A., & Horowitz, M. (Eds.). (1980). *Children under stress and in crisis*. Tel Aviv: Otsar Hamoreh [in Hebrew].

Raviv, A., Marshak-Pedhatzur, S., Raviv, A., & Erhard, R. (2002). The Israeli school psychologist: a professional profile. *School Psychology International, 23*, 283-306.

Raviv, A., Raviv, A., & Reisel, E. (1990). Teachers and students: two different perspectives?! Measuring social climate in the classroom. *American Educational Research Journal, 27*, 141-157.

Raviv, A., Raviv, A., & Reisel, E. (1993). Environmental approach used for evaluating an individual educational program. *Journal of Educational Research, 86*, 317-324.

Salmon, T. W. (1919). The war neuroses and their lesson. *New York State Journal of Medicine, 59*, 933-944.

Spearman, S., Buchner, N., & Friedman, Z. (1997). *Multi-professional therapeutic preparation for emergency: The "Open Line" unit at emergency.* Tel Aviv: City Guidance Center, Security and Emergency Wing, Tel-Aviv-Jaffa Municipality [in Hebrew].

Tatur, M. (1993). Psychological and educational work with a group of Arab parents of kindergarten children in Jaffa. In S. Levinson (Ed.), *Psychology in the schools and in the community* (pp. 105-113). Tel Aviv: Hadar publishing house [in Hebrew].

Teichman, J., Spiegel, Y., & Teichman, M. (1978). Crisis intervention with families of servicemen missing in action. *American Journal of Community Psychology, 6*, 315-325.

Wingenfeld, S., & Newbrough, J. R. (2000). Community psychology in international perspective. In J. Rappaport & S. E. (Eds.), *Handbook of community psychology* (pp. 779-810). Dordrecht, Netherlands: Kluwer Academic Publishers.

Zaki, M. (1987). *Toward a community model in school psychology.* Paper presented at the 21st scientific congress of the Israeli psychological association, Tel-Aviv [in Hebrew].

Zaki, M. (1990). *Consultation in school psychology: An alternative model in school settings.* Tirat Hacarmel: Municipal school psychology service [in Hebrew].

Zaki, M. (2000). *Child, school, and community: Selected chapters in school and community psychology.* Tirat Hacarmel: The psychology station [in Hebrew].

Ziv, A. (1980). The school psychologist in work. *Israeli Journal of Psychology and Counseling in Education, 12*, 25-33.

17
Community Psychology in Poland

ANNA BOKSZCZANIN, KRZYSZTOF KANIASTY,
AND MAŁGORZATA SZARZYŃSKA

Abstract

As of now, there is no formal professional psychological association or branch of academic psychology devoted exclusively to the topics and interests of community psychology in Poland. Consequently, the postulates and aims of community psychology are usually presented, if at all, within university courses covering applied and social psychology. This chapter is an attempt to shed some light on historical and political forces that thwarted the development of community psychology in Poland. We believe that because of political and societal changes initiated by the 1989 collapse of the communist system in Eastern and Central Europe, there are finally opportunities in Poland for community psychology to flourish.

Introduction

Community psychology (CP), with its own label as "psychologia społeczności," has only recently entered into Polish psychology. We could say that before 1989—that is before the collapse of the communist system in Eastern and Central Europe—the term "community psychology" did not exist in Polish psychological literature. Most psychology professionals would have had a hard time answering the question "what is community psychology?"

The lack of CP in Poland prior to 1989 creates an interesting historical paradox. If community psychologists seek to understand and to enhance quality of life for individuals, communities, and society, then why would a socialist society *not* invest in this field of psychology? After all, was the happiness of the collective not the ultimate goal for the governments subscribing to communist doctrines? The answer is simple: the communist and socialist societies did not have, nor could they have, social problems that community psychologists would try to react to, remedy, or prevent. A just communist society did not experience problems such as drug abuse, crime, unemployment, homelessness, poverty, or stigmatizing disease epidemics. And, even if the communist governments would have admitted to some of these issues—for example, alcohol abuse has always been considered a problem in Poland and the Soviet Union—the origin of these predicaments could not be attributed to the society and its communities because their (the communist regime's) social and political construction was almost perfect. Of course, most of the professionals and lay people realized that the official reports concerning, for example, the rates of crime, unemployment, or poverty were far from the reality. Frankly, many of these legal documents were routinely classified or, if publicly accessible, falsified. In other words, an accurate and factual diagnosis of the societal needs and well-being was not possible.

Instead of attributing social problems to the political system, such maladies were blamed on the weak and defective character of the individual. Thus, "blaming the victim" was a routine strategy in explaining away social problems and, in the process, protecting the communist ideals. People suffering from psychoses and alcohol or other substance abuse were usually forced into state-sponsored treatments, and only in 1994 did the Polish government endorse a decree requiring hospitals to obtain consent (from the patients or guardians) for psychiatric interventions. Prior to that change, it was quite easy for people of power or with influence to confine anyone to inpatient treatments without much ado. Incidentally, the very same framework was one of the reasons why many political dissidents in communist societies were incarcerated in prisons as criminals or in psychiatric hospitals as mentally ill. Simply, according to official conviction, only criminals and the mentally ill would rebel against a perfect society. Many of these people suffered long-term isolation, medically unjustified treatments, or even physical abuse.

These philosophical and political barriers made it difficult for community psychology to emerge in Poland during communism. In other words, if there are no societal problems, there is no need for community psychology. Even if people were unhappy or unhealthy, the problem was not societal; rather it was the individual that was the source of it, and, of course, the capitalist and imperialist governments to the west of the Berlin Wall.

This governmental stance does not mean that social scientists have not attempted to study these issues in the countries behind the Iron Curtain. However, researchers investigated them as social psychologists, clinical or health psychologists, or sociologists. An individualistic approach dominated these studies because global systemic approaches for studying societal problems were incompatible with the communist ideology. Only now, after the end of communism, is it possible for Poland to become a "great laboratory" for community psychologists. This transition to democracy has created fertile milieu for social interventions adopted in other parts of the world and their methodologically and ethically sound evaluations.

Empirical Assessment

In order to empirically substantiate our claims that the field of community psychology has not yet entered the working vocabulary of Polish psychologists, we conducted a Web-based survey with 11 questions attempting to assess familiarity with CP among academicians, professionals, and students. An invitation letter was sent to all departments of psychology in all major Polish universities and colleges, as well as to the most prominent psychological associations, organizations, and interest groups. Our cover letter asked for a wide distribution of the survey among the employees, members, and students. The actual survey was easily accessible on the Web for 4 weeks in January 2005. Reminder notes were sent, as well.

Only 41 respondents complied with the appeal and completed our short survey. Unfortunately, it is not possible to compute the response rate of our survey because we do not know how many potential respondents actually received (or read) our request for participation. We treated this exercise more as an informal reconnaissance for the purpose of writing this chapter rather than a methodologically governed empirical study. The introduction to the survey encouraged the recipients to forward the announcement to anyone they believe might be interested in sharing their opinions. Frankly, we thought that this method would secure a greater number of responses. In our opinion, the low number of the actual surveys completed is more evidence of lack of understanding or appreciation for CP in Poland.

Thirty-seven percent of 41 participants (n = 15) were academicians employed at universities or colleges, 54% were students of psychology (n = 22), and 10% were practitioners (n = 4). Sixty-six percent of the respondents were females (n = 27).

The first question of the survey asked the respondents to provide their own definition of community psychology without consulting any literature on the topic. To assess the fidelity of these definitions, we used as an anchor a broad definition of CP as a discipline seeking to "understand and to enhance quality of life for individuals, communities, and society" (e.g., Dalton, Elias, & Wandersman, 2001, p. 5).[1] Only 3 persons (6%) gave us a definition that we would consider "correct" according to how the field of community psychology has been defined in leading American textbooks in this field. Thirty respondents (73%), however, gave answers that were not necessarily wrong but were too general and fuzzy and did not discriminate CP from clinical, health, or social psychologies. Interestingly, seven respondents (15%) gave us

---

[1] We chose Dalton et al.'s definition because of its elegant inclusiveness of the multitude of aims and values generally associated with community psychology in the West. We hope that in the next updated edition of this volume published a few years from now, we will able to offer our own definition based on the consensus among Polish professionals.

a complete definition of social psychology. Such confusion might have resulted from the fact that in the Polish language, the term "psychologia społeczna" (social psychology) and the label "psychologia społeczności" (community psychology) are simply phonetically and lexically alike. Of course, in many languages "psychology" and "psychiatry" share the same problem yet are readily distinguishable for most professionals.

A couple of questions asked the respondents to nominate up to three journal papers and three books published in Poland that were in their opinion good examples of CP. The majority of the nominations were publications clearly pertaining to issues dealing with social psychology. Only one of all listed journal articles was directly CP relevant. Among the nominated books, three volumes broadly represented the values and topics close to CP. Two of them were monographs about large-scale studies investigating psychological and community consequences of the 1997 Polish Flood, and one was an edited book about coping with threats and trauma.

Forty-four percent of respondents (n = 18) claimed that they heard about CP, as it was briefly introduced during their courses on general, clinical, industrial–organizational, or social psychology. Just one person reported that he or she participated in a course devoted to CP during their pursuit of a psychology major.

We also asked if the respondents believed that Polish universities and colleges with programs in psychology should offer classes in CP. Sixty percent of the sample said "yes" to this question, and only two individuals said "no." The rest of the respondents had "no opinion" regarding that issue. Interestingly, among 29 individuals who would welcome community courses for psychology majors in Poland, 18 (62%) were students.

The last question of the survey assessed respondents' expectations concerning the future of CP in Poland. One-half of the sample (n = 22) believed that the chances for the growth of CP in Poland were rather slim. Forty percent of respondents (n = 16) estimated that these chances were good or very good.

Content Review

Our next empirical effort in this appraisal of the status of CP was a content review of the five most premier general psychology journals published in Poland. We evaluated the content of each article published in these journals since 1999 and identified those papers that, in our judgment, concerned topical issues dealing with the aims of CP. To aid our classification process, we compiled a list of key topics of articles published in the *American Journal of Community Psychology* in the past 5 years. Hence, we basically classified those Polish papers as "community psychology" items if their content would have been appropriate for a publication in AJCP. The inclusion criteria were broad (e.g., life satisfaction, social support, prevention, crime), and the papers that did not easily fall into the "community" rubric (because their titles and abstracts did not mention the "key words") were carefully read in their entirety by the first and third authors to achieve agreement.

Among 140 papers published in the past 5 years in *Studia Psychologiczne* ("Psychological Studies"), we were able to classify only 6 (4%) as dealing with community psychology topics. From the 130 articles that appeared in *Przegląd Psychologiczny* ("Psychological Review"), 20 (15%) earned "the community psychology-related" label.

In *Czasopismo Psychologiczne* ("Psychological Periodical"), 115 different articles were published, and 20 of them (17%) had some "community-psychology-related" content. For example, eight papers were labeled as dealing with "stress, coping, environment psychology, or SES," seven as devoted to "political psychology," three within "cross-cultural and ethnic issues," one dealt with "sexual harassment issues," and the final one was on "psychology and religion."

Eighteen articles (29%) had a community psychology connection out of the 63 papers published in *Kolokwia Psychologiczne* ("Psychological Colloquia"). Twelve were classified as on "stress, coping, environmental psychology, SES, and/or well-being," four were on "political psychology," and two focused on "cross-cultural and ethnic studies." Most of the 18 articles appeared in two special issues, both of which were quite relevant to CP (Vol. 7, 1999, "Oppression and support" and Vol. 10, 2002, "Psychology and contemporary social-cultural changes"). Finally, quite impressively, one-third of all papers published in *Polish Psychological Bulletin*, an English language journal, were judged by us as very relevant to CP (32 out of 98).

Our final effort was to review the most frequently used classroom textbooks concerning general psychology, clinical psychology, and social psychology. We did not find a direct mention of CP in any of them. Nevertheless, in some of these textbooks, topics and issues readily identifiable with CP, such as prevention, competence promotion, community mental health delivery, or interventions, were not only mentioned but discussed at some length.

All in all, the results of our informal survey and reviews of leading journals and textbooks in Poland supported our impression that Polish psychologists are not very familiar with the field of CP. Polish textbooks do not define CP and, therefore, the field of CP is infrequently introduced in many lecture halls. Yet, Polish researchers publish studies that might fit very well within major domains of CP as defined in the United States and elsewhere. These statements must be qualified by the fact that our reconnaissance did not include all psychological journals and periodicals available in Poland. For example, we did not sample professional newsletters or mass market psychological magazines. The sample included only peer-reviewed journals. In addition, we limited our search to the past 5 years because we believed that potential "community-oriented" studies initiated after the 1989 transition would only be able to surface as formal publications in most recent years.

Concluding Remarks

Although not formally defined in major textbooks nor yet institutionalized as an independent branch of psychology, we must not forget that there really is much community research and action in Poland. Many professional psychologists and advanced students are directly employed or in some other ways involved in prevention and intervention programs aimed at bettering psychological and social well-being of individuals and their communities. Although present before, in recent years programs attempting to prevent substance abuse, family violence, or controllable physical diseases have mushroomed in Poland since the country's slow, yet consistent, political democratization and movement toward a capitalistic economy in the last decade of the second millennium. Likewise, the number of intervention programs for people suffering from these as well as other problems (e.g., unemployment, homelessness, terminal illness) has been steadily increasing. As the country began to acknowledge the chronicity of crime and vulnerability to disasters, crisis intervention initiatives also evolved and become more accessible. Interestingly, and somewhat ironically, the impact of a severely devastating flood that affected large parts of southwestern Poland in summer 1997 exposed, for many Polish psychologists, a greater need for CP. Many practitioners and teachers of psychology immediately burst into action as providers and organizers during the crisis. Most importantly, however, past the immediate aftermath, psychologists have continued to develop research programs and engaged in other community-related activities that are most indicative of the spirit of CP.

In Poland, we still need to train community psychologists. We need textbooks and journals devoted to CP. Those psychologists that now work in the community with victims of violence, alcoholics, drug abusers, chronically ill, unemployed, poor, or disaster victims are most often people who were trained as clinical or general psychologists. Most likely they had to start with what they knew the best—a person-oriented approach. They learned about CP on the job, by trial and error. These professionals are a wonderful resource to be recruited as instructors and mentors into a formalized education of CP in Poland. Academic psychologists are now conducting studies on unemployment, homelessness, poverty, and disasters. More and more money is coming from the European Union for special educational and preventive programs. These programs are often well conducted yet not always formally evaluated. Thus, there is an abundance of vital opportunities in this part of the world for CP to flourish.

References

Dalton, J.H., Elias, M.J., & Wandersman, A. (2001). *Community psychology: Linking individuals and communities*. Stamford, CT: Wadsworth.

18
Moving but Not Yet Talking: Community Psychology in Turkey

Serdar M. Degirmencioglu

Abstract

Community psychology (CP), with its emphasis on the local and native processes, and its focus on empowerment, liberation, social justice, change, and action, has a lot to offer to the society in Turkey. Psychologists in Turkey have often adopted dominant models from the United States, and many faculty are trained in the United States. CP is not a dominant subfield in the United States and therefore has not been very familiar or appealing to psychologists in Turkey. CP is particularly valuable given the strong calls for culturally situated psychologies in Turkey—a country with a very rich history, geography, cultures, and communities. CP is emerging in Turkey, more in practice than in training or research. During the 1999 earthquake relief efforts and the following period, many psychologists personally experienced what community work has to offer and liked it. A few students are on their way to obtaining CP degrees outside of Turkey. The future, however, is uncertain. No department or organization has committed itself to fostering CP. Undergraduate courses and publications are rare. Work focused on advocacy and policy hardly exist. CP in Turkey is developing but not in a planned or deliberate manner. It will take time for CP to become a very active and vocal discipline in Turkey.

Introduction

One of the distinguishing features of developmental psychology is the light it has shed on the many contextual forces that jointly influence an individual's life, the potential for turning points, and how different individual trajectories might lead to the same outcome. As a developmental psychologist, I am very cognizant of how my own career path has intersected with community psychology (CP). The unplanned twists and turns in my career that led in the direction of CP might shed light on the state of CP in Turkey, which is in many ways in its infancy. CP in Turkey is developing but not in a formal, planned, or deliberate manner.

Just like most of the psychology faculty members in Turkey, I obtained my Ph.D. in the United States. Just like most of them, my doctoral training included no CP exposure or any real community work. The only CP course I ever took was an undergraduate course that Chris Gilleard, from Britain, was teaching at Middle East Technical University in Ankara. This course left a huge impression on me but not to the extent that I would consider CP as an option for a Ph.D. degree. None of my peers did. My career path led to an affiliation with CP because in my postdoctoral work at Northwestern's Institute for Policy Research, I recognized gaps in the sociological literature on neighborhoods: That literature focused on demography at the expense of community processes. The unplanned twists and turns in my career later included research at a community center in Ankara, where I was convinced that I should assume an active role at community centers. Later I ended up on the board of the foundation that operated this community center. More importantly, I had to assume a central role in organizing community-level work after a major earthquake hit Turkey in 1999 and the Turkish Psychological Association was pressed to start relief work at the community level.

These twists and turns, including the earthquake, were opportunities for me (and perhaps for others) to rediscover the value of community-level work. These experiences helped me consolidate my belief that CP has a lot to offer here in Turkey and elsewhere. What makes CP a unique subfield of psychology, strong enough to have worldwide appeal, to have produced journals and a division under APA, is its unique emphasis on the local, collective, indigenous processes and locating psychological processes within. To me, CP is a field that takes ecology and community seriously. In all this, what is particularly desirable and useful in the local context is the focus on empowerment, liberation, social justice, and dignity, the explicit acceptance of the role of scientist as a social agent and social action as part of science. This way of defining CP helps one see how CP is similar and yet different from social work.

Brief History of Psychology in Turkey

A short overview of psychology as a discipline is needed to understand where CP is in Turkey. Psychology in Turkey has existed for a relatively long time: The first chair of psychology was established in 1915 (Kagitcibasi, 1994). Important work was carried out before World War II in Ankara and Istanbul, and a few students of psychology emerged as leading scholars. Of these, the better known is Muzafer Sherif, whose work in many ways transformed the field of social psychology. Strong psychology departments emerged in the 1960s and 1970s. The number of departments increased almost exponentially in the 1990s, when private universities were founded and the demand for higher education pushed more and more students in the direction of psychology. The first psychology organization was started in the 1940s. This organization remained weak and after organizational diffi-culties and a period of domination by psychiatrists merged with another newer and more academic organization in 1976, resulting in the Turkish Psychological Association (TPA). TPA still has fewer than 5,000 members and does not have subdivisions focused on different branches of psychology, including CP. The majority of practicing psychologists are engaged in clinical work in various applied settings.

A Description of Community Psychology Activity in Turkey

Good description is often ignored in psychology, and that is why methods focused on rich and thick description are often not employed. Grand theories and minitheories often obscure the necessity of doing justice to the complex processes psychologists set out to explain. In Turkey, I have witnessed time and again how many psychologists and social scientists, as well as lay people, try to employ models imported from abroad (i.e., the West) to understand their very own lives and culture. Therefore, I find it important here to describe the state of CP in Turkey before I present my own assessment. For this purpose, I will use a number of basic indicators or markers that can be used to describe the status of any field. I hope these indicators will help the readers make their own assessments.

What's in a Name?

An important indicator that signifies that a field exists is that it has a relatively well-accepted name. That turns out to be an important issue for CP in Turkey because of the difficulty associated with the very term "community": There is not a well-accepted corresponding term for community in modern Turkish. The older word "cemaat" that best fits with the meaning of the term "community" has become a tainted word because it has long been associated with "religious communities." In the Ottoman Empire, religious communities were part and parcel of daily life and public administration. Once a religious community was officially recognized, it could enjoy a large degree of auton-omy in administrative terms as well as in its religious practices. When the Republic of Turkey was founded in 1923, public administration was quickly secularized and religious orders were soon outlawed. Since then, the issue of religion and religious communities has been a contentious and unresolved public matter. For most modern-minded people, religion and religious entities were categorically something of the past and had to be left behind. Particularly since the military seized power in 1980, however, religious orders, communities, and some underground organizations have gained in strength and are perceived as a major threat to the secular republic by many.

   "Cemaat" is now commonly used solely to refer to religion-based group-ings and the term has become difficult to use to refer to other types of communities. If "topluluk" is used instead, it could only do a poor job because it simply refers to a collective of people but not a human community with a history, geography, shared action, and so on (Degirmencioglu, 2004). "Commune" is another alternative but is also too narrow and sounds too left-ist a term to use. "Camia" perhaps is an alternative but often refers to some-thing larger and looser than a community. Therefore, the term "community psychologist" is difficult to use in Turkey. It is also difficult to translate CP: Some have tried "topluluk psikolojisi" but that sounds more like group psychology. The issue is yet to be resolved in any adequate way.

Self-Designated Affiliations

One of the simplest indicators to employ here would be self-designated affil-iation with the field of CP. To this day, I have never seen anyone affiliate with CP verbally or in writing in Turkey. This does not mean, of course, that there is no CP activity in the country. There are people in the field who do what CP practitioners do but they do not necessarily call their work CP or call them-selves community psychologists. Reviews on the development of psychology as a discipline in Turkey (e.g., Kagitcibasi, 1994) do not mention CP at all.

Another type of self-designated affiliation is membership in a CP organi-zation. To the best of my knowledge, there is only one member from Turkey (myself) in the U.S.-based Society for Community Research and Action. The European Community Psychology Association, which replaced the informal European Network on Community Psychology in 2005, also has only one member from Turkey (myself).

Training and Degrees

A major determinant of affiliation with a discipline is the degree the individ-ual has obtained. A key indicator as to whether CP is an existing field or a discipline is individuals holding CP degrees. There is no one in Turkey with an M.A. or Ph.D. in CP—or a Ph.D. with a minor in CP. The future, however, is more optimistic for CP in Turkey as there are doctoral candidates in CP programs in the United States and a handful of undergraduate students who are aspiring to enroll in CP programs.

Another stringent indicator of CP presence would be courses and any special training on CP that may lead to a degree. For this chapter, I have surveyed the undergraduate programs and the few graduate programs in the country and found no CP or community-focused courses. There have been occasional CP courses in select departments (one of which I took in 1987 from Chris Gilliard, a community psychologist from Britain), but these are courses offered when there is a visiting faculty. I have also asked psychology faculty members, via a country-wide e-mail group, to name any colleagues that have ever offered a CP course and only one name (who no longer is a faculty member) was mentioned. Therefore, except for the CP I have offered as an elective at Bilgi University, there are no CP courses—at least with this name—now in Turkey.

Conference Activities

Another indicator regarding CP presence is the sessions devoted to CP held at conventions, congresses, and other meetings. Conferences provide a unique setting for face-to-face contact with a large number of peers and colleagues and often involve discussions of new concepts and sometimes debates that never make it to professional journals. Such professional events are sometimes the setting where the very first public announcement of manifestos are made. Session titles could be examined for evidence of CP work in a given conference. The title might include the term "CP" or focus on core processes in the definition of CP or simply community-based work. When I examined the titles in the past 10 years, there appears to be an increase in the number of sessions related to CP. This increase is particularly evident in the conferences held after 1999— the year when a large number of psychologists were involved, mostly for the first time, in real community-level relief work. If, however, the number of sessions is the focus, it is clear that CP activity at conferences is rather small.

Publications in Turkey

Another important indicator of the presence of CP is the number of articles that include CP as a phrase or CP constructs as their main focus. This is a rather stringent indicator given the fact that new, non-mainstream or "radical" approaches are not received well in many mainstream journals where the existing scholarly paradigms dominate. As noted before, reviews of the development of psychology as a discipline in Turkey do not mention CP at all, which also indicates that CP publications were absent. During my 2-year co-editorship of the *Turkish Journal of Psychology*, the journal did not receive any CP submissions. There are few other journals of psychology in Turkey, and there is very little, if any, CP work published in them. If journals in fields like social work are examined, it is clear that community-level work outside of psychology is also not common. This is partly due to the fact that most CP work in Turkey is carried out by practitioners who tend not to do rigorous research or attempt to turn their work into publications. This is consistent with my later conclusion that CP is indeed budding in Turkey, but more in practice rather than in training or research.

Publications Outside of Turkey

CP work from Turkey has not appeared in CP journals published in English. An important insight might be gained by identifying work from Turkey that could be considered CP work published in professional journals (affiliated with psychology or otherwise) and examining the journals in which they were published. This examination reveals that some work focusing on community-level psychological dynamics (e.g., Bardo & Dökmeci, 1990, 1992) and particularly on immigrants and immigrant communities from Turkey in

Europe (e.g., Phalet & Hagendoon, 1996) have been published in psychology journals in Europe. But the journals in which they were published in were more or less social or general psychology journals.

Community Psychology in Turkey: A Field in Its Infancy

CP, with its emphasis on the local, on the native, and its focus on empowerment, liberation, social justice, social change, and social action, has a lot to offer to psychology and to the public in Turkey. Psychology has existed for a relatively long time in Turkey, and many psychologists are convinced that psychology can benefit the society in various ways (e.g., Kagitcibasi, 1995, 2002).

Psychologists in Turkey have often adopted, almost exclusively, dominant models from the United States (Gergen, Gülerce, Lock & Misra, 1996; Öngel & Smith, 1999) and most faculty members in prominent psychology departments are trained in the United States—the author not withstanding. CP, as a relatively young and clearly not a dominant subfield in the United States, has therefore not been very appealing to psychologists in Turkey. CP, however, can be particularly useful for psychologists worldwide who yearn for an indigenous psychology or indigenous psychologies (Adair & Diaz-Loving, 1999). CP is particularly valuable given the strong calls for culturally situated or indigenous psychologies in Turkey (Gergen et al., 1996; Öngel & Smith, 1999)—a country with a very rich history, geography, and cultures rooted in different communities dating sometimes back to the very first civilizations. CP inherently has the potential to meet the demands for culturally situated psychologies that matter for individuals and communities in Turkey.

The indicators I have employed above to describe the status of CP in Turkey suggest that CP is budding in Turkey, more in practice than in training or research. To use a developmental metaphor here, I believe that CP has recently been born in Turkey. Particularly with the 1999 earthquake relief work experience, many psychologists have personally tasted, in varying degrees, what CP has to offer and liked it. Some have been employed in community centers and engaged in community-level work where they faced the challenge of applied research. In an informal interview I conducted at a community center established after the earthquake, a clinical psychologist told me in length how they had come to that setting to deal with the earthquake trauma and as time passed started assisting the locals with their more essential problems. In one instance, a fight broke out among women in a tent camp because the more established and advantaged locals were very unhappy with the way poor and less educated newcomers, all migrant families who were pursuing jobs, were using the common areas in the camp. Someone called the newcomers "Kurds," and the tension turned into an ethnic problem. My colleague had to step out of her role as a clinical psychologist and work with the locals in a very different way to reframe and solve the problem. This she considered a very significant step in her career.

To continue with the developmental analogy, it is also clear that CP in Turkey is still in its infancy. There are students on their way to obtaining CP degrees outside of Turkey or aspiring to do so. However, the future is not certain. CP in Turkey does not have an established home nor a committed department or organization to foster the field. Students all around Turkey can now hear about local CP action as well as international CP opportunities, graduate programs, and even calls for papers via a listserve[1] but more undergraduate courses are needed to foster interest in CP.

CP in Turkey is moving, acting and enjoying its agency, but the field has not started to express itself verbally—in the form of publications, training, advocacy or even policy—and collectively. CP in Turkey is developing but not in a formal, planned, or deliberate manner. I certainly hope that CP will continue to grow in Turkey and become a very active and vocal discipline. That will certainly take time.

References

Adair, J.G. & Diaz-Loving, R. (1999). Indigenous psychologies: The meaning of the concept and its assessment: Introduction. *Applied Psychology: An International Review*, 48(4), 397-402.

Bardo, J.W. & Dökmeci, V. (1992). Modernization, traditionalism, and the changing structure of community satisfaction in two sub-communities in Istanbul, Turkey: A Procrustean analysis. *Genetic, Social & General Psychology Monographs*, 118(3), 273-293.

Bardo, J.W. & Dökmeci, V. (1990). Community satisfaction in two Turkish sub-communities: Further data on the significance of cultural differentation. *Genetic, Social & General Psychology Monographs*, 116(3), 325-337.

Degirmencioglu, S.M. (2004). Community. *Encyclopedia of Applied Developmental Science*. Thousand Oaks: Sage.

Gergen, K.J., Gülerce, A., Lock, A. & Misra, G. (1996). Psychological science in cultural context. *American Psychologist*, 51(5), 496-503.

Kagitcibasi, C. (1994). Psychology in Turkey. *International Journal of Psychology*, 29(6), 729-738.

Kagitcibasi, C. (1995). Is psychology relevant to global human development issues? Experience from Turkey. *American Psychologist*, 50(4), 293-300.

Kagitcibasi, C. (2002). Psychology and human competence development. *Applied Psychology: An International Review*, 51(1), 5-22.

Öngel, Ü. & Smith, P.B. (1999). The search for indigenous psychologies: Data from Turkey and the former USSR. *Applied Psychology: An International Review*, 48(4), 465-479.

Phalet, K. & Hagendoorn, L. (1996). Personal adjustment to acculturative transitions: The Turkish experience. *International Journal of Psychology*, 31(2), 131-144.

---

[1] This listserv is the largest academic psychology listserv in Turkey. Its members include psychology students, practitioners, and some faculty members. The listserv was established by Metin Özdemir, now a CP/developmental psychology doctoral student in the United States, and myself in 1999.

19
Community Psychology Initiatives in Greece

Sofia Triliva and Athanassios Marvakis

Abstract

In this chapter, we describe several community-focused initiatives that may be the stirrings of community psychology (CP) in Greece. Although CP has not 'officially' set hold in our country with regard to academic training, professional organizations, and journals, it may be accurate to say that its existence is evident through the many initiatives, programs, and actions that have been developed and applied in many communities throughout the country. It is the services offered by mental health centers, programming for parents, the prevention and health promotion initiatives made possible by the centers for prevention of drug use, and the community volunteer actions that focus on different social issues and community concerns that can be 'interpreted' as CP in Greece. The chapter describes the history of these community initiatives, their characteristics, their theoretical underpinnings, and how they relate to the discipline and the practices of CP as they are described in the international literature.

Introduction

When we were invited to write a chapter about community psychology (CP) in Greece, we both asked ourselves the same question: "Is there any semblance of what is described as CP in the literature in our country?" This question led to a great deal of thought and contemplation and to a convoluted path of discovery. Being that we live and work in a country with a long history, the path we followed seemed like a labyrinth. We began in a somewhat awkward fashion trying to excavate the psychological literature without the modern aids of databases (they do not exist in the Greek language), yet writings about psychology and community exist from the days of . . . Plato and Aristotle. Several of the underlying principles and conceptual tenets of CP may have had their origins in the writings and narrative accounts of

363

the ancient Greek philosophers. Ideas such as community and political consciousness and their connections to social and psychological well-being were integral concepts in the works of Aristotle and Plato. Moreover, these forefathers of many psychological concepts used the tools that we now call reflexivity and communal dialogues in developing understandings and in bolstering their arguments and worldviews. The idiosyncratic and tumultuous history of Greek society, culture, and the founding of psychology in Greece have impeded these philosophical inheritances from reaching ascendancy in modern-day research and practice in the field of psychology in this European nation (Dafermos, Marvakis, & Triliva, 2006). They are legacies that have remained enclosed in the treasure chests of the ancient philosophical writings to be discussed and debated in academic circles, mostly in departments of philosophy and classical studies, and hence have not infiltrated psychology curricula and, more importantly, the lives of most people living in Greece today.

The goal of this chapter is to describe what can be construed and/or interpreted as 'community psychology' in the Greek context, being that the field of psychology in general is in a neophyte stage of development and that 'community psychology' as it is defined by several influential texts in the international literature (Dalton, Elias, & Wandersman, 2001; Nelson & Prilleltensky 2005; Orford, 1992) has not yet emerged in Greece. A 'working' and implicit definition of CP for us is "a going into the community," an involvement of community stakeholders in defining what are the relevant issues for them and in delineating and participating in initiatives that can be applied to encounter these issues. Even though the field has not yet emerged within academic circles in the Greek context, a myriad of activities, interventions, and programming exists that could be 'interpreted' as CP. Many of these initiatives are person-centered. That is, one or a few charismatic or motivated individuals or groups who have an interest in the advancement of (psychological) applications within a specific context and who, through their own funding or efforts, began a 'center' where community services are offered to the public and professional training is made available to the mental health professionals who are interested (Tsegkos, in press; Vassiliou & Vassiliou, 1965; 1982).

Because there are no courses in 'community psychology' within the Greek academic curricula and only a handful of courses in what is called 'clinical-social psychology' at both the graduate and undergraduate level at three Greek universities, we will focus (more exemplary than exhaustively) on programming and interventions, which have emerged from and/or have been applied in community contexts, including those that were initiated by public institutions as well as by volunteers. In this description, we will try to focus on the history of each initiative and its (necessarily) implicit relation to CP principles.

Community Initiatives by Public Institutions

Community Mental Health Centers

Community initiatives exist in community mental health centers, centers for the prevention of substance abuse, school programming, and 'schools for parents.' There are 13 existing mental health centers founded in the mid-1980s that have as their objectives the "provision of psychosocial care, counseling intervention, and maintenance of the individual within the community; the provision of prevention initiatives, therapeutic help, and the restitution and psychosocial incorporation of the ailing person . . ." (Ministry of Health, Document no. 2E of the 59th meeting of the governing body, p. 1). The centers were linked to the psychiatric hospitals that existed in Greece and were one of the initiatives of the 'de-institutionalization campaign,' which started in Greece at that time and was made possible by the funds of the European Community.

The mental health centers (MHCs) have a 'social psychiatric' focus adopting the psychiatric reform notions of providing psychological, social, and psychiatric help within the community. In a sense, the centers were geared to act as filters for the psychiatric clinics, and along these lines their primary role has been to provide diagnostic and therapeutic services (Triliva & Stalikas, 2004). Some of the centers have developed primary prevention programming. While mental health centers appear to be an early sign of CP practice, they do employ top-down approaches. Thus far, they do not research the needs of the community nor evaluate the services they provide.

In summary, the MHCs exist within 13 different Greek communities but are 'not out in the community.' They in effect provide services by waiting for the community and individuals to attend 'their programs' or make use of 'their services.' This premise and mode of providing programming may appear simple and logical when taken from a Western perspective. In Greece, however, the use of services by *individuals-users* is not such a simple and *individual-focused* practice or initiative. There are complex family or collective decision-making processes on what constitutes help-seeking, who should seek help, from whom, and even what is 'problematic' behavior or state of being. This complexity becomes more obvious when we foreground and take into consideration what is (psychic) health in the Greek context, how the subjects involved try to achieve it, and which strategies and techniques (including seeking help from professionals or social networks) are applied and developed in one's attempt to deal with his or her problems. In Greece, individual (mental) health and well-being issues are not primarily perceived as being *private* matters to deal with individually by seeking help from professionals. Well-being is inextricably woven into the collective or social textile of ideas and identities. Research endeavors concerning people's points of view and understandings of what constitutes (psychic) health and the roads and strategies people use in dealing with the difficulties and the problems they face are sorely needed in Greece (Blue, 1999).

Substance Abuse Prevention and Therapy Programming

A second type of CP initiative focuses on drug use prevention. In this context, the Organization Against Narcotics (OAN), founded in 1993, has developed prevention programming in the larger prefectures all over Greece. Many community coalitions for drug abuse prevention have mushroomed throughout the country in the past 10 years. Although these organizations consist of a coalition of local members who represent the church, the governing bodies, health institutions, and other professional organizations, they are essentially operating by following the guidelines of the national Organization Against Narcotics. The local level of analysis is not very present in the analyses of needs and in the programming applied. This programming consists of primary prevention initiatives with the overriding goal of preventing drug use in the general community population and promoting well-being (Constitution of Rethymno Prefecture OAN). The activities involved in such an initiative are psycho-educational and experiential in nature, involve the participation in thematic-centered groups, and try to reach as many members of the prefecture/community as possible. The Advisory Council on Alcohol and Drug Education (TACADE) module, a British Organization (TACADE, 1999), is used in the programming, as are other program modules, which resemble this 'imported curriculum.'

Within the same organization there is also the Therapy Center for Dependent Individuals, which was founded in 1987 and focuses on drug addiction. It is a nonprofit, nongovernmental organization, which operates under the auspices of the Greek Ministry of Health and Welfare. The programs are modeled after the therapeutic community framework (KETHEA, 2001, 2005) that exists in the international literature. These programs try to bring about first-order and second-order change (Dalton, Elias, & Wandersman, 2001). They do this by setting up a community of support, in a sense of a system where the lines of expertise between the professionals who run the program and the individuals who seek help are not so rigid. The programs also reinforce the helping and support-giving skills of each individual taking part in the programming (mutual aid), as well as to help the person and his or her family in developing greater agency and autonomy in leading their lives.

Regardless of all the best intentions, perceptions, and definitions in expensive leaflets, what constitutes 'drugs' for these initiatives remains, for the most part, circumscribed to what in a sensationalized public discourse are named as "illegal drugs." In this fashion, the most widely used and abused substances in Greece (physician-prescribed psychotropic medications, nicotine, and alcohol) that have far ranging and catastrophic consequences on public health, compared with the illegal substances that are the center of the 'against drug use initiatives,' are hardly touched upon by initiatives and prevention campaigns (Piperopoulos, 1985). Elucidation, instruction, and information dispensation are often restricted to the dissemination of 'educational' materials. In connection to this it can be stated—with a bit of hyperbole—that *going into* the community is often reduced or confined to a form of dissemination or scattering of leaflets *in the streets* or *in localities* of the community, leaflets with superfluous information that simply litter the streets.

School Programming

School psychology is another area in which possible precursors to CP initiatives are being applied though very little development has occurred. Somewhat paradoxically, school community intervention initiatives have existed in Greece in an 'unofficial base' for many years. This field made an initial appearance in Greece in 1937 with the work of the well-known leftist intellectual Rosa Imvrioti on special-needs populations in the poor district of Kaisariani in Athens (Imvrioti 1939; Kalatzis 1985; Theodore et al. 2002). She founded the 'Model Special School of Athens' (Public Law 1049/1938), first opened during the 1937–1938 school year but ceased operation in autumn 1940 due to the war. Imvrioti and her colleagues included many newly developed and applied pedagogical initiatives in running the school, initiatives developed at that time in Europe. Unfortunately, her innovative initiatives did not lay the inroads for the development of the discipline of school psychology and the community services that could be offered by professionals specializing in this field. On the contrary, the barriers that have thwarted this development were many, including social-political upheaval,[1] the lack of licensing laws for psychologists until recently (Bouhoutsos & Roe, 1984; Nikolopoulou & Oakland, 1990; Theodore et al., 2002), the lack of specialization within psychology, weak social and political status of scientific and professional psychology, an 'entrenched' and inflexible educational system (Nikolopoulou & Oakland, 1990), the emulation and replication of the American 'School Psychology' within a very different cultural, systemic, political, and professional context (Theodore et al., 2002), and a lack of application of comprehensive mode that takes into consideration the cultural, organizational, and ethnic determinants of how services are delivered within the schools (Hatzichristou, 2003).

Due to these barriers outlined above, Greece has remained a nation in which there is very limited provision for psychological services within the

---

[1] Rosa Imvrioti was active in the 'National Resistance' during World War II and was held in different Greek concentration camps from 1948 until 1951. She was officially dismissed as the principal of the school after the end of World War II and many of the educational materials that had been produced and used in the school were destroyed, possibly as a way of wiping away all the evidence of this innovative initiative. This model school, even as a structure, slowly declined and now looks like more like a ruin.

centralized school system. In 1989, a limited number of psychologists were hired to work within 'special schools' and in 2000, the Centers of Diagnosis, Assessment, and Support Services were founded within many prefectures in the nation. These centers are not housed in schools and have mostly provided diagnostic services by applying individualistic and psycho-centric models.

The work of the Doksiadi Institute on abuse prevention, the work of Chimienti and Triliva (1995) and Triliva and Chimienti (1993, 1996) on conflict resolution, the published modules on mental health promotion (Triliva & Chimienti 1998, 2002), and the bias and prejudice sensitization work of Tsiakalos (2000) and Papas (1998) have been available in Greece, yet none have been integrated within the wider school system. Nor have they been widely used in the newly developed programming called 'health promotion initiatives.' In a sense, all of these practical and theoretical works have not been adopted by the school system, but have instead remained on the shelves of academic offices and not in the hands of practitioners. Most importantly, these works have not touched upon the lives of the children and educators that they were intended for.

Parent Education: 'Schools for Parents'

Programming with the aim of educating parents about child and adolescent development, discipline techniques, and conflict resolution has been in place within community settings for approximately 40 years in Greece. The theoretical underpinnings of these initiatives emphasize empowerment and self-determination, but the methodology imposes a paternalistic or 'right and wrong' perspective primarily because it is 'copied' from theories and applications that exist in other nations where more individualistic values predominate and collectivist values are in the background.

The Federation for Parent Education has developed such programming since the year 1978 under the auspices of UNESCO (Hourdaki, 1982, 1992). The format of this programming consists of lectures and educational activities that follow the theoretical tenet of 'logical consequences' espoused by Dreikurs (Dreikurs & Grey, 1970; Dreikurs & Soltz, 1964) and Dinkmeyer (Dinkmeyer & McKay, 1973, 1976, 1983) and the very detailed handbooks and step by step exercises that characterize their publications (these publications were translated into the Greek language). The emphasis of these works is on strengthening individual competencies in care-giving with a particular emphasis on discipline. Although these lectures, discussions, and guidance sessions have been in place for many years, a relatively small number of mostly women with young or adolescent children take part in the programming. No outcome or process evaluation studies as to the effectiveness of this programming has been conducted within the Greek cultural milieu and this makes it difficult to know how well it has rooted in the communities in which these programs are initiated.

Nonprofit Volunteer Initiated Programming

There are several volunteer organizations in Greece that provide community services that have CP values such as empowerment and self-determination. In the text that follows, we will describe only two characteristic examples of such programming in Greece, ventures in which we are personally involved.

Lyceum for Greek Women

One example of such programming is the Lyceum for Greek Women, an organization that has existed since 1911 and was founded by Siganou Paron, one of the earliest feminists in Greece. This organization's goals have been expanded through the years and now include the support of the bedrock of the Greek community, which is the family. In the Lyceum for Greek Women in Rethymno (on the island of Crete), there has been a family support program in place for the past 25 years. It is a community outreach program that has provided educational lectures on topics such as child development and health, the influence of the mass media on family life, and many topics on the psychosocial aspects of family living. In the past 5 years, the programming at the lyceum has become more experiential in nature, and the interventions have been derived from the explicitly expressed needs of the community members that attend and are involved. The interventions have also been evaluated (Triliva, 2004; Triliva, in press) within an action research paradigm. The weaving of traditional ways of knowing, understanding, and developing knowledge has been a part of the programming in the past few years, and the goal of the programming has been the empowerment of the individual members of the community regarding personal and relational well-being. In the upcoming year, the initiatives undertaken will have as a goal the collective well-being of the community members and the enhancement of their capabilities of becoming active change agents within the community.

Immigrants' Center Rethymno

Although the incorporation of various ethno-linguistic populations and the sending and receiving of migrants has been a constant feature in the modern Greek state during the long process of it formation into a nation-state in the 19th and 20th centuries, there still exists a very prevalent myth that it has historically been a homogeneous nation that only very recently (the past 15 years) has had an influx of immigrants. This myth is being used to describe, explain, or legitimize the political, practical, and social refusal of the 'system' to officially incorporate immigrants into the mainstream life of the communities in which they live and work. The legal system, as well as administrative practices, forces most migrants and their families to live in a state of permanent insecurity and dependence. Added to these obstacles are the everyday forms of discrimination and racism they experience. Very little has been put in place structurally to assist in the empowering of immigrant groups and aid local populations in welcoming them into their communities.[2] This lack of state-developed infrastructures for migrants and refugees—valid also for the other social marginalized or excluded groups in the country—is only partially being filled by initiatives of NGOs. Thus, organizations such as the Greek Council for Refugees, Caritas, the Red Cross, Doctors of the World, and others organize initiatives for the teaching and learning of the Greek language, providing food rations and clothing, offering medical and pharmaceutical care and psychological support as well as opening reception centers for refugees and including activities for those newly imprisoned.

Apart from this, there are some scattered local initiatives aiming to help empower immigrants and to offer them the chance of participating and articulating their needs. One example of the community initiatives in Greece, which has focused on immigrant and local cooperation and the development of mutuality, is the Immigrants' Center Rethymno on the island of Crete. We shall describe the physical setting, its social substructures, and the methodological underpinnings of this initiative: The immigrants' center is thought of as a 'meeting place' or a 'hangout.' It is a single-family dwelling with a small yard in the back that is leased by the local nonprofit association called Solidarity Initiative towards Immigrants. Immigrants, students, and other local participants put forth all of their mechanical and handcrafting know-how in order for the physical environment to take shape. The constructing materials for this endeavor came from donations provided by local merchants and businesses. This cycling of resources demonstrates one of the founding principles of the center, as does the interdependence that is cultivated by such initiatives. From a social or community perspective, the center is organized as an autonomously managed and operated public space in which a variety of social/community activities are organized on a volunteer basis. This public meeting place is open to activities and initiatives that can directly or indirectly contribute to the empowerment and adaptation of immigrants in the relatively small community of Rethymno as well as the community's adaptation to the changes precipitated by the influx of people from ethnically, geographically, and religiously diverse backgrounds. From a methodological perspective, we can characterize the immigrant's center as a 'real-experimental initiative' (in German: *Realexperiment*) or as an 'action research project' based on the underpinnings of solidarity movements. As a social movement, the center has the ongoing goal of bringing about a 'learning democracy' and 'collective socialization' of all the people who take part in the activities, whether they are immigrants, students, or local participants. Participation in this project and experiment in solidarity-socialization influences all of the participants, of course, differently depending on their social position, their

---

[2] See the contributions on this in Marvakis, Parsanoglu, and Pavlou (2001) and Pavlou and Christopoulos (2004).

subjectivities, and their evident and latent needs. It is hoped that ecological succession will be achieved and that the outcomes at the microlevel of the center will shine upon and influence the rest of the community of Rethymno.

Conclusion

In our attempt to locate and identify educational, professional, and programming endeavors in Greece that can be placed under the rubric of CP, we located a myriad of different initiatives that we have documented above and that exist in many communities all over the country. We did not find courses or degree programs at the university level that have a CP focus. The initiatives we did locate and described above have not been institutionalized in terms of professional organizations, journals, or programs. This state of affairs has brought about concomitant negative *and* positive side effects:

(a) The programming developed in Greece paralleled the reforms of the provision of (mental) health services (in the 1980s), and along with this the community mental health movement mushroomed and emulated mainstream North American and Western European psychology in theory, philosophy, and practice. Initiatives by public institutions are "copying" (following) North American or Western European practices, programming, and models, and hence, locally grown knowledge and understanding has yet to emerge. Basic or applied research is in a neophyte stage of development (needs analysis and evaluation is totally absent) and not 'grounded' in the social-psychological or local contexts. Initiatives and programs are developed and applied following Western 'modules' many times without any regard to the needs, wants, discourses, and understandings of the communities in which they are embedded.

(b) This 'un-institutionalized' and informal state of being opens the possibilities for community-centered forms of developments to take place because 'deconstruction' of solidified structures and prototypes will not need to occur for 'new' developments to take hold.

The initiatives described above are usually fragmented and scattered "unsystematically" all over the territory with no network(ing) and (systematic) communication between those that develop and run them. The volunteer initiatives are "captured" in (are busy with) trying to keep their good practices "alive" locally and have only few or no resources for evaluation, networking, and communication. Keeping in mind that there is substantially no continuous financial and other support, the only way towards "development" seems to be the starting and restarting from point zero each and every time. The building of sound community structures that endure the tests of time has not been easy in Greece.

The practices in the MHC centers, narcotics preventions meetings, and other initiatives by public institutions dubbed "interventions" are too often conceptualized as (individual, clinical) "treatment" or are even restricted to dispensing (individualistic) therapeutic language/vocabulary in the community and towards the contacted population. Through this form of outreach, they are promoting a kind of "discursive psychologization" (or psychologization of the public and lay discourses) rather than supporting reflexivity, communal understandings, and change within the community. Interventions are *for* the people not *of* and *by* the people (Martin-Baro, 1994), people have to go *to* the MHC centers, narcotics prevention meetings, or circles of intervention; very little of this takes place *in* the community and is of the people. Community-building, community participation, grassroots organizing, and social–political empowerment of people has not been part of the focus. Thus, it is more than understandable that the communities develop idiosyncratic ways of resistance to this kind of (culturally not adapted) "treatment," which is being expressed as resistance, reluctance, refusal, and mistrust towards these "offers." Moreover, because these initiatives are developed within non-governmental bodies though funded by the state, they are forced to function as a partial surrogate or substitute of the welfare state, and of course this is done in a haphazard manner.

In a nutshell, psychology in general is in a state of transition in Greece and CP in a state of formation. There are some structures and social policies in place that can potentially develop community initiatives that adhere to the values and principles on which CP was founded. It is crucial, however, if holistic, accountable, and transformative practices are to take hold, that the "Greek subject" is to be studied and understood and that his or her individual and collective voices are heard. The visions, needs, and actions of these subjects have to be adapted and understood within the "Greek context." It is the interplay of subject and context and how it is translated into practice that keeps us interested in CP.

References

Blue, A. V. (1999). *The making of Greek psychiatry*. Athens: Exandas [in Greek].
Bouhoutsos, J. C. & Roe, K. V. (1984). Mental health services and the emerging role of psychology in Greece. *American Psychologist,* 39(1), 57-61.
Chimienti, G. & Triliva, S. (1995). Cognitive and behavioral changes following social skills training with Greek and Lebanese elementary school children. *International Journal of Mental Health*, 23, 53-68.
Dafermos, M. & Marvakis, A., & Triliva, S. (2006). (De)Constructing psychology in Greece. *Annual Review of Critical Psychology, 5*. http://www.discourseunit.com/arcp/s.htm
Dalton, J. H., Elias, M. J., & Wandersman, A. (2001). *Community psychology - linking individuals and communities*. Belmont, CA: Wadsworth, Thomson Learning.
Dinkmeyer, D. & McKay, G. D. (1973). *Raising a responsible child*. NY: Simon & Schuster.
Dinkmeyer, D. & McKay, G. D. (1976). *Systemic training for effective parenting: Parent's handbook*. Circle Pines, MN: American Guidance Center.
Dinkmeyer, D. & McKay, G. D. (1983). *The parent's guide: STEP/Teen, systematic training for effective parenting of teens*. Circle Pines, MN: American Guidance Service.

Dreikurs, R. & Grey, L. (1970). *Parent's guide to child discipline*. New York: Hawthorn.

Dreikurs, R. & Soltz, V. (1964). Children: The challenge. New York: Duell, Sloan & Pearce.

Hatzichristou, S. (2003). Alternative school psychological services: Development of a model linking theory, research and service delivery. In N. M. Lambert, I. Hylander & J. Sandoval (Eds.), *Consultee-Centered Consultation: Improving the Quality of Professional Services in Schools and Community* (pp. 115-132). Mahwah, NJ: Lawrence Erlbaum.

Hourdaki, M. (1982, 1992). *Family Psychology*. Athens: Grigoris [in Greek].

Imvrioti, R. (1939). *Abnormal and retarded children – first year of the special needs model school*. Athens: Elliniki Ekdotiki Etaireia [in Greek].

Kalatzis, K. G. (1985). *Ston asterismo tou Dimitri Glinou*. Athina: Diptycho [in Greek].

Martin-Baro, I. (1994). *Writings for a liberation psychology*. Cambridge, MA: Harvard University Press.

Marvakis, A., Pavlou, M., & Parsanoglou, D. (2001) (Eds.), *Migrants in Greece*. Athens: Ellinika Grammata / Nikos Poulantzas Association on Policy Issues [in Greek].

Nelson, G. & Prilleltensky, I. (2005). *Community psychology in pursuit of liberation and well-being*. New York: Palgrave Macmillan.

Nikolopoulou, A. K. & Oakland, T. (1990). School psychology in Greece: An updated review. *School Psychology International*, 11, 147-154.

Orford, J. (1992). *Community psychology - theory and practice*. West Sussex, UK: John Wiley & Sons.

Papas, A. (1998). Intercultural Education and Didactics, Volume A. Athens: Athanasios E. Papas [in Greek].

Pavlou, M. & Christopoulos, D. (2004) (Eds.), *Greece of immigration: Social participation, rights, and citizenship*. Athens: Kritiki & KEMO [in Greek].

Piperopoulos, G. (1985). On the role of psychology in Greece: Comment on Bouhoutsos and Roe. *American Psychologist*, 40(4), 475.

TACADE, (1999). *Skills for the primary school children*. Athens, KETHEA. [Greek edition]

Theodore, L. A., Bray, M. A., Kehle, T. J., & Dioguardi, R. J. (2002). School psychology in Greece. A system of change. *School Psychology International*, 23(2), 148-154.

Triliva, S. (2004). A family support program that promotes 'positive psychology': Goals, community partnership and experiential learning. *The XIV IFTA: World Family Therapy Congress*, Istanbul, Turkey, March 17-24, Book of Abstracts, p. 153.

Triliva, S. (in press). Philosophical dialogues as paths to a more 'positive psychology'. *Journal of Community and Applied Social Psychology*.

Triliva, S. & Chimienti, G. (1993). The relationship between Greek 3rd and 4th grade students' behavior and their sociometric status. *Psychological Issues*, 6(1), 39-58.

Triliva, S. & Chimienti, G. (1996). The application of a program to enhance social and emotional skills in Greek elementary schools. *Psychological Issues*, 7(1), 52-65 [in Greek].

Triliva, S. & Chimienti, G. (1998). *Conflict resolution: A program for elementary school students*. Athens: Ellinika Grammata [in Greek].

Triliva, S. & Chimienti, G. (2002). *Self-discovery: Self-awareness, self-control, & self-respect. Emotional and social competence*. Athens: Pataki [in Greek].

Triliva, S. & Stalikas, A. (2004). The use of psychological tests and measurements by psychologists in the rold of counsellor in Greece. *Counseling Psyhology Review,* 19(4), 32-39.

Tsegkos, I. K. (in press). *Open psychotherapeutic center: Interventions and idiosyncrasies of 25 years of existence*. Athens: Enallaktikes Ekdoseis [in Greek].

Tsiakalos, G. (2000). A guide to anti-racist education. Athens: Ellinika Grammata [in Greek].

Vassiliou, G. & Vasiliou, V. (1982). Promoting psychological functioning and preventing malfunctioning. *Pediatrician*, 11(1-2), 90-98.

Vassiliou, G. & Vassiliou, V. (1965). Attitudes of the Athenian public towards mental illness. *International Mental Health and Research Newsletter*, 3(2), 12-17.

AFRICA

20
Community Psychology in South Africa

ARVIN BHANA, INGE PETERSEN, AND TAMSEN ROCHAT

Abstract

In this chapter, we describe the historical and contemporary forces that have shaped the development of psychology and community psychology (CP) in pre-apartheid and post-apartheid South Africa. In the evolution of CP in South Africa, we describe how resistance to the apartheid government is reflected in the call for relevance in the academies and how CP was viewed as an important part of the call for change and social justice. The parlous state of psychological services to the populace in general is highlighted. We reflect on how privileging biomedical care and clinical psychology has hindered the development of CP but at the same time spurred on a critical discourse of psychology and psychological practice in general. We then comment on the current status of CP in South Africa, which while broadly recognized and taught in tertiary institutions does not exist as an independent category of practice. We reflect on the impact of the new Mental Health Act and the compulsory community service for clinical psychologists and its implications for CP. Finally, we comment on the emergence and support of indigenous knowledge as an important vehicle for informing CP in the future.

Introduction

In this chapter, the informal historical roots of community psychology (CP) in South Africa are described, which are in turn very closely aligned with the political history of the country. This political history is also intimately linked with the development and history of psychology in general, from its academic roots to the professionalization of the field, notably in clinical, counseling, educational, and industrial/organizational psychology. Because there are very strong links in the language and ideologies of mainstream psychology between the United States, Europe, and South Africa, the terminology used in describing various disciplines and fields of practice, including CP, was readily adopted. Currently, CP in South Africa is both a well-recognized field of study and training but paradoxically is distinctly absent as a visible field of practice. Though its history as a formal field of study and practice is very recent, with discernable trends beginning in the late 1970s, one can generally refer to two distinct periods in the development of CP, namely, CP in the pre-apartheid era, and CP in post-apartheid South Africa, that is, following the first democratic elections in 1994. While the United States and Europe constituted the major sources of theoretical influence in the development of psychology and CP in South Africa, the a-contextual applications of these theories in South Africa's charged political climate came in for severe criticism and promoted calls for new understandings that would represent African perspectives.

In the Beginning . . .

As a former colony of Britain, South Africa gained its independence in 1961 when the then Prime Minister, H.F. Verwoerd (a psychologist himself), declared South Africa a republic after winning a whites-only referendum on the question of independence. Through its policy of separate development, various laws were passed that enforced racial segregation as best exampled by the Group Areas Act of 1950, which designated the area a person of a particular racial group was allowed to live in, do business, go to school, or seek health care. Black[1] Africans were further segregated into various tribal groups on the basis of language and ethnicity, such as Zulu, Xhosa, Venda, and so on, with the plan that each of these groups could be consolidated into "independent homelands." Most of these assigned areas, which constituted only 13% of South African land, were thoroughly degraded by overpopulation and soil erosion. Laws to further entrench segregation ultimately impacted on every imaginable facet of life, including separate health, education, sport and recreation, and transport facilities, leading ultimately to absurdities such as separate benches in parks and separate beaches for the various racial groups.

Against the backdrop of an increasingly draconian and authoritarian apartheid regime, South Africa saw an increase in the expression of resistance most dramatically captured by the death of 69 people demonstrating against carrying "passes" (a system devised to control the movement of black people) in Sharpeville in March 1960. This resulted in the banning of resistance movements and the introduction of detention without trial, which characterized

---

[1] The terms 'black,' 'white,' 'asian/indian,' and 'coloured' were terms used by the apartheid government to racially classify individuals into one of these four groups. The nomenclature persists to this day and serves an important purpose in dealing with issues of social redress. The terms in this chapter are presented in lower case so as to negate their use as racial categories; they are merely used as demographic markers.

much of the political landscape of the 1960s and 1970s. While these decades were marked by a sustained resistance against apartheid and innumerable human rights violations, a strong resurgence of resistance reemerged in the 1970s, particularly in June 1976 when school pupils in the largest township outside of Johannesburg (Soweto[2]) erupted in protest and mass action, followed by uprisings throughout the country. The immediate trigger for the uprising was that black schools were being forced to provide instruction in the language of Afrikaans, widely perceived as the language of a white oppressor. The symbolism of this act is apparent and generally perceived as an attempt to enforce the centrality of Afrikaner culture, but also to further marginalize black languages and identity. Given that psychology from as early as pre–World War II enthusiastically preoccupied itself with intelligence testing especially around 'mental hygiene,' 'race relations,' and 'the poor white problem' (Painter & Terre Blanche, 2004), it is not surprising that:

Psychology's response to these problems fell far short of being progressive. In both its active advocacy for apartheid policies based on the 'results' of mental testing and (increasingly after World War II) its apparent scientific neutrality with regard to matters of discrimination and social inequality (in industry, for example), psychology carved out its professional niche and invested its intellectual capital in the service of an explicitly racist–capitalist system. (Painter & Terre Blanche, 2004, p. 524)

Hence the historical development of CP was shaped both by the political pressures around it as well as the disaffection emerging from the academic community. which challenged the uncritical theory, method, and practice of psychology in South Africa (Berger & Lazarus, 1987; Seedat, Duncan & Lazarus, 2001; Seedat, MacKenzie & Stevens, 2004). Prior to South Africa's first democratic elections in 1994, the ready insertion of Euro-American psychology into South Africa was essentially made possible due to the fact that all institutions, including academic institutions, were controlled by whites. The politics of a racist and oppressive political system dictates that the 'superiority' of whites emanates from the 'superior' white races across the globe, especially Europe and America. Ideas and knowledge that flows from these continents are then privileged over all other forms of knowledge. In this context, local knowledge is considered to be of lesser value. Thus, much of the terminology emanating from European and American psychology forms part of the lexicon of South African psychology. In fact, in the 1970s and 1980s, students taking undergraduate psychology classes in most universities in South Africa would be reading out of a textbook written for American students. Thus, the historical base of academic and theoretical psychology and CP resides largely in Europe or North America. It is only in the past two decades that various South African authors have begun to address issues of

---

[2] SOWETO (South Western Townships) was established as a dormitory township to service the city of Johannesburg.

promoting local content and theory in psychology. Similarly, CP was adopted, together with its theoretical and historical foundations, almost exclusively from the United States.

A Brief History of Psychology in South Africa

Prior to the 1990s, the apartheid government had placed various restrictions on blacks wishing to train or study at historically white universities, including requirements that black students should apply for a permit to study at these institutions. This policy was in keeping with the ideological rationale for establishing black institutions, which was to only provide basic forms of tertiary-level training to blacks because most managerial or leadership positions were forcibly occupied by whites and in keeping with the apartheid principles of engineered white supremacy. There could never be a situation where a black person would have managerial oversight over a white person. These restrictions had the effect of creating a large pool of white psychologists (who were also largely urban-based) and a significantly small pool of black psychologists as no similar training facilities existed in the black institutions at the time. While the academic faculty at white institutions was exclusively white, white academics could also be found at black institutions and at some black institutions received special compensation. Ironically, the same historically black institutions created to enforce the apartheid systems' and labor policies became its most vocal and fiercest of critics as these institutions began attracting intellectuals and critical thinkers, gaining momentum especially in the 1980s and 1990s. The institutionalization of apartheid in separate educational facilities meant that black scholars were concentrated at black institutions, with this critical mass further fuelling and energizing the politics of resistance.

In the mid-1980s, apartheid South Africa was facing significant challenges both locally and internationally, and these challenges also began to find their voice in academia, including in psychology. The combined critical voice of psychology and its questioning of the nature of psychological practice and its relevance to the vast majority of South Africans emanated from these black institutions and those universities that were predominately English-speaking (in contrast with universities who were predominately Afrikaans-speaking) (Sigogo et al., 2004). The increase in the challenge to the apartheid government was paralleled by an increase in the dissatisfaction with the discipline and purpose of psychology as a whole. In fact, the professional association representing South African psychology went through a number of iterations before it finally rejected racial classification as a basis for membership when the Psychological Society of South Africa was first formed in 1994 (Duncan, Stevens & Bowman, 2004). The current skewed nature in the representation of previously disadvantaged groups in the profession with regard to its membership profile needs to be understood as a function of the system of apartheid education and institutionalization.

Professionalization of Psychology

Psychology, as a practice, was given statutory recognition as an auxiliary medical service in 1955. This was the first year that psychologists could register under the auspices of the South African Medical and Dental Council (SAMDC). The SAMDC, a professional registration and licensing authority with an overwhelming medical bias, comprised a number of professional boards to regulate the various health professions, with psychology as one such board. The medical emphasis of the registering authority also influenced the development and expectations of psychology and its subspecialties most notable in the dominance of clinical psychology (Henderson, 2004), which grew more rapidly than other registration categories with CP remaining relatively unknown and unheard of until the past decade. (This is not surprising at it was just emerging in the United States and United Kingdom at about this time). Along with the country's democratic political transformation in the mid-1990s, the SAMDC transformed into the Health Professions Council of South Africa (HPCSA) in 1998, in an attempt to give emphasis to a wider grouping of health professions, including psychology. As a statutory body, the HPCSA, the Professional Board for Psychology, regulates the profession through its system of licensing and certification (Louw, 1997). The minimum requirement to qualify as a practicing psychologist registered with the Professional Board of Psychology is an accredited master's degree at a university and a 1-year internship at a board-approved training site. Because of the close relationship between clinical psychology and the medical fraternity, almost all clinical psychology internships are in psychiatric hospitals and units. Given the historical dominance of biomedical care in South Africa and the historical relationship between clinical psychology and biomedicine, both theoretically (e.g., extensive focus on psychopathology and diagnosis) and in practice (within clinical settings, including psychiatric hospitals), the dominance of clinical psychology continues to this day, with over a third of psychologists registered in this category. The only other categories currently registered with the HPCSA are counseling, educational, industrial, and research psychology. The impact of the medical model on psychology as a profession is evident in the focus on providing curative hospital-based services within an individualist framework on a one-on-one basis. This is still the dominant model of the majority of psychological service provision in South Africa today, despite the acknowledgement that psychological services continue to be inaccessible to the vast majority of South Africans (Ratele, 2004; Stevens, 2003). Because CP requires a shift to a more collectivist approach, the development of more decentralized and community-based services currently plays a relatively small role in wider community-based settings.

A number of factors militated against the growth of CP in South Africa (Swartz & Gibson, 2001). Prior to the 1980s, professional practice issues in clinical and industrial or organizational psychology dominated academic discourse. Psychology as a profession and academic discipline functioned a-contextually, ignoring the political context as a defining force in the lives of most South Africans. Further, the majority of psychologists was white, middle class, and predominately trained to work with whites from similar backgrounds. While many white psychologists sought to engage with black clients, mainstream psychology was unable to have any meaningful impact on the lives of most South Africans as it represented the views and values of European or American whites. Further, the enormous chasm between the lives of black and white South Africans and an inability to communicate in an African language on the part of whites severely compromised the level and type of services that could be provided, let alone the possibility of addressing the larger sociopolitical challenges facing South Africa.

During the 1970s and especially during the 1980s, fissures began to emerge between progressive academic psychologists, usually from English-speaking universities, and academic psychologists from Afrikaans-speaking universities. The language classification of universities emerged out of the apartheid government's need to control academic institutions. Progressive academics began to challenge the a-contextual nature of psychology, both through academic writings as well as an activist agenda. With regard to the former, the birth of the 'alternative' journal *Psychology in Society* in 1983 gave voice to sociopolitical issues in psychology. CP was the second most frequent topic addressed in PINS between 1983 and 1993 (Painter & Terre Blanche, 2004).

The discipline of psychology was believed to be in crisis because of its inability to respond to the issues facing ordinary South Africans during the period of civil unrest. This criticism was most commonly expressed in the challenge of establishing the relevance of psychology. The "relevance debate," as it has come to be known, is related both to the content and form of psychology and, consequently, also to the development of CP. The general state of poverty, lack of resources, and various human rights abuses arising as a consequence of apartheid led to the rise of various proposals to more effectively address these issues, especially in the majority black population. One approach was to make various issues such as racism, sexism, and class oppression part of mainstream academic, teaching, and research activities (de la Rey & Ipser, 2004). A call for more direct intervention was argued by some, where psychologists were enjoined to become activists or act in ways that would be empowering of communities (Dawes, 1985; Seedat, 1997, de la Rey & Ipser, 2004). Given the focus on contextual influences on mental health, critical and community psychology came to be viewed by progressive academics and activists as vehicles for transforming psychology theory and practice as they encompassed models of social change.

Emphasis was particularly placed on transforming understandings of mental health, developing contextual understandings of the etiology and determinants of psychosocial and mental health problems, reconfiguring psychologists roles outside of the stereotypical and dominant medical models, and developing models of service delivery that were sensitive to contextual and cultural elements. CP was even considered in relation to psychodynamic ideas in an effort to encourage reflective thinking about the 'lives and concerns of the population as a whole' (Swartz, Gibson & Gelman, 2002, p. 5). These emerging foci were vital to transforming psychology towards a discipline associated with mental health and psychological service delivery in South Africa, in view of the historical racial, gender, and class inequalities and discrimination that had previously characterized it (Foster & Swartz, 1997; Freeman, 1991; Vogelman, Perkel & Strebel, 1992). For example, clinical psychology was deemed to be elitist on the one hand, serving a minority of white middle class individuals in costly one-on-one sessions, and oppressive on the other. Public sector mental health care for the vast majority of black Africans was largely confined to custodial biomedical care for patients diagnosed with serious mental disorders. The envisaged new roles would require that psychologists involve themselves in activities that would include resource mobilization for poor communities, advocacy, training of mental health workers offering social services as part of NGOs, and using networks to help support community initiatives (Berger & Lazarus, 1987; Lazarus & Seedat, 1996; Seedat, Duncan & Lazarus, 2001; Seedat, MacKenzie & Stevens, 2004).

Rise in Activism

In tandem with the increasing confrontation between the apartheid government and the general populace was the rise in activism among particular groups of academics and social activists. The dissatisfaction about the general failure of psychologists, doctors, nurses, social workers, and other social service providers coalesced into the development of a movement to try to address these concerns through social action. It was in 1983 that the first branch of a politically progressive mental health and social service group known as Organisation for Appropriate Social Services in South Africa (OASSSA) emerged (Hayes, 2000). The organization sought to develop more appropriate forms of social service practice in relation to service delivery, the political mobilization of psychologists and other social service workers, and the transformation of mainstream individualistic notions of mental health and illness towards more contextual understandings (Hayes, 2000). The movement readily appropriated central concepts from CP such as empowerment, community organization, and the active participation of communities in finding solutions in pursuit of these ideals. CP provided a theoretical base for engagement in social change activities as well as the development of more appropriate and accessible psychological services for traumatized communities. As an activist movement located largely within academic institutions, OASSSA responded to the needs of traumatized communities, particularly through its work of detainee counseling and training of lay counselors. It is less clear in how well the organization fared at redefining understandings of mental health and illness as well as the terrain of psychological practice

(Hayes, 2000). Nevertheless, at least theoretically, it furthered the development of CP in South Africa by arguing for the development of alternative models of service delivery, particularly through journals such as *Psychology in Society* and which served to reflect on debates that the mainstream and conservative journal *South African Journal of Psychology* tended to ignore. Given the enormous needs of a traumatized society and within the context of limited resources, not much attention was given to prevention and mental health promotion until the dawning of the post-apartheid democracy in 1994. OASSSA's role in arguing for an appropriate and responsive social service was deemed to be redundant in the context of the political changes in 1994. Many of the academics and activists centrally involved in the work of OASSSA began working with the representatives of the newly elected African National Congress (ANC) to help shape that government's desire to bring better social services to the wider society.

Status of CP in South Africa

Despite the changes described earlier in this chapter with regard to the restructuring of the Health Professions Council as a licensing authority, as well the emergence of a new Professional Association of Psychology, CP to date is not a formal category of registration. However, a significant number of tertiary-level training institutions include CP within their curricula and even have community-based training sites and internships. Recognizing the problems attendant on the provision of psychological services in the country, whether in the public or private sector, and the bias to urban-based settings while the needs of rural communities was poorly served, the Minister of Health established a compulsory period of 1 year of community service for clinical psychologists. In effect, an additional year was added to the training of psychologists and mandating that community-based placements be encouraged. The intention is that these periods of service are completed in outlying areas and usually close to hospitals serving rural communities.

However, there are numerous teething problems associated with this model, such as the lack of support for community service psychologists, the lack of equipment, language barriers, and absence of a supervisory structure, including a shortage of supervision from universities and training institutions with most citing resource constraints as a contributor to the inability to support trainees in the community service year. Perhaps of most concern, however, is the lack of clear practice guidelines for community service psychologists to include prevention and promotion activities. While compulsory community service for clinical psychologists may have the desired effect of providing better access to ameliorative psychological services, it is at risk of following a similar route to that of the community mental health movement in the United States in the 1960s where mental health services were made more accessible through the establishment of community mental health centers. The service rendered, however, remained strongly clinical and individually centered and was criticized for being 'old wine in new bottles' (Rappaport, 1977). While the newly established community service requirement runs a similar risk, it clearly acknowledges mental health issues and provides community-based services to rural areas. As such, the new Mental Health Act and the compulsory community service posts in South Africa currently constitutes the single most important development with regard to the practice of CP.

Professional Psychology: Race and Gender

In light of these interesting developments aimed at supporting the decentralization of psychological and psychiatric services and the fact that the critical need for trained black professionals has not abated, various attempts are being made to redress the fact that psychology continues to be dominated by whites. For example, the HPCSA requires that all universities ensure that at least 50% of the intake of students for training as professional psychologists are black. The need for training of black African psychologists is particularly great given that the majority of South Africans' mother tongue is an African language, with psychological interventions being very difficult to do through a translator. Increasingly, sharp gender distinctions have been drawn whereby psychology is constructed as "woman's work" or a "woman's profession" (Richter & Griesel, 1999), further restricting it as a career option, especially among black men. In an attempt to address the need to provide greater access to psychological services, the HPCSA, together with the various universities involved in training professional psychologists, introduced a new practice framework that introduced a middle-level professional category in 1999 called the bachelor of psychology (B. Psych), which is a 4-year degree-based qualification that includes a supervised practicum placement of 6 months. This development aims to introduce service learning components using community-based placements to encourage the transference and wider availability of general mental health care skills. However, without a concomitant development of posts for this category of psychological practitioner within the health and other sectors, there is a risk that this restructuring may, however, merely serve to provide an alternative route to professional registration for private practitioners rather than meeting the demand to increase access to psychological services. The introduction of this new category of psychological practitioner, therefore, runs the risk of reinforcing predominant views of psychology as an individual and clinically focused occupation (Wilson, Richter, Durrheim, Surendorff & Asafo-Agyei, 1999).

Theories of CP in South Africa

In keeping with political changes in South Africa, CP has gone through various theoretical shifts. Seedat (1997) provides a theoretical perspective describing the process that psychologists tended to undergo in the 1980s and

1990s. He argued that because of the disarray in psychology as an academic and professional discipline, many psychologists moved from disillusionment with the state of psychological theory to reactive critical engagement, constructive self-definition, to ultimately engaging in an emancipatory discourse and praxis. Psychologists would accordingly employ theoretical approaches that tended to match their level of engagement with this process. The result was a spectrum of theoretical approaches in the application of community psychology in South Africa, which ranged from 'mainstream' to 'liberatory' approaches.

More 'mainstream' approaches such as that represented by Rappaport's (1977, 1981) work on empowerment in the United States found favor with academics and activists alike. As a sociopolitical instrument, the apartheid system had denuded individuals of dignity and emphasized differences to maintain separation. Rappaport's (1977) early textbook on community psychology as well as later work expanding on empowerment (Rappaport, 1981, 1985) fell on fertile ground as he argued for dignity and the celebration of diversity. Specifically, the focus on rights, given that South Africa was emerging from a culture where the rights of oppressed groups were trampled, and an emphasis on developing a holistic and competency enhancement understanding of individuals helped provide an important alternative to the overly individual medical-centered and pathology bias of clinical psychology. Focusing on strengths rather than deficits had huge appeal both ideologically and theoretically.

Further, a major criticism of clinical psychology was its failure to take account of contexts. In South Africa, context was seen to be an intrinsic part of any meaningful analysis of the social conditions of individuals' lives. Bronfenbrenner's (1979) ecological model, which emphasized the interacting forces at the level of the macro-, meso-, and micro-systems, was widely used to provide critical insights into the way in which apartheid systems impacted on individual lives, but also helped provide critical commentary on how social systems adversely impacted upon the development of young South Africans (Dawes & Donald, 1994).

Similarly, the community mental health model and Caplan's (1964) description of primary, secondary, and tertiary prevention had a significant influence on conceptualizing the delivery of mental health services for post-apartheid South Africa. Rather than the development of community mental health centers, the integration of mental health into primary health care was mooted. The idea was that primary health care facilities would be the first contact that patients would have with the health care system, with these facilities located within communities. Primary health care personnel would be trained in the identification and basic counseling of common mental health problems and referral of treatment-resistant problems to specialist services at the district level, facilitating early detection and treatment of problems. Health care personnel at the primary level would also be responsible for tertiary prevention in the form of follow-up care of more serious mental disorders as well as primary prevention and mental health promotion. Patients requiring longer term in-patient treatment would be referred to specialist hospitals at a regional or provincial level (ANC, 1994; Robertson et al., 1997).

Because of the central position of racism and political oppression in South Africa at the time, many psychologists concerned with more 'liberatory' approaches to community psychology turned to the work emanating from Central America, which had a similar oppressive history. In particular, social-community psychology (Serrano-Garcia, Lopez & Rivera-Medina, 1987) formed a platform for the emergence of critical approaches to community psychology in South Africa. Further, the work of various other academic activists was drawn on, such as that of Bulhan (1985, 1989, 1990), Paulo Freire (1970, 1973), and Frantz Fanon (1968), all of whom referred to political and psychological oppression in their own countries.

CP in Post-apartheid South Africa

Further theoretical shifts are evident in post-apartheid South Africa (the period after the first democratic elections in 1994). With political freedom came an expectation from the general populace, academics and activists alike that the move towards an egalitarian society would help correct the injustices of the past. Thus, a key issue for CP immediately after the country's first democratic elections was a concern with addressing historical disadvantages. In practical terms, CP had to address itself to issues of access, redress, and equity. Significant proportions of South Africans continue to have limited access to resources, largely because of historical imbalances in psychological service provision. Identifying and developing mechanisms for ensuring access to previously denied resources is, thus, an important focus for CP in post-apartheid South Africa, particularly given the trauma experienced as a result of apartheid, poverty, and more recently HIV/AIDS (Petersen, 2005). It is not surprising therefore that CP has recently been criticized for having an ameliorative rather than transformative agenda in post-apartheid South Africa (Painter & Terre Blanche, 2004). The challenge for CP is, however, to redress historical imbalances in the distribution of power and resources, while at the same time retaining a transformative agenda, while not losing sight of the need to help empower communities to act on their own behalf. To this end, a number of training institutions have adopted 'liberatory' and critical theoretical models of CP such as those promoted by Nelson and Prilleltensky (2005).

Further, given widespread poverty as well as the AIDS pandemic in South Africa, which currently affects 11% (5 million) of its population, the need for prevention and health promotion interventions is increasingly gaining importance in post-apartheid South Africa. While mainstream prevention and promotion activities largely adopt individualistic models that focus on strengthening individual resilience, increasing attention is being given to approaches such as community health psychology that help promote social change towards more health-enabling socio-contextual environmental influences (cf. Campbell & Murray, 2004). In many ways, this approach is not unlike that of the Ghanaian approach to CP, namely that individual problems are largely a function of cultural beliefs, systems, and policies in that society (Akotia & Barimah, this volume). A holistic ecological understanding of individuals within their social context is therefore crucial to CP in South Africa and Ghana, even though they may have arrived at this point through different historical influences.

Community health psychology draws heavily on Freire's (1973) concept of conscientization with critical social analysis of social conditions that undermine a group's well-being as the first step in facilitating two processes. The first relates to the renegotiation of collective social identities that may undermine the groups' health towards health-enhancing alternatives. The second relates to empowering the group to engage in collective action for social change that will provide more health enhancing community contexts (Campbell & Murray, 2004).

The most salient criticism of CP in South Africa is that it has not engaged in systematically developing and building a theory of practice that is recognized as being South African. Indeed, even though CP in the United States is "described as largely anglo- and andro-centric scholarship" (Angelique & Culley, this volume), it has refocused its efforts in building theoretical models that specifically attempt to address these issues from a critical feminist standpoint and a return to ecological explanations to champion the cause of social justice. In fairness, this scholarship is only now beginning to emerge where community practice is helping to build theory that has contextual relevance for South Africa.

Despite these theoretical shifts, it is of concern that the integration of indigenous knowledge systems into the training and practice of CP is still marginal. This is despite the extensive network of indigenous healers who are recognized as vital to providing community-based health services through their understanding of cultural practices and beliefs that lead to ill health as well as the fact that indigenous healers are soon to be registered with the HPCSA and will have statutory and legal rights in treating individuals. CP in South Africa has generally eschewed indigenous knowledge systems in understanding and intervening with problems, showing a continued bias towards theories and models emanating from Europe, North America, Latin America, and even Asia. Indigenous knowledge systems in South Africa, particularly among blacks, have relied primarily on its oral tradition. Rapid urbanization and increasing literacy has created new opportunities for debating and understanding the various influences on ordinary people's lives. For example, much has been written about the extent of the orphan problem in sub-Saharan Africa, particularly in view of the number of parents succumbing to the AIDS virus. However, it is becoming apparent that the family systems modeled on Western standards fail to account for the role of multiple caregivers in any one household and that absent fathers are often not experienced as such. The complex relationships between children and their "social" parents have much more importance than their biological caregivers. Yet, even this relationship is beginning to change with urbanization. CP has to understand these complex relationships as it attempts to develop interventions in situations that address issues of risk and resilience for developing children and youth. It is these forms of knowledge that will assist in building a knowledge base that speaks to local contexts and cultures.

Conclusion

It is obvious that South Africa's political history and context has had a significant influence in shaping the development of CP in this country. During the apartheid era, community psychology provided a theoretical base for psychologists concerned with the provision of more appropriate and accessible psychological services to traumatized communities who could not access such services. It also provided a legitimate approach for psychologists to engage in social change activities under the apartheid regime to address sociopolitical factors impinging on the mental well-being of people and communities. These activities largely took place within activist NGO settings. Ironically, unlike the experience in Cameroon (Nsamenang, Fru, & Brown, this volume), which has relied extensively on building upon its indigenous and organizational spirit, CP in South Africa has tended to ignore such influences, focusing more on issues of class and oppression of disadvantaged groups. This perhaps needs to be understood as flowing from the political history of the country.

Post-apartheid, CP has grown as an academic field of study, spanning mainstream to more liberatory critical approaches, depending on the political persuasion of its advocates. It is likely that the academy will continue to promote multiple theoretical voices. Just as CP in South Africa was historically informed by a political context, it is likely that theoretical boundaries will shift to take account of indigenous knowledge systems, especially as more and more black intellectuals enter academia. However, the growth of CP in South Africa as an academic field has not been accompanied by a concomitant growth as a field of practice, even though the introduction of community service psychology posts presents an opportunity for expansion. This is perhaps a reflection of the continued hegemony of biomedical ideology, which still retains center stage and fits well with the political persuasion of the new democratic dispensation that foregrounds individualistic capitalist socioeconomic principles as an important vehicle for social change.

References

African National Congress (ANC) 1994. A National Health Plan for South Africa. Johannesburg: ANC.

Berger, S., & Lazarus, S. (1987). The views of community organisers on the relevance of psychological practice in South Africa. *Psychology in Society, 7*, 6-23.

Bronfenbrenner, U. (1979). *The ecology of human development. Experiments by nature and design.* Cambridge, MA: Harvard University Press.

Bulhan, H.A. (1985). *Frantz Fanon and the psychology of oppression.* New York: Plenum Press.

Bulhan, H.A. (1989). *Family therapy in the urban trenches. Dialectics of oppression and therapy.* Washington, DC: Basic Health Management Publication.

Bulhan, H.A. (1990). Afrocentric psychology: perspective and practice. In L.J. Nicholas & S. Cooper (Eds.), *Psychology and apartheid. Essays on the struggle for psychology and the mind in South Africa* (pp. 66-78). Johannesburg: Madiba Publication.

Caplan, G. (1964). *Principles of preventive psychiatry.* New York: Basic Books.

Campbell, C., & Murray, M. (2004). Community Health Psychology. Promoting analysis and action for social change. *Journal of Health Psychology, 9(2)*, 187-195.

Dawes, A. (1985). Politics and mental health: The position of clinical psychology in South Africa. *South African Journal of Psychology, 23(2)*, 53-58.

Dawes, A., & Donald, D. (1994). *Childhood and adversity: Psychological perspectives from South African research.* Cape Town: David Phillip.

de la Rey, C., & Ipser, J. (2004). The call for relevance: South African democracy ten years into democracy. *South African Journal of Psychology, 34(4)*, 544-552.

Duncan, N., Stevens, G., & Bowman, B. (2004). South African psychology and racism: Historical determinants and future prospects. In D. Hook (Ed.), *Critical psychology* (pp. 360-388). Lansdowne: UCT Press.

Fanon, F. (1968). *The wretched of the earth.* Harmondsworth: Penguin.

Foster, D., & Swartz, S. (1997). Introduction: policy considerations. In D. Foster, M. Freeman, & Y. Pillay (Eds.), *Mental health policy issues in South Africa* (pp. 1-22). Cape Town: Medical Association of South Africa, Multimedia Publications.

Freeman, M. (1991). Mental health for all – moving beyond rhetoric. *South African Journal of Psychology, 21*, 141-147.

Freire, P. (1970). *The pedagogy of the oppressed.* London: Penguin.

Freire, P. (1973). *Education for critical consciousness.* New York: Continuum.

Hayes, G. (2000). The struggle for mental health in South Africa: Psychologists, apartheid and the story of Durban OASSSA. *Journal of Community and Applied Social Psychology, 10*, 327-342.

Henderson, J. (2004). Getting "layed"?: *New professional positions in South African psychology.* Unpublished master's dissertation, Rhodes University, Grahamstown.

Louw, J. (1997). Regulating professional conduct Part I: Codes of ethics of national psychology association in South Africa. *South African Journal of Psychology, 27*, 183-188.

Nelson, G., & Prilleltensky, I. (Eds.). (2005). *Community psychology. In pursuit of liberation and well-being.* New York: Palgrave MacMillan.

Petersen, I. (2005). In search of transformative community practice [Review of the book *Reflective practice. Psychodynamic ideas in the community*]. *Psychology in Society (PINS), 32*, 89-91.

Painter, D., & Terre Blanche, M. (2004). Critical psychology in South Africa: Looking back and looking ahead. *South African Journal of Psychology, 34(4)*, 520-543.

Rappaport, J. (1977). *Community psychology: Values, research and action.* New York: Holt, Rinehart and Winston.

Rappaport, J. (1981). In praise of paradox: A social policy of empowerment over prevention. *American Journal of Community Psychology, 9*, 1-25.

Rappaport, J. (1985). The power of empowerment language. *Social Policy, Fall*, 15-21.

Ratele, K. (2004). About black psychology. In D. Hook (Ed.), *Critical psychology* (pp. 389-414). Lansdowne: UCT Press.

Richter, L.M., & Griesel, R.D. (1999). Women psychologists in South Africa. *Feminism & Psychology, 9*, 134-141.

Robertson, B., Zwi, R., Ensink, K., Malcom, C., Milligan, P., Moutinho, D., Uys, L., Vitas, L., Watson, R., & Wilson, D. (1997). Psychiatric service provision. In D. Foster, M. Freeman and Y. Pillay (Eds.), *Mental Health Policy Issues for South Africa* (pp. 69-93). MASA: Cape Town.

Seedat, M. (1997). The quest for liberatory psychology. *South African Journal of Psychology, 27(4)*, 261-272.

Seedat, M., Duncan, N., & Lazarus, S. (Eds.), (2001). *Community psychology. Theory, method and practice. South African and other perspectives.* Cape Town: Oxford University Press Southern Africa.

Seedat, M., MacKenzie, S., & Stevens, G. (2004). Trends and redress in community psychology during 10 years of democracy (1994-2003): A journal-based perspective. *South African Journal of Psychology, 34(4)*, 595-612.

Serrano-Garcia, I., Lopez, M., & Rivera-Medina, E. (1987). Toward a social-community psychology. *Journal of Community Psychology, 15*, 431-445.

Sigogo, T.N., Hooper, M., Long, C., Lykes, B., Wilson, K. & Zietkiewicz, E. (2004). Chasing Rainbow Notions: Enacting community psychology in the classroom and beyond in post-1994 South Africa. *American Journal of Community Psychology, 33(1-2)*, 77-89.

Stevens, G. (2003). Academic representations of 'race' and racism in psychology: Knowledge production, historical context and dialectics in transitional South Africa. *International Journal of Intercultural Relations, 27(2)*, 189-207.

Swartz, L., & Gibson, K. (2001). The 'old' versus the 'new' in South African community psychology: The quest for appropriate social change. In M.Seedat, S. Lazarus & N. Duncan (Eds.), *Community psychology: Theory, method and practice: South African and other perspectives* (pp. 37-50). Cape Town: Oxford University Press.

Swartz, L., Gibson, K., & Gelman, T. (Eds.). (2002). *Reflective practice. Psychodynamic ideas in the community.* Cape Town: Human Sciences Research Council Publishers.

Vogelman, L., Perkel, A., & Strebel, A. (1992). Psychology and the community: Issues to consider in a changing South Africa. *Psychology Quarterly, 2(2)*, 1-9.

Wilson, M., Richter, L., Durrheim, K., Surendorff, N., & Asafo-Agyei, L. (1999). Employment opportunities for psychology graduates in South Africa: A contemporary analysis. *South African Journal of Psychology, 29*, 184-190.

21
The Roots of Community Psychology in Cameroon

A. Bame Nsamenang, Francis Nkwenti Fru,
and Melissa Asma Browne

Abstract

In Cameroon, community psychology is still a work in progress, albeit a nascent one. Its root is a developmental process that is embedded in African antiquity but recognizable in four phases. First, there is an antiquated sense of community, by which members of the family and community engaged in self-supportive services and collective mutual assistance. Second, although colonialists met widespread community-based values and practices, they put in place a social Darwinian project as Europe's civilizing contribution to 'backward' Africa to replace them. Third, community psychology–related practices such as outreach professional services are embedded in or are maturing out of outreach services in agriculture, health sector, missionary work, and development education. Finally, human services psychology is evolving as an academic discipline for community-based practitioners. Indigenous precepts and strands of relevant psychosocial theories explain this developmental process.

Introduction

In this brief chapter, we endeavour to reconstruct a road map of collaborative or mutual efforts that are inbuilt into Cameroon's indigenous social thought and cultural practices, with the objective of identifying milestones and turning points on the long road to a budding but not yet fully established discipline of community psychology (CP). We are visualizing the future of CP in Cameroon from the nature, history, and lessons from indigenous community-based efforts to satisfy social security needs, sustain agricultural productivity, and other activities—collective efforts that pre-date the professional practice sectors and a slowly maturing profession of community psychology.

In it, we juxtapose an Africentric approach to serving social security needs through indigenous communitarian structures and cultural practices

392

with our conception of CP as an ivory tower professionalism (in need of more status and funding) that inspires outreach community services. As such, whether for good or bad, CP is elitist, indeed social Darwinian, in being advocacy-driven and essentially interventionist, for example, "advocating and promoting social change in disenfranchised communities" (Harper, 2003, p. 37) in the light of the Swampscott Conference. The advocacy factored into the *raison d'être* of community psychology goes beyond efforts at science-based influence of policy; it extends to action that endeavors to change the nature and type of institutions and services in communities perceived as underserved. Thus, CP embraces advocacy that attempts to activate and mobilize people into awareness and involvement in their own well-being, purportedly in new and more sustained ways. It engenders an instinctive devaluation if not dismissal of Africa's rich indigenous cultures and wisdom of her timeless traditions (Callaghan, 1998).

Thus, the nascent field of CP is an intervention in Cameroon, par excellence; because the communitarian spirit or efforts that are indigenous to a community to improve individual and collective destiny existed before the service sectors that manifest elements of community psychology were introduced by the colonial powers. A befitting example is education, about which Fafunwa (1974) pertinently clarifies: To understand the history of education in Africa, adequate knowledge of the indigenous educational systems that existed before the arrival of colonial education from Islamic and Western sources is required. Similarly, antiquated indigenous community processes have survived millennia of official neglect but today coexist usefully with what is budding as elements of CP practices, showing no signs of disappearing (Nsamenang, 2004a). Indigenous community processes differ from those of community psychology in their organizational coherence, ownership, centres of authority, and approach. They serve community needs from a supportive participatory mode while those of CP–like practices in agricultural extension and health care delivery, for example, are paternalistic, expert-driven, and organized from centralized government agencies and those of nongovernmental organizations (NGOs), as discussed later.

Indigenous Sense of Community: The Root of Community Psychology in Cameroon

In global perspective, we visualize CP as a collective community response or mutually supportive action to relieve or 'move' a group or community from an undesirable condition to a more desirable one in its own terms or to "assist others in the joy of turning tales of terror into tales of joy" (Rappaport, 2000, p. 1). The academic dimension of such a 'natural' process is to understand and build the body of knowledge and practices, especially the behavioral and social science (perhaps more appropriately, social justice) theories and principles that frame and undergird its nature and essence. However, the focus of the field today overwhelmingly is on 'quality training' to prepare psychologists to promote, primarily the ways European Enlightenment instigated the 'crafting' of community interventions or community change. There is real difficulty transcending mainstream psychology's primary focus on individual level of analysis. It is for this reason that we identify with Loomis's (2005) view of contemporary CP as an academic discipline and service sector that grew out of psychological science and thrives on advocacy. Loomis (1995) anchors her ecological stance on the person-in-context as one main tenet of CP to perceive a need to distinguish individual analysis, which is closely associated with the Freudian model of psychology, and social level analysis, which is more germane to social psychology and sociology. Integrating the sovereign individuation and ecological nicheness perspectives, that is, conceptualizing the person-in-context in 'social roles' (Levine & Perkins, 1987), satisfies two core values of community psychology: sense of community and empowerment (Loomis, 2001).

Elitist CP–like services conceived and introduced by colonialists and their successors were not in common evidence in Cameroon prior to colonization, as we will explain in this chapter. What is commonplace is communitarian practice, which was and still is an indigenous African precept of values and practices of the 'native soil' involving manipulation of "social relations between individuals and groups to ease the production process" (Nsamenang, 1998, p. 77). One practice of this precept required group members to engage in "a rotational system of self-help collective work by which they all worked on each member's farm until everyone's work was completed" (Nsamenang, 1998, p. 77). This and similar practices gave birth to the rotational system of thrift and loan schemes that characterize life in Cameroonian communities today, offering a more dependable financing outlet to ordinary citizens than the conventional banks.

The rest of this chapter attempts to reconstruct the nature of how such indigenous values and practices contributed to and kept societal development in the hands of the people and the discourse of how it has shifted to experts and elites to become more paternalistic. The polemics began from the moment the paradigm of developmentalism was forced in unwittingly to replace community-based efforts, therein permanently truncating, stunting, or distorting indigenous collective capacity, but not halting it.

In light of the above, what seems to be seeding in Cameroon today as CP is an indigenous sense of community, rooted in an African sense of collective security in mutual supportiveness. In this sense, CP is a new label for a set of ancient African practices in agricultural productivity, village water supply, the construction of bridges and provisioning of services like collective defense and child protection (Gumne, 1983, 2000). Thus, prior to the advent of interventionist paradigms, of which CP in its modern construal is intruding as an exemplar, the indigenous Cameroonian sense of community and associated values and practices were well alive and continue to persist.

A Colonial, Modernist Imprint on Communitarian Efforts

We wish to acknowledge the many positive contributions Eurocentric civilization has made and is offering to Africa. However, in this section, we largely highlight the negative because it is these consequences that mask Africa's realities today. For example, when colonialists experienced communitarian principles and practices everywhere in Africa, they conceived a social engineering project to replace them, ostensibly as Europe's burden to civilize "backward" peoples (Dussel, 1998). They, thus, unleashed social Darwinism unsolicited on Africa.

Modernist commitments and deficit models that were framed on the dismissal of and beliefs in Africa's incapability to manage itself (Nsamenang, 2005) lured colonial experts and successors of the post colony into negations, rejections, and inaccurate perceptions of and assumptions about African knowledge systems and indigenous community processes. Imperial agronomic science, for example, condemned at first sight the unfamiliar African cultivation practices, denigrated African polycropping but forcibly introduced monoculture (single crop farming), which spawned out an explosive population of weeds and pests, whose corrective, a massive application of pesticides and insecticides, was "a cure that turned out to be worse than the disease" (Scott, 1998, p. 280).

The colonizers articulately promoted the theory "that the African was an incompetent farmer, too idle to rotate his crops and conserve soil fertility or, by correct tilling, to prevent soil erosion" (Ford, 1971, p. 6). Armed with such a mindset, colonialists arrogated to themselves the burden to solve Africa's problems by bringing "development" to the Dark Continent. But Richards (1985) laments the ignorance of some of the foreign experts he observed at work in their "civilizing" mission in agricultural modernization. Because they were blinded by Darwinian theorization and civilizing values, if any, they failed to notice any worth in African collaborative ways and supportive spirit. In consequence, they introduced deficit models, which persist today, as Africa in general and Cameroon in particular dips deeper into crisis (Nsamenang, 2005), in spite of decades of development cooperation.

Richards (1985) further highlights how the Western experts who were sent to redeem Africa were more ignorant of how Africans faced the problems they were called upon to tackle than were African owners of the problems. In substantiation, Ford (1971), a leading researcher on the colonial trypanosomiasis program, forthrightly testifies: "We were feebly scratching at the surface of events we hardly knew, and if we achieved anything at all, it was often to exacerbate the ills of the societies we imagined ourselves to be helping" (p. 8). The colonial trypanosomiasis program like almost all others finally "left ... a legacy of ideas that had little relevance to the biological processes with which they had unwittingly interfered" (Ford, 1971, p. 8). Nsamenang (2004b) contends that certain interventions to redeem Africa, like strengthening Africa's productive capacity to produce raw materials for Western industries, are interferences that have left the continent worse off than it would have been had Africa focused on producing crops to feed itself.

Indeed, colonial experts, scientists, and their successors of the post colony overlooked the 'considerable achievements' of the indigenous peoples in overcoming the obstacles of their lives (Ford, 1971). In continuation, today, the UN system, like donors and international advocacy, bypass Africa's indigenous social capital and modes of dealing with its sorry state (Nsamenang, 2005). In fact, it is not unusual in Africa for experts and advocacy to derive policy decisions about what is seen as 'civilized' for 'backward' Africa by 'dead reckoning' and armchair theorization. Such strategies sideline the vast majority of Africans and their communitarian devices, "systems and procedures of which scientists in the 'formal' sectors are often quite unaware" (Richards, 1985, p. 118). Expectedly, "a common criterion applied to educational relevance in much of Africa, for example, "appears to be a 'modernity' index put forth by governments and advocacy rather than the local community" (Nsamenang, 2005, p. 278). There is no doubt that Africa's social thought and practices contain many clues from which experts, governments, donors, and community psychologists might benefit. Unfortunately, like the colonial experts of yesteryear, today's advocacy and budding African psychologists still do not expect 'backward Africans' to work out any relevant solution to their problems nor possess any lessons for them as purveyors of modernity and progress.

Community Psychology: An Important Facet of Social Darwinism

The foregoing paragraphs portray psychology in general and CP in particular as an important intellectual arm of Europe's civilizing mission that helped to illuminate its modernist agenda in Africa. Accordingly, Mignolo (1998) refers to the conspiracy of academic disciplines with colonial powers to reinforce or consolidate the colonial stranglehold on Africa. Moghaddam and Taylor (1985) substantiate that the social sciences, which include CP, are "the most important, systematized set of values and ideas that have been imported to assist the modern sectors of developing societies in achieving conceptual systems compatible with those" (p. 1145) of Europe and its 'occupying' populations in other people's ancestral lands. Similarly, Nsamenang (2005) considers the 2004–2005 British prime minister's initiative to give a fresh impetus to Africa's difficulties with development, like others before it, as proselyting Western models to which Africans should conform. Its focus is "almost exclusively . . . on issues that are more germane to Western social reality than to the harsh realities of life in African communities" (Nsamenang, 1992, p. 192). As such, it loses "sight of the soil out of which the existing [African] society has grown and the human values it has produced" (Wastermann, 2001, p. 34). The initiative cannot help Africa develop on its communitarian terms; its net impact will push Africa further into a more precarious dangling status within the conceptual systems and consumer values and lifestyles of Europe and colonies of Europeans elsewhere around the globe (Nsamenang, 2005).

The Community Development Motif

The interventionism, modernist theory, and the management models of Tony Blair's development initiative for Africa inspire and underlie much of the organizational principles applied in the community development motif in Cameroon and elsewhere in Africa. The *force majeure* of the community development paradigm is a mischievous Western belief that "primitive" Africans cannot work out any "relevant answers to their own problems" (Richards, 1985, p. 14); they must be 'civilized.' This attitude, whose remnants persist to this day, is destructive to indigenous community efforts because it confuses as well as fosters Africa's misunderstanding of itself and distrust of its own capabilities, therein stunting communal initiatives (Creekmore, 1986). It translates virtually into a view of indigenous African systems and practices, even African humanity, as primitive and unworthy of any attention if Africa would catch up with modernity.

The deficit models this attitude incited from the beginning of the slave trade are quite visible in what is now seeding in Cameroon as a Eurocentric community psychology. Because indigenous systems were so novel and entirely unfamiliar, colonialists did not find any of their facets, which could promote their aims and interests. As a result, they, "from an instinctive conservatism" (Richards, 1985, p. 40), compulsively transplanted Eurocentric patterns into Africa. The elitism of modernist community development efforts is evident today in centrally planned projects that are top-down and expert-driven, even with the so-called participatory approaches, imposed by governing elite and advocacy agents on communities by force of regulatory mechanisms couched in motives that reflect more of metropolitan values than stark local realities. African communities do not instinctively identify with such projects, which are few indeed as most stop on the fringes of urban settings and incorporate them as beneficiaries rather than authors and owners of their own responses. This is because, prior to the introduction of such strategies, African communities had known and practiced various forms of indigenous collaborations and supportive efforts, which were built into the fabric of cultural life and productive activities, like communal farming schemes that have been 'upgraded' into modern-day thrift and loan cooperatives mentioned earlier.

Emerging Community Development Training and Practice

In 1960, the UN declared the 1960s the "Development Decade," which was meant to reduce the gap between the rich and the poor nations (Gumne, 1983). Unfortunately, the gap between the two worlds has instead increased in spite of the spirited "civilizing" or development work that has since gone on in Africa. This is because "A theorist's view of development is closely tied to his or her view of human nature, a view intimately tied to his or her conception of how the universe works" (Nsamenang, 1992, p. 210). An African theory of the universe differs from that of the Western world (Serpell, 1994), which contributes the gold standards for developmentalism through CP.

It is common knowledge, from a Western perspective, that development has failed in Africa; a failure that tends to be interpreted as self-inflicted. However, in the history of developmentalism, an African precept can hardly be identified in development thinking, even with participatory efforts or contemporary community development work. Instead, indigenous African thought and praxes tend to be sidelined by national governments and fiercely excluded from policy planning and program development by international advocacy (Nsamenang, 2005), and by induction, local and national experts, and nongovernmental organizations as well as other agents of social Darwinism. As a result, indigenous African systems are best qualified as "informal" or "nonformal," if not primitive, "by those obsessive derogationists whose measuring rod is Eurocentric" standards (Nsamenang, 2005, p. 276).

Nsamenang (2004b) remarks: "Africa might have failed the litmus test of Eurocentric material progress, but it is straight A's in the development of the human spirit. Its core values are in abeyance, waiting to initiate a grand world order with great potential" (p. 25). Africa's hospitable heart and indomitable spirit, exemplified by Nelson Mandela's, are the preservatives for universal humanism, regardless of how they are reviled and exploited, even today in the sports arena and talent drain. Indeed, African humanism transcends the humanistic psychology espoused by Rogers (e.g., 1959) and Maslow (e.g., 1971).

Such a state of the field disempowers, disfranchises, and estranges the vast majority of Africa's peoples. This is because, beginning with the colonial experience in development work or social engineering and continuing today with the import of foreign experts for community development in the face of massive brain drain, this approach takes away ownership for the development and progress of Africa's communities from its peoples and not only transfers it to visiting elites, experts, and donors but simultaneously drains Africa of its most vibrant human capital. These interveners compulsively impose extraverted remedies on Africans and their world that starkly differs from the Western world, which inspires and drives developmentalism, as if Africa were a tabula rasa in community-based efforts.

Traditional community development processes in precolonial Cameroon consisted of activities aimed at evolving a sociocentric identity and meeting such basic societal needs as ensuring food security, providing shelter, constructing roads, protecting the common good, and so forth. But the developmentalism introduced by the colonialists increasingly focused on "things" (Gumne, 2000) and development indices, often with only marginal focus on the collective welfare of the peoples who provide the indices (Nsamenang, 2004b). For example, "development" work from its inception focused almost exclusively on increasing *per capita* income and other economic parameters rather than on the conditions that contribute to the fullness of life and human dignity.

Two Divergent Colonial Bequeaths to Community Development in Cameroon

In Cameroon, national community development planning inherited two colonial legacies of the community development paradigm from the two constituent federated states of West Cameroon, of which Britain was the imperial power, and East Cameroon, with France as its colonial metropolis.

Before the Second World War, the community development motif was introduced into English-speaking Cameroon as adult education and community reorganization, like a scientific production forest. This type of forest illustrates "the dangers of dismembering an exceptionally complex and poorly understood set of relations and processes in order to isolate a single element of instrumental value" (Scott, 1998, p. 21), for instance, given tree species or participatory development. As adult education, community development was placed within the boundaries of Native Authorities (Cameroon, 1981; Gumne, 2000). In the course of time, it was transferred to the Ministry of Interior, then that of Cooperative and Community Development. Adult education centers were systematically created in the emerging urban settings and plantation camps and gradually extended into village communities. At first, *ad hoc* courses for community development agents were organized at Man o' war Bay in Victoria to dispense skills in organizing community initiatives in self-help, acquisition of stamina and physical strength in the sense of military endurance. The colonial strategy ignored communal strategies, indigenous powerbases, and collaborative networks, thereby permanently disrupting the power structure and centres of control in communities. Instead of acknowledging an African presence of communitarianism in collaboration, mutuality, and hospitality, the colonizers emphasized centrally planned cooperation and cooperatives, which they placed under the auspices of Native Authorities, ostensibly to point to imperial acceptance of "native" ways, which was in effect the disorganization or halting of the native spirit.

Domestic science centers were established in Buea, Victoria, Kumba, Mamfe, and Bamenda. Soon adult education appeared to have taken a much more serious tone and cohesive outlook in English-speaking Cameroon than the despised and neglected communitarian efforts of the people. It placed special attention on the illiterate labor concentrations of the plantation camps, which cultivated cheap produce for European industries—and still does today. In 1968, the first professional training course was organized for frontline workers at the newly created Community Development Center in Kumba (Gumne, 2000). A second center for junior staff was opened later in Santa, but senior level community development personnel were/are trained at the Pan-African Institute for Development in Buea for English language Africans and in Douala for French language speakers.

The community development movement was introduced into French-speaking Cameroon as *Animation Rurale* ("Rural Mobilization") in the Ministry of Planning (Cameroon, 1981). The mission of the movement was to carry out village surveys and to promote the reorganization of villages into harmonious communities to stimulate self-help development that reflected the willingness of the rural population to improve their own standards of living not only through government assistance but also through their own personal efforts. It was transferred several times over from ministry to ministry, a process that destabilized the program. The program took off with 100 mobile teams, which were constituted, from agents of *Animation Rurale* and Agriculture, Forestry, and Social Welfare Administration. However, the program was soon aborted because it was plagued by strains and conflicts of interest of the participating sectors. It must be noted that, as in English-speaking Cameroon, the *Animation Rurale* ignored traditional village leaders on whom villagers relied and instead embarked on a training program for selected cadres, who soon lost credibility with the population. In addition, the training centers were scattered and the education of selected leaders was rather scholastic and too generic or universalistic to be meaningful and useful to the villagers. It was slim on the communitarian outlooks and existential realities of the people.

The Cameroon government thus inherited two divergent colonial orientations to community development. An attempt to extend the apparently more serviceable English-speaking model into the French-speaking territory met with stiff resistance, as the French-speaking majority population misinterpreted the motive. The suspicions and conflicts it stirred linger. Decree No. 76/256 of 1 July 1976 (Cameroon, 1981; Gumne, 1983), in principle, brought together the two models into a single national program and placed it in the Ministry of Agriculture. But confusion still reigns and bureaucracy stifles effective community-based work and outreach services, as it is quite elitist and highly centralized; core decision-making is in the government ministry, not in the community.

In the shadow of the 1965 Swampscott Conference, an important seminar on community development and local government was held in Buea in 1966 under the auspices of the United Nations (Cameroon, 1981). It recommended and stressed that:

(a) Communities would be assisted only if they begin self-help projects of their own.
(b) The women's program of the Ministry of Primary Education would be transferred to the Department of Community Development.
(c) The programs and activities of Community Development and *Animation Rurale* would be evaluated with the objective to harmonizing them.
(d) A Cameroonian definition of community development was necessary.

This definition placed emphasis on the social, cultural, and economic facets of community development, with the voluntary involvement of communities in a partnership between the people, the government, nongovernmental agencies, and possibly foreign technical and financial assistance (Gumne, 2000). Although the definition highlighted government commitment to encouraging communities to sustain and intensify their traditions of self-help efforts, framing community development work within a modernist ideology and governing bureaucracy limited and still limits the interventionist's scope to be inclusive of the community as owner and much less its indigenous organizational spirit and collaborative process. This has generated resistance and various levels of failure across communities.

Embeddedness of Community Psychology in the Professional Practice Sectors

Psychology, the intellectual roots of CP, is an inchoate discipline in Cameroon; it is not yet a full-fledge service domain (Nsamenang, 1995). Nevertheless, CP–related processes and practices, as sketched above, which are similar to the mutually supportive indigenous efforts in a community, are evident in the outreach services of some 'modern' sectors, like health, development education, agricultural extension, missionary work, and so forth. They may be regarded as 'received knowledge' and wisdom or social engineering to improve specific domains of or introduce social change into the community life of those who have failed "to develop from the primitive to the civilized" (Masefield, 1972, p. 75).

The pervasive paternalism in donor generosity and helping attitudes toward Africans stems from the perception of the African as "a desperate beggar imprisoned by evolution and incapable of any achievement" (Nsamenang, 2005, p. 282). Although these services are quite useful, they still lack the psychological principles and context-sensitive practitioners who should serve in a full-fledge discipline of CP. It is in this sense that the participatory and collaborative processes and practices of indigenous village communities cannot be regarded as CP, although they engender some of its rudimentary elements, which seminal academic work in Cameroon is beginning to 'structure' into a human services psychology.

Community Psychology: Beginning to Sprout as Human Services Psychology

The Bamenda University of Science and Technology (BUST) was inspired by the community-social psychology program of UMBC (University of Maryland Baltimore County; www.umbc.edu; 2003) to initiate an experiment to evolve a human services psychology (HSP) that is tuned to the Cameroonian context but does not lose sight of state-of-the art trends in the field. The HSP avoids the elitism that characterizes training programs and outgrows the restrictive Freudian model of psychology that focuses on the individual level of analysis to offer a curriculum that trains for critical, multiple, and interactive levels of analysis (Nsamenang, 2003). Accordingly, the main thrust of the HSP program, though its curriculum does not exclude the individual, focuses on community structures, social capital, human services policies and structures, and so forth, and the principles and innovative theorization they engender. It also concentrates on perceptions and the impact of services on the effective functioning of individuals and communities.

The goal of HSP is to produce academic and professional persons with a constructively critical but creative spirit who can guide the healthy development of individuals in their communities and offer solutions to problems in context. In order to render it consistent with our view of CP expressed earlier as an outgrowth from cultural roots, the program acknowledges and weaves together African 'theory' of the universe, stark ecological realities, and familial strengths and social capital into community resources and project patterns and humane productive values. It also endeavors to prepare graduates to cope with Africa's hybrid cultural character and global trends as they confront local imperatives to exacerbate the already precarious state of vulnerable individuals, fragile families, and the contradictions and disempowerment inherent in hybridism.

Conceptual Issues and Theoretical Roots of an Emerging Community Psychology

The theoretical roots of CP, as it is sluggishly emerging in Cameroon, are in an ancient indigenous principle of collective self-reliance and mutual supportiveness or the sense of community (Loomis, 2001) or being 'better together' (Rogoff, Turkanis, & Bartlett, 2001). African social thought promotes the view of 'better together'; if people can do something to help themselves, that is good in itself. Discourse on the processes and events that are shaping the local field and gradually transforming community practices into a discipline (Reiff, 1970, 1971) anchor onto the traditions of ecological and cultural theorizing. In addition, change theory and organizational and ecological models offer some correctives through focusing on group processes and resistance to change as matters of primary concern. Both the organizational and the ecological models draw on systems theories and group process theories to portray the community as the "unit of analysis" (Kelly, Ryan, Altman, & Stelzner, 2000).

However, it is often difficult and sometimes impractical to intervene at multiple levels simultaneously given the complex, context-bound, and hybrid dynamism of Africa's social problems, especially the unfamiliar, un-Western nature of African ways of thinking and acting that now coexist and are almost overwhelmed or distorted by imported versions. Cameroon's, like Africa's, hybridism is "a restive intermingling, like strands in a braid, of Eastern and Western legacies superimposed on a deeply resilient Africanity," a complexity that "has been little contemplated or theorized about. No existing theory fittingly explains it and no antecedent evolutionary template exactly corresponds with its triple-strand braid" (Nsamenang, 2005, p. 276). Thus, Africa's often posited primitivism is a misperception rather than an evolutionary reality. Such reductionism and wrongful niching of Africa in evolutionary history simplifies and misdirects CP practices, thereby exacerbating misunderstanding and failure.

We are positing the impetus to look at Cameroon and other African nations from a different perspective in the field of CP—to come with an abandonment, so to speak, of Western methodologies in exchange for the discovery of new methods, new ways of understanding, new concepts about development and community efforts (Ngaujah, 2003). We are invoking a learning posture or discovery mode, which is about how community psychologists and other interventionists "would do well to perceive of their role as first and always a learner" (Ngaujah, 2003, p. 9).

Psychology thus is challenged to bring to the center of its theorizing, research, and practice the psychosocial experiences and the voices of the peasantry, the bulk of its subject matter. Such a paradigm shift, one that embraces the sociopolitical and cultural changes, is necessary. It can facilitate the inclusion of both indigenous African social thought and knowledge systems, particularly the local knowledge that can only come from practical experience (Scott, 1998). The paradigm shift in general and HSP in particular can serve as a 'liberating project' to "Africanize knowledge systems and various methodologies for the African context" (Lo-oh, 2005, p. 115).

In the HSP program, we are aware that the uniqueness of many African psychosocial phenomena renders Euro-American theories and knowledge systems not entirely suitable for a relevant psychology for Africa (see, e.g., Hook, 2004; Nsamenang, 2000; Peltzer, 1990, 2000; Wexler & Katz, 1989). As a result, we situate the theoretical roots of HSP in the liberatory model or the framework for community praxis. Seedat (1997) broadly defines liberatory psychology as that which respects indigenous knowledge systems and practices, engages critically and constructively with Euro-American theory, and resists the hegemony of dominant institutional power structures. Liberatory psychology is at once radical, political, and critical and empowering, and has as primary aim a creative and innovative motive to develop psychological praxis that is geared towards instigating awareness and priming service that draws on humanistic psychology to acknowledge and accord positive regard and dignity to every human, and that creates and sustains social justice and respect of diversity (see Hook, 2004, for an extended discussion). As a liberatory tool, the central concern of CP ought to be "Whose reality counts" (Chambers, 1997). Every cultural community grapples in its own terms to understand human existence in its multiple dimensions of spirituality, reality, procreation, sense of community, and much more (Nsamenang, 2004b). This fact of culture highlights even masked denial or denigration and devaluation of a people's responsibility for or "initiative and dignity" (Segalowitz, 2003) in "their own development," which is a primordial value in community psychology, as a human rights issue.

References

Callaghan, L. (1998). Building on an African worldview. *Early Childhood Matters*, 89, 30-33.
Cameroon. (1981). *National plan for community development*. Yaounde, Cameroon: Directorate of Community Development.
Chambers, R. (1997). *Whose reality counts: Putting the first last*. London: Intermediate Technology Publications.
Dussel, E. (1998). Beyond Eurocentrism: The world-system and the limits of modernity (pp. 3-31). In F. Jameson & M. Miyoshi (Eds.), *The cultures of globalization*. Durham: Duke University Press.
Fafunwa, B. (1974). A History of Education in Nigeria. London: Allen and Unwin.
Ford, J. (1971). *The role of trypanosomiasis in African ecology*. Oxford: Clarendon Press.
Gumne, N.F.K. (1983). *Education and development in Cameroon, 1960-1962*. Unpublished master of education thesis, University of Manchester.
Gumne, N.F.K. (2000). A review of non-formal education practices in Cameroon. In T.M. Ndongko and I.L. Tambo (Eds.), *Educational development in Cameroon 1961-1999: Issues and perspectives* (pp. 205-219). Platteville, Wisconsin: Nkemnji Global Tech.
Harper, G.W. (2003). Reclaiming the dream: Training and social change in Latino/a communities. *The Community Psychologist,* 36(1), 36-40.
Hook, D. (Ed.). (2004). *Introduction to critical psychology*. Cape Town, South Africa: The University of Cape Town Press.
Kelly, J.G., Ryan, A.M., Altman, B.E., & Stelzner, S.P. (2000). Understanding and changing social systems. In J. Rappaport & E. Seidman (Eds.), *Handbook of community psychology* (pp. 133–159). New York: Kluwer.
Kishani, B.T. (2001). On the interface of philosophy and language in Africa: Some practical and theoretical issues. *African Studies Review*, 44(3), 27-45.
Levine, M. & Perkins, D.V. (1987). *Social roles. Principles of community psychology: Perspectives and applications* (pp. 113-123). New York: Oxford University Press.
Loomis, C. (1995). *Community psychology practiced through research*. Second Thought Paper, UMBC Community-Social Psychology Graduate Program.
Loomis, C. (2001). *Psychological sense of community and participation in an urban university: Prediction, trends, and multiple communities*. Ph.D. thesis, University of Maryland at Baltimore County, MD, USA.

Loomis, C. (2005, June 6). Scientific endeavour and ideological advocacy in Canadian and U.S. community psychology. Abstract submitted for the Symposium "Culture and Cognitive Development: Scientific Endeavor or Ideological Advocacy?" at the 26th International Congress of Applied Psychology. Athens, Greece.

Lo-oh, J.L. (2005). An Emerging Africentric Thought and Praxis. Review of 2004 A.B. Nsamenang, The Teaching Learning Transaction: An Africentric Approach to Educational Psychology. Bamenda, Cameroon: HDRC Publication. *Journal of Psychology in Africa*, 15(1), 115-116.

Masefield, G.B. (1972). *A history of the colonial agricultural service*. Oxford: Clarendon Press.

Maslow, A. (1971). *The farther reaches of human nature*. New York: Viking Press.

Mignolo, W.D. (1998). Globalization, civilization processes, and the relocation of language and cultures (32-53). In F. Jameson & M. Miyoshi (Eds.), *The cultures of globalization*. Durham: Duke University Press.

Mogdaddam, F.M. & Taylor, D.M. (1985). Psychology in the developing world: An evaluation through the concepts of "dual perception" and "parallel growth." *American Psychologist*, 40, 1144-1146.

Ngaujah, D.E. (2003). *An Ecocultural and social paradigm for understanding human development: A West African context*. Graduate Seminar Paper, Biola University, CA.

Nsamenang, A.B. (1992). *Human development in cultural context: A Third World perspective*. Newbury Park, CA: Sage Publications.

Nsamenang, A.B. (1995). Factors influencing the development of psychology in Sub-Saharan Africa. *International Journal of Psychology*, 30(6), 729-739.

Nsamenang, A.B. (1998). Work organization and economic management in Sub-Saharan Africa: From a Eurocentric orientation toward an Afrocentric perspective. *Psychology and Developing Societies*, 10(1), 75-97.

Nsamenang, A.B. (2000). Critical psychology: A sub-Saharan African voice from Cameroon. In Tod Sloan (Ed.), *Voices for critical psychology* (pp. 91-102). London: Macmillan.

Nsamenang, A.B. (2003, October). *The Human Services Psychology (HSP) Program at BUST*. Bamenda: BUST.

Nsamenang, A.B. (2004a). *The teaching-learning transaction: An Africentric approach to educational psychology*. Bamenda, Cameroon: HDRC Publication.

Nsamenang, A.B. (2004b). *Cultures of human development and education: Challenge to growing up African*. New York: Nova Science.

Nsamenang, A.B. (2005). Educational Development and Knowledge Flow: Local and global forces in human development in Africa. *Higher Education Policy*, 18, 275-288.

Peltzer, Karl. (2000). Psychotherapy in South Africa. *Journal of Psychology in Africa; South of the Sahara, the Caribbean & Afro-Latin America. Working Group for African Psychology, Nigeria* 10(2), 171-188.

Peltzer, K. (1990). Psychotherapy and psychoanalysis in Africa. In. S. Madu, P.K. Baguma, et al. (Eds.), *Cross-cultural dialogue on psychotherapy in Africa* (pp. 10-22). Sovenga, South Africa: UNIN Press.

Rappaport, J. (1987). Terms of empowerment/exemplars of prevention: Toward a theory of community psychology. *America Journal of Community Psychology*, 15, 121-144.

Rappaport, J. (2000). Community narratives: Tales of terror and joy. *American Journal of Community Psychology*, 28(1), 1-24.

Reiff, R.R. (1971). Community psychology in public policy. In J.C. Glidewell & G. Rosenblum (Eds.), *Issues in community psychology and preventive mental health* (pp. 33-54). New York: Behavioral Publications.

Reiff, R.R. (1970). Psychology and public policy. *Professional Psychology: Research & Practice,* 1(4), 315-330.

Richards, P. (1985). *Indigenous agricultural revolution: Ecology and food production in West Africa.* London: Hutchinson.

Rogers, C.R. (1959). A theory of therapy, personality and interpersonal relationships, as developed in the client-centered framework. In S. Koch (Ed.), *Psychology: A study of science* (pp. 184-256). New York: McGraw-Hill.

Rogoff, B., Turkanis, G.C. & Bartlett, L. (2001). *Learning together.* Oxford: Oxford University Press.

Scott, J.C. (1998). *Seeing like the state: How certain schemes to improve the human condition have failed.* New Haven: Yale University Press.

Seedat, M. (1997). The quest for liberatory psychology. *South African Journal of Psychology,* 27(4), 261-270.

Segalowitz, S.J. (2003). The concept of constructivism in developmental psychology and neuroscience. *ISSBD Newsletter*, 27(43), 2-4.

Serpell, R. (1994). An African social ontogeny: Review of A. Bame Nsamenang (1992): Human development in cultural context. *Cross-Cultural Psychology Bulletin,* 28(1), 17-21.

Wexler, A. & Katz, R. (1989). Healing and transformation: Lessons from indigenous people. In K. Peltzer and P.O. Ebigbo (Eds), *Clinical psychology in Africa (South of the Sahara, the Caribbean and Afro - Latin America).* Enugu, Nigeria: Chuka Printing Co.

22
History of Community Psychology in Ghana

Charity S. Akotia and Kofi B. Barimah

Abstract

This chapter traces the emergence and practice of community psychology in Ghana. We begin with a discussion of the early stages of the development of community psychology in the country. Having been foreshadowed by the activities of nongovernmental organizations (NGOs), community psychologists mainly use the classroom as a catalyst for promoting the values and principles of the field. The classroom is also used for sensitizing individuals about this field of psychology. The chapter also highlights the fertile psycho-social background that makes the acceptance of community psychology a natural fit in Ghana. We also discuss the challenges in the development and practice of community psychology as a formal discipline in one of the country's universities and conclude with optimism that the field has a promising future in Ghana.

Introduction

Community psychology (CP) is a field within psychology that is still developing and defining itself. According to Nelson and Prilleltensky (2005), "community psychology has been in the past different from what it is now and . . . that the field continues to change" (p. 4). In this paper, we will adopt the definition of CP given by Dalton, Elias, and Wandersman (2001), which states that "community psychology concerns the relationships of the individual to communities and society. Through collaborative research and action, community psychologists seek to understand and to enhance quality of life for individuals, communities and society" (p. 5). It is noteworthy, argued Dalton et al. (2001), that individuals in communities are understood in terms of their relationships rather than in isolation. This implies that there is some kind of connection between individuals and their environments that has an effect on the lives of individuals.

In this paper, two pioneers (current authors) of the development and practice of CP in Ghana provide a short history focused on CP's early stages of development and practice, the use of the classroom as a catalyst for development and practice, as well as some challenges and future prospects for community psychological practice in Ghana.

The Early Stages of CP in Ghana

CP as an academic discipline is not very familiar among Ghanaians. One reason for this perhaps is the fact that even to date, many of the most recent introductory to psychology textbooks do not mention CP when discussing the applied fields of psychology. However, when we look at CP in terms of the definition given above, and also as research and action for social change, which is focused on prevention, reduction of oppression, and the promotion of individual and societal well-being, we could perhaps say that the field is foreshadowed by the work of nongovernmental organizations (NGOs) in the country. Thus, in Ghana, many people and organizations may have been practicing some principles of CP without necessarily referring to them as CP.

NGOs have emerged from the vacuum in economic and social welfare provision left by shrinking government services in the wake of the country's economic decline and the sociopolitical crises of the 1970s and 1980s (Denkabe, 1994; Katsriku, 1997). The 1970s and 1980s also saw rapid social change due to industrialization and urbanization, which brought about many social consequences such as a breakdown of the extended family system, which used to be the anchor of society (Danquah, 1982). This change significantly increased social stress and unrest in the country, thus creating an urgent need for prevention in the field of mental health. According to Denkabe (1994), NGOs have found a firm foothold in Ghana as a result of their focus on poor, marginalized communities. Their activities have mainly centered on advocacy, empowerment, self-help projects, poverty reduction, health, capacity building, environmental degradation, and research with a bias toward the rural areas (Katsriku, 1997). NGOs thus work directly with individuals within communities and attempt to improve their quality of life. Prior to the activities of NGOs, however, some sectors of the government such as health and community development may have been practicing the principles and ideals of CP.

Though CP has been foreshadowed by the activities of NGOs in Ghana, it is only now beginning to emerge as a formal discipline in the country's universities. Prior to the early part of the 1990s, when a few students from Ghana gained admission to pursue a master's program in CP at Wilfrid Laurier University in Waterloo, Ontario, Canada, the field was not well-known among many Ghanaian psychologists. It was during this period that the authors of this chapter were trained in the field. The principal author graduated in 1992 while the second author graduated in 1993.

Several factors motivated us to pursue CP in Canada. Prominent among these was the realization that too many psycho-social problems abound in our communities and the consideration that we would never have enough mental health and NGO personnel to handle these problems. Secondly, the NGOs also seemed to focus on some specific areas such as poverty reduction, empowerment, self-help developmental projects, and so forth. It thus appeared that not much attention, for example, was being given to prevention. It was against this background that we developed an interest in pursuing a master's program in CP in Canada with the goal of returning to Ghana after completion and establishing CP and its principles in Ghanaian institutions. It was also considered that knowledge gained during our graduate years could be imparted to others and together we could make an impact on society as a whole. Since our graduation, a number of Ghanaian students have pursued postgraduate degrees in CP, both in the United States and in Canada. Wilfrid Laurier University, Ontario, Canada, for instance, has trained and continues to train Ghanaian community psychologists.

The Use of the Classroom as a Catalyst for the Development of CP

The principal author returned to the country to join the faculty at the Department of Psychology, University of Ghana, in September 1992. Upon her return and with the knowledge that not many individuals were acquainted with the values and principles of CP, and more importantly, knowing how valuable and relevant the principles are to our communities, she considered it important and a necessary first step to use the classroom as a base for consciousness raising and social change The main idea was to use the classroom to provide information that people do not have about CP so they could start sensitizing themselves and others about the field. Berger (1987) has extensively discussed the use of the classroom as a foundation of social intervention and change. According to him, "teachers and students appear to have a lot of time available for social change work. Many other potential bases seem to have much less social change time" (p. 35). University professors are also able to (overtly or covertly) negotiate for more time to engage in social intervention. Thus, the importance of the emergence of formal CP in Ghana in the university setting can therefore not be overemphasized.

The Practice of CP in Ghana

Touched by the many problems (such as poverty, HIV/AIDS epidemic, homelessness, unemployment, and so forth) in the country that could not be directly addressed by the central government, the principal author considered it imperative to introduce CP in the syllabus of the Department of Psychology. In 1996, with the support of some community psychologists in Canada, a course in CP successfully took off. This was the first ever CP class offered in the country. It is noteworthy that the theories and values espoused by CP in the United States and Canada are already a natural fit in the Ghanaian society. Indeed, many of these theories and values appear to be consistent with Ghanaian traditional values (see Opoku, 1978; Sarpong, 1974), For instance, the extended family system, coupled with communal living practiced among Ghanaians, has to a very large extent shaped the practice and understanding of CP in Ghana. Traditionally, the extended family system and other social networks serve as a cushion for individuals within communities. According to Roberts (2001), a typical Ghanaian considers ill-health and health to be a shared responsibility as opposed to being an individual affair. This makes the understanding of social problems and the use of ecological approach in preventing and solving problems a lot easier for those who deliver services. Thus, to understand a problem or illness in a traditional Ghanaian context, one needs to look beyond the individual and search for possible causes and explanations from significant others. Indigenous knowledge has therefore largely influenced the development and practice of CP in Ghana. Generally, Ghanaian traditional values also prescribe collectivism and social support for each other. It is not uncommon to overhear a Ghanaian saying "we are each other's keeper," which traditionally is very much encouraged in our societies. Every individual in the community has the social responsibility for the other person. The aged for instance are the responsibility of the whole community. Family members and others are expected to cater to their needs. The collectivist worldview is captured in the statement "I am because we are" (Naidoo, Olowu, Gilbert & Akotia, 1999). In doing this, social support and sense of community are provided to community members.

Similarly, prevention is another value espoused by CP that also seems a natural fit in a typical Ghanaian society. Ghana, just as many other developing countries, has very challenging social conditions. Many people live in poverty. Additionally, there are many diseases that abound in the country and yet resources and manpower are in acute shortage (Akotia, 2005). Though Ghana, as part of its poverty reduction strategy, is now introducing a National Health Scheme, this project is yet to start in many districts in the country. This makes it difficult especially for those in low-income groups to access health services. Thus, the health needs of many Ghanaians cannot be met. Prevention and health promotion interventions are therefore very much needed in our communities. Generally, community-wide approaches to solving problems espoused by CP, by and large, would be of much benefit to Ghanaian societies.

Another CP principle that fits the Ghanaian context is the issue of empowerment. We believe this value is also a good fit in our communities. We say this because in Ghana, just as in many developing countries, there are many people who are struggling for basic necessities of life. Women, particularly those from rural Ghana, form the majority of those in the poverty bracket.

This may be due to our cultural values and beliefs where various cultural practices combine to ensure that allocation of resources favour males, thereby worsening the vulnerable situation of the majority of women in Ghana (The Country Women in Development [WID] Profile, 1999). How then do we get women out of this situation? Empowering them to take control of their lives, through more access to economic services, reallocation of resources, and improvement in knowledge and technology, more generally, would go a long way to benefit both women and the nation as a whole (The WID Project, 1999).

While overall the U.S./Canada version of CP has been a surprisingly good fit in Ghana, there are some unique features based on the peculiar sociopolitical and cultural context. Unlike CP in the United States and Canada, which is largely pragmatic, CP in Ghana is more theoretical, using value-based principles that strive to improve quality of life. Perhaps, one reason for this difference is that unlike the United States and Canada, there are few community psychologists to do outreach and community work in Ghana. Because community psychologists are few, not much can be achieved in a pragmatic way as they have to concentrate on the little contribution they can make in the classroom. Additionally, there appears to be stronger social policies in the United States and Canada in terms of community development and social change compared with Ghana. This has implications for CP in Ghana: community psychologists would have to do a lot more education, advocacy, prevention, and health promotion in order to bring about social change. Consequently, we have accepted the challenge to work with social workers, politicians, NGOs, and other stakeholders for the promotion and implementation of appropriate social welfare policies.

With regard to theoretical orientation, what best suits the Ghanaian context is a holistic approach, ecological in nature, to improving the lives of individuals within communities. It is believed that individuals face problems not because of their personality but largely because of the cultural beliefs, systems, and policies that are put in place in our society. Understanding individuals within their social context is therefore crucial in Ghana for any effective intervention.

As community psychologists, we continue to use research and teaching to bring about change in the lives of community members. For example, the principal author's research work focuses on prevention issues (e.g., suicide prevention and HIV/AIDS). The second author also continues to apply the concept of empowerment (see Barimah & Nelson, 1994) to health as outlined by the World Health Organization (WHO). According to WHO (1978), for any person to achieve his or her fullest health potential, he or she should have absolute control over matters pertaining to his or her health. Thus, our capacity to control our health becomes ineffective when we cannot bring basic resources such as food, shelter, personal relationships, and conditions under control (Watt & Rodnell, 1988).

Some Challenges of CP Practice in Ghana

Even though there are more than 10 public and private universities in the country, CP has only been formalized as a final year undergraduate course in the Department of Psychology at the University of Ghana, in consultation with some faculty members at Wilfrid Laurier University, Ontario, Canada. The Department of Psychology at the University of Ghana has generally been very traditional with regards to ideals, orientation, and epistemology in psychology (Brookins, Bryant, Akotia, Watts, Emshoff & Moleko, 2003). Training in psychology in Ghana has therefore been strictly taught according to basic psychological frameworks and the scientific rigors that go with them. The initiation of CP, a field that holds the belief that knowledge is pluralistic (Dalton, Elias & Wandersman, 2001), was a challenge to incorporate into the department. With this kind of background and the bureaucracy that exists in the university as a whole, it was a challenge to introduce the course. Training is generally geared toward equipping students with the necessary skills that can be used to deal with problems in the communities. There is, however, no degree in CP as it is still taught as a single course in one semester. A point worthy of note is that students of CP, upon completion of their undergraduate program, usually work under different labels such as social workers, community development officers, project officers, and coordinators for NGOs. Some of these students have also proceeded to graduate schools in Western universities.

At the Catholic University College where the second author teaches, no formal CP program exists. Yet, he is able to teach social analysis with the focus on social problems and intervention. The basis for social change envisioned by the program is the use of the "small wins" concept (Weick, 1984). Thus, social intervention in Ghana is based on multifaceted cultural beliefs and values, many of which serve as "blocks" to any effective social change. By implication, social interventionists would have to attempt change in "small wins" to try and educate individuals within the community on those beliefs that negatively impact on development and change.

Future Prospects of CP in Ghana

Despite the long history and tradition of action research, preventive efforts, and promotion of mental health in our local communities, CP is still not professionalized in Ghana. For example, there are no professional bodies at the moment and also no journals can be credited to CP in Ghana. It is noteworthy, however, that mainstream psychology itself has only recently been professionalized. The Ghana Psychological Association is only about 6 years old (formed in 2001, after many years of effort). It is, therefore, not surprising that CP has not yet been professionalized in Ghana.

Even though CP is still largely an underdeveloped area of applied psychology in Ghana, it has a bright and promising future. Conditions in the country today are particularly ready for the acceptance of CP. Psychosocial problems abound and yet the government is not able to deal with them effectively. Little attention has been given to mental health issues in the country. This makes prevention, for example, an applicable and relevant principle in our communities (Akotia, 2005). It is believed that in due time, CP will be widely accepted, and many more programs will be established in various universities throughout the country. With the likelihood of new programs and trained community psychologists, we are optimistic about a move towards professionalization of the field in Ghana.

We will conclude by stating that though the development of CP seems to be slow, it has prospects for a bright future in nation building and development in Ghana.

References

Akotia, C. S. (2005). Values and principles of community psychology: Views from Ghana. In G. Nelson & I. Prilleltensky (Eds.), *Community psychology: In pursuit of liberation and well-being*. London: Palgrave Macmillan. pp. 20-22.

Brookins, C. C., Bryant, D., Akotia, C. S., Watts, R., Emshoff, E., & Moleko, A. (June, 2003). International Research Collaboration in Africa: Symposium presented at the 9th Biennial Conference for Community Research and Action. Las Vegas, Nevada.

Barimah, K. B., & Nelson, G. (1994). Empowerment in a supplementary food program in rural Ghana. *International Quarterly of Community Health Education, 14(2)*, 173-190.

Berger, S. D. (1987). Higher education as a base for social intervention: A comparative analysis. In E. M. Bennett (Ed.), *Social intervention: Theory and practice*. New York: The Edwin Mellen Press, pp. 31-55.

Dalton, J. H., Elias, M. J., & Wandersman, A. (2001). *Community psychology: Linking individuals and communities*. Stanford: Thomson Learning.

Danquah, S. A. (1982). The practice of behavior therapy in West Africa: The case of Ghana. *Journal of Behavior Therapy and Experimental Psychiatry, 13*, 5-13.

Denkabe, A. (1994). An overview of the non-governmental sector in Ghana. In F. K. Drah & S. M. Oquaye (Eds.), *Civil society in Ghana*. Accra: Friedrich Ebert Foundation.

Katsriku, B. (1997). The growth of NGOS in Ghana. *NGO Forum, 2(2)*, p. 2.

Naidoo, J. C., Olowu, A., Gilbert, A., & Akotia, C. (1999). Challenging Euro-centered psychology: The voices of African psychologists. In W. J. Lonner, D. L. Dinnel, D. K. Forgays, & S. A. Hayes, (Eds.), *Merging past, present, and future in cross-cultural psychology*. Lisse: Swets & Zeitlinger. pp. 124-134.

Nelson, G., & Prilleltensky, I. (2005). *Community psychology: In pursuit of liberation and well-being*. London: Palgrave Macmillan.

Opoku, A. K. (1978). *West African traditional religion*. Awka: Kucena Damian (Nig) Ltd.

Roberts, H. (2001). A report on mental health in Ghana. Unpublished report.

Sarpong, P. (1974). *Ghana in retrospect*. Tema: Ghana Publishing Corporation.

The Women in Development Project (WID). (1999). An unpublished report. Japan International Cooperation Agency. pp. 3-4.

Watt, A., & Rodnell, S. (1988). Community involvement in health promotion: Progress or panacea? *Health Promotion, 2*, 4-11.

Weick, K. L. (1984). Small wins: Redefining the scale of social problems, *American Psychologist, 39(1)*, 40-49.

WHO. (1978). Primary Health Care: Report of the international conference on primary health care. Alma Ata. Geneva: WHO.

Conclusion: History and Theories of Community Psychology Around the Globe

STEPHANIE M. REICH, MANUEL RIEMER, ISAAC PRILLELTENSKY, AND MARITZA MONTERO

While the task of trying to summarize the content of this book is a daunting one, we would be remiss to pass up the opportunity to reflect on the global themes, commonalities, and uniqueness of the history and development of community psychology (CP) in each of these countries. We would also lose the chance to reflect on our own process of editing this book and ways in which our privilege and power affected the final product. Thus, it is with the acknowledgment that we will not do the chapters justice that we embark on the task of writing a conclusion chapter.

Why Summarize?

After reading a text in which each chapter provided a brief conclusion, one may wonder why we included a conclusion chapter. Our reasons are manifold. First, one of our goals in editing this book was to open up a discourse about the prevalence and complexity of community psychology as well as dispel some of the ethnocentrism of its presentation in the West. Secondly, we would like to draw attention to elements that we found common across many of the chapters we edited that may indicate potential universalities of the field, necessities for development, and strong influences. Third, some countries had very unique experiences in their histories and practice of CP which we would like to highlight. Lastly, we hope that drawing attention to some elements of the chapters will entice those with little time to read to go back to chapters they may have overlooked.

Before trying to summarize this volume, we would like to acknowledge that we will not be able to do this task justice. We will not discuss all of the commonalities and differences that have been described in the chapters nor will we be able to cover those similarities and differences that we identify here to the extent that they deserve. The text is too rich and the space for this chapter is too short. Furthermore, this is just one way to compare and summarize these chapters, and you may not agree with our synthesis. We hope that this facilitates deeper thought into the history and development of CP and encourages further discussion on the topic. Thus, this chapter will highlight some elements of the book, draw attention to topics we expected to see more written about, identify some remaining questions, and suggest some future directions for the field, internationally.

Power in Editing

As part of the process of reflecting and concluding, we would like to acknowledge the power issues at play during this editing process. Throughout this project, we had complete power as to which countries were included, how much space each country was given, and the ability to request revisions before considering a chapter finished. While our goal was to provide a history through the eyes of people within their own country, we inevitably shaped the way the story was told. In many cases, we requested that chapters be trimmed down when they exceeded space limitation. This resulted in some information being excluded. In some instances, we requested elaborations from contributors. Thus, we facilitated the inclusion of information that may not have been presented otherwise. In one of the integrative conclusions at the end of a chapter, we found a critique to be somewhat disparaging of another contributor's work. We gave the authors of this comment the option to either delete the critique or provide space at the end of their chapter for a response from the recipient authors of the comment. The authors opted to delete the comment. Clearly, the process of editing inevitably holds immense power over the project. While we tried to be cognizant of this issue, we still maintained our power in the editing process. This privilege continues through this conclusion chapter, in which we have the final word. Our reflections here are not *the* final conclusions of the book, but simply the perspectives of four editors engaged in this process. These reflections are clearly colored by our cultural experiences and position in this project. Still, we hope they provide food for thought or at least an entry point for thinking about the myriad experiences present in this text.

Difficulties Translating CP

According to Tolan and colleagues (1990), the construction of knowledge in community psychology is best seen as a *conversation*. However, while developing a common language within a country is already a difficult endeavor, it becomes even more of a challenge when the conversation becomes international. This becomes apparent in the difficulty by several countries in translating the term *community psychology* and applying it in their country. While psychology seems to be a more or less universal term, translators struggle with the term *community*. In several countries, there is no direct translation for this word. Words that are related in the native language often have

a slightly different meaning, often more narrow in scope than English definition of the term *community*. In Japan, for example, the word *chi'iki shakai* is
limited to communities based on geographical area. In Norway, there is either
a word that would describe a local community in a geographical sense or one
that describes the society as a whole but none that would fit the English
meaning of the word *community* appropriately. The translation of community used in Germany, *gemeinde*, is mainly understood as referring to a
parish. Similarly, in Turkey the native word that best fits with the term
community is *cemaat*, which is associated with religious communities. Other
Turkish words are either too laden with political associations or too limiting
in their meaning, making it linguistically difficult to refer to a field of CP.

The absence of a native term that resembles the Anglo-American meaning
of community in these countries is interesting and important to consider when
reading and comparing the chapters in this book. First, to enable an exchange
among community psychologists from different countries and to make the
book readable to as many people around the globe as possible, we asked our
authors to write their chapters in the English language. In the process of translating there may be important cultural nuances lost or certain meanings
slightly altered. But, even in English-speaking countries, the term *community*
may have different local meanings. That is why it is important to pay attention
to the local context and history in understanding CP in these different countries and to not be misled by the fact that most authors use the same label.

CP Predating Swampscott

It is also important to note that while the term *community psychology*
appeared first in the context of the Swampscott conference in the United
States, many of the authors describe community practice and the development of community theory in their country long before this conference. The
New Zealand/Aotearoan scholar Beaglehole, for example, called for the
scientific study of "personality-in-culture" in his book, *Mental Health in New
Zealand*, 15 years prior to Swampscott. According to the authors of the
New Zealand/Aotearoa chapter, if the language were updated, this book
could easily pass as a contemporary manifesto for CP. But, even before this,
the Māori of Aotearoa had an elaborated understanding of the interrelatedness of people and their natural environment. Likewise, the authors of the
Cameroon chapter describe a communitarian practice that is deeply rooted in
the African traditions of the production process. Similarly, Marie Jahoda's
work as community activist in Austria and later in Scotland is another example of CP-like work predating Swampscott. The examples from the book are
too numerous to list here, but clearly, the Swampscott conference was not the
birthplace of CP. Rather it was a place where the name was formalized.
Perhaps this conference should be referred to as the baptism (or any other
form of name giving ceremony) of CP.

Definitions

When one compares the definitions of CP that each group of authors provided, it becomes clear that the there is a common ground and a common understanding of what the field of CP entails. Most authors agree with Dalton, Elias, and Wandersman (2001) that CP "concerns the relationships of the individual to communities and society. Through collaborative research and action, community psychologists seek to understand and to enhance quality of life for individuals, community, and society" (p. 5). Several authors expand on this basic definition especially with regard to the purpose of CP, the context in which it operates, the people that CP is working with and for, and the critical and political impetus for its existence. In Latin America, for example, the authors stress the importance of taking into account the historic, cultural, and social context of community. In this definition, they include the importance of social change and stakeholder participation in the process of redistributing power. This perspective is shared with the British authors who see CP "as a framework for working with those marginalised by the social system that leads to self-aware change with an emphasis on value-based, participatory work and the forging of alliances." The Indian authors emphasize the importance of understanding the needs of the people in the community and the resources available to meet those needs; while the Norwegian authors highlight the applied aspect of CP as well as its conceptual roots in ecological theory.

In deciding what to include as CP, many authors consider practices that are seen as CP such as prevention and community-based intervention. Multiple authors also refer to values such as social justice, equality, empowerment, and valuing diversity when defining CP. Some authors include a more direct call for actions toward transformative change in their definition, which is more radical than the wording used by Dalton and his colleagues. The Norwegian authors, for example, state in their definition that CP has "an ethical obligation to fight against macro arrangements that foster human indignity and injustice." Working from these rich definitions, the chapters took a variety of approaches for describing how CP has and is developing in their country and/or region. These approaches varied in their starting points, topics covered, and conclusions about the field of CP.

Starting Points

We found it quite interesting where each chapter decided to start their story of CP. For some, the history began with a description of the geographical region and cultural diversity (e.g., Canada, Latin America). This geographical description sometimes included an account of the political system (e.g., Norway), economic activity (e.g., Argentina/Uruguay), and oppressive history (e.g., New Zealand/Aotearoa). For some countries, a description of the political environment was a useful starting point with some describing political practices that hindered the development of social action (e.g., Hong Kong, Poland), especially those that were oppressive (e.g., Portugal, South Africa), and others noting how the political climate motivated awareness of social justice (e.g., Italy, Germany). Some chapters began with the current state of CP in their country (e.g., Australia, Japan) while others focused on the current lack of formalized CP (Great Britain, Ghana, Greece, Israel). The United States chapter gave a timeline of events while the Indian chapter focused on the development of psychology and community mental health. The Turkish chapter started off with a personal experience of being a community psychologist in Turkey while others identified theoretical contributions (intellectual thought, Spain; and indigenous theories, Cameroon). Each starting place grounded the discussion of history in a context: be it political, personal, or geographical.

Another interesting aspect of how the stories about CP were composed in these different chapters was the method the authors used to assess the status of the field in their country. Several of the chapters used survey methods to poll other people in the country about the existence, definition, or practice of the field (e.g., Australia, Poland, Turkey) and others used databases to identify work that might fall under the umbrella of CP (e.g., Israel, Japan, India).

Social Climate and the Development of CP

Irrespective of where the chapters began their tale, each included a description of the social and political climate of their country that was either ripe for the development of the field or barren for the cultivation of community practice. Throughout the book, political structures, ruling governments, social movements, and globalization are mentioned as substantial contributors to the growth or barriers to growth of the field of community psychology.

Oppressive Pasts

The political structure seemed to be a major contributor or hindrance to the development of CP in the majority of the countries included in this book. Many countries described an oppressive history of colonization, dictatorships, and racist practices. Numerous countries were colonized by the British, Spanish, or French. While rule by these imperialists has ended in most of these countries, the influence of their oppression still affects the development and practice of CP. For instance in South Africa, where British colonial rule was replaced by "a draconian and authoritarian apartheid regime," racial tension and injustice led the way for social movement, and eventually the development of CP. The oppressive political structure both prohibited the establishment of a field of CP and served as a catalyst for sparking interest in development of such an area of research and action. In Cameroon, colonization suppressed active communitarian practices as "the colonial strategy ignored communal strategies, indigenous powerbases and collaborative networks." Only now as an independent country is Cameroon developing ways to cultivate an Afrocentric CP based on indigenous knowledge.

Along the lines of colonial oppression, military dictatorships also impeded community action. Only when such tyrannical rule ended did social action, in general, and CP, in particular, begin to flourish. Portugal, for instance, saw a move towards social and community action with the end of its military dictatorship in 1974. Similarly, the end of Franco's dictatorship in Spain allowed for the free exchange of intellectual ideas around liberation, community organization, and participatory action.

Social Movements

Social movements were often described as the first signs of the development of CP. One common social movement was the community mental health movement and its efforts towards deinstitutionalization. Many countries (Argentina, Brazil, Chile, Germany, Greece, Japan, India, Israel, New Zealand/ Aotearoa, Norway, Portugal, Spain, Venezuela, United States) described community mental health activities prompting the development of CP. For others, it was the entrance of nongovernmental organizations (NGOs) that prompted social action. For instance, in Cameroon, Ghana, and Hong Kong, NGOs often engaged in community practices and demonstrated CP values. In Ghana, NGOs were "practicing some principles of CP without necessarily referring to it as CP." These activities "mainly centered on advocacy, empowerment, self-help projects, poverty reduction, health, capacity building, [and] environmental degradation." In other countries grassroots social movements layed the ground work for CP. In Germany, the student movement helped develop "new theoretical means to criticize the social, political and economic development in post-war Germany," and in Italy, the 1970s were full of "innovative collective" movement by students, women, mental health patients, and health professionals to move "educational, social and health services interventions from secondary and tertiary prevention to primary prevention, encourage citizens participation, network among the services, and above all, promote health and quality of life." The 1980s in Latin America experienced numerous social movements as well, aimed at increasing "occupation of the public space in order to make the people within communities' voices heard and their needs attended to."

Political Ideology

In addition to social movements and histories of oppression, the political ideologies of each country greatly affected if and how CP developed. In Poland, for example, communism denied the existence of societal problems and therefore prohibited any type of community level intervention to promote health and well-being. Conversely, in Hong Kong, capitalism acknowledged social problems but viewed them as individual issues that were only relevant to the *community* if they interfered with productivity. As such, "public spending grew only in proportion to GDP growth and dependence on the state was to be discouraged."

The negative influence of capitalism on community well-being was noted in several chapters as neoliberal politics gain prominence. For instance, in the River Plate region, neoliberal models appear to increase social injustice and inequality by "deregulating the labor market, and privatizing (in Argentina) or attempting to privatize (in Uruguay) state-owned companies." The Norwegian chapter cautioned that this laissez-faire swing may be the eventual demise (or at least dramatic change) of CP as "the recognition of these [CP] values is diminishing, due to globalization and the gradually stronger influence of neoliberalism." The British chapter also describes the negative impact of neoliberalism as the "collective influence of the working class was directly attacked and weakened, and the institutions of the welfare state subjected to an incessant regime of budgetary cuts, strengthened general management, and subsequently (from the mid-1980s) to the 'discipline of the market' with swathes of provision being cut or outsourced."

While neoliberal politics have and continue to be a threat to CP and community health, the influence of progressive governments was a pleasant commonality among many of the countries in this book. In New Zealand/ Aotearoa, the Labour party was able to institute "social security from the cradle to the grave" and in Norway the "welfare system has involved a high level of social security, free education and redistribution of wealth between regions." Similarly, in Canada, liberal governments through such things as "national health care, social welfare programs, an appreciation for cultural diversity, and an emphasis on social solidarity . . . have often supported or complemented the goals of CP."

Geography

Another aspect of the climate for the development of CP is the actual topography of the country in which is it developing. For instance, Australia is a large country with a largely unpopulated desert interior. This climate and expansiveness greatly affects how CP develops by limiting contact among community psychologists, distributing people throughout the country's perimeter, and increasing the size of the government that community psychologists hope to work with. Thus, the way in which CP develops and is practiced is affected by the sheer size and inhabitability of the country. Conversely, New Zealand/Aotearoa consists of two rather small connected islands. The easy transmission of ideas in this country allows for more networking among community psychologists and greater influence on the national government. Similarly, Puerto Rico, one of the smallest regions in Central America, developed CP sooner than its neighboring countries.

However, small countries do not develop CP in the same manner as exhibited by the informal presence of CP in Hong Kong, Great Britain, and Cuba.

Contributors and Antecedents to Development and Practice of CP

While the political and physical climate was an important part of the story of the development of CP, the intellectual climate and professional antecedents to the field were equally important. For some regions, CP grew out of another discipline or is still practiced under the umbrella of another field. The most commonly cited areas were social work, sociology, social psychology, and school psychology. For instance, in Spain, the development of CP was in line with the growth of social work until the 1970s when CP set to make the "transition from the inherited models of social work to more systematic and transformational models" of CP. In Brazil, Chile, Venezuela, Colombia, Costa Rica, Perú, El Salvador, and regions of Mexico, the majority of work in the community was conducted by anthropology, sociology, psychiatry, or adult education. However, it was social psychology that began to critically reflect on these practices. Thus, in Latin America, CP grew from social psychology to become what is currently social-community psychology.

In some countries, CP did not grow out of another discipline. Rather it is still practiced under the umbrella of another field. As mentioned above, CP work in Hong Kong, Ghana, and Cameroon is often conducted through NGOs without being called CP. Along these lines, in Israel, the label *community psychologist* does not exist. Instead, school psychologists engage in CP work. Similarly, in Turkey, there are few community psychologists per se, but there is community work being done by clinical and developmental psychologists. In Great Britain, some use the label of community psychologist while others in the region practice CP from such titles as educational psychologist, sociologist, or anthropologist.

A few of the chapters described how CP was influenced by or is currently working alongside other fields. These include feminism/feminist psychology, critical psychology, and liberation theology/psychology. Feminism and feminist perspectives were included in the history of some of the countries while largely ignored in others. For example, Australia, Canada, Great Britain, and Norway describe the shared experience of "swimming against the stream" for CP and feminism, with some programs of CP being strongly influenced by feminist theory. As the Norwegian chapter states, "feminist contributors have provided critical, important, and necessary voices about gender oppression in the Norwegian society." While some chapters acknowledged the creation of women's interests groups within CP organizations (e.g., Australia, United States), these countries noted the androcentric practices of CP, both historically and currently. As the Italian chapter states, "community psychologists as a group have not dealt so far with gender issues . . . CP needs to update the internal theoretical debate and deal with the critiques posed by feminist, cultural, and postcolonial perspective."

Similar to feminism/feminist psychology, critical psychology challenged the field of CP to questions its theories and practices but still remained a fringe contributor to the field. In Germany, for instance, the Frankfurt School challenged the field to "critically reflect on the current state of practice and theory of psychiatry, psychology, and other disciplines in the psychosocial field and to engage in social change." In some countries, such as Canada, the United Kingdom, and the United States, an explicit effort is being made to integrate critical and community psychology into critical community psychology. The signing of the Monterrey Declaration of Critical Community Psychology (in the United States) marks one concrete step towards integrating these two fields.

Liberation theology and liberation psychology were fields often cited as a contributor and/or antecedent to the development of CP internationally. For some countries, the role of liberation theology was in the creation of specific programs or ways of addressing specific societal issues. For instance, in Portugal the alphabetization program to combat illiteracy was founded on the liberatory principles of conscientization, and in South Africa, conscientization has promoted critical social analysis of social conditions. In the majority of the countries in Latin America, the theology and philosophy of liberation have been important contributors to how CP is defined and practiced. Liberation ideas have been present in such countries as Costa Rica, Colombia, Venezuela, Brazil, Chile, and El Salvador, creating mutual influences between CP and psychology of liberation. The current work of the Martin Luther King Jr. Memorial Centre in Cuba is one explicit example. For many countries, liberation theology and liberation psychology prompted different ways of thinking through social issues, implementing change, and mobilizing people.

Native Values, Theories, and Practices

Another important influence cited for the development of CP was the native values, practices, and theories of indigenous people. While all countries have indigenous people, only a few of the chapters explicitly discussed how their cultural heritage influenced how CP developed and how it is currently practiced. The chapter from Cameroon described how the imperialism of psychology and CP in particular dismissed and suppressed indigenous theories and practices. Only now are efforts being made to capitalize on the ancient knowledge and experience of the people to create an indigenous CP of the people and for the people. In Ghana, indigenous knowledge and values have greatly influenced the development of CP, as "Ghanaian traditional values also prescribe collectivism and social support for each other." In New Zealand/Aotearoa, indigenous beliefs predate CP, utilizing many of the same values and practices. Thus, the Māori traditions as well as Māori scholars have greatly influenced the development and practice of the field.

Intellectual Colonization

While colonization was discussed above as an important contributor to the political climate in which CP is developing, it was also mentioned throughout this text as an important part of the intellectual climate as well. Physical colonization of countries throughout the world had a profound influence on the development of CP. However, intellectual colonization has possibly had as strong an influence on the field. Intellectual colonization of CP includes the education of foreign researchers in U.S. and Canadian institutions, the abundant number of Western texts and journals, and the funding of interventions and research in non-Western countries. For some "colonized" countries, CP has developed in line with the Western version of CP. For instance, Japan's version of CP has been heavily influenced by the development of CP in the United States. As the authors write, "indigenous theories or formulations of research and action in CP that are unique to the Japanese society have yet to be explored vis-à-vis the CP models in the United States and other countries." The Australian chapter mirrors this sentiment with the question, "Australia is indeed 'so far away' from North America and Britain, but how much does it matter if our orientation is as close to theirs as this chapter implies, albeit with a local flavour?"

For other countries, the development of their own version of CP has been triggered by how poorly Westernized views of health and psychology fit their local context. India, for example, views health quite differently than many Western countries, and as such, U.S., Canadian, and British views of mental health and community well-being do not apply. Thus, Indian CP has moved away from "a Western paradigm to [a more] culturally relevant context." Similarly, Greece describes how its intellectual colonization has impeded its development of an native CP. "Initiatives by public institutions are "copying" (following) North American or Western European practices, programming, and models, and hence, locally grown knowledge and understanding has yet to emerge."

The Italian chapter describes how the first community psychologist was trained in the United States and returned to Italy to find that U.S. models did not fit the European context. As stated in the chapter, "European countries share broad cultural values as well as historical and political experiences, which are different from those of the United States. These differences emerge in their social representation of the world, which influences the formulation and diffusion of particular theories." The poor fit of U.S. theories and practices exemplified the need for and formation of the European Network of Community Psychology (ENCP).

Many of the contributors to this book note that they and many of their colleagues were trained either in the United States or Canada (e.g., Ghana, Italy, India, Japan, Turkey). While few reflect on how this intellectual colonization affects the practice of CP in their own countries, it is worthy of thinking about, especially for those actively involved in educating international scholars.

Formalization/Academization of CP

Each chapter was asked to describe whether they viewed the field of CP to be formalized in their country/region and, if so, to describe the processes and relevant occurrences of this formalization. Most of the chapters describe the presence or absence of professional organizations, journals, regular meetings/conferences, and educational tracks in CP.

Organizations and Journals

The majority of the countries included in this book either have a formalized field of CP (e.g., India, Japan, United States) or a branch of the national psychological association with a CP focus (e.g., Australia, Norway, Portugal). In Europe, there are national CP organizations as well as the international European Network of Community Psychology. Several countries described their field as nascent with no formal association or publication (e.g. Ghana, Greece, Cameroon).

Whether a country has a specific CP publication did not seem tied to whether it also has a formal organization of CP. For instance, in Great Britain, community psychologists tend to be members of the larger British Psychological Association, however the country has the *Journal of Community and Applied Social Psychology*. Similarly, in South Africa, to date, there is no formal branch of CP within the Professional Association of Psychology, but there is a CP-focused journal, *Psychology in Society*.

Perks and Hindrances of Formalization

Having a professional association and clear formalization of CP appears to be both a benefit and a detriment to many of the countries included in this book. On one hand, formalization provides legitimacy. For instance, in Italy, the compulsory inclusion of CP in all clinical and community programs ensured discipline-wide awareness of CP and helped establish the field. On the other hand, formalization restricts the flexibility and evolution of the field. In Australia, the membership requirements to the Australian Psychological Colleges have "undermined the inclusive values inherent in community psychology" as well as limited its ability to "attract or involve interested people unable to fulfill College membership criteria."

Education in CP

Formalization has also affected the teaching of CP in many regions of the world. The majority of the chapters state that CP is taught in at least some of the universities within their countries. Most commonly, CP is offered as a course as part of undergraduate training in psychology. Some countries provide graduate training in CP at both the master's and doctoral levels

(Australia, Brazil, Canada, Chile, Columbia, Ecuador, Italy, Japan, Mexico, New Zealand/Aotearoa, Puerto Rico, Portugal, Venezuela, United States). In regions where CP is highly formalized, CP curriculum is rather regimented. For instance, in Great Britain, the British Psychological Association "retains tight control of and scrutiny of the undergraduate and postgraduate curricula." Thus, formalization provides both credibility and barriers to the development of the field.

Practice as Path to Formalization

Many of the chapters described how community-based practice led to the desire for a field of CP. For some regions, community-based action was occurring without realization that others were working in similar areas, with similar goals and values. It was the coming together of practitioners that lead to the establishment of a field of CP. This pattern was common in many regions of Latin America where "private projects and social policies trying to respond with more or less success, to the demands and needs of the population." For instance, in Chile, CP practiced by nongovernmental institutions played an important role during the Pinochet dictatorship to "help the victims of political repression and aggression, to empower the communities in order to resist these sources of oppression and protect themselves, to keep active the political consciousness of the population, and to defend human rights." Similarly, projects in Argentina, Brazil, Colombia, Costa Rica, El Salvador, Mexico, Perú, and Venezuela were aimed at dealing with and solving social problems of communities in need. Through these applied practices, community-based researchers and practitioners were able to forge a new field. In Latin America, these applied practices transformed social psychology into social-community psychology.

Conferencing for Critical Mass

Another recurrent theme in the chapters was how professional conferences served as a catalyst for the development of CP. These professional meetings provided a forum for community-based practitioners to discuss their work, theories, frustrations, and goals. Seeing others working in the same areas provided a sense of critical mass for the establishment of a field of CP. In Portugal, "the organization of scientific meetings allowed Portuguese psychologists to confront their practice with the experience of other countries" and assisted in the formalization of the field. In Germany, the informal exchanges at academic forums helped establish the formal organization (Gesellschaft für gemeindepsychologische Forschung und Praxis) as well as the publishing of a regular newsletter. In Spain, a series of meetings helped promote "the incorporation of CP in the academic context . . . [and] the inclusion of CP principles and practices in different forms and different levels of academic activity." Along these lines, many countries in Europe

(Germany, Great Britain, Italy, Portugal, Poland, and Spain) also noted the benefit of the European Congress of Community Psychology in promoting the field of CP and the germination of ideas. The Interamerican Society for Psychology's congresses also played an important role for the sharing of ideas between Latin American countries and Spain.

Target Areas of Research and Practice That Transcend Borders

In comparing the application of CP to research and practice, we noticed that certain topic areas were mentioned in almost all chapters. For example, most countries describe community psychologists working on issues of mental health often with a specific emphasis on community-based provision of services, prevention, and empowerment of mental health service consumers. This may not be surprising considering that in many countries, CP evolved out the community mental health movement and many community psychologists have close links to clinical psychology.

Other target areas of research and practice that are mentioned in literally all chapters are issues of poverty, power, and inequality with a focus on transformative change. Of course, the manifestation of poverty and inequality differs significantly depending on the societal structure and culture, the political system, the degree to which the country experienced colonization, and the point in history. Thus, it is no surprise that the specific issues of inequality discussed in each chapter differ from country to country. In the United States, Canada, and Australia, for example, CP is actively trying to fight oppression based on gender and sexual orientation while in countries like South Africa, Cameroon, and New Zealand, CP is involved in addressing the long-term impact of colonization. CP in many countries attempts to address the unequal distribution of wealth and other issues of inequality. What is common in all of this is that CP relates the individual well-being to societal and cultural condition and the insight that those conditions need to change in a transformative way to accomplish individual, community, and societal well-being.

Other areas of interest and CP application that are mentioned are inclusion and diversity (e.g., United States), health promotion (e.g., Uruguay), community development (e.g., Canada, Germany), nongovernmental organizations (e.g., Ghana, Hong Kong), school-based interventions and programs (e.g., Norway), HIV and AIDS (e.g., India, South Africa, Puerto Rico), youth groups (e.g., Italy), community centers (e.g., Portugal), social networks including those beginning to evolve on the Internet (e.g., Colombia, Brazil, Venezuela, Argentina, Italy), immigration (e.g., Greece), indigenous issues (e.g., New Zealand/Aotearoa, Australia), and community interventions in catastrophes and wartimes (e.g., Turkey, Poland, Israel). While this list is not exhaustive, it clearly shows that CP is a diverse interdisciplinary field that is applied to many different areas of interest.

The list of focus areas above is certainly not extensive, and we encourage the readers to review each chapter carefully with an eye for areas of research and practice that overlap with their own interest to learn how this issue is addressed elsewhere and potentially find collaborators. In addition, one should look for issues that are not well covered in one's home country but may be relevant to his or her local context. In comparing their own with the CP of other countries, the Italian authors, for example, found that "Italian CP has, so far, dedicated little attention to different aspects of diversity, for instance, cultural, ethnic, and sexual diversity, disability, and therefore to the issues of racism and prejudice." We hope that readers, just like the authors and editors of this book, will experience similar insights as they make their way through the chapters of this volume.

Theories

In reading through the chapters of this book, theory seems to serve three major functions in CP. First, very similar to the critical theory of the Frankfurt School, it serves as a social theory oriented toward critiquing and changing societal conditions. The expectation is that theory as well as practice are contributing to transformative social change. This is seen as contrary to traditional theory in the positivistic psychological and social science, which is mainly oriented to understanding and explaining psychological and social phenomena. An illustrative example of this emancipatory expectation towards knowledge generation is how CP in Latin America was influenced, among others, by Kurt Lewin's idea of action research, Marx's economic and philosophical theories on society, the critical theory of the Frankfurt School, and the theory of dependency. In Latin America, these ideas were integrated with the concepts of conscientization and de-ideologizing based on Freire's adult education and Fals Borda's critical sociology. These led to a theory of liberation and a practice of participatory action research, both of which have been very influential to CP throughout the world.

A second function of theory in CP has been to describe community, its context, as well as its development. Two theories, sense of community and ecological theory, serve as examples here. Ecological theory and the importance of considering context and doing research at multiple levels of analysis is discussed in most, if not all, chapters. Taking the larger context into account is one of the key differences between traditional mainstream psychology and CP. Sense of community was first developed in the United States in the 1970s and 1980s but since then has been developed further and adapted to fit local understandings of community in other countries such as Italy and Australia.

A third function of theory is to provide guiding principles for practice as well as tools for structuring and reflecting on one's practice. This idea of "a theory of practice" is elaborated in the Italian chapter, for example. Francescato and her colleagues describe a series of guiding principles that describe what they refer to as a European community practice. These include deliberations in regard to problem attribution, interaction between person and context, the link between individual empowerment and collective political struggle, among others. In the United States, two internationally influential theories of practice, prevention theory and empowerment, "separate the field into two streams of scholarship." While the prevention camp maintains that prevention "represents the field's commitment to proactive rather than reactive interventions", Rappaport argues that this model is limited and fails "to view persons in a holistic manner." As an alternative he offers the empowerment approach, which would allow us to view people holistically, "as individuals with needs and rights." While Rappaport's empowerment approach is mentioned by several authors as an important theoretical influence in their country, it is also criticized as representing an individualistic and androcentric world view and failing to address important aspect of power structures in society. It would be interesting to discuss Rappaport's notion of viewing the person in a holistic manner in comparison with the Indian perspective on health where no distinction is made between physical, mental, and spiritual health. As noted by the Indian authors, "the Eastern holistic approach requires far more complex ways of evaluation."

Which of these functions theory serves for the individual varies across community psychologists and often changes over time with the individual's intellectual development. The chapter from South Africa describes this in the following way: "[. . .] many psychologists moved from disillusionment with the state of psychological theory to reactive critical engagement, constructive self-definition to ultimately engaging in an emancipatory discourse and praxis. Psychologists would accordingly employ theoretical approaches that tended to match their level of engagement with this process. The result was a spectrum of theoretical approaches in the application of community psychology in South Africa which ranged from 'mainstream' to 'liberatory' approaches."

In general, we found that most authors describe important theoretical roots of CP and discuss critical aspects of theory building in their country while putting less emphasis on elaborating existing indigenous theories or describing how theories from other countries have been adapted locally. Several of the authors, however, provide deliberations about the degree to which existing CP theories from other countries fit the local context, how these theories can be adapted to make them fit, or whether new indigenous theories need to be developed. The aforementioned holistic approach to health and the belief in Karma in India as well as the traditional communitarian practice in Cameroon are two examples of cultural traditions that are different from the Western perspectives where many CP theories have been developed. The authors from these countries describe the most important cultural features that newly developed theories would have to fit. Similarly, the Japanese chapter references the utility of a model for assessing the cross-cultural validity of CP research and action across two cultures. It will be interesting to look back 10 years from now (maybe in the context of the next edition of this book) and study the theories that will be developed in these as well as other countries and the process of their development.

Methods

One characteristics of CP is that it is "not wedded to any particular orthodoxy of method," as the British authors describe it. This sentiment is mirrored by many other authors when they point out the limitations and problems of methods that have been developed under the logical positivistic paradigm dominant in psychology and other related fields such as sociology. They warn that these methods are too individualistic and oriented towards the control of the research participants, which is clearly contradictory to the CP values of empowerment, participation, and transformative change as well as the ecological framework. Thus, many community psychologists turn away from positivist methods towards more qualitative and participatory ones. However, most authors favor methodological pluralism and do not feel that CP has to commit to one particular methodology. The Spanish authors, for example, discuss how the complete abandonment of neopositivist methodo-logy can be problematic: "The demonization of neopositive approaches, whose essence has been confused with their circumstances, has in many contexts made community work inoperative, producing a perverse effect whereby after lucid exercises of deconstruction and problematization, communities are condemned by absolute relativism, impotence, or refuge in a sterile intellectualism due to a lack of operative instruments of action."

Methods that utilize an ecological framework naturally lead CP towards multilevel research. Several authors describe turning to other disciplines to find methods that enable investigation at multiple levels. However, several authors note the difficulty in conducting research that is truly multilevel and contextual and find that it is easy to get caught at the individual level. For example, community mental health centres are a great improvement over res-idential care but most often they are still focused on individual clients and their immediate network.

One of the most prominent methods described by authors is participatory action research. This method, originally developed in Latin America, reflects many important values of CP. It emphasizes the participation of all relevant stakeholders in all aspects of the research process and, in the tradition of Kurt Lewin, tries to understand phenomena by changing them. The work of the educator Paulo Freire and of the sociologist Orlando Fals Borda was very important in transforming Lewin's action research into participatory action research. In Latin America, they have developed "participatory methods and modes of intervention responding to the needs of the communities, while incorporating those communities to the definition, solution of their prob-lems, or satisfaction of their needs."

While many countries noted the difficulties of using research methods that are not tied to individualistic approaches, few described innovative methodologies. One notable example was the Italian chapter, which has devel-oped methods for community profiling, network building, multidimensional organizational analysis, as well as affective and empowering training. Overall, few indigenous methods were discussed in detail.

Reflecting on Self-Critiques

Each chapter was asked to compare the development of CP in their country to the development in other regions of the world. In addition to integrating the text, the process allowed for self-reflection and critiques of what has or has not been addressed in each chapter. Because the topics covered in these conclusions are extensive, we will only discuss a couple here. One interesting pattern was the extent to which chapters discussed their efforts to include indigenous values and practices into CP. Some chapters described their efforts while others acknowledge the complete omission of indigenous traditions in their practice of CP. For some countries, especially those that were intellectually colonized, the role of indigenous knowledge has been essential for the development of a CP that is truly grounded in the community. For all three African countries, the role of indigenous knowledge and the diversity of the indigenous cultures were important components of how CP has developed, its current status, and where it is headed. While New Zealand/Aotearoa also acknowledged the need for incorporation of indigenous values and theories into the practice of CP, its neighboring country, Australia, has not included aboriginal values and theories into its development of the field. However, Australian CP has been actively involved in raising awareness around racism and the need for reconciliation. Few countries, especially those that have horribly oppressed their indigenous people, have been influenced by indigenous traditions. Canadian, Norwegian, and U.S. community psychologists may work with indigenous people but have not included their traditions, beliefs, or practices into the field of CP.

Another common self-critique across the chapter was the tendency of CP to rely on individualistic methods, approaches, or interventions. Many attributed this habit to traditional psychological roots that are focused on the individual. Others noted a paucity of community-based methods. While all countries wished to use collective approaches to CP, few felt that they were consistently applying them to address the social ecology of their countries. Most chapters reflected on the need to develop better ways to measure communities.

International Exchanges and Networks

Intellectual and personal exchange among countries has been described by many authors as crucial for the development of CP in their country. These international contacts facilitated the exchange of ideas, theories, and methods and often helped strengthen the visibility and position of CP in the respective countries. These exchanges happened in many different forms either on an individual basis or in larger networks.

In many countries (e.g., India, Japan, Germany, Italy, Turkey, Ghana), scholars learned about the ideas, theories, and practice of CP during their studies in countries with an already established field of CP such as Canada and the United States. After their training they returned to their own countries, shared these ideas with their colleagues, and began adopting them to the local needs and context. In other cases, visiting community psychologists from other countries helped the local development of CP by giving it a boost and a direction to head in (e.g., Mexico, Portugal).

Several authors mention the importance of international networks and conferences for the intellectual development of CP in their country as well as for building alliances that strengthen the position of CP within their country. The great influence of Latin American scholarship on their country's development of CP, for example, led the Spanish authors to the statement that "of great importance for this interchange have been the exchange forums for Latin American and Spanish professionals and academics as well as the setting up of interinstitutional collaboration conventions." Similarly, the Italian and German authors describe the development of a European approach to CP that was facilitated by the founding of the European Network of Community Psychology. The Latin American chapter also describes a very active exchange of ideas among the countries in this region.

Another form of exchange is the use of literature and textbooks from other countries. The frequent reference to Dalton, Elias, and Wandersman's (2001) textbook for the definition of CP in different chapters can be seen as an indicator that the use of this book has expanded beyond the borders of the home country of these authors. Another example is the influence of the scholarly writings by Martín-Baró, Freire, and Montero among many other Latin American authors for community psychologists in Spain as well as other countries. However, in a recent international symposium at the 2005 biennial conference of the Society for Community Research and Action, several international community psychologists raised the issue that the use of literature from other countries is somewhat limited by language barriers and is also often one-directional with a clear advantage for those countries who publish in either English and Spanish. They advocated for developing infrastructures and finding resources that would foster true exchange of scholarly work. We hope that after reading about the important and interesting contributions of community psychologists around the world described in this volume, readers will support this call for building further infrastructures for international sharing of ideas.

Some Additional Questions

After reading the fascinating contributions of each country, there are a few questions that came to mind often. Given the length of this conclusion chapter, we will only draw attention to three of them. One recurrent question is, What makes community psychology community psychology? While we allowed each contributor to define CP for themselves, the definitions were similar but not synonymous. Some described the characteristics of CP, others the areas it addresses, while others focused on the values that underlay it. Thus, as readers one is left wondering if CP is a profession, a field, a value-system, a world view, or perhaps all of the above.

A second question that emerged was, What is a community psychologist? This book provides numerous examples of people doing community-based work but does not specifically define who is a community psychologist. Is a school psychologist in Israel a community psychologist? How about a social worker in Germany or a nurse in a NGO in South Africa or a community activist in Great Britain? Does licensure make a community psychologist a community psychologist? How about specific training in CP, such as a doctoral program? Where are the lines drawn and do they need to be? For this chapter, we allowed contributors to decide whom they labeled community psychologists. In our invitation to contribute, we noted that some countries or regions may not refer to their field or area as CP. Instead, we defined CP as research and action for social change that is focused on the prevention of human suffering, the reduction of oppression, and the promotion of individual, relational, and societal well-being. Thus, we did not define what a community psychologist is nor did any chapter in this book. The British chapter warns of the "problem for a historian who wishes to focus on 'approved CP' without wishing to 'colonise' or rather 'appropriate' others' activities (with or without their consent)."

A final question we will raise here is about what role community psychology should play. Is CP a critical-political tool or an ameliorative component for clinical needs? Should CP be political? Should it focus on social transformation? These are not questions we will answer; they are simply questions that remain.

Future Directions

Overall, many authors view the future of CP with hope and optimism but also with caution. While countries with budding fields of CP stress the need for hard work and persistence to develop the field, several authors, (e.g., Germany, Hong Kong) express worries that CP is on the decline in their country. Regardless of how established CP is in each country, most, if not all, authors expressed the view that the further establishment and development of CP will require a lot of effort as the field faces major challenges. For instance, several chapters noted the benefits and detriments of defining a professional identity for CP and whether professionalization and formalization will help carry CP values forwards. As noted by the Australian authors, the formalization, such as becoming a chapter in a psychological society, can actually hinder important values by creating artificial boundaries that can be exclusionary.

Some of the challenges often noted in this text were issues of marginalization, legitimacy, lack of visibility, and related to these, the competition for resources. Even in countries where CP is well established such as Canada and the United States, marginalization is seen as one of the major challenges that CP is facing for the future. The interested reader is referred to the conclusion of the German chapter, which offers an analysis of this problem by comparing the situation in several countries to their own.

The change of the political situation especially towards neoliberal forms of capitalism as well as more conservative governments is also highlighted by several authors, especially from Europe, as a challenge for CP in the future. In a climate of privatization, individualization, and increased economic competition, "theoretical and practical concepts, which stress the connection between individual and societal responsibility, lose their attractiveness" as the German authors point out.

Another challenge mentioned by several authors is the need to diversify the ranks of scholars within CP academic programs. Several authors stressed the importance of being more vigilant in working towards inclusion and equality in academia. The United States and Italy, for example, expressed the need to work towards more gender equality. In Latin America, New Zealand/ Aotearoa, Australia, and Canada, the authors see a responsibility to be more inclusive toward the indigenous population, which is also seen as a great opportunity to tap into the wisdom of these groups.

Some authors mentioned opportunities for interdisciplinary partnerships and collaborations with fields that share similar values and/or share a common cause such as feminism (e.g., Italy, United States), cultural diversity and immigration (e.g., Greece, Israel), and public health (e.g., Canada). The Latin America chapter proposes the development of community clinical psychology while the authors in the U.S. chapter advocate for the development of critical community psychology. Common to these approaches is the idea that building alliances with other related fields does not only provide the opportunity for a rich exchange of ideas and methods but also helps to strengthen each other's positions by building critical mass. In addition, the ecological foundation of CP and, thus, the need for multilevel research naturally requires interdisciplinary collaboration. Some also see a bigger role for CP in public policy and politics (e.g., Australia, Latin America) as well as in addressing the widespread ramifications of globalized capitalism. Addressing these issues would require a type of knowledge that is not always readily available within CP and makes the collaboration with other disciplines attractive, if not necessary. This includes knowledge about how to address power issues that go beyond the idea of empowerment.

The development of more indigenous theories and methods is seen as a need and opportunity by several authors (e.g., Japan, India, Cameroon). This includes an assessment of the degree to which theories and methods developed in other countries, especially the United States, are applicable locally and where the gaps and mismatches lay.

In looking forward the Argentinian/Uruguayan authors express eloquently what many community psychologists around the globe probably feel: "A real difficulty for the full development of a community psychology epistemologically solid and fruitful in its applications is the current hegemony of the Cartesian and mechanistic conception of the human being and their social organisations. Due to the very nature of its object of study and of its practice, community psychology seems to demand that a new paradigm begin: the new paradigm of the sciences of life [. . .], which is based on a holistic, systematic, and ecologic conception of the human factor as nonessential part of the biosphere." The Indian holistic view of health, the Cameroon traditional "communitarian practice," and the Māori "profoundly ecological view of life" are just a few examples of the accumulated wisdom of indigenous cultures described in this book that it is worth learning from as we move this agenda forward.

Final Conclusion and Parting Words

This volume has been an incredible journey that lasted several years. As we conclude this final chapter, we feel relieved that this project finally comes to an end and sad that we cannot start over, incorporating all the things we have learned and adding more countries who have just begun their practice of CP. It is with joy that we look back over the past 3 years. Through this project, we got to know many interesting people from around the globe and learned many new things about our field. We are aware that we had high expectations for our contributing authors and we are thankful for their patience when we requested a third, fourth, or even sixth revision of their chapters. It has been an honor to work with these incredible people and we are proud to be the ones presenting their work.

We are also aware that we were not able to include all the countries and all the information that would have been of interest to the reader. We hope that this book is just one piece of a movement towards more global exchange about CP. The increased presence of international scholars at local or continental conferences, the recent international conference in Puerto Rico, and the upcoming special issue on international CP in the *American Journal for Community Psychology* are all indicators for a positive direction.

We are indebted to the contributing authors for sharing their incredible knowledge of the history and theories of CP in their country. We hope the reader profits as much as we did from learning about the development of CP around the world. We concur with the authors from New Zealand/Aotearoa that "without a thorough understanding of our past, our efforts to improve the future will at best be limited. *Me tiro whakamuri a kia hangai whakamua.* ('Look backward in order to move forward with purpose')."

References

Dalton, J. H., Elias, M. J., & Wandersman, A. (2001). *Community psychology: Linking individuals and communities.* Palo Alto, CA: Wadsworth.

Tolan, P., Keys, C., Chertock, F., & Jason, L. (Eds.). (1990). *Researching community psychology: Issues of theory and methods.* Washington, DC: American Psychological Association.

Index

New Zealand/Aotearoa, 7, 89, 124, 125, 127, 136, 140–158, 232, 417, 418, 420, 421, 423, 426, 427, 431, 434, 435
Nongovernmental organizations (NGO), 88, 188, 206, 393, 398, 407, 408, 420, 427, 433
North America, 54, 123, 124, 137, 221, 222, 379, 388, 424
Norway, 282–295, 417, 418, 420–422, 425, 427
Norwegian Psychological Association, 286, 288

O

Ontology, 82
Organisational change, 221
Organizational effectiveness, 292
Otherness, 83, 86

P

Pacific, 54, 120, 124, 141, 146
Paradigm, 21, 43, 44, 82, 83, 114, 120, 121, 148, 183, 186, 190, 222, 223, 394, 397, 399, 424, 430, 435
Paradigm shifts, 21, 43, 403
Participant conceptualizers, 39, 42, 169
Participatory action, 20, 25, 42, 53, 67, 84, 87, 309, 310, 420, 428, 430
Participatory Action Research, 20, 23, 25, 42, 53, 62, 67, 84, 87, 189, 193, 303, 310, 428, 430
Participatory development, 53, 188, 399
Partnerships, 28, 175, 231, 289, 326, 329, 434
Peace, 41, 100, 114, 125–127, 129, 302
Pedagogy, 303, 310, 319
Person-environment fit, 44, 132, 167, 174
Physical health, 191, 429
Planning, 111, 130, 145, 151, 156, 184, 187, 190, 193, 284, 288, 289, 302, 337, 342, 398–400
Politics, 29, 41, 82, 83, 147, 230, 239, 242, 243, 246, 266, 277, 284, 302, 318, 328, 330, 379, 380, 421
Portuguese Psychologists Association (Ordem dos Psicólogos), 324
Portuguese Society for Community Psychology, 324

Positivistic, 42, 428, 430
Postgraduate training, xx
Power asymmetries, 51, 62
Power imbalances, 42, 49
Practitioner, 8, 42, 123, 130, 131, 155, 191, 196, 208, 289, 385
Praxis, 53, 66, 72, 76, 85, 136, 137, 230, 305, 386, 403, 426, 429
Prejudice, 29, 129, 184, 186, 278, 311, 368, 428
Preventive work, 287, 289, 342
Primary prevention, 71, 73, 210, 241, 264, 339, 342, 344, 365, 366, 387, 420
Privatization, 277, 292, 338, 434
Privilege, 49, 127, 155, 299, 416
Problematization, 64, 85, 87, 313, 430
Professional organisations, 152, 153, 220, 265
Professionalization, 7, 22, 377, 381, 413, 433
Program evaluation, 17, 18, 20, 130, 175, 241
Protective factors, 21, 44
Psychological anthropology, 148
Psychological Society of South Africa, 380
Psychosocial difficulties, 289
Psychotherapy, 88, 169, 175, 226, 229, 245, 249, 256, 266, 345
Public health, 21, 27, 39, 45, 49, 62, 105, 106, 109, 112, 113, 134, 146, 165, 175, 212, 247, 257, 288, 289, 366, 434
Public mental health, 109, 242, 283, 304
Public sector planning, 288

Q

Qualitative research/methods, 19, 42, 53, 155,
Quality of Life, 14, 20, 71, 77, 83, 88, 169, 173, 188, 192, 206, 246, 264, 268, 271, 308, 321, 352, 408, 411, 418, 420
Quantitative research/methods, 121, 153, 251, 256, 292

R

Race, 8, 18, 24, 27, 41, 42, 51, 128, 146, 379, 385

Printed in the United States
116161LV00002B/49-54/A

9 780387 494999